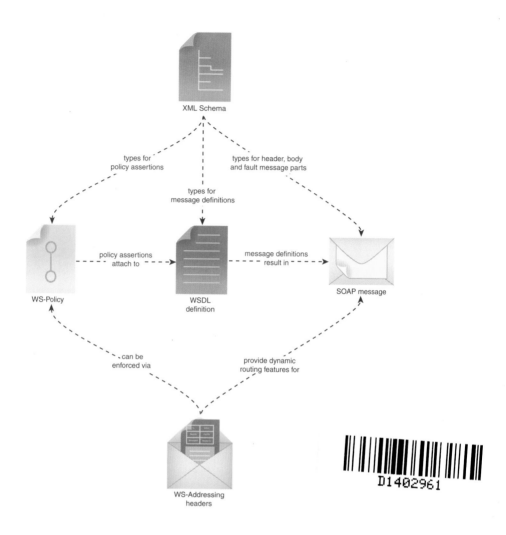

XML Schema

types for
policy assertions

types for header, body
and fault message parts

types for
message definitions

WS-Policy

policy assertions
attach to

WSDL
definition

message definitions
result in

SOAP message

can be
enforced via

provide dynamic
routing features for

WS-Addressing
headers

WSDL Definition

Abstract Description

Concrete Description

XML Schema Definition

Global Element
Complex Type
Complex Type
Complex Type
Simple Type
Simple Type

Global Element
Simple Type

WS-Policy Definition

Policy Expression
Policy Alternative
Policy Assertion
Policy Assertion

Policy Alternative
Policy Assertion
Policy Assertion

Policy Expression
Policy Assertion
Policy Assertion

SOAP Message Envelope

Header
Block   Block

Body

Fault

Praise for this Book

"This compendium is the new bible for WS-* design and SOA. The structured approach allows beginners, experts and executives to understand and execute successfully on an SOA Strategy. Thomas Erl and his team did once again a great job."

—*Sascha Kuhlmann*
Global Program Lead Enterprise Architecture, SAP

"A first-rate and in-depth dive into service contract and interface design that elaborates on the best book in the field, *SOA Principles of Service Design*. Over the years Thomas's books have provided a foundation for defining our SOA standards (for over 200 services) and contain the latest material and case studies which comprise the singular most important advice for those implementing large-scale SOAs."

—*Bob Hathaway*
Senior SOA Architect
SOA Object Systems, Starwood Hotels

"Anyone tasked with publishing and evolving Web services 'contract first' will welcome this book, packed full of authoritative explanations and advice from authors who truly understand their subject."

—*Paul Downey*
Chief Web Services Architect, BT

"This book is an excellent resource for anybody trying to get a comprehensive understanding of the technical foundation of Web services based service-oriented architecture. It is written by the experts who have worked on the development of the underlying world-wide standards."

—*Michael Bechauf*
Vice President of Standards Strategy and Developer Programs, SAP AG

Web Service Contract Design and Versioning for SOA

The Prentice Hall Service-Oriented Computing Series
from Thomas Erl aims to provide the IT industry with
a consistent level of unbiased, practical, and
comprehensive guidance and instruction in the areas
of service-oriented architecture, service-orientation,
and the expanding landscape that is shaping
the real-world service-oriented computing platform.

For more information, visit www.soabooks.com.

Web Service Contract Design and Versioning for SOA

Thomas Erl, Anish Karmarkar, Priscilla Walmsley,
Hugo Haas, Umit Yalcinalp, Canyang Kevin Liu,
David Orchard, Andre Tost, James Pasley

PRENTICE HALL

UPPER SADDLE RIVER, NJ • BOSTON • INDIANAPOLIS • SAN FRANCISCO

NEW YORK • TORONTO • MONTREAL • LONDON • MUNICH • PARIS • MADRID

CAPETOWN • SYDNEY • TOKYO • SINGAPORE • MEXICO CITY

PRENTICE
HALL

The publisher offers excellent discounts on this book when ordered in quantity for bulk purchases or special sales, which may include electronic versions and/or custom covers and content particular to your business, training goals, marketing focus, and branding interests. For more information, please contact:

> U.S. Corporate and Government Sales
> (800) 382-3419
> corpsales@pearsontechgroup.com

For sales outside the United States please contact:

> International Sales
> international@pearson.com

Visit us on the Web: www.informit.com/ph

Library of Congress Cataloging-in-Publication Data:

Web service contract design and versioning for SOA / Thomas Erl ... [et al.].

   p. cm.

  ISBN 0-13-613517-X (hbk. : alk. paper) 1. Web services. 2. Computer network architectures. 3. Computer architecture. I. Erl, Thomas. II. Title: Web service contract design and versioning for Service Oriented Architecture.

  TK5105.88813.E76 2008

  006.7'8—dc22

2008025188

ISBN-13: 978-0-13-613517-3
ISBN-10: 0-13-613517-X
Text printed in the United States on recycled paper at R.R. Donnelley in Crawfordsville, Indiana.
First printing September 2008

Editor-in-Chief
Mark L. Taub

Managing Editor
Kristy Hart

Copy Editor
Language Logistics

Development Editors
Dmitry Kirsanov
Songlin Qiu

Indexer
Cheryl Lenser

Proofreader
Williams Woods Publishing

Composition
Jake McFarland
Bumpy Design

Graphics
Zuzana Cappova
Tami Young

Photos
Thomas Erl
Johan Odendaal

"To my family for their continuing support."
– Thomas Erl

"Dedicated to my family: Aai, Baba, Chetan, Swati, Sidsel, and Leena. For making it possible and for making everything worthwhile."
– Anish Karmarkar

"To Doug, with love"
– Priscilla Walmsley

"To my wife, Nicole, for her endless support."
– Hugo Haas

"To my sister, Isik Boran."
– Umit Yalcinap

"To my children, Julia and Mark, who have made my life meaningful."
– Canyang Kevin Liu

"I want to thank my wife Silke and my sons Marc and Jonas for their constant help, support and understanding, not just with this project but with so many others throughout the years."
– Andre Tost

"To my wife Patricia and our children Rebecca, James, Robert, Hannah and Alyssa."
– James Pasley

Contents

PART I: FUNDAMENTAL SERVICE CONTRACT DESIGN

Chapter 8: Fundamental WSDL Part II: Concrete Description Design 197

PART II: ADVANCED SERVICE CONTRACT DESIGN

CHAPTER 12: Advanced XML Schema Part I: Message Flexibility, Type Inheritance, and Composition 309

CHAPTER 15: Advanced WSDL Part II: Message Dispatch, Service Instance Identification, and Non-SOAP HTTP Binding 445

CHAPTER 18: Advanced Message Design Part I: WS-Addressing Vocabularies 549

PART III: SERVICE CONTRACT VERSIONING

PART IV: APPENDICES

Foreword

I have often commented that learning the Web services set of specifications (WS-*) by reading them is like trying to understand the English language by reading Webster's dictionary. This is because every concept, every word is expressed in terms of other words that have yet to be understood, resulting ultimately in cyclical definitions. How could one effectively learn a verbal language that way?

Nearly ten years in the making, the WS-* specifications are the result of an industry-wide effort to define interoperable interfaces, transports, and metadata, using XML and XML Schema as the means for doing so. The specifications are intentionally broken up into small atomic units so that individual applications or infrastructure offerings from commercial vendors and open source may implement them in order to ease adoption and move us all closer to platform-independent interoperability. They are also composable with each other in that they may be used together. But how?

In all fairness, the WS-* specifications are self-explanatory enough to get a rough understanding of the purpose of each one if you read them long and hard enough. Through arduous scrutiny of jargon and angle brackets, eventually there is enough that sinks in to reach a critical mass of basic understanding.

Grasping their purpose and using the WS-* specifications as a reference for implementation is only the first level of knowledge. In fact most programmers and architects by now are familiar with the common trio (WSDL, XML Schema, and SOAP). This does not, however, imply that the use of these specifications is intuitively obvious. And what about the other specs in the stack? At last count, there were nearly 50. Can they all be learned together? How does one sort through them all and figure out which ones are the most important to pay attention to and which will have the most impact on their organization if used properly? What is the impact if used improperly? Even if the details are partially hidden behind an SOA platform, there are still architectural issues to be considered.

Enter this book. It is about technologies and practices related to designing and governing Web service contracts in support of SOA and service-orientation. Written by experts who have themselves contributed to the creation and development of the WS-* specifications, this book provides guidance to demonstrate how the most relevant Web service contract technologies work together as a framework—insight that all too often gets left behind on the cutting room floor after countless conference calls and face-to-face meetings among working groups, technical committees, task forces, and sub-committees. The book further helps the reader to understand how the WS-* technologies can be best leveraged and evolved in support of SOA and service-orientation.

This book provides the reader with common understanding across a broad range of WS-* technologies as they pertain to service contracts, service versioning, policy management, and SOA governance in order to enable the reader to leverage the full capabilities that are part of modern WS-* platforms. Issues such as the pros and cons and proper use of the many standardized interoperable message exchange patterns are explored, as well as how to take full advantage of WS-Addressing. In addition, this book provides in-depth discussion on governance issues, particularly as it pertains to service contract design, service versioning, and service policy. Insight and guidance is provided on when and how to design WSDL operations that are intelligently combined with XML Schema and WS-Policy statements to produce service contracts that are conducive to effective versioning.

We hope you enjoy this body of work. Your SOA projects are likely already under way or are about to begin. You are building new architectures for your organization that are going to be in place for decades to come. Many years of hard work have gone into the WS-* set of specifications, and this book will help you to reap the benefits of that work to create truly loosely-coupled and flexible service contracts that will mitigate the impact of change on your organization.

—*David A. Chappell, Technologist and author of several books and papers on interoperability,*
   SOA, and Enterprise Service Bus

Preface

After we completed this manuscript, I checked the schedule and noticed our original start date. From the initial kick-off call during which everyone was given the green light to begin writing their chapters to the day I had to hand over the manuscript to Prentice Hall for indexing spanned a period of about 32 months. I initially didn't think too much of it because I already knew this project had taken over two years. But when I looked at that number again sometime later, it struck me.

The time it has taken for this book to be developed and authored is actually comparable to the time it originally took for several of the XML and Web services-based technology specifications covered in this book to be developed into fully ratified standards.

Though a curious statistic, this comparison doesn't do the subject matter justice. The development processes these technology standards were subject to are on entirely different levels, in that they were vastly complex both from human and technology perspectives.

There's the human element that emerges in the technical committee that is tasked with the responsibility of producing a standard. Such a committee will be comprised of members with different agendas, different perceptions, and different personalities. So many differences can turn a standards development process into a rollercoaster of group dynamics, ranging from strong teamwork to stages of scrutiny, confrontation, and even raw tension. Trying to achieve a consensus in an active technical committee is not for the weak at heart.

And then there's the technology element, which is reflected in the deliverables produced by the committee. Technical specifications are meticulously crafted and worded and revised and reworded in continuous, patient, and sometimes mind-numbingly tedious cycles. But despite best efforts, creating a new language or vocabulary that will meet the ever-escalating needs and expectations of the industry as a whole is a daunting prospect. Not to mention that there is a constant possibility that the particular standard a committee might have spent a good part of their lives working on will be overshadowed by a competing effort or perhaps even rejected by the industry altogether.

But amidst these challenges, there have been many success stories. In a way, this book is a testament of this in that it documents a collection of respected and widely-recognized de facto standards that have established themselves as important IT milestones.

Ultimately, though, this book is about you, the reader. It was written for you to fully leverage what these technology standards have to offer. As successful as these technologies have been, what counts in the end is how effective they are for you.

—*Thomas Erl*

Acknowledgments

Special thanks to the following reviewers that generously volunteered their time and expertise (in alphabetical order):

Michael Bechauf

David Booth

Glen Daniels

Kevin P. Davis

Paul Downey

Florent Georges

Martin Gudgin

Bob Hathaway

Sascha Kuhlmann

Martin Little

Arthur Ryman

Linda Terlouw

Chapter 1

Introduction

1.1 About this Book

The notion of a contract is something most of us are very familiar with. It's an agreement between two parties on a set of terms usually to govern the exchange of something. Without contracts, the world (especially the business world) could not operate the way it does today. Each contract that two parties adhere to guarantees that an exchange is carried out predictably, as expected.

It is this type of predictability that we are very interested in when establishing contracts within technical environments. When we design two software programs to exchange information, we want to ensure that both follow the terms established by the technical contract every time. In fact, this makes predictability not just a preference but a requirement for software design.

But it's not just the terms of exchange that we want to have documented in some form; we also need to establish the interface used to carry out the exchange. As with contracts, interfaces are also part of everyday life.

A remote control, an automobile dashboard, a calculator, a computer keyboard—each of these items represents an interface into something. They are interfaces designed to be used by humans to issue commands into a machine or a device. As such, they establish a pre-defined, standardized means of issuing these commands.

They also represent and express the contract that we must comply to in order to get what we want from whatever it is we are interfacing with. If you don't press the right buttons on the remote control, you won't get to view what you're looking for. Similarly, if you don't turn the steering wheel in the right direction, the car won't go where you want it to.

Interfaces and the contracts they express are essential to just about everything we need to do in order to function in society. They are just as fundamental to software program design in the service-oriented computing world. Whereas older systems may have been designed as self-contained, monolithic programs with no need to expose technical interfaces, service-oriented solutions are naturally partitioned into sets of software programs (called "services") that must interface with each other.

But, there's more to it than that. When applying service-orientation to design software programs as services, most service contracts will need to facilitate interaction with not just one, but a range of potential programs. To realistically enable this level of flexibility within a technical interface means that its design will demand extra attention and care.

Requirements like this are nothing new. The aforementioned remote control and automobile dashboard are almost always built to accommodate numerous types of human users. The better designed these interfaces are, the more people will be able to use them effectively, and the more consistent and predictable the usage experience will be.

When building Web services for SOA, this is exactly what we need to accomplish. The services must have balanced, effective technical contracts that will allow numerous programs to use (and reuse) the functionality the services have to offer.

But, there's still more to it than that. Delivering a well-designed service contract is the first major step in a service lifecycle that can easily span years. During that period, change is inevitable. Although common SOA methodologies will help produce service contracts with increased longevity, their lifespans are, more often than not, limited.

We therefore need to be prepared for this eventuality by having solid governance practices in place that can help evolve a service through times of change. This will extend the lifespan of the service itself beyond the lifespans of its contracts.

This book is exclusively focused on the design and evolution of Web service contracts. The upcoming chapters have been authored by some of the top experts in the fields of SOA, Web service technologies, service contract design, and service versioning and governance.

1.2 Objectives of this Book

Collectively, these chapters were written with the following primary goals in mind:

- to document Web service contract-related technologies within the context of SOA

- to highlight proven contract-related techniques and patterns for contract design and versioning

- to demonstrate how first-generation Web service technologies (WSDL, SOAP, XML Schema) work together with WS-* technologies, such as WS-Addressing and WS-Policy

- to highlight how the application of various Web service technologies can be influenced by SOA design principles and patterns

1.3 Who this Book is For

This book can be used as a tutorial and a reference text and is intended for the following types of readers:

- developers who want to learn how to work with Web service technologies as part of SOA projects

- architects who want to learn how to design Web service contracts in support of SOA projects

- governance specialists who want to learn proven practices for service contract versioning

- SOA practitioners who want to better understand how to build Web service contracts in support of service-orientation

- IT professionals who want to gain a better insight into the concepts and mechanics that underlie modern Web service contracts and messages

1.4 What this Book Does Not Cover

This is a book about Web service contracts only. It explores a wide range of technologies and techniques that pertain to the development, design, and versioning of Web service contracts and related message design topics. However, this book does not get into the development or implementation of Web service programs. Therefore, wire-level topics, such as reliable messaging, security, and transactions, are not covered.

Similarly, while the overarching context of this book is SOA, there is only one chapter dedicated to explaining fundamental terms and concepts. If you are new to SOA, be sure to read the resources recommended in the following *Prerequisite Reading* section.

1.5 Prerequisite Reading

This book assumes you have a basic knowledge of fundamental XML concepts. If you have not yet worked with XML, you can begin catching up by reading some of the brief tutorials published at www.xmlenterprise.com.

If you are new to SOA, you can get a basic understanding of service-oriented computing, service-orientation, and related design patterns by studying the content at the following Web sites:

- www.whatissoa.com

- www.soaprinciples.com

- www.soapatterns.org

To further ensure that you have a clear understanding of key terms used and referenced in the upcoming chapters, you can also visit the online master glossary for this book series at www.soaglossary.com to look up definitions for terms that may not be fully described in this book.

Even if you are an experienced SOA practitioner, we suggest you take the time to have a look at these online resources. A great deal of ambiguity has surrounded SOA and service-oriented computing and these explanations and definitions will ensure that you fully understand key terms and concepts in relation to this book and the book series as a whole.

1.6 Supplementary Reading

Here are some recommendations for additional books that elaborate on key topics covered by this title:

- *SOA Principles of Service Design* – A comprehensive documentation of the service-orientation design paradigm with full descriptions of all of the principles referenced in this book.

- *SOA Design Patterns* – This book provides a comprehensive catalog of design patterns, many of which are specific to Web service contract design and versioning. You can look up concise descriptions for these patterns at www.soapatterns.org.

- *Definitive XML Schema* – This classic title provides complete coverage of the XML Schema language, including several advanced topics outside of the scope of the upcoming chapters dedicated to XML Schema-based message design.

- *Service-Oriented Architecture: Concepts, Technology, and Design* – The coverage of service-oriented analysis and design processes in this title supplements the technology-centric focus of this book with methodology-related topics.

The following titles are currently in development as part of the *Prentice Hall Service-Oriented Computing Series from Thomas Erl*:

- *SOA with .NET* – A book dedicated to building services and service-oriented solutions with .NET development tools and technologies, with an emphasis on Web services and REST services.

- *SOA with Java* – As with the previously listed title, this book is about developing service-oriented solutions with Web services and REST services, except the focus is on the use of Java technologies and platforms.

- *SOA Governance* – This book will explore a wide range of organizational and technological governance topics, including Web service contract versioning and evolution.

- *ESB Architecture for SOA* – Several of the policy-related topics covered in the upcoming chapters will be further explored in relation to ESB architectures in this title.

For the latest information regarding the release of these new books, visit www.soabooks.com.

1.7 How this Book is Organized

This book begins with Chapters 1 and 2 providing introductory content and case study background information, respectively. All subsequent chapters are grouped into the following parts:

- Part I: Fundamental Service Contract Design

- Part II: Advanced Service Contract Design

- Part III: Service Contract Versioning

- Part IV: Appendices

Part I: Fundamental Service Contract Design

Chapter 3: SOA Fundamentals and Web Service Contracts

We begin with an overview of key terms and concepts associated with SOA, service-orientation, and service-oriented computing in general as they pertain to Web service contract design.

Chapter 4: Anatomy of a Web Service Contract

This introductory chapter provides a visual exploration of Web service contract structures from both logical and physical perspectives. The focus is on establishing a conceptual understanding of the various parts that can comprise a Web service contract and the mechanics that make these parts work together.

Concepts pertaining to abstract and concrete descriptions are discussed in relation to message, operation, and port type (interface) definitions, along with different message parts, such as the body, header, and headerfault. Also covered are the binding, service, and port (endpoint) sections and how they relate to message parts (body, header, headerfault), envelope structure, and each other.

This chapter contains no code examples and only begins discussing the actual technologies used to build Web service contracts after the basics have been covered in abstract. The final section concludes the chapter with a series of guidelines.

Chapter 5: A Plain English Guide to Namespaces

As an integral part of the XML-based Web services framework, both custom and predefined namespaces are used to ensure that all of the technologies covered in this book can harmoniously work together. Therefore, before we get into the actual technology languages used to build Web service contracts, we first provide an informal but in-depth tutorial about namespaces.

Because the topic of namespaces represents a common point of confusion for many IT professionals, this chapter takes extra time to explain the concepts and applications of namespaces in plain English. A range of examples and perspectives are provided so that you are fully prepared for any namespace-related issues discussed in subsequent chapters.

Chapter 6: Fundamental XML Schema: Types and Message Structure Basics

We now begin to get into the details of contract design with a chapter dedicated to describing basic XML Schema topics, as they pertain to message design for Web service contracts. The emphasis is on different types of constraints for complex and simple types. Also provided is coverage of how XML Schema types can be customized and extended using type inheritance features.

This chapter also officially kicks off the case study by introducing a set of problems that are solved via the application of XML Schema features. The examples explored ultimately lead to the creation of a set of XML Schema types that will be used by message definitions in the following chapters.

Chapter 7: Fundamental WSDL Part I: Abstract Description Design

In this chapter we discuss all aspects of the Web Services Description Language (WSDL) 1.1 that relate to designing and building the parts that comprise the abstract service description. This includes the association of XML Schema types with message definitions, the organization of messages into operation definitions, and the grouping of operations within port type definitions. Also covered is the creation of message headers and the usage of the various namespaces required for different technologies to co-exist within a WSDL document.

Through a series of informal case study examples a complete abstract description is created, incorporating the XML Schema types that were defined in Chapter 6.

Chapter 8: Fundamental WSDL Part II: Concrete Description Design

We now move on to the design and development of the concrete description, the part of the WSDL document that binds the abstract description to actual transport and messaging protocols and also assigns it one or more physical network addresses.

This chapter covers all of the primary WSDL 1.1 language elements used to establish this binding, including the service and port definitions, as well as the important binding construct itself. A great deal of content is dedicated to exploring how these native WSDL elements are further supplemented via the use of extensibility elements from other languages, such as SOAP. How header and headerfault message parts are bound to actual SOAP message areas is also described.

The case study examples continue and culminate in the creation of a complete WSDL definition that includes both the abstract and concrete descriptions.

Chapter 9: Fundamental WSDL 2.0: New Features and Design Options

This book also covers the WSDL 2.0 standard, which introduces new features and imposes a series of syntactical changes to the WSDL 1.1 language. Through a series of examples, this chapter documents the differences between WSDL 1.1 and 2.0 as they pertain to both abstract and concrete descriptions, and then concludes with a complete WSDL 2.0 version of the WSDL document from Chapter 8.

Chapter 10: Fundamental WS-Policy: Expression, Assertion, and Attachment

Through the creation of policy assertions and policy expressions, the WS-Policy language provides various means of extending the technical interface that you can create with WSDL and XML Schema.

This chapter introduces the basics of how policies can be defined and expressed and then associated (attached) to different parts of a WSDL document. Topics include policy subjects, policy alternatives, composite policies, and embedded and external attachment options.

The examples again lead to a revised WSDL definition that includes a simple, attached policy expression.

Chapter 11: Fundamental Message Design: SOAP Envelope Structure and Header Block Processing

We now turn our attention to the SOAP technology language that is used to express the structure of messages as they exist "on the wire," when they are transmitted to and from Web services. Although this book is dedicated to the Web service contract only, it is important to understand how messages will be processed in order for us to design them effectively.

A primary topic in this chapter is the runtime usage of SOAP header blocks and the various roles and options that exist to carry out "targeted processing" where header blocks are designed to be accessed and used only by certain programs along a message path.

Note that this chapter does not explain the SOAP communications framework or any other topics that do not pertain directly to Web service contract design.

Part II: Advanced Service Contract Design

Chapter 12: Advanced XML Schema Part I: Message Flexibility and Type Inheritance and Composition

There are a variety of messages that a Web service will need to exchange, each with its own unique requirements. This, the first of two chapters dedicated to advanced XML Schema topics, explores the usage of wildcards, extension buckets, and content model groups and documents a variety of techniques that use these XML Schema features to accommodate different types of Web service message designs.

The chapter then continues with an explanation of type inheritance and composition and further discusses how cross-schema inheritance, as a concept, may have different implications than cross-service inheritance. Specifically, this part of the chapter provides examples that detail how abstract schemas can be created and how schemas in general can be extended.

Finally, a discussion of message design in support of CRUD-style Web service operations is provided. Individual Add, Get, Delete, and Update message designs are described, along with common granularity levels.

Chapter 13: Advanced XML Schema Part II: Reusability, Derived Types, Relational Design

The ability to share schemas across Web services is fundamental to establishing separate schema and contract architecture layers. This chapter delves into the various options by which schemas can be partitioned into reusable modules and then included or imported by different schemas (and, ultimately, different WSDL definitions). The creation of a common schema library is furthermore discussed and demonstrated.

Next are sections dedicated to explaining how relational data structures can be simulated using XML Schema features and also how narrative content can be added to supplement base schema content. Finally, the usage and incorporation of pre-defined industry schemas is explored along with several examples and techniques.

Chapter 14: Advanced WSDL Part I: Modularization, Extensibility, MEPs, and Asynchrony

Both WSDL 1.1 and 2.0 modularization features and techniques are covered and demonstrated in this chapter, along with issues pertaining to non-transitive limitations that also relate the reuse of XML Schema definitions across WSDL definitions. The use of WSDL import and include are compared, along with WSDL 2.0 interface inheritance design options.

This is followed by a comprehensive exploration of various WSDL extensibility elements and how they can be used and positioned within the WSDL definition structure, with an emphasis on the WSDL binding construct.

Subsequent sections discuss special message exchange patterns (including WSDL 1.1 outbound MEPs and the WSDL 2.0 Robust In-Only MEP) and various advanced techniques for asynchronous message exchanges involving HTTP, SOAP, and SMTP. Finally, a section dedicated to WS-BPEL related extensibility elements is provided along with recommendations as to how to best prepare WSDL definitions for eventual composition by WS-BPEL process definitions.

Chapter 15: Advanced WSDL Part II: Message Dispatch, Service Instance Identification, and Non-SOAP HTTP Binding

Various advanced WSDL techniques are explored in this chapter, including the use of new WSDL 2.0 features that allow for broad message coupling. A section dedicated to message dispatch design issues is also provided, along with guidelines as to how to leverage the SOAP Action value to support interpretation of WSDL definitions for dispatch purposes.

Additional topics include different approaches for Web service instance identification and creating header blocks, including the use of the header fault extension. Finally, the binding of WSDL to HTTP without SOAP is explored and demonstrated for both WSDL 1.1 and 2.0.

Chapter 16: Advanced WS-Policy Part I: Policy Centralization and Nested, Parameterized, and Ignorable Assertions

Continuing the coverage of the WS-Policy framework that began in Chapter 10, we now delve into various architectural issues, including the application of the Policy Centralization design pattern and different potential approaches for associating separate policy definition documents with WSDL definitions.

Subsequent parts of this chapter demonstrate the use of nested and parameterized policy expressions and then provide detailed coverage of ignorable policy assertions, including a comparison with optional policy assertions. The chapter concludes with an overview of concurrent policy-enabled Web service contracts.

Chapter 17: Advanced WS-Policy Part II: Custom Policy Assertion Design, Runtime Representation, and Compatibility

This chapter describes the design process and implications behind creating custom policy assertions. Various examples demonstrate different types of assertions and the pros and cons of customizing policies are further explained. A separate section is provided, dedicated to issues pertaining to the maintenance of custom policy assertion vocabularies.

Later in the chapter, the runtime representation or policy syntax is explored to provide insight as to how policy expressions and alternatives are streamlined into normalized representations. Finally, an intersection algorithm is explained to identify compatibility between service provider and consumer policies.

Chapter 18: Advanced Message Design Part I: WS-Addressing Vocabularies

WS-Addressing provides an industry-standard means of extending the base SOAP message design to accommodate a wide range of complex message exchange requirements.

This chapter formally introduces the WS-Addressing standard by individually describing the language elements and SOAP headers established by the Endpoint References (EPR) and Message Addressing Properties (MAP) vocabularies. The chapter provides numerous code samples and concludes with a case study example comprised of a complete set of WS-Addressing headers.

Chapter 19: Advanced Message Design Part II: WS-Addressing Rules and Design Techniques

Various, more specialized topics in relation to WS-Addressing are covered in this chapter, including EPR parameter mapping techniques, design issues relating to the binding of Endpoint References with WSDL definitions, and a detailed comparison of WS-Addressing Action values to alternative SOAP Action expressions. The chapter concludes with descriptions of policy assertions provided and standardized by the WS-Addressing specification.

Part III: Service Contract Versioning

Chapter 20: Versioning Fundamentals

Basic concepts and terminology associated with Web service contract versioning are established in this chapter, together with a detailed explanation of forward and backward compatibility from both technical and governance perspectives.

Version identification is then described and demonstrated through the use of annotated version numbers and namespace values. The chapter ends with sections that describe three primary versioning strategies (Strict, Flexible, Loose) that each support forward and backward compatibility to different extents. These strategies will be used for reference purposes throughout subsequent chapters.

Chapter 21: Versioning WSDL Definitions

This chapter explores different techniques for versioning different parts of a WSDL definition with an emphasis on the versioning of WSDL operations. Separate sections provide versioning guidance and examples for adding, renaming, and removing operations as well as modifying operation message exchange patterns and associated fault messages.

Also provided are techniques for versioning port type definitions and various parts of the concrete description. The last section describes what parts of the WSDL language can be used to potentially support forward compatibility.

Chapter 22: Versioning Message Schemas

The complex topic of XML Schema-based message versioning is tackled in this chapter, which groups techniques as per the three versioning strategies established in Chapter 20. Versioning approaches to adding, removing, renaming, and modifying existing XML Schema components are documented separately in relation to each versioning strategy.

Throughout these sections various XML Schema language features are explored, including the use of wildcards for forward compatibility and optional elements to accommodate backward compatibility. Another primary topic addressed throughout this chapter is the use of XML Schema namespaces for versioning purposes.

Chapter 23: Advanced Versioning

This final chapter provides a mixed bag of versioning guidelines, techniques, and design considerations. It starts off with versioning strategies specifically for WS-Policy expressions and assertions, and then continues with design methods that use policy assertions to express termination information and explore the utilization of custom attributes to express non-ignorable unknown elements (when using wildcards).

Various other versioning approaches are covered, several based on actual contract versioning design patterns, such as Partial Understanding. The chapter concludes with a series of tips for creating and customizing your own versioning strategy.

Part IV: Appendices

Appendix A: Case Study Conclusion

This appendix provides a brief summary and conclusion of the case study storyline, as it pertains to the Web service contracts designed within the ActionCon IT enterprise environment.

Appendix B: How Technology Standards are Developed

A concise overview of how the W3C organizes its technical committees is provided, along with descriptions of the processes and stages through which submitted specifications are developed into ratified standards.

Appendix C: Alphabetical Pseudo Schema Reference

Skeleton pseudo Schemas are supplied for all of the language elements explained in this book. These Schemas are listed in alphabetical order for quick reference purposes.

Appendix D: Namespaces and Prefixes Used in this Book

A reference list of the namespaces and associated prefixes used in previous chapters.

Appendix E: SOA Design Patterns Related to this Book

Concise descriptions of each of the design patterns referenced and discused throughout this book. Note that these pattern descriptions are also available online at www.soapatterns.org.

1.8 Symbols, Figures, and Style Conventions

Symbol Legend

This book contains a series of diagrams that are referred to as *figures*. The primary symbols used throughout all figures are individually described in the symbol legend located on the inside of the front cover.

How Color is Used

The color red is occasionally used to highlight text, especially within code samples. Generally, the highlighted code will be related to the current topic being discussed.

Summary of Key Points

Most primary sections in this book end with a concise summary of key topics presented in bullet form. Some of the smaller or more self-explanatory sections do not contain this additional summary.

1.9 Additional Information

The following sections provide supplementary information and resources for the *Prentice Hall Service-Oriented Computing Series from Thomas Erl.*

Official Book Series Site (www.soabooks.com)

The latest details about all books in this series and various supporting resources can be found at soabooks.com. Be sure to also check for updates, errata, and resources, such as supplementary posters.

Visio Stencil (www.soabooks.com)

Prentice Hall has produced a Visio stencil containing the color symbols used by the books in this series. This stencil can be downloaded at www.soabooks.com.

Community Patterns Site (www.soapatterns.org)

All of the pattern profile summary tables documented in this book are also published online at soapatterns.org, as part of an open site for the SOA community dedicated to SOA design patterns. This site allows you to provide feedback regarding any of the design patterns and to further submit your own pattern candidates.

Master Glossary (www.soaglossary.com)

To ensure constant content currency, a dedicated Web site at soaglossary.com provides a master online glossary for all series titles. This site continues to grow and expand with new glossary definitions as new series titles are developed and released.

Referenced Specifications (www.soaspecs.com)

The chapters throughout this book reference XML and Web services specifications and standards. The www.soaspecs.com Web site provides a central portal to the original specification documents created and maintained by the primary standards organizations.

Supplementary Posters (www.soaposters.com)

Color reference posters are available for free download at www.soaposters.com. The poster for this book is primarily comprised of the symbols and diagrams in Chapter 4 to provide an overview of how Web service contracts are structured.

The SOA Magazine (www.soamag.com)

The SOA Magazine is a regular publication provided by SOA Systems Inc. and Prentice Hall/PearsonPTR and is officially associated with the *Prentice Hall Service-Oriented Computing Series from Thomas Erl.* The SOA Magazine is dedicated to publishing specialized SOA articles, case studies, and papers by industry experts and professionals. The common criteria for contributions is that each explore a distinct aspect of service-oriented computing.

Referenced Specifications (www.soaspecs.com)

Various series titles reference or provide tutorials and examples of open XML and Web services specifications and standards. The www.soaspecs.com Web site provides a central portal to the original specification documents created and maintained by the primary standards organizations.

Notification Service (www.soabooks.com)

If you'd like to be automatically notified of new book releases in this series, new supplementary content for this title, or key changes to the previously listed Web sites, use the notification form at www.soabooks.com.

Case Study Background

2.1 How Case Study Examples are Used

This book contains numerous code examples and some case study content that relates back to the background information provided in this chapter. Most examples focus on the design of a specific set of Web service contracts, while others explore some inter-organization data exchange scenarios.

In order to more easily identify these examples, a special style element has been incorporated. Any portion of the book (beyond Chapter 2) that provides examples will contain a light gray background.

2.2 Case Study Background: ActionCon

The majority of examples in this book revolve around ActionCon, a relatively new company in the fast-paced world of video games. ActionCon manufactures a game console as well as the games that can be played on the console.

It releases a new model of the game console approximately every two years. There are currently two different models in the market, with the new 3Z console in the final stages of testing. Each game console has a number of features and optional accessories. They are assembled by ActionCon in their plant, mostly from smaller products purchased from other electronics manufacturing companies.

The majority of ActionCon's revenue, however, comes from its games. There are currently 45 games available, and new titles are being developed and released at a rate of approximately one per month. A particular game can only run on one console model and may require one or more of the additional accessories.

ActionCon's products are sold in a variety of retail store chains, as well as on its Web site. Both outlets are crucial to their sales.

History and Culture

ActionCon is only six years old and has experienced astronomical growth during that time. The company has a cowboy, startup culture with a constantly shifting organization chart and marketing message.

The overwhelming priority of ActionCon is to get new games out the door. The game developers are their most important asset, and nothing stands in their way of delivering new products. As a result, ActionCon has a culture where there is little red tape and almost no formal procedures. While this has allowed ActionCon to be nimble and respond to the constantly changing tastes in the video game market, it has also resulted in frequent confusion and disorganization.

Most of the examples in this book revolve around the adventures of Steve, who is both an architect and a developer. Steve is tasked with creating Web service contracts in order to fulfill various requirements. At the same time, he himself must learn about the required technologies and design techniques. For better or for worse, due to the lax nature of the IT culture, Steve has a great deal of freedom that allows him to experiment and investigate various design options and technologies.

Technical Infrastructure

ActionCon's technical infrastructure has expanded rapidly and is somewhat disorganized. Little thought or budget was given to infrastructure initially, and many of the initial information systems were thrown together by the game developers as a side project. Over time, new enhancements and fixes have been cobbled together based on initial systems that were not designed for change.

ActionCon's information systems fall into three major areas: game information, accounting and shipping, and inventory. The game information system consists of a small MySQL database with marketing and technical information about the games they sell. The main use for the game information database is to generate content for the Web site.

ActionCon's accounting system is also custom-developed. As the case study examples in upcoming chapters will explain, there will soon be a need for this system to facilitate the receipt of online purchase order documents from larger clients.

Business Goals and Obstacles

ActionCon has found themselves unexpectedly with a huge base of customers who are hungry for information about new products and games to which they want immediate access. It's critical to keep this clientele happy because they can be very fickle. ActionCon also wants to explore additional channels for expanding their customer base. Because the vast majority of their marketing is by word of mouth, they want to make it easier for people to share game information with others and have it distributed more widely over the Web.

It's equally important for ActionCon to keep their retailers satisfied. As with the online customers, retailers want up-to-the minute information about new games and marketing promotions. In addition, the larger retailers want robust automated systems for online ordering and payment. Some of the later case study examples explore design issues that arise when ActionCon attempts to establish a B2B relationship with one such large retailer called MegaEuroMart.

Part I

Fundamental Service Contract Design

As we established in Chapter 1, this is not a book about SOA, nor is it a book about Web services. Several books have been published over the past few years that address these topics individually. What we are focused on is the design and versioning of Web service contracts in support of service-oriented solution design. What this requires us to do is explore the marriage of Web service contract technologies with the service-orientation design paradigm and the service-oriented architectural model.

Chapter 3

SOA Fundamentals
and Web Service Contracts

As we established in Chapter 1, this is not a book about SOA, nor is it a book about Web services. Several books have been published over the past few years that address these topics individually. What we are focused on is the design and versioning of Web service contracts in support of service-oriented solution design. What this requires us to do is explore the marriage of Web service contract technologies with the service-orientation design paradigm and the service-oriented architectural model.

As a starting point, we first need to establish some fundamental terms and concepts associated with service-oriented computing and with an emphasis of how these terms and concepts relate to Web service contracts.

3.1 Basic SOA Terminology

This section borrows some content from SOAGlossary.com to provide the following term definitions:

- Service-Oriented Computing
- Service-Orientation
- Service-Oriented Architecture (SOA)
- Service
- Service Models
- Service Composition
- Service Inventory
- Service-Oriented Analysis
- Service Candidate
- Service-Oriented Design
- Web Service
- Service Contract
- Service-Related Granularity

If you are already an experienced SOA professional, then you might want to just skim through this part of the book. The defined terms are used here and there throughout subsequent chapters.

Service-Oriented Computing

Service-oriented computing is an umbrella term that represents a new generation distributed computing platform. As such, it encompasses many things, including its own design paradigm and design principles, design pattern catalogs, pattern languages, a distinct architectural model, and related concepts, technologies, and frameworks.

Service-oriented computing builds upon past distributed computing platforms and adds new design layers, governance considerations, and a vast set of preferred implementation technologies, many of which are based on the Web services framework.

In this book we refer primarily to the strategic goals of service-oriented computing as they tie into approaches for Web service contract design and versioning. These goals are briefly described in the *Service-Oriented Computing Goals and Web Service Contracts* section.

Service-Orientation

Service-orientation is a design paradigm intended for the creation of solution logic units that are individually shaped so that they can be collectively and repeatedly utilized in support of the realization of the specific strategic goals and benefits associated with SOA and service-oriented computing.

Solution logic designed in accordance with service-orientation can be qualified with "service-oriented," and units of service-oriented solution logic are referred to as "services." As a design paradigm for distributed computing, service-orientation can be compared to object-orientation (or object-oriented design). Service-orientation, in fact, has many roots in object-orientation and has also been influenced by other industry developments, including EAI, BPM, and Web services.

The service-orientation design paradigm is primarily comprised of eight specific design principles, as explained in the *Service-Orientation and Web Service Contracts* section. Several of these principles can affect the design of Web service contracts.

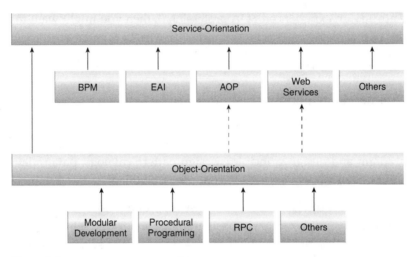

Figure 3.1

Service-orientation is an evolutionary design paradigm that owes much of its existence to established design practices and technology platforms.

Service-Oriented Architecture (SOA)

Service-oriented architecture represents an architectural model that aims to enhance the agility and cost-effectiveness of an enterprise while reducing the overall burden of IT on an organization. It accomplishes this by positioning services as the primary means through which solution logic is represented. SOA supports service-orientation in the realization of the strategic goals associated with service-oriented computing.

As a form of technology architecture, an SOA implementation can consist of a combination of technologies, products, APIs, supporting infrastructure extensions, and various other parts. The actual complexion of a deployed service-oriented architecture is unique within each enterprise; however it is typified by the introduction of new technologies and platforms that specifically support the creation, execution, and evolution of service-oriented solutions. As a result, building a technology architecture around the service-oriented architectural model establishes an environment suitable for solution logic that has been designed in compliance with service-orientation design principles.

NOTE

Historically, the term "service-oriented architecture" (or "SOA") has been used so broadly by the media and within vendor marketing literature that it has almost become synonymous with service-oriented computing itself.

Note that the following service-oriented architecture types exist:

- Service Architecture

- Service Composition Architecture

- Service Inventory Architecture

- Service-Oriented Enterprise Architecture

As you may have guessed, we are primarily focused on the service architecture in this book. However, the decisions we make regarding the design of Web service contracts will ultimately affect the quality of related composition and inventory architectures.

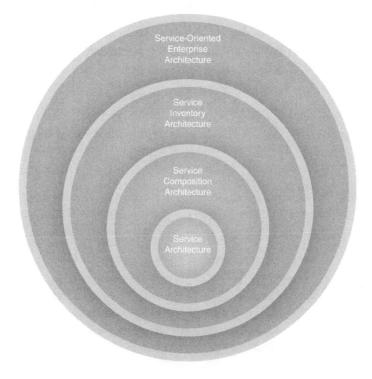

Figure 3.2

The layered SOA model that reveals how service-oriented architecture types can encompass each other. (These different architectural types are explained in Chapter 4 of the book *SOA Design Patterns.*)

Service

A *service* is a unit of solution logic to which service-orientation has been applied to a meaningful extent. It is the application of service-orientation design principles that distinguishes a unit of logic as a service compared to units of logic that may exist solely as objects or components.

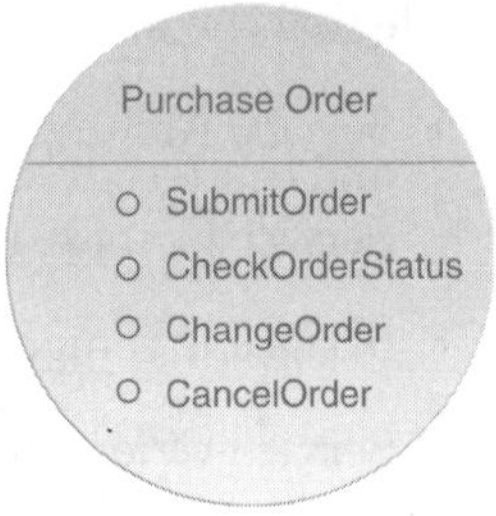

Subsequent to conceptual service modeling, service-oriented design and development stages implement a service as a physically independent software program with specific design characteristics that support the attainment of the strategic goals associated with service-oriented computing.

Purchase Order

○ SubmitOrder
○ CheckOrderStatus
○ ChangeOrder
○ CancelOrder

Figure 3.3

The chorded circle symbol is used to represent a service, primarily from a contract perspective.

Each service is assigned its own distinct functional context and is comprised of a set of capabilities related to this context. Therefore, a service can be considered a container of capabilities associated with a common purpose (or functional context). Capabilities are expressed in the service contract (defined shortly).

As we established earlier, this book is dedicated to the design of technical contracts for services built as Web services. Within a Web service contract, service capabilities are referred to as service *operations*.

Service Models

A *service model* is a classification used to indicate that a service belongs to one of several predefined types based on the nature of the logic it encapsulates, the reuse potential of this logic, and how the service may relate to domains within its enterprise.

The following three service models are common to most enterprise environments and therefore common to most SOA projects:

- *Task Service* – A service with a non-agnostic functional context that generally corresponds to single-purpose, parent business process logic. A task service will usually encapsulate the composition logic required to compose several other services in order to complete its task.

- *Entity Service* – A reusable service with an agnostic functional context associated with one or more related business entities (such as invoice, customer, claim, etc.). For example, a Purchase Order service has a functional context associated with the processing of purchase order-related data and logic. Chapter 13 has a section dedicated to Web service contract design for entity services.

- *Utility Service* – Also a reusable service with an agnostic functional context, but this type of service is intentionally not derived from business analysis specifications and models. It encapsulates low-level technology-centric functions, such as notification, logging, and security processing.

Service models play an important role during service-oriented analysis and service-oriented design phases. Although the just listed service models are well established, it is not uncommon for an organization to create its own service models. Often these new classifications tend to be derived from one of the aforementioned fundamental service models.

> **NOTE**
>
> Most of the service contract examples in this book are for entity services that are required to deal with core business-related processing and the exchange of business documents.

Agnostic Logic and Non-Agnostic Logic

The term "agnostic" originated from Greek and means "without knowledge." Therefore, logic that is sufficiently generic so that it is not specific to (has no knowledge of) a particular parent task is classified as *agnostic* logic. Because knowledge specific to single purpose tasks is intentionally omitted, agnostic logic is considered multi-purpose. On the flipside, logic that is specific to (contains knowledge of) a single-purpose task is labeled as *non-agnostic* logic.

Another way of thinking about agnostic and non-agnostic logic is to focus on the extent to which the logic can be repurposed. Because agnostic logic is expected to be multi-purpose, it is subject to the Service Reusability principle with the intention of turning it into highly reusable logic. Once reusable, this logic is truly multi-purpose in that it, as a single software program (or service), can be used to automate multiple business processes.

Non-agnostic logic does not have these types of expectations. It is deliberately designed as a single-purpose software program (or service) and therefore has different characteristics and requirements.

Service Composition

A *service composition* is an aggregate of services collectively composed to automate a particular task or business process. To qualify as a composition, at least two participating services plus one composition initiator need to be present. Otherwise, the service interaction only represents a point-to-point exchange.

Service compositions can be classified into primitive and complex variations. In early service-oriented solutions, simple logic was generally implemented via point-to-point exchanges or primitive compositions. As the surrounding technology matured, complex compositions became more common.

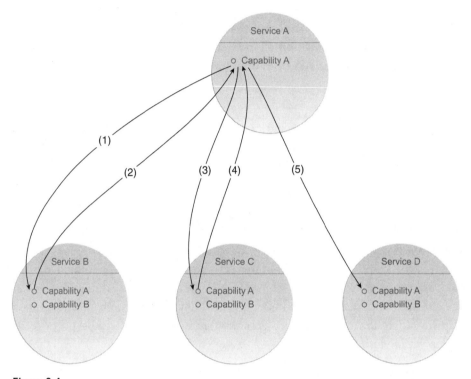

Figure 3.4

A service composition comprised of four services. The arrows indicate a sequence of modeled message exchanges. Note arrow #5 representing a one-way, asynchronous data delivery from Service A to Service D.

Much of the service-orientation design paradigm revolves around preparing services for effective participation in numerous complex compositions—so much so that the Service Composability design principle exists, dedicated solely to ensuring that services are designed in support of repeatable composition.

How service contracts are designed will influence the effectiveness and complexity potential of service compositions. Various contract-related granularity levels will determine the quantity of runtime processing and data exchange required—qualities that can end up hindering or enabling composition performance. Furthermore, techniques, such as those provided by the Contract Denormalization and Concurrent Contracts patterns, can help optimize composition designs. (These design patterns are briefly explained at the end of this chapter in the *SOA Design Patterns and Web Service Contracts* section.)

Service Inventory

A *service inventory* is an independently standardized and governed collection of complementary services within a boundary that represents an enterprise or a meaningful segment of an enterprise. When an organization has multiple service inventories, this term is further qualified as *domain service inventory*.

Service inventories are typically created through top-down delivery processes that result in the definition of *service inventory blueprints*. The subsequent application of service-orientation design principles and custom design standards throughout a service inventory is of paramount importance so as to establish a high degree of native inter-service interoperability. This supports the repeated creation of effective service compositions in response to new and changing business requirements.

It is worth noting that the application of the Standardized Service Contract principle is intended to be limited to the boundary of a service inventory, as are design standards-related patterns, such as Canonical Transport and Canonical Schema.

Service-Oriented Analysis

Service-oriented analysis represents one of the early stages in an SOA initiative and the first phase in the service delivery cycle. It is a process that begins with preparatory information gathering steps that are completed in support of a service modeling sub-process that results in the creation of conceptual service candidates, service capability candidates, and service composition candidates.

The service-oriented analysis process is commonly carried out iteratively, once for each business process. Typically, the delivery of a service inventory determines a scope that represents a meaningful domain or the enterprise as a whole. All iterations of a service-oriented analysis then pertain to that scope, with an end-result of a service inventory blueprint.

NOTE

Visit SOAMethodology.com for an explanation of the iterative service-oriented analysis process.

A key success factor of the service-oriented analysis process is the hands-on collaboration of both business analysts and technology architects. The former group is especially involved in the definition of service candidates with a business-centric functional context because they understand the business processes used as input for the analysis and because service-orientation aims to align business and IT more closely.

Service Candidate

When conceptualizing services during the service modeling sub-process of the service-oriented analysis phase, services are defined on a preliminary basis and still subject to a great deal of change and refinement before they are handed over to the service-oriented design project stage responsible for producing physical service contracts.

The term "service candidate" is used to help distinguish a conceptualized service from an actual implemented service. You'll notice a few references to service candidates in this book, especially in some of the early case study content.

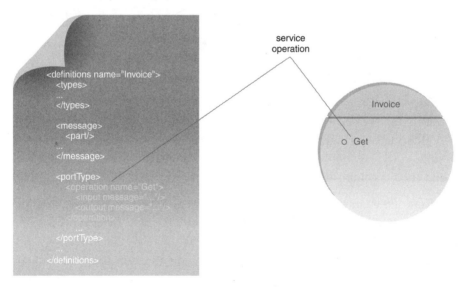

Figure 3.5
The chorded circle symbol (right) provides a simple representation of a service contract during both modeling and design stages. The Get operation (right) is first modeled and then forms the basis of the actual operation definition within a WSDL document (left).

Service-Oriented Design

The *service-oriented design* phase represents a service delivery lifecycle stage dedicated to producing service contracts in support of the well-established "contract-first" approach to software development.

The typical starting point for the service-oriented design process is a service candidate that was produced as a result of completing all required iterations of the service-oriented analysis process. Service-oriented design subjects this service candidate to additional considerations that shape it into a technical service contract in alignment with other service contracts being produced for the same service inventory.

There is a different service-oriented design process for each of the three common service models (task, entity, and utility). The variations in process steps primarily accommodate different priorities and the nature of the logic being expressed by the contract.

This book does not discuss the process of service-oriented design in detail, but there are references to some of the considerations raised by the "contract-first" emphasis of this process.

Web Service

A *Web service* is a body of solution logic that provides a physically decoupled technical contract consisting of a WSDL definition and one or more XML Schema and/or WS-Policy definitions. As we will explore in this book, these documents can exist in one physical file or be spread across multiple files and still be part of one service contract. Spreading them out makes them reusable across multiple contracts.

The Web service contract exposes public capabilities as operations, establishing a technical interface comparable to a traditional application programming interface (API) but without any ties to proprietary communications framework.

The logic encapsulated by a Web service does not need to be customized or component-based. Legacy application logic, for example, can be exposed via Web service contracts through the use of service adapter products. When custom-developed, Web service logic is typically based on modern component technologies, such as Java and .NET. In this case, the components are further qualified as core service logic.

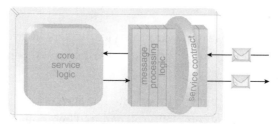

Web service acting as a service provider

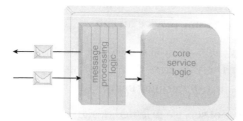

Portions of a Web service acting as a service consumer

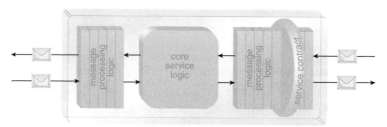

Web service transitioning through service consumer and provider roles

Figure 3.6

Three variations of a single Web service showing the different physical parts of its architecture that come into play, depending on the role it assumes at runtime. Note the cookie-shaped symbol that represents the service contract wedged in between layers of agent-driven message processing logic. This is the same chorded circle symbol shown earlier but from a different perspective.

Service Contract

A *service contract* is comprised of one or more published documents that express meta information about a service. The fundamental part of a service contract consists of the documents that express its technical interface. These form the technical service contract, which essentially establishes an API into the functionality offered by the service via its capabilities.

When services are implemented as Web services, the most common service description documents are the WSDL definition, XML schema definition, and WS-Policy definition. A Web service generally has one WSDL definition, which can link to multiple XML schema and policy definitions. When services are implemented as components, the technical service contract is comprised of a technology-specific API.

A service contract can be further comprised of human-readable documents, such as a Service Level Agreement (SLA) that describes additional quality-of-service features, behaviors, and limitations. As we discuss in the WS-Policy chapters, several SLA-related requirements can also be expressed in machine-readable format as policies.

Figure 3.7

The common documents that comprise the technical Web service contract, plus a human-readable SLA.

Within service-orientation, the design of the service contract is of paramount importance—so much so, that the Standardized Service Contract design principle and the aforementioned service-oriented design process are dedicated solely to the standardized creation of service contracts.

Note that because this book is focused only on technical contracts for Web services, the terms "service contract" and "Web service contract" are used interchangeably.

Service-Related Granularity

When designing services, there are different granularity levels that need to be taken into consideration, as follows:

- *Service Granularity* – Represents the functional scope of a service. For example, fine-grained service granularity indicates that there is little logic associated with the service's overall functional context.

- *Capability Granularity* – The functional scope of individual service capabilities (operations) is represented by this granularity level. For example, a GetDetail capability will tend to have a finer measure of granularity than a GetDocument capability.

- *Constraint Granularity* – The level of validation logic detail is measured by constraint granularity. The more coarse constraint granularity is, the less constraints (or smaller the amount of validation logic) a given capability will have.

- *Data Granularity* – This granularity level represents the quantity of data processed. From a Web service perspective, this corresponds to input, output, and fault messages. A fine level of data granularity is equivalent to a small amount of data.

Because the level of service granularity determines the functional scope of a service, it is usually determined during analysis and modeling stages that precede service contract design. Once a service's functional scope has been established, the other granularity types come into play and affect both the modeling and physical design of a Web service contract.

In this book you will especially notice references to constraint granularity because so much of contract design relates to the definition of validation logic constraints.

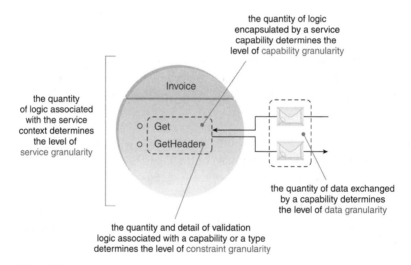

Figure 3.8

The four granularity levels that represent various characteristics of a service and its contract. Note that these granularity types are, for the most part, independent of each other.

Further Reading

As mentioned at the beginning of this section, all of these terms are defined at SOA-Glossary.com. More detailed explanations are available at WhatIsSOA.com and in Chapters 3 and 4 of *SOA: Principles of Service Design*. If you are not familiar with service-oriented computing, it is recommended that you read through these additional descriptions.

3.2 Service-Oriented Computing Goals and Web Service Contracts

It's always good to get an idea of the big picture before diving into the details of any technology-centric topic. For this reason, we'll take the time to briefly mention the overarching goals and benefits associated with service-oriented computing as they relate to Web service contract design.

Because these goals are strategic in nature, they are focused on long-term benefit—a consideration that ties into both the design and governance of services and their contracts. An understanding of these long-term benefits helps provide a strategic context for many of the suggested techniques and practices in this guide.

Here's the basic list of the goals and benefits of service-oriented computing:

- Increased Intrinsic Interoperability
- Increased Federation
- Increased Vendor Diversification Options
- Increased Business and Technology Domain Alignment
- Increased ROI
- Increased Organizational Agility
- Reduced IT Burden

Although it might not be evident, service contract design touches each of these goals to some extent.

Let's explore how.

Increased Intrinsic Interoperability

For services to attain a meaningful level of intrinsic interoperability, their technical contracts must be highly standardized and designed consistently to share common expressions and data models. This fundamental requirement is why project teams often must take control of their Web service contracts instead of allowing them to be auto-generated and derived from different sources.

Increased Federation

Service-oriented computing aims to achieve a federated service endpoint layer. It is the service contracts that are the endpoints in this layer, and it is only through their consistent and standardized design that federation can be achieved. This, again, is a goal that is supported by the ability of a project team to customize and refine Web service contracts so that they establish consistent endpoints within a given service inventory boundary.

Increased Vendor Diversification Options

For a service-oriented architecture to allow on-going vendor diversification, individual services must effectively abstract proprietary characteristics of their underlying vendor technology. The contract remains the only part of a service that is published and available to consumers. It must therefore be deliberately designed to express service capabilities without any vendor-specific details. This extent of abstraction allows service owners to extend or replace vendor technology. Vendor diversification is especially attainable through the use of Web services, due to the fact that they are supported by all primary vendors while providing a non-proprietary communications framework.

Increased Business and Technology Domain Alignment

The service layers that tend to yield the greatest gains for service-oriented environments are those comprised of business-centric services (such as task and entity services). These types of services introduce an opportunity to effectively express various forms of business logic in close alignment with how this logic is modeled and maintained by business analysts.

This expression is accomplished through service contracts and it is considered so important that entire modeling processes and approaches exist to first produce a conceptual version of the service contract prior to its physical design.

Strategic Benefits

The latter three goals listed in the previous bullet list represent strategic benefits that are achieved when attaining the first four goals. We therefore don't need to map the relevance of service contracts to each of them individually.

If we take the time to understand how central service contract design is to the ultimate target state we hope to achieve with service-oriented computing in general, it's clear to see why this book was written.

Further Reading

Formal descriptions for each of these strategic goals are available at WhatIsSOA.com and in Chapter 3 of *SOA: Principles of Service Design*. While it's good to have an understanding of these goals and benefits, it is not required to learn the technologies covered in this book.

3.3 Service-Orientation and Web Service Contracts

To understand SOA is to understand service-orientation, the design paradigm that establishes what is required in order to create software programs that are truly service-oriented.

Service-orientation represents a design approach comprised of eight specific design principles. Service contracts tie into most but not all of these principles. Let's first introduce their official definitions:

- *Standardized Service Contract* – "Services within the same service inventory are in compliance with the same contract design standards."

- *Service Loose Coupling* – "Service contracts impose low consumer coupling requirements and are themselves decoupled from their surrounding environment."

- *Service Abstraction* – "Service contracts only contain essential information and information about services is limited to what is published in service contracts."

- *Service Reusability* – "Services contain and express agnostic logic and can be positioned as reusable enterprise resources."

- *Service Autonomy* – "Services exercise a high level of control over their underlying runtime execution environment."

- *Service Statelessness* – "Services minimize resource consumption by deferring the management of state information when necessary."

- *Service Discoverability* – "Services are supplemented with communicative meta data by which they can be effectively discovered and interpreted."

- *Service Composability* – "Services are effective composition participants, regardless of the size and complexity of the composition."

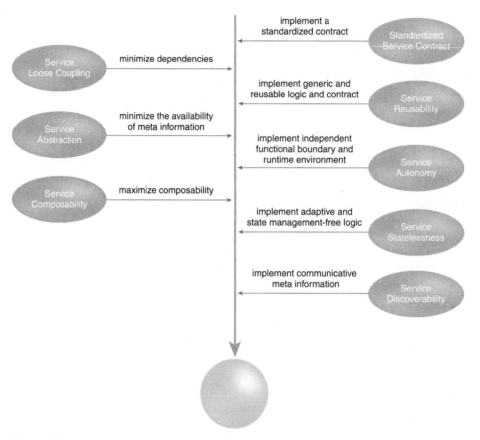

Figure 3.9
How service-orientation design principles can collectively shape service design.

Each of these design principles can, to some extent, influence how we decide to build a Web service contract. With regards to the topics covered in this book, the following principles have a direct impact.

Standardized Service Contract

Given its name, it's quite evident that this design principle is only about service contracts and the requirement for them to be consistently standardized within the boundary of a service inventory. This design principle essentially advocates "contract first" design for services.

Service Loose Coupling

This principle also relates to the service contract. Its design and how it is architecturally positioned within the service architecture are regulated with a strong emphasis on ensuring that only the right type of content makes its way into the contract in order to avoid the negative coupling types.

The following sections briefly describe common types of coupling. All are considered negative coupling types, except for the last.

Contract-to-Functional Coupling

Service contracts can become dependent on outside business processes, especially when they are coupled to logic that was designed directly in support of these processes. This can result in contract-to-functional coupling whereby the contract expresses characteristics that are specifically related to the parent process logic.

Contract-to-Implementation Coupling

When details about a service's underlying implementation are embedded within a service contract, an extent of contract-to-implementation coupling is formed. This negative coupling type commonly results when service contracts are a native part of the service implementation (as with component APIs) or when they are auto-generated and derived from implementation resources, such as legacy APIs, components, and databases.

Contract-to-Logic Coupling

The extent to which a service contract is bound to the underlying service programming logic is referred to as contract-to-logic coupling. This is considered a negative type of service coupling because service consumer programs that bind to the service contract end up also inadvertently forming dependencies on the underlying service logic.

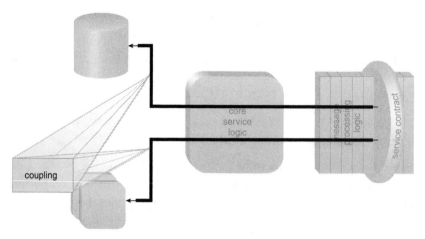

Figure 3.10

A Web service contract can be negatively coupled to various parts of the underlying service implementation.

Contract-to-Technology Coupling

When the contract exposed by a service is bound to non-industry-standard communications technology, it forms an extent of contract-to-technology coupling. Although this coupling type could be applied to the dependencies associated with any proprietary technology, it is used exclusively for communications technology because that is what service contracts are generally concerned with.

An example of contract-to-technology coupling is when the service exists as a distributed component that requires the use of a proprietary RPC technology. Because this book is focused solely on Web service contract technology, this coupling type does not pose a design concern.

Logic-to-Contract Coupling

Each of the previously described forms of coupling are considered negative because they can shorten the lifespan of a Web service contract, thereby leading to increased governance burden as a result of having to manage service contract versions.

This book is focused on providing the skills necessary to achieve high levels of *logic-to-contract* coupling by ensuring that the Web service contract can be designed with complete independence from the underlying Web service implementation.

Figure 3.11

The most desirable design is for the Web service contract to remain an independent and fully decoupled part of the service architecture, thereby requiring the underlying logic to be coupled to it.

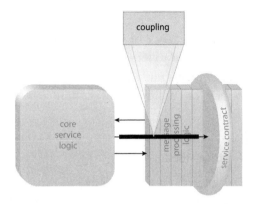

Service Abstraction

By turning services into black boxes, the contracts are all that is officially made available to consumer designers who want to use the services. While much of this principle is about the controlled hiding of information by service owners, it also advocates the streamlining of contract content to ensure that only essential content is made available. The related use of the Validation Abstraction pattern further can affect aspects of contract design, especially related to the constraint granularity of service capabilities.

Service Reusability

While this design principle is certainly focused on ensuring that service logic is designed to be robust and generic and much like a commercial product, these qualities also carry over into contract design. When viewing the service as a product and its contract as a generic API to which potentially many consumer programs will need to interface, the requirement emerges to ensure that the service's functional context, the definition of its capabilities, and the level at which each of its design granularities are set are appropriate for it to be positioned as a reusable enterprise resource.

Service Discoverability

Because the service contracts usually represent all that is made available about a service, they are what this principle is primarily focused on when attempting to make each service as discoverable and interpretable as possible by a range of project team members.

Note that although Web service contracts need to be designed to be discoverable, this book does not discuss discovery processes or registry-based architectures.

Service Composability

This regulatory design principle is very concerned with ensuring that service contracts are designed to represent and enable services to be effective composition participants. The contracts must therefore adhere to the requirements of the previously listed design principles and also take multiple and complex service composition requirements into account.

Further Reading

Design principles are referenced throughout this book but represent a separate subject-matter that is covered in *SOA Principles of Service Design*. Introductory coverage of service-orientation as a whole is also available at SOAPrinciples.com.

3.4 SOA Design Patterns and Web Service Contracts

Design patterns provide proven solutions to common design problems. SOA has matured to an extent where a catalog of design patterns has been established. Of interest to us are those that affect the design and versioning of service contracts, specifically:

- *Canonical Expression* – Service contracts are standardized using naming conventions.

- *Canonical Schema* – Schema data models for common information sets are standardized across service contracts within a service inventory boundary.

- *Canonical Versioning* – Service contracts within the same service inventory are subject to the same versioning rules and conventions.

- *Compatible Change* – Already implemented service contracts are revised without breaking backwards compatibility.

- *Concurrent Contracts* – Multiple contracts can be created for a single service, each targeted at a specific type of consumer.

- *Contract Centralization* – Access to service logic is limited to the service contract, forcing consumers to avoid negative contract-to-implementation coupling.

- *Contract Denormalization* – Service contracts can include a measured extent of denormalization, allowing multiple capabilities to redundantly express core functions in different ways for different types of consumer programs.

- *Decomposed Capability* – Services prone to future decomposition can be equipped with a series of granular capabilities that more easily facilitate decomposition.

- *Decoupled Contract* – The service contract is physically decoupled from its implementation.

- *Distributed Capability* – The underlying service logic is distributed, thereby allowing the implementation logic for a capability with unique processing requirements to be physically separated, while continuing to be represented by the same service contract.

- *Messaging Metadata* – The message contents can be supplemented with activity-specific metadata that can be interpreted and processed separately at runtime.

- *Partial Validation* – Service consumers are designed to validate a subset of the data received from a service.

- *Policy Centralization* – Global or domain-specific policy assertions can be isolated and applied to multiple services.

- *Proxy Capability* – When a service contract needs to be decomposed, the original service contract can be preserved, even if underlying capability logic is separated, by turning the established capability definition into a proxy.

- *Schema Centralization* – Select schemas that exist as physically separate parts of the service contract are shared across multiple contracts.

- *Service Messaging* – Services can be designed to interact via a messaging-based technology, which removes the need for persistent connections and reduces coupling requirements.

- *Termination Notification* – Service contracts are extended to express termination information.

- *Validation Abstraction* – Granular validation logic and rules can be abstracted away from the service contract, thereby decreasing constraint granularity and increasing the contract's potential longevity.

- *Version Identification* – Version numbers and related information is expressed within service contracts.

Web Services and the Decoupled Contract Pattern

It is worth singling out Decoupled Contract at this stage because a Web service contract is essentially an implementation of this pattern. When building services as Web services, service contracts are positioned as physically separate parts of the service architecture. This allows us to fully leverage the technologies covered in this book in order to design and develop these contracts independently from the logic and implementations they will eventually represent.

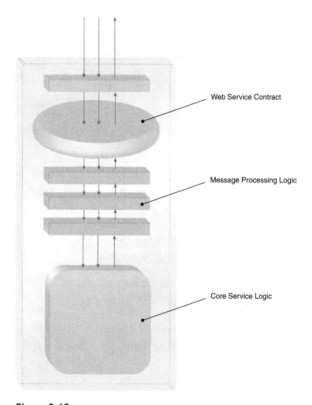

Figure 3.12
The Web service contract is a physically separated part of a Web service implementation.

Therefore, you may not see a lot of references to the Decoupled Contract pattern because it goes without saying that a Web service contract is naturally decoupled. However, it is always important to keep the coupling types explained earlier in the *Service-Orientation and Web Service Contracts* section in mind because although physically decoupled, the content of any Web service contract can still be negatively coupled to various parts of the service environment.

Further Reading

The previously listed design patterns are part of a larger design pattern catalog published in the book *SOA Design Patterns*. Concise descriptions of these patterns are also available at SOAPatterns.org.

Chapter 4

Anatomy of a Web Service Contract

W eb service contracts can range in content, depth, and complexity. To fully appreciate the intricacies and design options of how Web service contracts can be structured, we first need to decompose this structure in order to understand its individual parts and the mechanics that make these parts work together.

The purpose of this chapter is to explain the Web service contract from a conceptual and structural perspective without yet getting into the details of how the contract is actually developed through markup code.

We start exploring contract structure by breaking the contract down into a set of primary parts. This allows us to describe what these parts are, what technologies can be used to create them, and how they can relate to each other. Subsequent chapters will then drill down into each of the mentioned parts and technologies.

4.1 What is a Web Service Contract?

A Web service contract is essentially a collection of metadata that describes various aspects of an underlying software program, including:

- the purpose and function of its operations
- the messages that need to be exchanged in order to engage the operations
- data models used to define the structure of the messages (and associated validation rules used to ensure the integrity of data passed to and from the messages)
- a set of conditions under which the operations are provided
- information about how and where the service can be accessed

Several different and cooperating technologies are required to formally define this metadata, as explained later in the *Technologies Used to Create Web Service Contracts* section.

Fundamental Structure

Web service contracts are organized into a basic structure that reflects a relatively clear separation of "what," "how," and "where" as follows:

- **What** is the purpose of the service and its capabilities?
- **How** can the service be accessed?
- **Where** can the service be accessed?

When potential consumer program designers evaluate a service, they need to know *what* the service is capable of doing and under what conditions it can carry out its capabilities. If what's offered is what consumer designers need, then they must be able to determine *how* and *where* to access the service.

As illustrated in Figure 4.1, the service contract is organized into sections that individually address these three questions.

Figure 4.1

A Web service contract defines what a service offers and how and where it can be accessed.

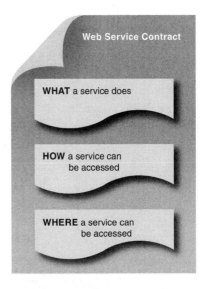

In addition to providing flexibility as to how a service can be located and consumed, this clean separation allows different parts of the contract to be owned and developed at different stages of the service delivery lifecycle by different members of a project team.

For example, architects and analysts can focus solely on the "what" part of a service when it is being conceptualized and designed. The "how" and "where" parts don't usually become relevant until developers actually build and deploy the contract as part of the overall service implementation.

Abstract and Concrete Descriptions

There are formal terms used to represent the three fundamental parts we just covered. As shown in Figure 4.2, the "what" portion of the Web service contract is referred to as the *abstract description*. This part is essentially responsible for expressing the contract's public interface (or API).

The balance of the Web service contract is represented by the *concrete description*, providing the implementation and communication details necessary for consumer programs to locate and use the service at runtime.

The concrete description encompasses the previously described "how" and "where" parts. An example of a characteristic that would be considered a "how" part is the wire format and protocol necessary to exchange messages with the service.

Figure 4.2

An abstract description establishes the technical interface independent of implementation details. A concrete
description adds deployment-specific details about
how and where to access a service.

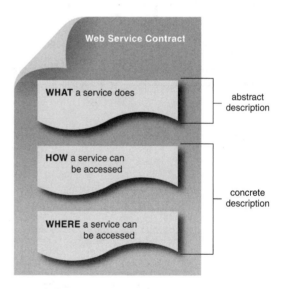

> **NOTE**
>
> The terms "abstract description" and "concrete description" originated
> with the W3C, the standards organization responsible for developing most
> of the technologies covered in this book. From an implementation per-
> spective, the abstract description is also very much concrete in that it
> ends up forming the actual physical interface that service consumer pro-
> grams end up connecting to.

SUMMARY OF KEY POINTS

- The term "abstract description" is commonly used to refer to the "what" part of the contract, whereas the term "concrete description" represents both the "how" and "where" parts.

- Abstract and concrete descriptions are frequently created during different stages of the service delivery lifecycle by different members of the project team.

4.2 The Parts of a Web Service Contract

Having just established a high-level structure of a Web service contract, let's drill down a bit to explore how abstract and concrete descriptions are further sub-divided into smaller parts.

> **NOTE**
>
> The following sections cover only the primary parts of the Web service contract. There are many other, more specialized definitions that will be introduced and explored in subsequent chapters.

Primary Parts of the Abstract Description

Figure 4.3 provides us with a *logical* view of the parts that comprise the abstract description. This means that when this section of a contract is actually created, these parts will be physically structured differently (as shown later in the *A Physical View of the Abstract Description* section).

The following sections are numbered to correspond with the numbers on Figure 4.3.

1. Port Type (Interface) Definition

The definition of the *port type* is the cornerstone of a Web service contract. Think of a port as a place of entry (such as a port used to receive ships for transferring cargo). A Web service contract can have one or more "types" of ports. Each port type essentially represents a technical interface or access point.

Note that for reasons we'll explain later, it is sometimes more appropriate to refer to the port type definition as the "interface definition."

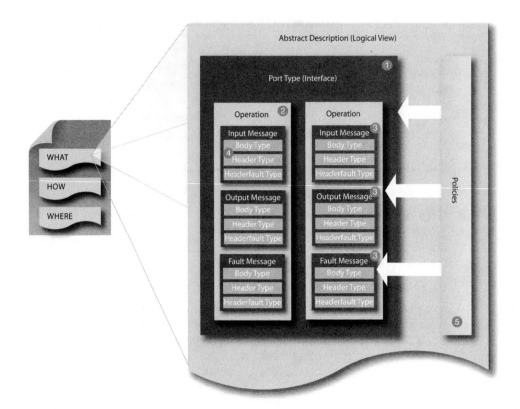

Figure 4.3
A logical view of the primary parts of an abstract description.

2. Operation Definition

For a Web service to be used by another program, it needs to expose externally consumable capabilities or functions. These are referred to as operations and are expressed as *operation definitions*.

A port type acts as a container for a set of related operations.

3. Message Definition

When a Web service is being invoked via one of its operations, the consumer program needs to exchange data with it in order for the Web service to perform the requested function. A *message definition* essentially establishes a "mini-structure" for the data to be transmitted.

There are three types of message definitions:

- *Input* – a message sent to the Web service by a consumer program
- *Output* – a message sent by the Web service to the consumer program
- *Fault* – an error notification message sent by the Web service to the consumer program

An operation can contain one or all of these message definitions but would generally not contain only an output or a fault message.

4. Type Definition

The data for a given input, output, or fault message needs to have a pre-defined structure of its own. That way, the Web service knows whether or not it is receiving or sending valid data. This data structure is established in a *body type definition*.

Messages further support the inclusion of message-specific metadata (information about the message that accompanies the message). For this form of supplementary data, a *header type definition* is also provided.

Finally, just as message transmissions can encounter error conditions, so can the processing of message metadata. Therefore, an additional *headerfault type definition* is available for when a response to a metadata-related error condition needs to be sent.

> **NOTE**
>
> The use of the headerfault type definition is not common in practice.

5. Policy Definition

All of the previous definitions in the abstract description have collectively defined the functional aspects of the Web service contract. *Policy definitions* can be created to extend the technical interface by expressing further behavioral requirements and characteristics of the service.

A Web service contract can have any number of supplementary policies. The horizontal arrows in Figures 4.3 and 4.4 indicate that polices can be specific to certain parts of the abstract description.

Note that polices can also be applied to parts of the concrete description.

A Physical View of the Abstract Description

So far we've been focusing on the logical view of the abstract description because it is conceptually important to understand it from this perspective. However, this is a book about technology, and the hundreds of pages that follow this chapter are all concerned with how Web service contracts are physically built.

Therefore, it's time that we start learning about how the organization of the various definitions we've described so far differs in a real-world contract document. As shown in Figure 4.4, the purpose behind the physical structure is to promote reuse in support of flexible and normalized Web service contracts.

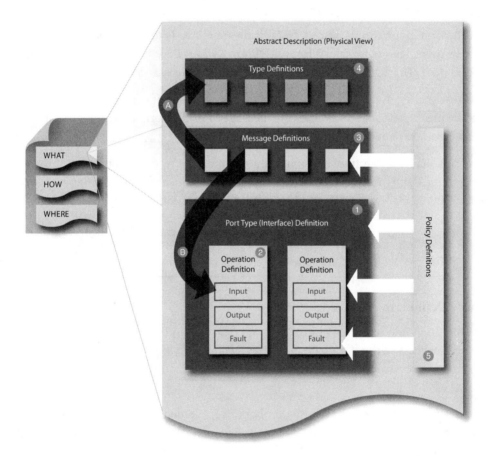

Figure 4.4

A physical view of the primary parts of an abstract description.

By following the numbers in Figure 4.4 we can trace back the actual location of the previously described definitions. While the port type definition (1) and policy definitions (5) are pretty much in the same place, we can see that the message definitions (3) and the type definitions (4) are no longer part of the port type or operation definitions (2).

Type and message definitions are positioned in separate parts of the contract so that they can be reused as follows:

A. Each type definition can be used by multiple message definitions.

B. Each message definition can be used by multiple operations (as input, output, and fault messages).

Although Figure 4.4 shows a series of available types, it does not make a distinction between a body, header, or headerfault type. All three types can exist as individual type definitions (4) but are then bundled together into one message definition (3). The body portion of this message is then associated with an input, output, or fault message as part of the operation definition (2).

> **NOTE**
>
> The header and headerfault parts are assigned to messages in the concrete description, the reason being that the messaging protocol to which the abstract description will be bound may or may not support their use.

WSDL 2.0 Changes to Physical View

We've intentionally avoided mentioning specific technologies so far in this chapter in order to establish as much of an abstract perspective of Web service contracts as possible. But it is worth noting that this book covers two different versions of the WSDL language used to express the Web service contract structure.

WSDL is explained later in this chapter. At this stage, we just need to point out that the physical view we just described complies with WSDL version 1.1. In version 2.0, the message definitions section (3) is removed, and operation definitions (2) refer directly to individual type definitions (4).

> **NOTE**
>
> In the upcoming sections dedicated to the parts of the concrete description, there is no distinction between a logical and physical view.

Primary Parts of the Concrete Description (Part I)

A concrete description supplements the abstract description with implementation-specific details required for the Web service to be invoked and communicated with by service consumer programs.

As we established earlier, the concrete description corresponds to the "how" and "where" sections of a Web service contract. We'll focus on these sections individually, starting with the "how" considerations addressed by the binding-related definitions illustrated in Figure 4.5.

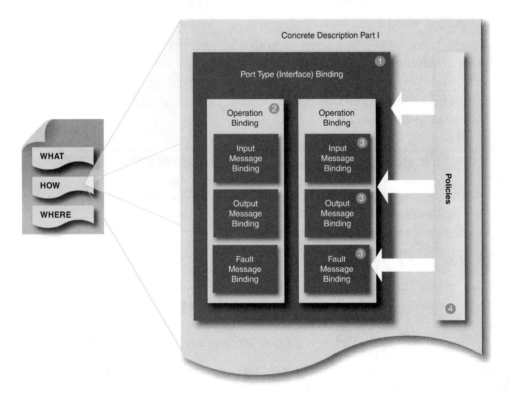

Figure 4.5

The primary parts of the binding portion of the concrete description. (Note that this represents both logical and physical views.)

The following sections are numbered to correspond with the numbers on Figure 4.5.

1. Port Type (Interface) Binding Definition

A *binding definition* details the communication technology that can be used by consumer programs to invoke and interact with the Web service.

A port type definition within an abstract description can be associated with one or more binding definitions, each of which contains the following two pieces of information:

- *Messaging Protocol Binding* – Defines a technology or industry standard (the message protocol) that specifies the format in which a message should be packaged by the sender and then unpackaged by the receiver.

- *Transport Protocol Binding* – Defines the communications technology (the transport protocol) with which the message should be transmitted across a network.

2. Operation Binding Definition

An *operating binding definition* represents the same type of binding definition as the port type binding, except that it is specific to the operation only. If the operation does not have this binding specified, it inherits the binding settings from its parent port type.

3. Message Binding Definitions

As with the operation binding, the *message binding definition* also represents a granular form of binding definition that, in this case, is specific to an input or output (or fault) message. If a message-specific binding is not provided, the message inherits the binding settings from its parent operation or its parent port type (if an operation binding is not present).

It is also here in the message binding definition that the header and headerfault parts of a message get associated with an input, output, or fault message that was defined in the abstract description. The reason again for making this association here is because not all message protocols support the use of header and headerfault parts.

4. Policy Definition

As with the definitions of an abstract description, policies can also be defined for the individual parts of a concrete description. Policies for binding definitions tend to be related to the configuration and runtime requirements of a particular messaging or transport protocol.

Primary Parts of the Concrete Description (Part II)

This final portion of the Web service contract structure focuses on the "where" section, as shown in Figure 4.6.

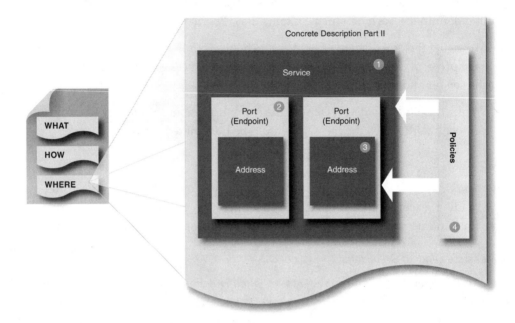

Figure 4.6

The primary parts of the service portion of the concrete description. (Note that this represents both logical and physical views.)

The following sections are numbered to correspond with the numbers on Figure 4.6.

1. Service Definition

The *service definition* simply groups related port (endpoint) definitions together. The port definition is explained shortly.

2. Port (Endpoint) Definition

Each binding definition needs to be associated with a port definition (also referred to as an endpoint definition), which simply acts as a container for the address definition (explained shortly). The same port definition can be used by different port type, operation, or message binding definitions.

3. Address Definition

An *address definition* establishes a physical network address. Depending on the communication technology (transport protocol) defined by the port type, operation, or message binding definition that is referencing the parent port definition for this address definition, the actual address value might be a Web URL, an email address, or some other type of transport-specific address.

4. Policy Definition

Policies can be created for address-related definitions in the concrete description. This may be necessary when certain requirements or characteristics specific to the network address need to be expressed.

How Parts of a Contract Relate to Each Other

As you may have already gathered, Web service contracts are highly modular. Let's take a minute to describe some of the relationships these parts can have:

- On a high level, one abstract description can have one or more associated concrete descriptions, each specifying a different messaging and/or transport protocol.
- One port type (interface) definition can have multiple operation definitions.
- Each operation definition can reference multiple message definitions.
- Each message definition can reference multiple type definitions.
- One port type (interface) definition can be associated with multiple binding definitions.
- Each binding definition can have multiple port (endpoint) definitions.
- A service definition can group multiple port (endpoint) definitions.
- Policies can be applied to most of these definitions.

Figure 4.7 illustrates these relationships by providing an example of one port type definition that is associated with two port type binding definitions (relationship A), each with its own port definition (relationship B).

Based on the numbers used in this diagram, we can further assume that the port type definition (1), the operation definition (2), and a message definition (3) each has its own corresponding binding definition. Also, the port type binding definition is associated with a port (4) that establishes its address.

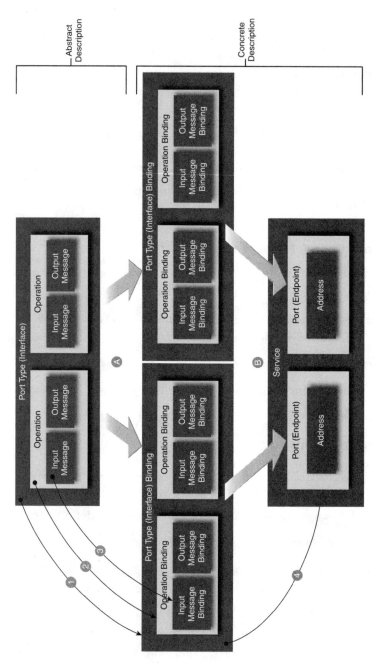

Figure 4.7

An example of how abstract and concrete descriptions can relate to each other.
(Note that fault messages have been omitted from this diagram.)

These relationships are discussed in detail in subsequent chapters. At this point it's just helpful for us to understand that various types of relationships can exist.

The Primary Parts of a Message

It's important to remember that building Web service contracts is more than just creating an interface to underlying service logic. The contract defines, in a very specific manner, the actual interaction requirements of the Web service. And, as you may have gathered from the previous two sections, both abstract and concrete descriptions express these interaction requirements by defining input and output messages and the technologies used to support the processing of these messages.

Let's therefore take the time to familiarize ourselves with the basic parts of a message. As shown in Figure 4.8, messages are wrapped in envelopes that have a basic structure of their own.

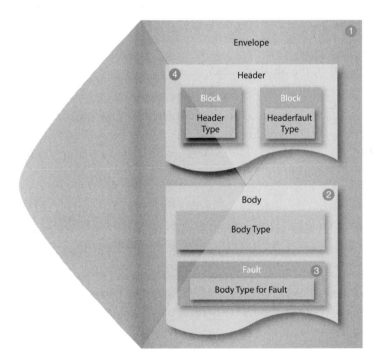

Figure 4.8
The fundamental structure of a message envelope.

Note that the following parts are not referred to as "definitions" because they represent an actual manifestation of what was established in the Web service contract definitions. In other words, runtime processors use the Web service contract definitions to generate these parts of the message (at runtime).

The following sections are numbered to correspond with the numbers on Figure 4.8.

1. Envelope

The scope of a message is defined by its *envelope*. This name is appropriate because it describes the message as a container of information. When discussing Web services, the terms "envelope" and "message" are frequently used interchangeably.

2. Body

The *body* represents a part of the message reserved for the data or the document being transported. Therefore, the type of information that usually resides within the message body is persistent in that its lifespan is greater than the time it takes for the message to be transmitted.

You'll notice the body part containing the *body type*. This relates back to the body type definition established in the abstract description. That type definition determined the structure for this portion of the message envelope.

Because a message exists as an actual body of data that is being transmitted somewhere, the body type in the message envelope would typically be populated with real data (like an invoice document) organized as per the body type definition from the message definition of the abstract description.

3. Fault

A message can be solely intended as a notification from the Web service to a consumer program that an error has occurred. The details of the error are housed in the fault part of the message envelope, which resides within the body section.

The fault part also has a type associated with it. This type corresponds to the fault type definition that was part of the abstract description's message definition.

4. Header

The *header* part of a message provides a location in which supplementary data about the message (metadata) can be stored. This data is usually temporary or non-persistent in nature in that its lifespan is generally equivalent to or shorter than the duration of the message transmission. A header allows metadata to be organized into sub-divided sections called *header blocks*.

Headers can contain many different types of header blocks, each dedicated to providing a distinct piece of supplementary data. This information is used by different programs to either help route a message or process its contents.

The first header block in Figure 4.8 is structured as per the header type definition that was established in the message definition of the abstract description. Similarly, the second header block is based on the headerfault type definition from the abstract description.

NOTE

Of all these parts, only the message envelope and the body are required. The header, header blocks, and fault parts are optional. Typically, only a body type or fault type is present within a given message (not both). Similarly, a message will either contain header types or headerfault types.As previously mentioned, whether the fault part is included in a message is based on which message definitions are present in the abstract description for a given operation.

With regards to header and headerfault parts, these do not always need to be defined as part of the Web service contract. In fact, in practice it has become more common for headers to be added, modified, and removed during the runtime processing of the message. This is explained in detail in Chapter 15.

SUMMARY OF KEY POINTS

- The primary parts of an abstract description are the port type, operation, message, type, and policy definitions.

- The primary parts of the concrete description are the port type binding, operation binding, message binding, service, port, and address definitions, as well as associated policy definitions.

- Definitions from abstract and concrete descriptions can have a variety of relationships.

- Abstract and concrete descriptions jointly define how real-life input and output messages are created.

4.3 Technologies Used to Create Web Service Contracts

Now that we've described the primary parts of a Web service contract and also how they can relate to each other, let's identify the development technologies suitable for creating these parts.

Each of these technologies shares the following characteristics:

- *Language* – Every part of a Web service contract is defined by writing code that conforms to a markup language. This is different from a traditional programming language, in that we do not compile our final results into a software program. We simply use the languages to create definitions that exist as textual documents; easy to access and read, but also reliant upon supporting platform programs for run-time processing.

- *XML-Based* – The markup grammar used to write these languages is expressed in XML. Therefore, you end up writing a Web service contract as a set of XML documents for the purpose of exchanging messages that also exist as XML documents and themselves carry data that is further represented with XML.

- *Vendor-Neutral* – Web service contract technologies were all developed by the same industry standards organization (the W3C) through rigorous, multi-year processes. Each was owned by a technical committee comprised of members from different vendor and practitioner organizations, and the final design of most of these language features required a consensus across this committee. Therefore, each of these technologies is also considered a legitimate industry standard.

More information regarding standards development processes, procedures, and stages is provided in Appendix B. Also note that these next sections only briefly introduce each technology; more in-depth coverage is provided in subsequent chapters.

"Element" vs. "Construct" vs. "Definition"

Before we introduce the technologies, let's first establish some additional terminology. If you are familiar with XML, you know that all of these XML-based languages are comprised of vocabularies of pre-defined elements, similar to those used in HTML (another Web language that was ratified into a standard through the W3C).

An additional term you'll see used in these next sections and throughout the remaining chapters is *construct* or *element construct*. A "construct" is a term used to refer to an element that contains nested child elements (in which case the element is implemented with an opening and closing tag). Think of a construct as an "element container."

For example, an HTML table exists as a table construct comprised of various nested elements (and nested constructs).

There are no rules as to when an element is referred to as a construct. It is just helpful at times to communicate that a particular part of a contract is represented as a container of elements.

The individual parts and definitions of a Web service contract that we've been explaining all exist as element constructs that contain further details. We make a distinction between a definition and a construct (or element) when we need to discuss how a part of a contract is implemented (coded) as opposed to designed.

So a definition, a construct, and an element can all refer to the same thing, just from different perspectives.

As we get into the details of these technology languages, we'll use a style convention whereby specific language element names are displayed in a different font. For example, we might state that the port type definition is created using the `portType` construct which is comprised of opening and closing `portType` tags.

Web Services Description Language (WSDL)

WSDL is considered to be the most fundamental and important technology for Web services development because it has become the de facto language for writing Web service contracts. Using WSDL, contract structure is defined and then further detailed and extended with the other technologies covered in this section.

As you may have gathered, we've already been discussing WSDL in this chapter. The basic Web service contract structure illustrated in previous diagrams has represented a WSDL definition, and the abstract and concrete descriptions are the fundamental parts of a WSDL structure (Figure 4.9).

Figure 4.9

The basic WSDL definition structure that we have been exploring throughout this chapter.

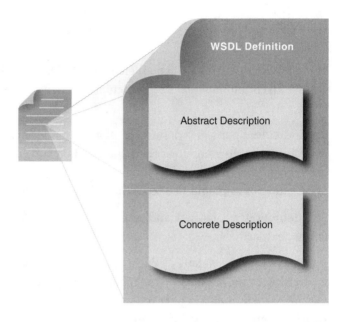

A WSDL document ends up acting as somewhat of a container in which elements from almost all other languages covered in this book converge. Chapters 7 and 8 introduce the WSDL language as it applies to abstract and concrete descriptions respectively. As you explore how these parts of the WSDL definition are assembled, you will be able to see just how much code in the WSDL document does *not* originate from the WSDL language.

Chapter 9 provides further WSDL coverage specific to the WSDL 2.0 standard, and Chapters 14 and 15 drill down into a wide range of advanced topics.

XML Schema Definition Language (XML Schema)

XML Schema provides a formal language for defining the structure and validation constraints of XML documents. Because XML is a native part of the WSDL language and because Web services operate by exchanging XML messages, XML Schema is a highly complementary technology for creating Web service contracts.

Schemas serve as the part of a contract that describes the detailed structure of messages. They define what elements and attributes may appear in the message, in what order, and what type of data they are allowed to contain.

All of the type definitions displayed in the previous figures are assumed to be created using the XML Schema language. The types section displayed earlier in the physical view of an abstract description (Figure 4.4) is technically part of the WSDL language, but its primary purpose is to house XML Schema elements.

XML Schema code can be embedded directly within WSDL documents or kept as separate documents and then referenced from the WSDL definitions. Each approach has its pros and cons.

When XML schemas exist as independent files, you can establish a many-to-many relationship between the schema documents and the WSDL message definitions. One schema might be used to describe several messages, particularly if they are related and share types. Similarly, each message definition can reference several different XML Schema types originating from different XML Schema documents.

> **NOTE**
>
> In case you're wondering why sometimes the word "schema" is capitalized and other times it isn't, this is explained in the "XML Schema" vs. "XML schema" section at the beginning of Chapter 6.

Most often, you will be designing your own schema from the ground up, based on your specific requirements. At other times, you will be using an industry schema that was developed by an industry organization, a vendor, or even a private corporation. When using an industry standard XML schema, you may wish to reuse only parts of it or extend it to meet your specific needs.

There are multiple ways to structure XML documents, just like there are a number of ways to design a database. Once you have decided on an XML structure (i.e. which elements and attributes you want to use) there is also more than one way to express that structure in an XML Schema definition.

Figure 4.10 provides a preview of common XML Schema constructs that we will be covering in Chapter 6. You will have the freedom to create a variety of different types based on XML Schema features that provide a series of built-in types and allow for the assembly of composite types commonly used to express complex structures and even entire business document structures.

Introductory XML Schema coverage is provided in the next chapter. Chapters 12 and 13 then delve into more advanced topics related to complex message design.

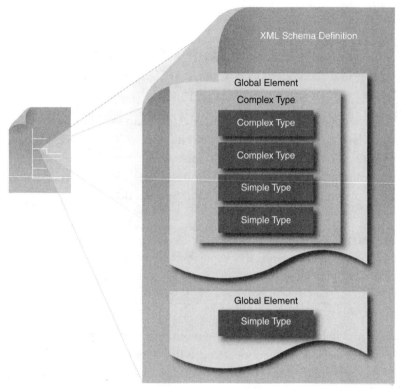

Figure 4.10

A logical view of a sample XML Schema definition structure comprised of different types that can then be used to define the structure of WSDL message definitions. Note the symbol on the left used to represent an XML Schema document.

WS-Policy Language

The WS-Policy standard specifies a policy framework specifically for Web services that enables behavior-related constraints and characteristics to be expressed as *machine-readable* metadata. This means that we can use this language to extend the base Web service contract provided by WSDL and XML Schema in order to add requirements or promote characteristics of the Web service that supplement the definitions in the abstract and concrete descriptions.

Figure 4.11 shows us that policy definition documents are just as modular as WSDL and XML Schema documents. As with XML Schema types, individual policy requirements (also referred to as policy assertions) can be combined or related to each other in order to form more complex composite policies (called policy expressions). You even have the ability to offer consumers a choice between two or more policies via the use of policy alternatives.

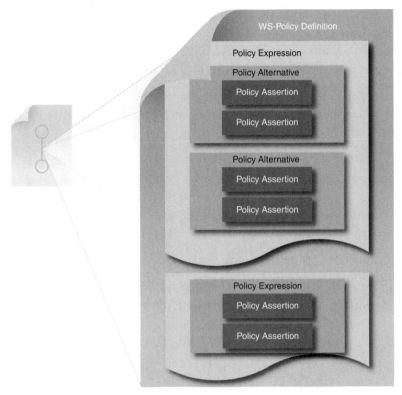

Figure 4.11

A sample WS-Policy definition with two composite policy expressions, each comprised of multiple policy assertions. Note the symbol on the left used to represent a policy document.

Another similarity that WS-Policy shares with XML Schema is how it relates to WSDL. Policies can also reside within or outside of the WSDL document. The related WS-PolicyAttachment language is used to associate (attach) policies to the various definitions in the abstract and concrete descriptions.

The WS-Policy and WS-PolicyAttachment languages are introduced in Chapter 10. More advanced topics are covered later in Chapters 16 and 17. Part of this coverage includes an exploration of how policy assertions are used by other languages to implement their features.

SOAP Language

SOAP provides a messaging format and mechanism that supports the standardized exchange of XML messages between software programs. SOAP has become the most prevalent messaging protocol used in conjunction with WSDL.

The SOAP language is used to express the structure of XML-based envelopes that host message definitions populated with actual data. Although at runtime SOAP language elements are usually auto-generated, SOAP is very much a technology related to the design-time creation of Web service contracts.

SOAP messages and message exchanges are fundamentally defined within the message and operation definitions of the WSDL document, and various SOAP language elements are further added to the concrete description in order to bind them to SOAP as a messaging protocol.

SOAP messages are most commonly:

- transmitted via HTTP

- described using XML Schema types

- associated with WSDL definitions in the concrete description

As shown in Figure 4.12, a standard SOAP message is divided into a set of parts. These parts are individually defined by XML Schema types via WSDL message definitions.

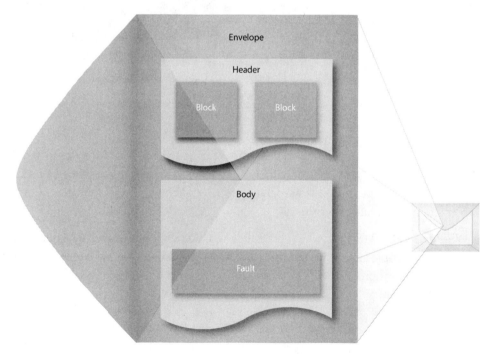

Figure 4.12

The SOAP message structure is defined by the SOAP standard and expressed with the SOAP language. Note the use of the symbol on the right to indicate a SOAP message in this book.

There are many supplemental technologies that extend SOAP messages via the use of SOAP header blocks. Many of these technologies are part of the WS-* specifications (also known as the second-generation Web services platform).

SOAP is introduced in Chapter 11. Advanced message design considerations are covered in Chapters 18 and 19 in relation to the WS-Addressing standard which provides fundamental routing and Web service instance identification header blocks.

Technologies for the Abstract Description

Figure 4.13 shows a high level mapping between the primary abstract description definitions and the related Web service technologies that can be used to create these definitions.

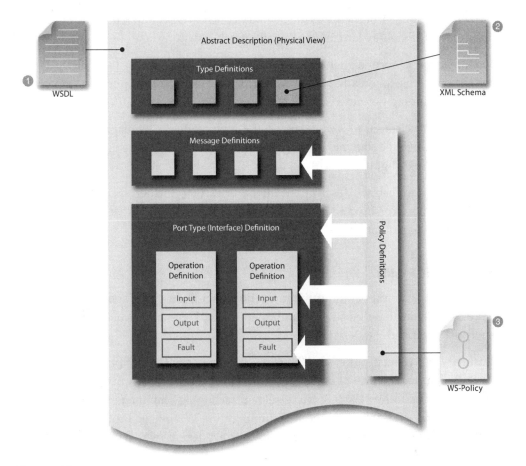

Figure 4.13

A high level mapping of the abstract description parts and related industry technologies.

What this figure tells us is that the overall structure of the abstract description (including the port type, operation, and message definitions) is created using WSDL (1).

The types part of a Web service contract is created collectively with WSDL and XML Schema (2) code in that the WSDL language provides a container construct wherein XML Schema code can be placed to express the various XML Schema types.

Finally, policy definitions can be separately created using the WS-Policy language (3). These policies can then be attached to the different WSDL definitions using the related WS-PolicyAttachment language.

Technologies for Concrete Descriptions

Let's now turn our attention to the technologies used to build a concrete description for a Web service. Figure 4.14 shows us the primary concrete description parts as they relate to three of the technology languages we just introduced.

In this depiction of a concrete description, we again establish how the WSDL (1) language is responsible for creating the overall structure, including the port type, operation and message binding definitions; as well as the service, port, and address definitions.

All of the constructs used to create these definitions can be further supplemented with special SOAP language statements (2) that allow the definitions to be directly associated with the SOAP messaging protocol.

And, as with the abstract description, all parts can be further supplemented with policy statements expressed using the WS-Policy language (3) as well as the related WS-PolicyAttachment language.

The WS-I Basic Profile

The Web Services Interoperability Organization (WS-I) develops specifications dedicated to establishing baseline interoperability between Web services using the technologies we just described.

The primary WS-I specification we'll be making reference to throughout this book is the Basic Profile, a document that essentially consists of a series of requirements and recommendations as to how Web services-related technology languages should be used together. Wherever appropriate, we'll be highlighting WS-I Basic Profile guidelines to supplement and provide further insight into contract design-related content.

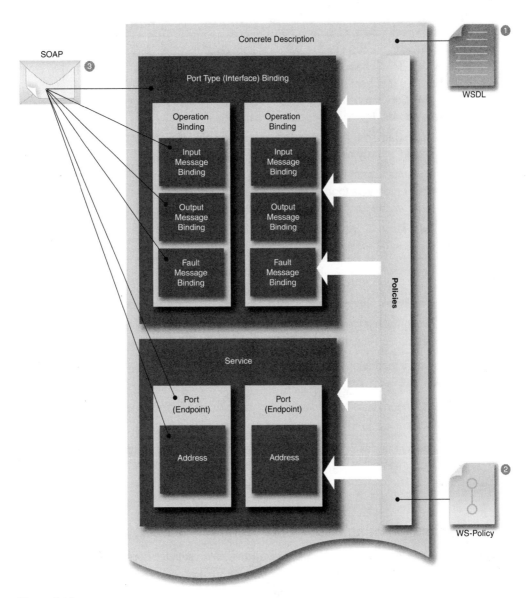

Figure 4.14

A look at the concrete description parts and the technology languages used to create them.

> **NOTE**
>
> In addition to the WS-I Profile, which is light on XML Schema guidelines, the W3C XML Schema Patterns for Databinding Working Group has documented a set of best practices for designing schemas for Web services. The XML Schema patterns are divided into two categories, basic and advanced, and there is a separate specification for each:
>
> - Basic patterns use only the basic features of XML Schema and should already be correctly implemented by all toolkits.
>
> - Advanced patterns are those that may still cause some tool interoperability problems today, but should be considered recommended patterns for the future.
>
> To view the actual specifications for any of the languages covered in this book, visit www.soaspecs.com.

SUMMARY OF KEY POINTS

- The primary technology languages used to create the abstract description are WSDL, XML Schema, and WS-Policy.

- The primary technology languages used to create the concrete description are WSDL, SOAP, and WS-Policy.

- A WSDL document will be comprised of code originating from all of these languages.

- XML Schema and WS-Policy definitions can optionally be placed into stand-alone documents that are then referenced from within the WSDL definition.

4.4 Guidelines for Using Web Service Contract Technologies

It is not difficult to learn the mechanics of building Web service contracts. Once you get to know the technologies we've been discussing in this chapter, you will be able to author custom contracts with relative ease.

As we already established, every primary technology we cover in this book exists as an XML-based, industry-standard, markup language. Even though each serves a different purpose, all share a common syntax and many common conventions.

While learning these languages is a fundamental requirement to customizing your Web service contracts, it is not the most important skill, nor is it the most challenging part of creating effective contracts

Writing a Web service contract and *designing* an effective Web service contract for a given service as part of a federated service inventory are two different things. This is where technology features, design philosophies, and business requirements converge. This book primarily attempts to help you with the first two items.

Keep in mind that these technology languages are merely tools. You can just as easily use them to build a bad Web service contract as you could a good one. It is therefore helpful to remember that the decisions you make when designing the different parts of a contract will eventually impact the usability, flexibility, and governance burden of your services.

Before we proceed to the series of chapters that explore these technologies in detail, here are a few guidelines to keep in mind.

Auto-Generation Tools

Many development tools allow you to generate XML code for Web service contract languages. While this is useful for learning purposes, it may not be suitable for designing standardized Web service contracts in support of service-orientation.

The Standardized Service Contract design principle requires that service contracts be designed in accordance with existing design standards. The Service Loose Coupling principle further explains that contracts generated from underlying parts of a service's implementation can inherit negative forms of coupling that will make the service burdensome to own and govern.

These considerations also tie directly into the Canonical Schema and Canonical Expression design patterns that promote the use of design standards within the boundary of a service inventory.

Flexibility vs. Restrictiveness

One common dilemma in XML-based design, and indeed in software engineering in general, is the tension between flexibility and restrictiveness. At one end of the spectrum, a contract could be highly flexible in that it might allow just about any consumer to send it any type of content. The advantage of this approach is that you will never have to change the service contract when the message structure changes.

However, this technique also has its weaknesses. If you don't define a message structure, you can't pre-define validation logic in the contract layer, and you have no formal documentation of what your service can do. Applications that process the messages will have no idea of what to expect.

On the other hand, you could write a very rigid schema for your contract that must be modified every time there is the slightest change or addition to the message definition. Such contracts are brittle and have a ripple effect on the solutions that consume and form dependencies on the service. You may want this kind of rigidity if you are implementing a service that processes messages requiring strict precision (such as bank transactions), but such rigidity often does more harm than good.

With service-orientation there is the tendency to be less restrictive with technical contracts than with traditional object and component interfaces. The priorities advocated by the Service Abstraction principle and the Validation Abstraction design pattern support this tendency. However, in the end, the ideal usually lies somewhere in the middle. The key is to identify the areas of the contract that require flexibility and to then design them so that they allow the necessary variation.

Modularity and Reuse

Reuse of software saves time and money, and programs that are reused are often more robust and better designed all around. The individual parts that comprise Web service contracts are no exception.

As you will learn in the upcoming chapters, there is plenty of opportunity for reuse within Web service contract languages. Leveraging language features that allow for the creation of modules and provide include mechanisms can significantly streamline all parts of the service contract (and can further end up saving a lot of time that would be spent writing redundant code).

Then, of course, there is the notion of reusing parts of a contract across different contracts. This is where standardization-related patterns, such as Canonical Schema, Schema Centralization, and Policy Centralization, prove extremely valuable in not only getting more ROI out of the service contract code, but—more importantly—ensuring that these key parts are consistent across all the service contracts that establish a federated endpoint layer within a service inventory.

As with anything, though, overuse of something can lead to the opposite of the intended effect. XML language modules and centralization techniques need to be carefully chosen. Over-modularizing code within or across service contracts will inevitably lead to an inhibitive and complex architecture.

> **NOTE**
>
> Ultimately, one of the biggest challenges to achieving reuse is not related to technology, but to organizational governance. This is an on-going area that is addressed by all levels of service-orientation and SOA and will be covered in the upcoming book *SOA Governance*.

Clarity and Ease of Processing

With their hierarchical structure, larger-sized Web service contracts can quickly become unwieldy. Although they are intended to be read by machines, it does not mean that it doesn't matter if they are difficult to interpret by humans (especially considering that you may not want to rely on auto-generation tools to create and maintain them).

People from both the service provider and consumer sides will need to discover, understand, and work with these contracts, and any misunderstandings will introduce risk. Furthermore, overly complex contracts lead to increased governance effort and a higher cost of ownership.

Of course contracts have a job to do and sometimes this job requires that they be designed to a degree of complexity and sophistication. However, never lose sight of the fact that others will end up having to use (and perhaps evolve) what you are building today. Good contract design requires that you strive for clarity and avoid complexity or ambiguity wherever possible.

Here are some guidelines:

- *Consistent Design* – Use the same name for parts of the contract that mean the same thing, and different names for parts that are conceptually different. Developing a naming standard (as per the Canonical Expression pattern) may be the only way to guarantee that contracts are consistent in how they express themselves. This includes choosing names that are human-readable and, ideally, provide a business context. Also, when possible, use a consistent order and structure for elements that tend to be reused.

- *Limited Depth* – Some structural elements can be very useful, but you should not introduce unnecessary constraints or nested levels into the data structures that underlie your contract types. As per the Service Abstraction principle, try to define a balanced level of constraint granularity.

- *Good Documentation* – Simply providing a name and a structure for elements is not enough for the contract to be communicative to a wide range of project team members. Use annotations to further document elements and types, as per the Service Discoverability principle. (There are tools that will generate human-readable documentation from schema annotations.)

SUMMARY OF KEY POINTS

- The use of auto-generation tools can make it challenging to author standardized Web service contracts.

- Granularity, reusability, and clarity are among the common Web service contract design considerations.

Chapter 5

A Plain English Guide to Namespaces

Before we begin describing the individual Web service contract technologies introduced in Chapter 4, we first need to establish *namespaces*, a part of both XML and Web service technology platforms that is so fundamental that their understanding is critical to designing, using, and governing Web service contracts.

Namespaces have traditionally been one of the most neglected design-time considerations, primarily because they have simply not been understood well enough. Therefore, we avoid "spec language" as much as possible in the upcoming sections, while also providing lots of examples. We start out by taking a conceptual look at the functionality namespaces offer and then dive into the technical details before linking back to how they relate to service contract design.

NOTE

Feel free to skip some or all of this chapter if you are already experienced with the use of namespaces. If you are familiar with namespaces but have not yet worked with them as part of Web service contracts, you may want to just skip to the *Namespaces and Web Service Contracts* section at the end of this chapter.

About the In Plain English Sections

In this chapter only, you will notice periodic *In Plain English* sections that explain some of the key topics with non-technical analogies. An on-going example of a school library allows us to draw comparisons between XML elements and books that need to be organized into genres (which are compared to namespaces).

5.1 Elements, Attributes, and Namespaces

Let's begin with a 60-second introduction to elements, attributes, and vocabularies so that we can set the stage for how namespaces fit into the XML world.

Elements

Whenever you ask someone to name the most fundamental parts of the XML language, chances are they will answer "elements and attributes." Of course, it's certainly true that an XML document is comprised of a number of elements, which exist as tags (text surrounded by angle brackets) as follows:

```
<some_element>
```

What's important about elements is that they can have content. This content can either be text or other elements, or both. Therefore, it is helpful to view elements as containers of information. To determine how big a given container (element) is, we need to know where it begins and ends. This is why elements are generally defined in pairs, where each pair is comprised of one opening and one closing element that together establish a construct.

As shown here, the closing element is identified by the forward-slash "/" that is placed after its first angle bracket:

```
<filter>some kind of filter</filter>
```

Attributes

In order to provide supplementary information about a specific element without having to add text or additional elements, you can simply stick an attribute name and its value between the angle brackets right after the element, as follows:

```
<filter productID="LD2343">
  some kind of filter
</filter>
```

Vocabularies

An XML *vocabulary* is simply a set of related elements and attributes. For example, you can create a series of elements and attributes that could be used to define the structure of an invoice document. This would likely constitute a vocabulary.

Similarly, you may be required to work with XML-based languages (such as XML Schema, WSDL, or SOAP). While these represent standardized technologies, they also exist as collections of related XML elements and attributes. Therefore, each is also considered a separate vocabulary.

Note that the use of the term "vocabulary" is subjective. Within an invoice vocabulary, you may have a set of related elements that are used to represent invoice line items. These could also be considered a vocabulary (or perhaps a sub or nested vocabulary).

What's Next

What we've been leading up to is an opportunity to gently introduce the concept of namespaces. As we discover throughout this chapter, a big part of what namespaces are used for is to enable us to combine elements and attributes from different vocabularies together into the same XML documents.

Namespaces and Elements

By just looking at an element, it can be difficult to understand what it is describing. For example, in a document where elements are used to represent products that can be bought in a hardware store, an element called `filter` could refer to one of several different types of filters, each with its own set of unique characteristics.

Figure 5.1 provides a sample XML element vocabulary for a store that sells appliances, heating equipment, and automotive parts. You'll notice on the third row of the element hierarchy that there are three elements named "filter," each used for a different purpose (a coffee machine, a heating furnace, and a car engine).

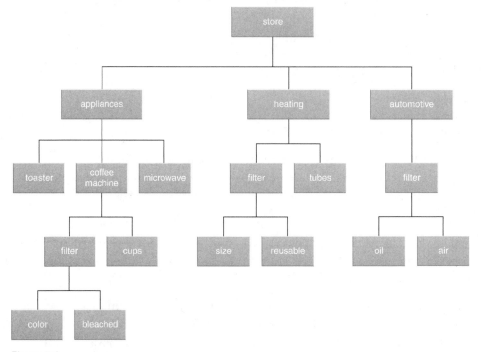

Figure 5.1

An XML element vocabulary for a hardware store.

Having different types of filter products that use the same `filter` element can pose a pretty significant data representation problem. For example, chances are that a coffee filter will need to be represented differently than a car filter.

So what can we do about this naming conflict? Well, the easy answer is to simply change the names. Why not just create separate `coffee_filter` and `car_filter` elements?

That's certainly one solution and an approach that is actually fairly common. But, what if you weren't the one naming the elements? Let's say you had to work with XML vocabularies that were pre-defined by standards organizations or different groups in your IT enterprise. In this case you might have an element named `filter` provided to you by the International Federation of Coffee Filter Makers (IFCFM) and another element named `filter` defined by the International Federation of Automobile Filter Makers (IFAFM).

To incorporate these elements into a single XML document will cause problems and confusion, without the use of some type of additional identifier. So how can we create, for example, a flexible Order document so that the auto mechanic with a caffeine addiction can purchase both a coffee filter and a car filter at the same time? The answer, as you might have guessed, is *namespaces*.

Namespaces were created by the W3C in a separate specification that supplements the XML standard and pretty much every technology standard associated with Web service contracts. (This specification is called "Namespaces in XML," and you can access it via www.soaspecs.com.)

A namespace simply gives us a way to organize related elements into groups. Within a group, each element name is ideally unique. This way, different types of elements can have the same name when they belong to different groups.

Let's create some groups to represent the three types of filter products that the store sells:

- CoffeeFilterNamespace
- AutoFilterNamespace
- HeatingFilterNamespace

We now need a practical way of associating each of these groups with an individual `filter` element. Namespaces provide a means of relating a group to an element by extending its name to include a reference to its group.

The following example adds a namespace to the `filter` element:

```
<cfn:filter productID="LD2343"
  xmlns:cfn="CoffeeFilterNamespace">
  Cone Filter (100 pack)
</cfn:filter>
```

You'll also notice the addition of a new attribute called "xmlns," short for "XML namespace." This attribute essentially allows us to establish a namespace by giving it a name ("CoffeeFilterNamespace") and a special identifier ("cfn") that acts as a reference to the namespace.

This identifier is called a *prefix* because it (together with the colon symbol) prefixes an element to indicate what namespace the element belongs to, as follows:

```
cfn:filter
```

With the prefix and the element combined, you now end up with a *qualified name* (also called the "QName").

Next is the corresponding example for the car filter, where the qualified name is `afn:filter`:

```
<afn:filter productID="XE9781" autoID="BMW"
  xmlns:afn="AutoFilterNamespace">
  Supreme Oil Filter
</afn:filter>
```

Because the use of a namespace allows us to create an entirely new element with the same name, we can give the `afn:filter` element an additional attribute that does not exist with the `cfn:filter` element.

Using qualified names allows us to place elements with the same name but that belong to different groups together into a single XML document. We'll be showing a lot of examples of this in subsequent chapters, but here's a preview of what the detail section of an order document might look like with three different qualified `filter` elements:

```
<order xmlns="OrderNamespace"
  xmlns:cfn="CoffeeFilterNamespace"
  xmlns:afn="AutoFilterNamespace"
  xmlns:hfn="HeatingFilterNamespace">
  ...
  <detail>
    <afn:filter productID="XE9781" autoID="BMW" >
```

```
      Supreme Oil Filter
   </afn:filter>
   <cfn:filter productID="LD2343">
     Cone Filter (100 pack)
   </cfn:filter>
   <cfn:filter productID="LD2346">
     Flat Bottom Filter (50 pack)
   </cfn:filter>
   <hfn:filter productID="TH7567">
     Boiler Filter 2000
   </hfn:filter>
  </detail>
</order>
```

In this example the xmlns attributes were moved to the root element so that we can have multiple occurrences of each qualified element without having to repeat this attribute (as demonstrated by the two cfn:filter elements).

Also, you might have caught the fact that the order and detail elements do not have a prefix. This is because we get to establish one "default" namespace for which we don't need to provide a prefix. We will explain prefixes and default namespaces in more detail shortly.

Figure 5.2 displays the XML element vocabulary that we have been gradually building. Within our store, we have identified three types of products that each require a filter element. To avoid naming conflicts, we created three separate namespaces to represent the filter elements (and their child elements).

NOTE

Although we've been focusing on namespaces as a means of avoiding element naming conflicts, there are several additional reasons as to why namespaces may need to be used. For example, namespaces can make an XML document more self-descriptive because a qualified element name has more context. How and why namespaces are used is explored further in this and subsequent chapters.

To get a different perspective on this, let's now turn our attention to an example more relevant to the case study we introduced in Chapter 2.

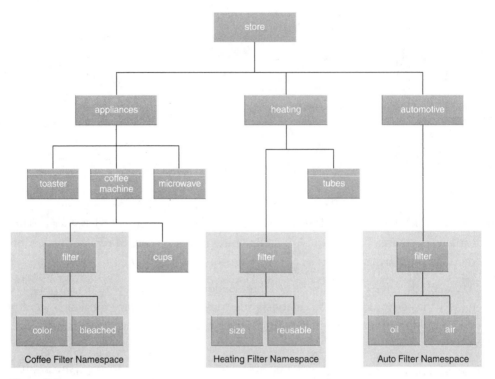

Figure 5.2
The conflicting `filter` elements and their respective child elements are added to separate namespaces.

Here we have a `game` element that was added to a namespace called
`"ActionconNamespace"`:

```
<ns:game productID="AY2344"
  xmlns:ns="ActionconNamespace">
  Service Blaster 2000
</ns:game>
```

In this example, we established the `ns:` namespace prefix, so the qualified element name
is `ns:game`. The `ns:` prefix does not have any particular meaning; we could have just as
easily used any other prefix value. Rather, it is the namespace value that the prefix is
mapped to that has relevance.

Namespaces and Attributes

Another interesting thing you can do with XML is associate a namespace with an attribute. This allows you to group related attributes into their own namespace just like you can with elements. In the following example, the `productID` attribute is in a different namespace than the `game` element:

```
<ns:game inv:productID="AY2344"
  xmlns:ns="ActionconNamespace"
  xmlns:inv="InventoryNamespace">
  Service Blaster 2000
</ns:game>
```

And, attributes and elements can belong to the same namespace:

```
<ns:game ns:productID="AY2344"
  xmlns:ns="ActionconNamespace">
  Service Blaster 2000
</ns:game>
```

IN PLAIN ENGLISH

In a school library, there are different types of books that students can borrow. To make it easier for students to find what they're looking for, all of the books are categorized into genres, such as Science, Literature, Biography, and so on. The library organizes the shelf display of the books according to these genres, with big signs indicating the categories.

Furthermore, the genres have codes that are used to record the books on paper forms and in the library's inventory management system. These codes also appear next to the titles when students use terminals to perform searches, or when the items being borrowed are displayed on the "check-out" cards students receive.

What does all of this have to do with namespaces? Well, the manner in which the library groups related books into genres is comparable to how you may choose to establish a namespace in order to group related elements. This avoids confusion if you should have identically named books and also provides a context for a book when its title doesn't indicate what it's about.

For example, you could have two books named "The Migration" where the first is an educational book about birds, and the second is a novel that tells the story of an immigrant. Associating the genre (Nature Studies or Fiction, in this case) allows both titles to co-exist harmoniously within the same library.

Working with Namespaces

Each element and attribute can only belong to a maximum of one namespace. Alternatively, an element or an attribute does not need to belong to any namespace at all. The very first code samples we showed at the beginning of the *Elements, Attributes, and Namespaces* section, for example, were still legitimate XML fragments with no association to namespaces.

However, in the world of Web service contract and message design, namespaces are everywhere you turn. You will encounter them in WSDL definitions, SOAP message definitions, and even policy definitions. Close down any of these documents and open an XML Schema definition, and there will be more namespaces, right in your face. Since you can't escape them, it's best to embrace them.

As mentioned earlier, some namespaces are forced on us by external standards organizations. These we often must work with "as-is," by building our Web service contract architecture around them. As for the others, though, their design is up to us.

Because namespaces eventually become so deeply and widely entrenched across all of your Web service contract-related XML documents, you should never allow them to be created "ad-hoc." Design conventions and a long-term namespace governance strategy are generally required.

One of the biggest design decisions you need to deal with first when coming up with a strategy is determining how many namespaces you should create. Because each element and attribute can only belong to one, you need to ensure that you define the right kinds of namespaces that establish groups and categories appropriately scoped to what they are supposed to represent.

Here are some things to consider:

- the number of business documents you are expecting to create or work with

- the service models you plan to use

- the scope and size of your planned service inventory (and whether other domain inventories will reside alongside it)

- other functional or business domains that may exist in your enterprise

- existing standards and conventions related to data and business modeling

---

NOTE

Some toolkits will generate structures in code that reflect namespaces. For example, if you implement your service logic using Java, you will likely end up with a package for each namespace that you have defined.

SUMMARY OF KEY POINTS

- The basic building blocks of XML are elements, attributes and namespaces.

- Namespaces help avoid name collisions and ambiguities among XML elements and attributes with different origins.

- Namespaces are most commonly associated with elements and attributes via the use of prefixes.

5.2 Namespace Terminology

Based on what we have described so far, we can now define some terms that are used within the industry to describe and work with namespaces.

Local Name

The *local name* is simply the name of an element or attribute without the namespace that it belongs to.

In the following example, "game" and "productID" are local names:

```
<ns:game ns:productID="AY2344"
  xmlns:ns="ActionconNamespace">
  Service Blaster 2000
</ns:game>
```

Expanded Name

The combination of an element or attribute name and its namespace is called the *expanded name*, as shown here:

```
ActionconNamespace.game
```

NOTE

We don't actually use expanded names in this book. As you may have gathered from the preceding examples, we use prefixes instead (which are explained next).

Namespace Prefix

Because namespace names can be quite long and can contain characters that are not allowed in XML names, it is not practical to always use expanded names. Instead, we can create an alias called the *namespace prefix*.

In the familiar example that follows, the `ns:` prefix is declared via the `xmlns` attribute and then used by the `game` element and the `productID` attribute.

```
<ns:game ns:productID="AY2344"
  xmlns:ns="ActionconNamespace">
  Service Blaster 2000
</ns:game>
```

If you look back at the sample Order document we showed in the *Namespaces and Elements* section, you'll see how we can place the `xmlns` attribute in a parent element so that numerous child elements can reuse it.

> **NOTE**
>
> Technically, `xmlns` is not considered an attribute, even though it looks like one. It is officially defined as a "namespace declaration." However, to keep things simple, we will continue to refer to it as an attribute throughout this book.

Default Namespace

As its name indicates, the *default namespace* represents the one namespace within an XML document that does not require a prefix (because it's the "default"). In other words, a namespace still exists, but elements belonging to it do not require a prefix because we are simply stating that "any elements without a prefix belong to this namespace."

```
<game productID="AY2344"
  xmlns="ActionconNamespace">
  Service Blaster 2000
</game>
```

The default namespace is most commonly used for convenience. In the upcoming chapters, you'll notice the default namespace used to represent the WSDL namespace so that WSDL-related elements in Web service contracts do not require a prefix.

Qualified Name

As we've already explained in the previous sections, the *qualified name* of an element is the combination of its local name and namespace (as represented by the prefix), as shown here:

```
<ns:game ns:productID="AY2344"
  xmlns:ns="ActionconNamespace">
  Service Blaster 2000
</ns:game>
```

In the listing, both `ns:game` and `ns:productID` are qualified names. If a default namespace has been declared, then the element name without a prefix is considered the qualified name.

Target Namespace

This is a special type of namespace that is used to establish a namespace value associated with a specific XML document. To understand how this works, we need to complete this chapter and then learn a bit about the XML Schema language in the next chapter. What the target namespace is and how it is used is then explained in the *Target Namespace* section in Chapter 6.

IN PLAIN ENGLISH

Revisiting the library analogy from the previous *In Plain English* section where we associated genres with namespaces, we can loosely associate these terms as follows:

- A book title (like "The Migration") would be a local name.

- The book title together with the genre would be comparable to an expanded name.

- The genre code can be considered the equivalent of a namespace prefix.

- The book title together with the genre code therefore becomes the qualified name.

Also, as explained earlier, elements and attributes don't need to belong to any namespace. For this, you could draw a comparison to recently donated books and materials that have not yet been categorized and made available to the public. These are placed in a central bin until someone has the time to process them. While in that state, they have no official genre.

SUMMARY OF KEY POINTS

- The local name is the name of the XML element or attribute without its namespace prefix.

- The default namespace allows elements to be associated with a namespace without the need for a prefix.

- The qualified name is the combination of an element or attribute and its namespace prefix.

5.3 What's in a Name(space)?

It's time now to get into some of the more technical details of how namespaces are named, structured, and applied. Let's start with naming and structural considerations.

A namespace is comprised of a string of characters, but it can't be just any string of characters you might want to use. The W3C namespace specification states that the name of a namespace must be a *Uniform Resource Identifier* or "URI." Needless to say, there is a separate specification for what a URI is, and there are even more specifications that define different types of URIs, such as *Uniform Resource Names* (URNs) and *Uniform Resource Locators* (URLs). You may have heard at least about the last one, given that this standard is used to represent Web addresses in general.

The *IRI vs. URI vs. URL vs. URN* section at the beginning of Chapter 7 explains each of these terms individually. For the purpose of this discussion, let's just say that a URI is used to identify a resource, a URN is used to give a specific name or identity to a resource, and a URL tells us where the resource is and how to get to it over a network. And while namespace names can be any URI, by far the most common form is the URL, which we'll use from hereon.

Getting back to our `ns:game` element example, let's change the namespace definition to a proper URL:

```
<ns:game ns:productID="AY2344"
  xmlns:ns="http://actioncon.com/schema/gameinfo">
  Service Blaster 2000
</ns:game>
```

Keep in mind that even though the namespace name we just picked looks like a Web address that we could use in a browser to retrieve a document, it isn't! It is merely a value that we picked to follow the industry convention of using URLs as namespaces.

The fact that a namespace is a URL is completely irrelevant as far as any XML processing goes. The namespace processor will not interpret the content of the namespace name in any way—it will simply treat it as a string. And the processor will *not* go out on the Internet to try to resolve the namespace URL.

Even though it may seem a bit odd to use URLs that look like legitimate Web addresses (but usually aren't) as namespace names, there are some notable benefits:

- URLs are more likely to be consistently unique because they include domain names that can be directly associated with the organization or enterprise in which they are used.

- URLs are naturally hierarchical, allowing you to add some common structure to different namespaces.

Assume, for example, that you want to establish a namespace naming convention for your enterprise. You could start out by defining that each namespace must begin with something like this:

```
http://actioncon.com
```

You might then identify top-level business domains (as the basis for soon-to-be-defined namespaces), simply by using the lines of business that your company may have:

```
http://actioncon.com/marketing
http://actioncon.com/sales
http://actioncon.com/development
...
```

Next, you could decide that you want to separate the data (and message) definitions from the actual service contract definitions because these data definitions might be reused across multiple services. For this, you could create IT-centric domains, resulting in namespaces such as these:

```
http://actioncon.com/development/contract
http://actioncon.com/development/schema
...
```

You have now arrived at a level where you determine whether you want to give each business domain element its own namespace and whether you want to give each service its own namespace. As we mentioned earlier, the outcome of this discussion depends on many factors, like the size of your organization, the number of documents you expect to create, and so forth.

For the examples listed next, we will assume that the next level in your namespace hierarchy is defined by the core business process that the related documents are part of:

```
http://actioncon.com/sales/contract/online_sales
http://actioncon.com/sales/contract/gameinfo
http://actioncon.com/marketing/schema/campaign
...
```

Keep in mind that the strategy you define can differ from what we have outlined here. For example, you may decide that you don't want to define namespaces according to your lines of business because the related constructs can be reused across the entire enterprise.

NOTE

You also have the option of including actual version numbers into a namespace definition, as follows:

```
http://actioncon.com/ordermgmt/schema/Order/v1.0
```

The advantage here is that each XML document carries with it information about its version, making it easier to identify version incompatibilities at both runtime and design time.

Practices and techniques for using namespaces in support of Web service contract versioning are covered in a separate set of chapters in Part III of this book.

IN PLAIN ENGLISH

Over time, the school library begins to grow, accumulating ever more books. The number of items in each of the original genres has therefore increased to such an extent that it is decided to create a more detailed genre structure that incorporates "sub-genres," as follows:

- The Science genre is split up into Computer Science, Natural Sciences and Mathematics.

- Natural Sciences gets further divided into Biology, Chemistry and Physics.

- The Literature genre is split into Science Fiction, Short Stories and Poetry.

Because there aren't many books and other items in the Biography and Kids genres, these are not changed.

> After this restructuring, one of the librarians realizes that there is a book that could fit into both the Kids genre as well as the new Literature/Short Stories sub-genre. However, due to a strict purchasing policy that allows the library to only own one copy of any given book, the librarian is forced to choose between the two options.
>
> The hierarchy of genres and sub-genres described here is similar to how we can define namespaces to reflect a hierarchy of XML elements. The same way a book can only belong to one genre, an XML element or attribute can only be in one namespace.

Industry Standard Namespaces

Many of the namespaces you will need to work with have been pre-defined in technology specifications produced by standards organizations, like the W3C and OASIS. These standardized namespaces pretty much all follow naming conventions like the one we just introduced in the previous section.

Let's have a look at some of the more common ones:

- WSDL = `http://schemas.xmlsoap.org/wsdl/`

- XML Schema = `http://www.w3.org/2001/XMLSchema`

- SOAP = `http://schemas.xmlsoap.org/wsdl/soap/`

Another type of standardized namespace is developed by industry-specific standards organizations. Do you remember the International Federation of Coffee Filter Makers (IFCFM) and the International Federation of Automobile Filter Makers (IFAFM) that we mentioned earlier? If these had actually been real organizations, they would have likely produced standards with their own specific namespaces.

For a real-life example, let's take a look at the ACORD standard (created by the Association for Cooperative Operations Research and Development), which provides an XML vocabulary specific to the insurance industry. This specification defines a number of namespaces including this one:

```
http://ACORD.org/Standards/Life/2
```

Or how about the Open Travel Alliance (OTA), a standards organization dedicated to the travel industry. There's a specification that introduces the following standardized namespace:

```
http://www.opentravel.org/OTA/2003/05
```

It goes without saying that the namespaces you choose for your specific business documents and domains should not be similar to any standardized namespaces you might also be using.

> **NOTE**
>
> Feel free to skip this next section if you're not that interested in learning about the characters allowed in namespace values.

Namespace and URL Encoding

When working with regular URLs, there are a number of reserved characters that have a special purpose, such as:

```
?   +   =   @   #   /
```

The hash character "#", for example, is used to identify a particular fragment within a document (like an HTML bookmark), whereas the question mark "?" character is used to delimit parameters added to an HTTP GET request string.

Therefore, the presence of these characters in a URL for any reason other than their special purpose requires that you *encode* them. Encoding means that you create an alias for a particular character so that you don't have to use the actual character. For URIs, *percent-encoding* is used, meaning that a character can be represented by the percent sign "%", followed by a two-digit hexadecimal value that contains the ASCII code of that intended character.

For example, the following URL containing a question mark character:

```
http://actioncon.com/ordermgmt/schema/Order/?amount
```

... would need to be subjected to encoding, which would replace the question mark with the value "%3F", as follows:

```
http://actioncon.com/ordermgmt/schema/Order/%3Famount
```

If a URL containing such an encoded character is sent to a program, this program must then *decode* the URL to find out what the character really should have been.

Based on this system, you would therefore assume that the preceding two strings would be considered equal. However, here is where a namespace name is different from an actual URL. When used in a namespace name, the two preceding examples are considered different. The reason is that namespace names do not support any form of encoding. They are always just considered a string of characters.

> **NOTE**
>
> This also means that namespace names are case-sensitive, whereas some URI parts are not (like the DNS name of a Web resource).

So, why do namespace names not follow the same rules as URLs? It is simply because their only purpose is to be a name. They don't indicate a protocol, or a location on a network, or reflect any kind of real hierarchy. (But to the uninformed observer, they sure look like they do.)

Therefore, when getting down to the details of defining namespace names, it's important to disassociate them from regular URLs, by following these guidelines:

* Never use an encoding technique to express a namespace name.

* Use URL reserved characters (as defined in the URI specification) if you want to, but be aware that there will never be any special processing applied to them.

* Avoid the use of the percent symbol because it might imply that you are using percent-encoding (when, in fact, you are not).

* Also avoid the use of the space character (' '), even though it is technically allowed.

Note also that while it is theoretically legal to use relative URLs for namespaces, like this:

```
/sales/contract/online_sales/1.0
```

…it is not recommended. It can lead to confusion and potential overlap with namespace names declared elsewhere. In fact, relative URL values are deprecated in version 1.1 of the W3C namespace specification.

> **NOTE**
>
> Also worth considering is that toolkits may try to generate programming code that uses namespace names. Some of the characters in your namespace may be considered illegal when applied to programming code (which may force you to define custom mapping rules).

Namespaces and Actual URLs

The preceding description of namespace names may seem somewhat contradictory: On the one hand, we use URLs as the name, but on the other, we say that there is no meaning whatsoever behind the URL because it is just a string.

So what should you expect if you copy a namespace name and paste it into the address field of a Web browser? The sweeping answer to this question in pretty much any IT environment of any organization in any country is: "It depends."

In some cases the namespace value will actually point to a Web site or Web page on the Internet, and in other cases it won't. If you are creating custom namespaces for your enterprise, it's up to you whether you want them to actually represent content on the Internet or your local intranet. Similarly, the namespaces developed by some standards organizations do point to documents (usually specifications related to the namespace), whereas others will get you a "Page Not Found" error.

For example, the standardized namespaces we listed earlier that represent the WSDL, XML Schema, and SOAP standards actually do point to online content (specifically, they will display the XML schema used to describe the respective language). The other namespaces we listed for the ACORD and OTA organizations have no Web content behind them.

The bottom line is that there are pros and cons to each approach. Here are some reasons as to why it can make sense to have your custom namespaces point to online content:

- It can be convenient for architects and developers working with your Web service contracts to be able to get immediate access to WSDL, XML Schema, or WS-Policy definitions, simply by following the URL that is displayed right in front of them. Without this type of system in place, they will be required to go through some form of discovery process that may involve a registry or several phone calls to others that know the location of these documents.

- It opens the door to a potential programmatic document retrieval tool that could extract and then use namespace values to retrieve corresponding documents or specifications.

Here, now, are some reasons as to why it may not be such a good idea:

- It may turn into a significant governance burden. In larger enterprises with multiple service inventories and a variety of Web service contracts, you could easily end up with dozens of namespaces. Trying to stay on top of how this entire environment evolves and ensuring that all namespaces continue to point to the correct or latest documents can require a great deal of effort. You would need to ensure that the value gained outweighs this effort.

- Besides the maintenance of online content, another governance consideration is ensuring the availability of this content. This is especially important if you decide to have some of your namespaces point externally to documents on the Internet.

- Yet another availability-related consideration is the propagation of a Web services-based solution across different internal environments. For example, if you have a namespace point to a WSDL document, will that document be available (and will it be the same?) across development, test, staging, and production environments? You certainly wouldn't want to change a namespace name merely to reflect the fact that a document was moved from one server to another.

- It may not always be possible to point every namespace to an actual document. Some namespaces just don't warrant anything more than a name identifier. In this case, you may end up with only a subset of the namespaces representing actual URLs, which will be confusing for some of the project team members required to work with them. (In the end, they may simply assume that none of the namespaces point to content, even when many still do.)

With regards to the last item, you can introduce a naming convention for your namespaces so that Web service contract authors can indicate (by the name or a special character or code in the name) whether a given namespace does or does not point to anything.

> **NOTE**
>
> Many tools will inadvertently identify namespaces as actual URLs and translate them into hyperlinks. Having "clickable" namespace names may or may not be a good thing, depending on which of the two previously described approaches you choose.

SUMMARY OF KEY POINTS

- Namespace naming conventions can be used to establish a structure within Web service contract documents. They can also reflect business domains and other characteristics of the documents.

- Namespace names are not subject to the encoding rules that are applied to URL values and therefore can use some special characters.

- Even though a namespace name commonly follows the syntax of a URL, it is just a string, without any of the meaning or structure of a real URL. Most namespace names (including the standardized ones) look like real URLs, but they don't point to any online content.

5.4 Namespace Syntax

So far, we've been exploring what namespaces are used for and how they can be named and structured. Now it's time to take a closer look at how elements and attributes in an XML document can actually be associated with namespaces.

Declaring a Namespace Prefix

You've seen how namespace prefixes get declared via the use of the special `xmlns` attribute, as shown again in our familiar example:

```
<ns:game ns:productID="AY2344"
  xmlns:ns="http://actioncon.com/schema/gameinfo">
  Service Blaster 2000
</ns:game>
```

In this case, the declaration of a prefix occurs within the `game` element. Once established, the prefix can be used inside that same element, as well as any of its child elements. And, of course, it can also be used with any attributes that exist in the element and any of the child elements.

Where in the element the namespace declaration happens does not matter. For example, in the preceding code sample, the attribute `productID` uses the `ns:` prefix, even though that prefix is declared after the attribute. This is still perfectly valid.

The following example shows how the namespace declaration also applies to a child element:

```
<ns:game ns:productID="AY2344"
  xmlns:ns="http://actioncon.com/schema/gameinfo">
  <ns:gtin>
    1234567890123
  </ns:gtin>
  <ns:title>
    Service Blaster 2000
  </ns:title>
</ns:game>
```

As you may have expected, both the `gtin` and `title` elements are part of the namespace called `http://actioncon.com/schema/gameinfo` because they carry the `ns:` prefix with them.

Overriding a Prefix

A prefix does not necessarily have to apply to an entire XML document. A child element can override a namespace declaration by mapping a prefix to a different namespace that then applies to a subset of the document.

Let's look at an example for this case:

```
<ns:game ns:productID="AY2344"
  xmlns:ns="http://actioncon.com/schema/gameinfo">
  <ns:gtin xmlns:ns=
    "http://actioncon.com/schema/gameinfo/detail">
    1234567890123
  </ns:gtin>
</ns:game>
```

Even though the element `gtin` is using the same prefix, it now belongs to a different namespace (bolded text) because the `ns:` prefix is "re-declared" with a new `xmlns` attribute.

This example would be less confusing if we simply established a new prefix instead of reusing the existing one, as follows:

```
<ns:game ns:productID="AY2344"
  xmlns:ns="http://actioncon.com/schema/gameinfo">
  <ns2:gtin xmlns:ns2=
    "http://actioncon.com/schema/gameinfo/detail">
    1234567890123
  </ns2:gtin>
  <ns:title>
```

```
       Service Blaster 2000
    </ns:title>
 </ns:game>
```

A namespace prefix applies only within the scope established by the element that contains its declaration. This means that in the preceding example, the `ns2:` prefix can only be used by the `gtin` element and any attributes or child elements that may fall within it.

The following example is therefore invalid:

```
<ns:game ns:productID="AY2344"
   xmlns:ns="http://actioncon.com/schema/gameinfo">
   <ns2:gtin xmlns:ns2=
     "http://actioncon.com/schema/gameinfo/detail">
     1234567890123
   </ns2:gtin>
   <ns2:title>
     Service Blaster 2000
   </ns2:title>
</ns:game>
```

Because the `title` element is not located within the `ns2:gtin` element, it cannot use the `ns2:` prefix.

However, this example is valid:

```
<ns:game ns:productID="AY2344"
   xmlns:ns="http://actioncon.com/schema/gameinfo">
   <ns2:gtin xmlns:ns2=
     "http://actioncon.com/schema/gameinfo/detail">
     <ns:value>
        1234567890123
     </ns:value>
   </ns2:gtin>
   <ns:title>
     Service Blaster 2000
   </ns:title>
</ns:game>
```

Even though we declared the `ns2:` prefix in the `gtin` element, this does not mean that all attributes and child elements must use this prefix. In fact, in most Web service contract documents you will see all kinds of elements from different vocabularies mixed together with different prefixes (as explained at the end of this chapter).

Therefore, it often makes the most sense to simply declare all of the namespace prefixes in the root element of a given document, as shown here:

```
<ns:game ns:productID="AY2344"
  xmlns:ns="http://actioncon.com/schema/gameinfo"
  xmlns:ns2="http://actioncon.com/schema/gameinfo/detail">
  <ns2:gtin>
    <ns:value>
       1234567890123
    </ns:value>
  </ns2:gtin>
  <ns:title>
    Service Blaster 2000
  </ns:title>
</ns:game>
```

> **NOTE**
>
> As we will see in the upcoming examples, this approach is the most common with Web service contracts.

For a visual representation of a sample namespace architecture, let's briefly revisit the hardware store example, where there are different types of filters. We originally created separate namespaces for the filters so that the same filter element could be used to represent different kinds of filter products.

We can now add new namespaces to establish the following domains within the logical data hierarchy:

- product line-specific namespaces for Appliances, Heating, and Automotive

- a root Store namespace that represents the scope of the entire store itself

Figure 5.3 shows how these new namespace definitions apply to the XML vocabulary, creating domains where some namespaces override others.

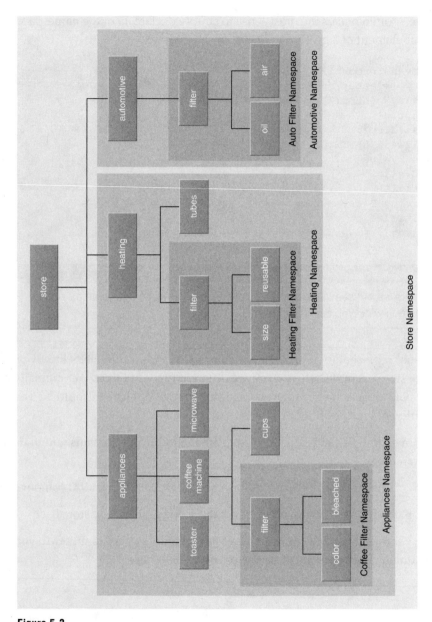

Figure 5.3
The scope of a namespace depends on where its prefix is applied. In this architecture, subsets of the overall model are based on more specific namespaces.

Valid Prefix Names

Let's briefly discuss the rules for naming prefixes. As you can probably guess by now, it makes sense to keep them short given their primary purpose is to act as a shortcut for the actual namespace value in order to reduce the length of the XML document as a whole.

The first character of a prefix must be a letter or the underscore ('_'). Allowed letters include alphabetical characters but not numbers or special characters like '(' or '&'. For the rest of the prefix, almost the same constraints apply, except that numbers, periods, and hyphens are allowed.

The following namespace prefixes are valid:

```
ns
_ns
ns123
abc.abc
abc.1.2
```

...and these are not valid:

```
&ns
12ns
abc:abc
```

The Default Namespace

Up until now, all of the examples have used prefixed elements and attributes. That is, they all had a namespace prefix. Earlier, in the *Namespace Terminology* section, we introduced the concept of a default namespace that allows us to pick one namespace value for which no prefix is required.

The default namespace is therefore declared using the xmlns attribute on its own, as follows:

```
<game productID="AY2344"
  xmlns="http://actioncon.com/schema/gameinfo">
  <gtin>
    1234567890123
  </gtin>
  <title>
    Service Blaster 2000
  </title>
</game>
```

As you can see, all of the prefixes are gone. Instead, a default namespace is established that applies to all elements.

One problem that can occur with this approach is when you need to extract parts of an XML document to use elsewhere. In this case, you may not be able to take the default namespace declaration with it.

For example, let's say we lifted the following fragment from the previous example:

```
<title>
   Service Blaster 2000
</title>
```

This extract carries no namespace information with it. If inserted into a different document, within an element that has a different default namespace, it will become part of that namespace, which could have unwanted side effects.

> **NOTE**
>
> It is worth mentioning that many XML-aware technologies automatically copy related namespace declarations when moving XML content from one document to another.

Therefore, if there is a chance that you will aggregate pieces of XML from a variety of sources, it is usually better not to depend on default namespace declarations. Having stated that, though, the use of default namespaces within Web service contracts is very common. Most often, the default namespace is assigned to elements from the WSDL language when displayed within a WSDL definition. As you will soon see in the upcoming chapters, this is the convention used throughout this book.

Can you use a default namespace and a namespace prefix together in the same document? Yes, you can, as shown next:

```
<game ns2:productID="AY2344"
    xmlns="http://actioncon.com/schema/gameinfo"
    xmlns:ns2="http://actioncon.com/schema/gameinfo/details">
  <gtin>
    1234567890123
  </gtin>
  <ns2:title>
    Service Blaster 2000
  </ns2:title>
</game>
```

Here again we have a document comprised of elements (and an attribute) originating from two different namespaces, but mixed together. The elements without a prefix, in this case, are simply associated with the default namespace.

Let's conclude this section with a brain teaser. Based on what you've learned so far, can you tell which namespace the elements and the attribute in this document belong to?

```
<game ns2:productID="AY2344"
    xmlns="http://actioncon.com/schema/gameinfo"
    xmlns:ns2="http://actioncon.com/schema/gameinfo/details">
  <gtin>
    1234567890123
  </gtin>
  <title
    xmlns="http://actioncon.com/schema/gameinfo/details">
    Service Blaster 2000
  </title>
</game>
```

The answer is:

- the productID attribute and title element belong to the http://actioncon.com/schema/gameinfo/details namespace

- the game and gtin elements belong to the http://actioncon.com/schema/ gameinfo namespace

If you're wondering why the title element is associated with the http:// actioncon.com/schema/gameinfo/details namespace when it does not have a ns2: prefix, then take a close look at the third xmlns attribute in the example.

No Namespace

At the very beginning of this chapter, we looked at an example that showed an element and an attribute with no default namespace and no namespace prefix. Here it is again:

```
<game productID="AY2344">
  Service Blaster 2000
</game>
```

So what does this mean with respect to namespaces? Well, it simply indicates that the element and the attribute in the example do not belong to one. Though this is not common in the world of Web service contracts, it is worth mentioning that it is legal.

The primary purpose of namespaces is to allow elements and attributes from different vocabularies or with identical names to be mixed together so that they can co-exist within the same document without causing conflicts. If you have your own set of elements and attributes that will never need to be combined with other vocabularies and that all have unique names (and always will), then you can certainly make a case for rejecting namespaces altogether.

But back to the real world now. Should you encounter "namespace-less" elements, the question might arise as to whether you can mix these with elements that do belong to a namespace. As shown in this example, the answer is "yes":

```
<ns:game ns:productID="AY2344"
  xmlns:ns="http://actioncon.com/schema/gameinfo">
  <gtin>
    123456789
  </gtin>
  <title>
    Service Blaster 2000
  </title>
</ns:game>
```

In this sample code, all of the red-colored elements have no namespace.

But wait—earlier we looked at an example where there was no prefix, even though the elements were still part of a namespace. As you probably recall (because we just covered it about five minutes ago), that was made possible by the special default namespace declaration.

So here's another interesting scenario: How can you combine elements with no namespace together with elements that belong to the default namespace? If you don't know the answer, don't worry about it. It's really not something you need to know for most Web service contract design work you'll be doing.

But, just in case you're interested, the answer is that you need to explicitly mark elements as not belonging to a namespace, as shown here:

```
<ns:game ns:productID="AY2344"
  xmlns:ns="http://actioncon.com/schema/gameinfo"
  xmlns="http://actioncon.com/schema/gameinfo">
  <gtin xmlns="">
    1234567890123
  </gtin>
  <title>
    Service Blaster 2000
  </title>
</ns:game>
```

In this example, we essentially declare a new default namespace within the `gtin` element, but that new default namespace has a value of an empty string. This "empty" namespace value indicates that there is no namespace at all.

Given that we spent the entire chapter so far talking about the value of namespaces and how to add elements and attributes to them, why would you ever want to explicitly declare that an element belongs to no namespace at all? Usually, the reason is to reduce the size and increase the simplicity of an XML document. Some XML documents can get large and verbose and can therefore consume excess bandwidth when transmitted as messages. You may run into a situation where extreme measures need to be taken in order to optimize the message design.

Another possible motivation is to accommodate toolkit behavior. Some development tools are not able to generate XML documents that use a default namespace, and will instead create their own prefixes for every element. In such a case, it may be acceptable to limit namespace bindings to a top-level element and have every element contained in that top-level element not have a namespace at all.

IN PLAIN ENGLISH

Some of the material that the school library offers cannot really be associated with any of the defined genres or sub-genres (like magazines, catalogs, and brochures). Additionally, the library is selling older books that can no longer be borrowed to students. These titles are disassociated with their original genres and placed into a box at the library's entrance where they are made available for sale. These items don't belong within the library's genre structure and therefore are analogous to elements that have no namespace.

SUMMARY OF KEY POINTS

- Prefixes apply to the element in which they are declared and all child elements and attributes, unless they are overwritten.

- By declaring a default namespace, elements can be bound to a namespace without using a prefix. The default namespace declaration also applies to the element in which it was declared and all its child elements (unless it is overwritten).

- Elements and attributes are not required to belong to a namespace. They can have no namespace if either none was declared or by explicitly being bound to a namespace definition with an empty value.

5.5 Namespaces and Web Service Contracts

Chapter 4 explained how a Web service contract is comprised of multiple technologies that are expressed by different XML-based standards and that the resulting contract definitions themselves are expressed using XML. When you have so many XML elements and attributes that originate from different vocabularies and now need to come together to define one Web service contract, you just know that namespaces are going to be a big part of the equation.

Let's investigate this further by grouping the types of namespaces involved in a Web service contract into the following two categories:

- namespaces that apply to the contract itself

- namespaces that apply to the wire-level messages that are exchanged when using the contract

Now let's add another dimension to this by adding two further categories:

- standardized namespaces that are pre-defined by Web service contract technology standards

- custom namespaces that are defined by you, the Web service contract designer

Both of the latter two namespace types apply to each of the former. In other words, you will use both standardized and custom namespaces to design the Web service contract and any related messages.

At this early stage in the book, we can't describe where these namespaces come from or how they are used. Subsequent chapters will introduce namespaces for new vocabularies and languages on an individual basis and provide further guidance for creating custom namespace values.

However, just to give you a sense of what's ahead, let's briefly preview some namespaces by showing code examples that include namespace prefix declarations for a WSDL definition and a SOAP message definition.

Common Namespaces in the Web Service Contract

Let's start with the following example showing a WSDL `definitions` element (explained in Chapter 7) containing a series of namespace declarations:

```
<definitions name="PurchaseOrder" targetNamespace=
  "http://actioncon.com/contract/po"
  xmlns:tns="http://actioncon.com/contract/po"
```

```
xmlns="http://schemas.xmlsoap.org/wsdl/"
xmlns:xsd="http://www.w3.org/2001/XMLSchema"
xmlns:soap="http://schemas.xmlsoap.org/wsdl/soap/"
xmlns:wsp="http://schemas.xmlsoap.org/ws/2004/09/policy"
xmlns:po="http://actioncon.com/schema/PurchaseOrder">
...
</definitions>
```

The bolded text highlights code that pertains to the target namespace, which is the one namespace-related topic that we did not cover so far because it is explained in detail in Chapter 6. We'll therefore take the easy way out and skip this part of the code.

WSDL Namespace

Both the abstract and the concrete descriptions that we introduced in Chapter 4 are defined using the Web Services Description Language (WSDL), which is comprised of a vocabulary of elements and attributes that are associated with this namespace:

```
xmlns="http://schemas.xmlsoap.org/wsdl/"
```

As explained earlier, a convention in this book is to make this the default namespace, which is why there is no declared prefix.

XML Schema Namespace

In Chapter 4 we showed how different types were defined using the XML Schema language. These types become the basis for message definitions (as explained in Chapter 6). Therefore, the following namespace is required for XML Schema elements that are used in the Web service contract:

```
xmlns:xsd="http://www.w3.org/2001/XMLSchema"
```

As you will see in future examples, this particular namespace declaration can be alternatively placed in a different location within the contract.

SOAP Namespace

Also explained in the previous chapter was how the binding part of a concrete description can be used to associate a Web service contract with an actual communication protocol. When we want to send input and output messages using the SOAP protocol, we need to indicate this in the binding part of the contract by adding elements from the SOAP language. This is why the following namespace is also needed:

```
xmlns:soap="http://schemas.xmlsoap.org/wsdl/soap/"
```

WS-Policy Namespace

You might recall that policies can be applied to various parts of the Web service contract. To express and attach these policies, we need to use elements from the WS-Policy vocabulary, which therefore introduces the need to also add this namespace:

```
xmlns:wsp="http://schemas.xmlsoap.org/ws/2004/09/policy"
```

Custom XML Schema Namespace

As we explain in the next chapter, you will be able to create your own XML schemas that provide custom types that can be used to define input, output, and fault messages for your service contract.

Each custom XML schema that you create can have its own namespace(s) which then need to be added to the Web service contract so that the types you want to use for message definitions can be incorporated.

This is an example of a custom namespace from a custom XML schema:

```
xmlns:po="http://actioncon.com/schema/PurchaseOrder"
```

When working with custom XML schemas, you are not limited to just one. You can have as many as you like, each of which can introduce its own namespace.

> **NOTE**
>
> The use of custom namespaces is not limited to custom XML schemas only. As explained in Chapter 7, you will also be creating custom namespaces for WSDL definitions.

Common Namespaces in the Message

After you invoke and interact with a Web service via its contract, input and output messages are usually generated and transmitted at runtime. When using the SOAP standard, these messages exist as individual XML documents that need their own set of namespaces and prefixes.

Here's an example of the Envelope element that establishes the root of a SOAP message and generally contains the required namespace prefix declarations:

```
<soap:Envelope
  xmlns:soap="http:www.w3.org/2003/05/soap-envelope"
  xmlns:wsa="http://www.w3.org/2005/08/addressing"
  xmlns:po="http://actioncon.com/schema/po">
  ...
</soap:Envelope>
```

SOAP Namespace

The structure of a SOAP message needs to be expressed using elements from the SOAP language, which is why the following namespace is provided:

```
xmlns:soap="http:www.w3.org/2003/05/soap-envelope"
```

Note that this namespace is different from the SOAP namespace we showed in the *Common Namespaces in the Web Service Contract* section. While that preceding namespace represented a modest vocabulary of elements used specifically for contract binding purposes, the SOAP specification defines a separate vocabulary for building the envelope structure of the message itself.

WS-Addressing Namespace

One of the message design technologies we cover in the latter half of this book is called WS-Addressing. It introduces a set of standardized SOAP headers that are expressed using elements from the WS-Addressing language, thereby requiring the presence of this namespace:

```
xmlns:wsa="http://www.w3.org/2005/08/addressing"
```

Custom XML Schema Namespace

Finally, because the SOAP message will be responsible for carrying actual business data and documents, we need the namespace of the custom XML schema that was created to define the types and structure for this business information.

This is why the same custom XML schema from the Web service contract is repeated in the SOAP message:

```
xmlns:po="http://actioncon.com/schema/PurchaseOrder"
```

> **NOTE**
>
> Even though a namespace may occur in both the service contract and the related SOAP message, it may use a different prefix in either one. Also, a given service contract can use more than one custom XML schema, each with its own namespace, resulting in the need for the SOAP message to use multiple prefixes to represent some types of message data.

Namespaces Used in this Book

Appendix D lists all of the prefixes and associated namespaces used in this book. Separate tables are provided for standardized namespaces that relate to industry standards and specifications and custom namespaces that were created in the code samples.

SUMMARY OF KEY POINTS

- When designing Web service contracts, you will need to work with namespaces that pertain to the contract as well as the wire-level messages.

- These namespaces will represent both custom XML vocabularies that you may need to create, as well as vocabularies that originate with industry technology standards.

- Both Web service contracts and generated messages will exist as XML documents that will typically require multiple namespaces to represent elements and attributes from multiple vocabularies.

Chapter 6

Fundamental XML Schema:
Types and Message Structure Basics

When you sit down to design an XML message using XML Schema, you will have probably completed the service-oriented analysis process and you will be looking at a conceptual service candidate with one or more capability candidates, each representing a potential Web service operation. Based on your analysis results and whatever else you will have documented in this service's profile, you will single out an operation and hopefully know enough about what you want its input and/or output messages to do.

The next step is designing the actual messages. This includes deciding exactly what data goes in each message and how it should be structured.

There are basic tenets when it comes to message design:

- flexible constraint granularity is desirable in most cases

- reuse and modularity are beneficial but must be used in moderation

- careful design tends to result in longer-lasting contracts

In this chapter, we examine how the XML Schema language can be used to define types for Web service messages. After an overview of element and attribute declarations, we will discuss simple and complex type definitions, facets, namespaces, and message structure design considerations.

Keep these tenets in mind when you move on to Chapter 12, where we build upon the basics covered in this chapter to explore how balanced message design can lead to increased flexibility and reuse.

"XML Schema" vs. "XML schema"

There are two spelling variations of this term. The word "schema" is capitalized when referring to the XML Schema language or specification and it is lower case when discussing schema documents.

For example, the following statement makes reference to the XML Schema language:

"One feature provided by XML Schema is the ability to…"

And this sentence explains the use of XML schema documents:

"*When defining an XML schema it is important to...*"

Note also that we often refer to XML schemas as just "schemas."

CASE STUDY BACKGROUND

The upcoming case study examples look at some of the design challenges ActionCon faces as they tackle their first service definition for the Game Information service. Steve uses basic XML Schema constructs to define a simple schema for describing game products to end users. He also designs a message that describes a purchase order document in support of the Purchase Order service they will also need to deliver soon.

NOTE

The following section provides background details for the case study relevant to this and subsequent chapters. If you are not interested in the case study, feel free to skip ahead to the *XML Schema Structure* section.

After completing the service modeling portion of the service-oriented analysis process, ActionCon has identified a series of service candidates that they intend to build as part of their planned service inventory.

The first service they tackle is one that will provide up-to-date game-related data to their retail and online customers. ActionCon also wants to create an online affiliates program, where third parties can create and market their own Web sites that sell ActionCon's games and earn a commission in return. Providing this game product data via a Web service will allow these affiliates to develop creative Web sites that always contain current game information without having to be recoded every time a new data item is added to the service.

ActionCon has tasked Steve with defining the message structure for the Game entity service. Steve already has a pretty good idea of what game-related information they want to provide to third parties.

Here is a look at the MySQL table called GAME (Table 6.1), which holds all the data about ActionCon game products.

Column Name	Type	Description
product_id	char(6)	unique ID of the game within ActionCon
gtin	char(13)	13-digit Global Trade Item Number assigned by GS1
title	varchar	title of the game
language	char(2)	natural language of the game and its descriptive information (currently only EN and ES are supported)
description	varchar	multi-paragraph description of the game
min_console_version	char(5)	minimum version of the console that is required to play this game
esrb_rating	char(4)	ESRB rating; EC, E, E10+, T, M, AO, or RP
retail_price	decimal(8,2)	suggested retail price
content_descriptors	varchar	descriptors as defined by ESRB (e.g. "mature humor," "strong lyrics"): multiple values separated by commas
version	integer	version
release_date	date	date of release of this version
genres	varchar	genres (e.g., puzzle, sports): multiple values separated by commas
min_num_players	integer	minimum number of players
max_num_players	integer	maximum number of players
joystick	boolean	whether a joystick is supported
joystick_req	boolean	whether a joystick is required
steering_wheel	boolean	whether a steering wheel is supported
steering_wheel_req	boolean	whether a steering wheel is required
hdtv	boolean	whether HDTV is supported
surround_sound	boolean	whether surround sound is supported

Table 6.1
Structure of the ActionCon GAME table.

Each game has a unique 6-character alphanumeric identifier (product_id) that is used on their Web site and in their internal accounting systems to identify games. Game records also have a 13-digit GTIN, which is a number assigned by GS1, the non-profit organization responsible for generating unique numbers for retail items (such as those used in point-of-sale systems). The rest of the columns in the table represent various features and descriptive information about the games.

This table has a fairly rigid design that has been built up gradually over time without a lot of planning. Therefore, although the database represents the general scope and data elements they want to include in the service, Steve realizes that they do not want to create a service contract that exactly maps to the database. Not only would this lead to negative contract-to-implementation coupling, Steve also remembers that the database will need to be redesigned in the near future (but not before they implement the service). Therefore, he firmly agrees that the service contract and the database table should not be tightly coupled.

Note that since the only current model of their game information is a single relational table that is not ideally designed, ActionCon would be well advised to develop a logical model (for example, in UML) of their game information. However, given that there are no resources for such an effort, Steve decides to move on directly to the design of the physical XML schema definition.

6.1 XML Schema Structure

The fundamental purpose of an XML schema is to declare elements and define their types. As we will shortly explain, there are different kinds of types we can create and different kinds of relationships we can establish between these types. Figure 6.1 hints at the three primary constructs that can be defined.

The structure of a given XML Schema definition can vary significantly. A schema document generally represents a scope associated with a vocabulary of related XML elements and types. As a result, in addition to defining types that formalize this vocabulary, the schema definition also establishes the structure of the vocabulary itself.

The most common type of vocabulary structure is that of a business document, such as the game record or purchase order that are the topics of several of the upcoming examples.

6.2 Elements and Attributes

An element is the core part of any XML document and pretty much all messages exchanged by Web services are expected to contain XML documents. Suppose we are designing the response message for the Game service that contains a set of requested game data. We will need a base element to represent each game record that is returned with the response message. Let's call this element "game."

Each game element will have a number of properties associated with it. For now, let's focus on the following:

- product ID

- GTIN

- title

These three properties plus the game element itself constitute a modest XML vocabulary.

Sometimes the easiest way to get started with designing an XML vocabulary is to create a sample instance of an XML document, as shown here:

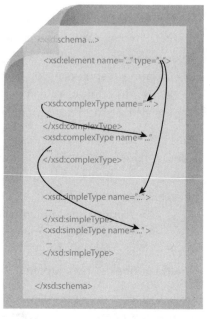

Figure 6.1

An XML Schema definition with element declarations and complex type and simple type definitions. The arrows indicate how these constructs can relate to each other, as further explored in this chapter.

```
<game xmlns="http://actioncon.com/schema/gameinfo"
    productID="AY2344">
  <gtin>1234567890123</gtin>
  <title>Service Blaster 2000</title>
</game>
```

Example 6.1

A simple XML document instance. The highlighted text represents an XML vocabulary comprised of three elements and one attribute.

Example 6.2 shows a schema that might be used to validate our instance. Its three element declarations and one attribute declaration assign names and types to the parts of the schema they declare:

```
<xsd:schema xmlns:xsd="http://www.w3.org/2001/XMLSchema"
  targetNamespace="http://actioncon.com/schema/gameinfo"
  xmlns="http://actioncon.com/schema/gameinfo"
  elementFormDefault="qualified">
<xsd:element name="game" type="GameType"/>
<xsd:complexType name="GameType">
  <xsd:sequence>
    <xsd:element name="gtin" type="xsd:string"/>
    <xsd:element name="title" type="xsd:string"/>
  </xsd:sequence>
  <xsd:attribute name="productID" type="xsd:string"/>
</xsd:complexType>
</xsd:schema>
```

Example 6.2

An XML schema that corresponds to the XML document instance from the previous example. The statements associated with the highlighted name attributes give us an idea of how an XML schema defines the structure of an XML document.

As you can see, XML schemas are themselves XML documents wherein elements share a common, pre-defined namespace (`http://www.w3.org/2001/XMLSchema`). We will explain all of the XML Schema elements and attributes used to create this schema in the upcoming sections.

The XML document instance in Example 6.1 contains three elements (`game`, `gtin`, `title`) and one attribute (`productID`). As a result, the XML schema contains three element declarations (which use the XML schema `xsd:element` element) and one attribute declaration (defined via the `xsd:attribute` element).

The `game` element declaration is considered *global* because it appears at the top level of the schema document (directly under the root `xsd:schema` construct). The other two element declarations, as well as the attribute declaration, are considered *local* because their scope is limited to the `GameType` construct in which they are declared. We'll be exploring the implications of global and local declarations further in the upcoming *Global vs. Local Declarations* section.

> **NOTE**
>
> Namespaces and the use of *prefixes* (the "`xsd:`" value located in front of parts of the schema code) were explained in Chapter 5.

Elements vs. Types

Each element and attribute is associated with a *type* which is a constraint that defines the nature of the data the element or attribute is allowed to contain. Sample types include integer and string, much like the data types used in programming languages. Other XML Schema types can be comprised of entire element structures. We'll be exploring the range of available XML Schema types shortly.

For now, it's important to understand that XML Schema provides a clean separation of the concept of elements and attributes from their types. This separation allows us to use different names for data that is structurally the same. In other words, we will be able to reuse one type for different purposes.

For example, we could write two element declarations, `consoleVersion` and `minimum-ConsoleVersionRequired`, which have the exact same structure, but different names. We would then only be required to define one type, `ConsoleVersionType`, and use it in both element declarations.

In addition to using different names, you can allow the corresponding elements to appear in different places in the schema definition, or in different schema definitions. A `minimumConsoleVersionRequired` element may only be relevant in the context of game information, while `consoleVersion` may appear only in purchase order documents.

You can also have two element declarations with the same name, but different types, in different contexts. For example, a `title` element within a `game` element can be an unconstrained string, while the `title` element within a `customerName` element might allow only the values "Mr.", "Ms.", "Mrs.", and "Dr.".

> **NOTE**
>
> In an object-oriented environment, types are analogous to classes, and elements are roughly comparable to variables that are instances of those classes.

Elements vs. Attributes

Each element in an XML document is described by an element declaration, as follows.

```
<xsd:element name="title" type="xsd:string"/>
```

Example 6.3
A single element declaration.

The `name` attribute specifies the element name that will be used in the XML message, whereas the `type` attribute indicates the type of the element. This example states that the `title` element can contain any string value because its type is `xsd:string`, one of the native built-in data types provided by the XML Schema language (as described in the section *Built-in Simple Types*).

> **NOTE**
>
> Names in XML must start with a letter or underscore and may contain only letters, digits, underscores (_), colons (:), hyphens (-), and periods (.). Although names can contain a wide range of characters, including letters from various character sets, some of these do not map cleanly onto common programming languages.
>
> In particular, non-ASCII characters and periods in names are supported by several Web services toolkits, but their use is not recommended as it can result in generated code that has convoluted names.

Attribute declarations have a similar syntax, but use the `xsd:attribute` element instead, as shown next. Like elements, attributes have names and types.

```
<xsd:attribute name="productID" type="xsd:string"/>
```

Example 6.4
The declaration for the `productID` attribute.

There are always base values that clearly belong in elements (like those representing an address, purchase order, claim, or any other kind of business document). But what about the supplementary values that are associated with these base values (like name, ID, total, etc.)?

When it comes to these secondary values, you can choose whether to place them within elements that are positioned as child elements of the parent base element or whether to locate them in attributes of the base element (or a combination of both).

This decision point is an often-discussed topic in the world of XML schema design. Although attributes are less verbose and result in smaller sized XML document instances, there are a number of important benefits of using child elements:

- You have more control over the rules of their appearance. For example, you can say that if a `game` element has a `joystickVersion` child element, it must also have a `joystickModel` child element. These types of dependencies are not possible for attributes.

- They can be repeated. A child element can appear multiple times within the construct of its parent element. For example, if you decide that a game can support multiple versions, you can allow a `version` child element to appear multiple times. Attributes, on the other hand, can only appear once per element.

- Elements are more extensible because attributes can later be added to them without affecting the processing of the document. For example, if you realize that you need to keep track of what currency a price is expressed in, you can declare a `currency` attribute in the `price` element declaration. If `price` is an attribute, this is not possible.

- For textual descriptions, it is useful to be able to contain other elements. For example, if you want to mark up a game description using XHTML (e.g., using b for bold), this is not possible if `description` is an attribute.

- There are a number of XML Schema features that can be used with elements but not attributes, such as substitution groups, type substitution, and nillable values.

- Tool support tends to be more robust for elements than attributes.

If you do choose to use both elements and attributes, you should be careful not to declare a child element and an attribute with the same name in the same complex type. In Example 6.2, we could technically have created an attribute named `gtin` as well as the child element with that name. However, this practice can confuse toolkits that generate code from the schemas.

Global vs. Local Declarations

> **NOTE**
>
> This section makes reference to complex types and the `xsd:complexType` element. We will cover these topics shortly in the upcoming *Types* section.

Element and attribute declarations can be either global or local. If they are global, they are placed at the top level of the schema as a child of the `xsd:schema` element. (In Example 6.2, the `game` element declaration is global.) Global element declarations must have names that are unique throughout the entire schema. They can then be referenced by name from within complex type definitions.

Local element declarations, on the other hand, appear entirely within the scope of a complex type definition and can only be used within that type definition, never referenced by other complex types. For this reason, it is possible to have multiple local element declarations with the same name, as long as they are within different complex types.

In Example 6.2, the element declarations for gtin and title, as well as the productID attribute declaration, are all local.

Example 6.5 shows how the type definition might be rewritten to declare the gtin and title elements globally. The element declarations, including their type attributes, are moved out from under the xsd:complexType element to the top level of the schema. These global element declarations are then referenced from within the GameType type using ref attributes on the xsd:element element.

```
<xsd:schema xmlns:xsd="http://www.w3.org/2001/XMLSchema"
   targetNamespace="http://actioncon.com/schema/gameinfo"
   xmlns="http://actioncon.com/schema/gameinfo"
   elementFormDefault="qualified">
   <xsd:element name="game" type="GameType"/>
    <xsd:complexType name="GameType">
     <xsd:sequence>
       <xsd:element ref="gtin"/>
       <xsd:element ref="title"/>
     </xsd:sequence>
     <xsd:attribute name="productID" type="xsd:string"/>
   </xsd:complexType>
   <xsd:element name="gtin" type="xsd:string"/>
   <xsd:element name="title" type="xsd:string"/>
</xsd:schema>
```

Example 6.5
gtin and title are declared as global elements.

When using XML schemas independently from Web services, there is limited benefit to using global element declarations. One advantage might appear to be that they can be shared and reused. However, as explained earlier, it is more useful to share types than elements. Reusing global types *and* global elements is usually overkill and in some toolkits can result in unnecessary classes being generated.

However, as part of Web service contracts, the WS-I Basic Profile requires that the root element referenced by a WSDL message definition always be globally declared. Otherwise, the processor will not know where to find the element declaration to start the validation process, because there could be several by that name. Chapter 7 discusses the relationship between XML schema types and WSDL message definitions and both Chapters 7 and 8 explore document-style message designs.

Element Granularity

Many data items have composite values, and it is sometimes unclear to what extent they should be broken down into separate elements. For example, suppose a product ID consists of two letters that represent its department, followed by a four-digit number. Should all six characters be modeled as one element, or should it be broken down into two sub-elements?

It depends on how that data item is to be used. The value should be split up if the individual parts:

- will be displayed separately

- will be sorted separately

- will be used separately in arithmetic operations

- have different data types

- need to be validated separately

- need to establish a higher level of constraint granularity

It is easier to concatenate two data values back together than it is to parse them apart, especially if the logic for splitting them is complex.

On the other hand, if the value is always used as a whole by service consumers, it can be kept together. It comes down to the functional nature of the service. For example, a service that simply provides product information for display might offer the product ID as one value, while a purchase order that needs to treat departments separately may split it up.

> **NOTE**
>
> Determining the granularity of elements will affect the constraint granularity and message granularity types explained in Chapter 3. There are various design patterns that will further influence the granularity of elements, including Contract Denormalization and Concurrent Contracts. In fact, for these two patterns in particular, having finer-grained elements can be beneficial in that it avoids having to create new types to accommodate new variations of the same operation. Instead, fine-grained types can be combined into a variety of composites.

SUMMARY OF KEY POINTS

- XML Schema separates the concepts of elements and attributes from their types.

- Attributes are limited to simple types, whereas child elements are more extensible and can contain further nested child elements.

- Elements and attributes can be declared locally or globally; global declarations are recommended for message structures.

6.3 Types

A type is used to describe and validate the content of an element and the values of its attributes. Types in XML Schema are either simple or complex.

Simple types describe elements that have textual content but no child elements or attributes. In Example 6.1, the `gtin` and `title` elements have simple types. Attributes, like `productID` in our example, always have simple types.

Complex types describe elements that may have child elements and/or attributes. The `game` element in our example has a complex type. An element that has attributes needs to have a complex type, even if it has no children. For example, if we added a `language` attribute to the `title` element, it would then need to be considered a complex type.

What's a Content Model?

Within an XML schema you can establish a variety of types. Some will have a specific structure associated with them, along with rules that determine the order, cardinality, names, and types of the child elements that reside with the construct. This structure is known as a *content model*. Many of the XML Schema features covered in this chapter relate to defining and organizing content models.

Named vs. Anonymous Types

Like element and attribute declarations, type definitions can be global or local. If a type is global, it is given a name that must be unique throughout the entire schema and is therefore referred to as a *named type*. If a type is local, it does not need a name because it cannot be reused elsewhere in the schema. As a result, it is then considered an *anonymous type*.

The benefit of named (global) types is that they may be defined once and used many times. For example, you may define a type named `ProductCodeType` that lists all of the valid product codes in your organization. This type can then be used in many element declarations in many schemas.

This has the advantages of:

- encouraging consistency throughout the organization

- reducing the possibility of error

- requiring less time to define new schemas

- simplifying maintenance (because new product codes need only be added in one place)

> **NOTE**
>
> An additional bonus is that straightforward names are used in generated code. Most code generation tools create a class for every complex type. If the type is named, that type name becomes the class name.

An anonymous type, on the other hand, can be used only in the element or attribute declaration that contains it. Certain advanced features of XML Schema (including redefinition, type derivation, union types, and list types) do not support anonymous types. This can seriously limit their reusability, extensibility, and their ability to change over time.

When generating code, the name of the class representing an anonymous type may be a confusing concatenation of several values, including the element's name, the element's parent's name, etc. This directly counters the objectives of the Standardized Service Contract design principle. For this reason, it is recommended that you always use global, named types in XML schemas that will be part of Web service contracts.

Built-in Simple Types

A set of simple pre-defined data types are provided by the XML Schema language and can be directly referenced within schemas that you create. They describe simple values such as strings, decimal numbers, and dates. (In Example 6.2, we used two built-in data types: `xsd:string` and `xsd:int`.)

Built-in data types are designed to be vendor and programming language-neutral, which means that toolkits will need to be used to map them to the proprietary data types used in individual programming languages.

Although there are 44 built-in types, only a handful of them are especially useful. Some examples are listed in Table 6.2:

Type Name	Description	Examples
xsd:string	unconstrained character string	Hello world!
xsd:double	double-precision 64-bit floating-point number	-INF, -5E2, 0, 24.5e-3, 12, 15.2, INF, NaN
xsd:float	single-precision 32-bit floating-point number	-INF, -5E2, 0, 24.5e-3, 12, 15.2, INF, NaN
xsd:decimal	decimal number	-5, +5.5, +.5, 5, 5.000
xsd:long	integer from -9223372036854775808 to 9223372036854775807	-9223372036854775808, 0, +3, 3
xsd:int	integer from -2147483648 to 2147483647	-2147483648, 0, 3, 2147483647
xsd:short	integer from -32768 to 32767	-32768, 0, 3, 32767
xsd:byte	integer from -128 to 127	-128, 0, 3, 100
xsd:date	date, in YYYY-MM-DD format (with optional time zone)	2004-04-12
xsd:time	time, in hh:mm:ss.sss format (with optional time zone)	15:20:00.000, 15:20:00Z, 15:20:00-05:00
xsd:dateTime	date and time, in YYYY-MM-DDThh:mm:ss.sss format (with optional time zone)	2004-04-12T15:20:00, 2004-04-12T15:20:00.000-05:00
xsd:language	natural language identifier	en, en-GB, en-US, es, fr
xsd:boolean	Logical	true, false, 0, 1
xsd:hexBinary	binary with hex encoding	0CD8, 0cd8
xsd:base64Binary	binary with base64 encoding	0CD8, 0cD8, +4
xsd:anyURI	URI (URL, URN, etc.)	http://www.actioncon.com, ../games.html, urn:example:org

Table 6.2

A list of sample built-in simple types predefined by the XML Schema specification.

Note that for service interoperability purposes, there are a few types that should be avoided:

- xsd:integer represents an arbitrarily large integer that may not be suitable for use in Web service contracts because, due to its unlimited size, it does not map cleanly onto commonly used data types of programming languages.

- xsd:unsignedLong, xsd:unsignedInt, xsd:unsignedShort and xsd:unsigned Byte are not recommended because they do not map well to Java types (although the JAXB specification does provide mappings for them).

It is often appropriate to use specific data types instead of just declaring everything a string. For example, if a data item is a date, the xsd:date type will ensure that received values are always valid dates. This also allows you to use the value directly in your code without having to cast it. The only consideration is that of constraint granularity.

Data types can be overused so that they unnecessarily lead to fragile Web service contracts that need to be prematurely versioned. Be sure to balance the benefit of data types with the governance implications as per the Service Abstraction design principle and the Validation Abstraction design pattern.

Types and Inheritance

The upcoming sections explore a range of specialized type definitions. It's worth highlighting two special elements used to create these type definitions, as they both provide a form of inheritance:

- xsd:restriction – As explained shortly in the *User-Defined Simple Types* section, this element allows you to take an existing type and customize it by making it more restrictive.

- xsd:extension – The *Complex Types* section introduces this element, which enables you to also start with an existing type definition and then extend it in different ways.

Each of these elements essentially inherits the qualities of a type and then further customizes it in some way.

User-Defined Simple Types

If you want a type that is more restrictive than those provided by XML Schema, you can define your own based on one of the built-in types.

For example, suppose that for the gtin element you only want to allow a string with 13 characters. You could define the simple type GTINType shown in Example 6.6 and assign it to the gtin element in its declaration. GTINType forces the length of the value to be 13 characters.

```
<xsd:simpleType name="GTINType">
  <xsd:restriction base="xsd:string">
    <xsd:length value="13"/>
  </xsd:restriction>
</xsd:simpleType>
```

Example 6.6
A user-defined simple type based on the built-in xsd:string type but augmented to include a length restriction.

As you can see, the xsd:simpleType element is used to define a simple type that is then customized (user-defined) through the use of the xsd:restriction construct that introduces a length limitation via the xsd:length element.

In this case, the xsd:string simple type is considered the *base type* as indicated by the xsd:restriction element's base attribute. The customization of the simple type (which is called "GTINType") is referred to as a *user-defined type*.

There is a wide variety of user-defined types that you can create. In fact, a base type can even be a previously created user-defined type that you then further customize. The only constraint is that when you define a new simple type, you must make it more restrictive than the base type. You cannot expand (loosen the constraint granularity of) a simple type.

> **NOTE**
>
> There is no requirement that type names have the word "Type" at the end. However, it is a common practice to distinguish type names from element names because this supports the objectives of the Standardized Service Contract principle. Conventions such as this also form the basis for the Canonical Expression design pattern.

Facets

The xsd:length element in the previous example is known as a *facet*, a special type of element that always appears as a child element of the xsd:restriction construct.

Facets can be used in combination with each other to express a wide range of validation logic by defining restrictions on the values allowed by a type. There are 12 facets in total, each of which is described in the remainder of this chapter.

Note that most tools that generate classes from schema definitions ignore user-defined simple types, with the exception of those that use enumerated lists of values described in the following section. In all other cases, the built-in type on which it is based is used instead. For example, an element of type GTINType would come to be a property of type xsd:string. However, it is still useful to define new simple types for the purposes of validation and documentation (as long as it doesn't give the impression that the validation will happen automatically in the generated code).

Enumerated Lists of Values

It is very common to require a specific list of allowed values for a type. A classic example of this is a list of country codes that is part of an address type.

Here is an example of an xsd:restriction construct in which code values are specified using a repeating xsd:enumeration facet.

```xsd
<xsd:simpleType name="ESRBRatingType">
  <xsd:restriction base="xsd:string">
    <xsd:enumeration value="EC"/>
    <xsd:enumeration value="E"/>
    <xsd:enumeration value="E10+"/>
    <xsd:enumeration value="T"/>
    <xsd:enumeration value="M"/>
    <xsd:enumeration value="AO"/>
    <xsd:enumeration value="RP"/>
  </xsd:restriction>
</xsd:simpleType>
```

Example 6.7

An enumerated list of values expressed through the repeated use of the xsd:enumeration facet.

Length Restrictions and Ranges

Example 6.6 showed how you can specify a length for a string value. You can also restrict a string to a range of lengths using the xsd:minLength and xsd:maxLength facets. Either of them (or both) may be incorporated within a simple type.

The type shown here might be used to ensure that a game title is at least 3 and at most 40 characters long:

```
<xsd:simpleType name="TitleType">
  <xsd:restriction base="xsd:string">
    <xsd:minLength value="3"/>
    <xsd:maxLength value="40"/>
  </xsd:restriction>
</xsd:simpleType>
```

Example 6.8

An example of how a value can be restricted to a range of lengths using the xsd:minLength and xsd:maxLength facets.

For numeric and date values, you can specify a range of allowed values using the xsd:minInclusive, xsd:maxInclusive, xsd:minExclusive, and/or xsd:maxExclusive facets. The type shown in the following example restricts the number of players to an integer between 1 and 5, inclusive.

```
<xsd:simpleType name="NumberOfPlayersType">
  <xsd:restriction base="xsd:int">
    <xsd:minInclusive value="1"/>
    <xsd:maxInclusive value="5"/>
  </xsd:restriction>
</xsd:simpleType>
```

Example 6.9

A simple type limited to a range of values using the two highlighted facets.

Decimal Precision and Scale

Decimal numbers can be limited by their total number of significant digits and their number of fractional digits using the xsd:totalDigits and xsd:fractionDigits facets, respectively.

This next example shows a type that restricts a price to 8 total digits, with up to 2 of those digits being fractional. The facet values specified represent the maximum number of digits, not the actual number.

```
<xsd:simpleType name="PriceType">
  <xsd:restriction base="xsd:decimal">
    <xsd:totalDigits value="8"/>
    <xsd:fractionDigits value="2"/>
  </xsd:restriction>
</xsd:simpleType>
```

Example 6.10

Facets used to define the precision and scale of decimals.

Formatting Patterns

Regular expressions can be used to specify a formatting pattern that a value must match. This is accomplished using an `xsd:pattern` facet. In the following example, the pattern `[A-Z]{2}[0-9]{4}` forces the value to consist of two uppercase letters followed by four digits.

```
<xsd:simpleType name="ProductIDType">
  <xsd:restriction base="xsd:string">
    <xsd:pattern value="[A-Z]{2}[0-9]{4}"/>
  </xsd:restriction>
</xsd:simpleType>
```

Example 6.11
A regular expression pattern facet.

XML Schema has its own regular expression syntax, but it is similar to those used in programming languages (Perl in particular). Table 6.3 provides some examples of typical expressions.

Regular Expression	Description	Matching Strings
ab | cd	ab or cd	ab, cd
(ab | cd)z	ab or cd, followed by z	abz, cdz
a?b+	An optional a followed by one or more b's	b, ab, bbbb, abbbb
a*b{2}	any number of a's followed by two b's	bb, abb, aaaabb
a{2,4}	between 2 and 4 a's	aa, aaa, aaaa
[abc]z	a or b or c, followed by z	az, bz, cz
[^abc]z	anything but a or b or c, followed by z	ez, fz
[a-f]*z	any number of letters a through f, followed by z	z, abcz, deaaadz
.{3}	any three characters	fe4
\d	a decimal digit	6
\s	a whitespace character (space, tab, newline, carriage return)	

Regular Expression	Description	Matching Strings
\p{Ll}	any lowercase character (as defined by Unicode)	a, b, c
\p{IsBasicLatin}	any character in the Unicode "Basic Latin" range	a, b, c

Table 6.3
A list of useful common expression patterns.

> **NOTE**
>
> One difference in the treatment of regular expressions in XML Schema is the fact that there is an implicit anchor at the beginning and end of the pattern. This means that in Example 6.11, the value must be six characters long and those six characters must match the pattern. In other regular expression syntaxes, a string might match that pattern as long as it contains (anywhere within it) six characters that match the pattern.

Complex Types

Complex types are used for elements that can have children and/or attributes. Like simple types, they can be global and named or local and anonymous. Only elements (not attributes) can have complex types. To fully understand complex types, we first need to learn about allowable *content* types.

Content Types

The "content" of an element is the text and child elements that are located within its opening and closing tags.

There are four types of content allowed by complex types (as also depicted in Figure 6.2):

- simple content
- element-only content
- mixed content
- empty content

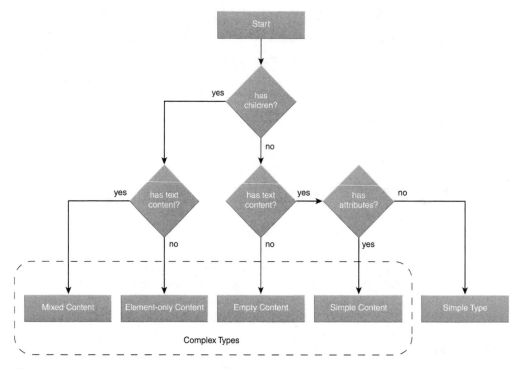

Figure 6.2
Content types as they relate to complex types.

NOTE
The content type is independent of attributes; all complex types allow attributes regardless of their content type.

The highlighted parts of this example reveal four elements with different content types.

```
<title language="en">Service Blaster 2000</title>

<numberOfPlayers>
  <minimum>1</minimum>
  <maximum>4</maximum>
</numberOfPlayers>

<rating value="EC"/>

<desc language="en">This is a <i>great</i> game.</desc>
```

Example 6.12
Elements with complex types.

All have complex types, but they each have a different content type, as follows:

- The `title` element has simple content because it contains only text.

- The `numberOfPlayers` element has element-only content because it has child elements, but no text content.

- The `rating` element has empty content because it does not have any content (just an attribute).

- The `desc` element has mixed content because it has both child elements and text content.

The next sections look at how we might define complex types to describe the first three of these elements. Mixed content is covered in Chapter 13.

Defining a Simple Content Complex Type

Complex types with simple content allow only text with no child elements. The sole difference between a simple type and a complex type with simple content is that the complex type allows attributes. If the `title` element in Example 6.12 did not have a `language` attribute, it could just have a simple type, as it was in Example 6.2.

A complex type definition that describes the `title` element with a `language` attribute is shown in Example 6.13. The base type in this case is `xsd:string`, meaning that the text content of `title` conforms to the simple type `xsd:string`. The type definition uses the `xsd:extension` element to extend `xsd:string` to add the `language` attribute.

```xsd
<xsd:complexType name="TitleType">
  <xsd:simpleContent>
    <xsd:extension base="xsd:string">
      <xsd:attribute name="language" type="xsd:language"/>
    </xsd:extension>
  </xsd:simpleContent>
</xsd:complexType>
```

Example 6.13
A complex type with simple content.

Defining an Element-only Content Complex Type

This represents by far the most common kind of complex type used in Web service messages. Complex types with element-only content are limited to containing child elements with no text content. Example 6.14 shows such a definition, which might be used to represent the `numberOfPlayers` element in Example 6.12. It also adds a required attribute.

```
<xsd:complexType name="NumberOfPlayersRangeType">
  <xsd:sequence>
    <xsd:element name="minimum" type="NumberOfPlayersType"/>
    <xsd:element name="maximum" type="NumberOfPlayersType"
      minOccurs="0"/>
  </xsd:sequence>
  <xsd:attribute name="limited" type="xsd:boolean"
    use="required"/>
</xsd:complexType>
```

Example 6.14
A complex type with element-only content.

For complex types that allow children, you need to formally specify a structure or content model. In this example, there can be two child elements: `minimum` and `maximum`. Both have the type `NumberOfPlayersType`, which we defined earlier in Example 6.9.

By default, a declared element must appear once and only once. However, you can use `minOccurs` and `maxOccurs` attributes on the element's declaration to change its cardinality.

The element declaration for `maximum` uses `minOccurs="0"` to indicate that the element is optional. The value of `minOccurs` can be any integer. The value of `maxOccurs` can be any integer, or the special value "`unbounded`," which means that the element can appear an unlimited number of times.

> **NOTE**
>
> Some development tools do not support specific integer values for the `minOccurs` and `maxOccurs` attributes, outside of "0" and "1." In this case, you may be required to use "`unbounded`" instead.

The type in Example 6.14 uses the `xsd:sequence` element, which means that the elements must appear in the XML message in the order they are declared in the schema. This is the most common type of model group, and it is the most appropriate for Web service messages because it makes the order of the elements more predictable, and it also maps more cleanly onto modeled service candidates.

> **NOTE**
>
> The two alternatives to `xsd:sequence` are `xsd:choice` and `xsd:all`.
> These elements are discussed in Chapter 12.

Example 6.14 also shows how you can declare an attribute in a type that has a content model. The attribute declaration must appear after the content model. Unlike elements, attributes are optional by default. You use a `use="required"` attribute setting (rather than `minOccurs`/`maxOccurs`) on an attribute declaration to make the attribute mandatory.

Defining an Empty Content Complex Type

To define a complex type with empty content you simply leave out the content model. Example 6.15 might be used for the `rating` element shown in Example 6.12. It consists only of an attribute declaration.

```
<xsd:complexType name="RatingType">
  <xsd:attribute name="value" type="ESRBRatingType"/>
</xsd:complexType>
```

Example 6.15
A complex type with empty content.

How Types are Used in Web Service Contracts

As you make your way through the upcoming chapters, you'll notice many references to XML Schema types. Figure 6.3 provides a brief preview as to how types tend to get used by different parts of the Web service contract.

Let's briefly explain each relationship:

1. XML Schema is used to define policy assertion types for both industry and custom policy assertions that are attached as extensions to the WSDL definition.

2. XML Schema is used to define the types associated with the message definitions (and their various parts) within a WSDL definition.

3. The XML Schema message types established via the WSDL definition form the basis of the SOAP message structure, including its optional header and fault message parts.

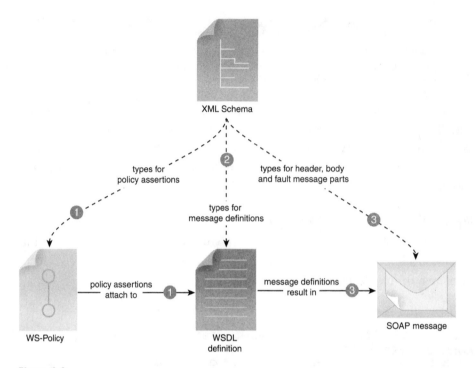

Figure 6.3
XML Schema types will usually make their way into all Web service contract-related documents.

Again, all of these relationships are explained throughout the remaining chapters in this book. At this stage, it is just important to acknowledge how fundamental the definition of XML Schema types is to Web service contract design in general.

SUMMARY OF KEY POINTS

- Simple types are for attributes and elements with no children and no attributes, while complex types are for elements with children and/or attributes.

- A number of built-in simple types are provided by the XML Schema language, such as xsd:string, xsd:int, and xsd:date.

- You can create new simple types that restrict values by ranges, lengths, enumerated lists, regular expressions, and other facets.

- Complex types have one of four content types: simple, element-only, mixed, and empty.

- To describe a complex type that allows children, you define a content model that identifies the names, order, and cardinality of the child elements.

6.4 Namespaces

As explained in Chapter 5, namespaces are used to disambiguate (uniquely identify) element names that are utilized in different contexts and for different purposes. Generally, a namespace name identifies the source of a particular XML vocabulary or language.

For example, the following value:

```
http://www.w3.org/2001/XMLSchema
```

...is the namespace for the XML Schema language vocabulary. You may have noticed that it was used in earlier examples, where we bound it with the `xsd:` prefix, which is common practice. Therefore, most examples that show an entire schema start with the following:

```
<xsd:schema xmlns:xsd="http://www.w3.org/2001/XMLSchema"
  ...>
```

Eventually, the elements that comprise your custom vocabulary will need to be incorporated within a WSDL definition so that they can be referenced by input and output message definitions that determine the interaction scenarios supported by WSDL operations.

Native elements from the WSDL and XML Schema languages will need to co-exist with each other and with custom vocabularies you created. Processors therefore need to figure out what element belongs to what source. As we explained in Chapter 5, namespaces and the use of prefixes make this possible.

NOTE

The use of namespaces is mandated by the WS-I Basic Profile.

There are many namespaces that represent pre-defined XML vocabularies and languages. When writing your own schema, you are effectively creating a custom vocabulary for which you can define a separate namespace. In fact, creating custom namespaces is required when building XML schemas for use in Web service contracts. These custom namespaces are called *target namespaces*.

The Target Namespace

To create a namespace for a custom vocabulary, you need to establish a target namespace for that vocabulary's schema. This namespace is different from the native XML

Schema namespace we highlighted earlier in this section, which traditionally relies on the use of the xsd: prefix.

The native XML Schema namespace is pre-defined and represents the industry standard XML Schema language. In an XML Schema definition, the target namespace (and its prefix) are determined by you to represent your custom vocabulary that you define using the XML Schema language.

NOTE
You can create a separate target namespace for the WSDL definition as well, as explained in Chapter 7.

The *targetNamespace* Attribute

To establish a target namespace, you need to populate the targetNamespace attribute of the xsd:schema element, as shown here:

```
<xsd:schema xmlns:xsd="http://www.w3.org/2001/XMLSchema"
  targetNamespace="http://actioncon.com/schema/gameinfo"
  xmlns="http://actioncon.com/schema/gameinfo">
  <xsd:element name="game" type="GameType"/>
  <xsd:complexType name="GameType">
    <xsd:sequence>
      <xsd:element name="gtin" type="xsd:string"/>
      <xsd:element name="title" type="xsd:string"/>
    </xsd:sequence>
    <xsd:attribute name="productID" type="xsd:string"/>
  </xsd:complexType>
</xsd:schema>
```

Example 6.16
An xsd:schema element with a targetNamespace attribute.

The target namespace definition causes all global elements and types that are declared in the schema to become part of that namespace. In the preceding example, the red text shows how the target namespace is established using the targetNamespace attribute. The bolded text then demonstrates how we assign this same namespace as the default namespace (using the xmlns attribute). As explained in Chapter 5, this allows us to refer to types defined in the schema, such as GameType, without using a prefix.

Let's see what an instance of an XML document following the schema from the previous example might look like:

```
<games:game productID="AY2344"
  xmlns:games="http://actioncon.com/schema/gameinfo">
  <gtin>
    1234567890123
  </gtin>
  <title>
    Service Blaster 2000
  </title>
</games:game>
```

Example 6.17

An XML document instance based on the previous XML schema. Note the use of the `games:` prefix to represent the target namespace.

In this example, the `games:` prefix indicates that the `game` element is part of the `http://actioncon.com/schema/gameinfo` namespace, which matches the target namespace definition in the schema. But the `productID` attribute, as well as the `gtin` and `title` elements, are not prefixed.

The reason for this is that the target namespace, as defined in the previous schema example, only applies to global elements. The `gtin` and `title` elements are declared as local elements, and therefore they have no namespace. If we decided to change them to be global elements, which are then referenced from within the complex type definition, the schema would look like this:

```
<xsd:schema xmlns:xsd="http://www.w3.org/2001/XMLSchema"
  targetNamespace="http://actioncon.com/schema/gameinfo"
  xmlns="http://actioncon.com/schema/gameinfo">
  <xsd:element name="game" type="GameType"/>
  <xsd:complexType name="GameType">
    <xsd:sequence>
      <xsd:element ref="gtin"/>
      <xsd:element ref="title"/>
    </xsd:sequence>
    <xsd:attribute name="productID" type="xsd:string"/>
  </xsd:complexType>
  <xsd:element name="gtin" type="xsd:string"/>
  <xsd:element name="title" type="xsd:string"/>
</xsd:schema>
```

Example 6.18

A different version of the schema in which three global elements are declared.

In the corresponding XML document instance created from this revised schema, the namespace is applied to all elements, because they have been made global:

```
<games:game productID="AY2344"
  xmlns:games="http://actioncon.com/schema/gameinfo">
  <games:gtin>
    1234567890123
  </games:gtin>
  <games:title>
    Service Blaster 2000
  </games:title>
</games:game>
```

Example 6.19
An XML document instance based on the previous schema. Because all three elements are global, they fall within the target namespace and must be prefixed accordingly.

NOTE
The productID attribute still has no namespace, because we didn't change it to be declared globally.

The previous XML schema (from Example 6.18) was designed to associate the XML Schema namespace to the default namespace. It is also possible to assign the target namespace to a prefix, as follows:

```
<xsd:schema xmlns:xsd="http://www.w3.org/2001/XMLSchema"
  targetNamespace="http://actioncon.com/schema/gameinfo"
  xmlns:games="http://actioncon.com/schema/gameinfo">
  <xsd:element name="game" type="games:GameType"/>
  <xsd:element name="gtin" type="xsd:int"/>
  <xsd:element name="title" type="xsd:string"/>
  <xsd:complexType name="GameType">
    <xsd:sequence>
      <xsd:element ref="games:gtin"/>
      <xsd:element ref="games:title"/>
    </sequence>
    <xsd:attribute name="productID" type="xsd:string"/>
  </complexType>
</schema>
```

Example 6.20
In this case, the target namespace is assigned to a prefix rather than being the default. As a result, the values of the ref and type attributes must use prefixes to refer to elements and types by their qualified names.

Target Namespace Format Conventions

You might recall that in Chapter 5 we highlighted the importance of setting namespace naming conventions as early as possible in the service-oriented design process. With Web services, it is especially crucial to separate schema target namespaces from WSDL target namespaces for clarity and governance purposes. See Part IV for an exploration of how namespaces tie into various contract versioning techniques.

At ActionCon, Steve and Kevin establish the following namespace conventions:

- All schema target namespaces must follow the format:
  `"http://actioncon.com"`+ `"/schema/"` + subject area

- All WSDL target namespaces must follow the format:
  `"http://actioncon.com"`+ `"/contract/"` + subject area

This pre-defined format becomes part of the official, custom design standards applied to all Web service contracts.

Namespace Prefixes and Runtime XML Document Generation

All of our examples have focused on schemas and XML documents that we will have defined at design time. It is worth noting that when incorporating these XML schemas with Web service contracts, the XML document instances will be created by the runtime platforms hosting the Web services and its consumer programs. These platforms will likely include SOAP engines that will automatically decide how to add, name, and assign namespace prefixes to XML documents packaged as SOAP messages.

Qualified and Unqualified Elements

We've explained how target namespaces apply to globally declared elements and attributes. But how can we define a schema where locally declared elements and attributes also become part of the target namespace? For this we need to turn to the following two special attributes of the `xsd:schema` element: `elementFormDefault` and `attributeFormDefault`.

The `elementFormDefault` *Attribute*

This attribute essentially allows us to override the rule that a schema's target namespace only applies to global elements.

The `elementFormDefault` attribute can be set to one of two values: "qualified" or "unqualified." The value of "unqualified" indicates that only global elements are associated with a target namespace. This value is the default (even when the `elementFormDefault` attribute is not used at all).

However, when set to "qualified," we introduce a requirement that all elements (global and local) are part of the target namespace, as shown here:

```
<xsd:schema xmlns:xsd="http://www.w3.org/2001/XMLSchema"
  targetNamespace="http://actioncon.com/schema/gameinfo"
  xmlns="http://actioncon.com/schema/gameinfo"
  elementFormDefault="qualified">
  <xsd:element name="game" type="GameType"/>
  <xsd:complexType name="GameType">
    <xsd:sequence>
      <xsd:element name="gtin" type="xsd:string"/>
      <xsd:element name="title" type="xsd:string"/>
    </xsd:sequence>
    <xsd:attribute name="productID" type="xsd:string"/>
  </xsd:complexType>
</xsd:schema>
```

Example 6.21
Because the `elementFormDefault` attribute is set to "qualified," all four elements are associated with the target namespace.

In the following XML document instance that is based on this schema, the `games:` prefix is used for references to all elements:

```
<games:game productID="AY2344"
  xmlns:games="http://actioncon.com/schema/gameinfo">
  <games:gtin>
    1234567890123
  </games:gtin>
  <games:title>
    Service Blaster 2000
  </games:title>
</games:game>
```

Example 6.22
An XML document where all elements belong to the same namespace. (Note how this example looks exactly like an earlier example, where the `gtin` and `title` elements were declared globally.)

Now that all of the elements in the document are in the same namespace, we could also use a default namespace declaration instead.

NOTE

In most circles, keeping the `elementFormDefault` attribute set to "qualified" is a recommended practice because unqualified schemas can become confusing and cause problems with some toolkits. Although, while some prefer to set this element to "unqualified" because it can increase readability (and also because there is an assumption that you can sufficiently structure the message by adding namespaces only to the top-level elements), others feel this can lead to confusion and can result in default namespaces becoming unusable.

The `attributeFormDefault` Attribute

What the `elementFormDefault` attribute is to elements, the `attributeFormDefault` attribute is to attributes. This attribute can also be set to the "qualified" and "unqualified" values, and, as with `elementFormDefault`, also defaults to "unqualified." The meanings of these attribute settings are also the same: a value of "unqualified" only binds global attributes to the target namespace, whereas the value of "qualified" binds both local and global attributes.

However, one difference worth noting when comparing this attribute to `elementFormDefault` is that `attributeFormDefault` simply does not get used as much. It is unusual for Web service contract designers to want to force an association with a namespace on attributes.

The `form` Attribute

Another related attribute that is worth knowing about is `form`. It allows us to choose specific local elements that we want to associate with the target namespace. The `xsd:element` element used to declare new elements can have a `form` attribute that can be set to "qualified" or "unqualified."

In the following example, we don't use the `elementFormDefault` attribute, which means that, by default, no local elements will be bound to the target namespace. However, the `form` attribute with a setting of "qualified" is added to the `gtin` element declaration, which ensures that this specific local element is, in fact, associated with the target namespace.

```
<xsd:schema xmlns:xsd="http://www.w3.org/2001/XMLSchema"
  targetNamespace="http://actioncon.com/schema/gameinfo"
  xmlns="http://actioncon.com/schema/gameinfo">
  <xsd:element name="game" type="GameType"/>
  <xsd:complexType name="GameType">
    <xsd:sequence>
      <xsd:element name="gtin" type="xsd:string"
        form="qualified"/>
      <xsd:element name="title" type="xsd:string"/>
    </xsd:sequence>
    <xsd:attribute name="productID" type="xsd:string"/>
  </xsd:complexType>
</xsd:schema>
```

Example 6.23
The form attribute is used with the gtin element declaration.

By now, you probably have a pretty good idea as to what the XML document instance for this schema will look like. Both the global game element and the local gtin element are prefixed with games: because they were both bound to the target namespace:

```
<games:game productID="AY2344"
  xmlns:games="http://actioncon.com/schema/gameinfo">
  <games:gtin>
    1234567890123
  </games:gtin>
  <title>
    Service Blaster 2000
  </title>
</games:game>
```

Example 6.24
In this XML document instance, the title element is not prefixed because the corresponding schema did not bind it to the target namespace.

Note that the form attribute can also be applied to attribute declarations in order to selectively choose which local attributes are bound to the target namespace, as follows:

```
<xsd:schema xmlns:xsd="http://www.w3.org/2001/XMLSchema"
  targetNamespace="http://actioncon.com/schema/gameinfo"
  xmlns="http://actioncon.com/schema/gameinfo">
  ...
    <xsd:attribute name="productID" type="xsd:string"
      form="qualified"/>
  </xsd:complexType>
</xsd:schema>
```

Example 6.25
The form attribute is used to associate the local productID attribute with the target namespace.

This then results in the requirement for us to prefix the attribute in the XML document instance:

```
<games:game games:productID="AY2344"
  xmlns:games="http://actioncon.com/schema/gameinfo">
  ...
</games:game>
```

Example 6.26
The productID attribute is prefixed with games: because of the use of the form attribute in the corresponding schema.

Namespaces and Schema Reuse

There is a many-to-many relationship among XML schemas, WSDL definitions, and namespaces. It is important to keep in mind that you can use the same target namespace for multiple schemas and (as discussed in the following chapter) for multiple WSDL definitions. This makes sense for related services, especially if they need to share the same type of data (and therefore also need to share the same schema content) or when they belong to the same business domain.

You can also design messages comprised of elements in multiple namespaces. This is useful when reusing an industry standard vocabulary or attempting to structure a large vocabulary. Combining schema documents from multiple namespaces is discussed further in Chapter 13.

SUMMARY OF KEY POINTS

- The target namespace of a schema identifies the namespace to which global (and possibly also local) elements and attributes in that schema belong.

- The `elementFormDefault`, `attributeFormDefault` and `form` attributes allow you to control which local elements or attributes within a given schema are bound to the target namespace.

- There is a many-to-many relationship among XML schemas, WSDL definitions, and namespaces.

CASE STUDY EXAMPLE
A Complete XML Schema Definition for the Game Service

Having worked through all of the previous examples, Steve manages to assemble the schema that describes the Game service's response message. An example XML document instance of the message content is shown in here:

```xml
<games xmlns="http://actioncon.com/schema/gameinfo">
  <game>
    <productID>AY2344</productID>
    <gtin>1234567890123</gtin>
    <title>Service Blaster 2000</title>
    <desc>This is a great game.</desc>
    <esrbRating>M</esrbRating>
    <msrPrice>29.99</msrPrice>
    <numberOfPlayers>
      <minimum>1</minimum>
      <maximum>4</maximum>
    </numberOfPlayers>
  </game>
  <!-- more games here -->
</games>
```

Example 6.27
The contents of the response message to be used by the Game service.

The full XML schema that corresponds to this response message is provided here:

```xsd
<xsd:schema xmlns:xsd="http://www.w3.org/2001/XMLSchema"
 targetNamespace="http://actioncon.com/schema/gameinfo"
 xmlns="http://actioncon.com/schema/gameinfo"
 elementFormDefault="qualified">
 <xsd:element name="games" type="GamesType"/>
 <xsd:complexType name="GamesType">
   <xsd:sequence>
     <xsd:element name="game" type="GameType"
       maxOccurs="unbounded"/>
   </xsd:sequence>
 </xsd:complexType>
 <xsd:complexType name="GameType">
   <xsd:sequence>
     <xsd:element name="productID" type="ProductIDType"/>
     <xsd:element name="gtin" type="GTINType"/>
     <xsd:element name="title" type="TitleType"/>
     <xsd:element name="desc" type="xsd:string"/>
     <xsd:element name="esrbRating" type="ESRBRatingType"/>
     <xsd:element name="msrPrice" type="PriceType"/>
     <xsd:element name="numberOfPlayers"
       type="NumberOfPlayersRangeType"/>
   </xsd:sequence>
 </xsd:complexType>
 <xsd:complexType name="TitleType">
   <xsd:simpleContent>
     <xsd:extension base="xsd:string">
       <xsd:attribute name="language" type="xsd:language"/>
     </xsd:extension>
   </xsd:simpleContent>
 </xsd:complexType>
 <xsd:complexType name="NumberOfPlayersRangeType">
   <xsd:sequence>
     <xsd:element name="minimum" type="xsd:short"/>
     <xsd:element name="maximum" type="xsd:short"
       minOccurs="0"/>
   </xsd:sequence>
 </xsd:complexType>
 <xsd:simpleType name="ProductIDType">
   <xsd:restriction base="xsd:string">
     <xsd:pattern value="[A-Z]{2}[0-9]{4}"/>
   </xsd:restriction>
 </xsd:simpleType>
 <xsd:simpleType name="GTINType">
   <xsd:restriction base="xsd:string">
     <xsd:length value="13"/>
   </xsd:restriction>
```

```
    </xsd:simpleType>
    <xsd:simpleType name="ESRBRatingType">
      <xsd:restriction base="xsd:string">
        <xsd:enumeration value="EC"/>
        <xsd:enumeration value="E"/>
        <xsd:enumeration value="E10+"/>
        <xsd:enumeration value="T"/>
        <xsd:enumeration value="M"/>
        <xsd:enumeration value="AO"/>
        <xsd:enumeration value="RP"/>
      </xsd:restriction>
    </xsd:simpleType>
    <xsd:simpleType name="PriceType">
      <xsd:restriction base="xsd:decimal">
        <xsd:totalDigits value="8"/>
        <xsd:fractionDigits value="2"/>
      </xsd:restriction>
    </xsd:simpleType>
</xsd:schema>
```

Example 6.28

The complete XML schema for the response message.

6.5 Message Structures

Just like database design, XML message design involves making choices among the many ways to represent and structure data. Earlier in this chapter, we looked at decisions regarding the use of elements versus attributes, the generic versus specific nature of elements, and the granularity of element content. When it comes to message definitions for Web service contracts, another key aspect is the actual design of element structures or, *structural elements*.

A structural element is a group of related elements that resides within a particular construct. For instance, in the previous example, the root games element established a parent construct with various nested child elements that collectively determined its overall structure. This is what makes the games element a structured element.

As with anything you design, you can create good or bad structures. Investing the effort to establish balanced and refined element structures is worthwhile. It can be beneficial in promoting reuse, organizing the messages and generated code more logically, simplifying mapping to existing systems, and allowing more expressive content models. These are all qualities that lead to flexible message designs.

CASE STUDY EXAMPLE

In addition to its Game service, ActionCon wants to get started on designing more complex services that allow the exchange of business documents, such as purchase orders and invoices. This will allow them to communicate with their suppliers and customers electronically, streamlining processes that have, at times, been inefficient and error-prone in the past.

Although Steve realizes that the design might have to change as part of the looming deal with MegaEuroMart, he is anxious to get started. He re-connects with Angela, ActionCon's accounting manager, with whom he collaborated to produce a variety of service candidates during the service-oriented analysis stage. They kick things off by digging up the original service profile document for the Purchase Order service candidate.

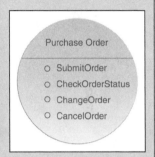

Starting with the `SubmitOrder` capability that they plan to eventually implement as a Web service operation, Steve and Angela begin to define the input request message that will need to represent the purchase order document being submitted to the service.

Figure 6.4

The original service candidate for the Purchase Order service that was modeled as part of a prior service-oriented analysis project.

After some further analysis, they determine that the following data items must be included:

- purchase order number

- purchase order date

- bill-to party (with an ID, name, and contact information)

- ship-to party (with an ID, name, and contact information)

- line items (with a product ID, product name, quantity, and price)

As with the Game service, Steve starts with a sample instance document to get a feel for how he might structure the purchase order vocabulary.

His first attempt is a fairly flat structure (shown in Figure 6.5 and followed by a sample document instance and schema). There are `lineItem` elements to group each line item together, but otherwise all of the data elements are at the same level.

Figure 6.5

A flat purchase order structure and an example of a relatively poor design.

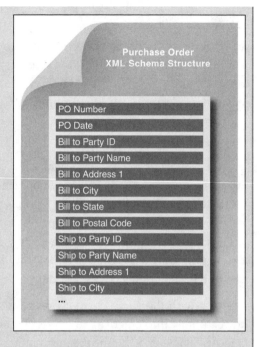

```
<purchaseOrder version="1.0"
  xmlns="http://actioncon.com/schema/po">
  <poNumber>12345</poNumber>
  <poDate>2006-10-15</poDate>
  <billToPartyID>444403</billToPartyID>
  <billToPartyName>
    MegaEuroMart
  </billToPartyName>
  <billToAddress1>123 Main St.</billToAddress1>
  <billToCity>Cleveland</billToCity>
  <billToState>OH</billToState>
  <billToPostalCode>37311</billToPostalCode>
  <shipToPartyID>444405</shipToPartyID>
  <shipToPartyName>NGS #233</shipToPartyName>
  <shipToAddress1>5100 Garfield Road</shipToAddress1>
  <shipToCity>Cleveland</shipToCity>
  ...
  <lineItem>
    <productID>AY2345</productID>
    ...
  </lineItem>
  <lineItem>
```

```
        <productID>BB1764</productID>
        ...
    </lineItem>
</purchaseOrder>
```

Example 6.29
The XML document instance for the flat structured input message.

The XML schema that describes this document is shown here:

```
<xsd:schema xmlns:xsd="http://www.w3.org/2001/XMLSchema"
  xmlns="http://actioncon.com/schema/po"
  targetNamespace="http://actioncon.com/schema/po"
  elementFormDefault="qualified">
  <xsd:element name="purchaseOrder" type="PurchaseOrderType"/>
  <xsd:complexType name="PurchaseOrderType">
    <xsd:sequence>
      <xsd:element name="poNumber" type="xsd:int"/>
      <xsd:element name="poDate" type="xsd:date"/>
      <xsd:element name="billToPartyID" type="xsd:int"/>
      <xsd:element name="billToPartyName" type="xsd:string"/>
      <xsd:element name="billToAddress1" type="xsd:string"/>
      <xsd:element name="billToCity" type="xsd:string"/>
      <xsd:element name="billToState" type="xsd:string"/>
      <xsd:element name="billToPostalCode" type="xsd:string"/>
      <xsd:element name="shipToPartyID" type="xsd:int"/>
      <xsd:element name="shipToPartyName" type="xsd:string"/>
      <xsd:element name="shipToAddress1" type="xsd:string"/>
      <xsd:element name="shipToCity" type="xsd:string"/>
      ...
      <xsd:element name="lineItem" type="LineItemType"
        maxOccurs="unbounded"/>
    </xsd:sequence>
    <xsd:attribute name="version" type="xsd:decimal"/>
  </xsd:complexType>
  <xsd:complexType name="LineItemType">
    <xsd:sequence>
      <xsd:element name="productID" type="ProductIDType"/>
      ...
    </xsd:sequence>
  </xsd:complexType>
</xsd:schema>
```

Example 6.30
The XML schema that corresponds to the previous message example.

The purchase order structure shown in the preceding example contains all of the required data, but its design has several weaknesses. The first is that it does not take advantage of reuse opportunities. The structure of the bill-to and ship-to parties is the same, but it is defined twice in the design. The schema describing this document has to declare each party name element twice, each city element twice, and so on. Since the element names are different, any code that handles party information (for example, to populate it or display it) also has to be written twice, once for each set of element names.

A better structure is depicted in Figure 6.6. In the sample XML document instance that follows (Example 6.31), we can see that two structural elements, `billToParty` and `shipToParty`, have been added to represent the bill-to and ship-to parties. The children of each of these elements are identical, which means that they can share the same `PartyType` complex type (shown in Example 6.32 with the revised `PurchaseOrderType` whose elements reference it). `PartyType` is not only reused twice in this message, but it may also be reused within other messages in different contexts.

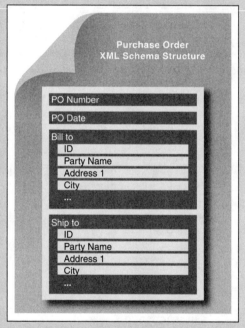

Figure 6.6

The purchase order document with an improved structure.

Steve shows his XML schema design to a data analyst for a second opinion. After a gasp and a stern lecture in data normalization from the analyst, Steve hurries back to his workstation to redesign the message type structure, as follows.

```
<purchaseOrder version="1.0"
  xmlns="http://actioncon.com/schema/po">
  ...
  <billToParty>
    <id>444403</id>
    <name>MegaEuroMart</name>
    <address1>123 Main St.</address1>
    <city>Cleveland</city>
```

```
      <state>OH</state>
      <postalCode>37311</postalCode>
    </billToParty>
    <shipToParty>
      <id>444405</id>
      <name>NGS #233</name>
      <address1>5100 Garfield Road</address1>
      . . .
    </shipToParty>
    . . .
</purchaseOrder>
```

Example 6.31
A better designed party information structure.

Here is the corresponding, improved XML schema:

```
<xsd:complexType name="PurchaseOrderType">
  <xsd:sequence>
    <xsd:element name="poNumber" type="xsd:int"/>
    <xsd:element name="poDate" type="xsd:date"/>
    <xsd:element name="billToParty" type="PartyType"/>
    <xsd:element name="shipToParty" type="PartyType"/>
    <xsd:element name="lineItem" type="LineItemType"
      maxOccurs="unbounded"/>
  </xsd:sequence>
  <xsd:attribute name="version" type="xsd:decimal"/>
</xsd:complexType>
<xsd:complexType name="PartyType">
  <xsd:sequence>
    <xsd:element name="id" type="xsd:int"/>
    <xsd:element name="partyName" type="xsd:string"
      minOccurs="0"/>
    <xsd:element name="contactName" type="xsd:string"
      minOccurs="0"/>
    <xsd:element name="phone" type="xsd:string"
      minOccurs="0"/>
    <xsd:element name="address1" type="xsd:string"/>
    <xsd:element name="city" type="xsd:string"/>
    <xsd:element name="state" type="xsd:string"/>
    <xsd:element name="postalCode" type="xsd:string"/>
  </xsd:sequence>
</xsd:complexType>
```

Example 6.32
The `PartyType` type is reused within the `PurchaseOrderType` type.

In addition to reuse, another benefit of this is that a code generation tool will be able to create a separate class to represent the party information. This tends to be more logical to the developer and can make it easier to integrate existing systems if, for example, the party information is part of a different service, legacy application, or database than the purchase order information. It can promote further reuse because the class written to handle party information can be reused in addition to the complex type.

Structural elements also allow for the creation of more robust content models. In this case, if the ship-to party is optional (for example in the case where it is the same as the bill-to party), you can make the entire `shipToParty` element optional.

You may then further specify that if the `shipToParty` *does* appear, it must have certain required children, such as `id` and `address1`. In the flat structure, the only option would have been to make all of the `shipToXxx` elements optional, which would be a much less expressive structure that would allow illogical or incomplete documents (such as one that contains a `shipToName` but not a `shipToID`).

NOTE

Technically, you could achieve this in XML Schema by embedding an optional `xsd:sequence` construct within your main `xsd:sequence` construct. However, code generation tools do not provide a lot of support for this kind of nested sequence structure.

Finally, the use of structural elements can increase extensibility and address versioning problems. If you later decide that there can be more than one ship-to party (for example, in the case of multi-shipment orders), you can simply increase the `maxOccurs` attribute on the `shipTo` element declaration without introducing a backward-incompatible change.

Structural elements can even be taken a step further in our purchase order scenario. In Example 6.33, yet another structural element, `address`, is added as a child of `billToParty` and `shipToParty`. The same benefits apply; the `AddressType` complex type and the underlying code that creates or processes it, can be reused in many contexts.

```
<purchaseOrder version="1.0"
  xmlns="http://actioncon.com/schema/po">
  ...
  <billToParty>
    <id>444403</id>
    <name>MegaEuroMart</name>
    <address>
      <line1>123 Main St.</line1>
      <city>Cleveland</city>
      <state>OH</state>
      <postalCode>37311</postalCode>
    </address>
  </billToParty>
  <shipToParty>
    <id>444405</id>
    <name>NGS #233</name>
    <address>
      <line1>5100 Garfield Road</line1>
      <city>Cleveland</city>
      ...
    </address>
  </shipToParty>
  ...
</purchaseOrder>
```

Example 6.33
Even more structured party information.

This example shows an appropriate level of structuring for the purchase order document. However, it *is* possible to have too many structural elements. Excessive levels of
nesting in an XML message can make the message structure difficult to understand and
overly lengthy. It can also make the schema and program code more difficult to
maintain.

Repeating Element Containers

A slightly different kind of structural element is a *container* element (or construct) that is
used to group lists of like elements together. In the "flat" purchase order example from
Example 6.29, all of the lineItem elements appeared at the top level of the purchase
order. It is common practice to place repeating elements into a container element whose
name is usually the plural of the name of the element being repeated. In the case of our

example, we would wrap our `lineItem` elements within a `lineItems` construct, as shown here:

```
<purchaseOrder version="1.0"
  xmlns="http://actioncon.com/schema/po">
  ...
  <lineItems>
    <lineItem>
      <productCode>AY2345</productCode>
      ...
    </lineItem>
    <lineItem>
      <productCode>BB1764</productCode>
      ...
    </lineItem>
  </lineItems>
</purchaseOrder>
```

Example 6.34
The `lineItems` element as a container for repeating `lineItem` elements.

This has some of the same benefits described in the previous section, namely extensibility and more expressive content models. It is more extensible because if you later decide to keep some other information about the list or change the contents of the list, you do not need to make a backward-incompatible change to the outer complex type (`PurchaseOrderType`).

> **NOTE**
>
> This approach also allows for a more expressive content structure if you choose to use the `xsd:all` construct instead of `xsd:sequence` in the outer part of the structure because it will get around the problem of the `xsd:all` construct not allowing repeating elements. The `xsd:all` element is explained in Chapter 12.

XML documents with container elements can be easier to process using some supplementary XML-based technologies like XSLT. Further, most mainstream toolkits will not generate a separate class for the `lineItems` element, assuming `lineItem` is the only possible child of `lineItems`. Instead, they will treat it like an array of `lineItem` values. This is the same behavior as when the `lineItems` element is not used. There is no special support in XML Schema for different kinds of arrays, such as lists, vectors, or hash maps. Most toolkits generate literal arrays (e.g. `LineItemType[]`) for repeating elements, regardless of whether they are in a separate container.

SUMMARY OF KEY POINTS

- Reusable patterns should be broken down into separate structural elements.

- Structural elements offer the benefits of promoting reuse, organizing messages more logically, simplifying mapping to existing systems, and allowing more expressive content models.

- Some advantages can be gained from placing repeating elements into their own containers.

CASE STUDY EXAMPLE
A Complete XML Schema Definition for the Purchase Order Service

After all of the lessons he learned throughout the process of creating and revising his XML Schema definition for a response message as part of the Purchase Order service, Steve settles on the following design.

```
<purchaseOrder version="1.0"
  xmlns="http://actioncon.com/schema/po">
  <poNumber>12345</poNumber>
  <poDate>2006-10-15</poDate>
  <billToParty>
    <id>444403</id>
    <partyName>MegaEuroMart</partyName>
    <contactName>Steve Smith</contactName>
    <phone>231-555-1122</phone>
    <address>
      <line1>123 Main St.</line1>
      <line2>Suite 300</line2>
      <city>Cleveland</city>
      <state>OH</state>
      <postalCode>37311</postalCode>
      <country>USA</country>
    </address>
  </billToParty>
  <shipToParty>
    <id>444405</id>
```

```
      <partyName>NGS #233</partyName>
      <contactName>Steve Smith</contactName>
      <phone>231-555-1122</phone>
      <address>
        <line1>5100 Garfield Road</line1>
        <city>Cleveland</city>
        <state>OH</state>
        <postalCode>37311</postalCode>
        <country>USA</country>
      </address>
    </shipToParty>
    <lineItems>
      <lineItem>
        <productID>AY2345</productID>
        <productName>
          Service Blaster 2000
        </productName>
        <quantity>12</quantity>
        <price>29.99</price>
      </lineItem>
      <lineItem>
        <productID>BB1764</productID>
        <productName>
          Service Blaster 5000 Special Edition
        </productName>
        <quantity>8</quantity>
        <price>19.95</price>
      </lineItem>
    </lineItems>
</purchaseOrder>
```

Example 6.35

A sample XML instance of the new Purchase Order message structure.

The complete XML schema code for this message design is as follows:

```
<xsd:schema xmlns:xsd="http://www.w3.org/2001/XMLSchema"
  xmlns="http://actioncon.com/schema/po"
  targetNamespace="http://actioncon.com/schema/po"
  elementFormDefault="qualified">
  <xsd:element name="purchaseOrder" type="PurchaseOrderType"/>
  <xsd:complexType name="PurchaseOrderType">
    <xsd:sequence>
      <xsd:element name="poNumber" type="xsd:int"/>
      <xsd:element name="poDate" type="xsd:date"/>
      <xsd:element name="billToParty" type="PartyType"/>
```

```
      <xsd:element name="shipToParty" type="PartyType"/>
      <xsd:element name="lineItems" type="LineItemsType"/>
    </xsd:sequence>
    <xsd:attribute name="version" type="xsd:decimal"/>
  </xsd:complexType>
  <xsd:complexType name="PartyType">
    <xsd:sequence>
      <xsd:element name="id" type="xsd:int"/>
      <xsd:element name="partyName" type="xsd:string"
        minOccurs="0"/>
      <xsd:element name="contactName" type="xsd:string"
        minOccurs="0"/>
      <xsd:element name="phone" type="xsd:string"
        minOccurs="0"/>
      <xsd:element name="address" type="AddressType"/>
    </xsd:sequence>
  </xsd:complexType>
  <xsd:complexType name="AddressType">
    <xsd:sequence>
      <xsd:element name="line1" type="xsd:string"/>
      <xsd:element name="line2" type="xsd:string"
        minOccurs="0"/>
      <xsd:element name="city" type="xsd:string"/>
      <xsd:element name="state" type="xsd:string"/>
      <xsd:element name="postalCode" type="xsd:string"/>
      <xsd:element name="country" type="xsd:string"/>
    </xsd:sequence>
  </xsd:complexType>
  <xsd:complexType name="LineItemsType">
    <xsd:sequence>
      <xsd:element name="lineItem" type="LineItemType"
        maxOccurs="unbounded"/>
    </xsd:sequence>
  </xsd:complexType>
  <xsd:complexType name="LineItemType">
    <xsd:sequence>
      <xsd:element name="productID" type="ProductIDType"/>
      <xsd:element name="productName" type="xsd:string"/>
      <xsd:element name="quantity" type="xsd:int"/>
      <xsd:element name="price" type="PriceType"/>
    </xsd:sequence>
  </xsd:complexType>
  <xsd:simpleType name="ProductIDType">
    <xsd:restriction base="xsd:string">
      <xsd:pattern value="[A-Z]{2}[0-9]{4}"/>
    </xsd:restriction>
```

```
    </xsd:simpleType>
    <xsd:simpleType name="PriceType">
      <xsd:restriction base="xsd:decimal">
        <xsd:totalDigits value="8"/>
        <xsd:fractionDigits value="2"/>
      </xsd:restriction>
    </xsd:simpleType>
  </xsd:schema>
```

Example 6.36

The complete schema for the purchase order message.

Chapter 7

Fundamental WSDL Part I: Abstract Description Design

In this chapter, we explain how to build the abstract description of a Web service contract using the WSDL 1.1 language, with several references to WSDL-related guidelines provided by the WS-I Basic Profile and occasional notes that highlight language changes in WSDL 2.0. (Full coverage of WSDL 2.0 is provided in Chapter 9.)

What, No `wsdl:` Prefix?

The convention used by this book requires that native elements from all documented markup languages be qualified using their corresponding prefixes when referenced within regular text. The one exception is WSDL language elements, which are referenced without a prefix because they are assigned the default namespace and therefore are not required to use a prefix. (Namespaces and prefixes were described in Chapter 5.)

IRI vs. URI vs. URL vs. URN

You'll see these acronyms used throughout this book. As we enter our coverage of the WSDL language it's probably a good time to point out what they mean and how they are different.

The Web started out by using URLs (Uniform Resource Locators) to locate and indicate how to retrieve Web pages using the format we are all familiar with:

```
http://www.soabooks.com/
```

The URL concept was generalized into URIs (Uniform Resource Identifiers) so that any number of things that may or may not have a physical presence on the Web could be identified. URLs are a subset of URIs, which means that all URLs are URIs, but not all URIs are URLs.

Here, for example, is a URI that is not a URL:

```
urn:isbn:0451450523
```

This URI is a URN (Uniform Resource Name), a less commonly used identifier. A URL differs from a URN in that it adds information about how to access the targeted resource, for example, by including protocol information.

URIs (and URLs) have a serious limitation due to the fact that they are expressed using a subset of standard US-ASCII characters. This means that Web addresses using URIs cannot contain special characters, such as accents from extended Latin alphabets or Asian and Cyrillic characters. Because the Web has grown worldwide, this has obviously become an issue. In response to this limitation, IRIs (Internationalized Resource Identifiers) were developed. An IRI is basically a URI that can contain a much larger set of characters. WSDL 1.1 and 2.0 support URLs and URIs, but only WSDL 2.0 supports IRIs.

NOTE

The following section establishes language elements applicable to both abstract and concrete descriptions. Therefore, this section is equally applicable to this and the next chapter.

7.1 WSDL Definition and Documentation

The `definitions` Element

All of the parts of the abstract and concrete descriptions are housed within a root element that establishes a parent construct called `definitions`. Whatever lies between the opening and closing `definitions` elements therefore represents the scope of a Web service contract.

```
<definitions name="PurchaseOrder" targetNamespace=
  "http://actioncon.com/contract/po" ...>
  ...
</definitions>
```

Example 7.1
The opening and closing `definitions` elements establishing the root construct that will contain the entire WSDL definition.

As shown in the example, this element has two optional attributes: `name` and `target-Namespace`. However, as indicated by the ellipsis after the `targetNamespace` attribute, there are additional attributes that can (also optionally) be added. These are `xmlns` attributes used to establish a range of prefixes for existing namespaces relevant to this contract. These prefixes are used to identify and distinguish elements from different origins (with different namespaces) residing in the same WSDL definition.

WSDL 2.0
The `definitions` element is renamed to `description` in the WSDL 2.0 specification.

The `targetNamespace` Attribute

Though technically optional, the `targetNamespace` attribute is actually very important. Analogous to the XML schema `targetNamespace` attribute, this attribute establishes the namespace value associated with all named elements defined within the WSDL document.

For example, the name of a `portType` element defined in the WSDL definition is automatically associated with this target namespace, and will therefore be distinguishable from identical names in different WSDL definitions (with different target namespaces).

Defining an appropriate namespace for a WSDL definition is as important as doing the same for an XML schema. Though WSDL 1.1 does not require a value for the `targetNamespace` attribute, it should always be defined.

WSDL 2.0
The WSDL 2.0 specification has adopted this practice and therefore makes the `targetNamespace` attribute required.

The `xmlns` Attribute

Like any other XML element, the `definitions` element can contain multiple variations of the `xmlns` attribute to establish a range of namespace prefixes. These prefixes are required when you need to mix elements from different origins into the same document.

A WSDL definition will basically always end up containing elements from languages other than WSDL (like SOAP and XML Schema) and different definitions (like types defined in other XML schema documents). All of this is really no different from the discussions about namespaces in Chapters 5 and 6.

```
<definitions name="PurchaseOrder" targetNamespace=
  "http://actioncon.com/contract/po"
  xmlns="http://schemas.xmlsoap.org/wsdl/"
  xmlns:tns="http://actioncon.com/contract/po"
  xmlns:wsdl="http://schemas.xmlsoap.org/wsdl/"
  xmlns:po="http://actioncon.com/schema/po"
```

```
xmlns:soap11="http://schemas.xmlsoap.org/wsdl/soap/"
xmlns:soap12="http://schemas.xmlsoap.org/wsdl/soap12/">
```

Example 7.2
The opening **definitions** element populated with sample prefix definitions.

This sample, borrowed from an upcoming case study example, shows just how many xmlns attributes can be required.

Let's briefly describe each one:

- The targetNamespace attribute is set to http://actioncon.com/contract/po, meaning that all named elements in the WSDL definition will belong to this namespace.

- The default namespace is set to the WSDL namespace, which means that the standard WSDL elements (types, portType, message, etc.) will not require any prefix when used in the document, as shown below:

```
<message name="msgPurchaseOrderRequest">
  <part name="PurchaseOrder" element="po:purchaseOrder"/>
</message>
```

- The prefix tns: is associated with http://actioncon.com/contract/po, which is also the target namespace. This allows referring to elements that belong to the target namespace in the WSDL document via this prefix.

For example, the following construct defines a WSDL portType element (we'll explain all of these elements in detail later):

```
<portType name="ptPurchaseOrder">
  ...
</portType>
```

This portType element will belong to the target namespace of the WSDL definition, namely http://actioncon.com/contract/po. Later in the WSDL document, as part of the concrete description, we define a binding element that refers to this portType:

```
<binding name="bdPO-SOAP11HTTP" type="tns:ptPurchaseOrder">
```

It can only refer to the correct `portType` element by using a prefix that is equal to the target namespace. This means that in any WSDL definition, you have to define a namespace prefix that is bound to the target namespace.

- The `po:` prefix allows referring to XML Schema elements that were declared in the `http://actioncon.com/schema/po` namespace, as shown here:

```
<message name="msgSubmitOrderRequest">
  <part name="PurchaseOrder" element="po:purchaseOrder"/>
</message>
```

- Finally, the prefixes named `soap11` and `soap12` are bound to the standard namespace for SOAP 1.1 and SOAP 1.2, respectively and are used exclusively within the concrete description.

Most WSDL editors and toolkits will generate a default list of namespace definitions and prefixes for you in the `definitions` element, so that you don't have to remember adding them manually for each new WSDL document.

You may have noticed that there is no prefix definition for XML Schema elements (for example, `xmlns:xsd="http://www.w3.org/2001/XMLSchema"`). The reason is that—as we will describe later—there is only one part of the WSDL contract in which XML Schema is used, and that is the `types` element. It usually includes a `schema` element, which then defines this namespace prefix (plus any additional namespace declarations that may be required in the schema).

In other words, the `xmlns` attribute that establishes the `xsd:` prefix can reside in either the `definitions` element, the `types` element, or within the `xsd:schema` element, as explained in the upcoming *The* `types` *Element* section.

For more information about the use of namespaces, refer back to Chapter 5 and the *Namespaces* section in Chapter 6.

The documentation Element

Any part of a WSDL definition can be annotated with human-readable comments via the use of the `documentation` element. It can be placed pretty much anywhere between other WSDL elements, and its content can be arbitrary text or even other XML elements (its data type corresponds to the XML schema "mixed" content type).

```
<documentation>
  This is an entity service responsible for purchase
  order-related processing only.
</documentation>
```

Example 7.3

A modest documentation construct with some comments.

It is common to use `documentation` constructs for the following reasons:

- to explain the purpose of a service

- to describe the functionality provided by individual service operations

- to explain a particular message or message exchange pattern

- to clarify the business context for which a service or an operation may be best used

- to supply contact names of the service owners or technical support professionals responsible for administering the service

- to express versioning information, such as version numbers (as explained in Part IV of this book)

The `documentation` element is one of the primary means by which the Service Discoverability principle is applied to Web service contract documents. Adding descriptive annotations fully supports this principle's objective of maximizing the communications quality of service contracts.

NOTE

An alternative means of annotating a WSDL document is the use of the standard comment notation that was popularized with HTML:

```
<!-- This is an entity service responsible for purchase
order-related processing only. -->
```

WS-I Guideline

The WS-I Basic Profile recommends that the `documentation` element be present as the first child element of any of the following WSDL elements: `definitions`, `types`, `import`, `message`, `part`, `interface`, `operation`, `input`, `output`, `fault`, and others.

CASE STUDY EXAMPLE

At ActionCon, Steve is tasked with defining interfaces for the Purchase Order service as well as the Game service. In Chapter 6, Steve investigated the existing database and designed XML schemas for the required messages. Now he is ready to move on to start the Web service contract design.

Because he knows that the looming deal with MegaEuroMart has been receiving all of his CTO's attention, Steve decides to get his hands dirty with the contract of the Purchase Order service first.

As established in Chapter 6, existing design standards at ActionCon require that the following conventions be applied:

- All XML schema target namespaces must use the format:
  `"http://actioncon.com"+ "/schema/"` + short description

- All WSDL target namespaces must use the format:
  `"http://actioncon.com" + "/contract/"` + short description

Following these namespace conventions, it doesn't take long for Steve to come up with the following:

`"http://actioncon.com/contract/po"`

Using this target namespace value, Steve proceeds to create the `definitions` construct, as shown here:

```
<definitions name="PurchaseOrder" targetNamespace=
  "http://actioncon.com/contract/po"
  xmlns="http://schemas.xmlsoap.org/wsdl/"
  xmlns:tns="http://actioncon.com/contract/po">
  <documentation>
    This is an entity service responsible for purchase
    order-related processing only.
  </documentation>
  ...
</definitions>
```

Example 7.4

The `definitions` construct further supplemented with annotations placed in a `documentation` construct.

SUMMARY OF KEY POINTS

- WSDL documents have a root `definitions` element that establishes the document's target namespace.

- The `targetNamespace` attribute is important as it declares a namespace associated with the WSDL definition as a whole.

- Also important are the various `xmlns` attributes that can be added to define prefixes for namespaces associated with other languages or documents from which elements need to exist in the WSDL definition.

- The `documentation` element can be used to annotate WSDL definitions in support of the Service Discoverability principle.

7.2 Abstract Description Structure

At the abstract level, a Web service is defined in terms of its public interface. The abstract description establishes this interface via a set of related element constructs.

Here is a recap from Chapter 4 as to how these elements relate to each other to establish the abstract description structure:

- Each `portType` element can contain one or more `operation` elements.

- Each `operation` element can contain one or more `message` elements.

- A `message` element can represent either an incoming (`input`) message or an outgoing (`output` or `fault`) message element for the operation.

These three parts of the abstract description also have the following characteristics:

- Messages are described through their associated type.

- The actual structure of a message is generally determined by an XML Schema complex type.

- The combination of input and output messages within a given operation definition determines that operation's message exchange pattern.

Figure 7.1 illustrates some of these relationships as they apply to element constructs defined by the WSDL language.

Figure 7.1

The primary constructs that comprise the abstract description. As indicated by the arrows, there are numerous relationships between these constructs, all of which will be explained in this and the next chapter.

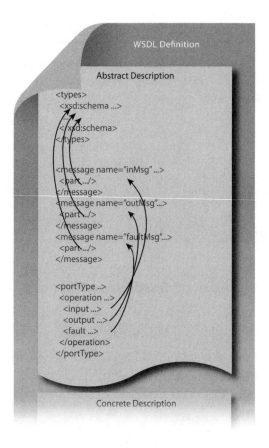

7.3 Type Definitions

The `types` Element

WSDL provides a construct specifically for the purpose of containing schema content used to define types for message definitions. This container is the `types` element, and it acts as a container for external type definitions provided primarily be XML Schema content, as shown here:

```
<types>
  <xsd:schema xmlns:xsd="http://www.w3.org/2001/XMLSchema"
    targetNamespace="http://actioncon.com/schema/powrapper">
    ...
  </xsd:schema>
</types>
```

Example 7.5

A `types` construct with a skeleton `xsd:schema` construct.

Inside the `types` construct, message type definitions in any schema language (including DTD, Relax NG, or even Java) can be embedded. However, by far the most common type language used is XML Schema. In fact, the WSDL 1.1 specification only provides XML Schema type examples and other schema languages are not explicitly addressed.

NOTE

The following section contains only a brief overview of how XML Schema types can be shared between schema documents. The *Reusable Schema Design* section in Chapter 13 elaborates on this topic with more detailed documentation and examples.

Embedded and External Types

A `types` construct can host entire XML schema definitions, embedded as part of the WSDL document. While this results in a nicely self-contained Web service contract, it doesn't necessarily lead to the most flexible data architecture when a Web service exists as part of a larger service inventory.

The Schema Centralization pattern advocates the sharing of XML schemas that represent common business documents, like invoices, claims, and (as per our case study examples so far), purchase orders. This relates directly to the use of the XML schema `xsd:import` and `xsd:include` elements in WSDL documents, which allow a WSDL definition to get access to types defined in schemas that exist in separate documents.

The following code sample (borrowed from the upcoming case study example) shows how the `types` construct can be populated with an XML schema definition comprised only of an `xsd:import` element.

```
<types>
  <xsd:schema xmlns:xsd="http://www.w3.org/2001/XMLSchema"
    targetNamespace="http://actioncon.com/schema/powrapper">
    <xsd:import namespace="http://actioncon.com/schema/po"
      schemaLocation="http://actioncon.com/schema/po.xsd"/>
  </xsd:schema>
</types>
```

Example 7.6
A `types` construct containing XML schema code with an `xsd:import` statement.

WS-I Guidelines

The WS-I Basic Profile imposes certain requirements upon the use of the `types` element and its values:

- The `targetNamespace` is required for all embedded schemas (unless the `xsd:schema` element has an `xsd:import` and/or `xsd:annotation` as its only child elements).

- The use of native SOAP data types (referred to as *encoding* types) is disallowed (the SOAP encoding array type was especially notorious for causing interoperability problems).

Furthermore, no two global `xsd:schema` elements within the same namespace can have the same name, regardless of whether they were embedded or imported (otherwise, runtime processes would not know which type to choose).

However, it is worth mentioning that duplicate declarations are not strictly prohibited when two declarations are in fact identical. In such a case, these declarations are just duplications that may not cause interoperability issues. Though not strictly prohibited, duplication adds no value and should always be avoided.

CASE STUDY EXAMPLE
Embedded XML Schema Types

Given that Steve has already designed all of the XML schemas he needs for the Purchase Order service contract, he now incorporates them into the WSDL document. The process was much easier than he expected; a simple copy and paste and he was pretty much done.

The result is a WSDL document that contains embedded XML schema types, as follows:

```
<definitions name="PurchaseOrder" targetNamespace=
  "http://actioncon.com/contract/po"
  xmlns="http://schemas.xmlsoap.org/wsdl/"
  xmlns:tns=" http://actioncon.com/contract/po"
  xmlns:po="http://actioncon.com/schema/po">
  <types>
  <xsd:schema xmlns:xsd="http://www.w3.org/2001/XMLSchema"
    xmlns="http://actioncon.com/schema/po"
    targetNamespace="http://actioncon.com/schema/po"
    elementFormDefault="qualified">
```

```xsd
<xsd:element name="purchaseOrder"
  type="PurchaseOrderType"/>
<xsd:complexType name="PurchaseOrderType">
 <xsd:sequence>
   <xsd:element name="poNumber" type="xsd:int"/>
   <xsd:element name="poDate" type="xsd:date"/>
   <xsd:element name="billToParty" type="PartyType"/>
   <xsd:element name="shipToParty" type="PartyType"/>
   <xsd:element name="lineItems" type="LineItemsType"/>
 </xsd:sequence>
 <xsd:attribute name="version" type="xsd:decimal"/>
</xsd:complexType>
<xsd:complexType name="PartyType">
 <xsd:sequence>
   <xsd:element name="id" type="xsd:int"/>
   <xsd:element name="partyName" type="xsd:string"/>
   <xsd:element name="contactName" type="xsd:string"/>
   <xsd:element name="phone" type="xsd:string"/>
   <xsd:element name="address" type="AddressType"/>
 </xsd:sequence>
</xsd:complexType>
<xsd:complexType name="AddressType">
 <xsd:sequence>
   <xsd:element name="line1" type="xsd:string"/>
   <xsd:element name="line2" type="xsd:string"
     minOccurs="0"/>
   <xsd:element name="city" type="xsd:string"/>
   <xsd:element name="state" type="xsd:string"/>
   <xsd:element name="postalCode" type="xsd:string"/>
   <xsd:element name="country" type="xsd:string"/>
 </xsd:sequence>
</xsd:complexType>
<xsd:complexType name="LineItemsType">
 <xsd:sequence>
   <xsd:element name="lineItem" type="LineItemType"
     maxOccurs="unbounded"/>
 </xsd:sequence>
</xsd:complexType>
<xsd:complexType name="LineItemType">
 <xsd:sequence>
   <xsd:element name="productID" type="ProductIDType"/>
   <xsd:element name="productName" type="xsd:string"/>
   <xsd:element name="quantity" type="xsd:int"/>
   <xsd:element name="price" type="PriceType"/>
 </xsd:sequence>
</xsd:complexType>
```

```
  <xsd:simpleType name="ProductIDType">
   <xsd:restriction base="xsd:string">
     <xsd:pattern value="[A-Z]{2}[0-9]{4}"/>
   </xsd:restriction>
  </xsd:simpleType>
  <xsd:simpleType name="PriceType">
   <xsd:restriction base="xsd:decimal">
     <xsd:totalDigits value="8"/>
     <xsd:fractionDigits value="2"/>
   </xsd:restriction>
  </xsd:simpleType>
 </xsd:schema>
</types>
...
</definitions>
```

Example 7.7

A `types` construct with embedded XML Schema type definitions.

As highlighted by the red text, the XML schema content in this `types` construct establishes a global `purchaseOrder` element that will be later assigned as the type associated with a `message` element. The `purchaseOrder` element is assigned the `PurchaseOrderType` complex type that contains a series of nested complex and simple types.

Included XML Schema Types

After finalizing his types definition (as per the previous example), Steve meets with a data analyst who quickly points out a fundamental problem with his design. He asks Steve, "What do you think will happen when another Web service needs to use the `PurchaseOrderType` complex type?" Steve realizes that embedded schema content can lead to unnecessary redundancy, especially for business documents (like purchase orders) that need to be shared across services.

Steve thanks the data analyst and retreats back to his workstation to revisit the WSDL definition. He moves the XML schema types into a separate `po.xsd` file located at `http://actioncon.com/schema/`.

He then adds the `xsd:include` element, as follows:

```
<definitions name="PurchaseOrder"
  targetNamespace="http://actioncon.com/contract/po"
  xmlns:tns="http://actioncon.com/contract/po"
  xmlns="http://schemas.xmlsoap.org/wsdl/"
  xmlns:po="http://actioncon.com/schema/po">
```

```
<types>
  <xsd:schema xmlns:xsd="http://www.w3.org/2001/XMLSchema"
    targetNamespace="http://actioncon.com/schema/po">
  <xsd:include
     schemaLocation="http://actioncon.com/schema/po.xsd"/>
  </xsd:schema>
</types>
</definitions>
```

Example 7.8
A types construct containing an xsd:include statement.

SUMMARY OF KEY POINTS

- The types construct within a WSDL definition allows for the data types used for messages to be defined.

- The types construct can contain entire XML schemas or references to separate schema documents.

- The use of the types construct is a primary factor when applying the Schema Centralization pattern.

7.4 Message Definitions

With the type definitions in place, message definitions can be created to reference these types and to provide a reference point for operation definitions. The following sections explain how the message construct establishes this link between XML Schema types and WSDL operations.

The message Element

The message element represents an abstract message that the service exchanges with a consumer program.

Here's what it looks like:

```
<message name="msgPurchaseOrderRequest">
  <part name="PurchaseOrder" element="po:purchaseOrder"/>
</message>
```

Example 7.9
The msgPurchaseOrderRequest message construct with a part child element. (The part element is explained in the following section.)

A WSDL document can contain any number of `message` constructs. Each must therefore have a name (as per the `name` attribute) so that it can be uniquely identified within the target namespace of the containing `definitions` construct. Specifically, the `name` value can be referenced from within one or more `operation` elements.

The `part` Element

A `message` construct can contain one or more `part` elements, each of which represents a piece of the information that the message will be delivering. The `name` attribute of a `part` element must also be populated with a unique name so that message parts can be clearly referenced.

There are two attributes that can be added to the `part` element:

- the `element` attribute
- the `type` attribute

A `part` element uses *one* of these two attributes to associate a type defined in the `types` construct with the message definition. Which attribute to add to the `part` element depends on how your XML schema types are structured, as follows:

> **NOTE**
>
> Prepare yourself, we're about to use the word "element" eight times in one sentence…

- If an XML Schema provides a global `element` element for a complex type, then you would use the `part` element's `element` attribute to associate the global `element` element by specifying the value of the `element` element's `name` attribute.

- If only the `complexType` construct is used, then you would use the `part` element's `type` attribute to specify the value of the `complexType` element's `name` attribute.

Note that there are other factors besides XML schema references that will influence the choice of attribute. For example, the attribute you choose will have a profound impact on the binding definitions in the concrete description (explained in Chapter 8).

WS-I Guideline

The WS-I provides the following recommendations pertaining to the choice of the `element` and `type` attributes for the `part` element:

- The `type` attribute can only be used with RPC-style binding, which means that messages are expected to contain granular, parameter data in order to emulate RPC data exchanges.

- The `element` attribute, on the other hand, is only to be used with document-style binding, which means that messages are expected to contain coarser-grained business documents.

Note that when document-style binding is used, a message may contain only one `part` element that binds to the SOAP `Body` element (as per the body type explained in Chapter 4). This means that additional `part` elements are allowed if they represent the header and headerfault types only. See the *Binding Definition* section in Chapter 8 for more details.

WSDL 2.0

The `message` element is not part of the WSDL 2.0 specification. The committee that developed this version of the WSDL language took WS-I recommendations into account and got rid of the `message` element altogether, thereby allowing the interface (port type) to directly reference XML Schema global elements.

CASE STUDY EXAMPLE

Steve proceeds to define a set of messages for the Purchase Order service. The first is an incoming request message for a purchase order document. The second is an acknowledgement message that responds to the consumer program by notifying it as to whether the purchase order was successfully received.

Coming from an RPC background, Steve is drawn to the use of the `part` element's `type` attribute. To ease into the coding of these constructs, he starts with the simpler task of defining the acknowledgement response message, as follows:

```
<message name="msgPurchaseOrderResponse">
  <part name="Acknowledgement" type="xsd:string"/>
</message>
```

Example 7.10
A `message` construct with a `part` child element.

This seems relatively straightforward and Steve is feeling pretty good about his mastery of WSDL. But, as he begins to define the request message responsible for delivering a purchase order document to the Web service, he starts to get a bit stressed.

Looking at the grammar of the `message` and `part` elements, Steve figures that there are different ways to define the message that contains a purchase order. He is a bit confused, especially with the choice of `element` and `type` attributes. Assuming he has provided a global element for each complex type, should he stick with the `type` or `element` attribute for all `part` elements? Can he use the `type` attribute for some of the `part` elements and the `element` attribute for others?

Given the XML schema for the purchase order document is already defined in Example 7.7, Steve decides to stick with the `type` attribute, which leads to the following definition:

```
<message name="msgPurchaseOrderRequest">
  <part name="PONumber" type="xsd:string"/>
  <part name="PODate" type="xsd:date"/>
  <part name="BillToParty" type="po:PartyType"/>
  <part name="ShipToParty" type="po:PartyType"/>
  <part name="LineItems" type="po:LineItemsType"/>
</message>
```

Example 7.11

A `message` construct with multiple `part` child elements.

After writing this construct out, Steve feels as though he was repeating a lot of the work he already did during the definition of the actual XML schema. He realizes that he can simplify his message design by just creating one `part` that references the `PurchaseOrderType` `complex` type, as shown here:

```
<message name="msgPurchaseOrderRequest">
  <part name="PurchaseOrder" type="po:PurchaseOrderType"/>
</message>
```

Example 7.12

The `message` construct now with only one `part` element referring to the complex type that represents the same sequence of elements as the previous example.

But before committing to the use of the `type` attribute, he decides to take a step back in order to investigate whether the `element` attribute is really any better. He begins by changing the attribute from `type` to `element` which results in a very similar message definition, as follows:

```
<message name="msgPurchaseOrderRequest">
  <part name="PurchaseOrder" element="po:purchaseOrder"/>
</message>
```

Example 7.13

A `message` construct with a `part` child element associated with the global `purchaseOrder` element.

He then reads up on how this attribute differs, and discovers the following:

- Using the `type` attribute will force the generation of a root element in the SOAP body that derives its name from the name of the operation. Although this may seem like a minor inconvenience, Steve is uncomfortable with this requirement, especially considering the many WSDL definitions he still has to write. With the `element` attribute, on the other hand, the content of the SOAP body becomes a direct instantiation of the schema type, which is more appealing.

- Using the `element` attribute also gives him complete control over the namespace of the SOAP body content. With the `type` attribute, the namespace would be taken from the SOAP binding definition, which is also less desirable.

- Finally, he learns that using the `element` attribute has become the industry norm.

All of these factors convince Steve to settle on the use of the `element` attribute, and he subsequently rewrites his original acknowledgement response message accordingly. To do this, though, he is required to add the following global element declaration to the XML schema:

```
<xsd:element name="acknowledgement" type="xsd:string"/>
```

Example 7.14

An `xsd:schema` element declaration for a simple response message.

The final results of his redesigned message definitions are shown in Example 7.15 (changes from the previous design are highlighed):

```
<definitions name="Purchase Order"
  targetNamespace="http://actioncon.com/contract/po"
  xmlns="http://schemas.xmlsoap.org/wsdl/"
  xmlns:tns=" http://actioncon.com/contract/po"
  xmlns:po="http://actioncon.com/schema/po">
  <types>
    <xsd:schema xmlns:xsd="http://www.w3.org/2001/XMLSchema"
      targetNamespace="http://actioncon.com/schema/po">
    <xsd:include
      schemaLocation="http://actioncon.com/schema/po.xsd"/>
    </xsd:schema>
  </types>
  <message name="msgPurchaseOrderRequest">
    <part name="PurchaseOrder" element="po:purchaseOrder"/>
  </message>
```

```
<message name="msgPurchaseOrderResponse">
  <part name="Acknowledgement" element="po:acknowledgement"/>
</message>
</definitions>
```

Example 7.15
Message definitions based on the use of the `element` attribute.

SUMMARY OF KEY POINTS

- A WSDL definition can contain multiple `message` elements, each of which represents a separate incoming or outgoing message supported by the Web service construct.

- `message` elements contain child `part` elements that establish the type of the message.

- `part` elements can reference the types established in the `types` construct.

7.5 Operation Definitions

Every WSDL definition needs at least one operation in order for an external consumer program to invoke it. Therefore, you are creating a piece of the public technical interface with every `operation` construct you build.

The `operation` Element

Now that we've defined input and output messages along with their corresponding XML schema types, it's time to put them to use by assigning them to operations. A WSDL definition can have one or more `operation` constructs, each of which corresponds to a specific capability or function offered by the Web service.

```
<operation name="opCheckOrderStatus" parameterOrder="...">
  <input message="tns:msgCheckOrderRequest"/>
  <output message="tns:msgCheckOrderResponse"/>
  <fault message="tns:msgCheckOrderFault"/>
</operation>
```

Example 7.16
The `operation` construct with child `input`, `output`, and `fault` elements.

As shown in this example, the `operation` construct can contain any of the following three child elements:

- `input` – an incoming request message sent by a service consumer program to the Web service

- `output` – an outgoing response message sent by the Web service to a service consumer program

- `fault` – a message sent out by the Web service when certain exception conditions occur

Each of these elements has a `message` attribute that is used to assign a message definition by referencing the `message` element's `name` attribute. As we know, each `message` element contains one or more `part` elements associated with an XML schema element or type.

Note also that the `operation`, `input`, `output`, and `fault` elements can all be uniquely identified via their respective `name` attributes.

Message Exchange Patterns (MEPs)

An `operation` construct can contain any combination of `input`, `output`, and `fault` elements. Within WSDL 1.1, the existence of `input` and `output` elements and the order in which they are organized establishes a specific *message exchange pattern* or *MEP* between a Web service and its consumers.

The WSDL 1.1 specification defines the following four MEPs:

- *Request-Response* – An operation receives an input message and returns a response or a fault message. Syntactically, an operation that implements this pattern looks like this:

```
<operation ...>
  <input .../>
  <output .../> and/or <fault .../>
</operation>
```

- *One-Way* – An operation receives an input message and returns nothing, which means that just one input element is required, as follows:

```
<operation ...>
  <input .../>
</operation>
```

- *Solicit-Response* – An operation sends out a message, and gets a response or a fault back. The structure is essentially the reverse of Request-Response, as shown here:

```
<operation ...>
  <output .../> and/or <fault .../>
  <input .../>
</operation>
```

- *Notification* – An operation only sends out a message and receives nothing in return, as follows:

```
<operation ...>
  <output .../> and/or <fault .../>
</operation>
```

The Request-Response and One-Way patterns are considered *inbound MEPs*, whereas the Solicit-Response and Notification patterns are referred to as *outbound MEPs*. Inbound MEPs are by far more common, and also the only ones endorsed by the WS-I Basic Profile. (For more information about outbound MEPs, see Chapter 14.)

WSDL 1.1 MEPs are not intended to cover all possible message exchange scenarios. In fact, because the `operation` element only allows a maximum of one `input` and/or `output` element, its ability to accommodate complicated message exchange requirements is limited.

For example, it is not possible to define a WSDL 1.1 operation that can receive multiple input messages in a pre-defined sequence. The WS-ReliableMessaging standard provides this type of functionality, but WSDL 2.0 is also capable of supporting more complicated MEPs (as discussed in Chapters 9 and 14).

The `parameterOrder` Attribute

You may have already noticed the `parameterOrder` attribute displayed within the `operation` element back in Example 7.16. We haven't yet mentioned it for a good reason.

Originally, when WSDL was developed in support of enabling RPC-style communication over HTTP, some people thought it would be useful to map an operation name to an RPC method call. `parameterOrder` is an optional attribute that is only applicable to operations based on the Request-Response and Solicit-Response MEPs and is intended solely for RPC binding.

Because RPC-centric communication is not really used within service-oriented solutions, this attribute is not recommended. It is further discouraged because it compromises the independence of the abstract description from the concrete description, thereby inhibiting the long-term evolution of the Web service contract.

According to the WSDL1.1 specification, `parameterOrder` may safely be ignored by those not concerned with RPC data exchange, and it is not required to be present even if the operation is to be used with an RPC-like binding. Chapter 14 covers some techniques for mapping a document-style binding to an RPC signature without using `parameterOrder`.

WSDL 2.0

The `parameterOrder` attribute was removed from version 2.0 of the WSDL specification.

Operation Overloading

Some programming languages allow method or operation overloading. For example, a C++ class may contain multiple member functions that have the same name, but with different parameters.

Because the WSDL 1.1 specification does not explicitly disallow more than one `operation` element under a `portType` construct to have the same name, some developers have tried to create overloaded operations by defining multiple operations that have the same name but with different message definitions.

Early implementations have proven that WSDL operation name overloading is ineffective because it can lead to unpredictable consequences, such as runtime message dispatch problems.

With RPC-style binding especially, the operation name is mapped to the name of the root element of the runtime message which is used to uniquely identify the runtime message. If multiple operations share the same name, it becomes hard for the receiving program to figure out where to dispatch an incoming message. As a best practice, a WSDL `portType` must have operations with distinct values for their `name` attributes. (Message dispatch issues are further explored in Chapter 15.)

WSDL 2.0

WSDL 2.0 supports this notion in that a message within a WSDL 2.0 definition is always defined using an XML Schema global element declaration with a unique name.

For the Purchase Order service, Steve needs to create an operation to allow external customers, such as MegaEuroMart, to submit a purchase order to ActionCon. He therefore defines an `opSubmitOrder` operation, as follows:

```
<operation name="opSubmitOrder">
  <input message="tns:msgSubmitOrderRequest"/>
  <output message="tns:msgSubmitOrderResponse"/>
</operation>
```

Example 7.17

An `operation` construct with `input` and `output` child elements.

Note the `message` attribute of the `input` and `output` elements. Each points to the name of a previously defined `message` element. The `tns:` prefix is used to indicate that the reference `message` construct was defined in this WSDL definition (in other words in "this namespace" or in the "target namespace").

The target namespace of the WSDL definition associates a unique identifier to the WSDL document, and therefore any element wanting to reference a definition that was newly established in this document needs to qualify the element with the `tns:` prefix.

SUMMARY OF KEY POINTS

- A WSDL definition can contain multiple `operation` constructs, each of which can represent a distinct capability of the service expressed via a set of message exchanges.

- The `operation` element can contain `child input`, `output`, and `fault` elements.

- The types and order of messages contained in an operation construct determine the operation's message exchange pattern.

7.6 Port Type Definitions

The official container for related operation elements is the `portType` construct, which establishes a self-contained interface for the Web service.

The `portType` Element

Now it's time to assemble all of the previously explained elements into an actual port type definition. As shown in this example, the `portType` construct can be comprised of one or more `operation` constructs.

```
<portType name="ptPurchaseOrder">
  <operation name="opSubmitOrder">
    <input message="tns:msgSubmitOrderRequest"/>
    <output message="tns:msgSubmitOrderResponse"/>
  </operation>
  <operation name="opCheckOrderStatus">
    <input message="tns:msgCheckOrderRequest"/>
    <output message="tns:msgCheckOrderResponse"/>
  </operation>
  <operation name="opChangeOrder">
    <input message="tns:msgChangeOrderRequest"/>
    <output message="tns:msgChangeOrderResponse"/>
  </operation>
  <operation name="opCancelOrder">
    <input message="tns:msgCancelOrderRequest"/>
    <output message="tns:msgCancelOrderResponse"/>
  </operation>
</portType>
```

Example 7.18
The `portType` construct containing a set of `operation` constructs.

Although it is by no means common in practice, it is worth mentioning that the WSDL `definitions` construct itself can contain more than one `portType` construct. This essentially allows you to define multiple interfaces for the same Web service within one contract document. However, a more accepted approach is to simply create a separate WSDL document when an alternative interface is required (as per the Concurrent Contracts design pattern). Also worth noting is that multiple `portType` constructs within the same WSDL definition can be used for versioning purposes, as explained further in Chapter 21.

WSDL 2.0
The WSDL 2.0 specification renames the `portType` element to `interface`.

7.7 A Complete Abstract Description

Steve completed his first set of definitions resulting in a Web service contract with a sole operation. He now feels sufficiently confident to study the full business requirements for this important entity service and subsequent to some further analysis determines that the following additional operations are required:

- `opCheckOrderStatus` – Retrieves the status of an existing order for a consumer program.

- `opChangeOrder` – Allows consumers to edit an existing order.

- `opCancelOrder` – Deactivates an existing order at the request of a consumer.

Being aware of the implementation issues imposed by RPC-style binding, Steve has decided to stay away from it wherever possible. Furthermore, before proceeding to add the additional required schema types, message definitions, and operation definitions, Steve familiarizes himself with the naming conventions established in the design standards specification produced by the ActionCon enterprise architecture group. These conventions help relate a message definition to its corresponding operation by requiring message definitions to be named as follows:

"msg" + "operation name" + "Request"/"Response"

After completing the message definitions and adding a the new `operation` elements to the `ptPurchaseOrder portType` construct, Steve now has a complete abstract description for the Purchase Order service:

```
<definitions name="PurchaseOrder" targetNamespace=
  "http://actioncon.com/contract/po"
  xmlns="http://schemas.xmlsoap.org/wsdl/"
  xmlns:tns="http://actioncon.com/contract/po"
  xmlns:po="http://actioncon.com/schema/po">
<types>
  <xsd:schema xmlns:xsd="http://www.w3.org/2001/XMLSchema"
    xmlns="http://actioncon.com/schema/po"
    targetNamespace="http://actioncon.com/schema/po"
    elementFormDefault="qualified">
  <xsd:element name="purchaseOrder"
    type="PurchaseOrderType"/>
  <xsd:element name="acknowledgement" type="xsd:string"/>
  <xsd:element name="poNumber" type="xsd:int"/>
  <xsd:element name="status" type="xsd:string"/>
```

```xsd
<xsd:complexType name="PurchaseOrderType">
 <xsd:sequence>
   <xsd:element ref="poNumber"/>
   <xsd:element name="poDate" type="xsd:date"/>
   <xsd:element name="billToParty" type="PartyType"/>
   <xsd:element name="shipToParty" type="PartyType"/>
   <xsd:element name="lineItems" type="LineItemsType"/>
 </xsd:sequence>
 <xsd:attribute name="version" type="xsd:decimal"/>
</xsd:complexType>
<xsd:complexType name="PartyType">
 <xsd:sequence>
   <xsd:element name="id" type="xsd:int"/>
   <xsd:element name="partyName" type="xsd:string"/>
   <xsd:element name="contactName" type="xsd:string"/>
   <xsd:element name="phone" type="xsd:string"/>
   <xsd:element name="address" type="AddressType"/>
 </xsd:sequence>
</xsd:complexType>
<xsd:complexType name="AddressType">
 <xsd:sequence>
   <xsd:element name="line1" type="xsd:string"/>
   <xsd:element name="line2" type="xsd:string" minOccurs="0"/>
   <xsd:element name="city" type="xsd:string"/>
   <xsd:element name="state" type="xsd:string"/>
   <xsd:element name="postalCode" type="xsd:string"/>
   <xsd:element name="country" type="xsd:string"/>
 </xsd:sequence>
</xsd:complexType>
<xsd:complexType name="LineItemsType">
 <xsd:sequence>
   <xsd:element name="lineItem" type="LineItemType"
     maxOccurs="unbounded"/>
 </xsd:sequence>
</xsd:complexType>
<xsd:complexType name="LineItemType">
 <xsd:sequence>
   <xsd:element name="productID" type="ProductIDType"/>
   <xsd:element name="productName" type="xsd:string"/>
   <xsd:element name="quantity" type="xsd:int"/>
   <xsd:element name="price" type="PriceType"/>
 </xsd:sequence>
</xsd:complexType>
<xsd:simpleType name="ProductIDType">
 <xsd:restriction base="xsd:string">
   <xsd:pattern value="[A-Z]{2}[0-9]{4}"/>
 </xsd:restriction>
```

```
  </xsd:simpleType>
  <xsd:simpleType name="PriceType">
   <xsd:restriction base="xsd:decimal">
     <xsd:totalDigits value="8"/>
     <xsd:fractionDigits value="2"/>
   </xsd:restriction>
  </xsd:simpleType>
 </xsd:schema>
</types>
<message name="msgSubmitOrderRequest">
  <part name="PurchaseOrder" element="po:purchaseOrder"/>
</message>
<message name="msgSubmitOrderResponse">
 <part name="Acknowledgement" element="po:acknowledgement"/>
</message>
<message name="msgCheckOrderRequest">
  <part name="PONumber" element="po:poNumber"/>
</message>
<message name="msgCheckOrderResponse">
 <part name="Status" element="po:status"/>
</message>
<message name="msgChangeOrderRequest">
  <part name="PurchaseOrder" element="po:purchaseOrder"/>
</message>
<message name="msgChangeOrderResponse">
 <part name="Acknowledgement" element="po:acknowledgement"/>
</message>
<message name="msgCancelOrderRequest">
  <part name="PONumber" element="po:poNumber"/>
</message>
<message name="msgCancelOrderResponse">
 <part name="Acknowledgement" element="po:acknowledgement"/>
</message>
<portType name="ptPurchaseOrder">
  <operation name="opSubmitOrder">
    <input message="tns:msgSubmitOrderRequest"/>
    <output message="tns:msgsubmitOrderResponse"/>
  </operation>
  <operation name="opCheckOrderStatus">
    <input message="tns:msgCheckOrderRequest"/>
    <output message="tns:msgCheckOrderResponse"/>
  </operation>
  <operation name="opChangeOrder">
    <input message="tns:msgChangeOrderRequest"/>
    <output message="tns:msgchangeOrderResponse"/>
  </operation>
```

```
      <operation name="opCancelOrder">
        <input message="tns:msgCancelOrderRequest"/>
        <output message="tns:msgCancelOrderResponse"/>
      </operation>
    </portType>
</definitions>
```

Example 7.19

A complete abstract description. Changes from the previous case study example are highlighted.

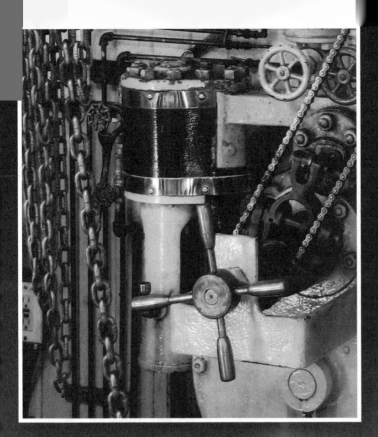

Chapter 8

Fundamental WSDL Part II: Concrete Description Design

8.1 Concrete Description Structure

8.2 Binding Definition

8.3 Service and Port Definitions

8.4 A Complete WSDL Definition
(Including the Concrete Description)

The abstract description we covered in Chapter 7 defines a public interface (or API) for a Web service in an implementation-neutral manner. We now get to dig into the details of how to assign a physical address to the abstract description and how it can be bound to transport and messaging protocols via the creation of a concrete description.

8.1 Concrete Description Structure

As we established back in Chapter 4, a concrete description is structured as follows:

- It is comprised of one or more binding and port definitions.

- Each binding specifies protocol details.

- Port definitions associate network addresses to binding definitions.

Because of the modularity in the structure of WSDL definitions, an abstract description can be offered to different consumers via multiple concrete descriptions providing access to the abstract description via different protocols and/or different locations. Therefore, the quantity of `binding` and `endpoint` constructs a WSDL definition will contain depends on whether the abstract description needs to support one or more communication technologies.

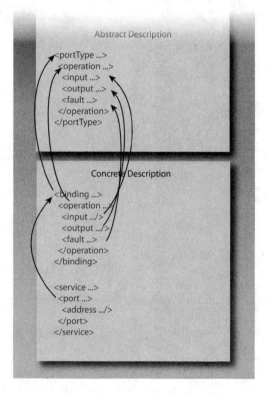

Figure 8.1

The figure displays the bottom half of the WSDL document from Figure 7.1 in Chapter 7. Here we can see the primary constructs of a concrete description and also how some of the binding-related elements are associated with elements in the abstract description.

Figure 8.1 displays the constructs that correspond to the definitions of a concrete description and further illustrates their relationship with corresponding portType, operation, and message elements.

8.2 Binding Definition

The purpose of a binding construct is to connect (bind) a portType element from an abstract description to a specific communications technology that will need to be used by consumer programs to access the port type's operations.

The binding Element

The structure of a binding construct mimics the structure of a portType construct, as shown in this example.

```
<binding ...>
  <-- extensibility element -->
  <operation ...>
    <-- extensibility element -->
    <input ...>
      <-- extensibility element -->
    </input>
    <output ...>
      <-- extensibility element -->
    </output>
    <fault ...>
      <-- extensibility element -->
    </fault>
  </operation>
</binding>
```

Example 8.1
A skeleton binding construct with a placeholder for extensibility elements (which will be described shortly).

Multiple `binding` constructs can exist within the same WSDL definition for the following reason:

- One abstract port type definition can be associated with multiple binding definitions in order to provide alternative means of communication.

- The WSDL definition can host multiple port type definitions, each with one or more binding definitions.

As with other WSDL elements, `binding` has a `name` attribute that can be used to uniquely identify one binding definition from another within the same namespace. Of greater interest is its `type` attribute, which is populated with the name of the `portType` element for which binding details are being defined.

Similarly, the `name` attributes of the `operation`, `input`, `output`, and `fault` child elements must be set to the fully qualified names of the corresponding `operation`, `input`, `output`, and `fault` elements of the `portType` identified by the parent `binding` element's `type` attribute.

WSDL 2.0

Because a `binding` element associates itself to a specific `portType`, WSDL 1.1 binding definitions are not reusable. In version 2.0 of the WSDL language, reusable binding definitions can be created by making their `interface` attributes optional (the name of the `portType` element was changed to `interface` in WSDL 2.0). To reuse a `binding` element, all you need to do is to omit the `interface` attribute and avoid specifying any operation-specific or fault-specific binding details.

WS-I Guideline

Can a `binding` construct leave some of the operations from the corresponding abstract description unspecified? The WSDL 1.1 specification is not explicit about whether or not this is allowed, but the WS-I Basic Profile clearly requires that a `binding` must have the same set of `operation` elements as the `portType` construct to which it refers.

This leads us to the question of whether a binding definition can leave any parts of the message definition within an operation unspecified. The WSDL 1.1 specification again does not address this, but the WS-I Basic Profile states that all child elements of an operation construct be fully specified.

Extensibility Elements

So far, a binding definition doesn't look a lot different from a port type definition, especially considering they share the same overall structure. With `binding` constructs things get real interesting once we add the actual protocol and transport details via the use of *extensibility elements.*

When we say that an abstract description is bound to a messaging protocol (like version 1.1 of SOAP), we mean that the messages defined in the abstract port type will be transmitted at runtime using the messaging format specified in the SOAP 1.1 standard. To achieve this binding, extensibility elements need to be added to the binding definition in order to determine:

- the actual wire transport technology used to deliver the message

- the format of the message as it exists on the wire

The latter part refers to a variety of options we have as to how the physical message should be structured. In the following example, you will notice the original `binding` construct now containing a series of extensibility elements. We'll step through these elements and their attributes to understand how they provide us with control over the design of physical messages.

```
<binding ...>
  <soap11:binding style="" transport=""/>
  <operation ...>
    <soap11:operation soapAction="" style=""/>
    <input ...>
      <soap11:body parts="" use="" encodingStyle=""
        namespace=""/>
      <soap11:header message="" part="" use=""encodingStyle=""
        namespace="">
        <soap11:headerfault message="" part=""
          use="" encodingStyle="" namespace=""/>
      </soap11:header>
    </input>
    <output>
      ... same idea as input ...
    </output>
    <fault>
      <soap11:fault name="" use="" encodingStyle="" namespace="">
    </fault>
```

```
  </operation>
</binding>
```

Example 8.2
The highlighted text indicates extensibility elements added to the `binding` construct.

What this example shows us is that different parts of the abstract port type can be associated with different extensibility elements.

> **NOTE**
>
> The use of the `soap11:` prefix refers to the SOAP 1.1 namespace that would have been established via an `xmlns` attribute of the `definitions` element.

The `binding` Element's `transport` Attribute

To assign a specific transport technology to a binding, the `transport` attribute is populated with a URI that represents the technology.

For example, to specify the HTTP binding of the SOAP 1.1 standard, the official URI for SOAP 1.1 over HTTP would be added as follows:

```
<binding... transport="http://schemas.xmlsoap.org/soap/http"/>
```

Example 8.3
The `transport` attribute of the `binding` element with a URI value that identifies the transport protocol.

The "Inheritance Rule"

The binding mechanism provided by WSDL 1.1 has a specific requirement as to how extensibility elements are processed. Essentially, those that are associated with `binding` elements at a higher level (in the overall `binding` construct hierarchy) are automatically carried over to (inherited by) child elements unless the child elements explicitly overwrite their parent extensibility elements via their own.

For example, the `transport` attribute can only be specified at the `portType` level and is therefore applied to all operations and messages within the port type. For example, the `style` attribute appears at both the port type and operation levels. It is required for the port type level, but it is actually optional for operation definitions. If an operation doesn't provide a value for `style`, it inherits this value from the port type level definition. If the `style` value is specified at both port type and operation levels, the operation level value overwrites the value from the port type level.

However, this form of inheritance does not apply to all settings. The previously described `transport` attribute is only definable for the parent `binding` element. This means that all operations within a given port type must share the same transport protocol.

WS-I Guideline

The official transport protocol endorsed by the WS-I Basic Profile is HTTP (or its secured variation HTTPS). It explicitly requires that a WSDL `binding` element reference the HTTP transport protocol together with a SOAP binding. Specifically, the `transport` attribute must have the following value:

```
http://schemas.xmlsoap.org/soap/http
```

Other URIs may still be used with the `transport` attribute to implement different transport protocols, such as SMTP, FTP, etc. However, neither WSDL nor SOAP specifications provide "standard" URIs for protocols other than HTTP. To use FTP, for example, the owners of the service and its consumers would need to agree on a URI value, and then make sure that the processors on both sides can be configured to recognize the custom URI value as the identifier for the FTP protocol.

The `soap11:operation` Element's `soapAction` Attribute

Version 1.1 of SOAP specifies a `soapAction` attribute that is added to the `soap11:operation` binding extensibility element. It is used to assign a value to the corresponding HTTP `SOAPAction` header that will be added when a SOAP message is transmitted via HTTP.

The following `soapAction` attribute value:

```
<soap11:operation soapAction=
  "http://actioncon.com/submitOrder/request" ... />
```

...will result in the following assignment of the `HTTP` `SOAPAction` header:

```
POST /ptPurchaseOrder HTTP/1.1
```

```
Host: www.actioncon.com
Content-Type: text/xml; charset="utf-8"
Content-Length: nnnn
SOAPAction: "http://actioncon.com/submitOrder/request"
```

Example 8.4

A `soap11:operation` extensibility element with a populated `soapAction` attribute.

NOTE

It is worth highlighting that a SOAP message represents an XML document that, when transported via HTTP, gets embedded within an HTTP message. Therefore, even though the above SOAP HTTP header is defined within the `soap11:operation` element, the value of its `soapAction` attribute does not become part of the SOAP message (nor do any of the other HTTP headers)—these headers are all part of the HTTP message.

This header provides a hint about the intention of the message that may be useful to the message receiver in order to figure out which operation to appropriately dispatch the message to.

Note that this attribute is actually required for the HTTP transport protocol to bind to SOAP. There is no default value, which means that it must be provided with a URI when HTTP is the transport protocol for the SOAP message, although you will often be able to simply populate it with an empty string (`soapAction=""`) without much problem.

The `soap11:binding` and `operation` Element's `style` Attribute

To generate a runtime message from an abstract description, certain rules need to be followed in order for the runtime processors to properly assemble the different pieces of the message.

One of these rules is established by the `style` attribute:

```
<binding name="bdPurchaseOrder" type="ptPurchaseOrder">
  <soap11:binding style="document" .../>
  <operation name="opSubmitOrder">
    <soap11:operation soapAction=
```

```
            "http://actioncon.com/submitOrder/request"/>
    ...
  </operation>
</binding>
```

Example 8.5

A sample `binding` construct containing a `soap11:binding` extensibility element and an `operation` construct with its own, `soap11:operation` extensibility element.

You'll notice that in the example only the `binding` element has a `soap11:binding` extensibility element with a `style` attribute. As mentioned earlier in the section *The "Inheritance Rule,"* settings in a parent extensibility element will be inherited by the child extensibility element unless that element overwrites it with its own setting. In the preceding example, the child `operation` extensibility element will inherit the style setting of the parent `binding` extensibility element unless the `operation` extensibility element sets its own style value.

In WSDL 1.1, there are two possible values for the `style` attribute: "document" and "rpc." Which value you choose will have implications on how a runtime SOAP message will be constructed in relation to its corresponding abstract WSDL message definition. Therefore, we'll explore these attribute values separately.

> **NOTE**
>
> If the `binding` element does not specify a `style` attribute, it is defaulted to "document."

When a binding style is set to "document" it essentially means two things:

- At design time, only one message `part` element will be bound to the SOAP body. In other words, a SOAP `Body` element (explained in Chapter 11) will contain at most the contents of one `part` element listed in the `parts` attribute.

- At runtime, an instance of the XML schema `element` element associated with the `part` element is sent as the child of the SOAP `Body` construct.

The `style="document"` setting is most commonly combined with the `use="literal"` setting on the SOAP `Body` extensibility element, which is explained in the upcoming *SOAP Extensibility Elements (and the `use` Attribute)* section.

Let's revisit the `opSubmitOrder` operation defined in Example 8.5 to preview how the runtime SOAP message document would look when the operation's `style` attribute is set to "document." To keep things simple, we'll focus only on the input message.

Here is the `binding` construct for the `opSubmitOrder` operation:

```
<binding name="bdPurchaseOrder" type="ptPurchaseOrder">
  <soap11:binding style="document" .../>
  <operation name="opSubmitOrder">
    <soap11:operation soapAction=
      "http://actioncon.com/submitOrder/request"/>
    <input message="tns:msgSubmitOrderRequest">
      <soap11:body parts="tns:PurchaseOrder" use="literal"/>
    </input>
    ...
  </operation>
  ...
</binding>
```

Example 8.6

A binding extensibility element associating a document-literal type message with an operation's input message.

This `binding` construct will generate the following runtime message:

```
POST /ptPurchaseOrder HTTP/1.1
Host: www.actioncon.com
Content-Type: text/xml; charset="utf-8"
Content-Length: nnnn
SOAPAction: "http://actioncon.com/submitOrder/request"
<soap:Envelope
  xmlns:soap="http://schemas.xmlsoap.org/soap/envelope/">
  ...
  <soap:Body>
    <purchaseOrder xmlns="http://actioncon.com/schema/po">
      <poNumber>po123456</poNumber>
      <poDate>10/30/2006</poDate>
      <billToParty> ... </billToParty>
      <shipToParty> ... </shipToParty>
      <lineItems> ... </lineItems>
    </purchaseOrder>
  </soap:Body>
</soap:Envelope>
```

Example 8.7

A SOAP message document containing the message produced by the previously displayed `binding` construct.

Let's now look at how the message structure changes when assigning a value of "rpc" to the style attribute:

- At design-time, the abstract WSDL message can have multiple part elements, and each is expected to represent a parameter or a return value of an RPC signature.

- At runtime, the following rules are used to determine how the message should be constructed:

  - The SOAP Body element is followed by a new wrapper element with a name that is identical to the operation name, and with a namespace value that equals the value of the namespace attribute of the Body element.

  - The message parts are then placed within this wrapper element. Each part is represented by an element with a name that is identical to the corresponding part element's name attribute value, and with a namespace value that is the same as the namespace attribute of the Body element.

The style="rpc" setting is often combined with the use="encoded" setting because both represent message structures that were more common during the early days of WSDL, when Web services were primarily used to emulate RPC exchanges. In the upcoming case study, the use attribute of the SOAP body extensibility element is set to "literal" instead. The implications of this are explained in the upcoming *SOAP Extensibility Elements (and the use Attribute)* section.

> **NOTE**
>
> In the upcoming section, you may notice that the capitalization will vary when we reference the `body` element. The XML vocabulary established for SOAP messages by the SOAP specification capitalizes this element name so that the element that represents the body of an actual SOAP message is `Body`. However, the extensibility element used to bind to SOAP within a WSDL definition is lower case, which is why you'll see it displayed as `body`. The same goes for other SOAP elements that relate to message types, such as `Header/header` and `Fault/fault`.

SOAP Extensibility Elements (and the use Attribute)

To fully understand how a SOAP 1.1 binding definition can impact the structure of a runtime message, we need to explain the SOAP extensibility elements and the related `use` attribute.

As we know, message-level binding definitions exist as `input`, `output`, or `fault` elements that reside under the binding `operation` construct. There are several available SOAP extensibility elements that can be added to these message definitions:

- `body` – Corresponds to the SOAP `Body` construct.

- `header` – Corresponds to a construct within the SOAP `Header` construct.

- `headerfault` – Corresponds to a construct within the SOAP `Header` construct, except that the header is populated with error details. (Note that this binding is rarely used in practice.)

- `fault` – Corresponds to the SOAP `Fault` construct.

Each represents a distinct section of a SOAP message, which means that each of these parts can be defined with a separate abstract message definition (and therefore a separate XML schema type).

> **NOTE**
>
> SOAP header sections are commonly pre-defined via the use of various WS-* technologies, such as WS-Addressing and WS-ReliableMessaging. You have the ability to create custom SOAP headers, but this chapter is focused on the SOAP body content only. More details regarding SOAP header blocks are provided in Chapter 11.

For now, we are primarily interested in the fact that every one of these four extensibility elements has the following attributes:

- a required `use` attribute

- an optional `encodingStyle` attribute

- an optional `namespace` attribute

These attributes are used to define how the extensibility element relates the wire message format to the corresponding abstract message definition.

```
<body use="" encodingStyle="" namespace="">
<header use="" encodingStyle="" namespace="">
<headerfault use="" encodingStyle="" namespace="">
<fault use="" encodingStyle="" namespace="">
```

Example 8.8
The same three attributes used by the `body`, `header`, `headerfault`, and `fault` SOAP extensibility elements.

Literal vs. Encoded

The `use` attribute can only have two possible values: "literal" and "encoded."

When set to "literal," an abstract message fully defines its corresponding runtime SOAP message, which essentially means that the SOAP message is defined by the XML schema types that underlie the abstract message definition.

A setting of "encoded" indicates that the abstract message is only one of the inputs that define the runtime SOAP message. Additional encoding rules provided by the SOAP specification are also incorporated. This setting was originally created to support different types of message data prior to the ratification of the XML Schema standard. It is therefore no longer common, especially in service-oriented solutions.

In order to understand possible message types, we will briefly explain the four different combinations of the `style` and `use` attributes:

- *Document-Literal* – An element referenced by a WSDL message `part` appears under the SOAP `body`, `header`, `headerfault`, or `fault` element at runtime and the message is fully defined by the corresponding XML Schema types.

- *RPC-Encoded* – The SOAP message includes the RPC wrapper element and is partially defined by the abstract WSDL message definitions and native SOAP encoding rules.

- *RPC-Literal* – The SOAP message includes the RPC wrapper element and is fully defined by the abstract WSDL message definitions and their corresponding XML schema types.

- *Document-Encoded* – This combination indicates that an element referenced by a WSDL message `part` will appear directly under the SOAP `Body`, `Header`, `Headerfault`, or `Fault` element at runtime. However, the instance XML message is derived from the XML Schema definition based on certain encoding rules. As a result, the runtime message may not always be valid with its corresponding XML Schema definition. (This combination makes little sense and is rarely ever used.)

WS-I Guideline

The WS-I Basic Profile disallows the use of the "encoding" value for the `use` attribute in order to foster interoperability across Web services. This also reflects the fact that the majority of Web services-based SOA products provide support for the document-literal message style.

Also (as earlier mentioned in Chapter 7) when the document-literal style is used, a `message` element is only allowed to contain one `part` element that binds to the SOAP `Body` element. Additional `part` elements can be present only if they bind to `header` or `headerfault` elements.

CASE STUDY EXAMPLE

In Chapter 7 Steve created an abstract operation called `opCheckOrderStatus` with an input message that was defined with the following XML Schema type:

```
<xsd:element name="poNumber" type="xsd:int"/>
```

Example 8.9
The `poNumber` XML Schema element declaration.

Steve decides to define a document-style literal binding for the input message of the `opCheckOrderStatus` operation by setting the `use` attribute of the SOAP `body` extensibility element to "literal." This forces the runtime instance of the `poNumber` element to be valid with the global element declaration of "`poNumber`."

The resulting SOAP request message looks like this:

```
<soap:Envelope
  xmlns:soap="http://schemas.xmlsoap.org/soap/envelope/">
```

```
<soap:Body>
  <po:poNumber xmlns:po="http://actioncon.com/schema/po">
    123456
  </po:poNumber>
</soap:Body>
</soap:Envelope>
```

Example 8.10
A SOAP message document based on a document-literal message type.

Don't worry too much about the new SOAP elements being displayed. These are all explained in Chapter 11. This next example shows the complete `binding` construct based on the use of the document-literal message type.

```
<binding name="bdPO-SOAP11HTTP" type="ptPurchaseOrder">
  <soap11:binding style="document"
    transport="http://schemas.xmlsoap.org/soap/http"/>
  <operation name="opSubmitOrder">
    <soap11:operation soapAction=
      "http://actioncon.com/submitOrder/request"/>
    <input>
      <soap11:body use="literal"/>
    </input>
    <output>
      <soap11:body use="literal"/>
    </output>
  </operation>
  <operation name="opCheckOrderStatus">
    <soap11:operation soapAction=
      "http://actioncon.com/checkOrder/request"/>
    <input>
      <soap11:body use="literal"/>
    </input>
    <output>
      <soap11:body use="literal"/>
    </output>
  </operation>
  <operation name="opChangeOrder">
    <soap11:operation soapAction=
      "http://actioncon.com/changeOrder/request"/>
    <input>
      <soap11:body use="literal"/>
    </input>
    <output>
      <soap11:body use="literal"/>
```

```
      </output>
    </operation>
    <operation name="opCancelOrder">
      <soap11:operation soapAction=
        "http://actioncon.com/cancelOrder/request"/>
      <input>
        <soap11:body use="literal"/>
      </input>
      <output>
        <soap11:body use="literal"/>
      </output>
    </operation>
</binding>
```

Example 8.11

A concrete description with SOAP 1.1 bindings based on the document-literal message type for the Purchase Order service contract.

Notice how in this example the `operation` elements do not have `style` attributes. This is because they inherit the `style` attribute value from the parent `binding` element (as explained earlier in the section *The "Inheritance Rule"*).

Binding to SOAP 1.2

So far, most of our examples have been based on the SOAP 1.1 binding extensibility elements. When WSDL 1.1 was developed, SOAP 1.2 didn't exist. Therefore, it's no big surprise that the WSDL 1.1 specification doesn't provide any binding extensions for SOAP 1.2.

The W3C recommends that SOAP 1.2 be used together with WSDL 2.0. However, the fact that WSDL 2.0 is not expected to be widely supported for some time makes it seem difficult for Web services to take advantage of the features in SOAP 1.2. It is possible (and increasingly common) for proprietary features to make it happen. However, the good news is that a newer W3C specification entitled *WSDL 1.1 Binding Extension for SOAP 1.2* has been under development, which provides a good amount of guidance as to how SOAP 1.2 bindings can be used with WSDL 1.1.

The grammar of a SOAP 1.2 binding is shown in the following example:

```
<binding ...>
  <soap12:binding style="" transport="" wsdl:required="" />
  <operation ...>
```

```
    <soap12:operation soapAction="" soapActionRequired=""
      style="" wsdl:required="" />
    <input>
      <soap12:body parts="" use="" encodingStyle=""
        namespace="" wsdl:required="" />
      <soap12:header message="" part="" use=""
        encodingStyle="" namespace="" wsdl:required="">
      <soap12:headerfault message=""
        part="" use="" encodingStyle="" namespace=""
        wsdl:required="" />
      </soap12:header>
    </input>
    <output>
      <!-- same as input -->
    </output>
    <fault>
      <soap12:fault name="" use="" encodingStyle=""
        namespace="" wsdl:required="" />
    </fault>
  </operation>
</binding>
<service ...>
  <port ...>
    <soap12:address location="" wsdl:required="" />
  </port>
</service>
```

Example 8.12

A binding construct highlighting SOAP 1.2 extensibility elements.

It's clear that a SOAP 1.2 `binding` construct mimics the SOAP 1.1 `binding` construct with only a few changes. Differences between SOAP 1.1 and 1.2 constructs are highlighted in the previous example and further explained here:

- *soap12: Prefix* – The SOAP 1.2 binding constructs are defined in the new namespace `http://schemas.xmlsoap.org/wsdl/soap12/`, as represented by the `soap12:` prefix in the previous example. This new URI can be used in binding definitions to indicate that an interface is bound to the SOAP 1.2 protocol.

- *soapActionRequired Attribute* – This optional attribute of the binding `soap12:operation` element provides a means of indicating whether a `soapAction` value is required.

NOTE

The XML schema for the SOAP 1.2 binding extension can be found at
http://schemas.xmlsoap.org/wsdl/soap12/wsdl11soap12.xsd.

The `wsdl:required` *Attribute*

The global `wsdl:required` attribute defined in the WSDL1.1 specification can be used with any extension element to indicate whether the extension is required or not. Although it is leveraged by SOAP 1.2 extension elements, this attribute is technically not new with SOAP 1.2 binding because it can also be used with SOAP 1.1 extensions (or any other extensions).

CASE STUDY EXAMPLE

Given that Steve has already created a `binding` construct with SOAP 1.1 extensibility elements, adjusting it to support SOAP 1.2 is pretty straightforward. The differences from Example 8.11 are highlighted in the following example:

```
<binding name="bdPO-SOAP12HTTP" type="ptPurchaseOrder">
  <soap12:binding style="document"
    transport="http://schemas.xmlsoap.org/soap/http"/>
  <operation name="opSubmitOrder">
    <soap12:operation soapAction=
      "http://actioncon.com/submitOrder/request"
      soapActionRequired="true" wsdl:required="true"/>
    <input>
      <soap12:body use="literal"/>
    </input>
    <output>
      <soap12:body use="literal"/>
    </output>
  </operation>
  <operation name="opCheckOrderStatus">
    <soap12:operation soapAction=
      "http://actioncon.com/checkOrder/request"
      soapActionRequired="true" wsdl:required="true"/>
    <input>
      <soap12:body use="literal"/>
    </input>
    <output>
      <soap12:body use="literal"/>
    </output>
  </operation>
  <operation name="opChangeOrder">
```

```
    <soap12:operation soapAction=
      "http://actioncon.com/changeOrder/request"
      soapActionRequired="true" wsdl:required="true"/>
    <input>
      <soap12:body use="literal"/>
    </input>
    <output>
      <soap12:body use="literal"/>
    </output>
  </operation>
  <operation name="opCancelOrder">
    <soap12:operation soapAction=
      "http://actioncon.com/cancelOrder/request"
      soapActionRequired="true" wsdl:required="true"/>
    <input>
      <soap12:body use="literal"/>
    </input>
    <output>
      <soap12:body use="literal"/>
    </output>
  </operation>
</binding>
```

Example 8.13

A binding construct with SOAP 1.2 extensibility elements.

SUMMARY OF KEY POINTS

- The `binding` construct is comprised of WSDL language elements and extensibility elements from other languages that are used to bind the contract to communication technologies.

- Within the hierarchy of a `binding` construct, the settings established by extensibility elements can be inherited by child elements unless child elements are assigned their own extensibility elements.

- An important consideration with the binding definition overall is combination of the settings for the `use` and `style` attributes.

8.3 Service and Port Definitions

Probably the simplest of all primary WSDL elements are the `service` and `endpoint` constructs. Their role, of course, is essential for a Web service to function, but their syntax is straightforward, as it focuses on establishing one or more addresses.

The `service` and `port` Elements

After a binding definition is completed, we need to assign it a physical network address that consumer programs will use to locate and invoke the Web service. The WSDL 1.1 elements used to establish this last part of the concrete description are `service` and `port`.

Here's what they look like:

```
<service name="svPurchaseOrder">
  <port name="purchaseOrder-http-soap11"
    binding="tns:bdPO-SOAP11HTTP">
    <soap11:address location=
      "http://actioncon.com/services/soap11/purchaseOrder"/>
  </port>
</service>
```

Example 8.14

A parent `service` construct with a `port` element.

The `port` element defines a physical location (often called an *endpoint*) for a binding definition. It identifies the binding definition via the required `binding` attribute. Note that a `port` can only reference one `binding` element which, in turn, can only reference one `portType` element. This means that a port essentially represents the deployed implementation of one single port type (interface).

The actual `port` element address value is defined via an extensibility element because each transport may have a different format for expressing the address. This extensibility element is located within the `port` construct, as follows:

```
<port name="purchaseOrder" binding="tns:bdPurchaseOrder">
  <soap11:address location=
    "http://actioncon.com/services/soap11/purchaseOrder"/>
</port>
```

Example 8.15

A sample `port` construct with a SOAP 1.1 `address` extensibility element.

A `port` construct cannot contain more than one address. If you have a set of related `port` elements, you can use the `service` construct to group them together.

NOTE

The naming of the `service` element can be confusing. The contents of this element by no means defines a Web service as a whole. You can think of the `port` element details more as invocation information required to create a service instance.

WS-I Guideline

When a `service` construct has multiple `port` elements, how are these ports supposed to be related to each other? Can the `port` elements implement different `portType` constructs? The WSDL 1.1 specification doesn't provide clear answers for these questions.

WSDL 2.0

The `port` element is renamed to `endpoint` in the WSDL 2.0 specification.

The WS-I Basic Profile (and WSDL 2.0) states that when a `service` construct hosts several `port` elements, that these ports should be related to the same `portType` (when the port type employs multiple binding definitions). So a best practice advocated by the WS-I is to not group `port` elements associated with different `portType` definitions into one `service` construct.

CASE STUDY EXAMPLE

In the previous examples, we've discussed how Steve at ActionCon wants to design the Purchase Order service to support both SOAP versions 1.1 and 1.2. To accomplish this, he needs to group the two `port` elements into a `service` construct, as follows:

```
<service name="svPurchaseOrder">
  <port name="purchaseOrder-http-soap11"
    binding="tns:bdPO-SOAP11HTTP">
    <soap11:address location=
      "http://actioncon.com/services/soap11/purchaseOrder"/>
  </port>
  <port name="purchaseOrder-http-soap12"
    binding="tns:bdPO-SOAP12HTTP">
    <soap12:address location=
      "http://actioncon.com/services/soap12/purchaseOrder"/>
  </port>
</service>
```

Example 8.16

A `service` construct with two `port` elements providing support for SOAP 1.1 and 1.2.

Just for fun, let's assume that Steve decides to implement this service with bindings for SOAP 1.1 over HTTP *and* SMTP. In this case, the `service` construct would resemble something like this:

```
<service name="svPurchaseOrder">
  <port name="purchaseOrder-http" binding="tns:bdPO-SOAP11HTTP">
    <soap11:address location=
      "http://actioncon.com/services/purchaseOrder"/>
  </port>
  <port name="purchaseOrder-smtp"
    binding="tns:bdPurchaseOrder-smtp">
    <soap11:address location=
      "mailto:purchaseOrderProcessing@actioncon.com"/>
  </port>
</service>
```

Example 8.17

A `service` construct with two `port` elements providing support for SOAP 1.1 via HTTP and SMTP.

SUMMARY OF KEY POINTS

- The elements used to define a concrete `binding` construct are `operation`, `input`, `output`, and `fault`.

- Binding extensibility elements for SOAP 1.1 are defined as part of the WSDL 1.1 specification, but not for SOAP 1.2.

- The WSDL 1.1 elements used to establish the physical location for a binding definition are `service` and `port`.

8.4 A Complete WSDL Definition (Including the Concrete Description)

In order to provide an end-to-end representation of a WSDL definition, the following example shows both completed abstract and concrete descriptions together.

CASE STUDY EXAMPLE

The first version of the WSDL definition assembled by Steve for the Purchase Order service is displayed here, complete with an abstract description that includes an embedded XML schema, and a concrete description with SOAP 1.1 and 1.2 binding definitions.

```
<definitions name="PurchaseOrder" targetNamespace=
  "http://actioncon.com/contract/po"
  xmlns="http://schemas.xmlsoap.org/wsdl/"
  xmlns:tns="http://actioncon.com/contract/po"
  xmlns:po="http://actioncon.com/schema/po"
  xmlns:soap11="http://schemas.xmlsoap.org/wsdl/soap/"
  xmlns:soap12="http://schemas.xmlsoap.org/wsdl/soap12/">
  <documentation>
    This is an entity service responsible for purchase
    order-related processing only.
  </documentation>

  <!-- BEGIN ABSTRACT DESCRIPTION -->
  <types>
  <xsd:schema xmlns:xsd="http://www.w3.org/2001/XMLSchema"
    xmlns="http://actioncon.com/schema/po"
    targetNamespace="http://actioncon.com/schema/po"
    elementFormDefault="qualified">
  <xsd:element name="purchaseOrder"
    type="PurchaseOrderType"/>
  <xsd:element name="acknowledgement" type="xsd:string"/>
  <xsd:element name="poNumber" type="xsd:int"/>
  <xsd:element name="status" type="xsd:string"/>
  <xsd:complexType name="PurchaseOrderType">
    <xsd:sequence>
      <xsd:element ref="poNumber"/>
      <xsd:element name="poDate" type="xsd:date"/>
      <xsd:element name="billToParty" type="PartyType"/>
      <xsd:element name="shipToParty" type="PartyType"/>
      <xsd:element name="lineItems" type="LineItemsType"/>
    </xsd:sequence>
    <xsd:attribute name="version" type="xsd:decimal"/>
  </xsd:complexType>
  <xsd:complexType name="PartyType">
    <xsd:sequence>
      <xsd:element name="id" type="xsd:int"/>
      <xsd:element name="partyName" type="xsd:string"/>
      <xsd:element name="contactName" type="xsd:string"/>
```

```xml
        <xsd:element name="phone" type="xsd:string"/>
        <xsd:element name="address" type="AddressType"/>
      </xsd:sequence>
    </xsd:complexType>
    <xsd:complexType name="AddressType">
      <xsd:sequence>
        <xsd:element name="line1" type="xsd:string"/>
        <xsd:element name="line2" type="xsd:string"
          minOccurs="0"/>
        <xsd:element name="city" type="xsd:string"/>
        <xsd:element name="state" type="xsd:string"/>
        <xsd:element name="postalCode" type="xsd:string"/>
        <xsd:element name="country" type="xsd:string"/>
      </xsd:sequence>
    </xsd:complexType>
    <xsd:complexType name="LineItemsType">
      <xsd:sequence>
        <xsd:element name="lineItem" type="LineItemType"
          maxOccurs="unbounded"/>
      </xsd:sequence>
    </xsd:complexType>
    <xsd:complexType name="LineItemType">
      <xsd:sequence>
        <xsd:element name="productID" type="ProductIDType"/>
        <xsd:element name="productName" type="xsd:string"/>
        <xsd:element name="quantity" type="xsd:int"/>
        <xsd:element name="price" type="PriceType"/>
      </xsd:sequence>
    </xsd:complexType>
    <xsd:simpleType name="ProductIDType">
      <xsd:restriction base="xsd:string">
        <xsd:pattern value="[A-Z]{2}[0-9]{4}"/>
      </xsd:restriction>
    </xsd:simpleType>
    <xsd:simpleType name="PriceType">
      <xsd:restriction base="xsd:decimal">
        <xsd:totalDigits value="8"/>
        <xsd:fractionDigits value="2"/>
      </xsd:restriction>
    </xsd:simpleType>
  </xsd:schema>
</types>

<message name="msgSubmitOrderRequest">
  <part name="PurchaseOrder" element="po:purchaseOrder"/>
</message>
```

```
<message name="msgSubmitOrderResponse">
  <part name="Acknowledgement" element="po:acknowledgement"/>
</message>
<message name="msgCheckOrderRequest">
  <part name="PONumber" element="po:poNumber"/>
</message>
<message name="msgCheckOrderResponse">
  <part name="Status" element="po:status"/>
</message>
<message name="msgChangeOrderRequest">
  <part name="PurchaseOrder" element="po:purchaseOrder"/>
</message>
<message name="msgChangeOrderResponse">
  <part name="Acknowledgement" element="po:acknowledgement"/>
</message>
<message name="msgCancelOrderRequest">
  <part name="PONumber" element="po:poNumber"/>
</message>
<message name="msgCancelOrderResponse">
  <part name="Acknowledgement" element="po:acknowledgement"/>
</message>

<portType name="ptPurchaseOrder">
  <operation name="opSubmitOrder">
    <input message="tns:msgSubmitOrderRequest"/>
    <output message="tns:msgSubmitOrderResponse"/>
  </operation>
  <operation name="opCheckOrderStatus">
    <input message="tns:msgCheckOrderRequest"/>
    <output message="tns:msgCheckOrderResponse"/>
  </operation>
  <operation name="opChangeOrder">
    <input message="tns:msgChangeOrderRequest"/>
    <output message="tns:msgChangeOrderResponse"/>
  </operation>
  <operation name="opCancelOrder">
    <input message="tns:msgCancelOrderRequest"/>
    <output message="tns:msgCancelOrderResponse"/>
  </operation>
</portType>
<!-- END ABSTRACT DESCRIPTION -->

<!-- BEGIN CONCRETE DESCRIPTION -->
<binding name="bdPO-SOAP11HTTP" type="tns:ptPurchaseOrder">
  <soap11:binding style="document"
    transport="http://schemas.xmlsoap.org/soap/http"/>
```

```
  <operation name="opSubmitOrder">
    <input>
      <soap11:body use="literal"/>
    </input>
    <output>
      <soap11:body use="literal"/>
    </output>
  </operation>
  <operation name="opCheckOrderStatus">
    <input>
      <soap11:body use="literal"/>
    </input>
    <output>
      <soap11:body use="literal"/>
    </output>
  </operation>
  <operation name="opChangeOrder">
    <input>
      <soap11:body use="literal"/>
    </input>
    <output>
      <soap11:body use="literal"/>
    </output>
  </operation>
  <operation name="opCancelOrder">
    <input>
      <soap11:body use="literal"/>
    </input>
    <output>
      <soap11:body use="literal"/>
    </output>
  </operation>
</binding>

<binding name="bdPO-SOAP12HTTP" type="tns:ptPurchaseOrder">
  <soap12:binding style="document"
    transport="http://schemas.xmlsoap.org/soap/http"/>
  <operation name="opSubmitOrder">
  <soap12:operation soapAction=
    "http://actioncon.com/submitOrder/request"
    soapActionRequired="true" wsdl:required="true"/>
    <input>
      <soap12:body use="literal"/>
    </input>
    <output>
      <soap12:body use="literal"/>
```

```
    </output>
  </operation>
  <operation name="opCheckOrderStatus">
  <soap12:operation soapAction=
    "http://actioncon.com/submitOrder/request"
    soapActionRequired="true" wsdl:required="true"/>
    <input>
      <soap12:body use="literal"/>
    </input>
    <output>
      <soap12:body use="literal"/>
    </output>
  </operation>
  <operation name="opChangeOrder">
  <soap12:operation soapAction=
    "http://actioncon.com/submitOrder/request"
    soapActionRequired="true" wsdl:required="true"/>
    <input>
      <soap12:body use="literal"/>
    </input>
    <output>
      <soap12:body use="literal"/>
    </output>
  </operation>
  <operation name="opCancelOrder">
  <soap12:operation soapAction=
    "http://actioncon.com/submitOrder/request"
    soapActionRequired="true" wsdl:required="true"/>
    <input>
      <soap12:body use="literal"/>
    </input>
    <output>
      <soap12:body use="literal"/>
    </output>
  </operation>
</binding>

<service name="svPurchaseOrder">
  <port name="purchaseOrder-http-soap11"
    binding="tns:bdPO-SOAP11HTTP">
    <soap11:address location=
      "http://actioncon.com/services/soap11/purchaseOrder"/>
  </port>
  <port name="purchaseOrder-http-soap12"
    binding="tns:bdPO-SOAP12HTTP">
    <soap12:address location=
```

```
            "http://actioncon.com/services/soap12/purchaseOrder"/>
      </port>
   </service>
   <!-- END CONCRETE DESCRIPTION -->
</definitions>
```

Example 8.18

The complete Web service contract for the Purchase Order service.

Chapter 9

Fundamental WSDL 2.0:
New Features and Design Options

9.1 WSDL 2.0 Document Structure

9.2 Interface Definition

9.3 Service and Endpoint Definitions

9.4 A Complete WSDL 2.0 Definition

This chapter is comprised of a series of concise sections that highlight differences between WSDL 2.0 and 1.1 supplemented with various examples. The chapter concludes with a WSDL 2.0 version of the WSDL 1.1 definition provided at the end of Chapter 8.

9.1 WSDL 2.0 Document Structure

As shown in Figure 9.1, the WSDL 2.0 language introduces some noticeable differences to the document structure of a WSDL definition, namely:

- The `definitions` element is renamed to `description`.

- The `portType` element is renamed to `interface`.

- The `port` element is renamed to `endpoint`.

Additionally, the `message` element is removed, as explained in the next section.

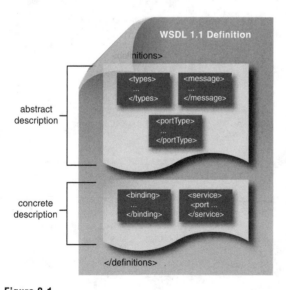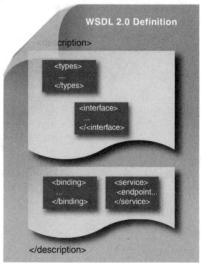

Figure 9.1

WSDL 2.0 inherits its overall structure from WSDL 1.1, but does make some changes to both abstract and concrete descriptions.

Elimination of the `message` Element

The WSDL 1.1 `message` element was mainly intended to serve as the bridge between message- and RPC-centric communication. As we established earlier in Chapter 7, it can be used to describe a document type message based on just one `part` element, or it can support RPC type (parameter-driven) messages based on multiple parts. However, its expressive power for RPC is limited. For example, it cannot describe a variable number of input parameters or a choice of responses. WSDL 2.0 addresses this industry shift by removing support for the `message` element altogether. It simply allows an operation to reference a type (such as an XML Schema element) directly.

9.2 Interface Definition

WSDL 2.0 not only changes the element name of an interface definition from `portType` to `interface`, it also expands the `interface` construct with a set of new elements and attributes, as shown in the highlighted parts of this example:

```
<interface name="..." extends="..." styleDefault="...">
   <fault name="..." element="..." />
   <operation name="..." pattern="..." style="..."
   wsdlx:safe="...">
     <input messageLabel="..." element="..." />
     <output messageLabel="..." element="..." />
     <infault ref="..." messageLabel="..." />
     <outfault ref="..." messageLabel="..." />
   </operation>
</interface>
```

Example 9.1
The WSDL 2.0 `interface` construct with possible child elements.

Let's explore these new elements and attributes more closely.

The `interface` Element's `extends` Attribute

Object-oriented programming introduced the concept of interface inheritance whereby a new interface can be derived from an existing interface by inheriting and then extending its operations.

The optional `extends` attribute of the `interface` element allows one interface to extend or inherit from one or more other interfaces. In such cases, the interface contains all the operations it extends plus the operations it defines directly.

Now let's have a look at an example of how the `extends` attribute works.

ActionCon introduces a requirement that any activities related to the processing of purchase orders must be logged in a storage center for auditing purposes. As shown here, Steve defines an interface for logging and then uses that interface in one of several purchase order-related interfaces.

```
<interface name="ifPurchaseOrderLog">
  <operation name="opLogOrder"
    pattern="http://www.w3.org/2006/01/wsdl/out-only">
    <output messageLabel="Out" element="po:orderLog"/>
  </operation>
</interface>
```

Example 9.2
An `interface` construct with one `operation` element.

The `ifPurchaseOrderLog` interface construct represents the operation that can be inherited by other interface constructs, and the `ifPurchaseOrder` interface construct is the interface that inherits it via the use of the `extends` attribute.

```
<interface name="ifPurchaseOrder" extends="tns:ifPurchaseOrderLog" >
  <operation name="opChangeOrder"
    pattern="http://www.w3.org/2006/01/wsdl/in-out">
    <input messageLabel="In" element="po:purchaseOrder "/>
    <output messageLabel="Out" element="po:acknowledgement"/>
  </operation>
  <operation name="opCancelOrder"
    pattern="http://www.w3.org/2006/01/wsdl/in-out">
    <input messageLabel="In" element="po:poNumber"/>
    <output messageLabel="Out" element="po:acknowledgement"/>
  </operation>
</interface>
```

Example 9.3
An `interface` construct that inherits from another `interface` construct as per the `extends` attribute.

As a result of the inheritance, the interface `ifPurchaseOrder` now contains three operations: `opLogOrder`, `opChangeOrder`, and `opCancelOrder`.

> **NOTE**
>
> This feature has one key limitation: Operation overloading is still not allowed, even when the interface is extended. Overloading refers to the situation when operations from two different interfaces have the same qualified name. With WSDL 2.0, if the definitions of the operations are exactly the same, they are considered to be the same operation (they are essentially collapsed into a single operation). If the two operations have the same qualified name but are not equivalent, an error is raised.

The `interface` Element's `styleDefault` Attribute

Styles define certain rules that are applied to operations. The `styleDefault` attribute can be used to set a default value for the `style` attributes of all operations under an interface.

```
<interface name="ifPurchaseOrderLog"
  styleDefault="http://www.w3.org/ns/wsdl/style/iri">
  <operation name="opLogOrder"
    pattern="http://www.w3.org/2006/01/wsdl/out-only">
    <output messageLabel="Out" element="po:orderLog"/>
  </operation>
</interface>
```

Example 9.4
The `interface` element's `styleDefault` attribute set to the IRI style.

The following pre-defined style values are provided:

- RPC Style (`http://www.w3.org/ns/wsdl/style/rpc`)

  Requires that all the operations within an interface must follow the rules for RPC-style messages.

- IRI Style (`http://www.w3.org/ns/wsdl/style/iri`)

  Places restrictions on message definitions so they may be serialized into something like HTTP URL-encoded.

- Multipart (`http://www.w3.org/ns/wsdl/style/multipart`)

  In the HTTP binding, for XForms clients, a message must be defined following this style and serialized as "Multipart/form-data."

The exact rules and restrictions of each style are documented in the WSDL 2.0 specification. `operation` elements can have individual `style` attribute settings that override the `styleDefault` setting of the parent `interface` element.

The `styleDefault` attribute is optional; if it's missing, it simply means no additional rules need to be followed.

The `wsdlx:safe` Global Attribute

This new attribute indicates whether an operation is considered to be "safe" as per the W3C Web Architecture specification, which states:

> *"...a safe interaction is one where the agent does not incur any obligation beyond the interaction. An agent may incur an obligation through other means (such as by signing a contract). If an agent does not have an obligation before a safe interaction, it does not have that obligation afterwards.*

> *Other Web interactions resemble orders more than queries. These unsafe interactions may cause a change to the state of a resource and the user may be held responsible for the consequences of these interactions. Unsafe interactions include subscribing to a newsletter, posting to a list, or modifying a database. Note: In this context, the word "unsafe" does not necessarily mean 'dangerous'..."*

In other words, if an operation performs something along the lines of a read-only function that doesn't permanently alter any part of the service environment or if it does not give the consumer any new obligations, then it is considered "safe."

> **NOTE**
>
> What is and is not actually "safe" is highly subjective, and it is up to each organization to establish this individually as part of its design standards.

This attribute is essentially a means by which a service contract can communicate that a particular operation has little risk associated with it. This can be valuable especially in support of the Service Discoverability principle, which encourages us to improve the communications quality of the contract. However, Service Abstraction considerations also need to be taken into account. In some cases, it may be deemed necessary not to allow this attribute at all.

If it is allowed, it is important that SOA governance procedures be in place to manage the potential change of this setting. If consumer programs become dependent on a service operation with the assumption that it is safe and then the underlying functionality of the operation changes so that it is no longer considered safe, then this may have a variety of negative impacts. It may also be required for this setting to be programmatically retrieved by certain consumers.

The default value of the `wsdlx:safe` attribute is "false." Therefore, if the attribute is not present or if it is explicitly set to false, then the consumer can assume the operation is "not safe."

> **NOTE**
>
> The `wsdlx:safe` attribute is classified as "global" because it is defined in a global XML Schema namespace (see http://www.w3.org/2007/06/wsdl/wsdl20-extensions.xsd) and can be used by any WSDL or XML document.

The `fault`, `infault`, and `outfault` Elements

With WSDL 2.0, the `fault` element is promoted to a first-level child element within the `interface` construct. This lifts `fault` to the same level as `operation`, allowing one fault message to be reused across different operations.

As shown in this example, a fault can be referenced by multiple operations via the `ref` attributes of their `infault` and `outfault` elements.

```
<types>
  <xsd:schema xmlns:xsd="http://www.w3.org/2001/XMLSchema"
    xmlns="http://actioncon.com/schema/po"
    targetNamespace="http://actioncon.com/schema/po"
    elementFormDefault="qualified">
  <xsd:element name="invalidOrder"
    type="invalidOrderType"/>
  <xsd:complexType name="invalidOrderType">
    <xsd:sequence>
      <xsd:element name="PODate" type="xsd:date"/>
      <xsd:element name="OrderID" type="xsd:string"/>
      <xsd:element name="Desc" type="xsd:string"/>
    </xsd:sequence>
  </xsd:complexType>
```

```
  </xsd:schema>
</types>
```

Example 9.5

The `types` construct establishing the `invalidOrderType` XML Schema type.

This `types` construct defines the `invalidOrderType` type that is subsequently reused as a fault message by the `opChangeOrder` and `opCancelOrder` operations via their respective `outfault` elements.

```
<interface name="ifPurchaseOrder" extends="tns:ifPurchaseOrderLog" >
  <fault name="invalidOrderFault" element="po:invalidOrder"/>
  <operation name="opChangeOrder"
    pattern="http://www.w3.org/2006/01/wsdl/in-out">
    <input messageLabel="In" element="po:purchaseOrder "/>
    <output messageLabel="Out" element="po:acknowledgement"/>
    <outfault ref="tns:invalidOrderFault" messageLabel="Out/>
  </operation>
  <operation name="opCancelOrder"
    pattern="http://www.w3.org/2006/01/wsdl/in-out">
    <input messageLabel="In" element="po:poNumber"/>
    <output messageLabel="Out"
      element="po:acknowledgement"/>
    <outfault ref="tns:invalidOrderFault" messageLabel="Out/>
  </operation>
</interface>
```

Example 9.6

The `outfault` elements within two `operation` constructs that reference the `invalidOrderType` type.

Defining faults at the interface level is especially beneficial for binding definitions. For example, a SOAP fault may have an error code (and sub-codes) in addition to its fault message details. By defining faults at the interface level, you can ensure that common error codes can be used across all operations that use the faults.

For example, when the interface in the following example is bound to SOAP 1.2, one can specify a SOAP fault code as "sender" for all invalid order errors.

```
<binding name="bdPurchaseOrder-SOAP12HTTP"
  interface="tns:ifPurchaseOrder" >
  <fault ref="tns:invalidOrderFault" soap12:code="soap12:Sender"/>
  <operation ref="tns:opChangeOrder" .../>
  <operation ref="tns:opCancelOrder" .../>
</binding>
```

Example 9.7

A `fault` element bound to the `binding` element that also contains two `operation` elements.

In this example, the `fault` element is bound to the `binding` element and therefore becomes applicable to both operations within the binding definition, allowing the operations to reuse the same fault code.

Given the structure of the interface and binding definitions, at runtime if an invalid order is found, the fault message returned to the sender will appear as something like this:

```
<soap:Envelope xmlns:soap=
  "http://www.w3.org/2003/05/soap-envelope"
  xmlns:po="http://actioncon.com/schema/po" ...>
  <soap:Body>
    <soap:Fault>
      <soap:Code>
        <soap:Value>soap:Sender</soap:Value>
      </soap:Code>
      <soap:Detail>
        <po:invalidOrder>
          <po:PODate>02-23-2008</po:PODate>
          <po:OrderID>1234</po:OrderID>
          <po:Desc>
            The required order party ID is missing.
          </po:Desc>
        </po:invalidOrder>
      </soap:Detail>
    </soap:Fault>
  </soap:Body>
</soap:Envelope>
```

Example 9.8

A sample runtime SOAP fault message.

The `pattern` and `messageLabel` Attributes

The WSDL 2.0 specification allows message exchange patterns (MEPs) to be defined in separate specifications and then brought into an `operation` definition via the new `pattern` attribute.

A related MEP specification establishes how many messages are exchanged and in what order. Each message can be identified with a message label and a direction ("in" or "out").

The operation that employs a particular MEP should provide a corresponding number of messages based on the following rules:

- For each message with a direction of "In," an `input` element needs to be defined with a `messageLabel` attribute set to "In."

- For each message with a direction of "Out," an `output` element is defined with a `messageLabel` attribute set to "Out."

- The order of the `input` and `output` elements should be the same as the order of their corresponding messages defined in the MEP specification.

WSDL 2.0 uses new terms to describe MEPs. For example, the "Request-Response" MEP from WSDL 1.1 is now "In-Out," and the "One-Way" MEP has been renamed to "In."

The `messageLabel` attribute of an operation's `input`, `output`, or `fault` element simply indicates the role played by the message in the MEP. For example, a setting of `message-Label="In"` for an "In-Out" MEP means that the message is the input message of an "In-Out" operation. (This may seem redundant because the `input` element's name already indicates that this is an input message.)

Here's an example that uses the `pattern` and `messageLabel` attributes for an operation based on the "In-Out" MEP.

```
<operation name="opChangeOrder"
  pattern="http://www.w3.org/2006/01/wsdl/in-out">
  <input messageLabel="In" element="po:purchaseOrder "/>
  <output messageLabel="Out" element="po:acknowledgement"/>
</operation>
```

Example 9.9
A WSDL 2.0 operation definition based on the In-Out MEP.

> **NOTE**
>
> WSDL 2.0 introduces a new MEP called "Robust In-Only," which is
> explained in Chapter 14. Also covered in that chapter is how you can
> create custom MEPs.

9.3 Service and Endpoint Definitions

In WSDL 2.0, a `service` element can only implement one interface via its `interface`
attribute as shown in the following example. What this means is that when a service has
more than one `endpoint` element, they will share an `interface` but employ different
bindings and addresses.

This is because they are alternatives in the sense that each endpoint can provide the
same behavior via different binding configurations. By allowing services to provide
alternative endpoints, consumers have more freedom to determine which port is the
best for a given purpose.

```
<service name="svPurchaseOrder" interface="ifPurchaseOrder">
  <endpoint name="purchaseOrder-http-soap12"
    binding="tns:bdPO-SOAP12HTTP" address=
    "http://actioncon.com/services/soap12/purchaseOrder"/>
</service>
```

Example 9.10
The `service` construct hosting an `endpoint` element.

> **NOTE**
>
> Another change introduced by WSDL 2.0 in the introduction of the
> `endpoint` element's `address` attribute, which eliminates the need for
> the address to be specified by a separate extensibility element.

9.4 A Complete WSDL 2.0 Definition

The following sample code shows the WSDL 1.1 definition from the end of Chapter 8, as
restructured into a WSDL 2.0 definition. The highlighted sections indicate where the
WSDL 2.0 language introduced changes.

```
<description targetNamespace="http://actioncon.com/contract/po"
  xmlns="http://schemas.xmlsoap.org/wsdl/"
  xmlns:tns="http://actioncon.com/contract/po"
  xmlns:po="http://actioncon.com/schema/po"
  xmlns:soapbind="http://www.w3.org/ns/wsdl/soap">

  <!- BEGIN ABSTRACT DESCRIPTION ->
  <types>
    <xsd:schema xmlns:xsd="http://www.w3.org/2001/XMLSchema"
      xmlns="http://actioncon.com/schema/po"
      targetNamespace="http://actioncon.com/schema/po"
      elementFormDefault="qualified">
      <xsd:element name="purchaseOrder" type="PurchaseOrderType"/>
      <xsd:element name="acknowledgement" type="xsd:string"/>
      <xsd:element name="poNumber" type="xsd:integer"/>
      <xsd:element name="status" type="xsd:string"/>
      <xsd:complexType name="PurchaseOrderType">
        <xsd:sequence>
          <xsd:element ref="poNumber"/>
          <xsd:element name="PODate" type="xsd:date"/>
          <xsd:element name="BillToParty" type="PartyType"/>
          <xsd:element name="ShipToParty" type="PartyType"/>
          <xsd:element name="LineItems" type="LineItemsType"/>
        </xsd:sequence>
      <xsd:attribute name="version" type="xsd:decimal"/>
      </xsd:complexType>
      <xsd:complexType name="PartyType">
        <xsd:sequence>
          <xsd:element name="ID" type="xsd:integer"/>
          <xsd:element name="PartyName" type="xsd:string"/>
          <xsd:element name="ContactName" type="xsd:string"/>
          <xsd:element name="Phone" type="xsd:string"/>
          <xsd:element name="Address" type="AddressType"/>
        </xsd:sequence>
      </xsd:complexType>
      <xsd:complexType name="AddressType">
        <xsd:sequence>
          <xsd:element name="Line1" type="xsd:string"/>
          <xsd:element name="Line2" type="xsd:string"
            minOccurs="0"/>
          <xsd:element name="City" type="xsd:string"/>
          <xsd:element name="State" type="xsd:string"/>
          <xsd:element name="PostalCode" type="xsd:string"/>
          <xsd:element name="Country" type="xsd:string"/>
        </xsd:sequence>
      </xsd:complexType>
```

```
      <xsd:complexType name="LineItemsType">
        <xsd:sequence>
          <xsd:element name="LineItem" type="LineItemType"
            maxOccurs="unbounded"/>
        </xsd:sequence>
      </xsd:complexType>
      <xsd:complexType name="LineItemType">
        <xsd:sequence>
          <xsd:element name="ProductID" type="ProductIDType"/>
          <xsd:element name="ProductName" type="xsd:string"/>
          <xsd:element name="Quantity" type="xsd:int"/>
          <xsd:element name="Price" type="PriceType"/>
        </xsd:sequence>
      </xsd:complexType>
      <xsd:simpleType name="ProductIDType">
        <xsd:restriction base="xsd:string">
          <xsd:pattern value="[A-Z]{2}[0-9]{4}"/>
        </xsd:restriction>
      </xsd:simpleType>
      <xsd:simpleType name="PriceType">
        <xsd:restriction base="xsd:decimal">
          <xsd:totalDigits value="8"/>
          <xsd:fractionDigits value="2"/>
        </xsd:restriction>
      </xsd:simpleType>
    </xsd:schema>
  </types>
  <interface name="ifPurchaseOrder">
    <operation name="opSubmitOrder"
      pattern="http://www.w3.org/2006/01/wsdl/in-out">
      <input messageLabel="In" element="po:purchaseOrder"/>
      <output messageLabel="Out" element="po:acknowlegement"/>
    </operation>
    <operation name="opCheckOrderStatus"
      pattern="http://www.w3.org/2006/01/wsdl/in-out">
      <input messageLabel="In" element="po:poNumber"/>
      <output messageLabel="Out" element="po:status"/>
    </operation>
    <operation name="opChangeOrder"
      pattern="http://www.w3.org/2006/01/wsdl/in-out">
      <input messageLabel="In" element="po:purchaseOrder "/>
      <output messageLabel="Out" element="po:acknowledgement"/>
    </operation>
    <operation name="opCancelOrder"
      pattern="http://www.w3.org/2006/01/wsdl/in-out">
      <input messageLabel="In" element="po:poNumber"/>
```

```xml
      <output messageLabel="Out" element="po:acknowledgement"/>
    </operation>
</interface>
<!-- END ABSTRACT DESCRIPTION -->

<!-- BEGIN CONCRETE DESCRIPTION -->
<binding name="bdPO-SOAP12HTTP" interface="ifPurchaseOrder"
  type="http://www.w3.org/2006/01/wsdl/soap"
  soapbind:protocol=
    "http://www.w3.org/2003/05/soap/bindings/HTTP">
  <operation ref="tns:opSubmitOrder"
    soapbind:mep=
      "http://www.w3.org/2003/05/soap/mep/request-response"
      soapbind:action=
        "http://actioncon.com/submitOrder/request"/>
   <operation ref="opCheckOrderStatus"
    soapbind:mep=
      "http://www.w3.org/2003/05/soap/mep/request-response"
      soapbind:action=
        "http://actioncon.com/checkOrder/request"/>
   <operation ref="opChangeOrder"
    soapbind:mep=
      "http://www.w3.org/2003/05/soap/mep/request-response"
      soapbind:action=
        "http://actioncon.com/changeOrder/request"/>
   <operation ref="opCancelOrder"
    soapbind:mep=
      "http://www.w3.org/2003/05/soap/mep/request-response"
      soapbind:action=
        "http://actioncon.com/cancelOrder/request"/>
</binding>

<service name="svPurchaseOrder" interface="ifPurchaseOrder">
  <endpoint name="purchaseOrder-http-soap12"
    binding="tns:bdPO-SOAP12HTTP" address=
      "http://actioncon.com/services/soap12/purchaseOrder"/>
</service>
<!-- END CONCRETE DESCRIPTION -->

</description>
```

Example 9.11

A complete WSDL 2.0 definition.

NOTE
There are tools available for converting WSDL 1.1 definitions to WSDL 2.0. For example, the W3C provides a simple on-line converter at www.w3.org/2006/02/WSDLConvert.html.

Chapter 10

Fundamental WS-Policy: Assertions, Expressions, and Attachments

Web service contracts can be extended with policies that express additional constraints, requirements, and qualities that typically relate to the *behaviors* of services. You can create human-readable policies that become part of a supplemental service-level agreement, or you can define machine-readable polices that are processed at runtime. The latter type of policy is the focus of this chapter and the technology we'll explore to create machine-readable policies is the WS-Policy language and related WS-Policy specifications.

There are many kinds of policies, some of which are pre-defined by industry specifications and others that can be customized by the Web service contract designer. For example, you can use policies to express interoperability and protocol constraints, as well as privacy, manageability, and quality of service (QoS) requirements. Furthermore, policies may be created for a single party, or they may apply to multiparty interactions.

From an architectural and contract design perspective, policies affect all levels of a service design. They can be applied to most parts of the abstract and concrete descriptions of a WSDL document, and they can be applied at different scopes. For example, one policy may pertain to a message definition while another is applied to the entire WSDL port type (or interface).

In this chapter, we first cover the essential aspects of policies and then introduce the fundamental parts of the WS-Policy language. Chapters 16 and 17 continue the exploration of the WS-Policy framework by documenting a range of advanced language features and design techniques.

The XML Schema and WSDL languages allow us to do little more than express the interaction requirements and constraints of a Web service. While this is, of course, fundamentally important for us to do anything useful with the Web service, it does not provide us with the opportunity to describe other aspects of the Web service, such as:

- Are there certain QoS requirements (reliability, security, etc.) that consumer programs will need to adhere to in order to work with the service?

- Are there any additional requirements as to how the service can or cannot be accessed?

- Are there properties or characteristics of the service that might be of interest to consumer programs?

- Are there certain rules that must be followed in order to interact with the service?

10.1 Policy Structure

The WS-Policy vocabulary is relatively simple in comparison to WSDL and XML Schema in that it contains only a modest amount of elements and attributes. However, policies introduce unique structural considerations that differ from the straightforward technical interface focus of WSDL and XML Schema. Because policies are about expressing behavioral qualities, they can range dramatically in size and in the nature of the policy content. Additionally, the flexibility and extensibility built in to the WS-Policy language allows its few elements and attributes to be combined into a variety of complex designs.

Before we learn more about the individual WS-Policy language elements, let's first introduce some basic terminology:

- The formal term for a policy is *policy expression.*

- A policy expression can be comprised of one or more elements that express specific policy requirements or properties. Each of these is called a *policy assertion.*

- In order to group policy assertions, we use a set of features from the WS-Policy language known as *policy operators.*

- Policy expressions can optionally be isolated into a separate document, referred to as a *WS-Policy definition.*

Among all of these parts of the WS-Policy framework, the most basic building block is the policy assertion.

> **NOTE**
>
> As discussed later in Chapter 16, support for policy definition documents can vary across different vendor platforms.

New Namespaces and Prefixes

Let's now take a minute to establish some new namespaces and prefixes associated with the WS-Policy language and common policies:

- `xmlns:wsp="http://www.w3.org/2006/07/ws-policy"` – This represents the actual namespace used for elements from the WS-Policy language.

- `xmlns:wsam="http://www.w3.org/2007/05/addressing/metadata"` – We will show some policy examples related to the WS-Addressing language, which is why this namespace comes up here. How the referenced WS-Addressing features actually work is covered in Chapter 18 and this particular policy assertion is further revisited at the end of Chapter 19.

- `xmlns:wsrmp="http://docs.oasis-open.org/ws-rx/wsrmp/200702"` – This namespace corresponds to the WS-ReliableMessaging policy assertion. Although WS-ReliableMessaging is not a technology covered in this book, there are a few references to one of its policy assertions in the examples.

- `xmlns:wsu="http://docs.oasis-open.org/wss/2004/01/oasis-200401-wss-wssecurity-utility-1.0.xsd"` – There is a special type of schema that is referred to as a "utility schema" in which generic and commonly used attributes are established. One such attribute is `wsu:Id`, a simple ID used to associate an identifier with an element. This and other chapters make occasional reference to this attribute.

Note that throughout the examples in this chapter we generally avoid displaying the previously listed `xmlns` values simply to avoid repeated clutter of policy definition code fragments.

Assertions, Expressions, and the `Policy` Element

The most important thing to understand about WS-Policy is that it is not a technology or language used to enforce policies. Its sole purpose is to provide a standardized syntax with which to express policies (hence the term "policy expression").

Policy Assertions

It all begins with a policy assertion, which, on its own, is simply a reference to a predefined XML Schema global element.

Here's an example of a simple policy assertion:

```
<wsrmp:RMAssertion><wsp:Policy/></wsrmp:RMAssertion>
```

Example 10.1
A policy assertion comprised of a policy assertion type that is defined via a corresponding XML Schema global element.

The `wsrmp:RMAssertion` element refers to an extensibility element defined in the WS-ReliableMessaging specification. This is therefore considered a WS-ReliableMessaging policy assertion.

The XML schema that defines this assertion looks like this:

```
<xsd:schema
  xmlns:tns="http://docs.oasis-open.org/ws-rx/wsrmp/200608"
  xmlns:xsd="http://www.w3.org/2001/XMLSchema"
  targetNamespace="http://docs.oasisopen.org/wsrx/wsrmp/200608"
    elementFormDefault="qualified"
    attributeFormDefault="unqualified">
  <xsd:element name="RMAssertion">
    <xsd:complexType>
      <xsd:sequence>
        <xsd:any namespace="##other" processContents="lax"
          minOccurs="0" maxOccurs="unbounded"/>
      </xsd:sequence>
      <xsd:anyAttribute namespace="##any"
        processContents="lax"/>
    </xsd:complexType>
  </xsd:element>
  ...
</xsd:schema>
```

Example 10.2

The XML Schema definition for the global **RMAssertion** element, as defined in the WS-ReliableMessaging specification.

We refer to what's defined in this schema as the *policy type*. Every assertion has an underlying policy type, which can be provided by an industry standard like WS-ReliableMessaging or you can custom define it by creating your own schema. All you need is a global element that can be referenced in the policy assertion syntax.

Beyond providing a standardized policy expression, WS-Policy has nothing to do with how policy assertions are actually processed. For example, what happens when the `wsrmp:RMAssertion` element is encountered at runtime is up to WS-ReliableMessaging related processors. All we use WS-Policy for is to associate this assertion with a WSDL definition.

Similarly, if you create your own custom policy assertions, you will need to provide the underlying processing logic that does something in response to encountering the policy assertion being processed at runtime.

NOTE

We don't cover the WS-ReliableMessaging standard in this book. But in case you are wondering what this assertion does, it simply indicates that the service consumer must support the reliable messaging features as defined in the WS-ReliableMessaging specification. For more details regarding this standard, visit www.soaspecs.com.

We're going to be using the `wsrmp:RMAssertion` element on and off throughout the WS-Policy chapters. Let's now take a look at another example:

```
<wsam:Addressing><wsp:Policy/></wsam:Addressing>
```

Example 10.3
A policy assertion from the WS-Addressing specification.

WS-Addressing (a technology we describe later in this book) provides a pre-defined `wsam:Addressing` extensibility element that can be used in the WSDL `binding` construct to associate WS-Addressing with the Web service.

As with `wsrmp:RMAssertion`, this assertion introduces the requirement that incoming messages support a particular technology; in this case, WS-Addressing.

Policy Expressions

On their own, the preceding policy assertion statements do not yet exist as standalone policies. In order create an actual *policy expression*, we need to wrap assertions in a `wsp:Policy` construct, as follows:

```
<wsp:Policy>
  <wsam:Addressing><wsp:Policy/></wsam:Addressing>
</wsp:Policy>
<wsp:Policy>
  <wsrmp:RMAssertion><wsp:Policy/></wsrmp:RMAssertion>
</wsp:Policy>
<wsp:Policy>
  <wsam:Addressing><wsp:Policy/></wsam:Addressing>
  <wsrmp:RMAssertion><wsp:Policy/></wsrmp:RMAssertion>
</wsp:Policy>
```

Example 10.4
Three separate policy expressions, each wrapping a different combination of the previously explained policy assertions.

Custom Policy Assertions

Let's now assume you want to create you own policy expression with an assertion that defines a response guarantee for a particular operation. Let's first create the XML Schema element that forms the basis of the required policy assertion.

```
<xsd:schema xmlns:xsd="http://www.w3.org/2001/XMLSchema"
  targetNamespace="http://actioncon.com/schema/respguarantee"
  elementFormDefault="qualified">
<xsd:element name="responseGuarantee"
  type="ResponseGuaranteeType"/>
<xsd:complexType name="ResponseGuaranteeType">
  <xsd:sequence>
    <xsd:element name="responseInMilliseconds"
      type="xsd:integer"/>
  </xsd:sequence>
</xsd:complexType>
</xsd:schema>
```

Example 10.5

The XML Schema global type definition for the **responseGuarantee** policy assertion. Note also how this policy assertion structure contains a nested element.

This is a good example of a custom-created QoS policy that can be added to a service contract so that consumers could retrieve the number of milliseconds within which the service promises to perform a particular task.

If you recall the ActionCon Purchase Order service, an assertion such as this could be used to indicate the amount of time the service will take to generate and return a purchase order document. Depending on the circumstances, the actual value of the assertion may differ, as shown in the following two assertion instances.

Assertion Instance #1

```
<argt:responseGuarantee>
  <argt:responseInMilliseconds>
    50
  </argt:responseInMilliseconds>
</argt:responseGuarantee>
```

Assertion Instance #2

```
<argt:responseGuarantee>
  <argt:responseInMilliseconds>
```

```
   30
 </argt:responseInMilliseconds>
</argt:responseGuarantee>
```

Example 10.6
Two different instances of a policy assertion, each providing different values.

Both assertions have the same assertion element, namely `argt:responseGuarantee`. However, each instance has a different value.

> **NOTE**
>
> This was an example of a parameterized policy assertion. Parameterized assertions are explained in Chapter 16.

SUMMARY OF KEY POINTS

- Policy assertions express granular constraints or characteristics via globally declared XML Schema elements.

- A policy expression represents one or more related policy assertions.

10.2 Composite Policies

In the previous example we created a simple policy assertion. On its own, this one assertion may be sufficient to warrant an entire, self-contained policy expression. However, more often than not, policies need to be assembled out of multiple policy assertions.

In order to combine policy assertion constructs into composite policy expressions, we need to use a new feature of the WS-Policy language known as *operators*. Specifically, we will need to work with the `wsp:ExactlyOne` and `wsp:All` elements and the `wsp:optional` attribute.

The `ExactlyOne` Element

This element groups a set of policy assertions from which only one can be used. In other words, it enforces a rule that "exactly one" of the listed assertions must be chosen.

Using the `wsp:ExactlyOne` element introduces the concept of *policy alternatives* as part of a policy expression. Each child element within this construct is considered a distinct alternative in the overall policy expression.

Consider the following example:

```
<wsp:Policy>
  <wsp:ExactlyOne>
    <wsam:Addressing><wsp:Policy/></wsam:Addressing>
    <wsrmp:RMAssertion><wsp:Policy/></wsrmp:RMAssertion>
  </wsp:ExactlyOne>
</wsp:Policy>
```

Example 10.7

A policy assertion structured with the **ExactlyOnce** construct, allowing only one of the two enclosed assertions to be used at a time.

Here, the WS-Policy expression contains two distinct alternatives. Each assertion, `wsam:Addressing` and `wsrmp:RMAssertion`, indicates a separate alternative.

> **NOTE**
>
> There is no significance as to how assertions are ordered within the `wsp:ExactlyOne` construct, and it is also possible for this content to be empty.

The `wsp:All` Element

The `wsp:All` operator element is the reverse of the `wsp:ExactlyOne` element. It imposes a rule that requires that *all* of the assertions within its construct be applied at the same time.

If we restructure the previous example using this element, it actually looks quite similar.

```
<wsp:Policy>
  <wsp:All>
    <wsam:Addressing><wsp:Policy/></wsam:Addressing>
    <wsrmp:RMAssertion><wsp:Policy/></wsrmp:RMAssertion>
  </wsp:All>
</wsp:Policy>
```

Example 10.8

A policy assertion structured with the **wsp:All** construct, requiring that both enclosed assertions be applied together.

As with the `wsp:ExactlyOne` construct, it does not matter in what order you decide to place the policy assertion type elements.

> **NOTE**
>
> When the `wsp:Policy` element is used without an operator element, it is the equivalent of using the `wsp:All` element. In other words, the requirement that all assertions be used within a given policy expression is the default.

The `wsp:optional` Attribute

The WS-Policy language provides a special Boolean attribute named `wsp:optional` that allows you to indicate that a policy assertion is not mandatory.

The following example shows this attribute used in conjunction with our previous `wsam:Addressing` assertion:

```
<wsp:Policy>
  <wsam:Addressing wsp:optional="true"/>
</wsp:Policy>
```

Example 10.9
A policy assertion that is not required.

> **NOTE**
>
> The default value of the `wsp:optional` attribute is "`false`," which means that if you don't use it, the policy assertion will be required.

This attribute is considered a "shortcut" because you can express the same policy logic in a more verbose manner using the previously described operator elements. The `wsp:All` element is essentially the same as specifying two distinct alternatives in a policy expression, as follows:

```
<wsp:Policy>
  <wsp:ExactlyOne>
    <wsp:All>
      <wsam:Addressing><wsp:Policy/></wsam:Addressing>
    </wsp:All>
    <wsp:All/>
  </wsp:ExactlyOne>
</wsp:Policy>
```

Example 10.10
Two `wsp:All` elements (one with an assertion and one without) wrapped in a `wsp:ExactlyOne` construct.

In this example, we have a `wsp:ExactlyOne` construct that houses two `wsp:All` elements. The second `wsp:All` element is highlighted. Unlike the first, which establishes a construct with one assertion, this second `wsp:All` element is empty.

According to the "exactly one" rule, we must choose one of the two alternatives. The first alternative is that the `wsam:Addressing` assertion is used because in this alternative, the assertion is wrapped in a nested `wsp:All` construct. The second alternative is that the second `wsp:All` element be chosen, and because it is empty, the result of this choice is that nothing happens. In other words, the use of the policy assertion is optional, as with the previous example that used the `wsp:optional` attribute.

This last example also hints at the more complex structures that can be built using nested operator elements and various other combinations, as described further in the next section.

SUMMARY OF KEY POINTS

- Operator elements can be used to define the structure and rules of policy expressions.

- The `wsp:Optional` attribute can be further added to policy assertions to indicate whether the assertion is required.

10.3 Operator Composition Rules

The rules of operator composition are often referred to as "operator algebra," but don't let that term give you flashbacks to high school math class. This section is really just a more involved discussion about the inherent properties of operator elements and how these properties can affect the structures you build.

It's important to understand these effects because you can combine operators in multiple ways to create highly complex policy expressions. In fact, one of the more interesting aspects of operator compositions is that you can produce composite policies comprised of policies created by yourself and others.

The WS-Policy defined operators `wsp:All` and `wsp:ExactlyOne` have the following properties that form the basis of operator composition rules:

- idempotent
- commutative

- associative

- `wsp:All` distributes over `wsp:ExactlyOne`

The following sections look at how these rules are applied in practice and further discuss the use of empty operator elements and how `wsp:Policy` compares to `wsp:All`.

NOTE

In the first three sections, we use the `wsp:All` operator as an example, but the same concepts also apply to `wsp:ExactlyOne`.

Idempotent Rule

Idempotency means that nesting multiple occurrences of operators within each other is equivalent to a single occurrence. In other words, applying the same operator to itself multiple times yields the same result.

This means that the following operator structure...

```
<wsp:All>
  <wsp:All>
    <wsp:All>
      <wsam:Addressing><wsp:Policy/></wsam:Addressing>
      <wsrmp:RMAssertion><wsp:Policy/></wsrmp:RMAssertion>
    </wsp:All>
  </wsp:All>
</wsp:All>
```

Example 10.11
Two policy assertions wrapped in multiple, nested `wsp:All` constructs.

...is equivalent to:

```
<wsp:All>
  <wsam:Addressing><wsp:Policy/></wsam:Addressing>
  <wsrmp:RMAssertion><wsp:Policy/></wsrmp:RMAssertion>
</wsp:All>
```

Example 10.12
Two policy assertions wrapped in a single `wsp:All` construct.

Commutative Rule

Commutativity means that the ordering of the children within the operator construct is insignificant.

In other words, the following operator structure…

```
<wsp:All>
  <wsam:Addressing><wsp:Policy/></wsam:Addressing>
  <wsrmp:RMAssertion><wsp:Policy/></wsrmp:RMAssertion>
</wsp:All>
```

Example 10.13

The wsam:Addressing policy assertion displayed before wsrmp:RMAssertion.

…is equivalent to:

```
<wsp:All>
  <wsrmp:RMAssertion><wsp:Policy/></wsrmp:RMAssertion>
  <wsam:Addressing><wsp:Policy/></wsam:Addressing>
</wsp:All>
```

Example 10.14

The wsrmp:RMAssertion and wsam:Addressing assertions displayed in a different order.

Associative Rule

This rule enables the streamlining of operator constructs by allowing for the removal of unnecessary nesting.

This means that the following operator structure…

```
<wsp:All>
  <wsam:Addressing><wsp:Policy/></wsam:Addressing>
  <wsp:All>
    <wsrmp:RMAssertion><wsp:Policy/></wsrmp:RMAssertion>
    <argt:responseGuarantee/>
  </wsp:All>
</wsp:All>
```

Example 10.15

One policy assertion positioned as the child element of the first wsp:All element, and two further assertions located within a nested wsp:All construct.

…is equivalent to:

```
<wsp:All>
  <wsam:Addressing><wsp:Policy/></wsam:Addressing>
  <wsrmp:RMAssertion><wsp:Policy/></wsrmp:RMAssertion>
  <argt:responseGuarantee/>
</wsp:All>
```

Example 10.16
With the nested `wsp:All` construct removed, all three policy assertions are grouped together.

`wsp:All` is Distributive Over `wsp:ExactlyOne`

This rule is primarily used for the normalization of policy expressions. It is very useful when constructing a set of alternatives at the top layers of an expression with further alternatives nested within the children. By applying the distributive property of `wsp:All`, we have obtained an equivalent expression with a distinct alternative that is expressed at the root.

What this means is that the following operator structure…

```
<wsp:All>
  <wsp:ExactlyOne>
    <wsam:Addressing><wsp:Policy/></wsam:Addressing>
    <wsrmp:RMAssertion><wsp:Policy/></wsrmp:RMAssertion>
  </wsp:ExactlyOne>
</wsp:All>
```

Example 10.17
Two policy assertions within an `wsp:ExactlyOne` construct establishing a policy alternative that is wrapped further within an `wsp:All` construct.

…is equivalent to:

```
<wsp:ExactlyOne>
  <wsp:All>
    <wsam:Addressing><wsp:Policy/></wsam:Addressing>
  </wsp:All>
  <wsp:All>
    <wsrmp:RMAssertion><wsp:Policy/></wsrmp:RMAssertion>
  </wsp:All>
</wsp:ExactlyOne >
```

Example 10.18
The individual assertions are wrapped in their own `wsp:All` constructs, both of which are wrapped in a `wsp:ExactlyOne` construct.

Let's take a more complex example to illustrate distribution. The following operator structure...

```
<wsp:All>
  <wsp:ExactlyOne>
    <wsam:Addressing><wsp:Policy/></wsam:Addressing>
    <wsrmp:RMAssertion><wsp:Policy/></wsrmp:RMAssertion>
  </wsp:ExactlyOne>
  <wsp:ExactlyOne>
    <argt:responseGuarantee/>
  </wsp:ExactlyOne>
</wsp:All>
```

Example 10.19
Two `wsp:ExactlyOne` operators wrapped in a `wsp:All` operator.

...is equivalent to:

```
<wsp:ExactlyOne>
  <wsp:All>
    <wsam:Addressing><wsp:Policy/></wsam:Addressing>
    <argt:responseGuarantee/>
  </wsp:All>
  <wsp:All>
    <wsrmp:RMAssertion><wsp:Policy/></wsrmp:RMAssertion>
    <argt:responseGuarantee/>
  </wsp:All>
</wsp:ExactlyOne>
```

Example 10.20
This time the `wsp:ExactlyOne` operator is the parent and the assertions are wrapped in `wsp:All` operators. Note the two occurrences of the `argt:responseGuarantee` assertion.

In the first example, each `wsp:ExactlyOne` construct establishes a policy alternative but the second has only one assertion. Because they are further wrapped in a `wsp:All` construct, the actual alternatives of the policy expression are:

Alternative #1: `wsam:Addressing` + `argt:responseGuarantee`

Alternative #2: `wsrmp:RMAssertion` + `argt:responseGuarantee`

This is more clearly conveyed in the second example due to the restructuring of the `wsp:ExactlyOne` and `wsp:All` elements.

We explore distributive operator concepts further in Chapter 16.

Empty Operators

Sometimes policy operators do not contain policy assertions. In this case, they are expressed as follows:

- `<wsp:All/>` indicates a policy with zero assertions.

- `<wsp:ExactlyOne/>` indicates a policy with zero policy alternatives.

Knowing this syntax is relevant because empty content can affect the meaning of an operator composition as follows:

```
<wsp:All>
  <wsp:ExactlyOne>
    <wsam:Addressing><wsp:Policy/></wsam:Addressing>
    <wsrmp:RMAssertion><wsp:Policy/></wsrmp:RMAssertion>
  </wsp:ExactlyOne>
  <wsp:ExactlyOne/>
</wsp:All>
```

Example 10.21
An operator composition containing an empty `wsp:ExactlyOne` element.

The policy expression in this example is essentially equivalent to a policy with zero policy alternatives because the empty operator statement (highlighted) has no assertions.

> **NOTE**
>
> This is a base rule that is not about distribution but rather indicates how zero policy alternatives compose with one or more alternatives to yield zero alternatives (similar to using a zero in multiplication).

Equivalence

So far, we've been studying the `wsp:All` and `wsp:ExactlyOne` operator elements. However, we have also seen the `wsp:Policy` element used with various child elements as well. You may be wondering how the `wsp:Policy` element fits into the composition rules.

A `wsp:Policy` element as an operator is equivalent to the `wsp:All` element. Therefore, an empty policy `<wsp:Policy/>` is equivalent to `<wsp:All/>`, a policy that contains zero assertions.

SUMMARY OF KEY POINTS

- There is a set of common rules associated with the application of policy operator elements that pertains to how the operators can be composed into different construct hierarchies.

- These rules relate to how policies and policy alternatives can and should be expressed and optimized.

10.4 Attaching Policies to WSDL Definitions

WS-Policy as a framework by itself would not be very useful without the ability to associate policy expressions to something. In this section we explore how policy expressions can be attached to different parts of a WSDL definition by using features from the WS-PolicyAttachment standard.

> **NOTE**
>
> With an understanding of how and why policies need to be explicitly associated with WSDL documents, we will also begin to appreciate how policy documents themselves can be defined and governed independently from WSDL documents. However, it is worth noting that the attachment mechanisms explained in this section are not limited to WSDL elements.

There are two ways of attaching policies to WSDL documents:

- The policy expression code can be embedded within the WSDL definition and then utilized via native references that can be attached directly to WSDL elements as child extensibility elements.

- Policy expressions can reside externally in a separate WS-Policy definition document, which is then referenced within the WSDL document via an external attachment mechanism.

> **NOTE**
>
> You might recognize from Chapter 6 that these two attachment options are similar to how XML schema types can be associated with WSDL definitions.

The *Attaching Policies to WSDL Definitions* section in this chapter and the *Reusability and Policy Centralization* section in Chapter 16 explain each of these options. But first, we need to cover a few basic attachment-related topics in the next two sections.

Policy Attachment Points and Policy Subjects

Whatever part of a WSDL definition we attach a policy to is referred to as a *policy attachment point*. For example, we could have a policy attached to an `operation` element and then another to one of that operation's `message` elements.

Within WSDL 1.1, the following elements represent common policy attachment points:

- `service` element
- `port` element
- `binding` element
- `portType` element
- `operation` element
- `message` element

The policy attachment specification organizes these policy attachment points into the following four distinct *policy subjects*:

- Service
- Endpoint
- Operation
- Message

Each policy subject represents a pre-defined scope within the overall WSDL definition. For example, one expression may apply to a particular message only, whereas another might have a scope that corresponds to an entire operation. In the latter case, the policy expression would be applicable to all message definitions that fall within that operation.

Let's discuss the policy subjects individually.

Service Policy Subject

This subject corresponds to the `service` element within the concrete description of a WSDL document. Therefore, a policy expression attached to the service subject will apply to all messages associated with the `port` constructs that fall within the `service` construct. This makes this subject the parent or master subject in that a policy expression attached at this level pretty much affects all message definitions within the WSDL document.

We haven't yet covered how polices get attached to parts of the WSDL definition, but at this stage, let's at least show the insertion point for the policy code so that we have a better idea as to how a policy can be attached to the service policy subject:

```
<service name="svPurchaseOrder">
  <!-- Insert Policy Expression Here -->
  <port name="purchaseOrder-http-soap11"
    binding="tns:bdPO-SOAP11HTTP">
    <soap11:address location=
      "http://actioncon.com/services/soap11/po"/>
  </port>
</service>
```

Example 10.22

A policy expression attached to the service policy subject is located directly beneath the opening `service` element.

Endpoint Policy Subject

The service policy subject seemed pretty straightforward, but things get a little more complicated with this one. The term "endpoint" in this case refers to the combination of the following three elements:

- `port`

- `binding`

- `portType`

So if you attach a policy expression to any one of these three elements, you have attached it to the endpoint policy subject.

To better understand this, first think about how these three elements are related in terms of messaging. A port type definition encompasses operations that have message definitions. But the port type needs to be bound to a concrete protocol via a corresponding binding definition which, in turn, needs an address provided by the port definition. In other words, all three elements are related to the same set of messages (those originally defined in the `portType` construct).

Because, as we stated earlier, policy expressions are all about establishing qualities and properties associated with messaging, grouping these three elements together as one policy subject makes a lot of sense.

Here's a look at where the policy code would go in the case of a `binding` element:

```
<binding name="bdPO-SOAP12HTTP" type="ptPurchaseOrder">
  <!-- Insert Policy Expression Here -->
  <soap12bind:binding style="document"
    transport="http://schemas.xmlsoap.org/soap/http"/>
```

```
<operation name="opSubmitOrder">
  ...
</operation>
...
</binding>
```

Example 10.23

A policy expression attached to the endpoint policy subject via the positioning of the policy expression beneath the opening `binding` element.

NOTE

Each of these three elements represents a potential policy attachment point and it doesn't matter which one you choose; in all three cases, you will have attached a policy to the endpoint policy subject.

Operation Policy Subject

You might have noticed that as we work through this list, the application scope of a policy gets smaller. Now we're moving down the ladder to the operation level.

Following the same rationale we just explained for the endpoint policy subject, you attach a policy to an operation policy subject when you attach it to either of the following two elements:

- the `operation` element of a `portType` construct

- the `operation` element of a `binding` construct

Again, this is because these two elements are so closely related and both represent the same set of message definitions.

Let's take a look at where the policy expression goes:

```
<operation name="opSubmitOrder">
  <!-- Insert Policy Expression Here -->
  <soap12bind:operation
    soapAction="http://action.com/submitOrder/request"
    soapActionRequired="true" required="true"/>
  <input>
    <soap12bind:body use="literal"/>
  </input>
  <output>
```

```
      <soap12bind:body use="literal"/>
   </output>
</operation>
```

Example 10.24
A policy expression attached to the operation policy subject by placing the policy expression code under the opening `operation` element.

Message Policy Subject

This last policy subject simply allows you to pinpoint a message definition with a policy expression. All of the preceding subjects grouped messages together, but there will be times when an expression is so specific that it only applies to a particular message.

Because a given message will be defined via `message` elements in the abstract and concrete descriptions, this subject represents any one of the following possible element pairs:

- the `input` element within the `operation` construct in the `portType` construct + the `input` element within the `operation` construct in the `binding` construct

- the `output` element within the `operation` construct in the `portType` construct + the `output` element within the `operation` construct in the `binding` construct

- the `fault` element within the `operation` construct in the `portType` construct + the `fault` element within the `operation` construct in the `binding` construct

In other words, if you attach the policy to one of the three message definitions in the abstract or concrete descriptions, you will have attached the expression to the message policy subject.

Again, this makes sense because the two (abstract and concrete) elements represent the same message. But just to hammer this point home, here's one more example:

```
<input>
   <!-- Insert Policy Expression Here -->
   <soap12bind:body use="literal"/> .
</input>
```

Example 10.25
A policy assertion attached to the message policy subject by locating the policy statement beneath the opening `input` element.

WSDL 2.0 Policy Subjects

WSDL 2.0 introduces a few changes as to how attachment points are organized into policy subjects, primarily related to fault definitions (Table 10.1 provides an overview).

WSDL Element	Policy Subject
`wsdl20:service`	service

`wsdl20:endpoint`
`wsdl20:binding`
`wsdl20:interface`
	endpoint

`wsdl20:binding/wsdl20:operation` `wsdl20:interface/wsdl20:operation`	operation
`wsdl20:binding/wsdl20:operation/wsdl20:input` `wsdl20:interface/wsdl20:operation/wsdl20:input`	message (for input message)
`wsdl20:binding/wsdl20:operation/wsdl20:output` `wsdl20:interface/wsdl20:operation/wsdl20:output`	message (for output message)

`wsdl20:binding/wsdl20:fault`
`wsdl20:interface/wsdl20:fault`
`wsdl20:binding/wsdl20:operation/wsdl20:infault`
`wsdl20:binding/wsdl20:interface/wsdl20:infault`
	message
	(for an input
	fault message)

`wsdl20:binding/wsdl20:fault`
`wsdl20:interface/wsdl20:fault`
`wsdl20:binding/wsdl20:operation/wsdl20:outfault`
`wsdl20:binding/wsdl20:interface/wsdl20:outfault`
	message
	(for an output
	fault message)

Table 10.1

The WSDL 2.0 attachment point elements and corresponding policy subjects.

NOTE

When you attach different policies to the same subject, the combination of policy expressions is called the *effective policy*. For example, if you have a policy expression attached to a `portType` element and then another to that `portType` element's corresponding `binding` element, you would have created an effective policy for the endpoint policy subject comprised of two different policy expressions. Chapter 17 explores the effects of applying multiple policies to the same subjects.

The `wsp:PolicyReference` Element

The `wsp:PolicyReference` element is the equivalent to an include statement in that it allows you to pull the contents of one policy expression into another. It contains a URI attribute that references the `wsu:Id` value of the policy expression to include.

```
<wsp:Policy>
  <wsp:PolicyReference URI="#reliability-policy"/>
  <wsam:Addressing><wsp:Policy/></wsam:Addressing>
</wsp:Policy>

<wsp:Policy wsu:Id="reliability-policy">
  <wsrmp:RMAssertion><wsp:Policy/></wsrmp:RMAssertion>
</wsp:Policy>
```

Example 10.26

The `wsp:PolicyReference` element performing an include of another policy expression.

In this example, the contents of the policy expression entitled "reliability-policy" are included into the top policy expression, which will result in a composite policy comprised of both `wsrmp:RMAssertion` and `wsam:Addressing` assertion types.

The use of the `wsu:Id` value was introduced at the beginning of this chapter in the *New Namespaces and Prefixes* section. It's a lot like an extensibility attribute in that it allows us to assign an identifier to the policy expression so that it can be referenced elsewhere.

> **NOTE**
>
> As an alternative to `wsu:Id`, you can use the `xml:Id` attribute, which provides the same overall function but is less common.

Embedded Attachments

To embed a policy expression within a WSDL document, we simply add the policy code into the WSDL `definitions` construct, along with the required namespace, as indicated by the highlighted sections in this example.

```
<definitions targetNamespace=
  "http://actioncon.com/contract/po"
  xmlns="http://schemas.xmlsoap.org/wsdl/"
  xmlns:tns="http://actioncon.com/contract/po"
  xmlns:po="http://actioncon.com/schema/po"
  xmlns:soap11bind="http://schemas.xmlsoap.org/wsdl/soap/"
  xmlns:soap12bind="http://schemas.xmlsoap.org/wsdl/soap12/"
  xmlns:wsp="http://www.w3.org/2006/07/ws-policy"
  xmlns:wsam="http://www.w3.org/2007/05/addressing/metadata"
  xmlns:wsrmp="http://docs.oasis-open.org/ws-rx/wsrmp/200702"
  xmlns:wsu="http://docs.oasis-open.org/wss/2004/01/oasis-
    200401-wss-wssecurity-utility-1.0.xsd">
    ...
    ...
    ...
  <wsp:Policy wsu:Id="composite-policy">
    <wsp:PolicyReference URI="#security-policy"/>
    <wsam:Addressing><wsp:Policy/></wsam:Addressing>
    <wsrmp:RMAssertion optional="true"/>
  </wsp:Policy>
  <wsp:Policy wsu:Id="security-policy">
    ...
  </wsp:Policy>
</definitions>
```

Example 10.27
Two policy assertions located inline within a WSDL definition.

You might have noticed the following extra line of code in the first embedded policy assertion of the previous example:

```
<wsp:PolicyReference URI="#security-policy"/>
```

Here we can see the `wsp:PolicyReference` element used again as an include mechanism between two separate policy expressions. Although the previous example showed this element incorporate policy content across policy expressions, it is also used when associating inline policy assertions to WSDL elements, as shown in the next example.

```
<binding name="bdPO-SOAP12HTTP" type="tns:ptPurchaseOrder">
  <wsp:PolicyReference URI="#composite-policy"/>
  <soap12bind:binding style="document"
    transport="http://schemas.xmlsoap.org/soap/http"/>
  <operation name="opSubmitOrder">
    <soap12bind:operation
      soapAction="http://action.com/submitOrder/request"
```

```
      soapActionRequired="true" required="true"/>
    <input>
      <soap12bind:body use="literal"/>
    </input>
    <output>
      <soap12bind:body use="literal"/>
    </output>
  </operation>
  ...
</binding>
```

Example 10.28

The `wsp:PolicyReference` element used to pull in the "composite-policy" policy expression.

Here, the WSDL `binding` construct contains an extensibility element comprised of the `wsp:PolicyReference` element that establishes the reference to the policy expression named "composite-policy."

Note that the code for the "composite-policy" expression could have simply been embedded directly within the WSDL `binding` construct. Because the `wsp:PolicyReference` element was used, this expression can now be shared elsewhere within the WSDL definition. For example, you'll notice that this example is comprised of a binding for SOAP 1.2. If the WSDL document also supported SOAP 1.1, the same policy assertion could have been reused by adding the same `wsp:PolicyReference` element to the SOAP 1.1 binding.

> **NOTE**
>
> External policy attachments are covered in Chapter 16.

SUMMARY OF KEY POINTS

- Policies are attached to policy subjects that represent parts of a WSDL definition.

- Each policy subject has a different scope and pertains to the message exchanges that can occur within that scope.

- Policy expressions can be embedded within the actual WSDL document or they can reside in an external document and then referenced from within the WSDL document.

10.5 A Complete WSDL Definition with an Attached Policy Expression

CASE STUDY EXAMPLE

One of the reasons that Steve originally designed the Web service contract for the Purchase Order service to include both SOAP 1.1 and 1.2 bindings is that the service could accommodate different types of consumers. Those capable of SOAP 1.2 tend to have more progressive platforms and can therefore support additional WS-* features.

Most notably, Steve has a requirement for the service to use WS-Addressing headers (explained in Chapter 18). However, after discussions with Kevin, the CTO, there is a reluctance to impose the requirement that all consumers support WS-Addressing. Therefore, Kevin and Steve decide that only those consumers that communicate with the service via SOAP 1.2 must also support the processing of the WS-Addressing headers that they will be designing.

To implement this new requirement, a simple policy expression is created and the WSDL definition is updated as per the highlighted code:

```
<definitions name="Purchase Order"
  targetNamespace="http://actioncon.com/contract/po
  xmlns:tns="http://actioncon.com/contract/po"
  xmlns:wsdl="http://schemas.xmlsoap.org/wsdl/"
  xmlns:po="http://actioncon.com/schema/po"
  xmlns:soap11="http://schemas.xmlsoap.org/wsdl/soap/"
  xmlns:soap12="http://schemas.xmlsoap.org/wsdl/soap12/"
  xmlns:wsp="http://www.w3.org/2006/07/ws-policy"
  xmlns:wsam="http://www.w3.org/2007/05/addressing/metadata"
  xmlns:wsu="http://docs.oasis-open.org/wss/2004/01/oasis-
    200401-wss-wssecurity-utility-1.0.xsd">
  <documentation>
    This is an entity service responsible for purchase
    order-related processing only.
  </documentation>
  <types>
    <xsd:schema xmlns:xsd="http://www.w3.org/2001/XMLSchema">
      <xsd:import namespace=
        "http://actioncon.com/schema/po"
        schemaLocation="http://actioncon.com/schema/po.xsd"/>
    </xsd:schema>
  </types>
  <message name="msgSubmitOrderRequest">
    <part name="PurchaseOrder" element="po:purchaseOrder"/>
  </message>
  <message name="msgSubmitOrderResponse">
```

```
      <part name="Acknowledgement" element="po:acknowledgement"/>
  </message>
  <message name="msgCheckOrderRequest">
    <part name="PONumber" element="po:poNumber"/>
  </message>
  <message name="msgCheckOrderResponse">
    <part name="Status" element="po:status"/>
  </message>
  <message name="msgChangeOrderRequest">
    <part name="PurchaseOrder" element="po:purchaseOrder"/>
  </message>
  <message name="msgChangeOrderResponse">
   <part name="Acknowledgement" element="po:acknowledgement"/>
  </message>
  <message name="msgCancelOrderRequest">
    <part name="PONumber" element="po:poNumber"/>
  </message>
  <message name="msgCancelOrderResponse">
    <part name="Acknowledgement" element="po:acknowledgement"/>
  </message>
  <portType name="ptPurchaseOrder">
    <operation name="opSubmitOrder">
      <input message="tns:msgSubmitOrderRequest"/>
      <output message="tns:msgSubmitOrderResponse"/>
    </operation>
    <operation name="opCheckOrderStatus">
      <input message="tns:msgCheckOrderRequest"/>
      <output message="tns:msgCheckOrderResponse"/>
    </operation>
    <operation name="opChangeOrder">
      <input message="tns:msgChangeOrderRequest"/>
      <output message="tns:msgChangeOrderResponse"/>
    </operation>
    <operation name="opCancelOrder">
      <input message="tns:msgCancelOrderRequest"/>
      <output message="tns:msgCancelOrderResponse"/>
    </operation>
  </portType>
  <binding name="bdPO-SOAP11HTTP" type="tns:ptPurchaseOrder">
    <soap11:binding style="document"
      transport="http://schemas.xmlsoap.org/soap/http"/>
    <operation name="opSubmitOrder">
      <input>
        <soap11:body use="literal"/>
      </input>
      <output>
        <soap11:body use="literal"/>
```

```
      </output>
    </operation>
    <operation name="opCheckOrderStatus">
      <input>
        <soap11:body use="literal"/>
      </input>
      <output>
        <soap11:body use="literal"/>
      </output>
    </operation>
    <operation name="opChangeOrder">
      <input>
        <soap11:body use="literal"/>
      </input>
      <output>
        <soap11:body use="literal"/>
      </output>
    </operation>
    <operation name="opCancelOrder">
      <input>
        <soap11:body use="literal"/>
      </input>
      <output>
        <soap11:body use="literal"/>
      </output>
    </operation>
  </binding>
  <binding name="bdPO-SOAP12HTTP" type="tns:ptPurchaseOrder">
  <wsp:PolicyReference URI="#addressing-policy"/>
    <soap12:binding style="document"
      transport="http://schemas.xmlsoap.org/soap/http"/>
    <operation name="opSubmitOrder">
    <soap12:operation soapAction=
      "http://actioncon.com/submitOrder/request"
      soapActionRequired="true" wsdl:required="true"/>
      <input>
        <soap12:body use="literal"/>
      </input>
      <output>
        <soap12:body use="literal"/>
      </output>
    </operation>
    <operation name="opCheckOrderStatus">
    <soap12:operation soapAction=
      "http://actioncon.com/submitOrder/request"
      soapActionRequired="true" wsdl:required="true"/>
      <input>
        <soap12:body use="literal"/>
```

```
        </input>
        <output>
          <soap12:body use="literal"/>
        </output>
      </operation>
      <operation name="opChangeOrder">
      <soap12:operation soapAction=
        "http://actioncon.com/submitOrder/request"
        soapActionRequired="true" wsdl:required="true"/>
        <input>
          <soap12:body use="literal"/>
        </input>
        <output>
          <soap12:body use="literal"/>
        </output>
      </operation>
        <operation name="opCancelOrder">
        <soap12:operation soapAction=
          "http://actioncon.com/submitOrder/request"
          soapActionRequired="true" wsdl:required="true"/>
        <input>
          <soap12:body use="literal"/>
        </input>
        <output>
          <soap12:body use="literal"/>
        </output>
      </operation>
    </binding>
    <service name="svPurchaseOrder">
      <port name="purchaseOrder-http-soap11"
        binding="tns:bdPO-SOAP11HTTP">
        <soap11:address location=
          "http://actioncon.com/services/soap11/po"/>
      </port>
      <port name="purchaseOrder-http-soap12"
        binding="tns:bdPO-SOAP12HTTP">
        <soap12:address location=
          "http://actioncon.com/services/soap12/po"/>
      </port>
    </service>
    <wsp:Policy wsu:Id="addressing-policy">
      <wsam:Addressing><wsp:Policy/></wsam:Addressing>
    </wsp:Policy>
</definitions>
```

Example 10.29

A basic policy expression with the `wsam:Addressing` assertion attached to the `binding` construct that represents the SOAP 1.2 binding for this WSDL definition.

Chapter 11

Fundamental Message Design: SOAP Envelope Structure, Fault Messages, and Header Processing

So far you've seen SOAP mentioned and discussed in previous chapters to various extents. Now we finally get the chance to fully explore this important technology by describing its features and limitations as they relate to Web service contract design. We start off by introducing the fundamental SOAP message structure and then begin a tutorial on the SOAP language.

As you may have already noticed from previous chapters, we are concerned with both versions 1.1 and 1.2 of SOAP in this book. Both variations of the SOAP language are very similar in their syntax and processing model, but there are some differences related to message structure and how SOAP, as a technology, can be put to use. Although the majority of examples in this chapter are based on SOAP 1.2, supplementary content is added to point out differences with SOAP 1.1 wherever appropriate.

> **NOTE**
>
> This chapter is focused on Web service contract design only, and therefore does not cover the entire SOAP framework. Topics pertaining to the wire-level transmission of SOAP messages and the overall mechanics behind SOAP communications are beyond the scope of this book.

What SOAP is Not

Before we get into the details of the language syntax and the messaging framework behind SOAP, let's first establish some clear facts about areas that SOAP does not address:

- SOAP is not a distributed object system and does not provide support for things like object-by-reference or distributed garbage collection.

- SOAP does not rely on persistent binary connections, such as those used by RPC frameworks, because it is strictly a messaging format that is most commonly deployed via the stateless HTTP protocol.

- The SOAP messaging framework does not provide QoS features typically found in vendor or platform-specific distributed messaging systems. For example, SOAP does not provide any specific features in the areas of security, reliability, transactions, conversations, addressing, correlation, etc. This does not mean that SOAP cannot be secure or reliable or that the SOAP applications cannot support transactions or routing. Such functionality has to be specified *within* the extensible SOAP message format. (Chapters 18 and 19 explore how SOAP is utilized specifically by WS-Addressing.)

CASE STUDY BACKGROUND

NOTE

The case study examples in this chapter are based on the XML Schema and WSDL definitions from Chapters 6, 7, and 8. Continuing with the Purchase Order service contract, the examples in this chapter will show how SOAP messages correspond to WSDL message definitions and will also provide a glimpse of how those messages manifest themselves on the wire.

Steve at ActionCon is feeling good these days. He followed a relatively thorough top-down process to deliver XML Schema types and a WSDL definition for his Purchase Order service (as explained in Chapter 7) and he is confident that he is well on his way to building a flexible, loosely-coupled service-oriented system.

He turns his attention to the data exchange requirements for his new service and realizes that pretty much all of the planned interactions will need to use SOAP messaging.

However, several questions arise:

- What should the structure of the messages look like beyond the business content they are required to transport?

- How should he go about debugging the message exchanges?

- What are the interoperability challenges?

- Should he use SOAP 1.1 or SOAP 1.2?

He knows that the message exchange requirements for MegaEuroMart will demand that his message designs adhere to the latest industry best practices. But ActionCon systems also need to talk to other partners in the future as well.

He suspects that some of these partner consumer programs will be a step behind MegaEuroMart in terms of sophistication and current technology. This can become a real challenge for the ultimate design of his Purchase Order service. To make the best technical decisions moving forward, he has to gain a solid understanding of SOAP technology.

Fortunately, Steve is able to enlist the help of Filip, an architect with a great deal of experience working with SOAP in various integration-centric implementations. Filip's first recommendation is that Steve enable the Purchase Order service to support both versions 1.1 and 1.2 of SOAP in order to facilitate the expected range of external partner consumers.

11.1 SOAP Message Structure

It's important to understand how the SOAP language allows us to consistently define a standardized message structure. This section explores the key language elements and discusses concepts and associated terms.

Figure 11.1 provides an overview of the SOAP language constructs that we are about to cover.

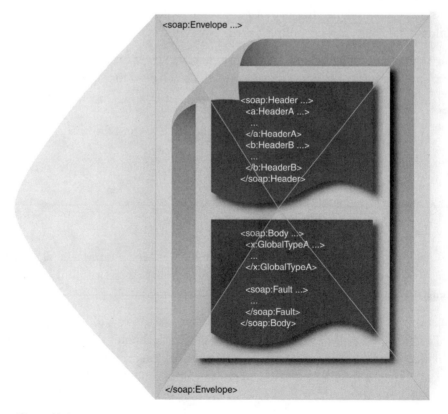

Figure 11.1

A SOAP message envelope is divided into two basic sections, each represented by its own construct.

The `soap:Envelope` Element

Each SOAP document begins with the `soap:Envelope` root element, which establishes the overall scope of the message.

Let's have a look at the `soap:Envelope` construct of a basic SOAP message as it exists after it has been generated "on the wire" for transport.

```
<soap:Envelope xmlns:soap=
  "http://www.w3.org/2003/05/soap-envelope">
  ...
</soap:Envelope>
```

Example 11.1
The `Envelope` construct with the SOAP namespace declaration.

This example ties back to the Purchase Order service that we discussed throughout Chapter 7. You'll notice the `xmlns` attribute that establishes the namespace value for the `soap:` prefix used to qualify the opening and closing `soap:Envelope` elements. This prefix will be used for all other native SOAP elements as well.

> **NOTE**
>
> Throughout this book the `soap11:` and `soap12:` prefixes are also used to distinguish between the versions of the SOAP language, especially in situations where support for a specific version needs to be indicated or when support for both versions within one contract is required.

Here are a few rules regarding the `soap:Envelope` element:

- A `soap:Envelope` construct always contains exactly one `soap:Body` construct that houses the primary business data the message is responsible for delivering.

- A `soap:Envelope` construct can also include an optional `soap:Header` construct that can contain zero or more additional constructs that exist as extensibility elements and are referred to as *header blocks* or *headers*.

Note that it is important to make a distinction between a SOAP envelope and a SOAP message. Whereas a SOAP message may be fully defined by its envelope, it can also encompass additional things, like attachments.

> **NOTE**
>
> SOAP 1.1 also allows additional elements (called "trailer elements") to be added after the `soap:Body` construct. This feature is not in wide use and can lead to interoperability issues as well as problems with migration to SOAP 1.2. (The WS-I Basic Profile disallows trailer elements.)

The `soap:Body` Element

The body of a message represents the main business data that the message is expected to deliver to an ultimate destination. A common term for this contained body of data is the *message payload*. The `Body` element essentially acts as a standardized wrapper for this data, which can exist as any combination of valid XML, including entire XML-based business documents.

Let's add the `Body` construct to the `soap:Envelope` construct we established in the previous example.

```
<soap:Envelope xmlns:soap="http://www.w3.org/2003/05/soap-envelope">
  <soap:Body>
    <po:poNumber xmlns:po="http://actioncon.com/schema/po">
      123456
    </po:poNumber>
  </soap:Body>
</soap:Envelope>
```

Example 11.2
A modest SOAP message containing a purchase order number.

This example shows the message from Chapter 7 that is responsible for delivering a purchase order number as the input for the `opCheckOrderStatus` operation of the Purchase Order service.

The `soap:Header` Element

Many consider the SOAP `soap:Header` element to be the cornerstone of the second-generation Web services framework. This is because it is capable of housing different types of header blocks, each dedicated to providing a distinct piece of supplementary data.

Header information is used by different programs to either help relay or forward a message or process its contents. Most of the WS-* specifications that extend the first-generation Web services platform are implemented as industry standard SOAP headers. The upcoming *SOAP Header Blocks and Targeting Processing* section provides some examples of WS-* SOAP header code.

So far the examples have provided a simple message structure comprised of the parent `soap:Envelope` construct with a nested `soap:Body` construct. Let's expand this message by adding a `soap:Header` construct that contains an extensibility element from the WS-Security standard that stores a digital signature used for security reasons to verify the origin of a message.

```
<soap:Envelope
  xmlns:soap="http://www.w3.org/2003/05/soap-envelope" ...>
  <soap:Header>
    <wsse:Security ...>
      <wsse:BinarySecurityToken ...>
        ...
      </wsse:BinarySecurityToken>
      <ds:Signature>
        ...
      </ds:Signature>
    </wsse:Security>
  </soap:Header>
  <soap:Body ...>
    <po:poNumber
      xmlns:po="http://actioncon.com/schema/po">
      123456
    </po:poNumber>
  </soap:Body>
</soap:Envelope>
```

Example 11.3
A SOAP message with a sample, security-related header block.

In this example, the digital signature contents are placed into a header block called "Security." We won't discuss the details of how this digital signature works; we are only interested in the fact that this represents one type of metadata that can be placed into a SOAP header block.

There are a variety of features and design considerations associated with header blocks. The upcoming *SOAP Header Blocks and Targeting Processing* section is dedicated to exploring different types of headers, and how different blocks can be targeted for processing by different recipients.

The `soap:Fault` Element

When a SOAP message is being processed or transmitted, various things can go wrong. Some error conditions can be anticipated so that if they occur, the affected programs can be notified. This is what SOAP fault messages are for.

Although the `soap:Fault` element is technically an optional child element of the `soap:Body` construct, for the message to be considered a SOAP fault message, this element is required and must be the only child element of `soap:Body`, as follows:

```
<soap:Envelope
  xmlns:soap="http://www.w3.org/2003/05/soap-envelope"">
  <soap:Body>
    <soap:Fault>
      ...
    </soap:Fault>
  </soap:Body>
</soap:Envelope>
```

Example 11.4
The location of the `soap:Fault` construct.

The SOAP standard includes a whole vocabulary of fault-related elements that are explained separately in the upcoming *Fault Messages* section.

SUMMARY OF KEY POINTS

- A SOAP message is primarily defined via the root `soap:Envelope` element, which contains a mandatory `soap:Body` element and an optional `soap:Header` element.

- The `soap:Header` construct establishes a location for supplementary metadata organized into header blocks.

- The `soap:Body` construct can further contain an optional `soap:Fault` element.

11.2 SOAP Nodes and Roles

Once a SOAP message is sent by a program, it becomes an independent unit of information that moves around a runtime environment with a specific destination in mind. Along the way, a message can find itself in all kinds of situations, several of which the original Web service contract designer did not anticipate.

For us to send a message from one location to another, we need software programs on the sending and receiving end of the transmission, but there is also the opportunity for additional software programs to get involved along the way.

What we just described is the fundamental basis of the SOAP communications framework. In order to formalize this framework, let's establish some key terms and concepts:

- The program responsible for sending a message to another program is called the *sender*.

- The program that receives a message sent to it by a sender is predictably named the *receiver*.

- A program that receives a message and then turns around to send the message to another program is effectively both a receiver and a sender, and therefore has the special title of *intermediary*.

- Because an intermediary is both a sender and receiver, we need a way to identify a program that is only the sender, and not the receiver. We therefore call it the *initial sender* because it is the program responsible for initiating the transmission of a message.

- Correspondingly, it is helpful to have a label for the program that will only receive a message and not send it. Given that this program represents the ultimate destination of the message, it is named the *ultimate receiver*.

- The route a message takes (starting with the initial sender, through intermediaries, and ending with an ultimate receiver) is called the *message path*.

- The sender, receiver, intermediary, initial sender, and ultimate receiver terms are temporary labels used to identify a software program based on its function within a given message path. A program that may be called an initial sender in one message path may actually be the ultimate receiver in another.

- It is important to note that it is not incorrect to refer to an intermediary as a receiver or a sender. It is a receiver when it receives a message and a sender when it sends the message. It is simply also classified as an intermediary because it performs both receiver and sender functions within a particular message path. As a result, an intermediary cannot be an initial sender or an ultimate receiver in a given message path.

- A message path may be dynamically determined when intermediaries are involved, because they may decide to route the message to different receivers depending on unpredictable runtime factors.

All of these terms are actually not that new. They are used in relation to Web services all the time as temporary roles that services assume when message exchanges are designed as part of service compositions.

However, we are not discussing Web services specifically in this section. Our focus is on SOAP messages and the underlying SOAP messaging framework. When designing a service-oriented solution from this perspective, we refer to any program along a message path that processes a SOAP message according to the rules of the SOAP standard as a *SOAP node*.

The difference between using these terms for SOAP nodes as opposed to Web services specifically is that a SOAP node is not limited to a Web service. It can be a legacy application capable of processing SOAP data or, more commonly, an event-driven agent that can transparently intercept and process messages.

Another reason we make this distinction is because there may be programs along a message path that also process a message but do not support SOAP. One example is an HTTP intermediary which may access or process HTTP header information, but does not touch any of the SOAP content.

NOTE

What exactly is an HTTP intermediary? As we will explore in detail in Chapter 14, the HTTP request-response message sequence typically uses a single connection between the user agent and the origin server. But, this does not always need to be the case. You have the option of positioning HTTP intermediaries along the request-response message path that enable request or response messages to go over multiple HTTP connections. Typically, HTTP intermediaries are used for caching, content filtering, authentication, and other security scenarios. HTTP intermediaries work at the HTTP protocol level and do not understand nor process SOAP envelopes.

How a SOAP node processes a message depends on the transport protocol associated with the message in the binding extensions of the WSDL definition. Each binding is like a set of rules that indicates how the message should be transmitted.

CASE STUDY EXAMPLE

Steve is facing a unique problem. MegaEuroMart architects have told him that every SOAP message that arrives and leaves the MegaEuroMart enterprise must be digitally signed. This allows MegaEuroMart to ensure that they accept messages only from sources that they trust. Steve likes the idea that the messages arriving from MegaEuroMart would be digitally signed. That way he has assurance that MegaEuroMart was the one who sent the message. But when he talked to the CTO of another partner he confirmed what he suspected: this partner has no plans to sign and verify messages. Setting up and maintaining the required security infrastructure is simply too expensive for them.

Steve does not want to build different point-solutions for each vendor. He would like his Purchase Order service to work exactly the same way regardless of the company that is interacting with it. He decides that if SOAP allows him to treat the two vendors the same, he is going to do just that.

He approaches Filip and asks if there is a simple way out of this. Filip introduces Steve to SOAP intermediaries. Filip's solution to the problem is to configure the infrastructure so that every SOAP message that travels to and from MegaEuroMart is always routed through a particular SOAP intermediary. Filip calls it the "signing intermediary." It verifies the signature and, if verified successfully, passes the message on to the Purchase Order service.

NOTE

One of the reasons SOAP nodes are important to understand is because they are closely related to the processing of header blocks. This relationship is explained in the upcoming *SOAP Header Blocks and Targeted Processing* section.

11.3 SOAP Header Blocks and Targeted Processing

We might be tempted to refer to the terms we just described as roles. This would be perfectly legitimate because they do, in fact, label a SOAP node based on the runtime role it assumes in a given situation. However, the SOAP standard assigns a very specific meaning to the term "role," so we'll stay true to this terminology. For clarity's sake, we'll refer to the particular types of roles described in this section as *SOAP roles*.

A SOAP role essentially indicates what a SOAP receiver is expected to do after it receives a message. The SOAP specification defines three fundamental roles, each of which is identified via a pre-defined URI that is assigned to SOAP nodes within a SOAP message path:

- *Next* – This SOAP role simply identifies the next SOAP node in a message path that is responsible for processing the header block.

  URI: `http://www.w3.org/2003/05/soap-envelope/role/next`

- *None* – In order to ensure that a particular header block survives all the way to the ultimate destination, this SOAP role can be used.

  URI: `http://www.w3.org/2003/05/soap-envelope/role/none`

- *ultimateReceiver* – This role is used when you want to identify the ultimate destination of a message, regardless of whether the next node in the path is actually the ultimate destination. Note that this is the default role if the `soap:role` attribute is absent.

  URI: `http://www.w3.org/2003/05/soap-envelope/role/ultimateReceiver`

Note that you are not limited to using these three pre-defined SOAP roles. You can create your own SOAP roles that are more specific to the nature of your message path. For example, you could define a "logger" role that indicates that the SOAP node will record data about certain messages it processes.

Here are a few guidelines to keep in mind with regard to how SOAP roles relate to SOAP nodes:

- A SOAP node can have multiple SOAP roles. For example, you can assign the "next" and "ultimateReceiver" SOAP roles to the same SOAP node. (In fact, for the ultimate receiver, when it receives the message, it would always also be assigned these two roles.)

- An intermediary is always assigned the "next" SOAP role because it cannot be an initial sender and therefore always follows (is next after) a previous SOAP node.

- An initial sender cannot be assigned the "next" or "ultimateReceiver" SOAP role.

> **NOTE**
>
> In SOAP 1.1, roles were called *actors*. Roles in SOAP 1.2 and actors in SOAP 1.1 mean exactly the same thing. SOAP 1.2 made this change to allow for a better description of the metaphor. It is much easier to say, for example, that a SOAP node *acts* in a particular *role* identified by a particular URI. How SOAP roles specifically related to header blocks is discussed next, as we learn about the `soap:role` attribute.

There are three key attributes that can be assigned to the `soap:Header` element within any SOAP header block:

- `soap:role`
- `soap:mustUnderstand`
- `soap:relay`

These attributes allow you to determine how the header will be processed at runtime. Let's take a look at each one individually.

The `soap:role` Attribute

SOAP roles are relevant to SOAP header blocks because the SOAP language actually allows us to assign a role value to a specific header. By doing so, we indicate that we want this block to be processed only by a SOAP node that matches the role.

For example:

- If the header block has a custom SOAP role of "logger" assigned to it, then we are saying that the information in this header block can be processed only by the SOAP node that assumes the logger role.

- If the SOAP role is that of "next," then we are saying that the next SOAP node in line can process that header block.

- If the SOAP role assigned to a header block is "ultimateReceiver," then only the SOAP node that is actually labeled as the ultimate receiver will process that header block.

NOTE

With regard to this last item, you might be wondering how a SOAP node can tell if it is an ultimate receiver? Well, typically a SOAP node is deployed for a specific purpose. It may be to process a purchase order, perform a logging function, or serve stock quotes. The main intent of the message is included in its body. The rule of thumb is that if a SOAP node processes the body of a SOAP message, then it is considered to fulfill the "ultimateReceiver" role.

So when we think about the Purchase Order service examples, the service that ultimately receives and accesses the purchase order document

> residing within the `soap:Body` construct is acting in the "ultimate-
> Receiver" role because the message path is considered to have ended at
> that point. One exception to this rule is when an intermediary that
> encrypts or decrypts the message is involved. In this case, the SOAP
> node will need to affect the message body content, while being consid-
> ered an intermediary.
>
> We will be introducing two different intermediary types toward the end of
> this chapter. The just described rule pertains to architectures that use
> forwarding intermediaries only. An active intermediary may decide to
> process message body contents and then still forward the message along
> its path.

What we get out of this whole system of SOAP nodes and roles is control over who processes header blocks along a message path. This is very important because some header blocks have specific purposes intended only for SOAP nodes designed to process their information.

A great example of this is security-related processing. If we have a SOAP message that includes a header block dedicated to hosting a digital signature, then we will want to indicate that this block should only be accessed by a SOAP node that is able to process the digital signature information in order to perform the required verification.

And what do you know, we do actually have such a SOAP message from our last example. Let's extract the skeleton `wsse:Security` header block and take a closer look at how a SOAP role is incorporated via the `soap:role` attribute:

```
<soap:Header>
  <wsse:Security soap:role=
    "http://megaeuromart.com/soap/roles/signature-verification" ...>
      ...
  </wsse:Security>
</soap:Header>
```

Example 11.5

A header block comprised of a `wsse:Security` element with a `soap:role` attribute.

In this example, the information in the `wsse:Security` header block will only be processed by a SOAP node that is assigned the role of "signature-verification."

Alternatively, we could have assigned the URI for the next SOAP role to the `soap:role` attribute, as shown in this example:

```
<soap:Header>
  <wsse:Security soap:role=
    "http://www.w3.org/2003/05/soap-envelope/role/next" ...>
    ...
  </wsse:Security>
</soap:Header>
```

Example 11.6

The same `wsse:Security` header block from Example 11.5, except the `soap:role` attribute value has been changed to "next."

Can you guess what the effect of this setting would be? Well, it means that the header block will get processed properly only if we get lucky. We are basically saying that we will allow whatever SOAP node comes next in the message path to access and work with the digital signature data. If the SOAP node is not designed to do this (but tries to access the SOAP header block anyway), we could end up with some problems. This means that the previously displayed header block statement is more appropriate.

Let's look at one more option. Do you remember the "none" SOAP role? How do you think the following header will get processed?

```
<soap:Header>
  <wsse:Security soap:role=
    "http://www.w3.org/2003/05/soap-envelope/role/none" ...>
    ...
  </wsse:Security>
</soap:Header>
```

Example 11.7

The `wsse:Security` header now with a `soap:role` setting of "none."

This would be a suitable setting for the `wsse:Security` element if a program that existed beyond the ultimate receiver SOAP node was going to process security information within its application logic. In this case, we use the "none" SOAP role to simply pass through the header information so that no one intermediary SOAP node can touch it.

> **NOTE**
>
> Because we are focused on the Web service contract and related topics associated with SOAP messages, we do not discuss how SOAP nodes are actually assigned SOAP roles. For the sake of this discussion, though, it is helpful to keep in mind that any one SOAP node can assume zero, one, or multiple roles.

CASE STUDY EXAMPLE

Steve is looking forward to implementing a service agent that will act as an intermediary SOAP node dedicated to providing digital signing functionality. Filip, though, makes him aware that if the SOAP header block containing the signature of a given message does not include a `soap:role` attribute, it would need to be processed by the ultimate receiver only, which in this case, is the Purchase Order service.

Steve would prefer to have the signature header targeted towards a signing intermediary because that would establish a much more flexible architecture. However, it would also require changing the messages that MegaEuroMart sends out.

Both Steve and Filip arrange a meeting with a senior architect from MegaEuroMart during which they explain the topology and architecture of the Purchase Order service. Filip proposes that they create a new role for targeting signature verification intermediaries so that digital signatures in messages received from MegaEuroMart can be processed by intermediaries prior to arriving at the Purchase Order service.

The MegaEuroMart architect asks Filip to explain how this would work. Filip jumps to the whiteboard and writes up how the `opCheckOrderStatus` operation request would look:

```
<soap:Envelope
  xmlns:soap="http://www.w3.org/2003/05/soap-envelope" ...>
  <soap:Header>
    <wsse:Security soap:role="http://megaeuromart.com/soap/roles/
      signature-verification" ...>
      <wsse:BinarySecurityToken ...>
        ...
      </wsse:BinarySecurityToken>
      <ds:Signature>
        ...
      </ds:Signature>
    </wsse:Security>
  </soap:Header>
```

```
    </soap:Header
    <soap:Body ...>
      <po:poNumber xmlns:po="http://actioncon.com/schema/po">
        123456
      </po:poNumber>
    </soap:Body>
</soap:Envelope>
```

Example 11.8

The same header block from Example 11.5 positioned within the overall envelope.

As highlighted in Filip's example, the signature verification role (and its associated URI) has been added to the `wsse:Security` header that contains the signature. This would allow the signing intermediary to perform the verification before passing the message onto the Purchase Order service.

The MegaEuroMart architect likes this idea quite a bit. In fact, he likes it so much that he decides that he wants all of his suppliers to include this new role in their message headers. He feels that having a signing and verification intermediary similar to ActionCon's is going to make their infrastructure more manageable and flexible.

The `soap:mustUnderstand` Attribute

A SOAP header block can be marked as mandatory or optional. This allows any SOAP node acting as a sender to specify whether it is necessary to process a given header block.

Even though we can use the `soap:mustUnderstand` attribute to state that it is mandatory for SOAP nodes to process a specific header block, this only applies to those SOAP nodes that match the role that is also assigned to the header block.

So going back to our `wsse:Security` header example, we can add this attribute to indicate that when this message encounters the SOAP node with the role "signature-verification," that this SOAP node must attempt to process the security header information. If it doesn't, or if it is unsuccessful, then an exception is raised.

```
<soap:Header>
  <wsse:Security soap:role=
    "http://megaeuromart.com/soap/roles/signature-verification"
    soap:mustUnderstand="true" ...>
    ...
```

```
    </wsse:Security>
  </soap:Header>
```

Example 11.9

The `wsse:Security` element with a `soap:mustUnderstand` attribute.

> **NOTE**
>
> The default value of the `soap:mustUnderstand` attribute is "false."

To make things a bit more interesting, let's expand the purchase order message to include header blocks for the WS-Addressing standard. Consider this a preview of things to come, as WS-Addressing will be explained in Chapter 18.

For now, we don't care about what WS-Addressing does or does not do. All we need to know is that it introduces the following new header blocks to the message:

- `wsa:Action` (specifies the overall intent of the message)

- `wsa:MessageID` (uniquely identifies the message)

These new headers are incorporated as follows:

```
<soap:Envelope ...>
  <soap:Header>
    <wsa:Action soap:mustUnderstand="1">
      http://actioncon.com/action/po
    </wsa:Action>
    <wsa:MessageID soap:mustUnderstand="1">
      uuid:246d44f9-5a2f-11d7-944a-006097b0abf
    </wsa:MessageId>
    <custom:ActivityID soap:mustUnderstand="0">
      39930
    </custom:ActivityID>
  </soap:Header>
  <soap:Body>
    <purchaseOrder version="1.0"
      xmlns="http://actioncon.com/schema/po">
      ...
    </purchaseOrder>
  </soap:Body>
</soap:Envelope>
```

Example 11.10

A SOAP message with three WS-Addressing header blocks with varying `soap:MustUnderstand` settings.

In the preceding example, the new header blocks have different settings when it comes to mandatory processing requirements. The `wsa:Action` and `wsa:MessageID` headers have a value of "1" assigned to their `soap:mustUnderstand` attributes, meaning that these headers must be accessed, understood, and processed by receiving SOAP nodes. Processing of the `custom:ActivityID` header, on the other hand, is completely voluntary because its `soap:mustUnderstand` attribute has the value of "0.0."

This means that if a SOAP node ignores the `wsa:Action` or the `wsa:MessageID` header, an error will be raised. If the `custom:ActivityID` header is ignored, life goes on as usual.

Another interesting characteristic about this revised sample message is that it doesn't assign a `soap:role` attribute to either header. This indicates that only the node acting as the ultimate receiver will have access to the header blocks.

> **NOTE**
>
> The `soap:mustUnderstand` attribute is similar to a pre-defined value used by the `soap:Code` element explained later, in the *Fault Messages* section. A key difference to note is that the header `soap:mustUnderstand` attribute always begins with a lowercase "m," whereas the `soap:Code` value is "MustUnderstand" (with an uppercase "M").

The `soap:relay` Attribute

SOAP defines a further header block attribute that can be used to indicate whether an intermediary SOAP node should forward the header if it decides not to process it. This is generally used to ensure that optional header blocks (with a `mustUnderstand` attribute value of "0") are preserved until they reach a SOAP node that is interested in processing them. Note that this attribute is of type `xsd:boolean` and its default value is "false."

> **NOTE**
>
> The use of the attributes we just described help determine how certain types of intermediary SOAP nodes will behave in relation to the processing of header blocks, as explained in the *SOAP Intermediaries* section.

Industry SOAP Header Block Examples

To give you a better sense as to the range of possible header blocks that can be used with SOAP messages, here is a set of samples mostly representing a cross-section of WS-* standards.

Resource Representation SOAP Header Block (RRSHB)

The RRSHB header block allows you to include a "resource representation" in a SOAP message, which is helpful especially if you are including a SOAP attachment to your message.

```
<soap:Envelope
  xmlns:soap="http://www.w3.org/2003/05/soap-envelope"
  xmlns:rep="http://www.w3.org/2004/08/representation"
  xmlns:xmlmime="http://www.w3.org/2004/11/xmlmime">
  <soap:Header>
    <rep:Representation
      resource="http://www.actioncon.com/photo">
      <rep:Data xmlmime:contentType="image/jpg">
      ...
      </rep:Data>
    </rep:Representation>
  </soap:Header>
  <soap:Body>
  ...
  </soap:Body>
</soap:Envelope>
```

Example 11.11
A SOAP message containing the `rep:Representation` header.

The header block `rep:Representation` represents the resource and its child element `rep:Data` contains the JPEG image (the actual resource).

WS-ReliableMessaging Sequence Header Block

In WS-ReliableMessaging, each message that is sent reliably has to identify the sequence in which the message is sent and the position of that message as it is ordered among others in the sequence.

In the following example, the `wsrm:Sequence` header identifies the sequence ID (`"http://actioncon.com/rm/123"`) using the `wsrm:Identifier` child element and the message number within that sequence, using the child element `wsrm:MessageNumber` (in this case "4").

```
<soap:Envelope
  xmlns:soap="http://www.w3.org/2003/05/soap-envelope"
  xmlns:wsrm="http://docs.oasis-open.org/ws-rx/wsrm/200702">
```

```
<soap:Header>
  <wsrm:Sequence>
    <wsrm:Identifier>
      http://actioncon.com/rm/123
    </wsrm:Identifier>
    <wsrm:MessageNumber>
      4
    </wsrm:MessageNumber>
  </wsrm:Sequence>
</soap:Header>
<soap:Body>
  ...
</soap:Body>
</soap:Envelope>
```

Example 11.12

A SOAP message containing the `wsrm:Sequence` header.

WS-Coordination Header Block

We've saved the biggest example for last. In the following code, we have a header block comprised of elements from two different WS-* specifications. The primary header construct originates from the WS-Coordination specification, which provides a context management framework that includes a set of pre-defined header blocks used to communicate between Web services involved in a coordinated activity (such as a transaction).

The example shows how a `wscoor:CoordinationContext` header is used to pass coordination information around to participating Web services.

Specifically, this header block contains:

- an activity identifier (`"http://actioncon.com/activity-1"`)

- the coordination type for the activity (`"http://docs.oasis-open.org/ws-tx/wscoor/2006/06"`)

- the expiration time of the activity (`4000 milliseconds`)

The `wscoor:CoordinationContext` construct further uses the `wsa:Address` element from the WS-Addressing standard, as shown here:

```
<soap:Envelope xmlns:soap="http://www.w3.org/2003/05/soap-envelope"
  xmlns:wscoor=
    "http://docs.oasis-open.org/ws-tx/wscoor/2006/06"
```

```
xmlns:wsa:"http://www.w3.org/2005/08/addressing" >
<soap:Header>
  <wscoor:CoordinationContext
    <wscoor:Identifier>
      http://actioncon.com/activity-1
    </wscoor:Identifier>
    <wscoor:Expires>
      4000
    </wscoor:Expires>
    <wscoor:CoordinationType>
      http://docs.oasis-open.org/ws-tx/wsat/2006/06
    </wscoor:CoordinationType>
    <wscoor:RegistrationService>
      <wsa:Address>
        http://actioncon.com/registration
      </wsa:Address>
    </wscoor:RegistrationService>
  </wscoor:CoordinationContext>
</soap:Header>
<soap:Body>
  ...
</soap:Body>
</soap:Envelope>
```

Example 11.13

A SOAP message containing the `wscoor:CoordinationContext` header block comprised of a variety of nested elements, including elements from the WS-Addressing standard.

SUMMARY OF KEY POINTS

- SOAP nodes represent any type of software program along a given message path that is capable of processing message content as per the SOAP standard.

- The `soap:role` attribute allows you to assign roles to header blocks so that only SOAP nodes that match those roles can process the header block information.

- The `soap:mustUnderstand` attribute enables you to require that a header block be processed by SOAP nodes that are allowed to do so.

- The `soap:relay` attribute can be used to tell intermediary SOAP nodes to pass on SOAP header blocks that were targeted toward the node but that it did not process.

11.4 SOAP Intermediaries

The SOAP protocol was always designed with intermediaries in mind. This is an important and distinguishing aspect of SOAP when comparing it to other messaging protocols.

There are native SOAP features that allow intermediaries to be targeted for processing parts of a message in a transport-independent manner and, as a direct consequence, SOAP provides an end-to-end model for processing messages beyond point-to-point message paths.

As you might recall from the *SOAP Nodes and Roles* section, SOAP intermediaries act as both senders and receivers of SOAP messages and regularly hang out along SOAP message paths. As a constant available part of a runtime's message framework, intermediaries can be enlisted to carry out a variety of functions.

Here are some of the more common things intermediaries are expected to do:

- load balancing

- routing (including content-based routing)

- logging or tracing

- caching

- exception handling

- SLA enforcement

- management functionality

- binding, message translation, or gateways

- security processing (confidentiality, authentication, authorization, integrity, non-repudiation)

- reliability

- payload transformation or transcoding

Depending on the type of processing that it needs to perform, an intermediary is generally classified as a *forwarding* or *active* intermediary.

Forwarding Intermediaries

This is a SOAP node that receives and then forwards a message. When a forwarding intermediary forwards a message, it typically removes from the message all header blocks that it itself processes. That's pretty straightforward. However, things get a bit more complicated when it comes to other header blocks.

A forwarding intermediary is generally expected to do the following to an incoming message:

- retain the SOAP body

- retain all the header blocks that were not targeted to it

- remove all the header blocks that were targeted to it and processed

- remove all the non re-transmittable header blocks that were targeted to it and were not processed

- retain all the re-transmittable header blocks that were targeted to it and were not processed

Keep in mind that the nature of processing a header block may require reinsertion of the same or other header blocks, removal of header blocks, modification of header blocks, or modification of SOAP body content, among other things. For example, when a header block related to decryption is processed it results in the SOAP body being decrypted.

The `soap:relay` attribute we introduced earlier is used to tell an intermediary that it should proceed to forward a header block if it does not process it. This is important because the default behavior of an intermediary is to remove headers that are targeted to it. Using this attribute is a way of extending the longevity of a header block, thereby maximizing the chance that some SOAP node along the message path will process it.

This is generally used to ensure that optional header blocks (with a `mustUnderstand` attribute value of "0") are preserved until they reach a SOAP node that is interested in processing them.

Active Intermediaries

An active intermediary performs additional processing not specified in the header blocks of the incoming message. Both forwarding and active intermediaries are legitimate SOAP nodes, but whereas the forwarding intermediary is always restricted to modifying, inserting (or reinserting), removing, or otherwise processing SOAP header blocks, the active intermediary is unconstrained as to which part of the SOAP message it processes and what it does with it.

> **NOTE**
>
> Although a forwarding intermediary is expected to limit its access to the SOAP header area, some in fact need to process the body content as well. For example, a logging header may require the intermediary to log the message somewhere and then reinsert the header back in the downstream message so as to enable logging at every node in the path. The golden rule, though, is that a forwarding intermediary does not change the existing SOAP body contents.

Another way to think of how forwarding and active intermediaries behave differently is in how they receive their instructions. A forwarding intermediary will look to the SOAP header to figure out what (if anything) it should do when it receives a message. The active intermediary may not care at all about the SOAP header, and may simply have its own, independent functions that it carries out.

Have a look at the following example. It seems like your average SOAP message with a header block and some body content. Now imagine that this is an outgoing message sent via a security processing intermediary that will receive this message and then encrypt and digitally sign it before it passes it on to the next node. Does that make it a forwarding or an active intermediary? Before you answer, study this code closely…

```
<soap:Envelope xmlns:soap=
  "http:www.w3.org/2003/05/soap-envelope">
  <soap:Header>
    <wsa:Action
      xmlns:wsa="http://www.w3.org/2005/08/addressing"
      soap:mustUnderstand="1"
      soap:role="http://actioncon.com/customRole">
        http://actioncon.com/action
    </wsa:Action>
  </soap:Header>
  <soap:Body>
    ...
  </soap:Body>
</soap:Envelope>
```

Example 11.14
An envelope containing a header block that is not processed.

The correct answer is that it is an active intermediary. Why? Because there is no header block telling it to perform those security functions. It simply does it on its own.

The only header block present is one that requires that the receiving SOAP node understand and support WS-Addressing. This again is intended for forwarding intermediaries. An active intermediary does not even need to acknowledge that header block and can ignore the `mustUnderstand="1"` setting. Also if the node does not play the role assigned to `wsa:Action`, then it won't process it even in the forwarding intermediary case.

Active Intermediaries as Threats

Although an active intermediary can be an effective way to consistently enforce the application of certain types of processing without a reliance on header blocks and other types of rules, the freedom with which they operate can also make them potentially dangerous.

If a message path spans certain uncontrolled zones (such as a partner domain or the Internet itself), it introduces the potential of including non-trusted intermediaries. This, in turn, introduces the risk that any one of those non-trusted intermediaries is malicious. So, if the payload data being transported by the SOAP message is considered sensitive, then the message needs to be secured from the very beginning in order to be protected against these risks.

This is where message-level security comes in. Traditional transport-level security measures (such as the use of SSL to encrypt an HTTP channel between two programs) do not protect message contents from malicious active intermediaries because the message content does not remain encrypted while in possession by the intermediary program.

This is where message-level security comes in, as provided by the WS-Security standard. Using the features of WS-Security related technologies, you can guarantee end-to-end message security by applying encryption and digital signing to the message in such a way that it stays with the message until only a certain pre-defined SOAP node receives it.

Ironically, the type of processing required to secure a message from active intermediaries can be provided by an active intermediary, such as the security intermediary we described earlier.

NOTE

WS-Security is not covered in his book. Visit www.soaspecs.com to learn more about the WS-Security specifications.

11.5 Fault Messages

The SOAP language provides a series of elements that help standardize the format and content of fault message data. The following section describes these elements individually and is then followed by a section that explains how SOAP faults are related to WSDL fault message definitions.

The SOAP Fault Vocabulary

SOAP in itself is not a large language. Its primary purpose, as just described in the *SOAP Message Structure* section, is to provide a standardized set of elements that organize a message into parts. However, curiously, it does provide a relatively detailed set of language elements dedicated solely to expressing information about fault conditions.

Most of this section is focused on describing the following SOAP 1.2 vocabulary:

- `soap:Reason`
- `soap:Node`
- `soap:Role`
- `soap:Text`
- `soap:Code`
- `soap:Detail`

> **NOTE**
>
> Many of these elements (and related values) were changed with version 1.2 of the SOAP language. Brief descriptions for the corresponding SOAP 1.1 elements are provided toward the end of this section.

The `soap:Reason` *Element*

This mandatory element provides the description of the fault condition. It may contain human readable text or it may be populated by the contents of the WSDL fault definition type, as explained in the upcoming *SOAP Faults vs. WSDL Faults* section.

The `soap:Node` *Element*

As explained earlier in the *SOAP Nodes and Roles* section, each SOAP-aware program along a message path is referred to as a SOAP node. This optional element is used to identify which node generated the exception condition that led to the fault.

The `soap:Role` Element

As explained in the *SOAP Header Blocks and Targeted Processing* section, there is a set of pre-defined roles that the SOAP standard associates with nodes. This is another optional element that can be set to the role of the node responsible for the fault.

The `soap:Text` Element

This optional element allows you to add further human readable description text for a given fault.

The `soap:Value` Element

This element can occur in two places: as a child of `soap:Code` or as a child of `soap:-Subcode`. In the former case, it acts as a container for one of the five predefined SOAP fault codes explained shortly in the section *The* `soap:Code` *Element*. As a child of the `soap:Subcode` element the `soap:Value` element is used as a container for a custom-defined sub-category of the fault code.

> **NOTE**
>
> Both the `soap:Reason` and `soap:Text` elements are intended to contain human-readable content. They are therefore often supplemented with the `xml:lang` attribute that allows you to set the language of the text. The setting you will notice in the upcoming examples is `xml:lang="en"`, which indicates that the language of the text is English. You can add further `xml:lang` attributes to identify different languages. For example, you could send the same fault text in both English and French as part of the same SOAP fault message. The allowed values for this attribute are defined here: http://www.ietf.org/rfc/rfc3066.txt.

The `soap:Code` and `soap:Detail` elements are explained in the next two sections, each of which introduces examples that demonstrate the use of the elements we just covered.

The `soap:Code` Element

This key element essentially represents the error code to identify the nature of the fault. `soap:Code` is a mandatory part of the `soap:Fault` construct and is limited to the following pre-defined values:

- `soap:VersionMismatch`
- `soap:MustUnderstand`

- `soap:Sender`

- `soap:Receiver`

- `soap:DataEncodingUnknown`

Note that this element can also contain a child `soap:Subcode` element, which is explained after the descriptions of the five `soap:Code` values.

soap:VersionMismatch

This fault is generated when an unexpected root element (other than the correct version of the SOAP envelope) is found. This may occur due to the use of a different namespace or a different local name for the root element. For example, if a SOAP 1.2 processor that does not support SOAP 1.1 encounters a SOAP 1.1 `Envelope` element, it would generate this fault:

```
<soap:Envelope xmlns:soap=
  "http://www.w3.org/2003/05/soap-envelope">
  <soap:Body>
    <soap:Fault>
      <soap:Code>
        <soap:Value>soap:VersionMismatch</soap:Value>
      </soap:Code>
      <soap:Reason>
        <soap:Text xml:lang="en">
          Version Mismatch
        </soap:Text>
      </soap:Reason>
    </soap:Fault>
  </soap:Body>
</soap:Envelope>
```

Example 11.15
The `soap:Code` element indicating a version mismatch error.

NOTE

Even though this type of fault can inform a sender that a receiver does not support the version of SOAP used in the message, it does not provide any information regarding what version(s) of SOAP the receiver *does* support. This type of information would allow the sender to resend the message with the appropriate version of SOAP. To address this need, SOAP 1.2 provides the `soap:Upgrade` header block that can be sent together with the fault message containing the `soap:VersionMismatch` code to indicate the version of SOAP that the receiver does support.

The syntax for the `soap:Upgrade` construct is as follows:

```
<soap:Upgrade ...>
  <soap:SupportedEnvelope qname="soap:Envelope"/>
</soap:Upgrade>
```

This header can contain one or more `soap:SupportedEnvelope` elements, each of which indicates a supported version of SOAP. The `qname` attribute specifies the qualified name of the supported `soap:Envelope` element. When there are multiple `soap:SupportedEnvelope` elements, they are considered to be listed in order of preference.

soap:MustUnderstand

When the recipient of a message encounters a header block that is targeted to the recipient and marked with the `mustUnderstand="true"` setting but which the recipient cannot understand, the `soap:MustUnderstand` fault will be raised. This particular fault is extremely important for the SOAP processing model because it ensures that if mandatory header blocks are not processed the message itself will not be processed either.

```
<soap:Envelope xmlns:soap=
  "http://www.w3.org/2003/05/soap-envelope">
  <soap:Header>
    ...additional details...
  </soap:Header>
  <soap:Body>
    <soap:Fault>
      <soap:Code>
        <soap:Value>soap:MustUnderstand</soap:Value>
      </soap:Code>
      <soap:Reason>
        <soap:Text xml:lang="en">
          Mandatory header(s) not understood
        </soap:Text>
      </soap:Reason>
    </soap:Fault>
  </soap:Body>
</soap:Envelope>
```

Example 11.16

The `soap:MustUnderstand` fault. Note the bolded `soap:Header` construct can provide further details as to why this fault occurred.

> **NOTE**
>
> For soap:MustUnderstand fault messages, a special soap:NotUn-
> derstood header block can also be used to contain information about
> which headers were not understood.

soap:Sender

This fault is generally used to indicate that the sender of the message did not include something that the receiver needed. Usually this pertains to missing or improperly formed message content and it is generally assumed that this type of problem will not be solved by immediately resending the message.

```
<soap:Envelope xmlns:soap=
  "http://www.w3.org/2003/05/soap-envelope">
  <soap:Body>
    <soap:Fault>
      <soap:Code>
        <soap:Value>soap:Sender</soap:Value>
      </soap:Code>
      <soap:Reason>
        <soap:Text xml:lang="en">
        Malformed message
        </soap:Text>
      </soap:Reason>
    </soap:Fault>
  </soap:Body>
</soap:Envelope>
```

Example 11.17
A fault that points to the sender of the message as the source of invalid message content that caused the exception.

soap:Receiver

The soap:Receiver fault is generated when there is a problem at the receiver's end. For example, the processing of the message may require a database connection that is unavailable or some other temporary resource constraint might occur. Typically, it is assumed that there is no problem with the message content itself and the message may be successfully processed if resent.

```
<soap:Envelope xmlns:soap=
  "http://www.w3.org/2003/05/soap-envelope">
  <soap:Body>
    <soap:Fault>
      <soap:Code>
        <soap:Value>soap:Receiver</soap:Value>
      </soap:Code>
      <soap:Reason>
        <soap:Text xml:lang="en">
          Resource Unavailable
        </soap:Text>
      </soap:Reason>
    </soap:Fault>
  </soap:Body>
</soap:Envelope>
```

Example 11.18

The soap:Code construct indicating that the receiver of the message raised the fault due to an unavailable resource it likely required to process the message.

soap:DataEncodingUnknown

The SOAP node will generate this fault when a message contains a header block or body content targeted at the node and the message contains data encoding (as specified by the encodingStyle attribute) that the node does not understand.

```
<soap:Envelope xmlns:soap=
  "http://www.w3.org/2003/05/soap-envelope">
  <soap:Body>
    <soap:Fault>
      <soap:Code>
        <soap:Value>soap:DataEncodingUnknown</soap:Value>
      </soap:Code>
      <soap:Reason>
        <soap:Text xml:lang="en">
          Unrecognized data encoding
        </soap:Text>
      </soap:Reason>
    </soap:Fault>
  </soap:Body>
</soap:Envelope>
```

Example 11.19

An unrecognized data encoding format causes a SOAP node to generate this fault message.

> **NOTE**
>
> This fault was introduced in SOAP 1.2 and does not exist in SOAP 1.1.

The `soap:Detail` Element

The `Detail` element is essentially used to provide application-specific SOAP fault information and can therefore contain child elements (called "detail entries") that represent and structure this custom fault data.

In the following example, the `Detail` element is used for an authentication-related fault and provides a detail entry listing for an unrecognized user name:

```
<soap:Envelope xmlns:soap=
  "http://www.w3.org/2003/05/soap-envelope"
  xmlns:sec="http://actioncon.com/security">
  <soap:Body>
    <soap:Fault>
      <soap:Code>
        <soap:Value>soap:Sender</soap:Value>
        <soap:Subcode>
          <soap:Value>sec:AuthenticationFailed</soap:Value>
        </soap:Subcode>
      </soap:Code>
      <soap:Reason>
        <soap:Text xml:lang="en">
          User name not recognized.
        </soap:Text>
      </soap:Reason>
      <soap:Detail>
        <sec:InvalidUsername>anonymous</sec:InvalidUsername>
      </soap:Detail>
    </soap:Fault>
  </soap:Body>
</soap:Envelope>
```

Example 11.20
A `soap:Detail` construct containing custom elements.

SOAP Faults vs. WSDL Faults

In Chapters 4 and 7 we introduced the WSDL fault message definition, which is one of three message definition types that you can create for a given WSDL operation. A common point of confusion when learning about Web service contract design is understanding the relationship between the WSDL fault message definition and the SOAP fault-related elements we just introduced.

A SOAP fault is what is described within the `soap:Fault` construct of a SOAP message. Parts of a SOAP fault may or may not have been pre-defined by a WSDL fault message definition. Similarly, if you choose to use a different message protocol instead of SOAP, you may end up binding your WSDL fault message to that protocol instead (which would result in a WSDL fault with no SOAP fault).

WSDL fault messages can be bound to SOAP fault elements as follows:

- *Binding WSDL 1.1 Faults to SOAP 1.2* – Most commonly, the WSDL fault message definition associated with a WSDL operation definition is bound directly to the `soap:Reason` element we described earlier. This means that whatever XML Schema type structure was created to define the WSDL fault message will end up being placed within a `soap:Reason` construct.

- *Binding WSDL 2.0 Faults to SOAP 1.2* – The WSDL 2.0 language actually introduces additional binding options, allowing us to bind the WSDL fault message to the `soap:Reason` or `soap:Subcode` elements.

But what about all of the remaining fault-related SOAP elements? If we can only bind the WSDL fault message definition to a specific set of those elements, then how are the others used?

Most commonly, the elements in the SOAP fault vocabulary are assembled into messages dynamically by runtime processors or service agents, or even the underlying platform or infrastructure responsible for hosting the Web services or providing the protocols for the transmission of the SOAP messages.

You can certainly also use these elements to create custom SOAP fault messages within your service logic, but the resulting message is different from what you would define as a WSDL fault message.

SOAP 1.1 Fault Elements and Values

Provided here are tables that show the difference in the naming of fault-related elements between versions 1.1 and 1.2 of the SOAP language. Table 11.1 provides a comparison of the primary fault elements, while Table 11.2 shows the predefined values for the `soap12:Code` and `soap11:faultcode` elements.

For a closer study of how the respective structures of SOAP 1.1 and 1.2 fault messages compare, see the `soap:Fault` pseudo-schemas provided in Appendix B for both versions of the SOAP language.

SOAP Version 1.2	SOAP Version 1.1
Code	Faultcode
Reason	Faultstring
Role	Faultactor
Detail	Detail
Node	--

Table 11.1
Native fault elements provided by the SOAP 1.1 and SOAP 1.2 languages.

SOAP Version 1.2	SOAP Version 1.1
VersionMismatch	VersionMismatch
MustUnderstand	MustUnderstand
Sender	Client
Receiver	Server
DataEncodingUnknown	--

Table 11.2
The allowable values for the `soap11:faultcode` and `soap12:Code` elements.

SUMMARY OF KEY POINTS

- The SOAP language provides a vocabulary of fault-related elements, most of which are assembled and populated dynamically at runtime into various fault messages.

- Depending on which version of WSDL is used, a WSDL fault message definition can be bound to one or more SOAP fault elements.

- SOAP 1.2 introduced significant naming changes to fault-related elements.

Part II

Advanced Service Contract Design

Chapter 12

Advanced XML Schema Part I: Message Flexibility, Type Inheritance, and Composition

Chapter 6 covered XML Schema features as they pertain to fundamental message design. It's time now to roll up our sleeves and expand on the basics to explore more complex message design issues and techniques over the next two chapters.

12.1 Message Flexibility and Constraint Granularity

Constraint granularity is usually ranked as the number one consideration when it comes to message design because it directly impacts how flexible messages can be. The ideal service contract has a structure that is well-defined enough to be useful but can also handle changes and variations gracefully. The degree of flexibility that is desirable depends on your requirements.

A banking transaction, for example, may need to disallow any extraneous or unexpected elements in a message, which means that less or no flexibility within the constraints would actually be preferable. At the other extreme, a service that is designed to send narrative content to a Web page should be very flexible because this type of content could be comprised of any combination of text.

The former scenario requires a higher level of constraint granularity, whereas the latter situation would benefit from coarse-grained message constraints. Most message designs lie somewhere in between. In this section, we look at a few techniques for improving flexibility by attaining a balanced level of constraint granularity.

Wildcards (`xsd:any` and `xsd:anyAttribute`)

One of the strengths of the XML meta-language compared to, for example, a comma-delimited format, is that you can insert elements into the middle of a document structure without throwing off the runtime processors.

When XML documents are defined with XML Schema, they are only extensible in this way if you write schema complex types to allow for these unexpected elements or attributes to be added. This is accomplished with the `xsd:any` and `xsd:anyAttribute` wildcard elements.

The `xsd:any` Element

The ultimate in loose constraint coupling is being able to design a part of a schema that basically translates into: "Pretty much any element can go here." This is essentially what the `xsd:any` element provides.

As shown in the following example, this element represents an *element wildcard*, which means that any elements in the target namespace are allowed to be added as a child of the `LineItemType` element (in this case, after the `productName` element). We'll refer to these new potential elements as *replacement elements*.

```
<xsd:complexType name="LineItemType">
  <xsd:sequence>
    <xsd:element name="productID" type="ProductIDType"/>
    <xsd:element name="productName" type="xsd:string"/>
    <xsd:any minOccurs="0" maxOccurs="unbounded"
      processContents="lax"
      namespace="http://actioncon.com/schema/gameinfo"/>
  </xsd:sequence>
</xsd:complexType>
```

Example 12.1

The `xsd:any` element establishing a wildcard as part of the `LineItemType` complex type.

NOTE

It is important to understand that the `xsd:any` element is not the same as using a CDATA section. You can add any element, not any *content*. Replacement elements must still represent valid XML.

Let's take a closer look at the `xsd:any` element's attributes.

The `minOccurs` and `maxOccurs` Attributes

These simply control the number of allowed replacement elements. If neither `minOccurs` nor `maxOccurs` attribute is used, the default number of allowed occurrences is one.

The `namespace` Attribute

The namespaces of the allowed replacement elements can be specified with this attribute, which can be set with the following pre-defined values:

- `##any` – (the default value) any namespace or no namespace

- `##other` – any namespace other than the target namespace

- `##targetNamespace` – the target namespace of the schema document

- `##local` – no namespace

- one or more specific namespaces, separated by whitespace

Only elements that belong to namespaces that fit into the value of this attribute can be used as replacement elements.

The `processContents` Attribute

This is an attribute used to control how strictly replacement elements are validated if the message is validated using a schema.

Its allowed values are:

- `skip` – No validation will be performed on the replacement elements.

- `lax` – The processor will look for declarations for those elements (based on their names) and if it finds them, it will validate them (if it doesn't find them, it will not raise an error).

- `strict` – (default) Elements must be declared and validated. If they are invalid or no declarations are found, an error is raised.

This example shows a `lineItem` element that has the `LineItemType` complex type shown in the previous example. It could be used to flexibly add any game information to any line item; for example to specify a particular version of the console that the person is ordering the game for.

```
<lineItem xmlns:game="http://actioncon.com/gameinfo">
  <productID>AY2345</productID>
  <productName>Service Blaster 2000</productName>
  <game:comment>This is a reorder.</game:comment>
  <game:consoleVersion>1.0</game:consoleVersion>
</lineItem>
```

Example 12.2
An instance of the `LineItemType` complex type containing two replacement elements (highlighted).

The `xsd:anyAttribute` *Element*

If you look closely at the next example, you'll notice the addition of the `xsd:anyAttribute` element, which is considered an *attribute wildcard*.

```
<xsd:complexType name="LineItemType">
  <xsd:sequence>
    <xsd:element name="productID" type="ProductIDType"/>
    <xsd:element name="productName" type="xsd:string"/>
    <xsd:any minOccurs="0" maxOccurs="unbounded"
      processContents="lax"
      namespace="http://actioncon.com/gameinfo"/>
  </xsd:sequence>
  <xsd:anyAttribute namespace="##other"/>
</xsd:complexType>
```

Example 12.3

The `xsd:anyAttribute` element establishing an attribute wildcard as part of the `LineItemType` complex type.

Using this type definition, an element of type `LineItemType` can have any attributes that are in a namespace other than the target namespace. As with attribute declarations, attribute wildcards must appear after the content model (the `xsd:sequence`, `xsd:choice`, or `xsd:all` group).

The `xsd:anyAttribute` element can have the `namespace` and `processContents` attributes, but not `minOccurs` or `maxOccurs`. An attribute wildcard always allows for any number of replacement attributes (zero, one, or many) to appear.

For example, the following `lineItem` element is valid according to how `LineItemType` was defined in the previous example:

```
<lineItem xmlns:game="http://actioncom.com/gameinfo"
  game:gameCategory="ACT">
  <productID>AY2345</productID>
  <productName>Service Blaster 2000</productName>
  <game:comment>This is a reorder.</game:comment>
  <game:consoleVersion>1.0</game:consoleVersion>
</lineItem>
```

Example 12.4

An instance of the `LineItemType` complex type containing both replacement elements and a replacement attribute (highlighted).

Wildcards and the UPA Rule

> **NOTE**
>
> The following is a brief introduction to XML Schema wildcards. This topic is discussed indepth as part of the versioning coverage in Chapter 22.

It is illegal in XML Schema 1.0 to place an `xsd:any` wildcard whose `namespace` attribute has the value `##any` or `##targetNamespace` directly after an element declaration that is optional (`minOccurs="0"`) because this violates the "Unique Particle Attribution" rule (as explained further in Chapters 20 and 22). Although not all tools report this problem, avoiding it will increase the interoperability of your schemas. Having the wildcard on its own in the `ExtensionType` content model (explained later in this chapter), rather than at the end of another content model, eliminates this problem.

Using Wildcards to Pass Through Data in Service Compositions

Before we describe the individual XML Schema elements that provide wildcard functionality, let's first demonstrate one of several applications this feature can have with Web service contracts.

Because wildcard elements can represent message content that is not pre-defined, this content is not validated at the contract level. Therefore, it allows you to add new elements at runtime that avoid validation until they encounter a certain body of service logic custom designed to check and parse the data.

Figure 12.1 shows a SOAP message being passed through two different Web services (Service 1 and Service 2) before it arrives at Service 3.

The message contains three sets of data in its body (A, B, C). Let's imagine B is represented by a wildcard. After the data is passed to Service 1, it processes A and C but doesn't touch B. It then creates a new message comprised of B and supplements it with two new sets of data (D and E). Service 2 then processes D and E but again preserves B and forwards it to Service 3, which finally contains the logic required to process B.

The benefits of this architecture are:

- Services 1 and 2 did not unnecessarily have to validate the data set represented by B, thereby increasing performance.

- Data set B could have been any combination of elements, as long as Service 3 (or whatever service acted as the ultimate receiver) would have been capable of processing.

- Alternatively, data set B could not have required any validation at all. For example, it may represent data that just needs to be passed on for display "as is" on a Web page.

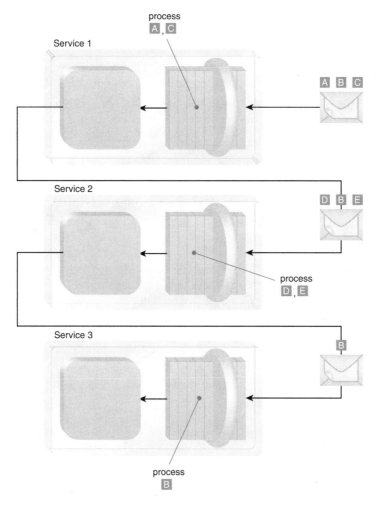

Figure 12.1

The "B" represents wildcard data that avoids validation as it is passed through until Service 3.

NOTE

This technique is focused on SOAP message body data only and should not be confused with the targeted header processing topics covered in Chapter 11.

Tool Support for Element and Attribute Wildcards

When working with some Web service development tools, using `xsd:any` or `xsd:any-Attribute` will result in a property of a class that is very generic. This generally works fine for data that does not need to be heavily manipulated. However, if you do want to process the data, you will have to manipulate it using the generic interfaces for XML elements and attributes rather than classes generated specifically for your data structure. This may mean extracting the names and values of the elements using the generic XML API and explicitly casting the data to the required type. For complex elements, it will further require traversing node trees using APIs like the DOM and can also increase the likelihood of raising runtime errors because the overall code is less type safe when parsing and handling generic content.

For this reason, it is best to use wildcards for the truly unexpected elements, rather than as a way to avoid listing all the possible elements in your content model. For example, if you know that all of the replacement elements are going to be properties of games and it is a finite set, you may be better off declaring them all (as optional).

Besides potentially inconsistent tool support, another disadvantage of the wildcard approach when you have specific replacement elements in mind is that you have no control over the number of occurrences of each element. For example, there could be several (or zero) `comment` elements and it would still be valid. There could be other global elements that were intended to appear in a different entity (say, `address`), but they can also validly appear in `lineItem`.

Not only does this limit validation, but it also limits the documentation of the structure because it is not easy to see what elements are intended to go in what constructs and how many of each are allowed.

Extension Buckets

When allowing for extensibility, it is good practice to create *buckets* for your extended elements so that they can be clearly identified. This means creating a generic element, for example `extension`, that acts as a container (bucket) for all of the replacement elements. As shown in Example 12.5, the `extension` element's `type` attribute points to the `ExtensionType` complex type, which itself declares an `xsd:any` wildcard element.

```
<xsd:complexType name="LineItemType">
  <xsd:sequence>
    <xsd:element name="productID" type="ProductIDType"/>
    <xsd:element name="productName" type="xsd:string"/>
```

```
    <xsd:element name="extension" type="ExtensionType"
      minOccurs="0"/>
  </xsd:sequence>
</xsd:complexType>
<xsd:complexType name="ExtensionType">
  <xsd:sequence>
    <xsd:any minOccurs="0" maxOccurs="unbounded"
      processContents="lax" namespace="##other"/>
  </xsd:sequence>
</xsd:complexType>
```

Example 12.5

The extension global element with a complex type that acts as an "extension bucket."

This approach adds another level to the document, as shown in Example 12.6, which slightly increases its size. However, there are several advantages:

- During the development process, the existence of the extension element makes project teams responsible for building both service and consumers more likely to plan for extensions.

- When using XSLT and other tools to process XML, an extension bucket can make it easier to identify and separate the replacement elements from the core ones.

- The extension element can be used to hold an attribute (for example, you might call it mustUse) that indicates whether the service processing the message must understand and process the replacement elements.

- You can avoid the Unique Particle Attribution problem described earlier.

Here is an XML document instance of the preceding LineItemType definition:

```
<lineItem xmlns:game="http://actioncon.com/gameinfo">
  <productID>AY2345</productID>
  <productName>Service Blaster 2000</productName>
  <extension>
    <game:comment>This is a reorder.</game:comment>
    <game:consoleVersion>1.0</game:consoleVersion>
  </extension>
</lineItem>
```

Example 12.6

An instance of the lineItem element within the extension construct acting as the "bucket."

Extension Buckets Using `xsd:anyType`

A different, but similar way of declaring an extension element that can contain any type of additional XML data is to use the `xsd:anyType` type. Note that while `xsd:any` is an element, `xsd:anyType` is a type. This means that it is used to identify that a particular element, which has a declared name in the schema, can contain any content. Such an element could be the extension element as we just described.

```xsd
<xsd:complexType name="LineItemType">
  <xsd:sequence>
    <xsd:element name="productID" type="ProductIDType"/>
    <xsd:element name="productName" type="xsd:string"/>
    <xsd:element name="extension"
      minOccurs="0" type="xsd:anyType"/>
  </xsd:sequence>
</xsd:complexType>
```

Example 12.7
The updated schema using the `xsd:anyType` type.

Note that the definition of the `ExtensionType` type is no longer necessary. Still, the document listed in Example 12.6 is a valid instance of this schema. The advantage here is that no additional type (like `ExtensionType`) needs to be defined. On the other hand, there are some disadvantages to using `xsd:anyType`:

- It does not allow you to make any statement about the expected namespace of the contained extension elements.

- It does not ever result in the contents being validated (while `ExtensionType` will allow for this, depending on the value of the `processContents` attribute).

- It will always allow both replacement elements and replacement attributes (while `ExtensionType` gives you finer control over which and how many replacement elements you want).

- It is not supported by all processors.

- `ExtensionType` can be later extended to support versioning scenarios, while `xsd:anyType` cannot.

An alternative to using `xsd:anyType` is to simply omit the type attribute, which has essentially the same effect as specifying it as `xsd:anyType`.

Generic vs. Specific Elements

Another way to achieve flexibility is to use more generic elements to structure your data. One case where this comes into play is when you have several data items that represent a particular "type" (or "class") of something, but each is a specific type (or a specialized class).

For example, in the Game service, each game has a number of features associated with it. The data used to represent each feature will be different, but all of these data items can be considered "types" of features.

On the most fundamental level, each feature has a name and a value. One way to represent this is by creating a different element for each feature, as shown here:

```
<game>
  ...
  <hdtv>true</hdtv>
  <surround_sound>true</surround_sound>
  <minPlayers>1</minPlayers>
  <maxPlayers>3</maxPlayers>
  <esrbRating>EC</esrbRating>
</game>
```

Example 12.8
The game construct with a set of different child elements, each of which represents a specific feature of the game.

The downside of using these specific element names is that they increase the rigidity of constraints. The resulting reduction in design flexibility means that every time a new feature comes along, the Game schema needs to be changed in order to incorporate a new element. These types of changes can easily break existing Web service contracts and introduce undesirable versioning requirements.

Also from a development perspective, any classes dependent on this schema will need to be regenerated and/or modified to account for the new element. Plus, the programming code that implements the logic of the service must be augmented to handle it also.

These issues can be avoided by adding a generic `feature` element that contains the value of the feature and puts the name of the feature in a `name` attribute, as in the following example:

```
<game>
  ...
  <feature name="hdtv">true</feature>
  <feature name="surround_sound">true</feature>
  <feature name="minPlayers">1</feature>
  <feature name="maxPlayers">3</feature>
  <feature name="esrbRating">EC</feature>
</game>
```

Example 12.9

The game construct with a set of the same `feature` child elements, each of which identifies a feature of the game via its name attribute.

This is far more flexible in that new features do not impose changes on the schema (or derived programming classes). The only impact will be on the service logic responsible for processing the `feature` elements.

There is a disadvantage to using generic elements, however. You cannot specify data types for their values because there is no way in XML Schema to express something like:

"If a `feature` element's `name` attribute is `minPlayers`, make the content `xsd:int`, and if it's `hdtv`, make it `xsd:boolean`."

This means that you are stuck with the type and structure associated with the element and you cannot take advantage of XML Schema features beyond that. For example, in the `game` construct you wouldn't be able to add a new attribute or change the data type of a `feature` element. This is not an issue when using specific elements because you can customize each element declaration as you like.

Another potential issue with generic elements is that you have no control over their order or whether they are required or repeating. You cannot force the existence of a `feature` element with the name "`maxPlayers`" and you also cannot specify that there can only be one `feature` element whose name is "`maxPlayers`." There can be zero, one, or many instances of any one type of feature element with the same `name` attribute, and they can appear in any order. Of course, you always have the option of enforcing these kinds of constraints within the service logic, but then it would not be part of the service contract.

Again this is not a problem when you use specific elements for each feature because you can use the `minOccurs` and `maxOccurs` attributes on individual element declarations.

Some considerations when determining whether to use generic or specific elements are:

- If there is little change, there is not much benefit to using generic elements. For example, if new features are rarely added.

- If they share similar characteristics, it can be easier to process a set of elements as generic elements. For example, this would allow the consumer of the Game service to simply turn a collection of `feature` elements into a Features table for display on a Web page.

- If they do not share similar characteristics, it can be easier to process them as specific elements. For example, if the service consumer needs to look up the game's maximum number of players, it is more convenient to simply call an operation like `getMaxPlayers` rather than retrieve all the features through a `getFeatures` operation and loop through the results until one called "`maxPlayers`" is found.

- If the content is likely to be significantly different for each feature, it is best to use specific elements so that you can adequately describe their structure in the schema (as when some features need to have differing multi-part or complex values).

- If it is important to validate message contents or the order or appearance of message data items, it is best to use specific elements because these constraints cannot be expressed with generic elements.

Another design alternative is to use a combination of generic and specific elements, as demonstrated in this next case study example.

CASE STUDY EXAMPLE

Steve needs to expand the Game schema he created earlier to include all relevant information about game products. When weighing the alternatives, he decides to go with a generic `feature` element rather than a specific element for each feature. The schema he creates is shown here:

```
<xsd:complexType name="GameType">
  <xsd:sequence>
    <xsd:element name="productID" type="ProductIDType"/>
    <xsd:element name="gtin" type="GTINType"/>
    <xsd:element name="title" type="TitleType"/>
    <xsd:element name="desc" type="DescType"/>
    <xsd:element name="msrPrice" type="PriceType"/>
    <xsd:element name="version" type="GameVersionType"/>
```

```
    <xsd:element name="onlinePreview" type="xsd:boolean"/>
    <xsd:element name="feature" maxOccurs="unbounded"
      type="FeatureType"/>
  </xsd:sequence>
</xsd:complexType>
<xsd:complexType name="FeatureType">
  <xsd:simpleContent>
    <xsd:extension base="xsd:string">
      <xsd:attribute name="name" type="xsd:string"/>
    </xsd:extension>
  </xsd:simpleContent>
</xsd:complexType>
```

Example 12.10

The `GameType` complex type with child elements that provide generic feature capabilities.

He bases this decision on a few factors. One is the fact that features change often. In their Game database table (defined in Chapter 6), there is a separate column for each feature, and every new feature requires a two-week development cycle to change the database and the code to accommodate it. He does not want to repeat this mistake.

Secondly, the data does not need to be validated. He knows that it is coming from a reliable source, so there would never be the risk of returning two `maxPlayers` features. The service consumers, which are generally third-party Web sites, simply display the features on a page; they do not individually process the features in any way, so they do not depend heavily on the data being present or valid. In fact, the feedback from these third parties is that it makes it much easier for them to allow searches on features if they are all structured identically in the XML.

Steve decides that data items like price, description, and version should not be treated like generic features because they are used differently, have a different structure, and are important to validate. He also decides to separate `onlinePreview`, an element that indicates whether the game can be played online, because consumers of the Game service will want to display games differently depending on the value of this element.

Steve then starts to wonder if he should take the use of generic elements up a level. ActionCon doesn't just sell games; it also sells consoles and accessories. Should there even be a `game` element? Or would it be better to have a generic `product` element instead that could represent any of the three categories of products that they sell? After comparing these options, he decides to continue using specific elements for games.

The main factor in this decision is that the content of a game element differs significantly from the content of an accessory element. Although they both have a product identifier and a price, there is not much in common beyond that. In addition, the likelihood of change is low. Unless ActionCon gets into a new industry or dramatically different product line, the three elements game, console, and accessory should cover their needs for the foreseeable future.

Content Model Groups (`xsd:choice`, `xsd:all`, and `xsd:sequence`)

So far, all of our examples have used xsd:sequence constructs, which means that the declared elements must appear in the XML message in the order they are declared in the schema. This section describes the xsd:choice and xsd:all constructs, which can be considered alternatives to using xsd:sequence.

> **NOTE**
>
> Because they are used to establish and organize groups of related elements, the xsd:choice and xsd:all constructs (as well as the xsd:sequence construct) are commonly referred to as "content model groups," or just "groups." The term "content model" was first described in Chapter 6.

The `xsd:choice` Element

An xsd:choice construct establishes a group wherein one of several choices is offered. A choice can represent an option between two or more individual elements or groups of elements.

This type of group can be used to represent the entire message content model, or it can be nested within an xsd:sequence construct (in which case it only represents a subset of the message content model). Any combination of nested xsd:choice and xsd:sequence groups is permitted.

This next example shows an xsd:sequence group that contains a nested xsd:choice group that allows the AddressType element enough flexibility to support different address formats.

```
<xsd:complexType name="AddressType">
  <xsd:sequence>
    <xsd:element name="line1" type="xsd:string"/>
```

```
    <xsd:element name="line2" type="xsd:string" minOccurs="0"/>
    <xsd:element name="city" type="xsd:string"/>
    <xsd:choice>
      <xsd:element name="state" type="xsd:string"/>
      <xsd:element name="province" type="xsd:string"/>
    </xsd:choice>
    <xsd:element name="postalCode" type="xsd:string"/>
    <xsd:element name="country" type="xsd:string"/>
  </xsd:sequence>
</xsd:complexType>
```

Example 12.11

A nested xsd:choice group that allows either a state or a province element to appear within the AddressType construct.

Tool Support for xsd:choice

Using the xsd:choice element may seem like the ideal way to flexibly define data models that can vary in different contexts or situations. However, several tools do not fully support xsd:choice groups. For example, some tools will more or less ignore the choice group in the previous example and treat the state and province elements the same way they treat optional elements.

This may not cause much of an issue, but as nested groups become more sophisticated, the chances that tools will cause problems increases.

For example, suppose you want to allow the lineItem elements in the purchase order to be intermingled with comment elements that apply to line items that follow it. In other words, some lineItem elements will be preceded by comment elements, whereas others will not. To create this type of structure, you could define a repeating xsd:choice group by adding a maxOccurs attribute and setting it to "unbounded," as shown in the next example. This effectively allows any number of comment and lineItem elements to appear in any order.

```
<xsd:complexType name="LineItemsType">
  <xsd:choice maxOccurs="unbounded">
    <xsd:element name="comment" type="xsd:string"/>
    <xsd:element name="lineItem" type="LineItemType"/>
  </xsd:choice>
</xsd:complexType>
```

Example 12.12

A complexType construct with a repeating xsd:choice group.

Most development tools will have a problem with this complex type and either generate an extremely generic structure for `LineItemsType` or generate a class that allows you to retrieve an array of comments and/or an array of line items but not preserve the order in which they appeared in the message. For this reason, in a Web service contract it is best to avoid using the `maxOccurs="unbounded"` attribute setting on the `xsd:choice` element.

Additionally, it is not desirable to make the position of an element within a group have meaning. In the previous example, the `comment` element is expected to always be displayed prior to the `lineItem` element for which it is providing a comment. This should be avoided because most toolkits do not treat order as significant and have a difficult time handling arrays that contain structures of different types (e.g., a single array that contains both comments and line items).

The `xsd:all` Element

The other alternative to using `xsd:sequence` is the `xsd:all` group. Don't be fooled by its name; it does not require that all elements within a group always be displayed. Instead, it establishes a rule that all elements appear by default. You can override this default setting on a per element basis by using the `minOccurs` attribute.

Its syntax is similar to the `xsd:choice` group:

```
<xsd:complexType name="LineItemsType">
  <xsd:all>
    <xsd:element name="comment" type="xsd:string"/>
    <xsd:element name="lineItem" type="LineItemType"/>
  </xsd:all>
</xsd:complexType>
```

Example 12.13

The `xsd:all` construct representing the `comment` and `lineItems` elements. Because neither child element has a `minOccurs` attribute, the default behavior of this group will require that both be displayed.

Here are some limitations to using the `xsd:all` group:

- It cannot allow a child to appear more than once.

- It cannot be combined with an `xsd:sequence` or `xsd:choice` group.

- It cannot be extended or restricted by other types.

The `xsd:sequence` *Element*

Besides better tool support than `xsd:choice` and `xsd:all`, a primary advantage to using `xsd:sequence` groups is that certain constraints cannot be expressed any other way.

For example, it is not possible to say that a `game` may have one `gtin`, one `title`, and up to three `desc` children, in any order. You could use an `xsd:all` group if you only want to allow each element once, or you could use the `xsd:choice` group if you do not mind there being more than one `gtin` or `title` element. In order to ensure that you will only have one `gtin` and one `title` and allow more than one `desc`, the best approach is to enforce the order by reverting back to the `xsd:sequence` element, as shown here:

```
<xsd:complexType name="GameType">
  <xsd:sequence>
    <xsd:element name="gtin" type="GTINType"/>
    <xsd:element name="title" type="xsd:string"/>
    <xsd:element name="desc" type="DescType" maxOccurs="3"/>
  </xsd:sequence>
</xsd:complexType>
```

Example 12.14
A standard `xsd:sequence` group that establishes a specific order.

NOTE

The use of XML Schema group elements is required. The child `xsd:element` elements within a `complexType` construct must be wrapped in a group element even if only one child element is present.

For example, the following construct would be invalid:

```
<xsd:complexType name="GameType">
  <xsd:element name="title" type="xsd:string"/>
</xsd:complexType>
```

SUMMARY OF KEY POINTS

- Coarse-grained constraint granularity can be achieved by using wildcards, namely `xsd:any` and `xsd:anyAttribute`. This is recommended for truly unexpected (or "non-predictable") elements, but it requires additional work to process these elements.

- Using generic element names can result in a more controlled level of flexibility. This is recommended for data that changes regularly and does not need to be strictly described or validated.

- Using `xsd:choice` and `xsd:all` groups can result in more flexible message content models. However, there is limited support for these elements in Web service development tools.

12.2 Type Inheritance and Composition

The XML Schema language emerged prior to the advent of service-orientation during a time when most distributed systems were designed according to component-based and object-oriented philosophies. Due to the modular nature of XML Schema (and other XML-based languages, like XSLT), several features were built into the language to support or align XML Schema technology with object-oriented design. These types of OOD-inspired extensions also made their way into Web service-related languages.

There are similarities between Web services and objects: both have interfaces (contracts) that have methods (operations) that encapsulate the underlying functionality. For very fine-grained utility services, this comparison is especially valid. Later in this chapter we describe CRUD-style operations for services with data access functions. These services might roughly resemble a typical object-oriented interface, with methods (operations) like `updateAppStatus` and `insertLogEvent`.

> **NOTE**
>
> A side-by-side comparison of object-orientation and service-orientation goals, concepts, and design principles has been documented in Chapter 14 of *SOA Principles of Service Design*.

Emulating Class Inheritance (`abstract` and `xsd:extension`)

Earlier in this chapter, we discussed the use of generic versus specific element names that can be used to create schema types that resemble generalized classes and specialized classes (or sub-classes).

We can take this concept a step further by taking advantage of an XML Schema feature called *type derivation* that allows us to create a base complex type from which other types can be derived (much like a base class).

For example, suppose we want to have separate elements for the three different kinds of products used by the Game service:

- `game`
- `console`
- `accessory`

All three product types have some information in common, such as:

- `productID`

- `title`

- `msrPrice`

The rest of their content is specific to their specialization (or sub-class), for example:

- A game might have a version number and an `onlinePreview` element indicating whether it can be previewed online.

- A console might also have a version number, but one that conforms to a different versioning scheme, as well as a choice of colors.

- An accessory might have a specific adapter type that would be used to connect it with different versions of games and consoles.

If we were to model these types as UML classes, it would look a lot like the class hierarchy displayed in Figure 12.2.

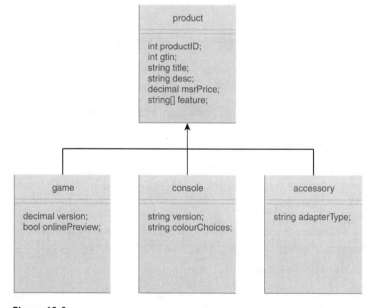

Figure 12.2
How the product generalization structure could be expressed via a traditional class hierarchy.

In this figure, the abstract (base) product class represents the properties that are common to all of the specialized classes (game, console, accessory). Each specialized class contains further properties that are specific to it.

So how do we establish this type of structure with XML Schema? Well, we define the base type as we would any complex type. We can optionally make the base complex type abstract, which means that its only purpose is to serve as the base type, and it cannot be used by any elements in an XML message instance.

To accomplish this, we use an attribute called `abstract`, as explained next.

The `abstract` *Attribute*

The `complexType` element we introduced in Chapter 6 has an optional attribute called `abstract` that can be used to establish a complex type as an abstract type, as follows:

```
<xsd:complexType name="ProductType" abstract="true">
  <xsd:sequence>
    <xsd:element name="productID" type="ProductIDType"/>
    <xsd:element name="gtin" type="GTINType"/>
    <xsd:element name="title" type="TitleType"/>
    <xsd:element name="desc" type="xsd:string"/>
    <xsd:element name="msrPrice" type="PriceType"/>
    <xsd:element name="feature" maxOccurs="unbounded"
      type="FeatureType"/>
  </xsd:sequence>
</xsd:complexType>
```

Example 12.15
A `complexType` element with an `abstract` attribute set to "true," thereby effectively establishing an abstract product type.

As an abstract type, the `ProductType` complex type will itself not be directly referenced by an element. Instead, it will be used as the basis of multiple other (specialized) complex types that will essentially inherit it.

The `xsd:extension` *Element*

The inheritance of a base type by a specialized type is carried out via the use of the `xsd:extension` element. This element basically tells the processor to pull in the contents of the referenced base type.

Here's an example of the `GameType` specialized complex type that extends (inherits) the contents of the `ProductType` abstract complex type:

```
<xsd:element name="game" type="GameType"/>
<xsd:complexType name="GameType">
  <xsd:complexContent>
    <xsd:extension base="ProductType">
      <xsd:sequence>
        <xsd:element name="version" type="GameVersionType"/>
        <xsd:element name="onlinePreview" type="xsd:boolean"/>
      </xsd:sequence>
    </xsd:extension>
  </xsd:complexContent>
</xsd:complexType>
```

Example 12.16

The `GameType` complex type using the `xsd:extension` element to reference the `ProductType` complex type.

As you can see in the definition of the `GameType` complex type, it further adds two new elements (`version` and `onlinePreview`), which represent the specialized content that applies only to games (and not to products in general).

A valid instance of `GameType` complex type is shown here:

```
<game>
  <productID>AY2344</productID>
  <gtin>1234567890123</gtin>
  <title>Service Blaster 2000</title>
  <desc>This is a <i>great</i> game.</desc>
  <msrPrice>29.99</msrPrice>
  <feature name="hdtv">true</feature>
  <feature name="surround_sound">true</feature>
  <feature name="minPlayers">1</feature>
  <feature name="maxPlayers">3</feature>
  <feature name="esrbRating">EC</feature>
  <version>1.1</version>
  <onlinePreview>true</onlinePreview>
</game>
```

Example 12.17

An instance of the `GameType` complex type. All highlighted parts are inherited.

> **NOTE**
>
> The order of the `game` element's child elements had to be changed from the earlier examples because the `feature` element is part of the inherited `ProductType` and therefore must appear before the `version` and `onlinePreview` elements, which are specific to `GameType`.

Let's now create a second specialized type to represent consoles (another kind of product). In the following example, the `ConsoleType` complex type contains the same `xsd:extension` element used to reference the abstract `ProductType` complex type:

```
<xsd:element name="console" type="ConsoleType"/>
<xsd:complexType name="ConsoleType">
  <xsd:complexContent>
    <xsd:extension base="ProductType">
      <xsd:sequence>
        <xsd:element name="version"
          type="ConsoleVersionType"/>
        <xsd:element name="colorChoices" type="xsd:string"/>
      </xsd:sequence>
    </xsd:extension>
  </xsd:complexContent>
</xsd:complexType>
```

Example 12.18
The XML schema for the derived console type.

Note how just like with `GameType`, `ConsoleType` also adds a `version` element. Why then didn't we just make the `version` element part of the base complex type? In this case, it wasn't possible because the `version` element for `GameType` is declared differently than the `version` element for `ConsoleType`. Because each needed the freedom to associate a different type to the `version` element, inheritance wasn't an option. Using locally declared elements, as we do here, allows the same element name to have different types in different contexts.

> **NOTE**
>
> To apply this inheritance feature across different schema documents, you will need to use the `xsd:include` or `xsd:import` elements described in Chapter 13. For example, an abstract type can be placed into its own schema and then included or imported into multiple specialized schemas.

Inheritance and Service-Orientation

As you were reading the *Emulating Class Inheritance* section so far, you might have realized that we've been discussing techniques that emulate a part of object-orientation that is generally omitted from service-orientation. You'd be right in this assumption. Although service-orientation has been heavily influenced by object-oriented design, its emphasis on maintaining a reduced level of coupling across services leaves little room for cross-service, ownership-based inheritance structures. Services need to exist autonomously so that they can be independently governed, evolved and, of course, composed.

While all of this is true, it pertains primarily to the design of a service as a whole. While service contracts are part of service design, XML schemas establish a data architecture layer that is ideally independent of—yet still fully capable of supporting—the service layer that is built over top of it.

As a result of this independence, you have some freedom as to how you design schemas. Although you may want to avoid any form of external dependency on certain schemas so that you don't constrict their ability to change or be evolved, there can be circumstances where type inheritance is effective.

As an example, let's turn our attention to the entity service model. The Web service contract for an entity service will be focused on a specific type of business document. As we already know, an entity service's functional context may have been based on multiple actual business entities. However, you may decide to create separate XML schemas that correspond to the business entities. In order to avoid having to create redundant types in each schema, you could decide to create an abstract schema and then allow each of the actual schemas to derive types from it (which, for those of you with an OO background, leads to opportunities for both inheritance and aggregation).

The benefit is that the abstract schema guarantees consistency across all specialized schemas, but the downside is that this consistency may turn into a problem one day when abstract types no longer apply to all derived schemas. So, although you do have the freedom to explore cross-schema inheritance, be sure to use it with caution and only when you're certain that the abstract types are very stable.

All of the types you establish via these schemas will form the basis of WSDL operation definitions to which (in the case of entity and utility services) many consumer programs will bind and form dependencies over time. You therefore want to avoid situations that force you to modify an established type in such a manner that it causes a ripple effect across all dependent consumer programs.

Tool Support for Derived Types

Most Web service development tools will treat complex type extensions like class inheritance. For example, they will generate a class named "GameType" that extends the class named "ProductType." GameType will inherit all methods from ProductType plus add new ones. Defining the common components once ensures that they are consistent and makes it easier to write and maintain the code that manipulates the common data. In addition, data items can be treated in the application code either generically as products or specifically as games or consoles, depending on the needs of the application.

XML Schema offers several other ways of representing class hierarchies, but they are generally not recommended for use in a Web services environment for the following reasons:

- Complex types can be derived by restriction (rather than extension) from other complex types. The derived type must allow only a subset of what the base type allows. This is of limited usefulness unless you are attempting to define a subset of another XML schema.

- Type substitution allows the same element name to be used for derived types (by extension or restriction). For example, we could declare a product element whose type is ProductType, and then in the message itself use the xsi:type attribute to indicate the derived type, as in <product xsi:type="GameType">. It is essentially casting an individual product element to a subtype, GameType, at runtime. While this can be an elegant way to achieve flexibility, it is not well supported in tools. For more interoperable schemas, it is best to declare separate elements (game, console, accessory) for each type (GameType, ConsoleType, AccessoryType), as shown earlier in this section.

- Substitution groups describe hierarchies of elements rather than types. They allow you to specify that one or more elements are substitutable for another element. For example, we could put the game, console and accessory elements in the substitution group of the product element. Then, anywhere product appears in a content model, any of the other three elements could appear instead. It is a more extensible alternative to choice groups. This is useful when describing narrative content, where you have less predictable structures. However, Web service messages are usually fairly predictable, so you are better off creating a hierarchy of *types* and explicitly stating where elements of each type can appear. Tool support of substitution groups is also limited.

Type Composition (`xsd:group`)

There is an alternative way to represent the fact that games, consoles, and accessories have properties in common. Through the use of *named model groups*, XML Schema allows you to identify shared content model fragments, allowing a type definition to be composed of product properties, plus have its own properties.

The `xsd:group` Element

Named model groups are defined using an `xsd:group` element in XML Schema. This next example shows a named model group called `ProductProperties` that contains a content model fragment describing all the generic product information:

```
<xsd:schema ...>
  <xsd:group name="ProductProperties">
    <xsd:sequence>
      <xsd:element name="productID" type="ProductIDType"/>
      <xsd:element name="gtin" type="GTINType"/>
      <xsd:element name="title" type="TitleType"/>
      <xsd:element name="desc" type="xsd:string"/>
      <xsd:element name="msrPrice" type="PriceType"/>
      <xsd:element name="feature" maxOccurs="unbounded"
        type="FeatureType"/>
    </xsd:sequence>
  </xsd:group>
</xsd:schema>
```

Example 12.19

An `xsd:group` is defined at the top level of the schema, as a child of `xsd:schema`.

Example 12.20 shows how `GameType` references the `ProductProperties` group. It also uses an `xsd:group` element, but this time with a `ref` attribute instead of a `name` attribute. The effect of referencing a group is as if you cut and pasted the content of the group into the place where it is referenced.

```
<xsd:complexType name="GameType">
  <xsd:sequence>
    <xsd:group ref="ProductProperties"/>
    <xsd:element name="version" type="GameVersionType"/>
    <xsd:element name="onlinePreview" type="xsd:boolean"/>
  </xsd:sequence>
</xsd:complexType>
```

Example 12.20

The GameType element pulls in the contents of the `ProductProperties` group via the use of the `ref` attribute of the `group` element.

The `ConsoleType` complex type could similarly reference the group to reuse the definition of the product properties. The instances of the `game` and `console` elements will look exactly the same as if we used a type extension in that there will be no `ProductProperties` element in the message content.

The primary benefit of this approach is its flexibility. When using named model groups, the shared portion can appear anywhere in the content model, not just at the beginning. This might be a consideration if the order matters (though, in most cases it doesn't). It's also more flexible in that you can include more than one group in a type structure. With type derivation, there is only single inheritance.

Either way, the same coupling-related considerations described in the *Inheritance and Service-Orientation* section can apply to the use of type composition as well because you are still effectively creating cross-schema dependencies.

> **NOTE**
>
> As with the inheritance approach, to apply type composition across different XML Schema documents requires the use of either the `xsd:include` or `xsd:import` elements described in Chapter 13.

Tool Support for Type Composition

Although the generic product elements are shared in the schema, most toolkits do not generate shared code or interfaces for these components. They will typically generate a `GameType` class that has all the generic product properties and a separate `ConsoleType` class that has separate definitions of the generic product properties. No separate `ProductProperties` class or interface will be generated; it will be as if the group did not exist.

Use of named model groups is most appropriate when the types represent different concepts that happen to have a few of the same child elements. However, if the types are really sub-classes of a more generic class, it is better to use type derivation because the generated code will be more useful and representative of the real model.

Another option for composition is to use a child element to contain the shared information. We could use the same `ProductType` complex type we defined before. Instead of deriving `GameType` from it, we could give `GameType` a child element named "productProperties" that has the type `ProductType`, as shown here:

```xsd
<xsd:complexType name="ProductType">
  <xsd:sequence>
    <xsd:element name="productID" type="ProductIDType"/>
    <xsd:element name="gtin" type="GTINType"/>
    <xsd:element name="title" type="TitleType"/>
    <xsd:element name="desc" type="xsd:string"/>
    <xsd:element name="msrPrice" type="PriceType"/>
    <xsd:element name="feature" maxOccurs="unbounded"
      type="FeatureType"/>
  </xsd:sequence>
</xsd:complexType>
<xsd:complexType name="GameType">
  <xsd:sequence>
    <xsd:element name="productProperties" type="ProductType"/>
    <xsd:element name="version" type="GameVersionType"/>
    <xsd:element name="onlinePreview" type="xsd:boolean"/>
  </xsd:sequence>
</xsd:complexType>
```

Example 12.21

A complex type that uses the `GameType` child element for composition.

In this case, the message instance *will* have an extra element in it, as follows:

```xml
<game>
  <productProperties>
    <productID>AY2344</productID>
    <gtin>1234567890123</gtin>
    <title>Service Blaster 2000</title>
    <desc>This is a <i>great</i> game.</desc>
    <msrPrice>29.99</msrPrice>
    <feature name="hdtv">true</feature>
    <feature name="surround_sound">true</feature>
    <feature name="minPlayers">1</feature>
    <feature name="maxPlayers">3</feature>
    <feature name="esrbRating">EC</feature>
  </productProperties>
  <version>1.1</version>
  <onlinePreview>true</onlinePreview>
</game>
```

Example 12.22

An instance of a document based on the derived `GameType` complex type.

One advantage of this approach is that it clearly identifies the shared information and provides a hook to access it. This can make it easier for the consumer of the message, especially if the message needs to be transformed via XSLT. It has an advantage over using named model groups because one class will be generated for the `productProperties` construct, so the code to process and generate that part of the message can be shared for both games and consoles.

The downside is that it adds an additional layer and therefore some additional complexity to the messages. When compared to the type inheritance method, this can make it slightly more difficult to write and maintain the code that implements the service and also makes the message more verbose.

SUMMARY OF KEY POINTS

- Service-orientation was influenced by object-orientation, but it generally does not support inheritance as part of service design. However, in the data architecture layer, type inheritance can be used to achieve consistency and reuse and to improve the usefulness of generated classes.

- Inheritance across schema types can be accomplished via the use of the `abstract` attribute and the `xsd:extension` element.

- An alternative for sharing related properties among types is the use of type composition via named model groups (`xsd:group`).

12.3 Common CRUD Messages Types

Service-oriented analysis approaches often result in the need for services to establish a standardized contract that represents information sets based on business documents or legacy repositories with proprietary APIs.

The two most common scenarios where this is required are:

- A service is based on the entity service model and therefore has a functional context that is associated with an information set (business document). Because these types of services are generally positioned as the sole or primary access point for the data associated with the information set (as per the Logic Centralization pattern), they are required to provide operations that perform various business functions, including generic data access.

- A service is based on the utility service model that is further shaped via the Legacy Wrapper pattern that gives the service a functional context based solely on the API of a legacy system or repository. The service's purpose in this case is simply to provide a standardized interface into a proprietary resource (which is often just one or a set of databases). As a result, this type of service will also need to supply operations with generic data handling functionality.

From a Web service contract perspective, these requirements typically translate into the need to provide operations based on the well-known CRUD (Create, Read, Update, Delete) functions that were popularized with component-based and object-oriented design approaches.

NOTE

Throughout the upcoming sections we replace "Create" with "Add" and "Read" with "Get" because these terms have become more common in SOA practice. So even though we'll continue to refer to the operations as CRUD-style, the actual acronym should be "AGUD" (for Add, Get, Update, Delete).

Before we explore how CRUD-style operations can affect message design, we'll first cover some related design factors.

The "Chatty" Factor

It is desirable, for reasons of performance, scalability, and reliability that a Web service not provide operations that are unnecessarily "chatty." Too many chatty operations lead to an overall chatty service. A chatty service is one to which multiple calls must be made, often synchronously, to get a useful result.

Instead, all the information the service needs to provide a commonly requested result should ideally be included in the same message. This means that information needed to accomplish several different (but related) actions may need to be bundled in one message.

For example, an incoming request message for the Purchase Order service might be designed to include:

- security credentials
- the status of the purchase order document
- what action needs to be performed next with it
- the format of the desired response or acknowledgement
- the location to send the response to

…and, of course, the purchase order document itself.

Some of this information will appear in the header, either via custom or industry standard SOAP header blocks. However, as the message is passed from service to service, it may be augmented and expanded, resulting in the accumulation of additional message body content, such as customer details or more detailed pricing and tax information for each of the ordered items.

While this applies to most service designs, it is of special importance to entity and wrapper utility services because they are often shouldered with the responsibility of defining and processing entire business records or documents and related vocabularies. Modeling the schemas together with these services therefore provides the opportunity to design CRUD-style operations with messages that can be equipped with a range of metadata (as previously listed).

> **NOTE**
>
> Design patterns such as Contract Denormalization and Concurrent Contracts allow for the definition of operations with overlapping functional contexts in support of providing both fine and coarse-grained message exchanges for a range of consumers. When applying these patterns, you therefore do not need to choose between creating CRUD operations with coarse or fine-grained message body content. However, you still don't avoid having to create the composite-style messages we just described.

The Agnostic Factor

Those of you familiar with CRUD-style design may be used to object or component-based design approaches that are centered on the delivery of parameter data. This was especially common in RPC environments where components shared a persistent connection within which granular pieces of data could be efficiently exchanged.

As just mentioned in the previous section about avoiding chatty services, the messaging-centric framework that underlies the Web services technology platform naturally leads to a tendency to decrease data granularity by encouraging the exchange of larger business documents in order to minimize the communications overhead associated with multiple service-to-consumer roundtrips.

We now need to add to this the fact that both entity and utility service models are expected to provide an *agnostic* functional context. To better understand what we mean by "agnostic," let's borrow the definition from SOAGlossary.com:

*"The term 'agnostic' originated from Greek where it means 'without knowledge.'
Therefore, logic that is sufficiently generic so that it is not specific to (has no knowledge of) a particular parent task is classified as agnostic logic. Because knowledge specific to single purpose tasks is intentionally omitted, agnostic logic is considered
multi-purpose. On the flipside, logic that is specific to (contains knowledge of) a single-purpose task is labeled as non-agnostic logic.*

*Another way of thinking about agnostic and non-agnostic logic is to focus on the
extent to which the logic can be repurposed. Because agnostic logic is expected to be
multi-purpose it is subject to the Service Reusability principle with the intention of
turning it into highly reusable logic. Once reusable, this logic is truly multi-purpose
in that it, as a single software program (or service), can be used to automate multiple
business processes.*

*Non-agnostic logic does not have these types of expectations. It is deliberately designed
as a single-purpose software program (or service) and therefore has different characteristics and requirements."*

Because entity and utility services are agnostic by nature, their CRUD-style operations
will generally need to be highly reusable. Agnostic service design considerations will
affect the Web service contract because of the emphasis on making each operation as
useful to as many types of consumers as possible. This influence in particular often leads
to a tendency to reduce levels of constraint granularity in order to increase flexibility.

NOTE

Just a reminder that we are focused on CRUD-style operations only in
these sections. It is important to acknowledge that entity services are
business-centric and will contain additional business logic beyond these
basic data access functions. Similarly, you can create a variety of different
utility services. In this section we only really explore wrapper utility services with generic data access functionality.

Common Message Types

Before we get into the details of CRUD-style service operations, let's first establish two
forms of common messages these operations tend to exchange.

Business Document Message

The document-centric messaging style often required by service-oriented solutions will tend to naturally result in more messages being passed around with entire business documents. The following is the message structure we established for the Game service in Chapter 6. As is discussed shortly, this type can be reused to facilitate different messages by different CRUD operations.

```xml
<xsd:schema xmlns:xsd="http://www.w3.org/2001/XMLSchema"
  targetNamespace="http://actioncon.com/schema/gameinfo"
  xmlns="http://actioncon.com/schema/gameinfo"
  elementFormDefault="qualified">
  <xsd:element name="games" type="GamesType"/>
  <xsd:complexType name="GamesType">
    <xsd:sequence>
      <xsd:element name="game" type="GameType"
        maxOccurs="unbounded"/>
    </xsd:sequence>
  </xsd:complexType>
  <xsd:complexType name="GameType">
    <xsd:sequence>
      <xsd:element name="productID" type="ProductIDType"/>
      <xsd:element name="gtin" type="GTINType"/>
      <xsd:element name="title" type="TitleType"/>
      <xsd:element name="desc" type="xsd:string"/>
      <xsd:element name="esrbRating" type="ESRBRatingType"/>
      <xsd:element name="msrPrice" type="PriceType"/>
      <xsd:element name="numberOfPlayers"
        type="NumberOfPlayersRangeType"/>
    </xsd:sequence>
  </xsd:complexType>
  <xsd:complexType name="TitleType">
    <xsd:simpleContent>
      <xsd:extension base="xsd:string">
        <xsd:attribute name="language" type="xsd:language"/>
      </xsd:extension>
    </xsd:simpleContent>
  </xsd:complexType>
  <xsd:complexType name="NumberOfPlayersRangeType">
    <xsd:sequence>
      <xsd:element name="minimum" type="xsd:short"/>
      <xsd:element name="maximum" type="xsd:short"
        minOccurs="0"/>
    </xsd:sequence>
```

```
      </xsd:complexType>
      <xsd:simpleType name="ProductIDType">
        <xsd:restriction base="xsd:string">
          <xsd:pattern value="[A-Z]{2}[0-9]{4}"/>
        </xsd:restriction>
      </xsd:simpleType>
      <xsd:simpleType name="GTINType">
        <xsd:restriction base="xsd:string">
          <xsd:length value="13"/>
        </xsd:restriction>
      </xsd:simpleType>
      <xsd:simpleType name="ESRBRatingType">
        <xsd:restriction base="xsd:string">
          <xsd:enumeration value="EC"/>
          <xsd:enumeration value="E"/>
          <xsd:enumeration value="E10+"/>
          <xsd:enumeration value="T"/>
          <xsd:enumeration value="M"/>
          <xsd:enumeration value="AO"/>
          <xsd:enumeration value="RP"/>
        </xsd:restriction>
      </xsd:simpleType>
      <xsd:simpleType name="PriceType">
        <xsd:restriction base="xsd:decimal">
          <xsd:totalDigits value="8"/>
          <xsd:fractionDigits value="2"/>
        </xsd:restriction>
      </xsd:simpleType>
</xsd:schema>
```

Example 12.23
The XML schema used to represent a complete Game document.

Acknowledgement Message

In the typical Request-Response MEP used by entity service operations, the delivery of a business document via a request message to or from the service is commonly followed by an acknowledgement response message that communicates whether the request message was successfully received and processed.

The actual structure of acknowledgement messages can vary, but often they are comprised of a sole code value that is represented by a simple type, as follows:

```
<xsd:schema xmlns:xsd="http://www.w3.org/2001/XMLSchema"
  targetNamespace="..." elementFormDefault="qualified">
  <xsd:element name="acknowledgement" type="xsd:string"/>
</xsd:schema>
```

Example 12.24
A simple acknowledgement message structure based on the `xsd:string` simple type.

Of course, more complex acknowledgement message structures can be designed, especially if there are custom contract design standards that require the inclusion of certain core elements.

> **NOTE**
>
> The acknowledgement messages discussed in these sections are custom-developed messages that are delivered by the Web service, usually via a request or output message that is part of the overall operation MEP. This is different from the kinds of acknowledgements that are issued on a transport level when using reliable messaging frameworks, such as those based on the WS-ReliableMessaging standard. To learn more about WS-ReliableMessaging, visit SOAspecs.com or read *Service-Oriented Architecture: Concepts, Technology, and Design.*

> **NOTE**
>
> The upcoming sections address different styles of operation message designs, three of which (Add, Update, Delete) will generally introduce issues around "transactionality" when the functionality they represent is incorporated into a service-oriented solution or composition architecture. Transaction-related implications are not discussed in this book due to its focus on Web service contract design only.

Add Operation Messages

Add operations commonly receive new business document instances from consumers and then create the corresponding records in databases and wherever else they need to exist in the underlying service implementation environment. These operations are typically labeled with the verb "Add," although "Create" and "Insert" are also used.

The typical processing sequence for this operation type is something like this:

1. Receive and validate new business document (Input Message).

2. Convert document into one or more native or proprietary formats and data models.

3. Insert records into one or more repositories.

4. Respond with a confirmation message (Output Message) or an error message (Fault Message).

Table 12.1 shows the common granularity levels of message definitions that are part of an Add operation.

Operation Message	Data Granularity	Constraint Granularity
Input Message	Coarse	Fine-Medium
Output Message	Fine	Varies

Table 12.1
Typical characteristics of Add operation messages.

Overall, an Add operation will have a coarse level of capability granularity due to the fact that it is usually required to deal with the processing of new and whole business documents.

The input message will often resemble the document in Example 12.22. The volume of information in the message gives it a coarse level of data granularity, whereas the amount of detailed validation logic typically applied can result in fine-grained constraint granularity. Often steps are taken (such as applying the Validation Abstraction and Rules Centralization design patterns) to reduce constraint granularity in order to prolong the lifespan of the type.

Furthermore, if supported by the underlying technology architecture (or, in the case of inter-organization exchange, if mutually supported by partner platforms), several of the techniques just covered in the *Message Flexibility and Constraint Granularity* section can be applied to reduce the fragility of the contract and make it less susceptible to change. This allows a business document to evolve over time (to an extent) while preserving the contract and postponing the need to introduce new versions.

> **NOTE**
>
> The chapters in Part IV of this book further explore the versioning and governance issues of contracts and messages.

The output message will generally be a positive or negative acknowledgement based on a type similar to what was shown in Example 12.24 in the *Acknowledgement Message* section.

Get Operation Messages

The most common function performed by a Get operation is reporting. This type of operation simply receives query criteria and then returns the results.

Here's a typical processing sequence:

1. Receive and validate query criteria (Input Message).

2. Convert query parameters into actual query syntax required to search for and retrieve data from repositories.

3. Compile query results into required report format.

4. Respond with report message (Output Message) or an error message (Fault Message).

Here's a look at the typical granularity levels for Get operation messages.

Operation Message	Data Granularity	Constraint Granularity
Input Message	Fine	Medium-to-Fine
Output Message	Fine-to-Coarse	Varies

Table 12.2
Typical characteristics of Get operation messages.

Because the results can vary dramatically, so can the overall level of a Get operation's capability granularity. As a rule of thumb, the more specialized the operation, the more granular the capability. For example, a GetOrderStatus operation will tend to perform less processing than a full blown GetOrder operation. (But then again, in some cases it might not.)

As explained in the sequence steps earlier, the role of the input message is to provide the criteria for the data to be retrieved. Therefore, the data granularity is usually high (less data) and the constraint granularity can vary depending on how this criteria is represented. It may be organized into its own complex type or perhaps just a simple type (such as xsd:string).

When it comes to the output message structure of a Get operation, the data granularity can vary dramatically. Often the capability granularity of the operation is an indication that the output message's data granularity will be low (more data), but that too can vary.

For example, you may have an operation that needs to query three different databases and perform various calculation routines in order to return just a single value. Whereas another operation with a finer-grained level of capability granularity may issue a simple query statement that ends up returning reams of records.

Due to the flexible reporting nature of Get operations, the constraint granularity of output messages can vary, meaning that detailed validation logic is not always embedded into the contract depending on the importance of service-side validation.

Document-Centric Update Operation Messages

Of all the CRUD-style operations, the one with the most unpredictable granularity levels is Update. This is because there are a variety of record types that can be updated and a variety of ways for the consumer to communicate what it would like updated.

The two most common options are the document-centric and parameter-centric update. The typical processing steps of the former approach are displayed next (the latter approach is explained in the following *Parameter-Centric Update Operations Messages* section).

The following common sequence assumes that the Update operation is responsible for updating one or more possible fields belonging to a database record that represents a business document or some other significant information set.

1. Receive and validate an entire business document containing one or more changed values (Input Message).

2. Compare entire document with the entire database record to identify changed values.

3. Perform the database update(s).

4. Respond with an acknowledgement message (Output Message) or an error message (Fault Message).

Note that Step 2 can be more streamlined when a convention is introduced to indicate "dirty" (changed) values within a submitted document. In this case, the service logic would only need to look for these values, thereby avoiding an entire comparison routine.

For example, the `NumberOfPlayersRangeType` type from the business document schema in Example 12.23 could be outfitted with an optional attribute that acts as a flag to indicate that the value in this type has been changed:

```xsd
<xsd:complexType name="NumberOfPlayersRangeType">
  <xsd:sequence>
    <xsd:element name="minimum" type="NumberOfPlayersType"/>
    <xsd:element name="maximum" type="NumberOfPlayersType"
      minOccurs="0"/>
  </xsd:sequence>
  <xsd:attribute name="dirty" type="xsd:boolean"
    use="optional"/>
</xsd:complexType>
```

Example 12.25
An optional attribute added to the `NumberOfPlayersRangeType` construct.

The primary benefit of this approach is that consumers remain loosely coupled from the Web service, especially if the constraint granularity of the type representing the input message is relatively coarse (meaning less or looser constraints). However, the downside is that we're inserting a technical implementation detail into a schema that is supposed to be dedicated to representing a business document.

An alternative approach is to create a separate schema that represents dirty element values only, as follows:

```xsd
<xsd:complexType name="DirtyUpdateType">
  <xsd:sequence>
    <xsd:any minOccurs="0" maxOccurs="unbounded"
      processContents="lax"
      namespace="..."/>
  </xsd:sequence>
</xsd:complexType>
```

Example 12.26
The `xsd:any` element being used to allow for one or more updated element values to be provided.

Supplementary schema designs like this can provide functional flexibility in how the document can evolve and in the extent of updates a consumer can embed within the input message, while also preserving the integrity of the official, centralized business document schemas.

The obvious downside to document-centric Update operations is the fact that they consume more bandwidth than they need to. An entire document is transmitted even if just one small value has changed. Also, if Step 2 does need to be performed, then the extra processing required to carry out the comparison will result in additional performance impact.

Here's a look at the typical granularity levels associated with this operation type.

Operation Message	Data Granularity	Constraint Granularity
Input Message	Coarse	Varies
Output Message	Fine	Varies

Table 12.3
Typical characteristics of document-centric Update operation messages.

Clearly the data granularity of the input message will be coarse when the Update operation is document-centric because it will expect to contain an entire business document (unless, of course, the document itself is small). Constraint granularity of the input message can range depending on whether some form of logic is used to pinpoint changed values or whether the entire document does indeed need to be validated and compared.

Output messages are generally acknowledgements, much like those described in the *Acknowledgement Message* section.

Parameter-Centric Update Operation Messages

While parameter-centric Update operations are more reminiscent of RPC-style communication, they are still appropriate in some cases, especially when Update operations are specialized. For example, an UpdateStatus operation may only warrant an input message with a modestly scoped complex type representing a few related values.

Regardless of the scope or size of the underlying types, here are the common steps:

1. Receive and validate a set of changed values (Input Message).

2. Perform the database update(s) with the changed values.

3. Respond with a confirmation message (Output Message) or an error message (Fault Message).

In this scenario, the use of wildcards or optional XML Schema elements can help accommodate a flexible parameter-centric input message definition.

From a communications perspective, this approach is more efficient because less data needs to be transported to perform the update. However, this performance gain can easily be lost when a Web service needs to be called repeatedly to perform a series of granular updates that could have been performed as part of a single, document-centric update (as per the previous discussion of chatty services).

Here's a look at the common, associated granularity levels:

Operation Message	Data Granularity	Constraint Granularity
Input Message	Fine	Fine
Output Message	Varies	Fine

Table 12.4
Typical characteristics of parameter-centric Get operation messages.

The data and constraint granularity levels of an input message for a parameter-centric Update operation will tend to be fine because, after all, we are designing this operation to receive specific parameter data.

Unlike the coarse input message of the document-centric variation from the previous example, here is what the entire XML schema may look like for the input message of operation type:

```xml
<xsd:schema xmlns:xsd="http://www.w3.org/2001/XMLSchema"
  targetNamespace="http://actioncon.com/schema/gameinfo"
  xmlns="http://actioncon.com/schema/gameinfo"
  elementFormDefault="qualified">
<xsd:element name="numberOfPlayers"
```

```
      type="NumberOfPlayersRangeType"/>
  <xsd:complexType name="NumberOfPlayersRangeType">
  <xsd:sequence>
    <xsd:element name="minimum" type="NumberOfPlayersType"/>
    <xsd:element name="maximum" type="NumberOfPlayersType"
      minOccurs="0"/>
  </xsd:sequence>
  </xsd:complexType>
</xsd:schema>
```

Example 12.27

The complete schema for a parameter-centric input message in which only the value of the NumberOfPlayers element is updated.

As with the document-centric Update operation, output messages tend to be acknowledgements.

> **NOTE**
>
> The use of the Contract Denormalization design pattern can support the co-existence of both document-centric and parameter-centric Update operations within one service, even when these operations provide over-lapping functionality. As a result, you may not need to choose between these two kinds of Update operations.

Delete Operation Messages

Delete operations are generally straightforward and usually do not require excess data to be communicated, as explained in the following sequence:

1. Receive and validate an identifier for the record to be deleted (Input Message).

2. Delete the corresponding record from the database(s).

3. Respond with a confirmation message (Output Message) or an error message (Fault Message).

In some extreme cases, a full business document is still sent as part of the input message and the service is required to confirm that the database record(s) it is about to delete matches this document in its entirety. But that requirement aside, the volume of data exchanged for a Delete operation is usually minimal.

As indicated in the following table, the small amount of data and the necessity for accuracy leads to the tendency to design fine granularity levels.

Operation Message	Data Granularity	Constraint Granularity
Input Message	Fine	Fine
Output Message	Fine	Varies

Table 12.5
Typical characteristics of Delete operation messages.

Because the data exchange requirements for Delete operations are typically command-driven in that the input message identifies what is to be deleted, and the operation then acts upon this data, granularity levels tend to be fine all around. There is usually little data involved, but constraints are strict to ensure that whatever data is exchanged is thoroughly validated before records are actually deleted.

As with the Add and Update operations, the output message tends to be an acknowledgement.

Message Types for Task Services

We've been focusing on CRUD-style operations for entity and utility service message types because they are common and can leverage several proven XML Schema features. But what about the task service model? The fact is that message types for task services are less predictable and more specific to the business requirements and environmental factors associated with carrying out a given task.

Task services tend to be positioned as the controllers of service compositions, which means that they contain the majority of composition logic. The only type of operations they consistently require are those that kick off this logic. Therefore, the nature of the message types required depends on the nature of the process logic represented by the task service.

For example, one task service may require just a simple ID value to carry out the processing of a parent business process, while another may need one or more entire business documents.

SUMMARY OF KEY POINTS

- Most entity and wrapper utility Web services commonly require CRUD-style operations, each of which has distinct characteristics and granularity levels.

- CRUD-style operations are primarily concerned with processing messages comprised of business documents and acknowledgements.

- Agnostic design considerations tend to advocate loosening constraint granularity in support of increased reuse.

Chapter 13

Advanced XML Schema Part II: Reusability, Relational Design, and Industry Schemas

13.1 Reusable Schema Design

How we design an XML Schema-based data representation architecture influences many aspects of the Web services that will depend on these schemas. The more well-defined and flexible this architecture is, the greater the potential we have of achieving key strategic SOA goals, including those related to reuse, interoperability, and agility. However, a poorly designed architecture with limited flexibility can seriously inhibit the evolution of an inventory of services. In other words, bad schema architecture can jeopardize an entire SOA initiative.

One of the fundamental influences of a data architecture in support of SOA originates from the Schema Centralization pattern, which essentially requires that schema types representing primary business documents be centralized and thereby established as official data models that should not be copied or otherwise redundantly defined. This, of course, pertains to entity-centric schemas based on business documents but can also affect other kinds of schemas as well.

To consistently apply Schema Centralization requires that we understand our options when it comes to determining how different types will be organized into different schema documents. Common data design concerns like normalization are combined with service design goals like reusability to form a distinct set of schema design considerations. In fact, reusability in schema design leads to a reduction of redundant schema content, which naturally results in normalization.

From a Web service contract perspective, the reusability of XML schemas relates to the definition of types that can be shared by multiple message definitions. The XML Schema language provides reuse features on several levels:

- Types can be reused by multiple elements within a schema.

- A schema can be broken down into smaller, modular schema documents that can be reused by other schemas.

- Entire schemas can be reused by multiple WSDL message definitions.

The first item in the list was covered in Chapter 6. Let's now explore the reuse of schema modules and entire schemas.

Reusing Schemas with the `xsd:include` Element

Depending on how you design your data architecture, you can have common sets of schemas where each set belongs to a specific business context. An example of a business context might be a broad business area, like accounting or claims. When grouping schemas in this manner, it is not uncommon for the business context to be associated with a namespace and for each group of related schemas to use that same namespace as their target namespace.

Even though the schemas are related by their business context (and namespace), they still exist in physically separate files. In this type of environment, it is not unusual to find common types that are shared by some or all schemas. To avoid redundant schema content, these types can therefore be isolated into their own schema document and can then be shared across multiple other schemas using the `xsd:include` element:

```
<xsd:include schemaLocation=
   "http://actioncon.com/schema/purchasingCommon.xsd"/>
```

Example 13.1

The `xsd:include` statement with a `schemaLocation` attribute pointing to the schema document to be included.

The `xsd:include` element is added to any schema document that needs to pull in types that reside within a separate schema document that has the same target namespace as the including document.

It provides a `schemaLocation` attribute that can be used to identify the physical location of the schema to include. The value of this attribute might be a full URL or a relative reference to a document on a file system or the Web. The location must point to a valid XML schema document whose root is `xsd:schema`.

A schema can contain multiple `xsd:include` elements, all of which must appear at the beginning of an `xsd:schema` construct, as follows:

```
<xsd:schema xmlns:xsd="http://www.w3.org/2001/XMLSchema"
   targetNamespace="http://actioncon.com/schema/purchasing"
   xmlns="http://actioncon.com/schema/purchasing"
   elementFormDefault="qualified">
   <xsd:include schemaLocation=
      "http://actioncon.com/schema/purchasingCommon.xsd"/>
```

```
   . . .
</xsd:schema>
```

Example 13.2
The `xsd:include` element positioned as the child element of the `xsd:schema` element.

Note in the previous example that the `xsd:schema` element establishes a target namespace value of:

```
http://actioncon.com/schema/purchasing
```

For the include statement to work, the purchasingCommon.xsd schema document must be using the same target namespace value. We can also guess that from its name, this included schema contains common types that apply to a business context associated with purchasing. It is likely, therefore, that this schema would not be used on its own, but would only ever serve as a *schema module* that is included into other schema documents.

CASE STUDY EXAMPLE

After learning about the include functionality provided by XML Schema, Steve reassesses his original Purchase Order schema (as displayed in its entirety back in Chapter 6). After some deep analysis, he realizes that this schema really does contain a number of types that are not specific to purchase order documents. If he continues to build all of his business document schemas in this manner, he will end up with a great deal of redundancy.

To help identify the best candidates for reuse, he digs up the Invoice schema that was created some time ago. Both Purchase Order and Invoice schemas have the same target namespace value because they were both classified as belonging to the purchasing business context.

After a side-by-side comparison, he pinpoints the following types as being common to both documents:

- `PartyType`
- `AddressType`
- `LineItemsType`

- `ProductIDType`

- `PriceType`

Following this discovery, he extracts the code for these types and places it into the following new Purchasing Common schema:

```
<xsd:schema xmlns:xsd="http://www.w3.org/2001/XMLSchema"
  targetNamespace="http://actioncon.com/schema/purchasing"
  xmlns="http://actioncon.com/schema/purchasing"
  elementFormDefault="qualified">
  <xsd:complexType name="PartyType">
    <xsd:sequence>
      <xsd:element name="id" type="xsd:int"/>
      <xsd:element name="partyName" type="xsd:string"
        minOccurs="0"/>
      <xsd:element name="contactName" type="xsd:string"
        minOccurs="0"/>
      <xsd:element name="phone" type="xsd:string"
        minOccurs="0"/>
      <xsd:element name="address" type="AddressType"/>
    </xsd:sequence>
  </xsd:complexType>
  <xsd:complexType name="AddressType">
    <xsd:sequence>
      <xsd:element name="line1" type="xsd:string"/>
      <xsd:element name="line2" type="xsd:string"
        minOccurs="0"/>
      <xsd:element name="city" type="xsd:string"/>
      <xsd:element name="state" type="xsd:string"/>
      <xsd:element name="postalCode" type="xsd:string"/>
      <xsd:element name="country" type="xsd:string"/>
    </xsd:sequence>
  </xsd:complexType>
  <xsd:complexType name="LineItemsType">
    <xsd:sequence>
      <xsd:element name="lineItem" type="LineItemType"
        maxOccurs="unbounded"/>
    </xsd:sequence>
  </xsd:complexType>
  <xsd:complexType name="LineItemType">
    <xsd:sequence>
      <xsd:element name="productID" type="ProductIDType"/>
      <xsd:element name="productName" type="xsd:string"/>
      <xsd:element name="quantity" type="xsd:int"/>
```

```
      <xsd:element name="price" type="PriceType"/>
    </xsd:sequence>
  </xsd:complexType>
  <xsd:simpleType name="ProductIDType">
    <xsd:restriction base="xsd:string">
      <xsd:pattern value="[A-Z]{2}[0-9]{4}"/>
    </xsd:restriction>
  </xsd:simpleType>
  <xsd:simpleType name="PriceType">
    <xsd:restriction base="xsd:decimal">
      <xsd:totalDigits value="8"/>
      <xsd:fractionDigits value="2"/>
    </xsd:restriction>
  </xsd:simpleType>
</xsd:schema>
```

Example 13.3

The new Purchasing Common schema with several common types that can be reused by other schemas.

Figure 13.1 provides an overview of how the new Purchasing Common schema relates to the Purchase Order and Invoice schema documents.

Figure 13.1

Both the Purchase Order schema (purchaseOrder.xsd) and the Invoice schema (invoice.xsd) include the contents of the Purchasing Common schema (purchasingCommon.xsd).
All schemas have the same target namespace, which indicates they belong to a common business context.

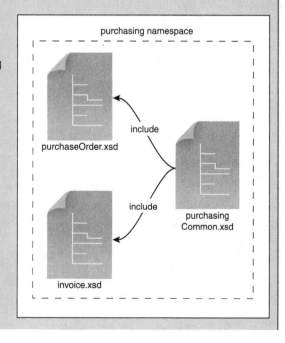

As shown next in Figure 13.2, the `PartyType` and `LineItemsType` elements are directly reused across the two message types represented by the Purchase Order and Invoice schemas. The other types listed previously are indirectly reused as they are used locally by the `PartyType` and `LineItemType` types.

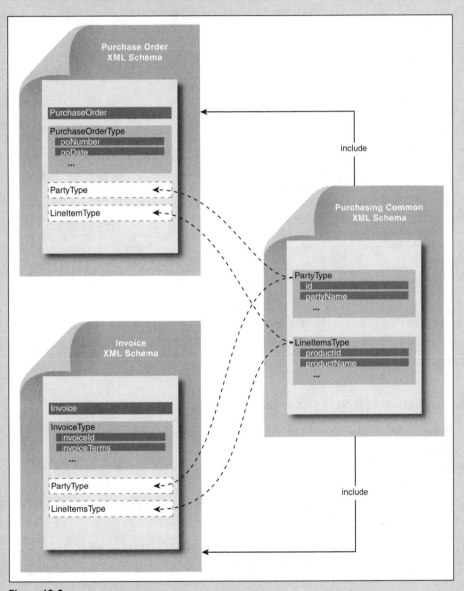

Figure 13.2

The Purchase Order and Invoice schemas sharing types from the Purchasing Common schema.

Here's the revised Purchase Order schema that now reuses types from the Purchasing
Common schema via the `xsd:include` element:

```
<xsd:schema xmlns:xsd="http://www.w3.org/2001/XMLSchema"
  targetNamespace="http://actioncon.com/schema/purchasing"
  xmlns="http://actioncon.com/schema/purchasing"
  elementFormDefault="qualified">
  <xsd:include schemaLocation=
    "http://actioncon.com/schema/purchasingCommon.xsd"/>
  <xsd:element name="purchaseOrder" type="PurchaseOrderType"/>
  <xsd:complexType name="PurchaseOrderType">
    <xsd:sequence>
      <xsd:element name="poNumber" type="xsd:int"/>
      <xsd:element name="poDate" type="xsd:date"/>
      <xsd:element name="billToParty" type="PartyType"/>
      <xsd:element name="shipToParty" type="PartyType"/>
      <xsd:element name="lineItems" type="LineItemsType"/>
    </xsd:sequence>
    <xsd:attribute name="version" type="xsd:decimal"/>
  </xsd:complexType>
</xsd:schema>
```

Example 13.4
The Purchase Order schema with an `xsd:include` statement that points to the Purchasing schema.

Note that in this example, because the included types are in the same namespace, and
that namespace is declared as the default in the schema, no prefix is required when
referencing them.

Reusing Schemas with the `xsd:import` Element

In Chapter 7 we briefly explained how a WSDL document can pull in types from a separate schema document by placing the `xsd:import` statement into its `types` construct.
If you take a closer look at the example in that chapter, you'll notice that the `xsd:import`
element is, in fact, wrapped within an `xsd:schema` construct. It's not as much about
importing types into a WSDL definition as it is importing types into a schema embedded within the WSDL document.

So why couldn't we just use the `xsd:include` element for this purpose? The answer has
to do with namespaces. As we just explained, `xsd:include` requires that the included

schema have the same target namespace value as the schema that contains the `xsd:include` statement.

With `xsd:import`, however, we don't have this limitation. This element is used specifically to import schemas that reside in a foreign namespace (which means they have a different target namespace value than the schema document that's doing the importing).

Let's first revisit the syntax we originally established in Chapter 7:

```
<xsd:import namespace="http://actioncon.com/schema/common"
  schemaLocation="http://actioncon.com/schema/common.xsd"/>
```

The `xsd:import` element has two attributes.

- `schemaLocation` – As with the `xsd:include` element, this optional attribute indicates the physical location of the schema document file being imported.

- `namespace` – The target namespace of the schema document being imported.

Another common requirement that the `xsd:import` element has with `xsd:include` is that it must also be located at the beginning of the `xsd:schema` construct.

> **NOTE**
>
> The `xsd:import` element provided by the XML Schema language should not be confused with the WSDL `import` element, which has similar syntax but is used to import one WSDL document into another WSDL document. The WSDL `import` element is described in Chapter 14.

Common Type Libraries

Before we can demonstrate how `xsd:import` works, we first need to establish a schema that we can import.

A proven use case for this feature is creating libraries of low-level "utility" types that can be used across different business contexts (by different kinds of business document schemas with different namespaces).

> **NOTE**
>
> The content of these schemas is often labeled as "common components" or "core components" because it contains both type and element declarations. To avoid confusion with component-based programs often used by Web services, we'll be referring to them as "common types" in this section (or "common elements" where appropriate).

Here are some good candidates for common types:

- identifiers (for example, product identifiers, customer identifiers, especially if they are made up of multiple parts)

- code lists such as departments, product types, currencies, natural languages

- measurement (i.e., an amount with a unit of measure)

- price (a price with an associated currency)

- personal information such as name, contact information and mailing address

These are the kinds of data structures that tend to be rewritten over and over again if there is no plan in place to centralize them in support of reuse. Having one definition for these low-level types can save a lot of time in developing and maintaining not only the schema, but the code that processes and/or generates the messages.

CASE STUDY EXAMPLE

After finishing his work on the Purchase Common schema, Steve realizes he hasn't yet taken into account the Game schema designed for the Game service. Upon reviewing this schema he notices more opportunities for reuse. Namely, the `PriceType`, `ProductIDType`, and `AddressType` types are duplicated across both the Game schema and the Purchase Common schema.

This frustrates Steve because he just finished moving those types into the Purchasing Common schema. However, now it appears as though that doesn't make sense anymore. The Game schema uses a different target namespace because it does not reside in the purchasing business context. Therefore, it cannot include these reusable types from the Purchasing Common schema using the `xsd:include` statement.

Steve now turns his attention toward the `xsd:import` element. He understands that he could force the reuse of these three types by removing them from the Game schema and then pulling them in via an `xsd:import` statement that references the Purchasing Common schema. But, that just doesn't seem right because the reusable types in the Purchasing Common schema are intended for purchasing-related schemas only.

He therefore thinks that these types are sufficiently generic that they should not be limited to any one business context. Instead, Steve decides to create the following new common library schema:

```
<xsd:schema xmlns:xsd="http://www.w3.org/2001/XMLSchema"
  targetNamespace="http://actioncon.com/schema/common"
  xmlns="http://actioncon.com/schema/common"
  elementFormDefault="qualified">
  <xsd:simpleType name="ProductIDType">
    <xsd:restriction base="xsd:string">
      <xsd:pattern value="[A-Z]{2}[0-9]{4}"/>
    </xsd:restriction>
  </xsd:simpleType>
  <xsd:simpleType name="PriceType">
    <xsd:restriction base="xsd:decimal">
      <xsd:totalDigits value="8"/>
      <xsd:fractionDigits value="2"/>
    </xsd:restriction>
  </xsd:simpleType>
  <xsd:complexType name="AddressType">
    <xsd:sequence>
      <xsd:element name="line1" type="xsd:string"/>
      <xsd:element name="line2" type="xsd:string"
        minOccurs="0"/>
      <xsd:element name="city" type="xsd:string"/>
      <xsd:element name="state" type="xsd:string"/>
      <xsd:element name="postalCode" type="xsd:string"/>
      <xsd:element name="country" type="xsd:string"/>
    </xsd:sequence>
  </xsd:complexType>
</xsd:schema>
```

Example 13.5
A common schema comprised of a library of common, reusable types.

Note how in this example the schema establishes a new target namespace that is different from either the Game service or the Purchase Order service. It is often advisable to put these common types in a separate namespace in order to further emphasize their generic and reusable nature. This is particularly true if you are designing a complex data architecture that will need to support many messages.

CASE STUDY EXAMPLE

Steve now needs to make the previously established common types available to the Game and Purchase Order schemas. He begins by mapping out the new inter-schema relationships, as shown in Figure 13.3.

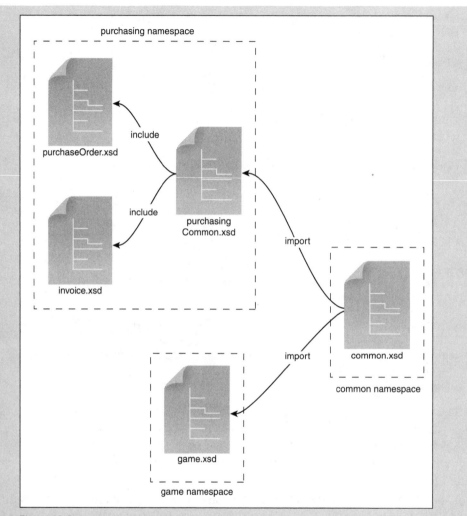

Figure 13.3
The Purchase Order and Game schemas sharing types from the new Common schema.

He immediately realizes that although the Game schema will be able to directly import the Common schema, it's a different scenario with the Purchase Order schema. The three types he extracted from the original Purchasing Common schema were not being reused directly by the Purchase Order schema; they were being used by the `PartyType` and `LineItemsType` elements within the Purchasing Common schema, and it was these two types that were directly referenced in the Purchase Order schema.

As a result, Steve's new Common schema needs to be imported by the Game schema and the Purchasing Common schema, while the Purchasing Common schema continues to be included by the Purchase Order and Invoice schemas.

A closer look at the imported subset of Figure 13.3 is displayed in Figure 13.4.

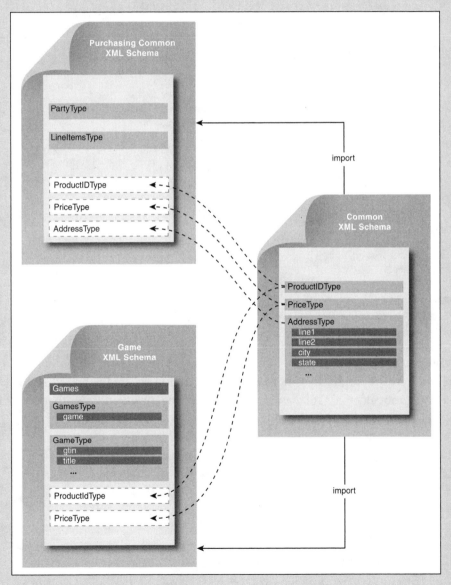

Figure 13.4
The Purchasing Common and Game schemas sharing types from the new Common schema.

Because the Purchase Order schema does not need to directly reference types in the Common schema, Steve does not need to add an xsd:import statement. Only the original xsd:include element is required with reference to the Purchasing Common schema defined earlier:

```
<xsd:schema xmlns:xsd="http://www.w3.org/2001/XMLSchema"
  xmlns="http://actioncon.com/schema/purchasing"

targetNamespace="http://actioncon.com/schema/purchasing"
  elementFormDefault="qualified">
  <xsd:include schemaLocation=
    "http://actioncon.com/schema/purchasingCommon.xsd"/>
  <xsd:element name="purchaseOrder" type="PurchaseOrderType"/>
  <xsd:complexType name="PurchaseOrderType">
    <xsd:sequence>
      <xsd:element name="poNumber" type="xsd:int"/>
      <xsd:element name="poDate" type="xsd:date"/>
      <xsd:element name="billToParty" type="PartyType"/>
      <xsd:element name="shipToParty" type="PartyType"/>
      <xsd:element name="lineItems" type="LineItemsType"/>
    </xsd:sequence>
    <xsd:attribute name="version" type="xsd:decimal"/>
  </xsd:complexType>
</xsd:schema>
```

Example 13.6
The Purchase Order schema reusing three types from the Purchasing Common schema.

Let's now have a look at a sample message instance of a purchase order document where the common: prefix that represents the Common schema is added to the purchaseOrder root element. You can identify each of the imported types that originated from the Common schema by locating the common: prefixes.

```
<purchaseOrder version="1.0"
  xmlns="http://actioncon.com/schema/purchasing"
  xmlns:common="http://actioncon.com/schema/common">
  <poNumber>12345</poNumber>
  <poDate>2006-10-15</poDate>
  <billToParty>
    <id>444403</id>
    <partyName>Neighborhood Game Stores, Inc.</partyName>
    <contactName>Steve Smith</contactName>
```

```
    <phone>231-555-1122</phone>
    <address>
      <common:line1>123 Main St.</common:line1>
      <common:line2>Suite 300</common:line2>
      <common:city>Cleveland</common:city>
      <common:state>OH</common:state>
      <common:postalCode>37311</common:postalCode>
      <common:country>USA</common:country>
    </address>
  </billToParty>
  ...
</purchaseOrder>
```

Example 13.7

A message instance containing elements from the common schema. Because these elements originated from a different namespace, they need to be prefixed with common:.

Note that the address element does not require a common: prefix because it was declared in the Purchasing Common schema (not in the Common schema), which has the same target namespace as the Purchase Order schema. The same is true of the productID and price elements.

Finally, let's check out the Invoice schema we've been hearing about. It too includes the Purchasing Common schema. Even though Invoice message has a slightly different structure from the Purchase Order message, it reuses a lot of the same common types:

```
<xsd:schema xmlns:xsd="http://www.w3.org/2001/XMLSchema"
  targetNamespace="http://actioncon.com/schema/purchasing"
  xmlns="http://actioncon.com/schema/purchasing"
  xmlns:common="http://actioncon.com/schema/common"
  elementFormDefault="qualified">
  <xsd:include schemaLocation="
    http://actioncon.com/schema/purchasingCommon.xsd"/>
  <xsd:import
    namespace="http://actioncon.com/schema/common"
    schemaLocation="http://actioncon.com/schema/common.xsd"/>
  <xsd:element name="invoice" type="InvoiceType"/>
  <xsd:complexType name="InvoiceType">
    <xsd:sequence>
      <xsd:element name="invoiceNumber" type="xsd:int"/>
      <xsd:element name="invoiceDate" type="xsd:date"/>
      <xsd:element name="totalAmount"
        type="common:PriceType"/>
      <xsd:element name="poNumber" type="xsd:int"/>
```

```
        <xsd:element name="poDate" type="xsd:date"/>
        <xsd:element name="billToParty" type="PartyType"/>
        <xsd:element name="lineItems" type="LineItemsType"/>
      </xsd:sequence>
      <xsd:attribute name="version" type="xsd:decimal"/>
    </xsd:complexType>
</xsd:schema>
```

Example 13.8

The Invoice schema including and then reusing the types from the Purchasing schema.

However, upon closer examination, we can see that the Invoice schema *does* need to import the Common schema. This is because it contains a `totalAmount` element with a type set to `common:PriceType`, which represents one of the types defined in the Common schema.

It's not enough that the Invoice schema includes the Purchasing Common schema that itself imports the types from the Common schema. Because the Invoice schema refers to a type from the Common schema by name, it must also explicitly import that schema as well.

This means that we need to update Figure 13.3 with a new import relationship, as shown in the red line in Figure 13.5.

NOTE

For descriptions on how to import XML schemas into WSDL documents, see Chapter 14.

SUMMARY OF KEY POINTS

- Schema Centralization is a fundamental part of establishing an effective schema architecture in support of Web services.

- Reuse in XML Schema can be achieved at several levels. Named types can be reused by many elements, a schema document can be reused in other schema documents, and schema documents can be reused in WSDL documents.

- In XML Schema, `xsd:import` is used to combine schema documents with different target namespaces, while `xsd:include` is used to combine documents with the same target namespace.

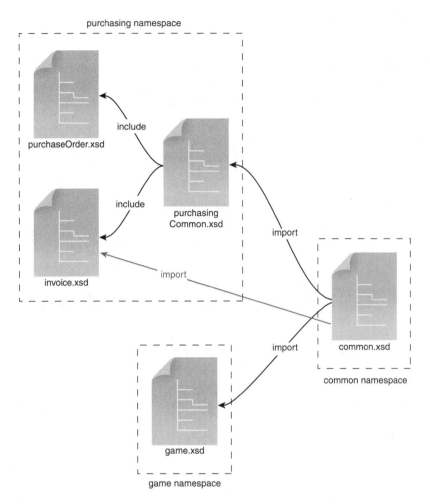

Figure 13.5
The Invoice schema needs to include the Purchasing Common schema and import the Common schema.

13.2 Representing Relationships in XML Schemas

In most enterprises, XML is the standard for runtime data exchange, but relational data-bases have remained the standard for the persistent storage of data. Modern database products do support native XML storage as well, but for the most part, the marriage of XML and relational data representation formats is something architects and data ana-lysts need to address.

For example, when you model a customer entity, you can decide on your definition of a customer, its unique identifier, and all of its attributes. You can also normalize all the relationships between customers and other entities; for example, a customer can have one to many addresses, and can be associated with zero to many purchases.

Much of the structured data stored in relational databases is modeled using entity relationships. When creating an entity relationship model, great care is usually taken to define what an entity is as opposed to how it is used in any particular context. An XML message, on the other hand, generally represents a particular usage or view of the data. Rather than being the definitive source for all information about an entity, it contains only the subset that is useful for the operation for which the message was defined.

For example, when modeling a purchase order entity, you may not want to include all of the customer information; perhaps you just need an identifier, name, and shipping address. For a line item in the purchase order, you may need to know a product's identifier, name, and price, but not its other attributes such as a long description or list of features.

NOTE

Another interesting aspect of relational schema design is that although XML is not inherently relational, one of the most common service models in use is in fact, very relational in nature. The entity service bases its functional context on relational, business-centric information sets, like customer, invoice, or claim. And the source of these entities is usually the same logical data model or entity relationship model created in support of database design.

Another means by which XML and relational data differ is in how they are structured. In a relational model there is no single starting point; entities exist and can be accessed independently of each other. In an XML hierarchy, one element must be at the root of the structure, and there is an implied relationship between all of the elements within that hierarchy.

Ideally, you will have a standardized data model that you can draw on for your XML message schemas. Just as in database design, in Web service message design there are benefits to using the same element names, types and relationships for the same data where possible, as advocated by the Canonical Schema pattern. For example, if your business entity model says that an address entity has the properties line1, line2, city, state, and zip, you can use the same definitions and names (or the relevant subset of them) for the elements in your message schemas.

It is important to point out that a business entity model represents a *logical* data model. You must avoid coupling your message schemas to any one physical database schema model. This inevitably leads to undesirable contract-to-implementation coupling that can inhibit the evolution of your Web service contract (as explained in the description of the Service Loose Coupling principle in Chapter 3).

One-to-Many Relationships

Most relationships in XML are simply modeled as parent-child structures, also known as *containment* relationships. For example, suppose each customer only has one address. In a relational model, there might be two separate tables: one for customer and one for address. This would be a good design if other entities (such as suppliers) have addresses also. In XML, this would simply be modeled as a parent-child relationship, where the `customer` element would contain a single `address` element.

A similar approach works if a customer can have more than one address. In a relational model, there would be a one-to-many relationship between the customer and the address. In XML, the `customer` element can simply contain more than one occurrence of the `address` element.

Many-to-Many Relationships

Many-to-many relationships are harder to represent directly with XML. In some cases, because an XML message represents a temporary view of the data, a one-to-many containment relationship is sufficient even if a many-to-many relationship exists in the real world. For example, a purchase order might represent orders for more than one product, and any one product can be ordered using many purchase orders, but for the purposes of the message you only need to follow the relationship in one direction: include all the products for this purchase order.

Sometimes there is a many-to-many relationship that *does* need to be fully represented in a message. Suppose that as part of the Game service, we want to include information about the consoles on which each game can run. A game may be able to run on more than one console version, and a console can run more than one game.

One way to represent this relationship is to repeat all the information about the console under each game, as shown in this next example. Because both games can run on the ActionCon X3T console, the properties (`ID`, `gtin`, and `title`) of that console are repeated more than once.

```
<games>
  <game>
    <productID>AY2344</productID>
    <gtin>1234567890123</gtin>
    <title>Service Blaster 2000</title>
    ...
    <consoles>
      <console>
        <productID>CC1567</productID>
        <gtin>1234567890456</gtin>
        <title>ActionCon X3T</title>
      </console>
      <console>
        <productID>CC1568</productID>
        <gtin>1234567890498</gtin>
        <title>ActionCon X3T Turbo</title>
      </console>
    </consoles>
  </game>
  <game>
    <productID>BB1764</productID>
    <gtin>1234567890124</gtin>
    <title>Interactive Service Magic</title>
    ...
    <consoles>
      <console>
        <productID>CC1567</productID>
        <gtin>1234567890456</gtin>
        <title>ActionCon X3T</title>
      </console>
      <console>
        <productID>CC1573</productID>
        <gtin>1234567890455</gtin>
        <title>ActionCon X3B</title>
      </console>
    </consoles>
  </game>
</games>
```

Example 13.9
A message instance that uses repeating constructs to represent many-to-many relationships.

This is a perfectly acceptable solution for low volumes of data with low repetition. However, if there were a lot of other information in the message about each console, and a console definition might be repeated dozens of times, this message could quickly become unnecessarily large.

The `xsd:key` and `xsd:keyref` Elements

An alternative to the previous approach is to keep information about games and consoles separate and use unique identifiers to specify the relationships. This approach is similar to using foreign keys in a database, as follows:

```
<gameinfo>
  <games>
    <game>
      <productID>AY2344</productID>
      <gtin>123456780123</gtin>
      <title>Service Blaster 2000</title>
      ...
      <consoleRefs>
        <consoleRef productID="CC1567"/>
        <consoleRef productID="CC1568"/>
      </consoleRefs>
    </game>
    <game>
      <productID>BB1764</productID>
      <gtin>1234567890124</gtin>
      <title>Interactive Service Magic</title>
      ...
      <consoleRefs>
        <consoleRef productID="CC1567"/>
        <consoleRef productID="CC1573"/>
      </consoleRefs>
    </game>
  </games>
  <consoles>
    <console>
      <productID>CC1567</productID>
      <gtin>1234567890456</gtin>
      <title>ActionCon X3T</title>
    </console>
    <console>
      <productID>CC1568</productID>
      <gtin>1234567890498</gtin>
      <title>ActionCon X3T Turbo</title>
    </console>
    <console>
      <productID>CC1573</productID>
      <gtin>1234567890455</gtin>
      <title>ActionCon X3B</title>
    </console>
```

```
    </consoles>
  </gameinfo>
```

Example 13.10
This message instance uses identifiers to emulate a many-to-many relationship between games and consoles.

In this case, the relationship from game to console is represented (in the `consoleRef` element) but not the relationship back from console to game. That's because only the game-to-console relationship is relevant to the Game service.

In your schema, you can use identity constraints to validate the relationship. The `xsd:key` and `xsd:keyref` elements are used for this purpose, as explained here:

- The `xsd:key` element defines the unique identifier of each console.

- Within it, `xsd:selector` identifies the element that needs to be unique (the console).

- Next, `xsd:field` specifies the element that contains the unique identifier (`productID`).

The `xsd:keyref` element is used to establish the foreign key relationship from the `consoleRef` element's `productID` attribute to the `console` element's `productID` child element. It uses a similar syntax to the `xsd:key` element, except that it also includes a `refer` attribute that indicates the key to which it refers.

Let's have a look at how all of this is organized into an element declaration:

```xml
<xsd:element name="gameinfo" type="GameInfoType">
  <xsd:key name="consoleIDKey">
    <xsd:selector xpath="consoles/console"/>
    <xsd:field xpath="productID"/>
  </xsd:key>
  <xsd:keyref name="consoleIDRef" refer="consoleIDKey">
    <xsd:selector xpath="games/game/consoleRefs/consoleRef"/>
    <xsd:field xpath="@productID"/>
  </xsd:keyref>
</xsd:element>
```

Example 13.11
An element with identity constraints established via the `xsd:key` and `xsd:keyref` elements.

> **NOTE**
>
> Those of you familiar with XPath probably noticed the use of XPath syntax in this example. A limited subset of XPath is allowed in the `xpath` attributes as a way to reference the elements and attributes of interest, relative to the `gameinfo` element. To learn more about XML, visit www.xmlenterprise.com.

Although the relationship can be expressed and validated using a schema, defining it in the schema will most likely not affect the class definitions generated by your tools. For example, for the `Game` class, it will not generate a `getConsole` method that will go out and get a related `Console` object. This makes it more difficult to write code to follow these relationships as compared to the containment relationships, where you *can* simply use a `getConsole` method.

Separate Relationship Element

Yet a third option is to use a separate relationship element that is outside the contents of either the game or the console, as shown here:

```
<gameinfo>
  <games>
  <game>
    <productID>AY2344</productID>
    <gtin>1234567890123</gtin>
    <title>Service Blaster 2000</title>
    ...
  </game>
  <game>
    <productID>BB1764</productID>
    <gtin>1234567890124</gtin>
    <title>Interactive Service Magic</title>
    ...
  </game>
  </games>
  <consoles>
    <console>
      <productID>CC1567</productID>
      <gtin>1234567890456</gtin>
      <title>ActionCon X3T</title>
    </console>
    <console>
      <productID>CC1568</productID>
```

```
        <gtin>1234567890498</gtin>
        <title>ActionCon X3T Turbo</title>
    </console>
    <console>
        <productID>CC1573</productID>
        <gtin>1234567890455</gtin>
        <title>ActionCon X3B</title>
    </console>
  </consoles>
  <game-consoles>
    <game-console>
        <gameRef productID="AY2344"/>
        <consoleRef productID="CC1567"/>
        <comment>requires memory upgrade</comment>
    </game-console>
    <game-console>
        <gameRef productID="AY2344"/>
        <consoleRef productID="CC1568"/>
    </game-console>
    <game-console>
        <gameRef productID="BB1764"/>
        <consoleRef productID="CC1567"/>
    </game-console>
    <game-console>
        <gameRef productID="BB1764"/>
        <consoleRef productID="CC1573"/>
    </game-console>
  </game-consoles>
</gameinfo>
```

Example 13.12

An instance of a message wherein reference ID values are used to associate `game` and `console` elements with `game-console` elements.

In this case, a `game-console` element is used for each relationship between a game and a console. This has the advantage of allowing you to represent the relationship in both directions in a compact way. It also provides a container for information about that relationship, such as the `comment` element shown in the first `game-console` element.

The disadvantage is that this is even more difficult to process using generated classes. It compounds the issues with the previous method by requiring yet a third unrelated element (`game-console`) that has to be retrieved.

SUMMARY OF KEY POINTS

- Compared to a relational data model, which defines the permanent representation of everything about an entity, an XML message is often a temporary view of that entity that contains only the information relevant to a particular operation.

- One-to-many relationships can be represented using containment (parent-child relationships). Many-to-many relationships can be represented using repetition, external elements referenced by identifiers, or decoupled elements with external elements aimed only to represent the relationship.

- The `xsd:key` and `xsd:keyref` elements can be used to enforce the integrity of relationships by emulating traditional relational concepts, such as primary and foreign keys.

13.3 Narrative Content

Narrative content represents human-readable text used, for example, to supplement business documents for presentation on Web pages. This type of content is generally far less structured and predictable than the data-centric message content we've been covering so far. A good example is the textual descriptions of the games that might be provided as part of the Game service.

In order to preserve the formatting that often needs to accompany narrative text, you may want to include HTML tags within the XML Schema declared elements, as shown with the `desc` element here:

```
<desc language="en">This is a <i>great</i> game</desc>
<desc language="en">This is a great game</desc>
<desc language="en"><b>This</b> is a <i>great</i> game</desc>
<desc language="en"><i>This</i> is <b>great</b> game</desc>
```

Example 13.13
A variety of legitimate values for the `desc` element. The highlighted text represents HTML formatting tags.

A mixed content complex type is used to describe an element like `desc` that can have both textual content as well as child elements. Mixed content types have syntax similar to their element-only counterparts, except that a `mixed` attribute set to "true" appears on the `xsd:complexType` element, indicating that textual content is allowed.

Mixed Content with a Repeating `xsd:choice` *Group*

NOTE
The `xsd:choice` element was explained in Chapter 12 in the *Content Model Groups* (xsd:choice, xsd:all, and xsd:sequence) section.

The type shown in Example 13.14 might be defined for the `desc` elements from the previous example. It allows the description to intermix text with optional `i` (italics) and `b` (bold) elements from the HTML language to format certain words or phrases.

```
<xsd:complexType name="DescType" mixed="true">
  <xsd:choice minOccurs="0" maxOccurs="unbounded">
    <xsd:element name="i" type="xsd:string"/>
    <xsd:element name="b" type="xsd:string"/>
  </xsd:choice>
  <xsd:attribute name="language" type="xsd:language"/>
</xsd:complexType>
```

Example 13.14
A complex type with mixed content.

In this case, `xsd:choice` is used instead of `xsd:sequence`. It may appear that it is allowing a choice between an `i` and a `b` element, until you look at the `minOccurs` and `maxOccurs` attributes of the `xsd:choice` element. The attributes allow the choice itself to be optional or repeating, so you can have any number of `i` or `b` elements (including zero, one, or both), in any order.

NOTE
XML Schema provides the built-in `xsd:language` type that can be used to indicate the natural language of text. It is usually applied to an attribute to describe the contents of an element, as per the previous example.

Tool Support for Narrative Content

Many code generation tools do not handle mixed content gracefully. Their unpredictable nature does not map easily onto existing programming models. Some tools would tend to keep track of all of the `i` and `b` elements, and the text, but not the order in which they appear. In these cases, a better approach is to use a completely generic type that uses a wildcard for its content model, such as the one shown here:

```
<xsd:complexType name="DescType" mixed="true">
  <xsd:sequence>
    <xsd:any minOccurs="0" maxOccurs="unbounded"
      processContents="lax" namespace="##other"/>
  </xsd:sequence>
</xsd:complexType>
```

Example 13.15
A complex type with mixed content and a wildcard. With this approach, some tools will give you an array of text and elements in the order they appear.

> **NOTE**
>
> Wildcard elements, such as `xsd:any`, are introduced at the beginning of Chapter 12 and more thoroughly covered in Chapter 22.

SUMMARY OF KEY POINTS

- Narrative content is best represented using mixed content types.

- When lack of tool support for mixed content is an issue, it is best to make the mixed content types as generic as possible.

13.4 Incorporating Industry Schemas

There are many pre-defined XML schemas that have been developed by standards bodies, industry groups, and even private corporations. The purpose of these schemas is usually to establish common XML-based data formats and data models for inter-organization data exchange. When partner organizations agree on the use of a common schema to send and receive business documents, they avoid having to introduce undesirable layers of transformation logic.

These standardized schema vocabularies might take the form of:

- generic software types (such as the UN/CEFACT core components specification)

- industry-specific vocabularies (such as XBRL for financial reporting)

- business document vocabularies (such as GS1, OAGIS, RosettaNet, and UBL)

Even if you don't need to exchange documents with external organizations, you might still want to consider reusing one of these industry schemas (or perhaps considering them as a starting point for your own custom schemas). If they are compatible with the types of business documents you are working with, then their use may save you a significant amount of development effort. Often, these schemas are also subjected to testing to ensure that tool support is also sufficient.

If you decide to adopt a standard schema exactly as it is defined, then it should be quite simple to incorporate it into your message designs. You can use the same `xsd:import` statement we described earlier in this chapter to import elements from the industry schema into your element structures, or even import the entire standard schema directly into your WSDL.

However, if the schema does not exactly meet your needs, then you will have to investigate adding new elements for information specific to your context, or you may want to actually further restrict elements from the standard schema vocabulary to better suit your constraint requirements.

The XML Schema language provides several features that can be used to extend or adapt a standardized schema vocabulary. Often it depends on how (and whether) the designers of the vocabulary intended for it to be extended. If a standard vocabulary does not have wildcards and does not define reusable types (like named types), it can limit the extent to which that schema can be customized. Some standards organizations provide users with guidelines for reusing and extending a vocabulary.

The most common approaches to working with industry schemas are to reuse specific industry schema types, add extensions or wildcards to industry schema types, or extend the industry schema itself with new types that intermingle custom elements with standard elements.

Let's discuss each approach individually.

Reusing Types

One possible scenario is that you are defining a new vocabulary that is very specific to your needs. You haven't found an industry standard XML vocabulary that will be useful without major revisions, so you decide to create your own. However, you want to use as many of the pre-defined building blocks from industry schemas as possible. This will help you to avoid having to reinvent types that have already been defined by a standards body, and will potentially increase the interoperability of your messages.

To achieve this, you can simply reference elements or types from the standard vocabulary in your own complex types, as shown here:

```
<xsd:schema xmlns:xsd="http://www.w3.org/2001/XMLSchema"
  xmlns="http://my-vocabulary.org"
  xmlns:std="http://standard.org"
  targetNamespace="http://my-vocabulary.org">
  <xsd:import namespace="http://standard.org"
    schemaLocation="http://standard.org/standard.xsd"/>
  <xsd:complexType name="MyNewType">
    <xsd:sequence>
      <xsd:element name="myVocabulary1" type="xsd:string"/>
      <xsd:element ref="std:standardVocabulary1"/>
      <xsd:element ref="std:standardVocabulary2"/>
      <xsd:element name="myVocabulary2" type="xsd:string"/>
    </xsd:sequence>
  </xsd:complexType>
  ...
</xsd:schema>
```

Example 13.16
A custom schema referring to elements from an industry schema (in another namespace).

As shown in this example, if an element is globally declared in the industry schema, you can use the `ref` attribute to refer to that element in one of your schema types.

If complex types are named (globally defined) in the industry schema, you can create your own new element and use the `type` attribute to refer to the named type. In either case, the value of the attribute will need to be prefixed to indicate that it's in the industry schema namespace, not your own.

CASE STUDY EXAMPLE

Steve at ActionCon is interested in adding more detail to the Game schema. He looks around for an industry standard electronic game vocabulary and comes across the GS1 business document vocabulary, which is a set of industry schemas used for electronic interchange.

GS1 has already defined a standard for electronic games with the help of experts in the entertainment and retail industries. ActionCon does not wish to adopt the entire set of GS1 schemas because they know that their partnership with MegaEuroMart will require them to use UBL (a competing standard) in the near future. However, Steve wants to take advantage of the several complex types that relate to electronic games, rather than invent new ones. To start with, he is interested in `ElectronicGamePlayer` `InformationType`, which describes the number and ages of the game players. It is defined in the ElectronicGamePlayerInformation.xsd schema shown here:

```
<xsd:schema version="2.2"
  xmlns:xsd="http://www.w3.org/2001/XMLSchema"
  xmlns:eg=
    "urn:ean.ucc:align:entertainment:electronic_games:2"
  attributeFormDefault="unqualified"
  elementFormDefault="unqualified"
  targetNamespace=
    "urn:ean.ucc:align:entertainment:electronic_games:2">
  <xsd:annotation>
    <xsd:documentation>
```

```
    </xsd:documentation>
  </xsd:annotation>
  <xsd:complexType name="ElectronicGamePlayerInformationType">
    <xsd:sequence>
      <xsd:element name="ageRangeDescription" minOccurs="0">
        <xsd:simpleType>
          <xsd:restriction base="xsd:string">
            <xsd:maxLength value="35"/>
            <xsd:minLength value="1"/>
          </xsd:restriction>
        </xsd:simpleType>
      </xsd:element>
      <xsd:element name="maximumNumberOfPlayers"
        type="xsd:integer" minOccurs="0"/>
      <xsd:element name="maximumPlayerAge"
        type="xsd:integer" minOccurs="0"/>
```

```
        <xsd:element name="minimumNumberOfPlayers"
          type="xsd:integer" minOccurs="0"/>
        <xsd:element name="minimumPlayerAge"
          type="xsd:integer" minOccurs="0"/>
    </xsd:sequence>
    </xsd:complexType>
</xsd:schema>
```

Example 13.17
The contents of the GS1 ElectronicGamePlayerInformation.xsd schema.

To incorporate these types into the ActionCon vocabulary, Steve simply imports the GS1 schema into the Game schema. He then refers to the `ElectronicGamePlayer InformationType` type by its qualified name, using a prefix mapped to the GS1 electronic games namespace:

```
<xsd:schema xmlns:xsd="http://www.w3.org/2001/XMLSchema"
  targetNamespace="http://actioncon.com/schema/gameinfo"
  xmlns="http://actioncon.com/schema/gameinfo"
  xmlns:common="http://actioncon.com/schema/common"
  xmlns:eg="urn:ean.ucc:align:entertainment:electronic_games:2"
  elementFormDefault="qualified">
  <xsd:import namespace=
    "urn:ean.ucc:align:entertainment:electronic_games:2"
    schemaLocation="ElectronicGamePlayerInformation.xsd"/>
  <xsd:import namespace="http://actioncon.com/schema/common"
    schemaLocation=
      "http://actioncon.com/schema/common.xsd"/>
  <xsd:complexType name="GameType">
    <xsd:sequence>
      <xsd:element name="productID"
        type="common:ProductIDType"/>
      <xsd:element name="gtin" type="GTINType"/>
      ...
      <xsd:element name="playerInformation"
        type="eg:ElectronicGamePlayerInformationType"/>
    </xsd:sequence>
  </xsd:complexType>
  ...
</xsd:schema>
```

Example 13.18
The `GameType` construct using a GS1 standard type.

Next is a valid XML message instance of the new schema:

```
<game:game xmlns:game="http://actioncon.com/gameinfo">
  <game:productID>AY2344</game:productID>
  <game:gtin>1234567890123</game:gtin>
  ...
  <game:playerInformation>
    <maximumNumberOfPlayers>2</maximumNumberOfPlayers>
    <maximumPlayerAge>15</maximumPlayerAge>
    <minimumNumberOfPlayers>1</minimumNumberOfPlayers>
    <minimumPlayerAge>10</minimumPlayerAge>
  </game:playerInformation>
</game:game>
```

Example 13.19
An instance of the Game type that uses GS1 elements.

One thing that may be surprising about this sample document is that the highlighted elements are not prefixed. That is because the GS1 schemas set the `elementForm Default` attribute to "unqualified," which means that locally declared elements are not associated with a namespace.

On the other hand, the remaining elements, such as `playerInformation`, are part of the `http://actioncon.com/gameinfo` namespace, and because the Game schema's `xsd:schema` element sets its `elementFormDefault` attribute to "qualified," the use of the `game:` prefix is required.

> **NOTE**
>
> More information about GS1 XML standards can be found at:
> http://www.gs1.org/productssolutions/ecom/xml/

Adding Wildcards

Some industry schemas are conveniently equipped with wildcards that act as extension points, allowing you to provide your own replacement elements that can be used to extend the base schema as you see fit.

To take advantage of these extension points, you can declare global elements that are used in place of the wildcards. For example, let's take a look at the Universal Business

Language (UBL), an OASIS standard for the exchange of business documents, such as orders, invoices, and bills of lading.

The standard provides UML models describing the structure of each message and the process in which it is used. It also defines a schema for each business document type.

In order to support custom extensions, the UBL vocabulary allows any business-document-level element to contain a UBLExtensions element as its first child. Example 13.20 shows a declaration for the UBLExtensions element (and its child element, UBLExtension).

```
<xsd:schema xmlns:xsd="http://www.w3.org/2001/XMLSchema"
  xmlns="urn:oasis:names:specification:
  ubl:schema:xs:CommonExtensionComponents-2"
  xmlns:cbc="urn:oasis:names:specification:
  ubl:schema:xs:CommonBasicComponents-2"
  targetNamespace="urn:oasis:names:specification:
  ubl:schema:xs:CommonExtensionComponents-2"
  elementFormDefault="qualified"
  attributeFormDefault="unqualified" version="2.0">
  ...
  <xsd:element name="UBLExtensions" type="UBLExtensionsType"/>
  <xsd:complexType name="UBLExtensionsType">
    <xsd:sequence>
      <xsd:element ref="UBLExtension" minOccurs="1"
        maxOccurs="unbounded"/>
    </xsd:sequence>
  </xsd:complexType>
  <xsd:element name="UBLExtension" type="UBLExtensionType"/>
  <xsd:complexType name="UBLExtensionType">
    <xsd:sequence>
      <xsd:element ref="cbc:ID" minOccurs="0"
        maxOccurs="1"/>
      <xsd:element ref="cbc:Name" minOccurs="0"
        maxOccurs="1"/>
      <xsd:element ref="ExtensionAgencyID" minOccurs="0"
        maxOccurs="1"/>
      <xsd:element ref="ExtensionAgencyName" minOccurs="0"
        maxOccurs="1"/>
      <xsd:element ref="ExtensionVersionID" minOccurs="0"
        maxOccurs="1"/>
      <xsd:element ref="ExtensionAgencyURI" minOccurs="0"
        maxOccurs="1"/>
      <xsd:element ref="ExtensionURI" minOccurs="0"
        maxOccurs="1"/>
```

```
        <xsd:element ref="ExtensionReasonCode" minOccurs="0"
          maxOccurs="1"/>
        <xsd:element ref="ExtensionReason" minOccurs="0"
          maxOccurs="1"/>
        <xsd:element ref="ExtensionContent" minOccurs="1"
          maxOccurs="1"/>
      </xsd:sequence>
    </xsd:complexType>
</xsd:schema>
```

Example 13.20

A UBL 2.0 schema containing extension definitions. Some schema annotations have been removed for brevity.

The `UBLExtension` construct can first contain any of several types of metadata about what the extension element represents. At the end of this structure is an element named `ExtensionContent` that implements the extension bucket concept described in Chapter 12.

The definition of `ExtensionContentType` is shown here:

```
<xsd:complexType name="ExtensionContentType">
  <xsd:sequence>
    <xsd:any namespace="##any" minOccurs="0" maxOccurs="1"
      processContents="skip"/>
  </xsd:sequence>
</xsd:complexType>
<xsd:element name="ExtensionContent" type="ExtensionContentType"/>
```

Example 13.21

The UBL `ExtensionContentType` complex type and the `ExtensionContent` global element.

Because its `processContents` attribute is set to "skip," you could use any elements you like (without declaring them) inside the `ExtensionContent` construct and they would still be valid according to the UBL schema. However, you are better off declaring the elements so that they can be documented and optionally generate class definitions for them.

CASE STUDY EXAMPLE

The new deal with MegaEuroMart is requiring ActionCon to rethink its design. MegaEuroMart has decided to use UBL 2.0, and they insist that their trading partners all use it as well. Despite the work that's already been done on the Purchase Order schema, Steve now needs to figure out how to incorporate a UBL-defined purchase order model into the mix.

Steve first decides to create a separate UBL structure to complement the ones that have already been created internally. The UBL purchase order has some of the same content as ActionCon's purchase order, but it introduces a different structure and new names. The following example represents a valid XML document based on the UBL Order element:

```
<Order xmlns:cbc="urn:oasis:names:specification:
  ubl:schema:xs:CommonBasicComponents-2"
    xmlns:cac="urn:oasis:names:specification:
  ubl:schema:xs:CommonAggregateComponents-2"
    xmlns="urn:oasis:names:specification:
  ubl:schema:xs:Order-2">
  <cbc:UBLVersionID>
    2.0
  </cbc:UBLVersionID>
  <cbc:CustomizationID>
    urn:oasis:names:specification:
    ubl:xpath:Order-2.0:sbs-1.0-draft
  </cbc:CustomizationID>
  <cbc:ProfileID>
    bpid:urn:oasis:names:draft:bpss:
    ubl-2-sbs-order-with-simple-response-draft
  </cbc:ProfileID>
  <cbc:ID>
    12345
  </cbc:ID>
  <cbc:IssueDate>
    2006-10-15
  </cbc:IssueDate>
  <cac:BuyerCustomerParty>
    <cbc:CustomerAssignedAccountID>
      444403
    </cbc:CustomerAssignedAccountID>
    <cac:Party>
      <cac:PartyName>
        <cbc:Name>Neighborhood Game Stores, Inc.</cbc:Name>
      </cac:PartyName>
```

```xml
        <cac:PostalAddress>
          <cbc:Room>300</cbc:Room>
          <cbc:StreetName>Main St.</cbc:StreetName>
          <cbc:BuildingNumber>123</cbc:BuildingNumber>
          <cbc:CityName>Cleveland</cbc:CityName>
          <cbc:PostalZone>37311</cbc:PostalZone>
          <cbc:CountrySubentity>OH</cbc:CountrySubentity>
          <cac:Country>
            <cbc:IdentificationCode>US</cbc:IdentificationCode>
          </cac:Country>
        </cac:PostalAddress>
        <cac:Contact>
          <cbc:Name>Steve Smith</cbc:Name>
          <cbc:Telephone>231-555-1122</cbc:Telephone>
        </cac:Contact>
      </cac:Party>
  </cac:BuyerCustomerParty>
  <cac:Delivery>
    <cac:DeliveryAddress>
      <cbc:StreetName>5100 Garfield Road</cbc:StreetName>
      <cbc:CityName>Traverse City</cbc:CityName>
      <cbc:PostalZone>49686</cbc:PostalZone>
      <cbc:CountrySubentity>MI</cbc:CountrySubentity>
      <cac:Country>
      <cbc:IdentificationCode>US</cbc:IdentificationCode>
      </cac:Country>
    </cac:DeliveryAddress>
  </cac:Delivery>
  <cac:OrderLine>
    <cac:LineItem>
      <cbc:ID>1</cbc:ID>
      <cbc:Quantity unitCode="EA">12</cbc:Quantity>
      <cac:Price>
        <cbc:PriceAmount currencyID="USD">
          29.99
        </cbc:PriceAmount>
      </cac:Price>
      <cac:Item>
        <cbc:Name>Service Blaster 2000</cbc:Name>
        <cac:SellersItemIdentification>
          <cbc:ID>AY2345</cbc:ID>
        </cac:SellersItemIdentification>
      </cac:Item>
    </cac:LineItem>
  </cac:OrderLine>
  <cac:OrderLine>
    <cac:LineItem>
```

```
      <cbc:ID>2</cbc:ID>
      <cbc:Quantity unitCode="EA">8</cbc:Quantity>
      <cac:Price>
        <cbc:PriceAmount currencyID="USD">
          19.95
        </cbc:PriceAmount>
      </cac:Price>
      <cac:Item>
        <cbc:Name>
          Extreme Composition - Special Edition
        </cbc:Name>
        <cac:SellersItemIdentification>
          <cbc:ID>BB1764</cbc:ID>
        </cac:SellersItemIdentification>
      </cac:Item>
    </cac:LineItem>
  </cac:OrderLine>
</Order>
```

Example 13.22

A purchase order document instance expressed with UBL 2.0.

Steve notices that a UBL purchase order document is naturally larger and more complex. There are a lot of extra structural elements that are designed to support variations in content other than those that will be used directly by ActionCon. Namespaces in UBL are also more varied because they are broken down not by subject area but by whether elements are considered to be "aggregate" or "basic."

Steve is reasonably happy with the UBL purchase order. He feels that the extra verbosity is a tradeoff for a more expressive vocabulary. He also sees a lot of benefit in using a standard vocabulary that has been adopted elsewhere in the industry and is also well-documented. This could carry over into benefits not just for ActionCon's relationship with MegaEuroMart, but also with other retailers. It can further spare Steve a lot of time designing and developing new schemas.

MegaEuroMart is mostly using standard UBL, but they also have defined a few extensions of their own. Because MegaEuroMart receives special deals for purchasing in high volumes, the prices for each item in the invoice may vary based on the quantity ordered so far that year. In order to make it clear to their manufacturers what policy they are using to determine the price, they add information to each order to indicate the quantity ordered and the price tier used.

The data analysts at MegaEuroMart weighed several options when deciding how to represent this information. They first attempted to express the data in standard UBL but found that they couldn't sufficiently represent order pricing details specific to their existing conventions and preferences.

The analysts next considered putting the data into another UBL element that they weren't using. For example, they thought they would store the cumulative quantity ordered in the `PriceChangeReason` element that can optionally appear as the child of `Price`. This would simplify the use of UBL by not requiring them to create a customized schema. However, the analysts (correctly) felt that this was bad design. It is confusing to consumers of the data to be tagging it with improper names, and in this case improper data types. In addition, MegaEuroMart may need the `PriceChangeReason` element in the future, or it may do business with a company that is already using that element for its intended purpose.

Finally, it is decided to customize the UBL schema. For each line item in the order, the analysts add two extra data elements:

- year-to-date quantity ordered (a quantity)

- price tier (an integer)

One immediate challenge is that UBL only allows customizations at the business document level (in the previously explained `UBLExtensions` construct), not at the line item level. Therefore, they need to define a structure that would match the custom data to individual line items in the order.

Here's an example of an Order schema that contains the customized elements:

```
<Order xmlns:cbc="urn:oasis:names:specification:
   ubl:schema:xs:CommonBasicComponents-2"
  xmlns:cac="urn:oasis:names:specification:
     ubl:schema:xs:CommonAggregateComponents-2"
  xmlns:ext="urn:oasis:names:specification:
     ubl:schema:xs:CommonExtensionComponents-2"
  xmlns:mmo="http://megaeuromart.com/order"
  xmlns="urn:oasis:names:specification:
   ubl:schema:xs:Order-2">
 <ext:UBLExtensions>
   <ext:UBLExtension>
     <ext:ExtensionContent>
       <mmo:PricingTerms>
         <mmo:PriceInfo>
```

```
              <mmo:LineItemID>1</mmo:LineItemID>
              <mmo:QuantityYearToDate unitCode="EA">
                255
              </mmo:QuantityYearToDate>
              <mmo:PriceTier>2</mmo:PriceTier>
           </mmo:PriceInfo>
           <mmo:PriceInfo>
              <mmo:LineItemID>2</mmo:LineItemID>
              <mmo:QuantityYearToDate unitCode="EA">
                415
              </mmo:QuantityYearToDate>
              <mmo:PriceTier>3</mmo:PriceTier>
           </mmo:PriceInfo>
         </mmo:PricingTerms>
      </ext:ExtensionContent>
   </ext:UBLExtension>
</ext:UBLExtensions>
<cbc:UBLVersionID>2.0</cbc:UBLVersionID>
...
```

Example 13.23
An XML purchase order document instance containing a mix of UBL and custom elements. The UBL elements appear either with no prefix or the `cac:`, `cbc:`, or `ext:` prefixes (mapped to UBL namespaces). The custom elements appear with the `mmo:` prefix.

This next schema declares the custom elements. It follows the same naming standards and schema structure as the core UBL schemas, which are themselves based on UN/CEFACT specifications. The custom schema also takes advantage of reusable types (namely the pre-defined numeric, identifier, and quantity types).

```
<xsd:schema xmlns:xsd="http://www.w3.org/2001/XMLSchema"
  xmlns="http://megaeuromart.com/order"
  targetNamespace="http://megaeuromart.com/order"
  xmlns:udt="urn:un:unece:uncefact:data:
    specification:
    UnqualifiedDataTypesSchemaModule:2">
  <xsd:import namespace="urn:un:unece:uncefact:data:
    specification:UnqualifiedDataTypesSchemaModule:2"/>
  <xsd:element name="PriceInfo" type="PriceInfoType"/>
  <xsd:element name="PriceTier" type="udt:NumericType"/>
  <xsd:element name="PricingTerms" type="PricingTermsType"/>
  <xsd:element name="LineItemID" type="udt:IdentifierType"/>
```

```
<xsd:element name="QuantityYearToDate"
  type="udt:QuantityType"/>
<xsd:complexType name="PriceInfoType">
  <xsd:sequence>
    <xsd:element ref="LineItemID"/>
    <xsd:element ref="QuantityYearToDate"/>
    <xsd:element ref="PriceTier"/>
  </xsd:sequence>
</xsd:complexType>
<xsd:complexType name="PricingTermsType">
  <xsd:sequence>
    <xsd:element ref="PriceInfo" minOccurs="0"
      maxOccurs="unbounded"/>
  </xsd:sequence>
</xsd:complexType>
</xsd:schema>
```

Example 13.24
The MegaEuroMart schema declaring custom purchase order elements.

This schema could be imported into the WSDL or into an outer schema in order to combine it with the UBL schema. However, when the instance shown in Example 13.23 is validated, it will not validate the elements because the xsd:any wildcard element in the ExtensionContentType construct has its processContents attribute set to "skip."

> **NOTE**
>
> XML Schema offers two other methods of extending schemas: substitution groups and redefinition.
>
> Substitution groups are a method of indicating that groups of elements are substitutable for each other. They can be useful in narrative XML where elements fall into certain categories. You can compare them to choice groups, except that they are more flexible and extensible.
>
> Redefinition allows you to include another schema document and basically replace the definitions of some or all of the included types or groups. This is accomplished using an xsd:redefine element, which contains the revised definitions of the types. Redefinition, unlike type derivation, does not require the use of the xsi:type attribute in instances. The redefined components have the same name as they had in the original definition.

Neither substitution nor redefinition is generally suitable for service contracts. They are sometimes not well supported by data binding tools and
redefinition in particular can have differing support among XML Schema
validating parsers. Also, redefining types can sometimes lead to side
effects because it may render types derived from the original definition
invalid.

SUMMARY OF KEY POINTS

- You can choose to adopt an industry schema or customize it to meet your data representation requirements.

- Customization options include the select reuse of schema types, the use of `xsd:any` wildcards, and `xsd:extension`.

- Some industry schemas are already designed with extension points that provide built-in wildcards.

Chapter 14

Advanced WSDL Part I:
Modularization, Extensibility, MEPs,
and Asynchrony

Although we've covered the fundamentals sufficiently for you to put together relatively complete Web service contracts, we've really only scratched the surface as to what you can do with the WSDL language.

Over the next two chapters, we explore features and techniques that can help you optimize WSDL definitions to accommodate special requirements and extend Web service contracts for increased sophistication.

14.1 Modularization Mechanisms

As we progressed through the fundamental WSDL concepts in Chapters 7, 8, and 9 you may have noticed the code samples grow in size when we neared showing the results at the end of each chapter. It is easy to imagine how, for a very complex service, a WSDL definition may expand to such an extent that it becomes unwieldy and burdensome to maintain. Additionally, the more bloated the contract, the greater the likelihood that redundant code is embedded, resulting in missed opportunities for reuse (and risking increased governance burden).

As with the XML Schema modularization features discussed in the previous chapter, there are features of the WSDL language that also support the creation of modules. Specifically, WSDL provides a way to import external definitions, which can lead to the following benefits:

- *Manageability* – Different parts of a definition can be maintained in different smaller documents by different project team members. The classic example is the separation of the abstract description from its concrete counterpart, where the former part is designed by an architect and the latter description is built by the development team. However, many more options for modularization exist.

- *Reusability* – Each independent part of a contract may be reused in a number of situations. For example, you may want to have the same abstract description implemented by different concrete descriptions.

Here we introduce the WSDL language features that enable modularization.

The `import` Element (WSDL 1.1, 2.0)

The WSDL 1.1 mechanism for importing WSDL definitions from one document into another is based on the use of the `import` element. This element is very similar to the XML Schema `xsd:import` element described in the previous chapter.

Let's have a look:

```
<import
  namespace="http://actioncon.com/contract/po"
  location="http://actioncon.com/contract/po.wsdl"/>
```

The `import` element requires specifying both a namespace and a location via the corresponding attributes.

Looking back at Chapter 7, you might recall that a WSDL document has a target namespace defined for its enclosed definitions, specified in the `targetNamespace` attribute of the `definitions` root element. The `import` element's `namespace` attribute points to the target namespace of the WSDL definition that is being imported. The `location` attribute then further sets the actual physical location of the WSDL document.

The `import` element must appear at the very beginning of the WSDL document, just below the opening `definitions` element. It can only be preceded by the `documentation` element or other elements that are outside the WSDL language.

WSDL 2.0 defines the same element but considers the `location` attribute a hint (a WSDL processor may already know where to find components associated with a particular namespace) and therefore makes it optional.

The fact that the WSDL `import` element is modeled after XML Schema's `xsd:import` element results in the requirement that imported namespaces must be foreign, meaning that they must be different from the target namespace of the importing document.

Non-Transitive Limitations

It is important to note that the WSDL import mechanism is not *transitive*, which means that if you import document C into your document A, and document C itself imports a separate document B, your original document A will only allow you to reference parts of the WSDL definition from document C. If you need to reference a part of document B, then you also need to import document B directly into document A. This scenario is depicted in Figure 14.1.

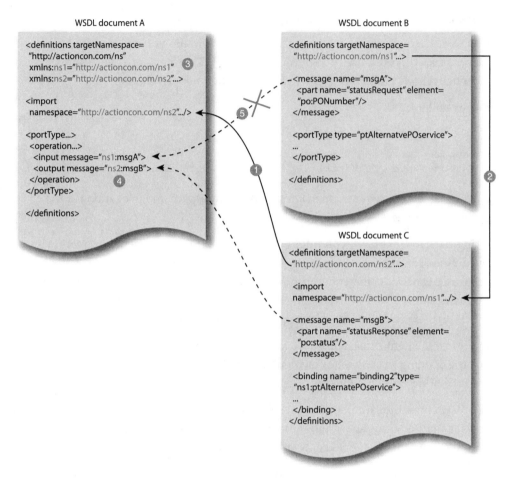

Figure 14.1

Due to the transitive limitation, this design won't work. WSDL document A is unable to reference a message definition from WSDL document B.

Let's sort out the namespaces in this example before we study it:

- WSDL document A – `http://actioncon.com/ns`

- WSDL document B – `http://actioncon.com/ns1`

- WSDL document C – `http://actioncon.com/ns2`

WSDL document A imports constructs from WSDL document C (1), which in turn imports constructs from WSDL document B (2). WSDL document A assigns the `ns1:` and `ns2:` prefixes to the two target namespaces used by WSDL documents B and C (3). It then sets the `message` attribute values of the `input` and `output` elements to `ns1:msgA` and `ns2:msgB` as part of the `operation` construct (4). This raises an error because `ns2:msgB` is not recognized (5).

Let's have a look at how this example needs to be changed in order to work.

Because WSDL document A now contains a new `import` element that points to WSDL document B directly (1), WSDL document A is able to reference `ns1:msgA` (2).

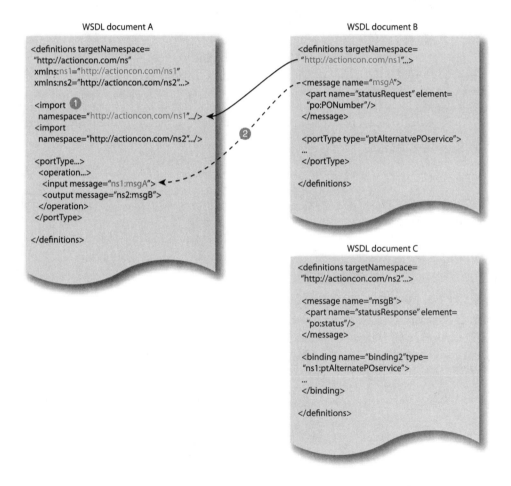

Figure 14.2

WSDL document A is now able to reference the message definition from WSDL document B.

CASE STUDY EXAMPLE
Split Concrete Descriptions Sharing the Same Abstract Description

Steve realizes that his Web service contract (shown at the end of Chapter 8), is starting to be very lengthy. He therefore decides to see what it would look like if he split it up as follows:

- The abstract description retains the `http://actioncon.com/contract/po` target namespace and is identical to original WSDL definition. Steve has made this document available at the same URL he used for the target namespace value, that is, `http://actioncon.com/contract/po`.

- He creates two concrete descriptions, one with bindings for SOAP 1.1 and the other for SOAP 1.2. Each of the two concrete descriptions is placed into its own WSDL document, and both documents import the same abstract description.

The bindings for the concrete descriptions are defined in the following namespaces:

- `http://actioncon.com/contract/POSoap11`

- `http://actioncon.com/contract/POSoap12`

...and each binds the `ptPurchase Order` portType construct defined in this namespace:

`http://actioncon.com/contract/po`

Figure 14.3 shows how the concrete and abstract descriptions exist as related WSDL documents, followed by entire markup code for each of the WSDL definitions containing the concrete descriptions.

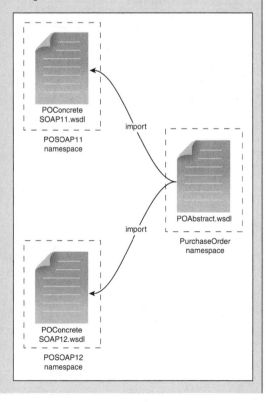

Figure 14.3
Two different concrete descriptions residing in two separate WSDL documents (left) both importing the same abstract description (right).

Here is the concrete description for the SOAP 1.1 binding:

```
<definitions targetNamespace=
  "http://actioncon.com/contract/POSoap11"
  xmlns:tns="http://actioncon.com/contract/POSoap11"
  xmlns:abs="http://actioncon.com/contract/po"
  xmlns="http://schemas.xmlsoap.org/wsdl/"
  xmlns:po="http://actioncon.com/schema/purchasing"
  xmlns:soap11="http://schemas.xmlsoap.org/wsdl/soap/">
  <import
    namespace="http://actioncon.com/contract/po"
    location="http://actioncon.com/contract/po"/>
  <binding name="bdPO-SOAP11HTTP" type="abs:ptPurchaseOrder">
    <soap11:binding style="document"
      transport="http://schemas.xmlsoap.org/soap/http"/>
    <operation name="opSubmitOrder">
      <input><soap11:body use="literal"/></input>
      <output><soap11:body use="literal"/></output>
    </operation>
    <operation name="opCheckOrderStatus">
      <input><soap11:body use="literal"/></input>
      <output><soap11:body use="literal"/></output>
    </operation>
    <operation name="opChangeOrder">
      <input><soap11:body use="literal"/></input>
      <output><soap11:body use="literal"/></output>
    </operation>
    <operation name="opCancelOrder">
      <input><soap11:body use="literal"/></input>
      <output><soap11:body use="literal"/></output>
    </operation>
  </binding>
  <service name="svPurchaseOrder">
    <port name="purchaseOrder-soap11http"
      binding="tns:bdPO-SOAP11HTTP">
      <soap11:address location=
        "http://actioncon.com/services/soap11/po"/>
    </port>
  </service>
</definitions>
```

Example 14.1

A WSDL definition containing a concrete description bound to SOAP 1.1 and importing an abstract description.

The concrete description for the SOAP 1.2 binding:

```
<definitions targetNamespace=
  "http://actioncon.com/contract/POSoap12"
  xmlns:tns="http://actioncon.com/contract/POSoap12"
  xmlns:abs="http://actioncon.com/contract/po"
  xmlns="http://schemas.xmlsoap.org/wsdl/"
  xmlns:po="http://actioncon.com/schema/purchasing"
  xmlns:soap11="http://schemas.xmlsoap.org/wsdl/soap/"
  xmlns:soap12="http://schemas.xmlsoap.org/wsdl/soap12/">
  <import
    namespace="http://actioncon.com/contract/po"
    location="http://actioncon.com/contract/po"/>
  <binding name="bdPO-SOAP12HTTP" type="abs:ptPurchaseOrder">
  <soap12:binding style="document"
    transport="http://schemas.xmlsoap.org/soap/http"/>
    <operation name="opSubmitOrder">
    <soap12:operation soapAction=
      "http://actioncon.com/submitOrder/request"
        soapActionRequired="true" required="true"/>
        <input><soap12:body use="literal"/></input>
        <output><soap12:body use="literal"/></output>
    </operation>
    <operation name="opCheckOrderStatus">
    <soap12:operation soapAction=
      "http://actioncon.com/submitOrder/request"
        soapActionRequired="true" required="true"/>
        <input><soap12:body use="literal"/></input>
        <output><soap12:body use="literal"/></output>
    </operation>
    <operation name="opChangeOrder">
    <soap12:operation soapAction=
      "http://actioncon.com/submitOrder/request"
        soapActionRequired="true" required="true"/>
        <input><soap12:body use="literal"/></input>
        <output><soap12:body use="literal"/></output>
    </operation>
   <operation name="opCancelOrder">
   <soap12:operation soapAction=
     "http://actioncon.com/submitOrder/request"
       soapActionRequired="true" required="true"/>
       <input><soap12:body use="literal"/></input>
       <output><soap12:body use="literal"/></output>
   </operation>
  </binding>
```

```
  <service name="svPurchaseOrder">
    <port name="purchaseOrder-http-soap12"
      binding="tns:bdPO-SOAP12HTTP">
      <soap12:address location=
        "http://actioncon.com/services/soap12/po"/>
    </port>
  </service>
</definitions>
```

Example 14.2
A WSDL definition containing a concrete description bound to SOAP 1.2 and importing the same abstract description as the previous definition.

The `include` Element (WSDL 2.0)

As with the WSDL `import` element, the XML Schema `xsd:import` element is used with the assumption that the externally imported content resides within a different namespace.

However, there are times when we don't want or need to use different namespaces for separated definitions. For this reason, the XML Schema language provides the `xsd:include` element, which works just like `xsd:import`, except there is no `namespace` attribute because the namespace of the included content is expected to be the same as the target namespace of the document that is doing the importing.

So why are we rehashing XML Schema topics when we should be focusing on WSDL? It's because WSDL 2.0 introduces an `include` element that works the same as `xsd:include`.

Here's what it looks like:

```
<include location=
  "http://actioncon.com/contract/PO-abstract.wsdl20"/>
```

Example 14.3
The WSDL 2.0 `include` element.

Figure 14.4 shows the `include` element in action as WSDL document A pulls in content from WSDL document B with both documents having the same target namespace.

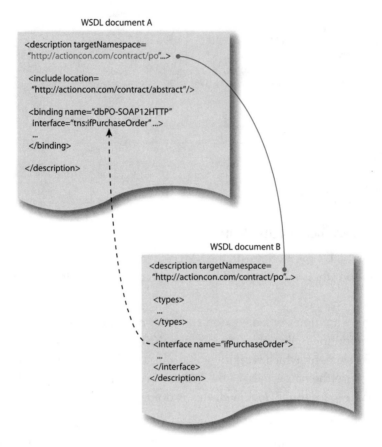

Figure 14.4

A WSDL document defining a concrete description (top) includes a WSDL document
defining the abstract description (bottom).

When Should `include` be Used Instead of `import`?

The answer is, as you might have guessed, related to the context of the included content.
If the content is specific to one WSDL document, then there may be no need to introduce
a separate namespace because only that document is ever expected to include the content. This makes a case for using the `include` element.

However, if the content has reuse potential, then you will want to assign it a separate
target namespace. This way, it can more easily exist independently from other WSDL
documents, which leads to the need for the `import` element.

If we look at some of the common SOA design patterns we can find circumstances that warrant each approach:

- The Redundant Implementation pattern advocates creating duplicate deployments of a service for scalability and load balancing purposes (and sometimes for other reasons as well). In this case, a different `service` construct is required for each implementation in order to establish the different service locations (via the child `port` constructs). Each service could have a separate WSDL document with its own `service` construct, and both documents could include the same abstract description and `binding` constructs. Because these parts of the contract are not being shared across different services (only by different implementations of the same service), they can exist in the same namespace.

- The Proxy Capability pattern supports the decomposition of a coarse-grained service into two or more fine-grained services by allowing the original service operations to remain as proxies to wherever the logic has been relocated to. In this case, the service contracts required for the new, fine-grained services will likely need to exist in separate namespaces, but perhaps the new abstract description belonging to the new service will still need to be shared by the old Web service contract (in order to maintain the proxy capabilities). In this case, the abstract description will need to be imported into the old contract because it will have a foreign namespace.

You might be wondering, if the `include` element is specific to WSDL 2.0, how a WSDL 1.1 document can include another. Technically, it cannot. Although you could try to use the `xsd:include` element, it will likely not be supported by many WSDL processors. This means that there is a simple limitation within WSDL 1.1 when it comes to modularized or physically partitioned WSDL content. Each WSDL document needs to establish a different namespace so that it can be composed back together using the WSDL import mechanism.

Can the WSDL `import` Element be Used to Import an XML Schema?

The WSDL 1.1 specification is unclear about the scope of the `import` element's application and technically allows it to be used to import both WSDL and XML Schema documents. However, the WS-I Basic Profile clearly states that it may only be used to import WSDL content, so the answer is generally "No."

XML Schema definitions should therefore only be imported via XML Schema's own `xsd:import` element, and the WS-I Basic Profile further requires that XML Schema imports be done from only within the WSDL `types` construct and that the `xsd:import` element be positioned as the child element of the `xsd:schema` element (as already discussed in Chapter 13).

How WSDL Documents are Merged

You might be wondering what a WSDL document looks like after it has imported an external WSDL definition. For instance, what happens to the `definitions` element of the WSDL document being imported? Does it simply get pulled into the importing document, resulting in a nested `definitions` construct? Not really.

The type of merging process carried out by a WSDL processor in response to encountering a WSDL `import` or `include` element is usually more intelligent than your standard C# include statement. The WSDL processor does not simply pull in all of the contents of a WSDL document to wherever the `include` or `import` element is located. Instead, it merges the individual content models from both (importing and imported) WSDL documents into one.

The resulting document therefore will likely be organized into the same abstract and concrete descriptions as a regular WSDL document, except that each description will be larger because it will contain content from both documents.

Importing XML Schemas

WSDL 2.0 uses different rules than WSDL 1.1 when it comes to importing XML schemas. These rules relate to the visibility of the imported schema content. In order to understand how the rules differ, we need to look at each scenario separately.

import with *WSDL 1.1 (High Visibility)*

The regular syntax used with the WSDL 1.1 language positions the `import` element within an `xsd:schema` construct and makes all imported XML Schema types visible (available) to the rest of the WSDL definition.

```
<definitions ...>
  <types>
    <xsd:schema xmlns:xsd="http://www.w3.org/2001/XMLSchema">
      <xsd:import namespace=
        "http://actioncon.com/schema/purchasing"
        schemaLocation=
        "http://actioncon.com/schema/purchaseOrder.xsd"/>
        <!-- imported types can be used here... -->
```

```
    </xsd:schema>
  </types>
  <!-- ...and here -->
</definitions>
```

Example 14.4
A WSDL 1.1 `types` definition with an `xsd:import` element wrapped in an `xsd:schema` construct.

import **with WSDL 2.0 (Constrained Visibility)**

If we use the WSDL 1.1 syntax in a WSDL 2.0 definition, we end up limiting the visibility of the schema content within the confines of the `xsd:schema` construct, which means other parts of the WSDL definition will not be able to reference the schema types.

```
<description ...>
  <types>
    <xsd:schema xmlns:xsd="http://www.w3.org/2001/XMLSchema">
      <xsd:import namespace=
        "http://actioncon.com/schema/purchasing"
        schemaLocation=
        "http://actioncon.com/schema/purchaseOrder.xsd"/>
      <!-- imported types can be used here... -->
    </xsd:schema>
  </types>
  <!-- ...but not here -->
</description>
```

Example 14.5
A WSDL 2.0 `types` definition with an `xsd:import` element wrapped in an `xsd:schema` construct.

import **with WSDL 2.0 (High Visibility)**

To achieve a high level of visibility in WSDL 2.0 requires that we remove the opening and closing `xsd:schema` tags so that the `xsd:import` element is a direct child of the `types` element, as shown here:

```
<description ...>
  <types>
    <xsd:import namespace=
      "http://actioncon.com/schema/purchasing"
      schemaLocation=
      "http://actioncon.com/schema/purchaseOrder.xsd"/>
```

```
  </types>
  <!-- imported types can be used here -->
</description>
```

Example 14.6

A WSDL 2.0 `types` definition with a child `xsd:import` element.

---

include with *WSDL 2.0 (High Visibility)*

Another way to bring in XML Schema content that is available to all parts of the WSDL document is via the `xsd:include` element. In this case, the element does need to be wrapped in `xsd:schema` elements, as follows:

```
<description ...>
  <types>
    <xsd:schema xmlns:xsd="http://www.w3.org/2001/XMLSchema"
      targetNamespace=
        "http://actioncon.com/schema/purchasing">
      <xsd:include schemaLocation=
        "http://actioncon.com/schema/purchaseOrderDetail.xsd"/>
      <!-- imported types can be used here... -->
    </xsd:schema>
  </types>
  <!-- ...and here -->
</description>
```

Example 14.7

A WSDL 2.0 `types` definition with an `xsd:include` element wrapped in an `xsd:schema` construct.

> **NOTE**
>
> The reasoning behind this syntactical change is to model the import and include mechanisms more closely around how they are already established in the XML Schema language. In a regular XML schema, the content within the `xsd:schema` construct is limited in scope (visibility) to that schema only. Therefore in WSDL 2.0 by adding the opening and closing `xsd:schema` elements we are indicating that we want to establish the same kind of scope.

XML Schema Definitions and Non-Transitive Limitations

When it comes to importing content that already has imported content, the same limitations that apply to WSDL documents importing other WSDL documents also apply to WSDL documents importing XML schemas.

In other words, if WSDL document B imports type definitions from XML schema A, and WSDL document A imports WSDL document B, WSDL document A will still not be able to reference the types in XML schema A. For WSDL document A to access the types from XML schema A, it must explicitly import them via the use of its own `xsd:import` statement.

Let's now relate the concept of importing XML schemas into WSDL definitions back to our case study example from Chapter 13.

CASE STUDY EXAMPLE

Steve now finally gets a chance to associate the modest XML Schema architecture he created earlier with the WSDL definitions he already established for the Purchase Order and Game services.

Figure 14.5 illustrates the resulting relationships between WSDL and XML Schema documents, which can be summarized as follows:

1. The Purchase Order WSDL definition (purchaseOrder.wsdl) imports the Purchase Order schema in order to directly reference its global elements within the `element` attribute of its message definitions.

2. The Purchase Order WSDL definition also imports the Common schema (common.xsd) in order to also directly reference its global elements within the `element` attribute of its message definitions.

3. The Game WSDL definition (game.wsdl) imports the Game schema in order to directly reference its global elements within the `element` attribute of its message definitions.

The Game WSDL definition does not have to import the Common schema because it does not need to reference any of its global elements.

Note that the numbers in the previous list correspond to the numbers used in the figure.

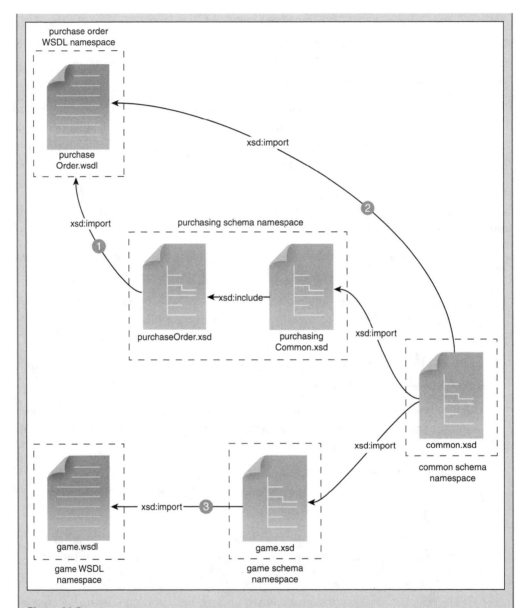

Figure 14.5

The XML Schema definitions from Chapter 13 now being imported into WSDL definitions. Note that the Invoice.xsd schema was removed because it is not relevant to the Purchase Order or Game service.

Note also the following about this new combined WSDL and XML Schema contract architecture:

- All of the displayed import and include statements are from the XML Schema language, which is why they are all prefixed with `xsd:`. WSDL import and include statements are not used because there is no WSDL document importing another.

- There are five different namespaces being used across the six documents. You can see how `xsd:import` is always used to cross namespace boundaries and how, in the one case where documents share a namespace, `xsd:include` is used instead.

- The Purchase Order WSDL definition does not have to explicitly import the Purchasing Common schema even if it needs to directly reference its global elements. This is because the Purchasing Common schema has the same target namespace as the Purchase Order schema which the Purchase Order WSDL definition does import. In other words, the transitive limitation does not apply here.

With regard to the last item on this bullet list, it is also worth mentioning that the WSDL 2.0 inclusion mechanism also is not affected by the transitive limitation because, again, you are still combining content within the same target namespace.

Multiple XML Schema Documents in a WSDL Document

All the examples of WSDL documents that we have seen so far import or embed a single XML Schema document. It is not uncommon to have to import multiple schema documents into the same WSDL definition, especially with Web services that have a coarser level of service granularity (which means they have a broader functional context and tend to provide a wider range of functionality).

Let's take a Claim entity service for example. As first explained in Chapter 3, this service's functional context is sometimes derived from a set of related business entities (like Claim, ClaimHistory, and ClaimType), which would make it a coarser-grained entity service. However, the canonical schemas it may be required to use (as per the Canonical Schema pattern) may be finer-grained where each schema corresponds to one business entity (such as one schema dedicated to ClaimHistory) and has its own namespace. In this case, the WSDL definition for the Claim service will be required to import all three claim-related XML schemas in order to access types from the different namespaces.

Associating multiple XML schemas with one WSDL document is usually no problem. You simply import (or, if you like, embed) the XML schemas into the `types` construct, as shown in our Purchase Order service example:

```
<types>
  <xsd:schema xmlns:xsd="http://www.w3.org/2001/XMLSchema">
    <xsd:import namespace=
      "http://actioncon.com/schema/purchasing"
      schemaLocation=
      "http://actioncon.com/schema/purchaseOrder.xsd"/>
    <xsd:import namespace=
      "http://actioncon.com/schema/common"
      schemaLocation=
      "http://actioncon.com/schema/common.xsd"/>
  </xsd:schema>
</types>
```

Example 14.8

A `types` construct importing two XML Schema definitions. Types from both XML Schema documents will become available to the rest of the WSDL document.

However, one clarification needs to be made about how these schema documents relate. Every XML schema is logically independent. In other words, while the types that they provide are visible throughout the enclosing WSDL document, they are not visible to the other enclosed XML Schema documents. Should one schema need to refer to definitions from another schema, then it would need to explicitly import those definitions via the `xsd:import` element.

CASE STUDY EXAMPLE

Steve decides to experiment with the two XML schemas he created in Chapter 13. These had the following namespaces:

- `http://actioncon.com/schema/purchasing`
- `http://actioncon.com/schema/common`

> **NOTE**
>
> As you might recall, the Purchase Order schema imports common types from the Common schema via the use of the `xsd:import` element.

In order to test transitive limitations, Steve wants to try out embedding those two XML Schema definitions into the WSDL document instead of importing them. He soon discovers that in order to do this, he needs to ensure that the Purchase Order schema retains its `xsd:import` statement that references the Common schema.

Without the `xsd:import` element present in the Purchase Order schema, that schema's complex types cannot reference the types from the Common schema (because they remain in different namespaces).

The following example shows the resulting WSDL document:

```
<definitions targetNamespace=
  "http://actioncon.com/contract/po"
  xmlns:tns=" http://actioncon.com/contract/po"
  xmlns="http://schemas.xmlsoap.org/wsdl/"
  xmlns:po="http://actioncon.com/schema/purchasing"
  xmlns:xsd="http://www.w3.org/2001/XMLSchema">
  <types>
    <xsd:schema targetNamespace=
      "http://actioncon.com/schema/common"
      xmlns="http://actioncon.com/schema/common"
      elementFormDefault="qualified">
    <xsd:simpleType name="ProductIDType">
      <xsd:restriction base="xsd:string">
        <xsd:pattern value="[A-Z]{2}[0-9]{4}"/>
      </xsd:restriction>
    </xsd:simpleType>
    <xsd:simpleType name="PriceType">
      <xsd:restriction base="xsd:decimal">
        <xsd:totalDigits value="8"/>
        <xsd:fractionDigits value="2"/>
      </xsd:restriction>
    </xsd:simpleType>
    <xsd:complexType name="AddressType">
      <xsd:sequence>
        <xsd:element name="line1" type="xsd:string"/>
        <xsd:element name="line2" type="xsd:string"
          minOccurs="0"/>
        <xsd:element name="city" type="xsd:string"/>
        <xsd:element name="state" type="xsd:string"/>
        <xsd:element name="postalCode" type="xsd:string"/>
        <xsd:element name="country" type="xsd:string"/>
      </xsd:sequence>
    </xsd:complexType>
  </xsd:schema>
  <xsd:schema targetNamespace=
    "http://actioncon.com/schema/purchasing"
    xmlns="http://actioncon.com/schema/purchasing"
    xmlns:common="http://actioncon.com/schema/common"
    elementFormDefault="qualified">
```

```xml
        <!-- This import statement is required. -->
        <xsd:import namespace=
          "http://actioncon.com/schema/common"/>
        <xsd:element name="purchaseOrder" type=
          "PurchaseOrderType"/>
        <xsd:complexType name="PurchaseOrderType">
          <xsd:sequence>
            <xsd:element name="poNumber" type="xsd:int"/>
            <xsd:element name="poDate" type="xsd:date"/>
            <xsd:element name="billToParty" type="PartyType"/>
            <xsd:element name="shipToParty" type="PartyType"/>
            <xsd:element name="lineItems"
              type="LineItemsType"/>
          </xsd:sequence>
          <xsd:attribute name="version" type="xsd:decimal"/>
        </xsd:complexType>
        <xsd:complexType name="PartyType">
          <xsd:sequence>
            <xsd:element name="id" type="xsd:int"/>
            <xsd:element name="partyName" type="xsd:string"/>
            <xsd:element name="contactName"
              type="xsd:string"/>
            <xsd:element name="phone" type="xsd:string"/>
            <xsd:element name="address"
              type="common:AddressType"/>
          </xsd:sequence>
        </xsd:complexType>
        <xsd:complexType name="LineItemsType">
          <xsd:sequence>
            <xsd:element name="lineItem" type="LineItemType"
              maxOccurs="unbounded"/>
          </xsd:sequence>
        </xsd:complexType>
        <xsd:complexType name="LineItemType">
          <xsd:sequence>
            <xsd:element name="productID" type=
              "common:ProductIDType"/>
            <xsd:element name="productName"
              type="xsd:string"/>
            <xsd:element name="quantity" type="xsd:int"/>
            <xsd:element name="price"
              type="common:PriceType"/>
          </xsd:sequence>
        </xsd:complexType>
      </xsd:schema>
```

```
    </types>
</definitions>
```

Example 14.9
Multiple schema definitions embedded in a WSDL `types` element. The highlighted `xsd:import` statement allows one schema to reference types that reside in the other. Note that the `xsd:import` element does not have a `schemaLocation` attribute because the WSDL processor automatically knows where to find the definitions for types in this namespace (they are embedded in the same WSDL document).

More About Interface Inheritance (WSDL 2.0)

Beyond splitting WSDL definitions into logical parts, WSDL 2.0 allows an interface to be extended. As already introduced in Chapter 9, this is achieved by using the `extends` attribute of the `interface` element, as follows:

```
<interface name="ifPurchaseOrderAdmin"
  extends="tns:ifPurchaseOrder">
  <operation name="opListOrders"
    pattern="http://www.w3.org/ns/wsdl/in-out">
    <input element="po:poListRequest"/>
    <output element="po:poListResponse"/>
  </operation>
</interface>
```

Example 14.10
The `ifPurchaseOrderAdmin` `interface` element with an `extends` attribute pointing to the `tns:ifPurchaseOrder` `interface` element.

This mechanism allows you to define an interface as an extension of a set of existing interfaces. The resulting, extended interface is composed of:

- the operations it defines
- the operations defined by the interfaces it extends (including the operations that those interfaces may themselves be inheriting from others)

Figure 14.6 illustrates an interface inheritance scenario.

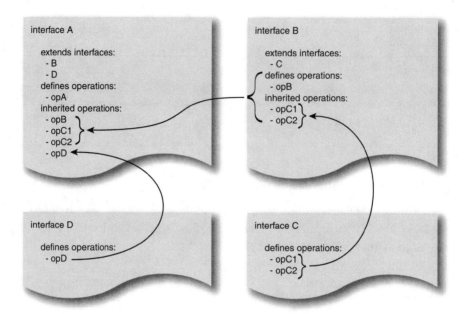

Figure 14.6

The WSDL interface A extends interfaces B and D. It defines operation opA and inherits operations opB, opC1, and opC2 from interface B and operation opD from interface D. opC1 and opC2 were inherited from interface C by interface B.

NOTE
Operations cannot be overloaded. If an operation is defined twice—that is, if an interface defines an operation with the same name as an operation from one of the interfaces it imports—that operation must be identical to the original one.

Inter-Service and Intra-Service Inheritance

Interface inheritance supports the extension of interfaces within the same WSDL document as well as across WSDL documents. In other words, you can have one WSDL definition with two interface constructs, whereby one extends the other—or—you can have one WSDL definition that is part of a Web service implementation and another that is independently deployed as part of a separate Web service implementation, and you can still have one interface extend another across these two services.

Although interface inheritance may seem like a sophisticated way of adding operations to existing interfaces without needing to recreate existing operations, any form of cross-service inheritance needs to be applied with caution.

Service-orientation was heavily influenced by object-oriented design approaches, but it intentionally does not share its affinity with inheritance structures. Services are delivered as standalone and self-contained software programs that can be independently evolved and governed. This is a key requirement that allows services to be freely recomposed (and versioned) over time. While interface inheritance does not oppose service-orientation when it is applied within the confines of a service, we look to avoid most forms of cross-service dependencies. However, as with anything, there may be valid exceptions to the rule.

For example, let's consider the Concurrent Contracts pattern that allows one Web service implementation to have two separate WSDL documents (each intended for a different type of consumer program). When the situation warrants only exposing a subset of the service's operations to some consumers, interface inheritance may provide a clean approach for reusing and maintaining the base set of operations that are shared across both services.

Emulating Interface Inheritance with WSDL 1.1

The `extends` attribute is new with WSDL 2.0. Therefore, WSDL 1.1 does not officially support interface inheritance. However, there is somewhat of a workaround.

If you have a `portType` element with a set of base operations, you can create a new `portType` construct within the same WSDL definition that introduces new operations. You can then bind the new port type to the same `port` element used by the original `portType` element. This effectively allows one abstract description to extend another. However, it is obviously less elegant than the WSDL 2.0 interface inheritance feature because the abstract description is split into two different interfaces.

SUMMARY OF KEY POINTS

- You can use the WSDL 1.1 and 2.0 `import` element to import WSDL definitions from a foreign namespace and the WSDL 2.0 `include` element to include WSDL definitions from the same target namespace.

- The WSDL import mechanism is non-transitive, meaning that a WSDL document can only import WSDL or XML Schema content from a document that it explicitly references via the `import` element.

- WSDL 2.0 enables interface inheritance via the use of the `extends` attribute. Although an option for intra-service interface inheritance, this feature needs to be used with caution when considering cross-service inheritance.

14.2 Extending the WSDL Language

So far, we have been presenting the features of WSDL that are part of the core language or directly explained in the WSDL specification. We will now begin discussing how to use WSDL to describe contracts that go beyond simple message exchanges with SOAP and HTTP.

Extensibility of the SOAP Binding Extensions

As we've already established, WSDL is most commonly used to describe services that depend on message exchanges via SOAP over HTTP. Therefore, the underlying binding elements will typically need to be extended using SOAP extensibility elements.

However, those SOAP binding extensions can themselves be further extended. This provides an opportunity to describe the use of SOAP over different underlying protocols. Let's take a closer look at how this is accomplished with both WSDL 1.1 and 2.0.

Specifying an Alternative Underlying Protocol (WSDL 1.1)

The `soap11:binding` and `soap12:binding` extensibility elements in WSDL 1.1 provide a `transport` attribute that can be used to set a URI that represents the actual transport protocol with which the SOAP message will be delivered.

Past examples in this book have been focused on the use of the HTTP binding, which is represented as follows:

```
<soap:binding... transport=
  "http://schemas.xmlsoap.org/soap/http">
```

You can indicate the use of other SOAP bindings by adding a different value to the `transport` attribute. Here is a list of the most common transports:

- SOAP 1.1 over HTTP – `http://schemas.xmlsoap.org/soap/http`

- SOAP over JMS – `http://www.soapjms.org/2007/08/soap/bindings/JMS/`

- SOAP over SMTP – `http://schemas.pocketsoap.com/soap/smtp`

The *Inherently Asynchronous Binding* section in this chapter shows an example of a Web service that uses SOAP over SMTP instead of HTTP.

Specifying an Alternative Underlying Protocol (WSDL 2.0)

The WSDL 2.0 SOAP binding extension can describe both SOAP 1.1 and SOAP 1.2 bindings and provides a feature that is similar to the WSDL 1.1 `transport` attribute, except that it is now called the `soap:protocol` attribute.

Here's what it looks like:

```
<binding... soap:protocol=
  "http://www.w3.org/2003/05/soap/binding/HTTP">
```

Other SOAP protocol bindings may be specified with different values of the `soap:protocol` attribute. Here are some common URI values for this attribute:

- SOAP over JMS – `http://www.soapjms.org/2007/08/soap/bindings/JMS/`

- SOAP 1.2 over HTTP – `http://www.w3.org/2003/05/soap/bindings/HTTP/`

- SOAP 1.1 over HTTP – `http://www.w3.org/2005/05/soap11/bindings/HTTP`

You may have noticed that the SOAP over JMS URI is the same for SOAP 1.1 and 1.2. This is, in fact, correct.

NOTE

Of all of the provided transport and protocol settings, only those for HTTP have been truly standardized industry-wide.

Non-Standard and Custom Transports

The transport identifiers listed in the previous section are used by WSDL processors to figure out how to process and transmit messages at runtime. As just mentioned in the note, some of these URI values are industry standard (which means pretty much all of the WSDL processors should recognize them), while support for the others may be limited to certain vendor platforms.

It can be helpful to keep in the back of your mind that you are not limited to these URIs and their corresponding transports. You do have the option of creating custom identifiers for which you can then build custom runtime processing logic. One reason you may want to do this is if you decide that a different transport protocol should be used to deliver your SOAP messages. For example, one option might be to use raw TCP as the delivery medium.

The option is there, but you need to make sure that any proprietary programming you add will not inhibit the use of your services. One of the key goals of an SOA initiative is to deliver services that are highly interoperable and reusable. Therefore, any non-standard transports you decide to enable also need to be supported by the programs that will need to use (or reuse) the service.

> **NOTE**
>
> Whenever considering more than one standard binding format, be sure to read up on the Canonical Protocol and Dual Protocols patterns.

Custom WSDL Extensions and the `wsdl:required` Attribute

The WSDL language was defined as an extensible XML vocabulary. It is said to have an "open-content model," which means that elements and attributes from other languages (or vocabularies) with different namespaces can be inserted into a WSDL document to provide additional functionality. It is up to those external languages to explain the purpose and function of extensibility statements.

As we established throughout Part I, these external elements are referred to as "extensibility elements." The examples we've seen so far (including the examples from this chapter) have focused on pre-defined extensibility elements. However, you can create your own, custom extensibility elements (and attributes) that can also be inserted throughout the WSDL definition, as long as you provide the custom logic to process them as well.

For example, using the following simple element in a WSDL document may specify that all messages include a certain type of security header:

```
<custom:SecurityHeaders/>
```

Using the `wsdl:required` *Attribute*

Let's take a minute to introduce the `wsdl:required` global attribute that originated with WSDL 1.1 and continues to be used with WSDL 2.0. This attribute can be added to a variety of different extension elements from different languages. As you may have guessed, when the `wsdl:required` attribute is set to "true" for a given element, the use of that element is required and when it is set to "false," it is optional.

So why is this important to us? Well, it's a matter of perspective. From the point of view of the Web service, all extensions—required or optional—must be honored. By including them in the contract, the service indicates that it supports the use of these extension elements.

From the point of view of the consumer, however, things are different:

- Required extensions become mandatory in that they represent functionality that is needed for the consumer to communicate with the Web service. If the consumer program does not know a particular extension or does not support it, it cannot interact with the service (and should not attempt to).

- Optional extensions are, as their name indicates, not required. The consumer may or may not comply with them (either because it does not support them or because it chose not to).

Let's revisit our previous custom example to add this attribute.

```
<custom:SecurityHeaders wsdl:required="true"/>
```

Now consumers must include security headers in all messages sent to the Web service and must also be prepared to receive those same headers in messages received from the service. Of course, this attribute is not limited to custom elements. In the upcoming sections and chapters, you'll notice it used with a variety of pre-defined extensibility elements, including the `wsam:Addressing` element introduced in Chapter 10.

SUMMARY OF KEY POINTS

- Existing SOAP binding extensions can be used to describe services using SOAP over a protocol other than HTTP.

- Additional functionality may be described by inserting custom or pre-defined extensibility elements and attributes into a WSDL document.

- The `wsdl:required` feature is itself an extensibility attribute that can be applied to custom and pre-defined extensibility elements.

14.3 Special Message Exchange Patterns

Chapter 7 introduced the four basic message exchange patterns that WSDL 1.1 supports and Chapter 9 provided a glimpse into the one new MEP from WSDL 2.0. Of all of these MEPs, only the WSDL 1.1 Request-Response and One-Way patterns are widely used (in fact, you can assume that their usage represents about 99.99% of all Web service implementations).

However, it's time now to take a closer look at the lesser known MEPs, some of which are becoming obsolete and one that has potential. In this section, we also study WSDL 2.0 mechanisms for defining composite patterns.

What Happened to Outbound MEPs?

Of the four MEPs explained in Chapter 7, the Request-Response and One-Way patterns are considered inbound because they both begin with a Web service receiving an input message from a consumer.

The other two MEPs, solicit-response and notification, are classified as outbound because, as you may have guessed, they start off with the transmission of a message from the Web service to the consumer.

Although part of the WSDL 1.1 standard, these two outbound MEPs were not adopted by the industry and ultimately were disapproved by the WS-I Basic Profile. To understand why this happened, we need to figure out why they were added to the standard to begin with.

How Outbound MEPs were Supposed to Work

The rationale behind the Solicit-Response and Notification MEPs was to allow for complex MEPs to be created. The assumption was that a consumer could first initiate contact with a Web service via an inbound MEP, during which it would pass the Web service its location and a request that it be contacted (solicited or notified) in the future.

This type of communication mechanism is similar in concept to a call-back routine in some programming languages and similar in execution to how event-driven architectures are designed. The Web service retains the location of the original consumer along with the consumer's original request, and whenever something happens (an event occurs) that is of relevance to the consumer, the Web service logic responds by initiating contact with the consumer.

As an example, let's try to relate an outbound MEP to the Purchase Order service we have been discussing. Assuming a new operation existed allowing a consumer to forward its location and interest in being notified of the status change of a pending purchase order, another operation could be added with either the Notification or Solicit-Response MEP to automatically communicate to the consumer when the status does change.

Why Outbound MEPs are Not Widely Supported

What we just explained here is actually the basis of the well-known publish-and-sub-scribe model. The concept of subscribing to events and then being notified of when they happen is, in fact, widely supported. Only these specific WSDL outbound MEPs were rarely used to implement this and other event-driven messaging models.

The very role a Web service assumes by default is that of service provider. Via its service contract, the Web service offers its capabilities to others to consume. It's awkward to think of a Web service, which is often defined by the very existence of its WSDL contract, as a program that initiates contact with others.

That's not to say that the core service logic that underlies a typical Web service implementation cannot initiate contact with another program. If fact, for service compositions to work, most Web services must transition through service provider and service consumer roles in order to perform intermediary processing and relay data to other composition participants. But services are usually designed to carry out this interaction via a series of inbound MEPs.

Because outbound MEPs are simply the reverse of inbound MEPs, they may seem quite straightforward in concept. However, in practice, this concept was difficult to apply. While a Web service's endpoint address is generally well-published and known to all consumer programs that are designed to work with the service, the reverse was not true. A service cannot have a way of knowing the endpoint addresses of all its consumers without some form of callback mechanism whereby consumers first contact the service to provide it with an address the service then can use for a later (outbound) data exchange. This type of callback functionality was never standardized and therefore not commonly implemented.

This simple fact led many platform and tool product vendors to decide against supporting outbound MEPs. Furthermore, because the WS-I Basic Profile is focused on the HTTP binding which does not natively support outbound patterns, the WS-I Basic Profile only endorses inbound MEPs as a means of guaranteeing cross-service interoperability. And, even though the WSDL 2.0 specification originally expanded the amount of outbound MEPs from two to four, in the end the committee decided not to include any outbound MEPs in the final, ratified standard.

The WSDL 2.0 Robust In-Only MEP

Time now to take a look into the future, namely at a new MEP that holds some promise. As you might recall from Chapter 9, WSDL 2.0 supports the Request-Response and One-Way MEPs but renames them to In-Out and In-Only respectively.

The Robust In-Only MEP is similar to In-Only except for the fact that a fault may be sent back to the consumer by the Web service after receiving the input message.

Let's use a fresh example to demonstrate this. Imagine a Weather service that receives regular updates from consumer programs that each represent a temperature sensor. The role of a sensor program is to issue a temperature update every hour. This is a one-way communication in that the sensor program (consumer) sends a SOAP message containing the temperature to the Web service via the In-Only MEP.

However, there are times when the service is too busy to receive and process this update. When this happens, the consumer program should attempt to resend the message after a short period. Given that the message is sent via an In-Only MEP, the consumer has no way of knowing that the Weather service chose not to process its message.

> **NOTE**
>
> This type of resending behavior could be provided natively by an underlying protocol. The use of this MEP guarantees that it will occur, regardless of the transport protocol used.

Using the Robust In-Only MEP, the Web service has the option of responding to the consumer only when it decides that it cannot process the original message. Therefore, the consumer only needs to resend its update if it receives this fault message.

Let's have a look at an `operation` construct based on this MEP:

```
<operation name="updateTemperature" pattern=
  "http://www.w3.org/ns/wsdl/robust-in-only ">
  <input element="weather:updateTemperature"/>
  <outfault element="weather:updateTemperatureFault"/>
</operation>
```

Example 14.11
An operation defined with the Robust In-Only MEP.

The input message maps to the `weather:updateTemperature` type. There is no output message but only an `outfault` message element that maps to the `weather:update TemperatureFault` type. The sending of the outfault message is optional, and at the discretion of the programming logic that underlies the `updateTemperature` operation.

> **NOTE**
>
> In this scenario, the fault is programmatically generated by the core Web service logic. This is different from various runtime exceptions that may occur when message delivery to the service fails. In these cases, some form of automatic notification may be sent back to the consumer.

WSDL 2.0 Custom MEPs

As pointed out earlier in the *Extending the WSDL Language* section, operations in WSDL 2.0 can be customized to support new message exchange patterns. These custom patterns are essentially proprietary within a given environment (such as the boundary established by a service inventory) because they rely on correspondingly custom logic within the service and perhaps also within consumers of the service as well.

So it's time to create our own custom MEP. First, we need to assign the MEP a custom identifier that will be used by the service logic to recognize it and to then carry out the required processing. As we initially explained in Chapter 9, the WSDL 2.0 `operation` element provides a `pattern` attribute that is assigned a URI. When we populate this attribute with any one of the pre-defined URIs provided by the WSDL 2.0 specification, runtime processors will respond by carrying out built-in logic used to support the MEP that corresponds to that URI. However, if we enter our own value into this attribute, then it's up to us to provide the programming logic needed to execute the MEP as we designed it.

> **NOTE**
>
> Even though you have flexibility as to what you place in the `pattern` attribute, it is recommended that you stick to using a URI value preceded with "http://" and to then host a document explaining the custom MEP at the address to which the URI points.

Let's step through a simple case study example to see how a custom MEP can be defined.

> **CASE STUDY EXAMPLE**
>
> Steve needs to build the `opOrderStatusNotification` operation of the Purchase Order service to provide publish-and-subscribe type of functionality. After studying the WSDL 2.0 standard, he notices the absence of the outbound MEPs he would

normally have used for this operation. He therefore realizes that he will need to build something custom.

Steve begins by defining his requirements:

- The operation must allow one input message in order for a consumer to subscribe to a particular purchase order document.

- The operation must also support the issuance of multiple output messages after the one input message has been received. Further, these output messages may occur over a period of time, ranging from seconds to days.

Using the MEP naming convention established by WSDL 2.0, he calls it the "In-Multiple-Out" MEP. Next, following the URI format used for XML Schema and WSDL definitions, Steve chooses to create an identifier by combining the following parts:

`http://actioncon.com` (the base value of all WSDL-related URIs)

- `/mep/` (to identify it as a URI for an MEP)

- `in-multiple-out` (the MEP name)

...which results in this URI value:

`http://actioncon.com/mep/in-multiple-out`

Steve then goes ahead and modifies the WSDL 2.0 version of the Purchase Order abstract description to add this new operation:

```
<operation name="opOrderStatusNotification"
  pattern="http://actioncon.com/mep/in-multiple-out">
  <input element="po:subscribe"/>
  <output element="po:status"/>
</operation>
```

Example 14.12

The definition of the custom In-Multiple-Out message exchange pattern. Note that because tools will not recognize custom MEPs, this is not a very portable solution.

Although on the surface this looks like a regular In-Out MEP, the URI helps us recognize that this is not the case. Steve works with developers to build the core service logic so that it responds to this URI value by allowing the service to issue the output message defined by `po:status` repeatedly, as required, every time there is a change in the purchase order a consumer is subscribed to.

SUMMARY OF KEY POINTS

- Outbound MEPs (such as Notification and Solicit-Response) have not been widely adopted by the industry, discouraged by the WS-Basic Profile, and are not part of WSDL 2.0.

- The Robust In-Only MEP is new with WSDL 2.0 and provides a variation of In-Only that allows for the optional response of a fault message.

- WSDL 2.0 allows you to create custom MEPs by defining a custom URI identifier.

14.4 Designing Asynchronous Operations

A common point of confusion with WSDL is how it can be used to describe asynchronous interactions. To fully understand this requires that we investigate what asynchrony means to a Web service contract and how asynchronous services are designed in general.

> **NOTE**
>
> In the upcoming sections you'll see the term "request-response" used a number of times, except that you'll notice that it is spelled with lower-case letters. We only capitalize this term when referring to the WSDL Request-Response MEP.

The Asynchronous Web Service

Here are some interesting statements:

- Because Web services are based on a messaging framework they are naturally *asynchronous*.

- Because the HTTP protocol is based on a request-response communication mechanism, Web services that exchange messages via HTTP are inherently *synchronous*.

So what is it then? We know that the vast majority of Web services rely on communication via HTTP, but that this communication is usually carried out via SOAP messages.

The fact is, though, that these statements are all true. We have the freedom to create Web services capable of both synchronous and asynchronous communication patterns. But it is the latter type that requires some further explanation.

What is Asynchrony?

Because Web services emerged during the RPC era, they were often required to continue emulating synchronous data exchanges. This is one of the reasons that synchronous communication remains the common default for most services today.

But in order to maximize the extent of loose coupling between the moving parts of a service-oriented solution, we need to understand how to leverage asynchrony wherever appropriate. Similarly, we need to realize when asynchronous data exchanges introduce unnecessary risk and design complexity. Either way, it all starts with how we design the Web service contract.

So, again, what exactly is asynchrony? Synchronous and asynchronous communication are both concerned with data exchange, but each approaches it in a different way. How they differ depends on where you stand:

- From a developer's perspective, an asynchronous transaction may be one where program A sends program B a request, and then the instance of program A is destroyed until program B responds and re-invokes program A. The synchronous transaction, on the other hand, would simply involve one call from program A in which it issues the request, and its instance remains in memory until it receives a (hopefully immediate) response.

- From a networking point of view, an asynchronous interaction may be one where program A establishes one connection to send program B some data, and then program B creates a second connection in order to respond. A synchronous interaction would require only one connection to complete this data exchange.

- From an abstract view, we may simply state that asynchronous communication is such that the response to a request does not come immediately after the request and may not come at all.

These are all valid ways of looking at asynchrony. Just to get one more opinion, here's how the W3C Web Services Glossary defines it:

> *"An interaction is said to be asynchronous when the associated messages are chronologically and procedurally decoupled. For example, in a request-response interaction, the client agent can process the response at some indeterminate point in the future when its existence is discovered. Mechanisms to do this include polling, notification by receipt of another message, etc."*

When it comes to Web services, there are several ways to model and design asynchronous data exchanges. Let's explore some of the more common approaches.

Polling

A particular data exchange requirement may be designed at the abstract level to be asynchronous. For example, a query may demand a long response time due to the processing requirements that come with accessing legacy repositories and consolidating data results. Knowing this in advance, you, as the service owner, may want to make this behavior clear to potential consumers by offering two operations:

- The first allows the consumer to submit the query request.

- The second allows the consumer to get the answer to the request at a later point.

This forms the basis for data exchange via polling.

In a polling scenario, a slow request-response operation is split into two: a request operation and a response operation, as follows:

1. *Request Operation* – The consumer sends its request to the Web service which only responds with an identifier (an ID value).

2. *Response Operation* – The consumer sends a polling request containing the identifier it was given from Step 1. The service either responds with the response if it is ready, or tells the consumer to try again later.

Figure 14.7 illustrates the dynamics of a polling data exchange. Note that the numbers from the previous list correspond to the numbers in the figure.

There are many additional parameters that can be applied to the polling technique. For example, an interval time can be specified to determine when exactly a consumer program is allowed to issue its polling requests. Overall, the main drawback of this approach is that it can result in heavy runtime loads on the service, especially in high concurrency environments. Moreover, it is simply more work for both the service and consumer developers to build and work with two separate operations.

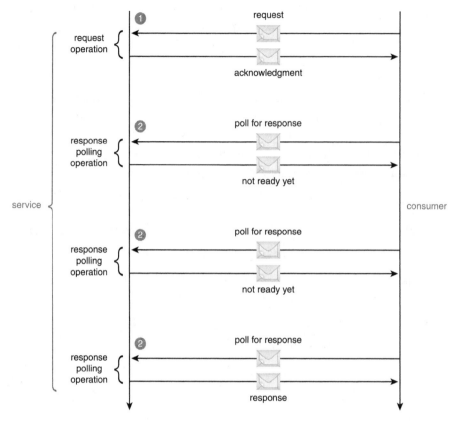

Figure 14.7

In a polling scenario, the consumer may repeatedly attempt to retrieve the response of its original request.

Asynchronous Protocol Binding

Another way to model asynchrony is at the binding level. Whether it is synchronous or asynchronous, an interaction between a Web service and its consumer can still be modeled as a related set of input and output messages as part of a single operation.

As we already know from our discussions about WSDL MEPs, a standard Request-Response (or In-Out) operation is defined by organizing the input and output message definitions in a particular sequence (input first, then output).

Regardless of the interaction scenarios they are involved in, SOAP messages are always one-way messages. Therefore, from an abstract perspective, two one-way SOAP messages arranged into a particular sequence are not procedurally coupled.

However, because the corresponding SOAP binding definitions dictate how SOAP messages must appear on the wire, they can introduce dependencies that relate (couple) one SOAP message to another. And since different bindings can have different properties, you may need to employ different strategies to handle asynchronous communication.

Let's first consider the case of a SOAP binding that is naturally asynchronous, and we'll then look into asynchrony with other types of bindings.

Inherently Asynchronous Binding

Certain bindings are natively asynchronous. The most common example is SOAP over SMTP. As you may know, SMTP is the protocol used to carry emails on the Internet. It is therefore naturally asynchronous because when somebody sends an email, an immediate answer is not expected. Therefore, when binding an abstract description to a SOAP over SMTP binding, the concrete description automatically becomes asynchronous by nature.

Figure 14.8 illustrates the data exchange between a Web service and consumer as two separate emails containing SOAP messages.

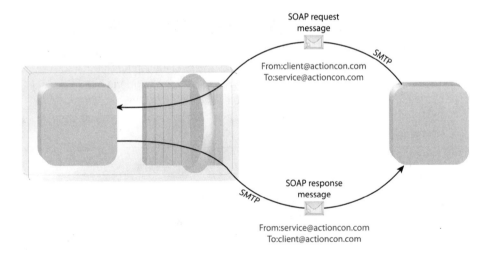

Figure 14.8

The consumer sends a SOAP request message via email to the service. Whenever the service is ready, it responds with an email message that contains the response SOAP message.

The SOAP over SMTP binding is established in the `transport` attribute of the `soap11:binding` element, as follows.

```
<binding name="bdPO-SOAP11HTTP" type="tns:ptPurchaseOrder">
  <soap11:binding style="document" transport=
  "http://schemas.pocketsoap.com/soap/smtp"/>
    ...
  <operation name="opChangedOrderStatus">
    <input>
      <soap11:body use="literal"/>
    </input>
    <output>
      <soap11:body use="literal"/>
    </output>
  </operation>
</binding>
```

Example 14.13
An operation element that is part of a portType construct that is bound to the SOAP over SMTP transport protocol.

Note in this example that besides the setting of the transport attribute, the rest of the binding is identical to the SOAP over HTTP binding.

> **NOTE**
>
> The implementation of the SMTP binding for SOAP 1.1 is not common, and there is no widely reviewed SMTP binding specification for SOAP 1.2. Therefore, be sure to confirm that your runtime platform supports this binding option before considering it. The specification for defining an SMTP binding extension for SOAP 1.1 is available at www.pocketsoap.com/specs/smtpbinding.

WS-Addressing

HTTP, the most widespread transport protocol used for SOAP messages, is naturally a request-response protocol. An HTTP request is sent by a consumer to an HTTP server, and an HTTP response is then sent back using the same TCP connection. If you recall our initial views on asynchrony at the beginning of this section, you could make a case that, especially from a networking perspective, HTTP is synchronous in nature.

For this reason, the SOAP over HTTP binding relates one SOAP message sent as an HTTP request to another SOAP message, which is received as the corresponding HTTP response. As a result, when using the SOAP over HTTP protocol to bind a request-response operation, the input and output messages are coupled.

Figure 14.9 illustrates the execution of a WSDL Request-Response MEP via SOAP over HTTP.

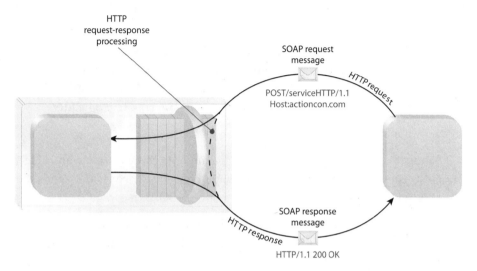

Figure 14.9

A consumer accesses a Web service's Request-Response operation by sending the request (input message) via an HTTP request and then receives the response (output message) via the corresponding HTTP response. The dashed line indicates the runtime processing performed by the platform to maintain the context of the HTTP request before generating the HTTP response.

Ok, well, that's interesting, but we're actually supposed to be discussing asynchronous communication in this section. What we're leading up to is a common situation where HTTP is the desired transport protocol for an interaction scenario that may not allow synchronous data exchange.

At times, it can take seconds for the response output message to be sent back to the consumer, which raises a problem within typical network environments where idle TCP connections are terminated. As previously stated, there is an expectation that the HTTP response be delivered via the same TCP connection established for the original request message.

In order to make HTTP suitable for scenarios that require longer response periods, we need the help of a separate set of SOAP extensibility elements. This is where WS-Addressing comes in. Although we cover WS-Addressing in detail in Chapters 18 and 19, let's briefly highlight how it helps enable asynchrony even if the transport protocol binding being used does not natively support it.

WS-Addressing provides a `wsa:ReplyTo` element that is placed into a SOAP header block (similar in concept to the reply-to header used in regular email). This little piece of metadata essentially tells the Web service not to return the response back to its requestor, but to send it to a different destination instead.

In the case of SOAP over HTTP and a Request-Response operation, it may be used by the consumer (in a request) to tell the service that the response should not be returned in the HTTP response; instead, the Web service is instructed to respond to the address and via the transport indicated in the WS-Addressing `wsa:ReplyTo` header.

Here's how it all happens:

1. The input SOAP message is sent by the consumer to the service via an HTTP request. The runtime environment in which the Web service resides sends the consumer an HTTP response but without a response SOAP message.

2. After the request has been processed by the Web service, it sends the output SOAP message via a separate HTTP request to the address provided by the `wsa:ReplyTo` header. The consumer receives the request and the HTTP mechanism automatically issues an HTTP response back to the service.

These steps correspond with the numbers in Figure 14.10.

The interesting aspect to this scenario is that it is the consumer that's telling the Web service what to do because it is the one responsible for populating the `wsa:ReplyTo` header block.

While this may be a valid design option for certain situations, we are focused on Web service contract design. How then, using WS-Addressing, can we design the contract so that it is the one fully responsible for determining the interaction requirements? The solution is for the Web service contract to tell the client that it must use this WS-Addressing feature.

As introduced in Chapter 10 and further explained at the end of Chapter 19, the `wsam:Addressing` policy assertion can be created to indicate the required use of WS-Addressing. By making this assertion mandatory and attaching it to the Request-Response operation, we can force the consumer to send WS-Addressing headers.

The WS-Addressing language pre-defines two additional child elements for `wsam:Addressing` that further help define the assertion:

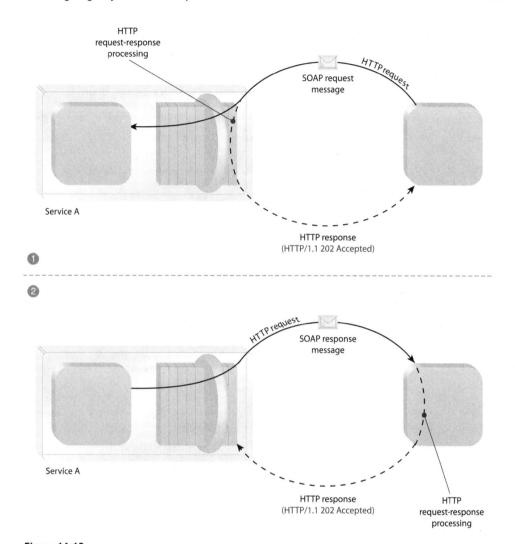

Figure 14.10

An operation with a Request-Response MEP that uses two separate HTTP requests (1 and 2) with the WS-Addressing `wsa:ReplyTo` header.

- `wsam:AnonymousResponses` – The presence of this element indicates that the service supports sending responses via the normal channel of a binding. This means that in a standard HTTP request-response exchange, the service expects that the response will be delivered via HTTP. The element has this name because WS-Addressing uses the concept of an anonymous recipient to talk about the normal channels for responses (as explained in Chapter 18).

- `wsam:NonAnynomousResponses` – This element may alternatively be used to indicate that the service supports sending responses via other channels. So, in the case of the HTTP request-response exchange, the response can be delivered via either a separate HTTP request or an alternative transport protocol, such as SMTP.

A synchronous request-response binding may therefore be described as asynchronous in a service description with the following WS-Policy statement:

```
<operation name="opChangedOrderStatus">
  <wsp:Policy wsdl:required="true">
    <wsam:Addressing>
      <wsp:Policy>
        <wsam:NonAnonymousResponses/>
      </wsp:Policy>
    </wsam:Addressing>
  </wsp:Policy>
  <input message="tns:msgCheckOrderRequest"/>
  <output message="tns:msgCheckOrderResponse"/>
</operation>
```

Example 14.14
An `operation` construct containing an embedded policy definition comprised of the `wsam:Addressing` element.

In this sample code, WS-Addressing is used by the Web service contract to achieve an asynchronous interaction with SOAP over HTTP. Specifically, the contract requires that consumers must use WS-Addressing in their requests to the service and that they must specify a reply-to address.

You may also notice in this example that the `wsp:Policy` element is using the `wsdl:required` attribute we described earlier in this chapter. The setting of "true" ensures that consumers do not ignore the policy assertion and are aware that WS-Addressing must be used.

Furthermore, the absence of `wsam:AnonymousResponses` does not mean that the service will reject requests with anonymous `wsam:ReplyTo` headers. The client may send such headers, but the service may send a WS-Addressing fault in response (as explained in Chapter 18). The statement guarantees that non-anonymous requests are allowed, though it does not specify the type of addresses that are accepted (e.g., an HTTP request message requesting an answer via SMTP).

NOTE

The WS-Addressing specification defines the `wsam:Addressing` policy assertion to indicate that WS-Addressing is supported or required. It is a convention to use the `wsam:` prefix for this element and the `wsam:AnonymousResponses` and `wsam:NonAnynomousResponses` elements.

Also note that `wsam:Addressing` is defined as a nested policy assertion, which means it always requires the child `wsp:Policy` element, even in the case where `wsam:AnonymousResponses` and `wsam:NonAnynomousResponses` are not specified, as follows:

```
<wsp:Policy>
  <wsam:Addressing>
    <wsp:Policy/>
  </wsam:Addressing>
</wsp:Policy>
```

For more details regarding nested assertions, see Chapter 16.

Guidelines for Using Asynchronous Patterns

When should asynchronous interactions be used? There are at least two good reasons:

- *Overcome Transport Protocol Limitations* – As previously mentioned, a TCP connection used by HTTP may be torn down by a router if it stays idle too long. Using the previously described techniques, asynchronous communication can be used to circumvent this limitation.

- *Increase Service Scalability* – If a particular operation takes a long time to complete, all of the connections and corresponding state data are kept active and will continue to consume memory resources. This can significantly tax services and surrounding runtime platforms (and supporting server hardware).

Forcing synchronous data exchange with every inter-service interaction can result in unnecessary runtime processing and bandwidth consumption. Strategically using asynchronous patterns can help optimize cross-service communication and streamline the overall design of service compositions.

SUMMARY OF KEY POINTS

- An operation at the abstract level is neither synchronous nor asynchronous by nature.

- Certain SOAP bindings, such as the SMTP binding, are inherently asynchronous.

- WS-Addressing can be used to enable sophisticated asynchronous functionality.

NOTE

The following section does not introduce or explain the WS-BPEL language. It is only focused on how the use of WS-BPEL can affect and extend the design of WSDL definitions. If you are unfamiliar with WS-BPEL or are not required to work with it, feel free to skip this part of the book. Introductory coverage of the WS-BPEL language is provided in the book *Service-Oriented Architecture: Concepts, Technology, and Design.*

14.5 WS-BPEL and WSDL

The WS-BPEL specification defines a language specifically for expressing business process logic carried out by the composition of Web services. In practice, this means that you can use the WS-BPEL language to implement Web services that make calls to other Web services. As part of the WS-BPEL specification, a number of extensibility elements are defined for WSDL (as explained in upcoming sections).

The WS-BPEL specification also imposes a few minor restrictions on how to structure WSDL definitions that are referenced by WS-BPEL process definitions:

WS-I Basic Profile Compliance

A note is included in the WS-BPEL specification that all WS-BPEL implementations should be able to participate in WS-I Basic Profile conforming interactions. While this leaves open the possibility of a WS-BPEL implementation supporting a WSDL definition that is not WS-I Basic Profile-compliant, in practice this form of compliance is highly recommended.

Probably the most important aspect of this is the use of literal style WSDL bindings. The WS-I Basic Profile states that literal bindings should be used instead of RPC-encoded bindings (as explained in Chapter 7). Because WS-BPEL uses XPath as its expression language, the variations in XML allowed for in the RPC-encoded WSDL binding make it very difficult to construct appropriate XPath expressions.

Restrictions Relating to Operations and Faults

The WS-BPEL specification explicitly bans the use of overloaded operation names in port types as well as the use of Solicit-Response or Notification MEPs in operations (which are also outside the WS-I Basic Profile).

Furthermore, WS-BPEL requires that all faults within a target namespace have a unique name. WSDL 1.1 only requires that faults used by an individual operation are named differently to each other. This means that in WSDL 1.1 it is necessary to specify a port type name, an operation name, and the fault name in order to uniquely identify a fault. The WS-BPEL language's fault handling mechanism requires that faults can be referred to by a qualified name consisting of the WSDL definition's target namespace and the fault name.

The WSDL language allows different faults to be defined using the same data type. In this case, some bindings will result in fault messages which can be indistinguishable from each other. The WS-BPEL specification defines some rules to dictate which exception definition should be chosen in the event that such a fault is received. This is based on the order in which the fault definitions appear in the WSDL definition. Typically the order of definitions in WSDL is not significant, so this could cause some confusion for developers. It is best to avoid this situation by ensuring that each fault is based on a different XML Schema element declaration.

> **NOTE**
>
> Because both the WS-BPEL 2.0 and WSDL 2.0 specifications were being developed at the around same time, the WS-BPEL language was based solely on the use of Web service contracts that comply with version 1.1 of the WSDL language.

WS-BPEL Extensions to WSDL

The WSDL extensibility elements defined by WS-BPEL are:

- `plnk:partnerLinkType`
- `bpws:property`
- `bpws:propertyAlias`

These elements will be explained shortly. Some are required in the WSDL definition for any Web service that is referenced from a WS-BPEL process definition. So even if your Web service is not initially implemented as part of a WS-BPEL composition, it might be worth including them as a convenience to WS-BPEL authors who might choose to compose your service at a later point. However, it is worth noting that WS-BPEL tools do provide good support for the creation of these extension elements, so their absence will not prevent their use by a WS-BPEL definition.

Programming languages are usually designed with specific use cases in mind and this can result in particular emphasis being placed on individual aspects of a language. Two such use cases considered in the design of WS-BPEL were asynchronous message exchanges and the correlation of new messages with any state stored as a result of previous message exchanges. It is these aspects of the WS-BPEL language that surfaced as extensions to the WSDL language.

So why did the authors of the WS-BPEL specification define extensions for WSDL? Wouldn't it have been better to simply place this information in the WS-BPEL definition itself and not go complicating WSDL with it? The answers to these questions are really quite simple. These extensions relate to the Web service interface, so in many ways the WSDL definition is the natural place to put them. WSDL (just like most other specifications) provides an extension mechanism specifically designed to allow it to be used in this way.

The presence of these extension elements should not cause any problems as any applications unaware of WS-BPEL should ignore them. However, if you prefer not to have these extensions in your WSDL definition, you can choose to place them in a separate WSDL document that imports the WSDL document that describes your Web service. This way you can point WS-BPEL tools at one WSDL document and everything else at the other. Some WS-BPEL editors automatically follow this technique in order to avoid the need to modify the original WSDL definitions when creating extensions.

Asynchronous Message Exchanges

The WS-BPEL specification provides a straightforward way to describe a situation where two services (called *partners*) communicate with each other using contracts. For this purpose, the `plnk:partnerLinkType` extension element for WSDL 1.1 was created. It essentially allows two port types to be grouped together to indicate that they are used for peer-to-peer communication.

In the following example, one `portType` is implemented by each partner. A role name is associated with each `portType` (via the use of the `plnk:role` element) to indicate which `portType` is implemented by the WS-BPEL process definition itself and which is provided by the other partner:

```
<plnk:partnerLinkType name="VendorPartnerLinkType"
  xmlns:plnk=
    "http://schemas.xmlsoap.org/ws/2003/05/partner-link/">
  <plnk:role name="serviceProvider">
    <plnk:portType name="po:POService"/>
  </plnk:role>
  <plnk:role name="client">
    <plnk:portType name="po:POServiceCallbacks"/>
  </plnk:role>
</plnk:partnerLinkType>
```

Example 14.15
A `partnerLinkType` construct that references two `portType` constructs. (This code resides in the WS-BPEL process definition, not in the WSDL definition.)

For consistency, the WS-BPEL language makes use of `plnk:partnerLinkType` definitions even where peer-to-peer messaging is not used. In this case, the `plnk:partner LinkType` construct contains a reference to a single `portType`. Again, the role name is used to indicate whether it implements that `portType` or intends to invoke on it:

```
<plnk:partnerLinkType name="VendorPartnerLinkType"
  xmlns:plnk=
    "http://schemas.xmlsoap.org/ws/2003/05/partner-link/">
  <plnk:role name="serviceProvider">
    <plnk:portType name="po:POService"/>
  </plnk:role>
</plnk:partnerLinkType>
```

Example 14.16
A `partnerLinkType` construct that references a single `portType` construct.

Correlation

WS-BPEL implementations store data associated with message exchanges. Messages received may need to be correlated with data relating to previous messages.

Correlation could be handled at the transport level, perhaps using identifiers within WS-Addressing headers and most WS-BPEL implementations facilitate this approach. However, the WS-BPEL specification takes the view that most business documents already contain meaningful identifiers. Rather than mandate the use of a second identification mechanism based solely on the needs of the technology, the WS-BPEL language facilitates the use of these business identifiers to achieve the correlation of incoming messages with the stored data.

The rules for correlating messages are implemented within the WS-BPEL process itself, the details of which are beyond the scope of this book. However, some portions of this surface as extensions to the WSDL definition via the `bpws:property` and `bpws:propertyAlias` elements.

In the WS-BPEL language, *properties* are a way to highlight important values that appear within messages. For example, you might define a property for a purchase order number. All properties are simple types, so a property declaration appears in a WSDL definition as just a name and a simple data type, as shown here:

```
<bpws:property
  xmlns:bpws="http://schemas.xmlsoap.org/ws/2003/03/business-process/"
  name="PONumber" type="xsd:integer"/>
```

Example 14.17
A property declaration of type `xsd:integer`.

A value such as a purchase order number might appear in a number of different messages. It could be in the purchase order document itself, but it might also be in an acknowledgement message for the receipt of that purchase order, or perhaps in a request for the status of the purchase order.

Property aliases allow you to specify in the WSDL definition how the value for such a property can be extracted from a variety of messages. This is achieved by specifying an XPath expression that is applied to one of the message parts.

The `bpws:propertyAlias` element can be defined for each message that the property can appear in. This means that a property alias definition consists of four things:

- a reference to the property
- a reference to the WSDL message
- the part name
- the XPath expression identifying the location of the value

Here's an example:

```
<bpws:propertyAlias
  xmlns:bpws="http://schemas.xmlsoap.org/ws/2003/03/business-process/"
  messageType="po:msgSubmitOrderRequest"
  part="PurchaseOrder"
  propertyName="po:PONumber"
  query="/po:purchaseOrder/po:poNumber"/>
```

Example 14.18

A `bpws:propertyAlias` element being used to find the value for the `PONumber` property in the `msgSubmitOrderRequest` message.

Properties and property aliases can also be used within a WS-BPEL definition simply to highlight important or commonly accessed values within documents. This can be a convenience for process designers as it saves them having to create the XPath expressions to access these values. However, the most common use of these elements is as part of message correlation.

CASE STUDY EXAMPLE
A WSDL Definition with WS-BPEL Extensibility Elements

An architect from MegaEuroMart contacts Steve to ask if he would be willing to assist in a beta project. Essentially, the architect would like to experiment with the use of WS-BPEL to build an executable business process to handle the exchange of purchase orders with ActionCon. Steve agrees and is subsequently sent the WS-BPEL process definition.

After studying the code and learning about the WS-BPEL extension requirements for WSDL definitions, Steve assembles a separate WSDL definition that imports his Purchase Order WSDL document (from Chapter 8), as follows:

```
<definitions
  targetNamespace="http://actioncon.com/ns-bpel"
  xmlns:bpws="http://schemas.xmlsoap.org/ws/2003/03/business-process/"
  xmlns:plnk="http://schemas.xmlsoap.org/ws/2003/05/partner-link/">
  <import .../>
  <bpws:property
    name="PONumber" type="xsd:integer"/>
  <bpws:propertyAlias
    messageType="po:msgSubmitOrderRequest"
    part="PurchaseOrder"
    propertyName="po:PONumber"
```

```
      query="/po:purchaseOrder/po:poNumber"/>
  <plnk:partnerLinkType name="VendorPartnerLinkType">
    <plnk:role name="serviceProvider">
        <plnk:portType name="po:ptPurchaseOrder"/>
    </plnk:role>
  </plnk:partnerLinkType>
</definitions>
```

Example 14.19

An abbreviated WSDL definition that highlights the extensibility elements introduced by the WS-BPEL language.

SUMMARY OF KEY POINTS

- The WS-BPEL language introduces the `plnk:partnerLinkType`, `bpws:property`, and `bpws:propertyAlias` extensibility elements for WSDL 1.1.

- The presence of some or all of these extensibility elements is required for Web services to be composed by WS-BPEL process definitions.

- Their primary purpose is to support asynchronous data exchanges and message correlation.

Chapter 15

Advanced WSDL Part II: Message Dispatch, Service Instance Identification, and Non-SOAP HTTP Binding

This chapter covers a variety of topics, ranging from complex to the obscure. This is therefore not a chapter you necessarily need to read sequentially. Feel free to jump to the sections that are of most interest to you.

Our focus in most of the upcoming sections is on doing more with the extensibility features we've introduced, including the use of protocols other than SOAP.

15.1 Extreme Loose Coupling with WSDL 2.0

One of the most intriguing features introduced by WSDL 2.0 is the option for input, output, and fault message definitions of an operation to allow *any* kind of message containing well-formed XML. This essentially allows you to increase the coarseness of input and output constraint granularity to the extent that you can blow away constraints altogether for a given operation.

The #any Attribute

The `element` attribute of the `input`, `output`, and `fault` elements has traditionally been assigned an XML Schema type that establishes the body structure of the SOAP message.

For example, here is the familiar `opSubmitOrder` `operation` construct that allows the Purchase Order service to receive new purchase order documents:

```
<operation name="opSubmitOrder"
  pattern="http://www.w3.org/ns/wsdl/in-out">
  <input messageLabel="In" element="po:purchaseOrder"/>
  <output messageLabel="Out"
    element="po:acknowledgement"/>
</operation>
```

Example 15.1

The original WSDL 2.0 version of the `opSubmitOrder` operation.

We can remove dependencies between operation messages and XML Schema types by setting the `element` attribute to the value of "#any," as shown here:

```
<operation name="opSubmitOrder"
  pattern="http://www.w3.org/ns/wsdl/in-out">
  <input messageLabel="In" element="#any"/>
  <output messageLabel="Out"
    element="po:acknowledgement"/>
</operation>
```

Example 15.2

The revised opSubmitOrder operation with the element attribute of the input element set to "#any."

Valid #any Messages

The sole criteria that messages being sent to or from an operation that uses the #any value must meet is that they must exist as a well-formed XML document with a single top element. To understand this better, let's take a look at a few SOAP messages that would and would not work.

The following message, for example, would not be acceptable because the message body does not contain a root XML element (the soap:Body element does not count):

```
<soap:Envelope xmlns:soap=
  "http://www.w3.org/2003/05/soap-envelope">
  <soap:Body>
    I can do anything.
  </soap:Body>
</soap:Envelope>
```

Example 15.3

A SOAP message with a soap:Body construct that does not contain a well-formed XML construct.

However, this message would be accepted:

```
<soap:Envelope xmlns:soap=
  "http://www.w3.org/2003/05/soap-envelope">
  <soap:Body>
    <ToDo>
      I can do anything.
    </ToDo>
  </soap:Body>
</soap:Envelope>
```

Example 15.4

A SOAP message with a soap:Body construct that does contain a well-formed XML construct.

...as would the following:

```
<soap:Envelope xmlns:soap=
  "http://www.w3.org/2003/05/soap-envelope">
  <soap:Body>
    <ToDo/>
  </soap:Body>
</soap:Envelope>
```

Example 15.5
Another example of a well-formed XML document (comprised solely as a single element) within the `soap:Body` construct.

...and this variation as well:

```
<soap:Envelope xmlns:soap=
  "http://www.w3.org/2003/05/soap-envelope">
  <soap:Body>
    <ToDo>
      <Icandoanything/>
    </ToDo>
  </soap:Body>
</soap:Envelope>
```

Example 15.6
Another legitimate XML document in the SOAP body.

But if you open your old XML textbooks to look up the rules of well formed XML syntax, then you would find that a message like this one would not work because it is still missing a parent root element:

```
<soap:Envelope xmlns:soap=
  "http://www.w3.org/2003/05/soap-envelope">
  <soap:Body>
    <ToDo/>
    <ToDo/>
  </soap:Body>
</soap:Envelope>
```

Example 15.7
An XML document that is not well formed within the SOAP body.

Architectural Considerations

Although a simple change, the use of the #any value can have a major impact on the role of a Web service contract. By allowing an operation to receive any kind of input message, we are essentially agreeing to allow incoming data to bypass contract-level validation.

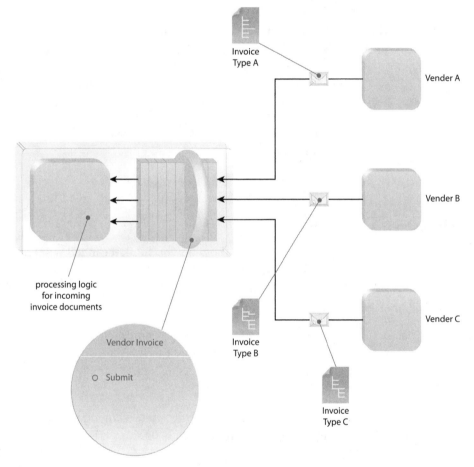

Figure 15.1

A Web service capable of receiving a range of invoice documents based on different schemas. Although flexible, this forces all of the validation processing upon the underlying service logic.

On the one hand, this feature fully supports the Service Loose Coupling and Service Abstraction design principles because we are dramatically reducing the dependency a consumer needs to form on a given service, and we are also not revealing (any) validation logic for incoming messages.

The downside is that we are not leveraging the powerful features of the XML Schema language for our Web service contracts. By accepting any input messages, we move the entire responsibility of having to validate those message contents into the core service logic.

WSDL #any and XML Schema xsd:any

The WSDL #any value was introduced with WSDL 2.0, but has its roots in XML Schema. As you might recall from Chapters 6 and 12, the WSDL #any value is conceptually similar to the XML Schema ##any namespace value as well as the xsd:any and xsd:anyAttribute elements. However, in practice, the WSDL #any value is applied differently from these XML Schema features.

If we wanted to create a statement in XML Schema that resembles a type comparable to the #any value, it would look something like this:

```
<xsd:any namespace="##any" processContents="skip" />
```

15.2 Message Dispatch Challenges

When a Web service is deployed and running, how do you think it can tell what operation an incoming message relates to? Well, you might say, it probably attempts to map the incoming input SOAP message with an operation that has an input message with a corresponding, matching type.

This runtime decision-based logic is referred to as *message dispatch* logic. It's pretty much what most Web service engines go by when carrying out this mapping. But what if more than one operation contains input messages with the same type? That's when things can get iffy.

Of course fundamentally, the WSDL language encourages reuse among its various definitions. For example, you can create multiple operations that each accept a purchase order document and then do something different with it. One may store it, the other may retrieve information based on values within the document, while a third may simply forward it elsewhere. In all three cases, the different operations could be designed to share the same underlying PurchaseOrderType XML Schema complex type.

Therefore, the runtime processor that will need to figure out which operation to give an incoming purchase order document to will run into a problem because the input message for all three operations is the same.

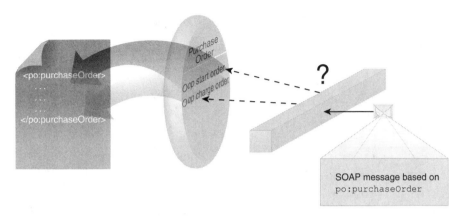

Figure 15.2

Message dispatch logic is usually taken care of by runtime system agents that parse and then route the SOAP message to the appropriate operation. However, custom message dispatch processing can also be added to the service logic.

NOTE

Although we are primarily concerned with input messages, it is important to acknowledge that this problem can also exist for outbound messages. For example, a single Web service contract can contain multiple operations with output message definitions that share exactly the same type. It is then the consumer program that needs to dispatch the messages without ambiguity.

CASE STUDY EXAMPLE

Steve built a sample consumer program to test his Purchase Order service and he is running into some problems. He can submit or change an order just fine. However, every time he tries to cancel an order, instead of a code confirming that the order was cancelled, he gets the order status back. Of course the consumer program does not expect a status message in response to an order cancellation request, and a runtime error predictably results.

Steve decides to talk to Kevin to figure out what is going on. Kevin says that it's probably because his operations are sharing the same underlying message types.

They both take a good look at the current WSDL code and discover the following:

- The `opCheckOrderStatus` and `opCancelOrder` operations accept the same input message (the `po:poNumber` element).

- The `opSubmitOrder` and `opChangeOrder` operations also accept the same input message (the `po:purchaseOrder` element).

That's a bit of a mystery. Kevin expected to find out that `opCheckOrderStatus` and `opCancelOrder` operations shared the same underlying type because that would explain why message dispatch logic is getting confused and sending an incoming message to the wrong operation.

What he doesn't understand is why this is not a problem for the `opSubmitOrder` and `opChangeOrder` operations, which also share the same underlying type. At first he thinks it must be just dumb luck that these operations work. But closer investigation reveals that there is some logic that helps figure out what goes where.

Specifically, the service has a decision routine that looks for the purchase order document's `po:purchaseOrder` element. If it contains the purchase order number (`po:poNumber`), then this means the corresponding record is already in the system, which makes it route the message to the `opChangeOrder` operation. If it isn't present, then `opSubmitOrder` is invoked instead.

But what can they do about the `opCheckOrderStatus` and `opCancelOrder` operations? Both accept just a purchase order number as input, and there is therefore no way to differentiate between the incoming messages, which look like this:

```
<soap:Envelope
  xmlns:soap="http://schemas.xmlsoap.org/soap/envelope/"
  xmlns:po="http://actioncon.com/schema/purchasing">
  <soap:Body>
    <po:poNumber>123456</po:poNumber>
  </soap:Body>
</soap:Envelope>
```

Example 15.8

An incoming SOAP message that is suitable for both the `opCheckOrderStatus` and `opCancelOrder` operations.

There are three common ways of solving this problem:

- Creating Unique Message Types
- Using the SOAP Action Header
- Using WS-Addressing Headers

Let's discuss each approach.

Creating Unique Message Types

This easiest and most recommended way to ensure the reliable dispatch of messages at the Web service end is by using a different qualified name for every input message.

How we achieve this depends on which version of WSDL we're using:

- *WSDL 1.1* – No two operations can use the same message `part` elements for their input message definitions.

- *WSDL 2.0* – No two operations can use the same global element declaration for their input message definitions.

As stated previously, the WSDL language does not prohibit reusing message types, but that doesn't necessarily make it a good idea.

CASE STUDY EXAMPLE

After talking to Kevin, Steve decides to use different XML element type names for the `opCheckOrderStatus` and `opCancelOrder` operations, as follows:

```
<xsd:element name="checkOrder" type="PONumberMsgType"/>
<xsd:element name="cancelOrder" type="PONumberMsgType"/>
<xsd:complexType name="PONumberMsgType">
  <xsd:sequence>
    <xsd:element ref="poNumber"/>
  </xsd:sequence>
</xsd:complexType>
```

Example 15.9
Two different global elements reusing the same underlying complex type.

Note that because he uses global element declarations, he can reuse the existing `PONumberMsgType` complex type while still establishing a separate global element for use by the operations. He then proceeds to change the `element` attributes of the `part` elements that are used by the two operation definitions:

```
<message name="msgCheckOrderRequest">
  <part name="PurchaseOrder" element="po:checkOrder"/>
</message>
<message name="msgCancelOrderRequest">
  <part name="PONumber" element="po:cancelOrder"/>
</message>
```

Example 15.10

The global element declarations from Example 15.9 assigned to `part` elements for two different messages.

Now that it's done, the messages look different on the wire. For example, a message to check the status of an order looks like this:

```
<soap:Envelope
  xmlns:soap="http://schemas.xmlsoap.org/soap/envelope/"
  xmlns:po="http://actioncon.com/schema/purchasing">
  <soap:Body>
    <po:checkOrder>
      <po:poNumber>123456</po:poNumber>
    </po:checkOrder>
  </soap:Body>
</soap:Envelope>
```

Example 15.11

An instance of the input SOAP message from Example 15.9.

Steve has fixed the problem, but he is still not completely satisfied.

He is uncomfortable with the fact that the `opSubmitOrder` and `opChangeOrder` operations still share the same underlying type. Even though the service logic works it out right now, it still doesn't feel like the best design to have identical incoming messages for these two operations. This leads him to investigate the use of SOAP Action headers (as explained next).

NOTE

Remember the `#any` statement we introduced at the beginning of this chapter? What if two or more operations have their input messages set to this value? In this case, other strategies need to be used, as explained in the upcoming sections.

HTTP SOAP Action Header

Another way to differentiate SOAP messages with `Body` constructs defined by the same underlying type is by using the SOAP Action setting.

SOAP Action was introduced in Chapter 11 as the `soapAction` attribute of the `soap:binding` element. It essentially allows an additional "action" value to be associated with the message as a hint as to what or who the message is for.

The syntax for defining the SOAP Action differs across versions of WSDL and SOAP, as follows:

SOAP Action in WSDL 1.1 with SOAP 1.1

```
<binding ...>
  <operation ...>
    <soap11:operation soapAction=
      "http://actioncon.com/action/submit" .../>
  </operation>
</binding>
```

Example 15.12
The `soapAction` attribute of the `soap11:operation` extensibility element assigned a SOAP action value.

SOAP Action in WSDL 1.1 with SOAP 1.2

For the SOAP 1.2 binding, the syntax is similar, except for the fact that SOAP 1.2 makes the use of a SOAP Action setting optional. It accomplishes this as follows:

- It retains the `soapAction` attribute but makes its presence optional.

- It introduces a new `soapActionRequired` attribute to indicate whether it requires a SOAP Action.

Note that you can only use the `soapActionRequired` attribute if you are also using the `soapAction` attribute.

Here's an example:

```
<binding ...>
  <operation ...>
    <soap12:operation
      soapAction="http://actioncon.com/action/submit"
      soapActionRequired="true" ... />
```

```
    </operation>
</binding>
```

Example 15.13
The soapAction attribute of the soap12:operation extensibility element assigned a SOAP action value and the soapActionRequired attribute set to "true."

NOTE

Unlike soapAction and soapActionRequired, which are attributes defined by the SOAP 1.2 language, the wsdl:required attribute is from WSDL 1.1. As explained in Chapter 14, it indicates that the soap12:operation element cannot be ignored, which means that if it is not recognized, the message delivery should fail. You can further add the wsdl:required attribute to help support the use of the SOAP attributes in particular.

SOAP Action in WSDL 2.0 with SOAP 1.1 or SOAP 1.2

With WSDL 2.0 the syntax differs in that the soapActionRequired attribute is no longer used, as follows:

```
<binding ...>
  <operation soapbind:action=
    "http://actioncon.com/action/submit" ...>
    ...
  </operation>
</binding>
```

Example 15.14
The soapbind:action extensibility attribute set to a SOAP Action value.

In this case, a SOAP binding automatically requires that you add a SOAP header when the optional soapbind:action attribute has a value. Let's take a look at an example with a SOAP 1.1 binding:

```
<binding name="bdPO-SOAP11HTTP" type="tns:ptPurchaseOrder">
  <soap11:binding style="document"
    transport="http://schemas.xmlsoap.org/soap/http"/>
  <operation name="opSubmitOrder">
    <soap11:operation
```

```
        soapAction="http://actioncon.com/action/submit"/>
     <input>
        <soap11:body use="literal"/>
     </input>
     <output>
        <soap11:body use="literal"/>
     </output>
   </operation>
   <operation name="opCheckOrderStatus">
      <soap11:operation
        soapAction="http://actioncon.com/action/check"/>
     <input>
        <soap11:body use="literal"/>
     </input>
     <output>
        <soap11:body use="literal"/>
     </output>
   </operation>
   <operation name="opChangeOrder">
      <soap11:operation
        soapAction="http://actioncon.com/action/change"/>
     <input>
        <soap11:body use="literal"/>
     </input>
     <output>
        <soap11:body use="literal"/>
     </output>
   </operation>
   <operation name="opCancelOrder">
      <soap11:operation
        soapAction="http://actioncon.com/action/cancel"/>
     <input>
        <soap11:body use="literal"/>
     </input>
     <output>
        <soap11:body use="literal"/>
     </output>
   </operation>
</binding>
```

Example 15.15

Updated SOAP 1.1 binding elements with populated soapAction attributes.

The result is four messages, each marked with a different SOAP Action URI. This now allows for easy identification and dispatch of each message.

Note that the overall syntax for this example would be identical for SOAP 1.2, except that the value of the `soap:version` attribute, the namespace prefix, and the binding name settings would need to be changed to corresponding values for the SOAP 1.2 specification.

The Actual HTTP Headers

The examples so far in this section have focused on how to set SOAP Action values as part of the WSDL `binding` construct. But, as we know, the purpose of making these settings to the binding definition is to generate an HTTP header that contains the SOAP Action value.

Let's therefore take a minute to see what SOAP Action headers look like when they are part of a generated, runtime message:

The `opSubmitOrder` operation from the previous example would result in the following HTTP header:

```
SOAPAction: "http://actioncon.com/action/submit"
```

...and when SOAP 1.2 is used, the header is expressed in a media-type format that looks like this:

```
Content-Type: application/soap+xml;action=
"http://actioncon.com/action/submit"
```

WS-Addressing SOAP Action Header

Specifying a SOAP Action value for each operation can be tedious. Also the actual transport of SOAP Action values may not be supported by all SOAP bindings. This is why WS-Addressing provides a `wsa:Action` header element that can carry a similar value inside the SOAP envelope.

To generate the `wsa:Action` header block as part of the header section in a SOAP message, we need to add some WS-Addressing extensibility code to the WSDL abstract description.

As with other WS-Addressing elements, `wsa:Action` is implemented as a policy assertion. Before we can add it, we first need to attach the basic `wsam:Addressing` assertion to the port type (or interface), as follows:

```
<portType... >
  <wsp:Policy wsdl:required="true">
    <wsam:Addressing><wsp:Policy/></wsam:Addressing>
  </wsp:Policy>
  ...
</portType>
```

Example 15.16
The `wsam:Addressing` policy assertion associated with a `portType` element.

The `wsa:Action` SOAP header block we eventually want to create will correspond to an attribute of the same name but with a different namespace prefix. It is called `wsaw:Action` (note the extra "w" in the prefix name), and it is added directly to the message definition. Specifically, it is implemented as an attribute of the `input`, `output`, and/or `fault` elements within an `operation` construct, as shown here:

```
<portType... >
  <operation ...>
    <input wsaw:Action=
      "http://actioncon.com/action/submit" .../>
  </operation>
  ...
</portType>
```

Example 15.17
The `wsaw:Action` attribute added to the abstract input message definition.

Here's the important part: it's the value to which the `wsaw:Action` attribute is set that will become the value of the `wsa:Action` header element.

So this means that a WSDL definition like this:

```
<definition targetNamespace=
  "http://actioncon.com/contract/po" ...>
  ...
  <portType name="ifPurchaseOrder">
    <operation name="opSubmitOrder">
      <input message="tns:msgSubmitOrderRequest"
        wsaw:Action=
          "http://actioncon.com/action/opSubmitOrder"/>
      <output message="tns:msgSubmitOrderResponse"
```

```
       wsaw:Action="http://actioncon.com/action/
           opSubmitOrderResponse"/>
    </operation>
  </portType>
  ...
</definition>
```

Example 15.18

The populated `wsaw:Action` attribute as part of an `input` element.

Would generate a request message like this:

```
<soap:Envelope
   xmlns:soap="http://www.w3.org/2003/05/soap-envelope"
   xmlns:wsa="http://www.w3.org/2005/08/addressing">
   <soap:Header>
     <wsa:To>
       http://actioncon.com/services/soap12/purchaseOrder
     </wsa:To>
     <wsa:Action>
       http://actioncon.com/action/opSubmitOrder
     </wsa:Action>
   </soap:Header>
   <soap:Body>
     <tns:msgSubmitOrderRequest>
       ...
     </tns:msgSubmitOrderRequest>
   </soap:Body>
</soap:Envelope>
```

Example 15.19

The resulting SOAP message with the corresponding `wsa:Action` header block containing the same value of the `wsaw:Action` attribute.

It can be time-consuming to associate this attribute with each and every message definition, which is why there is a neat feature that kicks in when you choose not to add the `wsaw:Action` attribute. As long as WS-Addressing is being used (as per the `wsam:Addressing` policy assertion), the `wsa:Action` header element will be populated with an auto-generated default URI value based on how the abstract WSDL definition is structured.

In case you're curious how this default value is created, here are the details:

- For input or output messages described with WSDL 1.1:

  `[target namespace]/[port type]/[operation]/[input|output name]`

- For fault messages described with WSDL 1.1:

  `[target namespace]/[port type]/[operation]/fault/[fault name]`

- For input or output messages described with WSDL 2.0:

  `[target namespace]/[interface]/[operation]/[message direction]`

- For fault messages described with WSDL 2.0:

  `[target namespace]/[interface]/[operation]/[fault name]`

> **NOTE**
>
> If the target namespace is a URN, the slashes (/) delimiting each part are replaced by colons (:).

For WSDL 2.0, the `[message direction]` part of the value is created as follows:

- "`Request`" for the input message of the In-Out and In-Optional-Out message exchange patterns.

- "`Response`" for the output message of the In-Out and In-Optional-Out message exchange patterns.

An empty string for one-way message exchange patterns.

These default values were cleverly thought up by the WS-Addressing committee so that each message can receive a unique `wsa:Action` header value without you having to do any real work.

> **NOTE**
>
> Regardless of whether you manually set the `wsaw:Action` attribute or if you rely on the auto-generated default values, a WSDL 1.1 definition and a WSDL 2.0 definition of the same service need to provide identical `wsa:Action` values (because they represent the same service).

> **NOTE**
>
> If both the `soapAction` attribute and the WS-Addressing `wsa:Action` attribute are in the same message, the values must be identical.

SUMMARY OF KEY POINTS

- To avoid message dispatch problems, different message types can be created for each input and output message exchanged by a service.

- SOAP Action and WS-Addressing provide alternative means of facilitating the runtime dispatch of messages.

15.3 Messages that Point to Service Instances

Service vs. Service Instance

Most of the scenarios discussed so far in this book revolve around a consumer program invoking and then interacting with a Web service. A request is issued, the service processes it and sends a response, and the service then removes itself from memory.

But what about a situation where you want to intentionally keep a Web service in memory? For example, suppose that in order to carry out a particular task, a service needs to perform a function twice in a row. Maybe it is, resource-wise, simply less expensive for it to remain in memory while repeatedly carrying out the function, rather than being invoked twice on separate occasions.

We'll refer to a service that is in memory as a *service instance*.

Now let's introduce the notion of context into this scenario. What if, when the service performs this function the first time, it retrieves data that only means something to the consumer program (which gives it a specific context)? In this case, the Web service remains in memory in anticipation of another request *from the same consumer*.

We'll refer to any data that the service instance retains in memory as *state data*. Therefore, a service instance retaining state data can be further qualified as a *stateful* service.

That's all well and fine, but how does the consumer contact that stateful service instance the second time around? Using the standard address established in the WSDL `port` or `endpoint` construct will only give it the ability to invoke a new service instance. This is of no use to the consumer because the *new* service instance will not have the context-specific state data it wants to access.

So, to deal with this situation, we need to give the service consumer the ability to interact with an existing service instance. That's what this section is all about.

NOTE
Although this feature supports keeping services stateful, the Service Statelessness design principle advocates minimizing a stateful condition when possible.

WSDL `wsdlx` and `wsdli` Extensibility Attributes

An interesting new feature introduced with WSDL 2.0 allows a Web service to issue a message containing an identifier that represents a service instance. The consumer program receiving this identifier will be able to send messages to that service instance.

The prefixes `wsdlx:` and `wsdli:` are used to identify a special set of WSDL 2.0 extensibility attributes. These attributes are not limited to service instance identification, but that's what we'll be focusing on here.

Essentially, the means by which a Web service can communicate the instance identifier is by sending a message based on a special XML Schema type that is decorated with `wsdlx:` and `wsdli:` attributes, which then help processors populate the `type` elements with the identifier value.

As with most things in the Web services world, this instance identifier is typically expressed as a URL. Here's an example:

```
http://actioncon.com/services/soap11/order/po123456
```

To send this value to the consumer program, we need to create an XML Schema type. The following example declares the `acknowledgement` element with a simple type of `xsd:anyURI` along with a series of extensibility-related content:

```
<xsd:element name="acknowledgement" type="xsd:anyURI"
  xmlns:abs="http://actioncon.com/contract/po"
  xmlns:wsdli="http://www.w3.org/ns/wsdl-instance"
  xmlns:wsdlx="http://www.w3.org/ns/wsdl-extensions"
  wsdli:wsdlLocation="http://actioncon.com/contract/po
    http://actioncon.com/contract/po"
  wsdlx:binding="os:bdPO-SOAP12HTTP"/>
```

Let's explain the prefix declarations first:

```
xmlns:abs="http://actioncon.com/contract/po"
xmlns:wsdli="http://www.w3.org/ns/wsdl-instance"
xmlns:wsdlx="http://www.w3.org/ns/wsdl-extensions"
```

This `os:` prefix represents the target namespace that corresponds to the WSDL document's target namespace value (which is required so that we can refer to the WSDL `binding` element) and the `wsdli:` and `wsdlx:` prefixes represent namespaces used for the following pre-defined extensibility attributes:

```
wsdli:wsdlLocation="http://actioncon.com/contract/po
  http://actioncon.com/contract/po"
wsdlx:binding="os:bdPO-SOAP12HTTP"
```

> **NOTE**
>
> The `wsdli:wsdlLocation` element has two arguments: the first is a namespace URI, and the second is the location of the WSDL document describing this namespace. In this case, both URIs are the same, meaning that `http://actioncon.com/contract/po` is the URI of the WSDL document describing the `http://actioncon.com/contract/po` namespace.

The `wsdli:wsdlLocation` and `wsdlx:binding` attributes are essentially used to identify the `binding` construct to which the `acknowledgement` element will be bound. As you can see here, their values correspond to the target namespace and binding name values:

```
<description targetNamespace=
  "http://actioncon.com/contract/PurchaseOrder"
  xmlns="http://schemas.xmlsoap.org/wsdl/"
  xmlns:tns="http://actioncon.com/contract/po"
  xmlns:po="http://actioncon.com/schema/purchasing"
  xmlns:soapbind="http://www.w3.org/ns/wsdl/soap">
  ...
  <binding name="bdPO-SOAP12HTTP"
    interface="tns:ifPurchaseOrder"
    type="http://www.w3.org/2006/01/wsdl/soap"
    soapbind:protocol=
      "http://www.w3.org/2003/05/soap/bindings/HTTP">
    <operation ref="tns:opSubmitOrder" soapbind:mep=
      "http://www.w3.org/2003/05/soap/mep/request-response"
      soapbind:action=
        "http://actioncon.com/submitOrder/request"/>
```

```
    ...
  </binding>
  ...
</description>
```

The end result is a response message sent by the Web service that contains an `acknowledgement` element populated with the service instance identifier. Here's an example of what the SOAP message might look like:

```
<soap:Envelope>
  <soap:Body>
    <po:acknowledgement>
      http://actioncon.com/services/soap11/order/po123456
    </po:acknowledgement>
  </soap:Body>
</soap:Envelope>
```

So, let's imagine that the consumer would like to contact the stateful service instance in order to carry out a status check on the purchase order in question. It would then send a message like this:

```
<soap:Envelope>
  <soap:Body>
    <po:checkOrder>
      <po:poNumber>
        123456
      </po:poNumber>
    </po:checkOrder>
  </soap:Body>
</soap:Envelope>
```

... to the following address:

```
http://actioncon.com/services/soap11/order/po123456
```

Applications of this Feature

Our simple example demonstrated one service sharing its identifier so that a consumer could continue interacting with that service instance. There are additional scenarios for which service instance identifiers can be used, the foremost example of which is one where a Web service issues an identifier that points to an instance of a *different* Web service. This may be an entirely separate service, or it may be a duplicate deployment of the same service, but located elsewhere (as per the Redundant Implementation design pattern).

These options allow for a variety of creative applications whereby services can essentially (and perhaps dynamically) control portions of message paths when redirection to service instances is required.

NOTE
The WS-Addressing language provides an alternative means of identifying service instances via the use of endpoint reference header blocks. This is explained in Chapter 18.

SUMMARY OF KEY POINTS

- A Web service can issue messages that contain identifiers used to represent service instances.

- The service contract can describe the XML Schema type that underlies those messages using the `wsdlx:binding` and `wsdlx:interface` attributes.

15.4 Custom Header Blocks and Header Faults

In Chapter 4 we introduced how header blocks and faults are defined as part of the overall WSDL document structure. Chapter 7 referenced the header and headerfault SOAP extensibility elements used to bind XML Schema types to the header portion of a SOAP message. In Chapter 10 we then discussed header processing from a SOAP perspective, where we also got to see some examples of what common, pre-defined industry headers look like.

We haven't yet, though, talked about creating our own custom header blocks and header faults.

The Header and Header Fault Types

Let's begin by creating a set of XML Schema types that we'll use to define the structure of a custom request header, response header, and header fault:

```
<types>
  <xsd:schema xmlns:xsd="http://www.w3.org/2001/XMLSchema"
    xmlns="http://actioncon.com/schema/purchasing"
    targetNamespace="http://actioncon.com/schema/purchasing"
    elementFormDefault="qualified">
    <xsd:element name="purchaseOrder"
```

```
      type="PurchaseOrderType"/>
    <xsd:element name="purchaseOrderResponse"
      type="PurchaseOrderResponseType"/>
    <xsd:element name="headerElement"
      type="HeaderType"/>
    <xsd:element name="responseHeaderElement"
      type="ResponseHeaderType"/>
    <xsd:element name="headerFaultElement"
      type="HeaderFaultType"/>
    <xsd:complexType name="PurchaseOrderType">
      ...
    </xsd:complexType>
    <xsd:complexType name="PurchaseOrderResponseType">
      ...
    </xsd:complexType>
    <xsd:complexType name="HeaderType">
      ...
    </xsd:complexType>
    <xsd:complexType name="ResponseHeaderType">
      ...
    </xsd:complexType>
    <xsd:complexType name="PurchaseOrderType">
      ...
    </xsd:complexType>
    ...
  </xsd:schema>
</types>
```

Example 15.20

The three global element declarations representing the header-related types.

This XML schema establishes five elements with types that will be used for two message definitions (an input and an output message). Of these five elements, the three highlighted ones are header-related.

Let's take a look at how the five types are associated with the `part` elements of the two `message` constructs:

```
<message name="msgPurchaseOrderRequest">
  <part name="PurchaseOrder" element="po:purchaseOrder/>
  <part name="HeaderPart" element="po:headerElement"/>
</message>
<message name="msgPurchaseOrderResponse">
  <part name="PurchaseOrderResponse"
    element="po:purchaseOrderResponse/>
  <part name="ResponseHeaderPart" element=
```

```
      "po:responseHeaderElement"/>
   <part name="responseHeaderFaultPart" element=
      "po:headerFaultElement"/>
</message>
```

Example 15.21

The three header-related global elements assigned to the `element` attributes of `part` elements.

The three highlighted elements represent those assigned to message `part` elements that will define the header portions of the SOAP message. The bolded text represents the names assigned to the header-related part elements. These name values will be referenced shortly within the `binding` construct.

Next, let's have a look at the `portType` construct that contains the `opSubmitOrder` operation that will use these two messages.

```
<portType name="ptPurchaseOrder">
   <operation name="opSubmitOrder">
      <input message="tns:msgPurchaseOrderRequest"/>
      <output message="tns:msgPurchaseOrderResponse"/>
   </operation>
   ...
</portType>
```

Example 15.22

The three global element declarations representing the header-related types.

Now it's time to move on to the `binding` construct, where the real action will take place. Here you specify for each `message` element which part will define the SOAP body, which type will define the SOAP header, and which type will define the header fault.

```
<binding name="bdPurchaseOrder" type="ptPurchaseOrder">
<soap11bind:binding style="document" .... >
   <operation name="opSubmitOrder"
      soapAction="http://actioncon.com/submitOrder/request">
      <input message="tns:msgSubmitOrderRequest">
         <soap11bind:body parts="tns:PurchaseOrder"
            use="literal"/>
         <soap11:header message="msgPurchaseOrderRequest"
            part="HeaderPart"/>
      </input>
      <output message="tns:msgSubmitOrderResponse">
         <soap11bind:body parts="tns:PurchaseOrderResponse"
            use="literal"/>
         <soap11:header message="msgPurchaseOrderResponse"
```

```
              part="ResponseHeaderPart">
              <soap11:headerfault message="msgPurchaseOrderResponse"
               part="ResponseHeaderFaultPart"/>
           </soap11:header>
        </input>
     </operation>
     ...
</binding>
```

Example 15.23

The binding construct hosting SOAP binding extensibility elements that are used to assign the part elements from the message definitions to the header portions of input and output SOAP messages.

Note that in this example the red text indicates the SOAP extensibility elements we introduced in Chapter 7. It is these elements that allow us to associate message part elements to the header section of the SOAP message. Not highlighted are the soap11bind:body extensibility elements that tie our other previously declared elements to the body of the input and output messages.

The bolded text highlights the message part elements that we established earlier, in Example 15.20. As we can see, the input message will contain one custom SOAP header block (headerPart), and the output message will contain a different SOAP header block (responseHeaderPart) as well as a header fault (responseHeaderFaultPart).

What the headers actually end up looking like depends on the structure of the corresponding XML Schema types.

If a header-related exception should occur, then the po:headerFaultElement that underlies the part of the message bound by soap11:headerfault would be populated with error information that would reside within a separate header block.

In other words, header-related fault information is stored and transported within the SOAP Header construct. This is different from a regular fault message where the fault data is placed into the SOAP Body construct.

CASE STUDY EXAMPLE
A Custom Security Header Block

Steve has been assigned new business requirements that introduce the need for security details to be included within messages sent to the Purchase Order service. He naturally begins investigating the use of WS-Security for this purpose, but was quickly told by his CTO that due to budget limitations, there is not enough funding to support the platform upgrades required for a WS-Security framework.

Steve therefore decides to design his own security header that will allow consumers that want to use the Purchase Order Web service to carry a secret token used for authentication purposes.

He starts by creating an XML Schema element for the custom security header comprised only of the `xsd:string` simple type.

```
<xsd:element name="securityType" type="xsd:string"/>
```

For simplicity's sake, Steve decides to define his header in the same target namespace as the rest of his Purchase Order service WSDL definition. Next, he associates the security element with a message `part` element of a message definition, as shown here:

```
<message name="msgSubmitOrderRequest">
  <part name="SecurityHeader" element="po:securityType"/>
  <part name="PurchaseOrder" element="po:purchaseOrder"/>
</message>
<message name="msgSubmitOrderResponse">
  <part name="Acknowledgement" element="po:acknowledgement"/>
</message>
```

Example 15.24

The msgSubmitOrderRequest message definition with a SecurityHeader part element that will be assigned to the SOAP header section.

Finally, he updates his concrete description by adding the `soap11:header` extensibility element to the `binding` construct. Specifically, he binds the `SecurityHeader` part element to the `opSubmitOrder` operation's `input` element, as follows:

```
<binding ...>
  <operation name="opSubmitOrder">
    <input>
      <soap11:body use="literal" part="PurchaseOrder"/>
      <soap11:header message="tns:msgSubmitOrderRequest"
        part="SecurityHeader" use="literal"/>
    </input>
    <output>
      <soap11:body use="literal"/>
    </output>
  </operation>
  ...
</binding>
```

Example 15.25

The binding construct with a SOAP extensibility header element used to assign the SecurityHeader part to the input message of the opSubmitOrder operation.

As a result, the input message for the `opSubmitOrder` operation contains two parts, one for the SOAP `Body` construct (`PurchaseOrder`) and the custom security type for the SOAP `Header` construct (`SecurityHeader`).

The resulting SOAP input message now has a custom header block that provides the security secret required for the consumer to access the Web service:

```
<soap:Envelope
  xmlns:soap="http://schemas.xmlsoap.org/soap/envelope/" ...>
<soap:Header>
  <po:security
    xmlns:po="http://actioncon.com/schema/purchasing">
      secret
  </po:security>
</soap:Header>
<soap:Body>
  ...
</soap:Body>
</soap:Envelope>
```

Example 15.26

The highlighted text represents the `po:securityType` construct that represents the header block as it might exist in an actual SOAP message.

Defining SOAP Header Blocks in WSDL 2.0

The syntax for defining a custom SOAP header block with WSDL 2.0 is slightly different when it comes to the SOAP extensibility element.

```
<soap:header element="po:securityType" mustUnderstand="true"
  wsdl:required="true"/>
```

Instead of the `message` and `part` attributes, the header `element` attribute now points directly to the global XML Schema element declaration.

A `mustUnderstand` attribute has been added to indicate whether the header is marked as mandatory. (This attribute was explained in Chapter 10.) Finally, the `wsdl:required` attribute indicates whether consumers must include this header block in all of their request messages or whether it is optional.

> **NOTE**
>
> The WSDL 1.1 specification is unclear about whether SOAP headers
> described in a WSDL document must be included by consumers or not.
> The WS-I Basic Profile made it mandatory for consumers to include them,
> but WSDL 2.0 provides the choice as to whether consumers should be
> forced to include them or not.

15.5 Binding to HTTP Without SOAP

As explained previously, the WSDL language allows an abstract description to be accessed
via protocols other than SOAP. Although SOAP remains, by far, the most common means
of interacting with Web services, it is good to know about the available alternatives.

Several binding options were already listed in Chapter 14 in the *Extensibility of the SOAP
Binding Extensions* section, but those were all specific to the use of SOAP messages. What
if you wanted to make your operations available to consumers that are either unable to
support the SOAP message format or simply don't want to?

This is when you can use pure HTTP. In this case, instead of describing the content of a
SOAP header and a SOAP body, the binding definitions describe the content of an HTTP
header and an HTTP message body.

> **NOTE**
>
> Before we proceed, keep in mind that you are not required to choose
> between SOAP over HTTP and just HTTP. As you might recall from Chap-
> ter 4, Web service contracts are organized into abstract and concrete
> descriptions that are further categorized via the "What," "How," and
> "Where" sections. This clean separation allows you to define an abstract
> description (the "What" part) and make it available via multiple concrete
> descriptions (representing the "How" and "Where" portions). In other
> words, you can offer the same operations via SOAP over HTTP and via
> HTTP only.

HTTP as a Messaging Protocol

HTTP is the protocol of the World Wide Web, which represents a global communications
framework with its own distinct architecture. Let's take a moment to compare the architecture of the Web with the architecture of Web services.

From a Web service contract perspective, a typical service-oriented architecture that is
comprised of one or more service inventories, each with a limited amount of service contracts, will have the following characteristics:

- a limited number of resources (services)
- a large number of custom operations (a collection of operations associated with each service)

The Web architecture, on the other hand, consists of the following:

- a large number of resources (anything that can be accessed via a URL)
- a small number of pre-defined methods

Here's a quick look at the four common HTTP methods:

- GET – retrieve content from a resource (read a file)
- PUT – update the value of a resource (create/copy a file)
- DELETE – delete a resource (delete a file)
- POST – this method is more difficult to characterize; it is sometimes used to create new resources on the Web or to do some special processing which does not fit into the GET/PUT/DELETE methods

The WSDL language was created specifically to describe Web services, not Web resources in general. It is therefore not always well-suited for the descriptions of arbitrary HTTP Web services. But, let's find out what is possible when we marry WSDL with just HTTP.

Figure 15.3

You can think of an HTTP message as a wrapper (or an envelope) that can carry an XML document on its own or within a SOAP envelope.

Binding to HTTP with WSDL 1.1

> **NOTE**
>
> The HTTP extensibility elements are typically prefixed with `httpbind:`
> instead of `http:` so as to not conflict with the use of "`http:`" in URLs.

The `httpbind:binding` *and* `httpbind:operation` *Elements*

The structure of the HTTP binding definition in WSDL 1.1 looks a lot like a SOAP binding definition, as shown here:

```
<binding name="bdPO-HTTP" type="abs:ptPurchaseOrder">
  <httpbind:binding verb="POST"/>
  <operation name="opSubmitOrder">
  <httpbind:operation location="submit"/>
    <input>
      ...
    </input>
    <output>
      ...
    </output>
  </operation>
</binding>
```

Example 15.27

The `httpbind:binding` and `httpbind:operation` extensibility elements used to bind the port type and operation, respectively.

As shown in the previous example, the `verb` attribute on the `httpbind:binding` element specifies what HTTP method is used on the HTTP requests of all operations in the port type.

"GET" and "POST" are the common values, though others are allowed. With GET, the message contents are incorporated into the request URL string, whereas with POST, the message becomes part of the HTTP message body (we'll show an example of an HTTP message shortly).

> **NOTE**
>
> In WSDL 1.1, only one HTTP method can be bound to a port type, which
> is a major limitation if you want to do serious things with HTTP messaging.

The `httpbind:operation` element's `location` attribute is explained in the next section because it relates to the `location` attribute of the `address` element that resides in the `port` construct.

The `httpbind:address` Element

The next example shows the HTTP extensibility element `httpbind:address` used to indicate the location of the service via the `location` attribute as part of the `port` construct:

```
<service name="svPurchaseOrder">
  <port name="purchaseOrder-http" binding="tns:bdPO-HTTP">
  <httpbind:address location=
    "http://actioncon.com/services/http/po/"/>
  </port>
</service>
```

Example 15.28
The `httpbind:address` extensibility element with a `location` attribute indicating the point of contact for this service.

The `location` Attribute

You might have noticed that both the `httpbind:operation` and `httpbind:address` elements have a `location` attribute. Even though `httpbind:operation` and `httpbind:address` reside in different parent constructs (`binding` and `service` respectively), they are closely related via this attribute.

The value of the `location` attribute in the `httpbind:address` element that resides within the `port` construct establishes the actual physical network address of a port type for a Web service.

The `httpbind:operation` element's `location` attribute determines the physical location of an operation within this port type by setting a value that simply extends (is relative to) the value of the `httpbind:address` element's `location` attribute.

This means that given the following setting (borrowed from the previous example) in the `port` construct:

```
<httpbind:address location=
  "http://actioncon.com/services/http/po/"/>
```

...and the following setting in the `operation` construct:

```
<httpbind:operation location="submit"/>
```

...the address of the operation becomes:

```
http://actioncon.com/services/http/po/submit
```

Note that you could also establish a completely new (absolute) URL value in the `httpbind:operation` element's `location` attribute that would be separate from (and therefore not relative to) the `httpbind:address` element's `location` attribute. However, because port types are generally self-contained, there is little reason to do so.

> **NOTE**
>
> With regards to the upcoming section, serialization (in the context of Web services) is the process of transforming a message from its WSDL-defined XML format to the actual, real-world format on the wire. When received, the message is then *deserialized*, which means the wire format is converted back into an XML format that conforms with how the message is defined in the WSDL document. The serialization rules for the HTTP binding specify how an XML message is mapped to an HTTP request or response.

MIME Serialization

HTTP messages can also leverage the MIME binding using extensibility elements to represent the types of information they are required to transport (because there is no expectation that an HTTP message will deliver XML formatted data).

As shown in this example, the `content` extensibility element is represented by the `mimebind:` prefix (which is declared in a MIME-specific namespace):

```
<operation name="opSubmitOrder">
  <httpbind:operation location="submit"/>
  <input>
    <mimebind:content type="text/xml"/>
  </input>
  <output>
    <mimebind:content type="text/xml"/>
  </output>
</operation>
```

Example 15.29
Both input and output messages are bound to the standard text/xml MIME content type.

The `mimebind:content` element is used to indicate that both input and output messages will be serialized from whatever the native format is (as determined by the `type` attribute value) to the HTTP message format, and then back again.

The "text/xml" setting represents the standard format for XML formatted data and is therefore very common. You can also use the `type` attribute of the `mimebind:content` element to indicate different media types, thus making it possible, for example, to return images or other binary data.

Let's take a brief look at some of the other MIME serialization options. Suppose that the message being serialized has a part a whose value is "`foo`" and a part b whose value is "`bar`". Then the following rules apply:

- `httpbind:urlEncoded` – This element is used with an input message to serialize the message in the request URL for the GET method. The following form is used: `?a=foo&b=bar`, or it is posted as form data via the POST method.

- `httpbind:urlReplacement` – This element is used on input messages to serialize message content in the request URL using a pattern indicated in the `location` attribute of the `httpbind:operation` element where elements to be replaced are specified within parentheses. The following form is used: `location="(a)/(b)"` which produces "`foo/bar`", which is used as a relative URL to the `httpbind:address`.

CASE STUDY EXAMPLE
A WSDL 1.1 Definition Bound to HTTP

One of Steve's coworkers, Joe, really likes HTTP and wants to debug services using a lightweight HTTP library in Perl instead of what he calls "a bulky IDE." He wants to start by running simple HTTP requests to interact with the service. Steve therefore decides to expose his service as XML over HTTP using HTTP POST. He begins by reusing the Purchase Order abstract service description and exposes the service online at the following location:

`http://actioncon.com/services/http/po/`

At first, he runs into some message dispatch problems with the `opCheckOrderStatus` and `opCancelOrder` operations. He recalls having similar issues with his SOAP binding definitions (as discussed earlier in the *Message Dispatch Challenges* section).

However, HTTP does not have a concept like SOAP Action and does not support WS-Addressing. In HTTP, different functions are supposed to have different addresses. Steve therefore realizes that he needs to use the `location` attribute to assign different URLs to the operations.

Below is the final WSDL definition containing a complete concrete description bound to HTTP only:

```
<definitions targetNamespace=
  "http://actioncon.com/contract/poHttp"
  xmlns:tns="http://actioncon.com/contract/poHttp"
  xmlns:abs="http://actioncon.com/contract/po"
  xmlns="http://schemas.xmlsoap.org/wsdl/"
  xmlns:po="http://actioncon.com/schema/purchasing"
  xmlns:httpbind="http://schemas.xmlsoap.org/wsdl/http/"
  xmlns:mimebind="http://schemas.xmlsoap.org/wsdl/mime/">
  <documentation>
    HTTP version of the Purchase Order service.
  </documentation>
  <import
    namespace="http://actioncon.com/contract/po"
    location="http://actioncon.com/contract/po"/>
  <binding name="bdPO-HTTP" type="abs:ptPurchaseOrder">
    <httpbind:binding verb="POST"/>
    <operation name="opSubmitOrder">
      <httpbind:operation location="submit"/>
      <input>
        <mimebind:content type="text/xml"/>
      </input>
      <output>
        <mimebind:content type="text/xml"/>
      </output>
    </operation>
    <operation name="opCheckOrderStatus">
      <httpbind:operation location="status"/>
      <input>
        <mimebind:content type="text/xml"/>
      </input>
      <output>
        <mimebind:content type="text/xml"/>
      </output>
    </operation>
    <operation name="opChangeOrder">
      <httpbind:operation location="change"/>
      <input>
```

```
            <mimebind:content type="text/xml"/>
        </input>
        <output>
            <mimebind:content type="text/xml"/>
        </output>
    </operation>
    <operation name="opCancelOrder">
        <httpbind:operation location="cancel"/>
        <input>
            <mimebind:content type="text/xml"/>
        </input>
        <output>
            <mimebind:content type="text/xml"/>
        </output>
    </operation>
  </binding>
  <service name="svPurchaseOrder">
    <port name="purchaseOrder-http"
        binding="tns:bdPO-HTTP">
        <httpbind:address location=
            "http://actioncon.com/services/http/po/"/>
    </port>
  </service>
</definitions>
```

Example 15.30

A complete WSDL 1.1 definition of the Purchase Order service with an imported abstract description bound to HTTP only.

Notice in this example, the new namespaces established in the definitions element that correspond to the new `httpbind:` and `mimebind:` extensibility elements.

After the Web service is up and running with this new version of the WSDL definition, Joe runs a test to check the status of an order by sending the following message with his custom program:

```
POST /services/http/po/status HTTP/1.1
Host: actioncon.com
Content-Type: text/xml; charset="utf-8"
    ...
<poNumber xmlns="http://actioncon.com/schema/purchasing">
    123456
</poNumber>
```

Example 15.31

A simple HTTP request message sent to the Web service.

This message solely consists of some HTTP headers and the XML formatted message body content. After the service processes the request, Joe's program receives the following response:

```
HTTP/1.1 200 OK
Content-type: application/xml
...
<status xmlns="http://actioncon.com/schema/purchasing">
  Pending
</status>
```

Example 15.32
A simple HTTP response message sent by the Web service.

Binding to HTTP with WSDL 2.0

WSDL 2.0 has a more complete HTTP binding syntax that resolves a few of the ambiguities from WSDL 1.1. In particular, it allows us to describe the following:

- HTTP headers

- HTTP authentication methods

- the use of cookies

Furthermore, its support for input and output serialization is more flexible and better defined. It also removes the limitation that WSDL 1.1 has where it can only bind a port type to one HTTP method.

Let's take a closer look at binding to HTTP using WSDL 2.0. One of the biggest changes you'll notice in the upcoming examples is that WSDL 2.0 does not require separate extensibility elements to establish the HTTP binding. Instead, special attributes are inserted right into native WSDL elements.

The `whttp:methodDefault`, `whttp:location`, *and* `whttp:method` *Attributes*

The `abs:ifPurchaseOrder` interface is bound to HTTP by setting the `binding` element's `type` attribute to the new namespace, as shown here:

```
<binding name="bdPO-HTTP" interface="abs:ifPurchaseOrder"
  type="http://www.w3.org/ns/wsdl/http" whttp:methodDefault="POST">
  <operation ref="tns:opSubmitOrder"
```

```
      whttp:location="submit"/>
  <operation ref="opCheckOrderStatus"
      whttp:location="status" whttp:method="GET"/>
  <operation ref="opChangeOrder"
      whttp:location="change"/>
  <operation ref="opCancelOrder"
      whttp:location="cancel"/>
</binding>
```

Example 15.33

A `binding` construct with child `operation` elements. Each element in this construct is extended with HTTP-specific attribute values.

You can probably tell by its name that the `whttp:methodDefault` attribute of the `binding` element allows you to set the default HTTP method to be used by operations within the interface. You'll notice the `opCheckOrderStatus` operation override this default by setting its own method via the `whttp:method` attribute.

The `whttp:location` attribute values indicate the physical location of each operation. The address value of this attribute is relative to the address of the interface itself. See the *The location Attribute* section earlier in this chapter for an example of how relative address values are structured.

The `address` *Attribute of the* `endpoint` *Element*

In the next example we can see how the `address` attribute added to the `endpoint` element establishes the physical network location of the concrete definition so that consumer programs know where to look specifically to find the HTTP version of this service.

```
<service name="svPurchaseOrder"
  interface="abs:ifPurchaseOrder">
  <endpoint name="purchaseOrder-http"
    binding="tns:bdPO-HTTP" address=
      "http://actioncon.com/services/http/po/"/>
</service>
```

Example 15.34

The `endpoint` element sets the address to which HTTP messages can be sent.

MIME Serialization

In WSDL 2.0, the MIME serialization format is indicated by specifying a media type in one of the following three attributes:

- `whttp:inputSerialization`

- `whttp:outputSerialization`

- `whttp:faultSerialization`

Consider the following message (similar to the message used as an example to demonstrate serialization options in the *MIME Serialization* sub-section of the *Binding to HTTP with WSDL 1.1* section):

```
<message>
  <a>foo</a>
  <b>bar</b>
</message>
```

The following serialization rules apply:

- GET Input Messages – The default `application/x-www-form-urlencoded` format is used for both the URL replacement and encoding concepts introduced by WSDL 1.1. The elements present in the `whttp:location` attribute on the operation are replaced (`whttp:location="{a}"` produces "foo") and the rest of the message is serialized as query parameters (`?b=bar`). This produces a location of "foo?b=bar". It is, basically, a combination of WSDL 1.1's `httpUrlEncoded` and `httpUrlReplacement` rules.

- POST Input Messages – The `multipart/form-data` format is used to indicate form submission. With this form, URL replacement rules also apply. Again, it corresponds to a combination of WSDL 1.1's `httpUrlEncoded` and `httpUrlReplacement` rules for POST.

- Input, Output, and Fault Messages – The `application/xml` format (which is the default for input messages using POST) serializes the messages as XML documents in the HTTP message body.

> **NOTE**
>
> The `application/xml` form is used instead of `text/xml` for XML messages that are part of a WSDL 1.1 HTTP binding. This is because the XML community in general has moved from `text/xml` to `application/xml` for XML documents since the publication of WSDL 1.1. While both are valid for XML documents, `application/xml` is preferred.

Steve decides to try out WSDL 2.0 for his HTTP service in order to study its differences and similarities. This example shows the results:

```
<description targetNamespace=
  "http://actioncon.com/contract/poHttp"
  xmlns:tns="http://actioncon.com/contract/poHttp"
  xmlns:abs="http://actioncon.com/contract/po"
  xmlns="http://www.w3.org/ns/wsdl"
  xmlns:whttp="http://www.w3.org/ns/wsdl/http">
  <documentation>
    HTTP version of the Purchase Order service.
  </documentation>
  <import
    namespace="http://actioncon.com/contract/po"
    location="http://actioncon.com/contract/po"/>
  <binding name="bdPO-HTTP" interface="abs:ifPurchaseOrder"
    type="http://www.w3.org/ns/wsdl/http"
    whttp:methodDefault="POST">
    <operation ref="tns:opSubmitOrder"
      whttp:location="submit"/>
    <operation ref="opCheckOrderStatus"
      whttp:location="status" whttp:method="GET"/>
    <operation ref="opChangeOrder"
      whttp:location="change"/>
    <operation ref="opCancelOrder"
      whttp:location="cancel"/>
  </binding>
  <service name="svPurchaseOrder"
    interface="abs:ifPurchaseOrder">
    <endpoint name="purchaseOrder-http"
      binding="tns:bdPO-HTTP" address=
        "http://actioncon.com/services/http/purchaseOrder/"/>
  </service>
</description>
```

Example 15.35

A complete WSDL 2.0 HTTP binding of the Purchase Order service.

The first thing Steve notices is how much smaller the resulting WSDL definition is. If he did not have message dispatch issues with his service before and did not have to specify different locations for different operations, the binding definition would have actually been even smaller.

> ### NOTE
>
> In this example the serialization format is not explicitly set because it auto-
> matically defaults to `application/xml`.

Additional WSDL 2.0 HTTP Binding Features

Here's a brief list of other features that might be of interest to you if you are exploring
the use of HTTP binding with WSDL 2.0:

- Authentication parameters may be indicated with the `whttp:authentication`
  `Type` and `whttp:authenticationRealm` attributes. `whttp:authenticationType`
  refers to the type of HTTP authentication used (`basic` or `digest`), and the security
  realm is set by `whttp:authenticationRealm`.

- The required use of cookies can be indicated with `whttp:cookies`.

- HTTP headers are declared in a way similar to SOAP headers, with an
  `whttp:header` element. The `name` attribute specifies the name of the HTTP header,
  the `type` attribute declares its XML type definition, and `required` specifies
  whether the use of the header is mandatory.

- When faults occur, the list of possible HTTP error codes returned by the service is
  specified with the `whttp:code` attribute in the `fault` element. For example, an
  authentication fault may result in a 401 HTTP error message.

- The `wsdlx:safe` attribute that was first explained in Chapter 8 can also be used
  with WSDL operations bound to HTTP methods to indicate whether the use of the
  method can have harmful side effects.

- URL replacement and encoding problems with WSDL 1.1 have been addressed in
  WSDL 2.0 with operation styles. Essentially, an IRI is established to declare that a
  certain operation follows a number of restrictions that make it suitable for being
  serialized in the `application/x-www-form-urlencoded` format. (IRIs were first
  introduced at the beginning of Chapter 6.)

Chapter 16

Advanced WS-Policy Part I: Policy Centralization and Nested, Parameterized, and Ignorable Assertions

Though a simple and small language, WS-Policy allows for complex representations of policies. This chapter explores new design-time options for building sophisticated policy expression structures and entire policy definition architectures, and also discusses the implications of these designs by runtime processors.

16.1 Reusability and Policy Centralization

We concluded Chapter 10 with a look at policies that are embedded within a WSDL definition and also attached to policy subjects. Those embedded policy expressions can be reused within the scope of a WSDL definition by having multiple `wsp:PolicyReference` elements reference the same `wsp:Policy` construct via its `name`, `wsu:Id` or `xml:Id` attribute.

We can consider this a form of intra-document reuse, where the scope of reusability is limited to one WSDL definition. In this section, we will be exploring the physical centralization of policy expressions into separate policy documents that we'll refer to as *policy definitions*.

> **NOTE**
>
> The following sections focus on the "controlled reuse" of policies within pre-defined service inventory boundaries. While this is a common approach to sharing policies across WSDL definitions, it does not preclude you from simply reusing policies to whatever extent you choose, regardless of centralization considerations.

Policy Centralization and Policy Definitions

As you might recall, you can establish many-to-many relationships between WSDL definitions and XML schemas where one XML schema is reused (imported or included) within multiple WSDL definitions, and/or a single WSDL definition can reference and pull in content from multiple XML schemas. This flexibility allows you to establish a Web service contract architecture that can leverage and foster reuse.

Similar reuse opportunities are available when exploring relationships between WSDL definitions and policy definitions. In fact, grouping common policy expressions within separate policy definition documents is the basis of an SOA design pattern called Policy Centralization, which we explain shortly.

In Chapter 14 we introduced the notion of creating reusable schemas that contained common types. Some of those types were limited to a domain (like the purchasing-specific types in the Purchasing Common schema), while others were useful on a global basis (such as with the generic types in the Common schema).

When it comes to creating physically separate policy definition documents, we have the same options, as follows:

Domain Policy Definition

You can create policy expressions that apply to a subset of the services within a given service inventory. These policies are still reusable because they are applicable to multiple Web service contracts, but they are limited in scope to a particular domain. As with creating domain-specific common schema types, domain-level policies are often also related to a business domain. However, it is up to you to create your own domains based on whatever requirements you have. For example, you could establish a policy domain specific to a transport protocol.

> **NOTE**
>
> In the upcoming case study example, we will be creating a domain policy definition that contains policy expressions for the purchasing domain only.

Global Policy Definitions

Global policies are expected to apply to all services within a particular governance boundary. Therefore, global policy definitions often contain very broad and generalized policy expressions.

The scope implied by the use of the term "global" depends on the scope of the underlying service inventory. As explained early on in Chapter 3, you can establish pools of services (service inventories) that are independently standardized and governed. Sometimes, an inventory is enterprise-wide, whereas other times it only represents a domain within the enterprise.

In the latter case, a global policy definition would be applicable to just the scope of the domain inventory. A domain policy definition would then apply to a subset of the service contracts within the domain inventory. So again, when we call a policy definition "global," we mean that it is global within one service inventory boundary only.

> **NOTE**
>
> You can also look into creating policies that span multiple domain service inventories. This may or may not be a good idea, depending on how complex the architecture becomes and also on the governance impact this may result in. However, if this is something you do decide to explore, you can further qualify these types of polices as "master global policies" or just "master policies."

Policy Centralization

This pattern (which is similar in concept to the Schema Centralization pattern) simply advocates creating the domain and global policy definitions we just described. It results in a system whereby policies can be consistently enforced across several Web service contracts. This reduces redundant policy content within a service inventory and further allows policies to be centrally maintained.

An added benefit is that the policy documents can more easily be owned by custodians that do not necessarily have to be involved with the governance of the WSDL definitions. This type of freedom is conducive to evolving technical policies in tandem with actual business policies and also provides policy custodians the option to use their own, preferred tools.

> **NOTE**
>
> The techniques in this section can also be applied to WSDL definition-specific policies. Instead of embedding non-reusable policy expressions within WSDL documents, you can also isolate them in separate policy definition documents to allow them to be maintained in a physically separate file.

Designing External WS-Policy Definitions

Several approaches exist for establishing a relationship between a WSDL definition document and a separate WS-Policy definition document. However, not all approaches are supported by all vendor platforms, and some platforms may not support external policy reuse at all. Therefore, it is very important that you investigate the environment in which you plan to deploy external policy definitions before deciding on any of the techniques described in the upcoming sections.

Policy Processors

Unlike XML and WSDL processors that are widely established, runtime programs that perform WS-Policy-specific processing have not been formally defined and their behavior can therefore vary across vendor platforms. In some cases, it may be a dedicated event-driven agent that carries policy processing out, whereas other times this logic may exist as an extension of the overall Web services toolkit and runtime platform. It's therefore helpful to keep this in mind whenever you see the term "policy processing" used in this book.

Using the `wsp:PolicyAttachment` *Element*

A common means of sharing policy expression code is to place into its own WS-Policy definition via the `wsp:PolicyAttachment` element, as shown here:

```
<wsp:PolicyAttachment>
  ...
  <wsp:Policy>
    <wsam:Addressing><wsp:Policy/></wsam:Addressing>
    <wsrmp:RMAssertion optional="true"/>
  </wsp:Policy>
</wsp:PolicyAttachment>
```

Example 16.1
A `wsp:PolicyAttachment` construct containing a policy expression. This code presumably resides in a separate policy definition document.

Here we can see that the `wsp:PolicyAttachment` construct simply wraps around an existing policy expression. The ellipsis at the top indicates room for any of the following additional child elements:

- `wsp:AppliesTo` – This element is used to indicate what part of the WSDL document the policy expression applies to.

- `wsp:Policy` or `wsp:PolicyReference` – These elements have been previously explained. As child elements to `wsp:PolicyAttachment`, they designate the specific policy expression that will be applied to the policy subject identified in the `wsp:AppliesTo` element.

The content of a `wsp:AppliesTo` element can be any element. This makes the external referencing mechanism quite powerful in that you can technically target any part of a

WSDL definition. This element uses a further `wsp:URI` element that allows for the identification of the target element via a URL statement.

In the following example we've populated the `wsp:PolicyAttachment` construct with `wsp:AppliesTo` and `wsp:URI` child elements that indicate that the policy expression at the bottom of the `wsp:PolicyAttachment` construct will be applied to the `endpoint` element of the WSDL 2.0 binding for the Purchase Order service.

```
<wsp:PolicyAttachment>
  <wsp:AppliesTo>
    <wsp:URI>
      http://actioncon.com/purchaseOrder.wsdl20
      #wsdl.endpoint(PurchaseOrderService/Endpoint)
    </wsp:URI>
  </wsp:AppliesTo>
  <wsp:Policy>
    <wsam:Addressing><wsp:Policy/></wsam:Addressing>
    <wsrmp:RMAssertion optional="true"/>
  </wsp:Policy>
</wsp:PolicyAttachment>
```

Example 16.2

The `wsp:AppliesTo` and `wsp:URI` child elements with a URL that identifies the target element of the policy.

NOTE

A key architectural consideration with this approach is that it places control of what WSDL definitions and subjects the policy applies to in the hands of the policy definition owner. This differs from upcoming alternatives where policies exist in separate documents but their application is determined within WSDL definitions instead.

Using the `wsp:PolicyURIs` *Attribute*

An alternative attachment method documented in the WS-Policy specification is the use of the `wsp:PolicyURIs` attribute which can simply be added (as an extensibility attribute) to any valid policy attachment point within a WSDL definition, as shown here:

```
<portType name="ptPurchaseOrder"
  wsp:PolicyURIs="custom:commonPolicies.xml">
  <operation name="opSubmitOrder">
    <input message="tns:msgSubmitOrderRequest"/>
    <output message="tns:msgsubmitOrderResponse"/>
  </operation>
  ...
</portType>
```

Example 16.3
The portType element is extended with the wsp:PolicyURIs attribute.

In this example, the ptPurchaseOrder portType element is attached to the policies residing in the commonPolicies.xml document. Note that the wsp:PolicyURIs attribute can contain a list of URI addresses that point to multiple physically separate policy definition documents.

Using the Name and URI Attributes

The WS-Policy language provides a Name attribute that allows you to assign a separate ID value to a wsp:Policy element specifically for external references. Even though this attribute is called "Name," the value needs to be an IRI.

A wsp:PolicyReference element located in a separate document (most likely a WSDL definition) can then point to the external policy expression via a URI attribute that is populated with the same value as the wsp:Policy element's Name attribute.

So let's imagine that the following policy expression is located in a document called commonPolicies.xml:

```
<wsp:Policy Name="http://actioncon.com/policies/common">
  <wsam:Addressing><wsp:Policy/></wsam:Addressing>
</wsp:Policy>
```

Example 16.4
A wsp:Policy construct residing within a separate policy definition document. The Name attribute provides the policy expression with an externally "referenceable" identifier.

The value of the Name attribute gives this wsp:Policy construct a reference ID that can be used by wsp:PolicyReference elements to point to and reuse the policy expression.

For example, the following `wsp:PolicyReference` statement may reside in a WSDL definition document:

```
<wsp:PolicyReference
  URI="http://actioncon.com/policies/common"/>
```

Example 16.5
A `wsp:PolicyReference` element that points to the previously displayed `wsp:Policy` construct via the `URI` attribute.

> **NOTE**
>
> The mechanics behind performing the actual inclusion of the policy expression into the WSDL definition is up to your runtime and service hosting platform. If you intend to use this approach, be sure to confirm that your policy processors support these attributes. You may also want to consider using (or you may be required to use) XPointer to enable cross-document inclusion.

Wrapping Policies Within WSDL Definitions

An alternative means of creating common policy definition documents is to place the reusable policy expressions into a separate WSDL definition document. This is by no means an "official" approach documented in the WS-Policy specifications, but should instead be considered a possible workaround if support for the preceding techniques is not provided by your platform.

With this approach, you may be able to simply use the existing WSDL `import` or `include` elements to pull in the contents of the external WSDL document containing the policy expressions.

In this case, you would place the policy expression within a WSDL `definitions` construct as follows:

```
<definitions targetNamespace=
  "http://actioncon.com/policies/common">
  <wsp:Policy wsu:Id="addressing-policy">
    <wsam:Addressing><wsp:Policy/></wsam:Addressing>
  </wsp:Policy>
  ...
</definitions>
```

Example 16.6
A WSDL `definitions` construct that acts as a container for common policies.

As shown here, you can optionally assign the WSDL definition its own target namespace value.

> **NOTE**
>
> In this case we used the value assigned to the wsp:Policy element's Name attribute from the previous example as the target namespace value. However, this is just incidental. You can create whatever namespace value you like.

Within the WSDL definition that needs to pull in this policy, you can then add a standard WSDL import element that points to the WSDL definition acting as the policy definition, as follows:

```
<definitions targetNamespace=
  "http://actioncon.com/contract/PurchaseOrder" ...>
  <import
    namespace="http://actioncon.com/policies/common"
    location="http://actioncon.com/policies/common"/>
  ...
  <wsp:PolicyReference URI="#addressing-policy"/>
  ...
</definitions>
```

Example 16.7

An example of a WSDL definition that includes a wsp:PolicyReference statement that points to an imported wsp:Policy construct. If you check back to the *Attaching Policies to WSDL Definitions* section from Chapter 10, you can see that this code resembles the same syntax used for local references within a WSDL document.

Note how the wsp:Policy element from Example 16.6 does not use a Name attribute. This is because it is not expecting to be externally referenced. Via the WSDL import mechanism, the policy expression is brought into the WSDL definition and then referenced as though it was a local part of the document. This is also why the URI attribute of the wsp:PolicyReference element contains only a local pointer (based on the convention of using the hash mark: "#").

> **NOTE**
>
> One potential problem with this approach is the enforcement of the "uniqueness" of the wsp:Policy element's xml:Id or wsu:Id attribute value across multiple WSDL documents. If this issue cannot be resolved by your platform, the use of XML Include or XPointer may need to be considered.

CASE STUDY EXAMPLE

Soon after refining his Web service contracts with some of the more advanced XML Schema and WSDL features, Steve is called into a meeting with the Kevin, the CEO, and Donna, the president of ActionCon.

This meeting concerns Steve. It's unusual to have a formal meeting with Kevin, and he hasn't even met Donna yet. His first thought is that his department is being downsized and Steve begins to think about how he should update his resume as he heads toward the meeting room.

However, his fears soon disappear when he hears the news. Apparently, there have been some recent security breaches resulting in stolen corporate financial data and one attempted malicious attack on the ActionCon data warehouse that was luckily caught and countered in time.

As a result of these events, Steve is told that all Web services that handle financial data must be fully secured and must also require that outside consumers comply with the use of certain security options. Steve is informed that an external security consulting company has been hired to perform an audit and that they will soon be providing him with a list of requirements that will impact the design of his Web services.

Subsequent to the meeting, Steve begins to re-investigate the use of the WS-Policy framework. In his previous work with policies (from Chapter 10), Steve successfully attached a policy to one of his Web service contracts. But given the scope of the upcoming security requirements, he now turns his attention to establishing a centralized policy architecture, the initial draft of which is displayed in Figure 16.1.

He knows that there will be the need for security policies that affect Web services that process financial information. As shown on the right side of Figure 16.1, he establishes a logical finance domain that will be supported by a domain policy definition comprised of policy expressions that will apply to all Web services that handle financial data. Currently, both his Purchase Order and Invoice services would fall within this domain.

The following example shows a basic skeleton outline of the policy expression that will reside in the financePolicies.xml document:

```
<wsp:Policy Name="http://actioncon.com/policies/finance">
  <!-- finance-related policy assertions -->
</wsp:Policy>
```

Example 16.8

The start of a domain policy definition containing finance-related assertions.

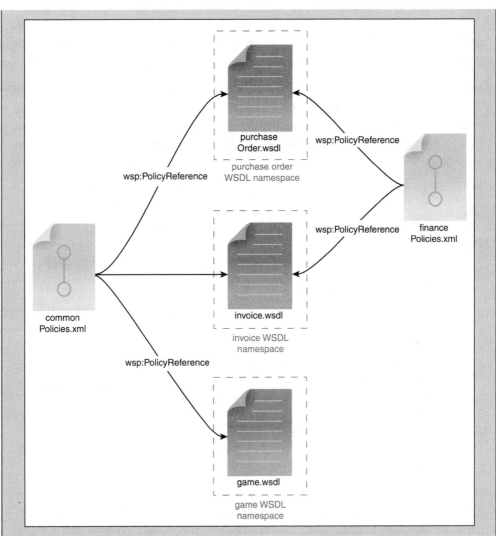

Figure 16.1

A domain policy definition (right) associated with finance-related Web services, and a global policy definition (left) providing common policies that apply to all services.

NOTE

The contents of the financePolicies.xml domain policy definition are developed in the upcoming *Case Study Example: Nested and Parameterized Assertions* section.

As indicated by the left side of his policy centralization architecture, Steve decides that he might as well also establish a global policy definition that will provide general policy expressions that apply to all Web services within his planned inventory.

Based on a recent enterprise design standard handed down by the CTO, Steve already knows that one global policy will be to require that all Web service contracts contain an assertion that requires consumer programs to support WS-Addressing headers. Therefore, his initial policy expression for the commonPolicies.xml global policy definition looks like this:

```
<wsp:Policy Name="http://actioncon.com/policies/common">
  <wsam:Addressing><wsp:Policy/></wsam:Addressing>
</wsp:Policy>
```

Example 16.9

By virtue of the fact that this simple policy expression is part of a global policy definition, it is expected to extend all Web service contracts within Steve's planned service inventory.

Common Policy Centralization Challenges

In order to facilitate such a centralized policy architecture, a number of considerations need to be taken into account, several of which might impose significant challenges upon an IT department:

- New governance processes are required to ensure that global and domain policy definitions are maintained and to further guarantee that changes to these policies will not negatively impact any of the Web service contracts they apply to.

- Standard processes are required for project teams to reliably obtain domain and global WS-Policy definition documents. This means that a discovery process ordinarily geared toward WSDL documents will now need to extend to WS-Policy definitions.

- Conflicts may exist between overlapping policies, such as when a global policy introduces a constraint that is contrary to a constraint provided by a domain-level policy. These conflicts need to be taken into account whenever new domain or global polices are added or modified.

- One centralization challenge related in particular to the use of the WS-PolicyAttachment mechanism is that the infrastructure needs to know where to get the policies from. Often, a middleware platform, such as an ESB, is required (as explained shortly).

Finally, as mentioned in the previous section, not all service runtime platforms support external referencing to WS-Policy definitions that exist as standalone XML documents. Without robust support for sharing policies, it is difficult to achieve meaningful centralization.

NOTE

An additional design-related challenge to achieving a centralized policy architecture is knowing in advance where to attach policies to. Because policies can be associated with different attachment points within different policy subjects, it's impossible to know ahead of time what a domain or global policy will apply to. When manually maintaining policy-enabled WSDL definitions in a centralized architecture, one approach is to "pre-attach" a `wsp:PolicyReference` element to some or all potential attachment points in a WSDL `definitions` construct and for most of these elements to initially point to empty policy expressions (`wsp:Policy` constructs with no assertions).

This establishes a relationship between the WSDL document and a series of centralized policy definition documents and allows policy custodians to add new expressions without having to revisit the WSDL definitions. However, this is not a common or recommended practice. It can result in an awkward architecture, and in some environments, it may add runtime processing cycles as the platform hosting the Web services may try to resolve and check for external policies that aren't there each time the service is invoked. Furthermore, conflicts can arise when empty and non-empty policies are combined across policy attachment points.

Policy Centralization and ESBs

Several platforms (especially those provided by modern Enterprise Service Bus products) are equipped with built-in support for policy centralization. You simply fill out a form to associate a centralized policy expression with your services, and the platform takes care of the rest. This can be an extremely convenient and powerful means of achieving an effective centralized policy architecture; however, it often comes with the trade-off that your Web service contracts must form dependencies on proprietary features that may be difficult to move away from if you ever want to change or diversify your service inventory architecture.

SUMMARY OF KEY POINTS

- Policy expressions can be isolated into policy definition documents that can be shared and reused across WSDL documents, just like XML Schema definitions.

- One approach involves using the wsp:Policy element's Name attribute to establish an externally referenceable identifier. However, you need to ensure that the service inventory architecture supports this type of external references.

- Another approach is to create policy definition documents as WSDL definitions that are then imported into other WSDL definitions. This technique can be used when there is insufficient product support for regular external references.

16.2 Nested and Parameterized Assertions

In Chapter 10 we covered simple assertions, operators, and expressions. In this section, we'll take a look at how these parts can be further combined and extended. Specifically, we'll explore how policy expressions can be nested within each other and how they can be designed to accept and respond to parameter data provided by the consumer.

Nested Policy Assertions

Policy assertions can be structured around parent-child relationships whereby a child policy assertion is nested within a parent assertion. As shown in the following example, assertion ex:Assertion2 is nested within ex:Assertion1:

```
<wsp:Policy>
  <wsp:ExactlyOne>
    <wsp:All>
      <ex:Assertion1>
        <wsp:Policy>
          <wsp:ExactlyOne>
            <wsp:All>
              <ex:Assertion2/>
            </wsp:All>
          </wsp:ExactlyOne>
        </wsp:Policy>
      </ex:Assertion1>
```

```
    </wsp:All>
   </wsp:ExactlyOne>
</wsp:Policy>
```

Example 16.10
One assertion nested within another.

So, why would you want to nest a policy assertion? There's a simple, two-part answer.

An assertion needs to be nested when:

- the behavior of the nested assertion is dependent on the parent assertion (or vice versa), and/or

- the parent and child assertions apply to the same targets (attachment points)

Sometimes a policy assertion will be defined to *extend* an existing assertion. In this case, it will likely need to be nested within the existing assertion because it is directly dependent on the assertion it is extending. Furthermore, for this type of structure to make sense, both parent and child assertions need to be targeting the same policy subject within the WSDL definition.

As you may have noticed in the previous sample code, the syntax requirement for nesting assertions is that the child assertion be wrapped in its own `wsp:Policy` construct. You may be wondering why this is actually required.

For example, why can't you just do this:

```
<wsp:Policy>
  <wsp:ExactlyOne>
    <wsp:All>
      <ex:Assertion1>
        <ex:Assertion2/>
      </ex:Assertion1>
    </wsp:All>
  </wsp:ExactlyOne>
</wsp:Policy>
```

Example 16.11
An attempt at nesting an assertion that does not result in an actual, nested assertion.

The reason the approach in this example doesn't result in a nested assertion has to do with how runtime policy processors work. (Specifically, this is related to how these processors perform "policy matching.") The policy processor looks for the `wsp:Policy` element and when it finds it, it only cares about the first assertion element it encounters.

To the processor, `ex:Assertion1` represents the policy assertion and it has no interest in what lies within the `ex:Assertion1` construct (unless there happens to be a nested `wsp:Policy` or `wsp:PolicyReference` element). Therefore, to communicate to the processor that there are actually two separate policy assertions, we need to add two separate `wsp:Policy` constructs (as we did in Example 16.10).

Parameterized Assertions

Even though we just dismissed Example 16.11 as not representing a nested policy, it does actually demonstrate another important type of policy structure. Because the `ex:Assertion2` element is not its own policy, it is considered a parameter of `ex:Assertion1`. This means that whatever part of the runtime environment will be responsible for processing the `ex:Assertion1` policy will receive the value of `ex:Assertion2` as input.

There are, of course, other ways to create parameterized assertions. In fact, we previewed one in Chapter 10. You might recall the following example:

```
<wsp:Policy>
  <argt:responseGuarantee>
    <argt:responseInMilliseconds>
      50
    </argt:responseInMilliseconds>
  </argt:responseGuarantee>
</wsp:Policy>
```

Example 16.12
A parameterized `argt:responseGuarantee` policy assertion.

In this case, all of the contents of the `argt:responseGuarantee` construct are considered parameters. Given that this is a custom policy assertion (not one that originated with an industry standard), there will need to be custom service logic that processes these parameters at runtime. Also, development tools will likely not be able to check for policy compatibility using these custom assertions.

Let's now check out a more detailed case study example with both nested and parameterized policy assertions based on industry standards.

> **NOTE**
>
> Unlike nested assertions for which support is quite common, not all plat-
> forms provide support for parameterized assertions.

CASE STUDY EXAMPLE
Nested and Parameterized WS-SecurityPolicy Assertions

> **NOTE**
>
> The following case study example makes references to the WS-Security
> and WS-SecurityPolicy languages, which are not explained in this book.
> You do not need to be familiar with these standards to understand this
> example. You can ignore the security-related terminology and just focus
> on the highlighted assertions that demonstrate nested and parameterized
> structures. (If you are interested in learning more about this standard, be
> sure to visit www.soaspecs.com.)
>
> Note also that in this example we will use the `sp:` prefix to represent
> assertions that are defined in the WS-SecurityPolicy specification.

Earlier (in Chapter 14) Steve was told that there were insufficient funds to establish
the infrastructure to support a WS-Security framework. Due to the recent security
breaches, establishing this framework has now become a priority.

Specifically, the security audit carried out by the external consultants produces the
following security requirements that affect all Web services that process financial
data:

- Consumers must now access all Web services using transport or message-level
  security.

- For transport-level security, Web services need to be accessed via SSL with
  transport-level tokens.

- For message-level security, Web services need to be accessed using X509 tokens
  for authentication and all messages must be signed and encrypted.

In response to these requirements, Steve decides to design a policy alternative for his
newly created domain policy definition that gives consumers a choice between using
either transport- or message-level security. He uses two pre-defined assertions from
the WS-SecurityPolicy language to express these options, as follows:

```
<wsp:Policy Name="http://actioncon.com/policies/finance">
  <wsp:ExactlyOne>
    <sp:TransportBinding/>
    <sp:SymmetricBinding/>
  </wsp:ExactlyOne>
</wsp:Policy>
```

Example 16.13

The policy expression from the domain policy definition now comprised of a policy alternative offering a choice between two security-related assertions.

Steve looks at his newly created policy expression and thinks to himself, "It can't be that easy..." He begins reading the WS-SecurityPolicy specification and soon finds out that it isn't.

He discovers that for both assertions additional properties need to be defined. For example, ActionCon requires a specific transport token (https) for transport level security which relies on timestamps to be present in the security header of a SOAP envelope. Additionally, a specific algorithm suite (Basic264) for cryptography needs to be supported.

All of these required properties are defined as three additional nested assertions as per the highlighted parts of this example:

```
<wsp:Policy Name="http://actioncon.com/policies/finance">
  <wsp:ExactlyOne>
    <sp:TransportBinding>
      <wsp:Policy>
        <sp:TransportToken>
          <wsp:Policy>
            <sp:HttpsToken>
              ...tokens...
            </sp:HttpsToken>
          </wsp:Policy>
        </sp:TransportToken>
        <sp:IncludeTimestamp/>
        <sp:AlgorithmSuite>
          <wsp:Policy>
            <sp:Basic256/>
          </wsp:Policy>
        </sp:AlgoritmSuite>
      </wsp:Policy>
    </sp:TransportBinding>
```

```
  . . .
</wsp:Policy>
```

Example 16.14

The sp:TransportBinding policy assertion containing three nested policy assertions.

Steve now turns his attention to the sp:SymmetricBinding assertion that represents the message-level security alternative. This assertion actually contains *seven* nested assertions within three nested wsp:Policy layers, as follows:

```
<wsp:Policy Name="http://actioncon.com/policies/finance">
  <wsp:ExactlyOne>
    . . .
    <sp:SymmetricBinding>
      <wsp:Policy>
        <sp:ProtectionToken>
          <wsp:Policy>
            <sp:X509Token sp:IncludeToken=
              "http://schemas.xmlsoap.org/ws/2005
              /07/securitypolicy/IncludeToken/Never">
              <wsp:Policy>
                ...details of X509 token...
              </wsp:Policy>
            </sp:X509Token>
          </wsp:Policy>
        </sp:ProtectionToken>
        <sp:AlgorithmSuite>
          <wsp:Policy>
            <sp:Basic256/>
          </wsp:Policy>
        </sp:AlgorithmSuite>
        <sp:Layout>
          ...layout details...
        </sp:Layout>
        <sp:IncludeTimestamp/>
        <sp:OnlySignEntireHeadersAndBody/>
      </wsp:Policy>
    </sp:SymmetricBinding>
  </sp:ExactlyOne>
</wsp:Policy>
```

Example 16.15

The sp:SymmetricBinding policy assertion containing seven nested policy assertions.

As a result of this exercise, all of the nested assertions required to fully provide the two security-related policy alternatives are established. But what about parameterized assertions? Some of the nested assertions shown in the previous example are, in fact, also parameterized.

This next example displays the entire policy expression with both policy alternatives. The highlighted parts represent parameters for parameterized assertions:

```
<wsp:Policy Name="http://actioncon.com/policies/finance">
  <wsp:ExactlyOne>
    <sp:TransportBinding>
      <wsp:Policy>
        <sp:TransportToken/>
          <wsp:Policy>
            <sp:HttpsToken>
              ...tokens...
            </sp:HttpsToken>
          </wsp:Policy>
        </sp:TransportToken>
        <sp:IncludeTimestamp/>
        <sp:AlgorithmSuite>
          <wsp:Policy>
            <sp:Basic256/>
          </wsp:Policy>
        </sp:AlgoritmSuite>
      </wsp:Policy>
    </sp:TransportBinding>
    <sp:SymmetricBinding>
      <wsp:Policy>
        <sp:ProtectionToken>
          <wsp:Policy>
            <sp:X509Token sp:IncludeToken=
              "http://schemas.xmlsoap.org/ws/2005
              /07/securitypolicy/IncludeToken/Never">
              <wsp:Policy>
                ...details of X509 token...
              </wsp:Policy>
            </sp:X509Token>
          </wsp:Policy>
        </sp:ProtectionToken>
        <sp:AlgorithmSuite>
          <wsp:Policy>
            <sp:Basic256/>
          </wsp:Policy>
        </sp:AlgorithmSuite>
```

```
      <sp:Layout>
       ...layout details...
      </sp:Layout>
      <sp:IncludeTimestamp/>
      <sp:OnlySignEntireHeadersAndBody/>
     </wsp:Policy>
   </sp:SymmetricBinding>
  </sp:ExactlyOne>
</wsp:Policy>
```

Example 16.16
A policy expression comprised of two security-related policy alternatives.

The italicized text shows where some of the parameter data would be placed, but for simplicity's sake it's been omitted. Note how the `sp:X509Token` element incorporates assertion parameters via attributes. How parameter data is defined and represented within a given assertion depends solely on the design of the underlying policy assertion type.

SUMMARY OF KEY POINTS

- Policy expressions can be nested within each other, thereby allowing for the creation of complex constructs with multiple policy assertions.

- When policy assertion elements are nested or contain data values determined at runtime, the policy is considered to be parameterized.

16.3 Ignorable Assertions

No part of the WS-Policy language has resulted in as much debate as the use of ignorable assertions. In a nutshell, this feature allows you to express a behavior of a Web service as an assertion that consumer programs can simply choose to disregard.

Here's what an ignorable assertion looks like:

```
<wsp:Policy>
  <custom:TraceMessage wsp:Ignorable="true"/>
</wsp:Policy>
```

Example 16.17
A policy expression containing an ignorable policy assertion.

In this little example, `custom:TraceMessage` represents a custom assertion, but the setting of `wsp:Ignorable="true"` makes consumer-side processing of the assertion purely voluntary, meaning that consumers don't need to perform extra processing in order to communicate with the service.

To better understand this attribute, let's begin by comparing it to the `wsp:Optional` attribute we introduced in Chapter 10.

`wsp:Ignorable` vs. `wsp:Optional`

As you might recall, the `wsp:Optional` attribute can also be used to label a policy assertion as not being required. How then is `wsp:Ignorable` different from `wsp:Optional`? The difference between these two attributes has to do with the types of assertions they are applied to.

Applying the `wsp:Optional` Attribute

The `wsp:Optional` attribute is generally used as a form of "short hand" to define the equivalent of a policy alternative that offers the consumer a choice of whether to process an assertion or not process anything at all.

Therefore, this attribute tends to communicate to the consumer that:

> "You can choose to comply with the assertion and do the corresponding processing, or you can choose not to and then no assertion-related processing will occur."

A good example of this is when a technology is supported by a Web service, but its use is not mandatory by all consumers, as follows:

```
<wsp:Policy>
  <wsam:Addressing wsp:Optional="true"/>
</wsp:Policy>
```

Example 16.18
A policy assertion with the `wsp:Optional` attribute.

In this case, the Web service indicates that it supports WS-Addressing headers, but consumers don't need to use them if they don't want to.

Applying the `wsp:Ignorable` *Attribute*

What the `wsp:Ignorable` is most often used to communicate about a Web service is some behavior that will be carried out, regardless of whether the consumer program acknowledges or processes it.

In other words, this attribute conveys to the consumer that:

"By the way, you should be aware of the fact that the Web service will be doing this thing regardless of whether or not you will do anything in response to it."

The `custom:TraceMessage` assertion example we provided at the beginning of this section is appropriate for this attribute. It basically states that incoming messages from the consumer will be traced either way.

Other common applications for this attribute include:

* communicating messaging-related behaviors (stating that messages are being logged or that message details will be retained in memory as state data)

* communicating assurances (such as response time or availability guarantees, or promising non third-party or intermediary involvement)

In fact, you can express anything you like with ignorable assertions. However, this feature does need to be used with caution. See the *Considerations for Using Ignorable Assertions* section for some guidelines.

What About Using `wsp:Optional` *and* `wsp:Ignorable` *Together?*

Here's a brain teaser. The `wsp:Ignorable` attribute is supposed to indicate assertion behavior that will always occur, while the `wsp:Optional` attribute is intended to indicate that an assertion behavior does not have to occur.

So what happens when we create an assertion like this:

```
<wsp:Policy>
  <custom:TraceMessage
    wsp:Ignorable="true"
    wsp:Optional="true"/>
</wsp:Policy>
```

Example 16.19

A policy assertion with both `wsp:Ignorable` and `wsp:Optional` attributes.

A good way to understand the implications of this is to reorganize the assertion into a set of policy alternatives, as follows:

```
<wsp:Policy>
  <wsp:exactlyOne>
    <wsp:All>
      <custom:TraceMessage wsp:Ignorable="true"/>
    </wsp:All>
    <wsp:All/>
  </wsp:exactlyOne>
</wsp:Policy>
```

Example 16.20

The policy expression from Example 16.19 is restructured into a policy alternative.

What we end up with is a policy alternative with no required assertions, which is very similar to just using the `wsp:Optional` attribute on its own. Therefore, this combination is usually considered inappropriate unless the underlying runtime platform provides some proprietary processing that requires the presence of these two attributes or unless there are requirements that the `wsp:Ignorable` attribute be added simply for communication purposes.

> **NOTE**
>
> Another difference between how these two attributes are processed relates to the use of the normal form, which is explained in the *Runtime Policy Representation* secion in Chapter 17. The `wsp:Optional` attribute is not retained after the normal form is applied (because it is turned into an alternative), whereas the `wsp:Ignorable` attribute remains part of the normal form, as an attribute of the assertions.
>
> Incidentally, when we restructured the policy expression from Example 16.19 into the policy alternative displayed in Example 16.20, we applied normalization.

Using `wsp:Ignorable` to Target Consumers

Because it is the consumer program's responsibility to either ignore or understand and respond to ignorable assertions, you can use this feature to provide policy assertions that are specifically targeted to different types of consumers. This is especially useful when creating custom policy assertions that not all consumers will understand.

For example, you may have an agnostic Web service that gets reused a lot as part of different service compositions. A new composition may require that the service express an assurance that communicates its availability to other services, as follows:

```
<wsp:Policy>
  <custom:Available wsp:Ignorable="true">
    <start>5:00</start>
    <end>23:00</end>
  </custom:Available>
</wsp:Policy>
```

Example 16.21

A parameterized instance of an ignorable policy assertion that states that the Web service is available between 5 AM and 11 PM.

This allows those other services (which act as consumers when they invoke your Web service) to first check the availability assurance assertion prior to attempting invocation.

In this example, the use of the custom:Available assertion is only required by that one service composition. All of the other compositions and solutions that reuse the Web service to automate different business processes may not understand or require knowledge of this assertion. And, most importantly, even though the assertion was added well after the Web service has been in production, because it is ignorable, its presence has no effect on any of the existing service consumers (disregarding the fact that consumers who attempt to access this service between 11:00 PM and 5:00 AM will certainly be affected).

CASE STUDY EXAMPLE
Adding an Ignorable Domain Policy Expression

Another recommendation that was part of the security audit report (explained in earlier examples) was that all incoming messages containing financial data be logged. These logs will provide a valuable record of service usage and can help trace back any attempted attacks or misuse of a Web service. As an added bonus, the logged data can further be used for diagnostic purposes, fault detection, and will also help provide usage statistics.

When first hearing of this new requirement, Steve boldly asks, "Why can't we just add logging functionality to the service logic without having to advertise it in the service contract?" It's a valid point, thinks Steve, especially considering that this functionality is supposed to be added for security purposes.

The security consultants inform Steve that they would like nothing more than to see the logging function be added transparently in the background. However, other ActionCon architects have pointed out that certain service consumer programs sometimes need to send messages with highly sensitive data. In these cases, these consumers require the option of not accessing a Web service that logs incoming messages.

Steve now gets the picture and proceeds to expand his original finance domain policy definition with the ignorable `custom:LogMessage` assertion, as follows:

```
<wsp:Policy Name="http://actioncon.com/policies/finance"
  ...>
  <wsp:All>
    <custom:LogMessage wsp:Ignorable="true"/>
    <wsp:ExactlyOne>
      <sp:TransportBinding>
        ...
      </sp:TransportBinding>
      <sp:SymmetricBinding>
        ...
      </sp:SymmetricBinding>
    </sp:ExactlyOne>
  </wsp:All>
</wsp:Policy>
```

Example 16.22

The ignorable `custom:LogMessage` assertion is added to the finance domain policy definition from the previous case study example.

With this ignorable assertion in place, it is now up to consumer programs to check for its existence to determine whether they want to send a Web service within the finance domain a message or not.

Considerations for Using Ignorable Assertions

You can use the `wsp:Ignorable` attribute as an extension to the Web service contract to communicate pretty much anything you want about a Web service, but that doesn't necessarily always make it a good idea.

As with any part of a Web service contract, you need to respect the Service Loose Coupling design principle to avoid inadvertently allowing implementation details to make their way into the WSDL definition.

For example, an ignorable assertion like this:

```
<wsp:Policy>
  <custom:MyDatabaseIsDB2 wsp:Ignorable="true"/>
</wsp:Policy>
```

Example 16.23
An ignorable policy assertion of questionable value.

…is just not a good idea. Even if there was an immediate requirement to communicate the underlying database product to consumers, using the technical interface is the last place you'd want to do it.

This is an extreme example of a negative type of coupling called Contract-to-Implementation coupling. The problem this leads to is that consumer programs may be developed to bind and process these very implementation-specific assertions, and as soon as you change the implementation, a change to the assertion name will impact the consumers.

Of course, you could parameterize this assertion as follows:

```
<wsp:Policy>
  <custom:Database wsp:Ignorable="true">
    DB2
  </custom:Database>
</wsp:Policy>
```

Example 16.24
A parameterized version of the preceding policy assertion.

…but again, following the Service Loose Coupling principle (as well as the Service Abstraction principle), implementation details should really be kept private.

There will certainly be less controversial usages for this attribute for which you may be tempted to express configuration, environmental, or deployment characteristics of a Web service.

The number one question you need to raise when considering any of these types of assertions is: "What are the governance implications?" In other words, you need to weigh how useful an ignorable assertion may be to consumers against the impact of having to maintain and perhaps change this assertion in the future.

> **NOTE**
>
> When maintaining policies using proprietary vendor platform features, you may be required to create various types of ignorable assertions (or these assertions may be created for you automatically by the vendor tools) that *do* express implementation details. This is especially the case when most consumers (which, of course, can also be Web services) are being built and deployed in the same vendor environment. Be sure to assess the long-term impact of using proprietary features before committing to them.

SUMMARY OF KEY POINTS

- A policy assertion can be tagged as "ignorable" in order to communicate that the assertion that will be in effect does not need to be acknowledged by the consumer.

- Ignorable assertions are primarily used for information purposes to convey to consumers that a certain type of processing will occur on the service-side, regardless of whether the consumer performs any special processing in response to the assertion.

- Ignorable assertions are different from optional assertions and the `wsp:Ignorable` attribute is almost never used together with the `wsp:Optional` attribute.

16.4 Concurrent Policy-Enabled Contracts

The Concurrent Contract design pattern provides a design option whereby the same underlying service logic can expose two or more different contracts. When services are built as Web services, this pattern is more easily implemented because of the fact that Web service contracts are physically decoupled from their underlying implementation.

When designing policy alternatives for Web service contracts, you can end up with some very complex and elaborate structures. While these may be justified, it is worth understanding that you can also apply the Concurrent Contracts pattern as a means of establishing multiple Web service contracts that each express a policy expression (or perhaps a subset of the overall policy alternatives). In other words, creating multiple contracts may be a viable alternative to policy alternatives.

One reason in particular to consider this approach is when a Web service needs to accommodate both trusted and non-trusted consumer programs. You, as the service owner, may not want to expose a detailed set of policy alternatives to the non-trusted consumers because some of the alternative policy expressions may include private or business-related assertions that should only be made available to trusted parties.

NOTE
You can consider the approach of having concurrent policies as a specialized implementation of the Concurrent Contracts design pattern.

In the *Case Study Example: Split Concrete Descriptions Sharing the Same Abstract Description* section from Chapter 14, we demonstrated how two different WSDL concrete descriptions each imported the same abstract description for reuse purposes.

Let's revisit this example now to add a different policy expression to each concrete description:

The concrete description for the SOAP 1.1 binding with an ignorable assertion:

```
<definitions targetNamespace=
  "http://actioncon.com/contract/POSoap11"
  xmlns:tns="http://actioncon.com/contract/POSoap11"
  xmlns="http://schemas.xmlsoap.org/wsdl/"
  xmlns:wsp="http://www.w3.org/2006/07/ws-policy"
  xmlns:abs="http://actioncon.com/contract/po"
  xmlns:po="http://actioncon.com/schema/purchasing"
  xmlns:custom="http://actioncon.com/policy/custom"
  xmlns:soap11="http://schemas.xmlsoap.org/wsdl/soap/">
  <import
    namespace="http://actioncon.com/contract/PurchaseOrder"
    location="http://actioncon.com/contract/PurchaseOrder"/>
  <binding name="bdPO-SOAP11HTTP" type="abs:ptPurchaseOrder">
  <soap11:binding style="document"
    transport="http://schemas.xmlsoap.org/soap/http"/>
    <operation name="opSubmitOrder">
      <input><soap11:body use="literal"/></input>
      <output><soap11:body use="literal"/></output>
    </operation>
    <operation name="opCheckOrderStatus">
      <input><soap11:body use="literal"/></input>
      <output><soap11:body use="literal"/></output>
    </operation>
    <operation name="opChangeOrder">
      <input><soap11:body use="literal"/></input>
      <output><soap11:body use="literal"/></output>
    </operation>
```

```
   <operation name="opCancelOrder">
     <input><soap11:body use="literal"/></input>
     <output><soap11:body use="literal"/></output>
   </operation>
 </binding>
 <service name="svPurchaseOrder">
   <wsp:Policy>
     <custom:LogMessage wsp:Ingorable="true"/>
   </wsp:Policy>
   <port name="purchaseOrder-soap11http"
     binding="tns:bdPO-SOAP11HTTP">
     <soap11:address location=
       "http://actioncon.com/services/soap11/purchaseOrder"/>
   </port>
 </service>
</definitions>
```

Example 16.25

A WSDL definition with an embedded, ignorable policy assertion.

The concrete description for the SOAP 1.2 binding with one required and one ignorable assertion:

```
<definitions targetNamespace=
  "http://actioncon.com/contract/POSoap12"
  xmlns:tns="http://actioncon.com/contract/POSoap12"
  xmlns="http://schemas.xmlsoap.org/wsdl/"
  xmlns:wsp="http://www.w3.org/2006/07/ws-policy"
  xmlns:wsam=" http://www.w3.org/2007/05/addressing/ metadata"
  xmlns:custom="http://actioncon.com/policy/custom"
  xmlns:abs="http://actioncon.com/contract/po"
  xmlns:po="http://actioncon.com/schema/purchasing"
  xmlns:soap11="http://schemas.xmlsoap.org/wsdl/soap/"
  xmlns:soap12="http://schemas.xmlsoap.org/wsdl/soap12/">
  <import
    namespace="http://actioncon.com/contract/PurchaseOrder"
    location="http://actioncon.com/contract/PurchaseOrder"/>
  <binding name="bdPO-SOAP12HTTP" type="abs:ptPurchaseOrder">
  <soap12:binding style="document"
    transport="http://schemas.xmlsoap.org/soap/http"/>
  <operation name="opSubmitOrder">
    <soap12:operation soapAction=
      "http://actioncon.com/submitOrder/request"
      soapActionRequired="true" required="true"/>
      <input><soap12:body use="literal"/></input>
      <output><soap12:body use="literal"/></output>
  </operation>
```

```
        <operation name="opCheckOrderStatus">
        <soap12:operation soapAction=
          "http://actioncon.com/submitOrder/request"
            soapActionRequired="true" required="true"/>
          <input><soap12:body use="literal"/></input>
          <output><soap12:body use="literal"/></output>
        </operation>
        <operation name="opChangeOrder">
        <soap12:operation soapAction=
          "http://actioncon.com/submitOrder/request"
          soapActionRequired="true" required="true"/>
          <input><soap12:body use="literal"/></input>
          <output><soap12:body use="literal"/></output>
        </operation>
        <operation name="opCancelOrder">
        <soap12:operation soapAction=
          "http://actioncon.com/submitOrder/request"
          soapActionRequired="true" required="true"/>
          <input><soap12:body use="literal"/></input>
          <output><soap12:body use="literal"/></output>
        </operation>
      </binding>
      <service name="svPurchaseOrder">
        <wsp:Policy>
          <wsp:All>
            <wsam:Addressing><wsp:Policy/></wsam:Addressing>
            <custom:LogMessage wsp:Ingorable="true"/>
          </wsp:All>
        </wsp:Policy>
        <port name="purchaseOrder-soap11http"
          binding="tns:bdPO-SOAP11HTTP">
          <soap11:address location=
            "http://actioncon.com/services/soap11/purchaseOrder"/>
        </port>
        <port name="purchaseOrder-http-soap12"
          binding="tns:bdPO-SOAP12HTTP">
          <soap12:address location=
            "http://actioncon.com/services/soap12/purchaseOrder"/>
        </port>
      </service>
</definitions>
```

Example 16.26

A different version of the WSDL definition with an embedded policy expression comprised of required and ignorable policy assertions.

You might recall that the two versions of the concrete descriptions were created to accommodate different types of consumers. Those that support SOAP 1.2 are now also being asked to support WS-Addressing headers as per the new `wsam:Addressing` assertion.

The alternate concrete description that exposes operations via SOAP 1.1 is intended for external partner organizations with less progressive technology platforms. Therefore, the `custom:LogMessage` assertion is added for informational purposes only. Any consumers incapable of working with WS-Policy will not be affected by the presence of this assertion because it is ignorable.

SUMMARY OF KEY POINTS

- When the Concurrent Contracts pattern is applied to a Web service, it provides a design option whereby a single body of service logic is exposed via multiple Web service contracts.

- Instead of creating elaborate policy alternatives, you can consider applying this pattern to provide alternate Web service contracts where each contains a different policy expression or a different set of policy alternatives.

- This technique is most commonly used to accommodate different groups of consumers and also to release alternate versions of Web service contracts for security reasons.

Chapter 17

Advanced WS-Policy Part II: Custom Policy Assertion Design, Runtime Representation, and Compatibility

A big part of leveraging the WS-Policy framework is creating your own vocabulary of custom policy assertions. About half of this chapter is dedicated to this topic, while the remaining sections discuss policy compatibility issues and explain how policies you create at design time are structurally transformed at runtime.

17.1 Designing Custom Policy Assertions

The WS-Policy framework is highly extensible, allowing you to create a variety of custom policy assertions through which you can express highly detailed (or intentionally vague) business policies that have unique meaning to your enterprise. This section provides a series of insights and guidelines for developing effective custom assertions.

Custom Assertion Schemas

Throughout previous chapters, we've seen policy assertions only as they exist within policy expressions:

```
<wsp:Policy
  xmlns:wsam=" http://www.w3.org/2007/05/addressing/metadata">
  <wsam:Addressing><wsp:Policy/></wsam:Addressing>
</wsp:Policy>
```

Example 17.1
The standard `wsam:Addressing` assertion we've been using in many examples.

It is important to acknowledge that behind each assertion there is an XML Schema global element declaration that defines the exact structure of a policy assertion. From this perspective, the definition of a policy assertion is no different from a message definition.

Industry standard assertions have their own, pre-defined XML schemas that are part of the specifications produced by technical committees. For example, here is the W3C XML Schema that defines various WS-Addressing types, including the global element declaration used for the `wsam:Addressing` assertion:

```xml
<?xml version="1.0" encoding="utf-8" ?>
<!DOCTYPE xsd:schema (View Source for full doctype...)>
<!-- W3C XML Schema defined in the Web Services Addressing 1.0 - Metadata specification
http://www.w3.org/TR/ws-addr-metadata Copyright © 2007 World Wide Web Consortium,
(Massachusetts Institute of Technology, European Research Consortium for Informatics
and Mathematics, Keio University). All Rights Reserved. This work is distributed under
the W3C® Software License [1] in the hope that it will be useful, but WITHOUT ANY
WARRANTY; without even the implied warranty of MERCHANTABILITY or FITNESS FOR A PARTICULAR
PURPOSE. [1] http://www.w3.org/Consortium/Legal/2002/copyright-software-20021231 $Id:
ws-addr-metadata.xsd,v 1.1 2007/05/15 15:03:00 plehegar Exp $ -->
<xs:schema xmlns:xs="http://www.w3.org/2001/XMLSchema"
  xmlns:tns="http://www.w3.org/2007/05/addressing/metadata"
  xmlns:wsp="http://www.w3.org/2006/07/ws-policy"
  targetNamespace=
    "http://www.w3.org/2007/05/addressing/metadata"
  blockDefault="#all" elementFormDefault="qualified"
  finalDefault="" attributeFormDefault="unqualified">
  <xs:element name="ServiceName"
    type="tns:ServiceNameType" />
  <xs:complexType name="ServiceNameType" mixed="false">
    <xs:simpleContent>
      <xs:extension base="xs:QName">
        <xs:attribute name="EndpointName" type="xs:NCName"
          use="optional" />
        <xs:anyAttribute namespace="##other"
          processContents="lax" />
      </xs:extension>
    </xs:simpleContent>
  </xs:complexType>
  <xs:element name="InterfaceName"
    type="tns:AttributedQNameType" />
  <xs:complexType name="AttributedQNameType" mixed="false">
    <xs:simpleContent>
      <xs:extension base="xs:QName">
        <xs:anyAttribute namespace="##other"
          processContents="lax" />
      </xs:extension>
    </xs:simpleContent>
  </xs:complexType>
  <xs:attribute name="Action" type="xs:anyURI" />
  <!-- WS-Policy assertions -->
  <xs:element name="Addressing">
    <xs:complexType mixed="false">
      <xs:sequence>
```

```
              <xs:element ref="wsp:Policy" />
          </xs:sequence>
          <xs:anyAttribute namespace="##other"
            processContents="lax" />
        </xs:complexType>
    </xs:element>
    <xs:element name="AnonymousResponses">
      <xs:complexType mixed="false">
        <xs:anyAttribute namespace="##other"
          processContents="lax" />
      </xs:complexType>
    </xs:element>
    <xs:element name="NonAnonymousResponses">
      <xs:complexType mixed="false">
        <xs:anyAttribute namespace="##other"
          processContents="lax" />
      </xs:complexType>
    </xs:element>
</xs:schema>
```

Example 17.2

The W3C XML Schema definition that provides the element declaration for the `wsam:Addressing` policy assertion. Note the use of the `xs:anyAttribute` element that allows for extensibility attributes, such as `wsp:Optional` or `wsp:Ignorable`, to be added when required. (You can access this schema at: http://www.w3.org/2007/05/addressing/metadata/.)

NOTE

In the preceding example, the `xs:` prefix was used for XML Schema elements and attributes only to retain the original manner in which this specification was authored by the W3C. We will continue to use the `xsd:` prefix for all of the custom examples provided by this book.

In order for you to create your own custom policy assertions, you need to declare its underlying XML Schema element yourself and then ensure that the target namespace of this XML schema is referenced in the `wsp:Policy` element that establishes the prefix used for your policy assertion.

As an example, let's revisit the ignorable `custom:TraceMessage` assertion from Chapter 16:

```
<wsp:Policy ...>
  <custom:TraceMessage wsp:Ignorable="true"/>
</wsp:Policy>
```

Example 17.3
The `custom:TraceMessage` assertion from the *Ignorable Assertions* section in Chapter 16.

This assertion can be defined as a flag that indicates whether or not messages will be traced. Therefore, we could put together a simple global element declaration, as follows:

```
<xsd:schema xmlns:xsd="http://www.w3.org/2001/XMLSchema"
  targetNamespace="http://actioncon.com/policy/custom">
  <xsd:element name="TraceMessage">
    <xsd:complexType mixed="false">
      <xsd:anyAttribute namespace="##other"
        processContents="lax" />
    </xsd:complexType>
  </xsd:element>
</xsd:schema>
```

Example 17.4
A simple XML Schema that defines the type for the `TraceMessage` global element.

To associate this global element with the custom policy assertion, we then need to properly declare the namespace, as shown here:

```
<wsp:Policy
  xmlns:custom="http://actioncon.com/policy/custom">
  <custom:TraceMessage wsp:Ignorable="true"/>
</wsp:Policy>
```

Example 17.5
The completed policy expression, now including the namespace used to reference the target namespace of the XML schema for the `TraceMessage` global element.

Custom Assertion Processing Logic

As we explained earlier, the WS-Policy runtime processor does not care about the XML schemas that define policy assertion types. It is only concerned with the proper structuring and expression of policy assertions, not how the assertions themselves are processed.

That responsibility lies with technology-specific runtime processors that need to kick in when it's to do something with the assertion. The runtime processors capable of working with pre-defined industry policy assertions like `wsam:Addressing` are generally supplied by vendor platforms and products. But when you create custom policy assertions, you will then be the one responsible for providing the corresponding runtime processing logic (outside of the validation of the assertion structure performed automatically by the XML Schema processor).

The type of logic can vary, depending on the nature of the policy assertion. For an ignorable assertion, such as the `custom:TraceMessage` assertion we just described, you may not be required to add any processing logic at all. The assertion may simply be used to tell consumers about the existence of internal message tracing logic that is already there.

But what if we wanted to create a different kind of tracing policy assertion? Instead of one that communicates that the service will be doing some tracing processing on its own, this new assertion would provide a more detailed feature tracing details for the consumer's benefit. For example, it could provide a tracing ID value and perhaps a code that indicated the extent to which an incoming message would be traced within the service's environment.

Let's call this new assertion `custom:TraceMessageDetail`. Here's what it could look like:

```
<wsp:Policy
  xmlns:custom="http://actioncon.com/policy/custom">
  <custom:TraceMessageDetail wsp:Optional="true"/>
</wsp:Policy>
```

Example 17.6
The optional `custom:TraceMessageDetail` assertion. (This is a separate example from Example 17.5, meaning that this assertion is not related to the `custom:TraceMessage` assertion we explained earlier.)

Note how this is an optional assertion (as opposed to an ignorable one) because in this case we've given the consumer the choice as to whether it wants its messages to be traced at all.

Here's a sample XML Schema type we can create for this assertion:

```
<xsd:schema xmlns:xsd="http://www.w3.org/2001/XMLSchema"
  targetNamespace="http://actioncon.com/policy/custom"
  xmlns="http://actioncon.com/policy/custom"
  elementFormDefault="qualified">
  <xsd:element name="TraceMessageDetail" type="TraceType"/>
  <xsd:complexType name="TraceType">
    <xsd:sequence>
      <xsd:element name="TraceID" type="xsd:int"/>
      <xsd:element name="TraceCode" type="xsd:string"/>
    </xsd:sequence>
    <xsd:attribute name="TimeStamp" type="xsd:dateTime"/>
    <xsd:anyAttribute namespace="##other"
      processContents="lax" />
  </xsd:complexType>
</xsd:schema>
```

Example 17.7

An XML schema that corresponds to the XML document instance from the previous example. The statements associated with the highlighted **name** attributes give us an idea of how an XML schema defines the structure of an XML document.

This kind of assertion is considered to be *parametric*, which means that the assertion is comprised of a type that will be populated with values at runtime. Consumers will need to be designed to include additional mechanisms to communicate with the service when they need to use this assertion.

Alternatively, different contracts can be used as described in the *Concurrent Policy-Enabled Contracts* section at the end of Chapter 16. This may help in determining which Web service contracts support tracing.

CASE STUDY EXAMPLE
Creating a Custom Assertion Schema

In order to implement the `custom:LogMessage` policy assertion that Steve was planning to make part of his finance domain policy definition, he creates an XML Schema document called financeCommon.xsd that includes the global element and complex type required to define the underlying policy type, as follows:

```
<xsd:schema xmlns:xsd="http://www.w3.org/2001/XMLSchema"
  targetNamespace="http://actioncon.com/policy/custom">
  <xsd:element name="LogMessage">
    <xsd:complexType mixed="false">
      <xsd:anyAttribute namespace="##other"
        processContents="lax" />
    </xsd:complexType>
  </xsd:element>
</xsd:schema>
```

Example 17.8

The XML Schema definition for the `custom:LogMessage` assertion.

He then associates the global element from this schema definition with the policy expression that resides in the financePolicies.xml document by adding the namespace reference to the `wsp:Policy` element, as shown here:

```
<wsp:Policy Name="http://actioncon.com/policies/finance"
  xmlns:custom="http://actioncon.com/policy/custom"
  xmlns:wsp="http://www.w3.org/2006/07/ws-policy"
  ...>
  <wsp:All>
    <custom:LogMessage wsp:Ignorable="true"/>
    <wsp:ExactlyOne>
      <sp:TransportBinding>
        ...
      </sp:TransportBinding>
      <sp:SymmetricBinding>
        ...
      </sp:SymmetricBinding>
    </wsp:ExactlyOne>
  </wsp:All>
</wsp:Policy>
```

Example 17.9

The WS-Policy definition for the `custom:LogMessage` assertion.

In the resulting architecture, the financeCommon.xsd XML Schema document is associated with the financePolicies.xml domain policy definition document (as shown in Figure 17.1). Steve will now be able to add further types to this schema in support of other policy assertions that apply to the finance policy domain.

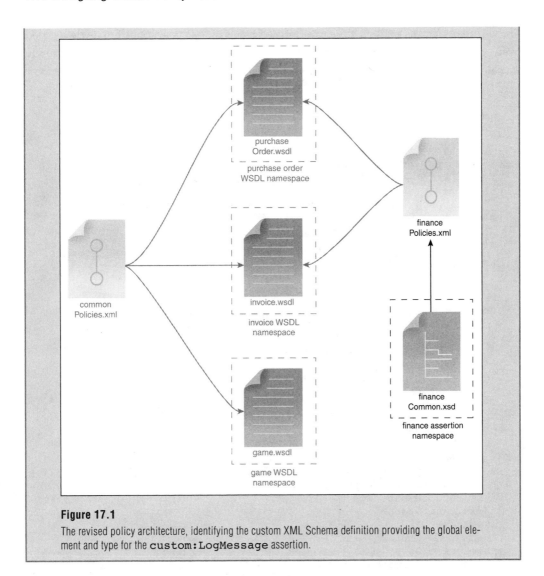

Figure 17.1

The revised policy architecture, identifying the custom XML Schema definition providing the global element and type for the **custom:LogMessage** assertion.

Not displayed in Figure 17.1 are the XML Schema definitions that provide the underlying types for the `sp:TransportBinding` and `sp:SymmetricBinding` assertions that were added back in the case study example from the *Nested and Parameterized* assertions section in Chapter 16. Also not shown is the XML Schema definition for the `wsam:Addressing` assertion that formed the basis of the global policy definition document (commonPolicies.xml) from Chapter 16's case study example in the *Reusability and Policy Centralization* section.

These three policy assertions have pre-defined types that are part of schemas developed in support of the WS-SecurityPolicy and WS-Addressing industry standards. We already revealed the XML Schema definition for `wsam:Addressing` earlier, in Example 17.2.

Let's reveal the WS-SecurityPolicy schema that defines the `sp:TransportBinding` and `sp:SymmetricBinding` assertions:

```xml
<?xml version="1.0" encoding="utf-8" ?>
<xs:schema targetNamespace=
  "http://schemas.xmlsoap.org/ws/2005/07/securitypolicy"
  xmlns:tns=
    "http://schemas.xmlsoap.org/ws/2005/07/securitypolicy"
  xmlns:wsp=
    "http://schemas.xmlsoap.org/ws/2004/09/policy"
  xmlns:xs="http://www.w3.org/2001/XMLSchema"
  elementFormDefault="qualified"
  blockDefault="#all">
  ...
  <xs:complexType name="NestedPolicyType">
    <xs:sequence>
      <xs:element ref="wsp:Policy" />
      <xs:any minOccurs="0" maxOccurs="unbounded"
        namespace="##other" processContents="lax" />
    </xs:sequence>
    <xs:anyAttribute namespace="##any"
      processContents="lax" />
  </xs:complexType>
  ...
  <xs:element name="TransportBinding"
    type="tns:NestedPolicyType">
    <xs:annotation>
      <xs:documentation xml:lang="en">
        8.3 TransportBinding Assertion
      </xs:documentation>
    </xs:annotation>
  </xs:element>
  ...
  <xs:element name="SymmetricBinding"
    type="tns:NestedPolicyType">
    <xs:annotation>
      <xs:documentation xml:lang="en">
        8.4 SymmetricBinding Assertion
      </xs:documentation>
    </xs:annotation>
  </xs:element>
  ...
</xs:schema>
```

Example 17.10

Some excerpts from the OASIS WS-SecurityPolicy XML Schema definition for the `sp:TransportBinding` and `sp:SymmetricBinding` assertions.

Figure 17.2 gives us a sense of how these industry schemas fit into the overall policy architecture:

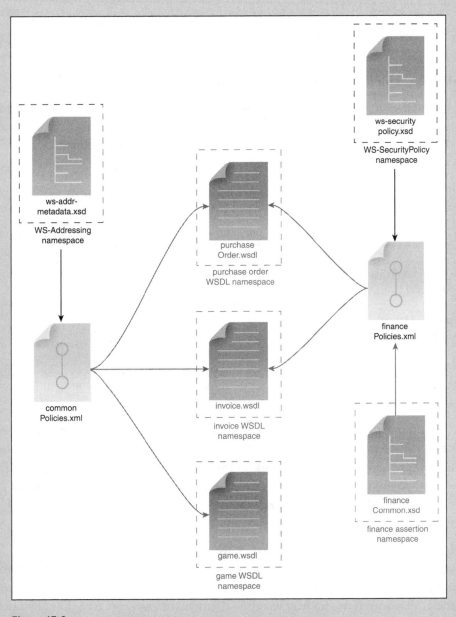

Figure 17.2

An expanded view of the policy architecture, showing the industry XML schemas required to implement industry policy assertions.

NOTE

As with the WS-Addressing XML Schema example from earlier in this section, the `xs:` prefix in the preceding WS-SecurityPolicy schema is only used to maintain content of the original version of the actual specification. Elsewhere in this book, the `xsd:` prefix is used instead.

Custom Assertion Attributes

You can, in theory, create custom extensibility attributes that extend pre-defined industry policy assertions. This is because the XML Schema type definition for many industry assertions includes an `xsd:anyAttribute` element that allows additional attributes to be added.

For example, you can, syntactically, extend the `wsam:Addressing` element as follows:

```
<wsp:Policy
  xmlns:wsam=" http://www.w3.org/2007/05/addressing/metadata"
  xmlns:custom="http://actioncon.com/policy/custom">
  <wsam:Addressing custom:ActionconMetadata="true"/>
</wsp:Policy>
```

Example 17.11

The `wsam:Addressing` assertion being extended by a custom attribute.

Although this type of extension may be possible, it is generally not recommended for the following reasons:

- The runtime processors may not be designed to accommodate this and may simply raise an error. For example, even though the complex type that underlies the `wsam:Addressing` assertion allows multiple, undefined attributes to be added, the actual WS-Addressing processor may be specifically designed to only look for and parse the WS-Policy `wsp:Optional` and `wsp:Ignorable` attributes. The processor may consider any other attributes invalid.

- Using this approach you cannot explicitly state whether the processing of the attribute is required or optional. In the previous example, even if the WS-Addressing processor ignored the presence of the `custom:ActionconMetadata` attribute, the attribute itself has no way of expressing whether its processing by consumers is optional or ignorable.

Assuming the custom attribute shown in Example 17.11 was optional, a more familiar way of expressing it would be to simply create a separate custom assertion, as follows:

```
<wsp:Policy
   xmlns:wsam=" http://www.w3.org/2007/05/addressing/metadata"
   xmlns:custom="http://actioncon.com/policy/custom">
   <wsam:Addressing><wsp:Policy/></wsam:Addressing>
   <custom:ActionconMetadata wsp:Optional="true"/>
</wsp:Policy>
```

Example 17.12

A policy expression containing the wsam:Addressing assertion along with the optional
`custom:ActionconMetadata` assertion.

Custom Policy Assertion Checklist

Provided here is a checklist of design considerations that you can take into account for each custom policy assertion you need to design:

- *What is the assertion behavior?* – Clearly define the behavior of the assertion and what this behavior does and does not apply to. This will help you determine the best name and type for the assertion and also whether it should be optional, ignorable, or neither.

- *Does the assertion require consumer participation?* – Make sure you understand whether the assertion requires participation by consumers or whether consumer participation is voluntary. This further helps clarify whether it should be ignorable.

- *What is the granularity of the assertion behavior?* – It is important to determine ahead of time which WSDL policy subjects the assertion is most appropriate for.

- *Does the assertion have associated and dependent assertions?* – Especially when creating complex nested assertions, all dependencies should be figured out so that the proper wsp:Policy structure and supporting assertion types can be designed.

- *Does the assertion introduce special service processing requirements?* – The assertion may just be communicating an existing behavior that already exists within the service logic, or the assertion may require that additional logic be added to the service (as with parametric assertions).

- *Does the behavior require special processing for determining compatibility of consumer and provider policies?* – This relates to the WS-Policy intersection considerations explained later in this chapter.

- *Does the custom assertion need to co-exist with other custom or industry assertions?* – This is especially important when applying policy centralization to create layers of overlapping assertions via domain and global policy definitions. This consideration leads to an analysis to determine any potential conflict within the merged policies (or within the effective policy).

- *Is the assertion clearly explained in a description document?* – The use of the previously explained description documents is an important convention that supports both implementation and governance of policy assertions.

Also be sure to read up on the use of standard policy profiles for documenting assertions, as explained in the upcoming *Assertion Description Documents* section.

> **NOTE**
>
> Be sure to check out the *"Web Services Policy 1.5 – Guidelines for Policy Assertion Authors"* document produced by the W3C technical committee responsible for the WS-Policy standard. It provides a series of best practices for authoring custom policy assertions that further extend or complement what was covered in this section. Visit the WS-Policy section at www.soaspecs.com to access this document.

SUMMARY OF KEY POINTS

- To design a custom policy assertion, you need to create an XML Schema global element, which usually requires defining a corresponding type.

- For parametric assertions that need to provide runtime-generated values or perform some other form of runtime processing, additional service logic will also need to be developed.

- Typically, additional consumer logic is not required when adding ignorable assertions for informative reasons only.

17.2 Maintaining Custom Policy Assertions

This section provides supplementary guidelines for establishing and documenting a standardized vocabulary of custom policy assertions.

Canonical Policy Vocabularies

For a policy assertion to be useful, it needs to be understood both by the Web service that provides it as well as by whichever consumers it is intended for. Industry policy assertions, such as the assertions from WS-Addressing and WS-SecurityPolicy we've already described, are established and widely recognized and supported. It's a different story when designing custom assertions, however.

SOA places a great deal of emphasis on standardizing the schemas that define data models for message payloads. The Canonical Schema pattern is, in fact, dedicated to establishing common messaging data models throughout service inventory boundaries.

Each time you create a new custom policy assertion, you introduce a new global element into your Web service contracts. Depending on the nature and purpose of individual assertions, the global elements that define policy assertions can arguably be viewed as extensions of the basic messaging data models. Therefore, the schemas used to define and represent custom policy assertions need to be as rigorously standardized as those that define message payload data.

Within the scope of a given service inventory boundary, different project teams delivering different services may end up creating a range of custom policy assertions. Some may be unique, while others will overlap in scope and purpose. Without design standards in place, redundant policies can become common, resulting in a poor policy architecture that is difficult and expensive to govern.

However, more to the point of attaining the strategic goals of SOA, redundant and nonstandardized policy assertions can actually inhibit the interoperability and reusability of services.

For example, imagine that Project Team A adds the `custom:LogMessage` policy assertion to the Web service contract of a reusable entity service, like an Invoice service. The assertion will work fine for the solution being built by Project Team A, but along comes Project Team B that wants to reuse the same Invoice Web service to automate part of its new application.

Project Team B disregards the existing assertion (because it's ignorable) and adds its own ignorable assertion called `unique:Logger`. The assertion does pretty much the same thing as `custom:LogMessage` (it just communicates the fact that automated logging functionality is present within the service), but Project Team B wants to own this assertion so that it can evolve it separately from Project Team A's custom assertion.

Later, Project Team C wants to reuse the Invoice service and notices that it has two similar ignorable assertions. This project team is just as interested in having its consumer programs respond to this logging assertion, but they are unsure of which of the two existing assertions to use. Rather than risk choosing the wrong one, the team adds their own. And so on...

In the end, these types of situations can result in some pretty convoluted and ugly Web service contracts. By applying the Canonical Policy Vocabulary pattern, we avoid these issues because an inventory-wide design standard is introduced and (hopefully) enforced. That is why it is common to support this approach by having a designated policy custodian who is responsible for issuing and maintaining the entire vocabulary of policy assertions for a service inventory.

In the described scenarios, following the Canonical Policy Vocabulary pattern, each project team would have allowed the policy custodian to either create a new custom policy assertion or assign them an existing, standardized policy assertion.

> **NOTE**
>
> For more information about the Canonical Policy Vocabulary pattern, visit SOAPatterns.org.

Assertion Description Documents

Policy assertions can be created by different project teams for different purposes, but as extensions to Web service contracts, they require the same (or more) attention when it comes to documentation and governance.

It is therefore very helpful to introduce a convention whereby each policy assertion is documented using a standardized template. These types of documents can be referred to as *assertion descriptions* or *assertion profiles*.

An assertion description document will generally include the following fields and types of information:

- assertion name

- assertion namespace

- assertion XML Schema definition (or a pointer to the schema document)

- a list of dependent or associated assertions (and whether the assertion is nested)

- a description of how alternatives with dependent or related assertions can be composed

- an explanation of whether (or under what circumstances) the assertion can be made optional or ignorable

- details as to whether the assertion can be extended by other assertions

- the scope of the assertion and to what extent it is centralized (as part of domain or global policy definitions)

- the assertion's target policy subjects (including explicit information as to which attachment points the assertion is *not* suitable for)

- an explanation of any processing logic that the Web service provides in support of the assertion (including a description of possible parameters and their meaning)

- references to additional, related materials, such as protocol specifications

- any relationship between the assertion and quality assurances made in the Web service's Service Level Agreement (SLA)

SUMMARY OF KEY POINTS

- The naming and typing of custom policy assertions needs to be standardized and governed, as per the Canonical Policy Vocabulary pattern.

- Individual policy assertions also need to be documented in a consistent manner using standardized policy description documents.

17.3 Runtime Policy Representation

All of the examples we've been exploring so far represent policies as we would author them at design time. The following section is focused on how the structures of policy expressions change when they are processed at runtime.

You might be tempted to ask, "Who cares?" As policy designers we should be focused on the design-time representation of our policy expressions and let runtime processors do whatever they need to, right? Well, as with any software program we build, we need to have an interest in what happens at runtime because that's what we are designing the program for.

Runtime representation is especially important with policy design because of the potentially fragmented and inconsistent means by which policy expressions can be designed and grouped throughout a WSDL definition or an entire policy definition architecture.

The upcoming *Normalization of Policies* section explains how processors tend to "flatten out" nested policy expressions into a standardized format. The following *Merging Policies* section then provides some insight as to how combining multiple, overlapping policies together helps us determine how a policy-enabled Web service will behave when it is contacted by a consumer program. Specifically, it helps us confirm whether individual, overlapping policies are compatible or not.

Normalization of Policies

Regardless of how you decide to design your policy expressions, most programs that end up processing them will translate your structure into a standardized representation format called the *normal form*. This makes the runtime presentation of policies consistent and predictable across most industry tools and processors.

As we will shortly see, a policy expression based on the normal form will tend to be more verbose than the custom structures that policy designers usually create. Therefore, these design-time representations are said to be based on the *compact form*. Note also that the process of applying the normal form to a policy expression based on the compact form is often referred to as *normalization*.

It is important to understand that applying normalization does not change what assertions within a policy expression do or how they relate; it only changes the construct structure in which they are expressed.

> **NOTE**
>
> The *wsp:All is Distributive Over wsp:ExactlyOne* section in Chapter 10 hinted at how normalization can be applied.

The normal form of a policy expression is based on the following structure:

```
<wsp:Policy ...>
  <wsp:ExactlyOne>
    <wsp:All>
      <Assertion>
        ...
      </Assertion>
    </wsp:All>
  </wsp:ExactlyOne>
</wsp:Policy>
```

Example 17.13

The standard structure of a `wsp:Policy` construct when presented in normal form. (Note that the `wsp:Exactly One` construct can contain multiple `wsp:All` child elements, as originally explained in Chapter 10.)

> **NOTE**
>
> For a full description of the normal form structure, see the pseudo schema in Appendix C. For those of you with a background in mathematics, the normalized policy format is based on the "disjunctive normal form."

The Normalization Process

An interesting aspect of the normal form is that it considers all policy expressions as a set of policy alternatives, regardless of whether the expression even has any alternatives. It does so because policy alternatives provide a fundamental means of organizing policy assertions within the WS-Policy language. Within the normal form, each policy alternative is defined as a list of assertions that are grouped together using wsp:All.

This affects the structure of nested assertions in particular, as it will tend to "flatten out" a policy expression by moving all nested alternatives to the same level, as direct child constructs of the parent wsp:Policy construct.

For example, the following policy expression contains nested assertions and alternatives:

```
<wsp:Policy ...>
  <wsam:Addressing wsp:Optional="true"/>
  <custom:Available24by7>
    <wsp:Policy>
      <wsp:ExaclyOne>
        <custom:ResponseGuarantee>
          6
        </custom:ResponseGuarantee>
        <custom:ResponseGuarantee>
          24
        </custom:ResponseGuarantee>
      </wsp:ExactlyOne>
    </wsp:Policy>
  </custom:Available24by7>
  <custom:Logging wsp:Ignorable="true"/>
</wsp:Policy>
```

Example 17.14

A policy expression in compact form.

… would be restructured as follows in normal form:

```
<wsp:Policy ...>
  <wsp:ExactlyOne>
    <wsp:All>
      <wsam:Addressing><wsp:Policy/></wsam:Addressing>
      <custom:Available24x7>
        <wsp:Policy>
          <wsp:ExactlyOne>
            <wsp:All>
              <custom:ResponseGuarantee>
                6
              </custom:ResponseGuarantee/>
            </wsp:All>
          </wsp:ExactlyOne>
        </wsp:Policy>
      </custom:Available24x7>
      <custom:Logging wsp:Ignorable="true"/>
    </wsp:All>
    <wsp:All>
      <wsam:Addressing><wsp:Policy/></wsam:Addressing>
      <custom:Available24x7>
        <wsp:Policy>
          <wsp:ExactlyOne>
            <wsp:All>
              <custom:ResponseGuarantee>
                12
              </custom:ResponseGuarantee>
            </wsp:All>
          </wsp:ExactlyOne>
        </wsp:Policy>
      </custom:Available24x7>
      <custom:Logging wsp:Ignorable="true"/>
    </wsp:All>
    <wsp:All>
      <custom:Available24x7>
        <wsp:Policy>
          <wsp:ExactlyOne>
            <wsp:All>
              <custom:ResponseGuarantee>
                6
              </custom:ResponseGuarantee>
            </wsp:All>
          </wsp:ExactlyOne>
        </wsp:Policy>
      </custom:Available24x7>
```

```
      <custom:LogMessge wsp:Ignorable="true"/>
   </wsp:All>
   <wsp:All>
     <custom:Available24x7>
       <wsp:Policy>
         <wsp:ExactlyOne>
           <wsp:All>
             <custom:ResponseGuarantee>
                12
             </custom:ResponseGuarantee>
           </wsp:All>
         </wsp:ExactlyOne>
       </wsp:Policy>
     </custom:Available24x7>
     <custom:Logging wsp:Ignorable="true"/>
   </wsp:All>
 </wsp:ExactlyOne>
</wsp:Policy>
```

Example 17.15
The previous policy expression now in normal form.

As you can see, the normal form forces all alternatives into separate `wsp:All` constructs. Also note how the `wsp:Optional` attribute is also removed so that optional assertions are structured as alternatives.

Another way of thinking about normalization is to imagine a policy expression with nested assertions and alternatives as a tree with various branches that can have further branches (an analogy used for many XML-related structures). A normalized policy expression essentially forces all the branches to the spine of the tree (the root of the XML document), whereby each branch represents a policy alternative.

NOTE
The upcoming *Merging Policies* section will provide a further example of how policy expressions are transformed into normal form.

Because the normal form is the standard runtime representation of policy expressions, you as the policy designer are not required to author normalized policy expressions. However, you should understand how normalization affects policy structures so that you can work with programs and tools that do perform the transformation of compact to normal form. If you are specifically interested in the steps followed to transform a policy expression into normal form, the normalization algorithm is explained in the WS-Policy specification, which you can access via www.soaspecs.com.

Merging Policies

In the *Effective Policies* section from Chapter 10 we explained how applying more than one policy to the same subject results in a combined policy labeled the "effective policy."

Let's just briefly recap:

- Using WS-PolicyAttachment features, you can associate a policy expression with a number of different attachment points within a WSDL definition.

- Attachment points are grouped into policy subjects that represent areas of the WSDL definition where policy expressions associated with different attachment points will affect the same message exchanges.

- As a result, you can easily create individual policy expressions at design time that will overlap at runtime when they are combined and then applied together to the same messages.

- All of the overlapping policies are combined together to represent the effective policy.

If you replace the word "combined" in the last two bullet items with the term "merged," then you will understand exactly what this section is all about. The more policy expressions that overlap, the more complex the merging considerations and the resulting effective policy.

If we don't pay attention to how policies will be merged at runtime, we risk inadvertently creating policies that may be in conflict when combined. This can, at minimum, inhibit messaging between a service and its consumers. However, more likely, conflicted policies will raise a variety of undesirable errors and can grind communication to a halt.

The Merging Process

Let's first learn about merging policies from a syntactical perspective. For each `wsp:Policy` element that is attached to a WSDL attachment point, the effect of merging is to replace that `wsp:Policy` element with a `wsp:All` element. This makes sense because we are, in fact, applying multiple policies together.

Each merged policy expression is represented as a child of a parent `wsp:Policy` construct. For example, suppose we created policies for the following WSDL 1.1 attachment points (all of which are part of the endpoint policy subject):

- `portType`
- `binding`
- `port`

Let's now assume that there are three policy expressions attached to each of these elements as shown in the following examples.

Policy expression attached to port element:

```
<definitions ...>
  ...
  <service ...>
    <port ...>
      <wsp:Policy>
        <wsp:ExactlyOne>
          <ex:Assertion1/>
          <ex:Assertion2/>
        </wsp:ExactlyOne>
      </wsp:Policy>
    </port>
  </service>
</definitions>
```

Example 17.16

A policy assertion alternative attached to a `port` element, providing a choice between `ex:Assertion1` and `ex:Assertion2`.

Policy expression attached to binding element:

```
<definitions ...>
  ...
  <binding ...>
    <wsp:Policy>
      <wsp:ExactlyOne>
        <ex:Assertion3/>
      </wsp:ExactlyOne>
    </wsp:Policy>
  </binding>
</definitions>
```

Example 17.17

The `ex:Assertion3` policy assertion attached to the `binding` element.

Policy expression attached to `portType` element:

```
<definitions ...>
  ...
  <portType ...>
    <wsp:Policy>
      <wsp:ExactlyOne>
        <ex:Assertion4/>
      </wsp:ExactlyOne>
    </wsp:Policy>
  </portType>
</definitions>
```

Example 17.18

The `ex:Assertion4` policy assertion attached to the `portType` element.

As we explained in Chapter 10, each policy subject can have multiple attachment points but, in the end, they all can affect the same message exchanges. Therefore, even though we have three policy assertions attached to different parts of the WSDL definition, all three will apply to the same message exchanges that are associated with the port type (which is further implemented via its binding and port definitions).

As a result, the policy that is applied at runtime (when the messages that are defined within this port type are actually received and transmitted) is the effective (merged) policy.

For example, the effective policy that results from the merging of the three previously displayed policy expressions would look like this:

```
<wsp:Policy>
  <wsp:All>
    <wsp:ExactlyOne>
      <ex:Assertion1/>
      <ex:Assertion2/>
    </wsp:ExactlyOne>
  </wsp:All>
  <wsp:All>
    <ex:Assertion3/>
  </wsp:All>
  <wsp:All>
```

```
    <ex:Assertion4/>
  </wsp:All>
</wsp:Policy>
```

Example 17.19

The effective policy is comprised of three required assertions, one of which is part of a policy alternative.

Note again that what this example displays is not something we pre-define. This is a computed, runtime view of the results of a policy merge as they would apply to a given message.

Normalizing Merged Policies

Earlier we explained the normalization algorithm that is used to standardize the runtime representation of policy expressions. When carrying out a policy merge, a processor may actually represent the previously displayed policy expression in the normalized form, which would result in the following effective policy:

```
<wsp:Policy>
  <wsp:ExactlyOne>
    <wsp:All>
      <ex:Assertion1/>
      <ex:Assertion3/>
      <ex:Assertion4/>
    <wsp:All/>
    <wsp:All>
      <ex:Assertion2/>
      <ex:Assertion3/>
      <ex:Assertion4/>
    </wsp:All>
  </wsp:ExactlyOne>
</wsp:Policy>
```

Example 17.20

Example 17.19 restructured into normal form.

Inter-Policy Compatibility

One aspect of merging policies we have not addressed is that of inter-policy compatibility. Unfortunately, the WS-Policy framework does not provide any features or guidance for conflict resolution between merged policies. Therefore, it's up to you to make this a priority when designing overlapping policy expressions. What is usually required is a thorough analysis process during which a range of message exchange scenarios is studied in order to identify when overlapping policy expressions can cause problems.

SUMMARY OF KEY POINTS

- Multiple policy expressions can be associated with the different attachment points within a policy subject. This results in all of these policies being applied together to the same message exchanges that fall within the scope of the policy subject.

- At runtime, these individual policies are merged into a single (most likely, normalized) policy expression. The combination of merged policies is the effective policy.

- Taking policy compatibility into account is important in order to determine how merged policy expressions will relate to each other at runtime (if at all).

17.4 Intersection and Consumer-Service Policy Compatibility

We've just been focusing on merged policy expressions and the compatibility of individual policies. It's now time to focus on the compatibility of policies with the consumers that will need to comply with them.

As we know, a service contract can contain a range of policies and policy alternatives. Similarly, a service can have a range of consumer programs that access it for different reasons. Therefore, it is not uncommon for any one consumer to not be capable of supporting all of the policy assertions within a given Web service contract.

Furthermore, you can have consumers that themselves have policy requirements. In this case, there is always the possibility that a consumer's policy requirements will not be compatible with the policy requirements of a service.

Whatever extent to which a consumer program's functionality and requirements are compatible with the policies of a Web service contract represents the extent to which the consumer and service are compatible from an interoperability perspective.

You can view a consumer's policy support and requirements as one sphere and a Web service's policy requirements as another sphere. Where they overlap (intersect) determines their compatibility. This is why we refer to this aspect of WS-Policy design as *intersection*. To help consumer designers and service owners determine compatibility and choose the most appropriate policy assertions for a given message exchange, WS-Policy provides the *intersection algorithm*. The basis of this algorithm are the effective policies of a service's policy subjects and whatever policy alternatives are present within these effective policies.

Compatibility Levels

Carrying out the intersection algorithm requires that the consumer itself provide its own set of polices as actual WS-Policy expressions. This allows for a direct comparison of the consumer's policy requirements with those of the service contract.

For example, a consumer designer may create a policy expression that indicates the following:

- The consumer program is capable of supporting message exchanges based on WS-Addressing, and…

- …the consumer program actually requires that services it exchanges messages with support WS-Addressing.

Therefore, the consumer designer may issue the following policy expression:

```
<wsp:Policy>
  <wsam:Addressing><wsp:Policy/></wsam:Addressing>
</wsp:Policy>
```

Example 17.21
A policy expression provided by the consumer containing the **wsam:Addressing** policy assertion.

This expression is not attached to a WSDL definition and is generally not programmatically implemented. It's just a means of communicating the consumer's policy requirements.

However, because the policy is expressed using the same language that Web service contracts use to define their policies, the consumer's policy expression can be used as input for an intersection algorithm that performs a direct comparison of consumer and service compatibilities.

Specifically, this comparison is carried out at two levels:

- assertion compatibility
- alternative compatibility

Let's explain each level separately.

Assertion Compatibility

As we established in Chapter 10, the global element used to represent the assertion has a type associated with it. Assertions are considered to be compatible when they have the same underlying type. At runtime this means that for assertions to be compatible, they must exist as instances of the same global element declaration.

In relation to the `wsam:Addressing` assertion provided by the consumer (from Example 17.21), this simply means that for a Web service contract to be compatible requires it to also contain a policy expression with the following policy assertion:

```
<wsam:Addressing><wsp:Policy/></wsam:Addressing>
```

Beyond type matching, the WS-Policy framework does not perform any further comparisons. For example, the intersection algorithm will not be able to tell whether the parameters that lie within matching service and consumer assertion types are also compatible. That responsibility lies within whatever programming logic processes the parameters.

This also means that even if you have matching assertion types, you may discover that the service and consumer policies are still incompatible (or that they will require custom standardization to enable compatibility). Therefore, the intersection algorithm can represent the first of several steps in a complete compatibility assessment.

NOTE

In order for nested assertions to be considered compatible, *both* consumer and service must support the corresponding nested expressions. Furthermore, an alternative in one assertion must be compatible with the corresponding alternative in the other. If a consumer or service uses a parameterized assertion, it is not guaranteed that the compatibility of the assertion can be determined in an interoperable manner.

Note also that the order of assertions within alternatives and the order of the alternatives themselves have no relevance from a compatibility perspective.

Alternative Compatibility

A consumer's policy alternatives are compatible with a service's policy alternatives as long as each contains at least one alternative with fully compatible assertions.

There are two ways of measuring this level of compatibility: *lax* and *strict*.

Strict compatibility essentially requires that for policy alternatives to be compatible, both consumer and service have exactly matching alternative assertion sets.

For example, consider the following two policy expressions, each with two alternatives:

```
Service Policy:
<wsp:Policy>
  <wsp:ExactlyOne>
    <wsp:All>
      <ex:Assertion1/>
      <ex:Assertion2/>
      <ex:Assertion3/>
    </wsp:All>
    <wsp:All>
      <ex:Assertion4/>
      <ex:Assertion5/>
      <ex:Assertion6/>
    </wsp:All>
  </wsp:ExactlyOne>
</wsp:Policy>
```

Example 17.22
The policy alternative provided by the Web service contract.

```
Consumer Policy:

<wsp:Policy>
  <wsp:ExactlyOne>
    <wsp:All>
      <ex:Assertion7/>
      <ex:Assertion4/>
      <ex:Assertion8/>
    </wsp:All>
    <wsp:All>
      <ex:Assertion2/>
      <ex:Assertion1/>
      <ex:Assertion3/>
    </wsp:All>
```

```
    </wsp:ExactlyOne>
</wsp:Policy>
```

Example 17.23
The policy alternative provided by the consumer program designer.

In these two examples, the first alternative in the service policy is compatible with the second alternative in the consumer policy.

In the lax mode, only assertions that are not marked ignorable within one alternative are compared with assertions from the other alternative. As a result, ignorable assertions do not contribute to compatibility. In strict mode, on the other hand, ignorable assertions are compared, which means that despite the fact that they have been tagged as ignorable, consumers are expected to understand them. (In other words, the `wsp:Ignorable` attribute actually gets ignored!)

There are various tools and products that can automatically perform an intersection analysis on two separate policy expressions. When these tools find no compatible policy assertions, they will simply indicate that no compatible policy alternatives are available. From the perspective of a consumer and a provider, this means that they cannot exchange messages. However, when compatibility is found, the intersection will result in a list of compatible consumer/service alternative pairs that will be used to determine the most appropriate, effective runtime policy.

Let's revisit the earlier examples where we compared service and consumer policy alternatives. After subjecting these two alternatives to the intersection algorithm, the following results are produced:

```
<wsp:Policy>
  <wsp:ExactlyOne>
    <wsp:All>
      <ex:Assertion1/>
      <ex:Assertion2/>
      <ex:Assertion3/>
      <ex:Assertion2/>
      <ex:Assertion1/>
      <ex:Assertion3/>
    </wsp:All>
  </wsp:ExactlyOne>
</wsp:Policy>
```

Example 17.24
The results of carrying out the intersection algorithm on the previous two examples.

Because of how the intersection process groups both consumer and service assertions, each is repeated twice. This expression is equivalent to the following:

```
<wsp:Policy>
  <wsp:ExactlyOne>
    <wsp:All>
      <ex:Assertion1/>
      <ex:Assertion2/>
      <ex:Assertion3/>
    </wsp:All>
  </wsp:ExactlyOne>
</wsp:Policy>
```

Example 17.25
After some editing, the three compatible policy assertions are clearly displayed.

NOTE

You are not required to use the intersection algorithm provided by WS-Policy to determine policy compatibility. There may be analysis and development tools that apply different approaches to performing policy comparisons that may be more suitable for your requirements.

SUMMARY OF KEY POINTS

- The WS-Policy framework provides a formal process for assessing the compatibility between two policy expressions called the "intersection algorithm."

- Intersection can be used to assess policy-related compatibility between a service and a consumer as long as the consumer provides its policy requirements via actual WS-Policy expressions.

- The intersection algorithm evaluates compatibility on the assertion and alternative levels.

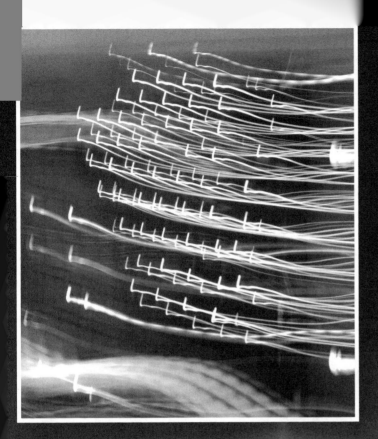

Chapter 18

Advanced Message Design Part I: WS-Addressing Vocabularies

W S-Addressing has emerged as a fundamental building block of the Web services framework, almost as important as SOAP itself for enabling communication between and across Web services that need to go beyond the regular WSDL Request-Response exchanges. This chapter continues where Chapter 11 left off, by exploring how the design of SOAP messages can be expanded with the standardized headers provided by the WS-Addressing language.

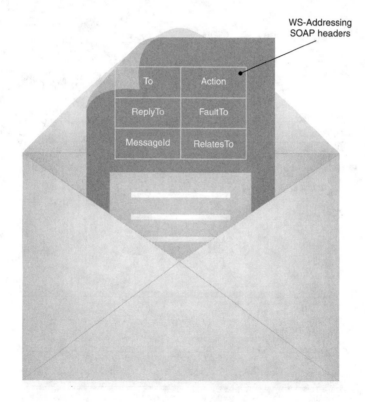

Figure 18.1

The majority of WS-Addressing features explained in this book are implemented using SOAP header blocks.

SOAP was designed as an intentionally simple and lightweight messaging protocol. As such, it is not equipped with the type of built-in infrastructure features that are common within communication frameworks used for traditional distributed systems. These types of capabilities are needed to build and run sophisticated service-oriented solutions comprised of complex compositions of services.

The WS-Addressing standard was developed to add these types of features as extensions to the SOAP messaging framework. Specifically, WS-Addressing provides a series of standardized headers that support:

- complex synchronous and asynchronous message exchange patterns

- service compositions involving multiple transports and/or transfer protocols

- messaging functionality used to deliver, route, identify, and correlate messages

- communication with and between consumers and stateful service instances

> **NOTE**
>
> The WS-Addressing standard is documented across three W3C specifications: Web Services Addressing Core, SOAP Binding, and Metadata, all of which were made part of versions 1.2 and 2.0 of the WS-I Basic Profile. Their features are furthermore used by several WS-* specifications, including WS-ReliableMessaging, WS-Coordination, WS-Trust, and WS-SecureConversation. To access any of these documents, visit www.soaspecs.com.

18.1 EPRs and MAPs

The WS-Addressing language is focused on expressing characteristics about a message that relate to its runtime processing and delivery. It accomplishes this primarily by defining a set of header blocks, each of which represents message characteristics in such a manner that they can be combined in a variety of creative ways.

We'll be explaining each of these headers shortly in the upcoming sections, but let's first focus on what lies at the heart of WS-Addressing: the *endpoint reference*.

Endpoint References (EPRs)

From a WS-Addressing perspective, an "endpoint" refers to the point of access whereby a Web service can be contacted, invoked, and communicated with. Most often, an endpoint will represent or be related to the Web service contract.

Without WS-Addressing, you can figure out the address to a Web service contract (endpoint) simply by studying the WSDL definition and locating the address value in its concrete description. This allows you to design a consumer program that can then send messages to that address (which represents the location of the endpoint).

With WS-Addressing, you can supplement this address with further parameter values. These parameters can be any type of information that is meaningful to the Web service (the endpoint) that they are being sent to. The combination of the endpoint address and these supplemental parameter values (as well as optional metadata) constitutes an endpoint reference or "EPR."

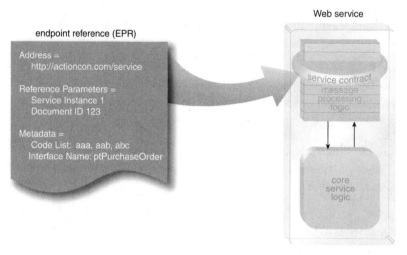

Figure 18.2
An EPR is a set of data that points to a specific Web service contract (endpoint).

The term "EPR" is loosely meant to refer to any XML element that is of type `wsa:EndpointReferenceType`. Some of the WS-Addressing headers we will explore in this chapter are based on this type, in which case the header itself is considered to contain an EPR.

There are two common use cases for EPR parameters:

• *Service Instance Routing* – EPR parameters are used to identify Web service instances.

- *State Messaging* – EPR parameters are used to hold and express supplemental context or state data that has special meaning to the Web service, thereby supporting the Service Statelessness principle by allowing the Web service to reduce or eliminate its own state data.

There are many other applications for EPRs that will allow you to create a variety of creative message designs that can tie into intermediary agent architectures to provide elaborate and complex message paths.

For example, the `wsa:EndpointReferenceType` type defined by the WS-Addressing specification can be utilized within SOAP headers pre-defined by other WS-* standards. The WS-Eventing specification uses this type to define the endpoint where notifications are to be sent, and WS-ReliableMessaging incorporates this type to pinpoint where message acknowledgements are transmitted to.

Message Addressing Properties (MAPs)

Message addressing properties or *"MAPs"* have been described as "e-mail for Web services," and if you ever get a chance to look at the headers that accompany an e-mail message you'll be able to get a good understanding of how MAPs work and why they were developed. In fact, we'll be drawing comparisons between WS-Addressing MAP elements and common e-mail SMTP headers (like To, From, Reply-To, Message-ID, and In-Reply-To) throughout the upcoming sections.

MAPs essentially allow you to add processing and delivery instructions into the SOAP message itself, enabling the message to become more of an independent unit of communication. An MAP-enabled message will be able to dictate how it should be routed, responded to, or otherwise processed. This type of message is more intelligent and independent when compared to traditional SOAP messages that relied almost entirely on the underlying runtime environment, transport protocols, and recipient programs to figure out how they should be processed.

> **NOTE**
>
> Message addressing properties were formerly called "message information headers."

MAPs and EPRs

As we were introducing MAPs, you might have been wondering how exactly they relate to the EPRs we just covered in the previous section. The remainder of this chapter will explore this relationship in detail, but here's a quick preview:

- The WS-Addressing language provides a set of MAP-related elements that are used to create SOAP headers (each of which is explained in the section *The MAP Vocabulary*).

- As we know, an EPR is an XML element that expresses a Web service's endpoint address, reference parameters, and other types of metadata. The EPR is pre-defined by the WS-Addressing specification via the XML Schema `wsa:EndpointReferenceType` complex type and the `wsa:EndpointReference` element declaration.

- Of all the MAP elements, three (`wsa:From`, `wsa:ReplyTo`, and `wsa:FaultTo`) are also of type `wsa:EndpointReferenceType`, which means that each of these MAP headers can be assigned an entire EPR.

Again, all of these details are explained in the upcoming sections.

MAPs and Transport-Independence

A key aspect of MAPs that will become more evident as you learn about the individual MAP elements is that they establish a means of controlling message communication dynamics without any reliance on a particular transport protocol.

If you are familiar with the intrinsic features of transport technologies like HTTP and SMTP, you will recognize similar features expressed via MAP elements as SOAP headers. By abstracting basic communication commands (like From and To and Reply To, etc.) into SOAP headers, the SOAP message itself naturally becomes less dependent on any particular transport technology, thereby allowing you to establish message paths comprised of multiple transports, if necessary.

Note that while this is an important consideration to keep in mind, SOAP is most widely used with the HTTP protocol (as discussed back in Chapter 15). The examples in the remainder of this chapter are therefore focused only on SOAP messages delivered via HTTP.

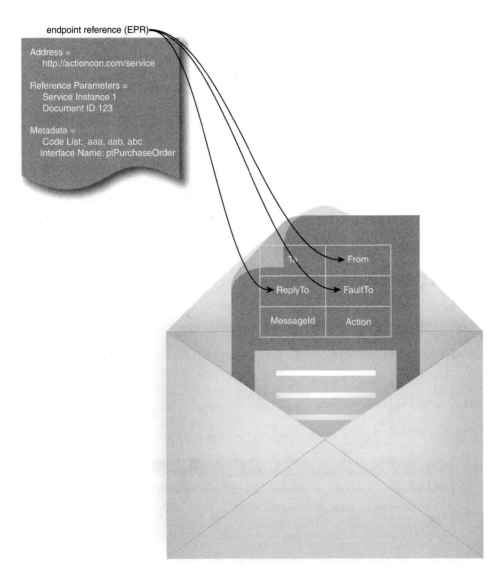

Figure 18.3
The EPR can be assigned to different MAP headers.

SUMMARY OF KEY POINTS

- WS-Addressing provides a set of features used to express characteristics about a message that pertain to its runtime processing and delivery.

- Endpoint references represent the address of a Web service contract along with supplementary parameters and metadata values that are meaningful to the endpoint and can be used to design sophisticated data exchange patterns that may require the involvement of intermediary agents.

- Message addressing properties represent a set of industry SOAP headers (inspired by e-mail functions) that allow a message to be equipped with a series of processing and delivery instructions.

18.2 The EPR Vocabulary

The WS-Addressing language provides a modest vocabulary for expressing EPRs, comprised of the following elements:

- `wsa:EndpointReference`

- `wsa:Address`

- `wsa:ReferenceParameters`

- `wsa:Metadata`

> **NOTE**
>
> The following sections make reference to the acronyms "IRI" and "URI." You may want to revisit the *IRI vs. URI vs. URL vs. URN* section in Chapter 7 if you don't recall their meaning.

Let's explain each element separately.

The `wsa:EndpointReference` Element

Every EPR is individually wrapped in this parent element. Each `wsa:EndpointReference` construct is comprised of a required `wsa:Address` element and can also include optional `wsa:ReferenceParameters` and `wsa:Metadata` elements.

As explained earlier, the term "EPR" most commonly refers to an instance of this element or an instance of an element that is of type `wsa:EndpointReferenceType`.

Here's a skeleton EPR construct:

```
<wsa:EndpointReference
   xmlns:wsa="http://www.w3.org/2005/08/addressing">
   ...
</wsa:EndpointReference>
```

Example 18.1
The parent `wsa:EndpointReference` construct. The opening tag establishes the `wsa:` prefix used by child elements from the WS-Addressing language.

The `wsa:Address` Element

This element simply establishes the address for the target Web service using an IRI value, as follows:

```
<wsa:EndpointReference
   xmlns:wsa="http://www.w3.org/2005/08/addressing">
   <wsa:Address>
     http://actioncon.com/service
   </wsa:Address>
</wsa:EndpointReference>
```

Example 18.2
The `wsa:Address` element containing the address value of the Web service issuing the EPR.

The value of the `wsa:Address` element usually corresponds to the value of the `soap:Address` element's `location` attribute, or the value of the `address` attribute of the WSDL 2.0 `endpoint` element. However, this element can also be populated with special pre-defined values provided by the WS-Addressing language, as follows:

Anonymous Address

When using SOAP over HTTP, this value indicates that the response to a SOAP message containing an EPR must be carried out synchronously using the HTTP request-response mechanism (described in Chapter 15).

In other words, when a service request message, sent by the consumer program, contains the anonymous value in its `wsa:ReplyTo` element, the service is required to send its response message via the HTTP response channel that is automatically provided by the underlying HTTP protocol. (The `wsa:ReplyTo` element is explained later in this chapter.)

This is comparable to responding to a message (that does not use WS-Addressing) as part of a regular WSDL Request-Response MEP where the response is automatically routed (via HTTP) back to the endpoint where the request message originated from.

Here's the pre-defined anonymous address value:

```
<wsa:Address>
  http://www.w3.org/2005/08/addressing/anonymous
</wsa:Address>
```

Example 18.3
A pre-defined address value used to indicate the anonymous value.

The use of this value can be forced by a WS-Addressing-specific policy assertion. See the *WS-Addressing Policy Assertions* section in Chapter 19 for details.

> **NOTE**
>
> This interpretation of the anonymous value is specific to the use of WS-Addressing messages via SOAP over HTTP. Other potential bindings can provide their own definitions for what this assertion means.

None Address

A further pre-defined URI exists to represent no address at all. This value is used to indicate that messages designated for a particular endpoint must be discarded.

For example, you could use this value with one of the MAP headers (explained in the upcoming *MAP Vocabulary* section) to intentionally communicate that response or fault messages for a particular EPR-enabled message should not be sent.

Here's the URI that represents a "none" value for the `wsa:Address` element:

```
<wsa:Address>
  http://www.w3.org/2005/08/addressing/none
</wsa:Address>
```

Example 18.4
The URI for the "none" value used to indicate that messages sent to a specific endpoint will actually not go anywhere.

The `wsa:ReferenceParameters` Element

With the optional `wsa:ReferenceParameters` element we finally get to add the details that will be used to supplement and extend the address with parameters.

Here's a simple example:

```
<wsa:EndpointReference
  xmlns:wsa="http://www.w3.org/2005/08/addressing"
  xmlns:act="http://actioncon.com/referenceIDs">
  <wsa:Address>
    http://actioncon.com/service
  </wsa:Address>
  <wsa:ReferenceParameters>
    <act:Instance>
      1
    </act:Instance>
  </wsa:ReferenceParameters>
</wsa:EndpointReference>
```

Example 18.5
The `wsa:ReferenceParameters` construct containing a custom child element with a parameter value.

You'll notice that in this example, the `wsa:ReferenceParameters` construct is populated with custom elements. The contents of this construct are always defined by the issuer of the EPR and are opaque to the EPR consumer. As stated earlier, these values are often generated at runtime.

You can place pretty much any element structure you like within the opening and closing `wsa:ReferenceParameters` tags. For example, you could add a new parameter as follows:

```
<wsa:ReferenceParameters>
  <act:Instance>
    1
  </act:Instance>
  <act:ClientID>
    id-123-456-abc:01:23
  </act:ClientID>
</wsa:ReferenceParameters>
```

Example 18.6
The new `act:ClientID` element is added, constituting a new parameter.

If you do provide more than one parameter, the order in which they appear has no significance.

The `wsa:Metadata` Element

Sometimes there will be additional information you want to associate with an EPR, beyond just the Web service address and related reference parameters. That's what this optional element is for. It can be used to provide supplementary details, such as descriptions or constraints related to the endpoint.

Here's an example:

```
<wsa:EndpointReference
  xmlns:wsa="http://www.w3.org/2005/08/addressing"
  xmlns:act="http://actioncon.com/referenceIDs"
  xmlns:po="http://actioncon.com/contract/po">
  <wsa:Address>
    http://actioncon.com/service
  </wsa:Address>
  <wsa:ReferenceParameters>
    <act:Instance>
      1
    </act:Instance>
  </wsa:ReferenceParameters>
  <wsa:Metadata>
    <wsam:InterfaceName>
      po:ifPurchaseOrder
    </wsam:InterfaceName>
  </wsa:Metadata>
</wsa:EndpointReference>
```

Example 18.7

A `wsa:ReferenceParameters` construct with a nested `wsa:Metadata` construct containing the `wsam:InterfaceName` element.

In this example, the `wsa:Metadata` construct contains the `wsam:InterfaceName` element used to identify the port type or interface of the endpoint's WSDL definition. This special child element is described in the *EPRs and WSDL Binding* section in Chapter 19.

SUMMARY OF KEY POINTS

- EPRs provide a standard way to express parameters and supplementary information (beyond an address value) that is meaningful to an endpoint.

- The `wsa:EndpointReference` construct is comprised of a required `wsa:Address` element and optional `wsa:ReferenceParameters` and `wsa:Metadata` elements.

- The `wsa:ReferenceParameters` element is a core part of WS-Addressing, as it can host a variety of custom elements that represent parameters used during the runtime processing of a message.

18.3 MAP Vocabulary

Let's now take a closer look at each of the elements that comprise the WS-Addressing MAP vocabulary, all of which establish (or relate to) SOAP header blocks:

- `wsa:To`
- `wsa:From`
- `wsa:ReplyTo`
- `wsa:FaultTo`
- `wsa:Action`
- `wsa:MessageId`
- `wsa:RelatesTo`
- `wsa:ReferenceParameters`

Note that when designing WS-Addressing-enabled messages, some of these elements are always required, whereas others are only required under certain circumstances related to how a given message is involved in a WSDL message exchange pattern (MEP). The rules that dictate how MAP elements are used together with certain WSDL MEPs are explained in the *MEP Requirements for MAP Elements* section in Chapter 19.

The `wsa:To` Element

This element establishes a SOAP header that simply specifies the target address of the message recipient. The value for the `wsa:To` element is often automatically set using the address information from the WSDL 1.1 `port` or WSDL 2.0 `endpoint` element (which will usually correspond to the SOAP address value).

Here's what a populated `wsa:To` SOAP header block looks like:

```
<soap:Header>
  <wsa:To>
    http://megaeuromart.com/client
  </wsa:To>
</soap:Header>
```

Example 18.8
The `wsa:To` element with a value indicating the address of the consumer to which the message is being sent.

The `wsa:To` element must contain a valid URI or IRI, and when its value is not defined at design time, it automatically defaults to the anonymous URI value we described earlier in the section *The `wsa:Address` Element*.

Note that you cannot assign an EPR to the `wsa:To` element directly. We explain how WS-Addressing SOAP headers, including `wsa:To`, are constructed when messages need to be based on an EPR in the *Mapping EPR Reference Parameters to MAP Headers* section in Chapter 19.

The `wsa:From` Element

You can use the optional `wsa:From` element to indicate the address and endpoint information about the sender of a message. Unlike the `wsa:To` element, you can actually assign an entire EPR to this element. It is therefore most commonly used when a Web service issues a message to a consumer in order to provide it with its endpoint details for future communication purposes.

Notice how in the following example, the `wsa:From` address value is wrapped in the `wsa:Address` element that was described earlier as part of the EPR vocabulary:

```
<soap:Header>
  <wsa:To>
    http://megaeuromart.com/client
  </wsa:To>
  <wsa:From>
    <wsa:Address>
      http://actioncon.com/service
    </wsa:Address>
```

```
    </wsa:From>
</soap:Header>
```

Example 18.9
The **wsa:From** construct containing a **wsa:Address** element with an address value that represents the Web
service from where the message originated.

The wsa:From element is one of only three MAP elements based on the XML Schema
wsa:EndpointReferenceType complex type, allowing it to be assigned the contents of
an entire wsa:EndpointReference construct. The preceding example assumes that this
construct only contains the wsa:Address element. An example that includes additional
EPR elements will be provided later in this section.

The wsa:ReplyTo Element

Using this element, you can tell message recipients where they should send response
messages to. This feature is often used to introduce asynchronous functionality.

Here's an example:

```
<soap:Header>
  <wsa:To>
    http://megaeuromart.com/client
  </wsa:To>
  <wsa:From>
    <wsa:Address>
      http://actioncon.com/service
    </wsa:Address>
  </wsa:From>
  <wsa:ReplyTo>
    <wsa:Address>
      http://actioncon.com/service/reply
    </wsa:Address>
  </wsa:ReplyTo>
</soap:Header>
```

Example 18.10
The **wsa:ReplyTo** header element indicating that the recipient of this message should, in fact, respond to a different address than from where this message originated.

As with the `wsa:From` element, the `wsa:ReplyTo` element must also contain an EPR. However, it does not need to be the same EPR as assigned to `wsa:From`. This allows you to create a variety of complex message paths. For example, when using EPRs for service instance routing, you could have one service instance send a consumer a SOAP message instructing it to respond to an instance of a different service altogether.

When not provided, the `wsa:ReplyTo` value defaults to an EPR with the anonymous address value explained earlier in the *Anonymous Address* section.

The `wsa:FaultTo` Element

You can use the `wsa:FaultTo` element to tell the message recipient where to send fault messages that communicate errors that may occur as a result of processing the message.

Here's an example:

```
<soap:Header>
  ...
  <wsa:FaultTo>
    <wsa:Address>
       http://actioncon.com/service/fault
    </wsa:Address>
  </wsa:FaultTo>
</soap:Header>
```

Example 18.11
The `wsa:FaultTo` element being assigned an EPR comprised of just a `wsa:Address` element value.

This optional element is also assigned an EPR as its value. When not provided, it defaults to the value of the `wsa:ReplyTo` element.

The `wsa:Action` Element

In Chapters 8 and 15 we discussed how you can communicate the Action value of a SOAP message via the use of the WSDL language's SOAP binding extensibility elements that set the HTTP Action header value. The `wsa:Action` element provides an alternative means of expressing the Action value via a standardized SOAP header.

This element is always required and must contain an IRI value which indicates the overall intent of the message, as shown here:

```
<soap:Header>
  ...
  <wsa:Action>
    http://actioncon.com/service/poprocess
  </wsa:Action>
</soap:Header>
```

Example 18.12
The required `wsa:Action` element containing a URI that indicates a hint as to the purpose or intent of the message.

Note the following regarding this MAP element:

- There are various requirements and preferences as to how the `wsa:Action` element relates to other Action headers and settings.

- Custom `wsa:Action` values also can be defined right within a WSDL definition.

See the *WS-Addressing and Action Values* section in Chapter 19 for details regarding both of these points.

The `wsa:MessageId` Element

This element essentially associates an identifier with the message that can be used for various purposes, including tracking and correlation with other messages.

```
<soap:Header>
  ...
  <wsa:MessageId>
    urn:uuid:246d44f9-5a2f-11d7-944a-006097b0abf
  </wsa:MessageId>
</soap:Header>
```

Example 18.13
The `wsa:MessageId` element containing a unique ID value.

The `wsa:RelatesTo` Element and the `RelationshipType` Attribute

Whereas the `wsa:MessageId` element can be used to identify a message, the `wsa:RelatesTo` element is used to indicate *how* a message relates to another message.

This optional element is populated with two IRIs:

- The value assigned to the element itself identifies the `wsa:MessageId` value of the message that this relationship refers to.

- The `RelationshipType` attribute of the `wsa:RelatesTo` element is then assigned a value that indicates the nature of the relationship.

Here's an example:

```
<soap:Header>
  ...
  <wsa:RelatesTo RelationshipType=
    "http://www.w3.org/2005/08/addressing/reply">
    urn:uuid:a46d54f9-5d2f-21d7-944a-106097bf065
  </wsa:RelatesTo>
</soap:Header>
```

Example 18.14

The `wsa:RelatesTo` element containing the identifier of a separate message that this message relates to.

You can set the value of the `RelationshipType` attribute to a custom URI to express different kinds of relationships. In the preceding example, the attribute is assigned the following value pre-defined by the WS-Addressing standard:

```
http://www.w3.org/2005/08/addressing/reply
```

This value is used to indicate that the relationship between the two messages is based on a standard Request-Response MEP exchange. When no value is provided for the `wsa:RelatesTo` element, it will default to the "reply" URI.

NOTE

The `wsa:To`, `wsa:From`, `wsa:ReplyTo`, `wsa:MessageID`, and `wsa:RelatesTo` elements are comparable to the SMTP To, From, Reply-To, Message-ID, and In-Reply-To values, respectively.

SUMMARY OF KEY POINTS

- The `wsa:Action` MAP element is always required with any WS-Addressing-enabled message. If `wsa:To` is not specified, it defaults to a value of "anon."

- The `wsa:From`, `wsa:ReplyTo`, and `wsa:FaultTo` MAP elements are based on the XML Schema `wsa:EndpointReferenceType` complex type, which means that they can be assigned entire EPRs.

- Many MAP elements have default URIs that are automatically assigned when values for the elements are not explicitly defined.

CASE STUDY EXAMPLE
A Complete Message with MAP Headers

Steve manages to assemble the header section of his SOAP message so that it now includes a set of MAP header elements.

```
<soap:Envelope
  xmlns:soap="http:www.w3.org/2003/05/soap-envelope"
  xmlns:wsa="http://www.w3.org/2005/08/addressing">
  <soap:Header>
    <wsa:To>
      http://megaeuromart.com/client
    </wsa:To>
    <wsa:ReplyTo>
      <wsa:Address>
        http://actioncon.com/service/reply
      </wsa:Address>
    </wsa:ReplyTo>
    <wsa:FaultTo>
      <wsa:Address>
        http://actioncon.com/service/fault
      </wsa:Address>
    </wsa:FaultTo>
    <wsa:Action>
      http://actioncon.com/service/poprocess
    </wsa:Action>
    <wsa:MessageId>
      urn:uuid:246d44f9-5a2f-11d7-944a-006097b0abf
    </wsa:MessageId>
```

```
  </soap:Header>
  <soap:Body>
    ...
  </soap:Body>
</soap:Envelope>
```

Example 18.15

A message from the Purchase Order endpoint containing an EPR for use by the consumer program.

NOTE
The `wsa:ReplyTo` and `wsa:FaultTo` elements in this sample message represent EPRs that are only comprised of `wsa:Address` elements. We will be exploring MAP headers that are assigned more complex EPRs (with reference parameters) in the following chapter.

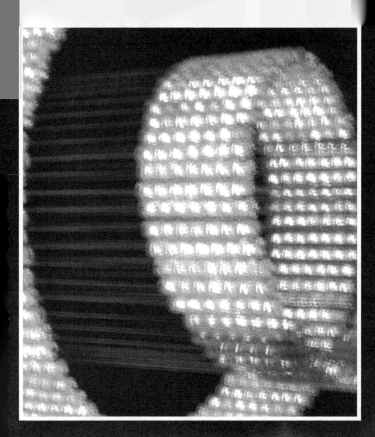

Chapter 19

Advanced Message Design Part II: WS-Addressing Rules and Design Techniques

The following explores a range of supplementary and advanced topics associated with the EPR and MAP vocabularies established in Chapter 18.

19.1 WS-Addressing Messaging Rules

The WS-Addressing standard requires that messages be designed differently depending on how they relate to a given message exchange pattern. The following sections explore these requirements and conclude with a summary table.

SOAP Header Structure

As you might recall from the *EPR Vocabulary* section, the `wsa:ReferenceParameters` element is an optional child element of the `wsa:EndpointReference` construct. We just covered three MAP elements (`wsa:From`, `wsa:ReplyTo`, `wsa:FaultTo`) that are based on the same XML Schema type as `wsa:EndpointReference`, and can therefore be assigned an entire EPR, including a `wsa:ReferenceParameters` construct populated with custom parameter elements.

We haven't showed this in the MAP examples so far because there are certain rules as to how child elements of `wsa:ReferenceParameters` are organized into SOAP header blocks.

Let's revisit the `wsa:ReferenceParameters` values we established back in Chapter 18:

```
<wsa:ReferenceParameters>
  <act:Instance>
    1
  </act:Instance>
  <act:ClientID>
    id-123-456-abc:01:23
  </act:ClientID>
</wsa:ReferenceParameters>
```

Example 19.1
The `wsa:ReferenceParameters` construct, as defined as part of an EPR.

The following two sections describe how the `act:Instance` and `act:ClientID` elements can be represented differently within SOAP headers.

Reference Parameters in a Message Sent from an Endpoint

When the Web service responsible for generating the EPR sends a message with these parameters, this entire construct will be assigned as a nested child element of any one of the three MAP elements (`wsa:From`, `wsa:ReplyTo`, `wsa:FaultTo`) that are of type `wsa:EndpointReferenceType` (as explained in the *EPRs and MAPs* section in Chapter 18).

In the following example, the `wsa:ReferenceParameters` construct is part of the `wsa:ReplyTo` element:

```
<soap:Header>
  <wsa:To>
    http://megaeuromart.com/client
  </wsa:To>
  <wsa:From>
    <wsa:Address>
      http://actioncon.com/service
    </wsa:Address>
  </wsa:From>
  <wsa:ReplyTo>
    <wsa:Address>
      http://actioncon.com/service/reply
    </wsa:Address>
    <wsa:ReferenceParameters>
      <act:Instance>
        1
      </act:Instance>
      <act:ClientID>
        id-123-456-abc:01:23
      </act:ClientID>
    </wsa:ReferenceParameters>
  </wsa:ReplyTo>
</soap:Header>
```

Example 19.2

The ERP containing the `wsa:ReferenceParameters` construct is assigned to a `wsa:ReplyTo` element.

For this example, let's assume the endpoint is sending the consumer a message with its own EPR details in the `wsa:ReplyTo` element to indicate that the consumer should use this specific EPR (including the specific reference parameters) when responding to this message. We don't know if the EPR represents the original sender of the message; all we know is that the message recipient should send a reply there.

This may seem like a relatively straightforward representation of the `wsa:Reference Parameters` construct values from the preceding example. However, things change in the structure of the message that the consumer must respond with, as explained next.

Reference Parameters in a Message Sent to an Endpoint

Back in the *MAP Vocabulary* section of Chapter 18 we explained that, unlike the `wsa:From`, `wsa:ReplyTo`, and `wsa:FaultTo` elements, the `wsa:To` element is not based on the `wsa:EndpointReferenceType` complex type. Instead of being able to contain an EPR, it can only be assigned a URI.

When a consumer program needs to send a message containing reference parameters to a Web service endpoint, it must specify the destination in the `wsa:To` element. Because the EPR itself cannot be assigned to this element, specific representation rules are used.

Essentially, for a program to send a message that contains reference parameters, the `wsa:ReferenceParameters` construct must be split apart and restructured according to the following rules:

1. The `wsa:ReferenceParameters` element is removed and not included in the SOAP message.

2. The value of the EPR `wsa:Address` element is assigned to the MAP `wsa:To` header element.

3. Each custom child element of the `wsa:ReferenceParameters` element establishes its own SOAP header block.

Therefore, the `soap:Header` construct of a message sent in response to the SOAP headers received in the previous example would look like this:

```
<soap:Header>
  <wsa:To>
    http://actioncon.com/service/reply
  </wsa:To>
  <wsa:From>
    http://megaeuromart.com/client
```

```
  </wsa:From>
  <act:Instance wsa:isReferenceParameter="1">
    1
  </act:Instance>
  <act:ClientID wsa:isReferenceParameter="1">
    id-123-456-abc:01:23
  </act:ClientID>
</soap:Header>
```

Example 19.3

The complexion of the response SOAP message changes significantly, as the `wsa:ReferenceParameters` element is stripped away and elements representing custom parameters become individual, peer-level SOAP header blocks. The bolded text highlights the address that was originally in the EPR's `wsa:Address` element and is now assigned to the `wsa:To` element.

You might have noticed the `wsa:isReferenceParameter` attribute pop up in this example. Because the new header blocks are no longer wrapped in a WS-Addressing defined construct, the recipient of the message may have no way of knowing that these headers pertain to endpoint reference values (because they essentially appear as custom headers).

It is for this reason that the `wsa:isReferenceParameter` attribute was added. Recipient processors can look for this attribute to identify and then process these headers as part of the overall WS-Addressing MAP values.

> **NOTE**
>
> Because the sender of a SOAP message is responsible for including header blocks and is expected to understand the implications of these inclusions, it must also determine the values of the `mustUnderstand`, `actor/role`, `relay`, and `reinsert` attributes for those headers. Instead of being able to wrap all child values of a `wsa:EndpointReference` construct into one header block to which these attributes apply collectively, they now must be set for each header individually.

Sending a Reply to a Message from an Endpoint

After a Web service generates an EPR and then sends a message containing the MAP header values, the consumer receiving that message may be expected to send its own WS-Addressing-enabled message. It is therefore important to understand how values from the service's message make their way into the message that the consumer sends.

Of primary importance is how the consumer's reply message will have its wsa:To element populated because that will determine where the message will actually be sent to. Figure 19.1 illustrates the decision process that WS-Addressing processors go through to determine this value.

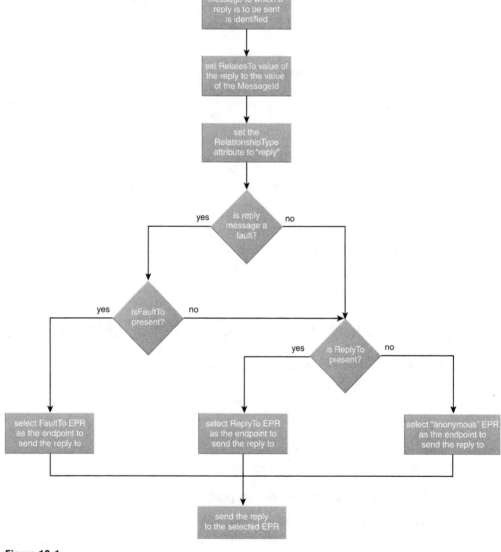

Figure 19.1

The decision process involved in determining the wsa:To value of a consumer's reply message.

Additionally, as explained earlier in this chapter, the value of the `wsa:RelatesTo` element in the consumer's message will be set to the value of the service message's `wsa:MessageId` element. If a message to which a WS-Addressing-enabled reply needs to be sent does not contain the `wsa:MessageId` property, an error is raised and a fault must be generated.

> **NOTE**
>
> You may have asked yourself why there is no mention of the `wsa:ReferenceParameters` element in this section, since it also imposes structural changes when sending a message to an endpoint. The rules that pertain to how reference parameters are represented are applied *regardless* of whether the message being sent to the endpoint is or is not a reply.

MEP Requirements for MAP Elements

As explained in the *MAP Vocabulary* section in Chapter 18, whether some of the MAP elements are required or optional within a given SOAP message depends on the message exchange pattern that they are involved with.

The following reference table provides an overview of these inclusion requirements along with other usage requirements that also vary based on the MEP.

MAP	Input Message in a One-Way/ In-Only MEP	Input Message in a Request-Response/ In-Out MEP	Output Message in a Request-Response/ In-Out MEP
`wsa:To`	not required (value set to a default if element is not provided)	required	required
`wsa:From`	not required	not required	not required
`wsa:ReplyTo`	not required	not required (if not specified, the value is the anonymous EPR)	not required

MAP	Input Message in a One-Way/ In-Only MEP	Input Message in a Request-Response/ In-Out MEP	Output Message in a Request-Response/ In-Out MEP
`wsa:FaultTo`	not required	not required (if not specified, the value is the same as `wsa:ReplyTo`)	not required
`wsa:Action`	required	required	required
`wsa:MessageId`	not required	required (used in the `wsa:RelatesTo` header of the response message)	not required
`wsa:RelatesTo`	not required	not required	required (the `RelationshipType` attribute is set to "http://www.w3.org/ 2005/08/addressing/ reply" and uses the `wsa:MessageId` value of the request (or "in") message

Table 19.1

Summary and comparison of how involvement in different MEPs introduces requirements upon some MAP elements.

CASE STUDY EXAMPLE

Comparison of Different WS-Addressing Messages

As part of his mandate to adopt WS-Addressing, Steve needs to learn about the different rules that apply to the messages that are sent to and from his Purchase Order Web service. This will allow him to fine-tune his message designs and also any potential issues that may arise with some of the message paths that will need to be accommodated between his service and external consumers.

He performs a test by sending a message to the Purchase Order service using a consumer program that pretends to be acting on behalf of ActionCon's client, MegaEuroMart. He then let's the Purchase Order service (acting as the endpoint) issue a response containing an EPR.

Here are the results:

```
<soap:Envelope
  xmlns:soap="http:www.w3.org/2003/05/soap-envelope"
  xmlns:wsa="http://www.w3.org/2005/08/addressing">
  <soap:Header>
    <wsa:To>
      http://megaeuromart.com/client
    </wsa:To>
    <wsa:ReplyTo>
      <wsa:Address>
        http://actioncon.com/service/reply
      </wsa:Address>
      <wsa:ReferenceParameters>
        <act:Instance>
          1
        </act:Instance>
        <act:ClientID>
          id-123-456-abc:01:23
        </act:ClientID>
      </wsa:ReferenceParameters>
    </wsa:ReplyTo>
    <wsa:FaultTo>
      <wsa:Address>
        http://actioncon.com/service/fault
      </wsa:Address>
      <wsa:ReferenceParameters>
        <act:ClientID>
          id-123-456-abc:01:23
        </act:ClientID>
      </wsa:ReferenceParameters>
    </wsa:FaultTo>
    <wsa:Action>
      http://actioncon.com/service/poresponse
    </wsa:Action>
    <wsa:MessageId>
      urn:uuid:246d44f9-5a2f-11d7-944a-006097b0abf
    </wsa:MessageId>
  </soap:Header>
  <soap:Body>
    ...
  </soap:Body>
</soap:Envelope>
```

Example 19.4

A message from the Purchase Order endpoint containing an EPR for use by the consumer program.

Steve designed his dummy consumer program to issue a reply message as he would expect that the MegaEuroMart consumer would.

Here's what the reply message looks like:

```
<soap:Envelope
  xmlns:soap="http:www.w3.org/2003/05/soap-envelope"
  xmlns:wsa="http://www.w3.org/2005/08/addressing">
  <soap:Header>
    <wsa:To>
      http://actioncon.com/service/reply
    </wsa:To>
    <wsa:Action>
      http://actioncon.com/service/posubmit
    </wsa:Action>
    <wsa:RelatesTo>
      urn:uuid:246d44f9-5a2f-11d7-944a-006097b0abf
    </wsa:RelatesTo>
    <act:Instance wsa:isReferenceParameter="1">
      1
    </act:Instance>
    <act:ClientID wsa:isReferenceParameter="1">
      id-123-456-abc:01:23
    </act:ClientID>
  </soap:Header>
  <soap:Body>
    . . .
  </soap:Body>
</soap:Envelope>
```

Example 19.5

A message that replies to the previous message that contained the EPR.

Finally, Steve tests out an error condition by having the consumer program send a fault response message, simulating a situation whereby the MegaEuroMart consumer program encounters an error when trying to process and reply to the message sent by the service:

```
<soap:Envelope
  xmlns:soap="http:www.w3.org/2003/05/soap-envelope"
  xmlns:wsa="http://www.w3.org/2005/08/addressing">
  <soap:Header>
    <wsa:To>
      http://megaeuromart.com/service/fault
    </wsa:To>
```

```
    <wsa:Action>
      http://actioncon.com/service/posubmitfault
    </wsa:Action>
    <wsa:RelatesTo>
      urn:uuid:246d44f9-5a2f-11d7-944a-006097b0abf
    </wsa:RelatesTo>
    <act:ClientID wsa:isReferenceParameter="1">
      id-123-456-abc:01:23
    </act:ClientID>
  </soap:Header>
  <soap:Body>
    ...
  </soap:Body>
</soap:Envelope>
```

Example 19.6

A sample fault message sent as a reply by the consumer instead of the message in the previous example.

Steve studies these three messages to pinpoint how key values were copied, retained, and represented:

- The value of the `wsa:To` message in Message 2 is set to the value from the `wsa:Address` child element of the `wsa:ReplyTo` construct from Message 1. (See red text in Examples 19.5 and 19.4.)

- The value of the `wsa:RelatesTo` element in Message 2 is set to the value of the `wsa:MessageId` element from Message 1. (See bolded text in Examples 19.5 and 19.4.)

- The value of the `wsa:To` message in Message 3 is set to the value from the `wsa:Address` child element of the `wsa:FaultTo` construct from Message 1. (See red text in Examples 19.6 and 19.4.)

- The value of the `wsa:RelatesTo` element in Message 3 is set to the value of the `wsa:MessageId` element from Message 1. (See bolded text in Examples 19.6 and 19.4.)

- The two custom client elements of the `wsa:ReferenceParameters` construct from the `wsa:ReplyTo` element in Message 1 established individual SOAP header blocks in Message 2. (See italicized code in Examples 19.4 and 19.5.)

- The `wsa:FaultTo` header element in Message 1 had a `wsa:Reference Parameters` construct with only one custom client element, which was then its own SOAP header in Message 3. (See italicized code in Examples 19.4 and 19.6.)

> **NOTE**
>
> In the previous two examples the `wsa:RelatesTo` element did not provide a `RelationshipType` element, which set the relation type to "http://www.w3.org/2005/08/addressing/reply" by default.

SUMMARY OF KEY POINTS

- When sending a message with EPR reference parameters to an endpoint, the `wsa:ReferenceParameters` construct is subject to special structural rules.

- When replying to a message from an endpoint, additional rules are used to determine the value of MAP header elements, namely the `wsa:To` element.

- Certain MAP header elements may or may not be required, depending on how a message participates in an MEP.

19.2 EPRs and WSDL Binding

Both the WSDL and WS-Addressing languages have the ability to specify endpoint details and message content. The WS-Addressing standard provides a series of binding-related features that allow you to connect these two languages together.

Specifically, the WS-Addressing WSDL binding defines:

- rules for embedding references to parts of the WSDL definition within an EPR

- rules for embedding EPRs within a WSDL definition

The following two sections explore these rules.

Embedding WSDL References Within an EPR

As explained earlier in Chapter 18, an EPR can contain an optional `wsa:Metadata` element. It is possible to use this element in order to embed the following WSDL-related information within the EPR:

- WSDL 1.1 `portType` or WSDL 2.0 `interface` element name

- WSDL 1.1 or WSDL 2.0 `service` element name

- WSDL 1.1 `port` or WSDL 2.0 `endpoint` element name

WS-Addressing provides the following two child elements for the `wsa:Metadata` construct that are used to contain these WSDL element name values:

- `wsam:InterfaceName` – Used to assign the name of either the WSDL 1.1 `portType` element or the WSDL 2.0 `interface` element.

- `wsam:ServiceName` – This element is specifically to contain the name of the WSDL 1.1 or WSDL 2.0 `service` element. The `wsam:ServiceName` element further provides an `EndpointName` attribute that can be optionally added to indicate the WSDL 1.1 `port` or WSDL 2.0 `endpoint` element associated with the `service` element.

Here's an example:

```
<wsa:EndpointReference ...>
  <wsa:Address>
    http://actioncon.com/service
  </wsa:Address>
  <wsa:Metadata>
    <wsam:InterfaceName>
      act:ptPurchaseOrder
    </wsam:InterfaceName>
    <wsam:ServiceName>
      act:svPurchaseOrder
    </wsam:ServiceName>
  </wsa:Metadata>
</wsa:EndpointReference>
```

Example 19.7

This EPR contains a `wsa:Metadata` construct that has references to the `portType` and `service` elements from the Purchase Order WSDL definition described in Chapter 8.

Note how in the preceding example the `wsam:ServiceName` element does not have an `EndpointName` attribute. Let's now take another look at what the source `act:svPurchaseOrder` construct in the WSDL definition at the end of Chapter 8 contains:

```
<service name="svPurchaseOrder">
  <port name="purchaseOrder-http-soap11"
    binding="tns:bdPO-SOAP11HTTP">
    <soap11:address location=
      "http://actioncon.com/services/soap11/purchaseOrder"/>
  </port>
  <port name="purchaseOrder-http-soap12"
    binding="tns:bdPO-SOAP12HTTP">
    <soap12:address location=
      "http://actioncon.com/services/soap12/purchaseOrder"/>
  </port>
</service>
```

Example 19.8

The entire service contract from the concrete WSDL description that was built in Chapter 8.

The text highlighted in red reveals that there are actually two `port` elements, each providing a means of accessing the Web service via a different version of SOAP. This means that both of these `port` elements are provided as access points for the endpoint represented by this EPR.

However, if we want to limit this EPR so that recipients of the SOAP message containing the WS-Addressing EPR values would only be limited to accessing the Web service via version 1.1 of SOAP, we could add the `EndpointName` attribute as follows:

```
<wsa:EndpointReference ...>
  ...
  <wsa:Metadata>
    <wsam:InterfaceName>
      act:ptPurchaseOrder
    </wsam:InterfaceName>
    <wsam:ServiceName
      EndpointName="act:purchaseOrder-http-soap11">
      act:svPurchaseOrder
    </wsam:ServiceName>
  </wsa:Metadata>
</wsa:EndpointReference>
```

Example 19.9

The `EndpointName` attribute is added to limit access to the Web service endpoint to a specific port.

Note that you can also add the `wsdli:wsdlLocation` attribute to the `wsa:Metadata` element to provide a more explicit pointer to the WSDL document that contains the definitions of `act:ptPurchaseOrder` and `act:svPurchaseOrder`, as shown here:

```
<wsa:EndpointReference ...>
  <wsa:Metadata
    xmlns:wsdli="http://www.w3.org/ns/wsdl-instance"
    wsdli:wsdlLocation="http://actioncon.com/contract/po">
    ...
  </wsa:Metadata>
</wsa:EndpointReference>
```

Example 19.10

The `wsdli:wsdlLocation` attribute is added to the `wsa:Metadata` element.

The `wsdli:wsdlLocation` attribute was explained in the *Messages that Point to Service Instances* section in Chapter 15.

> **NOTE**
>
> One interesting feature that originally existed in the WS-Addressing specification was the ability to embed an entire WSDL definition into the `wsa:Metadata` construct as follows:
>
> ```
> <wsa:EndpointReference ...>
>     <wsa:Metadata>
>         <wsdl:definitions ...>
>             ...
>         </wsdl:definitions>
>     </wsa:Metadata>
> </wsa:EndpointReference>
> ```
>
> This feature was removed from the final version of the standard due to lack of industry support.

Embedding EPRs in a WSDL Document

So far we've been focusing on how to embed information about a WSDL definition into a WS-Addressing-enabled SOAP message. It is also possible to do the opposite by embedding EPR values directly into the WSDL definition.

As shown in the following example, the `wsa:EndpointReference` construct is added as a child extensibility element of the WSDL 1.1 `port` element (or, alternatively, the WSDL

2.0 `endpoint` element), and the values of the EPR `wsa:Address` and `wsa:Reference Parameters` elements are already pre-set.

```
<definitions ...>
  ...
  <service name="svPurchaseOrder">
    <port name="purchaseOrder-http-soap11"
      binding="tns:bdPO-SOAP11HTTP">
      <soap11:address location=
        "http://actioncon.com/services/soap11/purchaseOrder"/>
      <wsa:EndpointReference xmlns:act="...">
        <wsa:Address>
          http://actioncon.com/services/soap11/purchaseOrder
        </wsa:Address>
        <wsa:ReferenceParameters>
          <act:Instance>
            1
          </act:Instance>
        </wsa:ReferenceParameters>
      </wsa:EndpointReference>
    </port>
  </service>
</definitions>
```

Example 19.11

An entire `wsa:EndpointReference` construct, embedded within a WSDL `service` construct, as an extensibility element for the `port` element.

Embedding EPR values into the WSDL definition can be an effective means of predefining reference parameters that must be sent with any message targeting the address represented by the WSDL `port` (or `endpoint`) element.

In the preceding example, every message sent to the address specified by the `port` element must contain the following SOAP header block:

```
<act:Instance>1</act:Instance>
```

NOTE

When following this approach, the value of the `wsa:Address` element and the `soap:address` element's `location` attribute must be the same.

CASE STUDY EXAMPLE
Designing a Self-Descriptive Message

While Steve is working on incorporating support for WS-Addressing into his message designs, he is contacted by Filip who has a request. With the tracing and logging features that have been recently added (as per the new policy assertions explained in Chapters 16 and 17), the administrators would really like for the messages to be more self-descriptive. This would help a great deal with troubleshooting and also the archival of logged data.

Steve begins looking at the acknowledgement message that is sent by the Purchase Order service after its opSubmitOrder operation receives a valid purchase order document. He decides that he wants this message to be explicitly associated with its WSDL definition so that administrators can easily locate and use the WSDL definition (and any associated policy expressions) for troubleshooting purposes.

After exploring his options, Steve figures that the simplest way to achieve this is to utilize the wsa:From header block, which can be used to identify the source WSDL definition in which the message was first defined (as an output message of the opSubmitOrder operation). Steve then further decides to include the WSDL port type, service, and port names using the wsam:InterfaceName and wsam:ServiceName elements. He adds the wsa:MessageId and wsa:RelatesTo headers to uniquely identify the message and correlate it to other messages.

With these additions, the acknowledgement message is expanded as follows:

```
<soap:Envelope
  xmlns:soap="http:www.w3.org/2003/05/soap-envelope"
  xmlns:wsa="http://www.w3.org/2005/08/addressing"
  xmlns:wsam="http://www.w3.org/2007/05/addressing/metadata">
  <soap:Header>
    <wsa:From soap:mustUnderstand="1">
      <wsa:Address>
        http://actioncon.com/service
      </wsa:Address>
      <wsa:Metadata xmlns:po=
        "http://actioncon.com/contract/po"
        xmlns:wsdli="http://www.w3.org/ns/wsdl-instance"
        wsdli:location=
          "http://actioncon.com/contract/po">
      <wsam:InterfaceName>
        po:ptPurchaseOrder
      </wsam:InterfaceName>
```

```
            <wsam:ServiceName
              EndpointName="purchaseOrder-http-soap12">
              po:svPurchaseOrder
            </wsam:ServiceName>
        </wsa:Metadata>
      </wsa:From>
      <wsa:To soap:mustUnderstand="1">
        http://megaeuromart.com/partner/ActionCon/reply
      </wsa:To>
      <wsa:Action soap:mustUnderstand="1">
        http://actioncon.com/action/poresponse
      </wsa:Action>
      <wsa:RelatesTo soap:mustUnderstand="1">
        urn:uuid:a46d54f9-5d2f-21d7-944a-106097bf065
      </wsa:RelatesTo>
      <wsa:MessageId>
        urn:uuid:246d44f9-5a2f-11d7-944a-006097b0abf
      </wsa:MessageId>
    </soap:Header>
    <soap:Body>
      <acknowledgement
        xmlns="http://actioncon.com/schema/po"
        version="1.0">
        ...
      </acknowledgement>
    </soap:Body>
  </soap:Envelope>
```

Example 19.12

An acknowledgement message sent by the Purchase Order Web service with additional `wsa:Metadata` elements that make the message more descriptive.

SUMMARY OF KEY POINTS

- Using the `wsam:InterfaceName` and `wsam:ServiceName` elements within the `wsa:Metadata` construct, you can embed WSDL definition references within an EPR.

- You can also embed the `wsa:EndpointReference` construct within a WSDL definition, thereby making it an actual extension of the Web service contract.

19.3 WS-Addressing and Action Values

Probably the most common point of confusion when working with WS-Addressing is the `wsa:Action` element. As we've already established in previous chapters that covered the WSDL and SOAP languages, there are existing ways of expressing the Action value for a SOAP message in order to provide a hint or indication as to the message's overall purpose.

Along comes the WS-Addressing with yet another way of representing the Action value and not only do we have to figure out which of the available representation options is the most suitable, we also have to understand how they can or should co-exist to avoid conflicts.

The following sections explore the use of the `wsa:Action` element and provide a series of comparisons and guidelines.

> **NOTE**
>
> In the upcoming sections, be sure to notice the difference between the `wsa:Action` element and the `wsam:Action` attribute.

Why is `wsa:Action` Always Required?

As we mentioned earlier, the `wsa:Action` element must always be present in any WS-Addressing-enabled SOAP message. But why is the `wsa:Action` element mandatory, especially when we already have HTTP Action values that can be pre-set within the WSDL definition? As we explained in Chapter 15, the Action value is used to provide a hint as to the intent of a given SOAP message. This hint is considered an important piece of supplementary information used by runtime processors and also custom solution logic to decide how a message may need to be dispatched, routed, or otherwise processed.

The technical committee responsible for producing the WS-Addressing standard introduced this requirement to help promote industry-wide interoperability across different vendor platforms, by moving the representation of Action values toward a transport-neutral representation format, namely the SOAP header. By forcing its usage in all WS-Addressing-enabled messages, the `wsa:Action` element establishes itself as an industry standard representation for the Action hint, without ties to or dependencies on HTTP.

Various WS-* specifications (such as WS-ReliableMessaging) already rely on the WS-Addressing `wsa:Action` element and further provide pre-defined and standardized Action values used for specific message types.

The `wsa:Action` Element and WSDL

As already discussed in the *Message Dispatch Challenges* section in Chapter 15, there are several primary ways to use WSDL to specify the value of the `wsa:Action` element.

The `wsam:Action` attribute can be specified on any input, output, or fault message in the WSDL definition. This attribute contains an absolute IRI, which eventually sets the value for the `wsa:Action` MAP element for that message.

Alternatively, the `soapAction` attribute used in WSDL with the SOAP binding extensibility elements specifies the value of the `SOAPAction` HTTP header and has pretty much the same structure as the `wsa:Action` MAP element (except that `wsa:Action` is an IRI and `SOAPAction` is not).

As previously explained, if the value of the `soapAction` attribute is not empty, then it must match the value of the `wsam:Action` attribute, if present. If the `wsam:Action` attribute is not specified but the `soapAction` attribute is specified, then the value of the `wsa:Action` MAP element is determined by the value of the `soapAction` attribute.

If neither the `wsam:Action` or the `soapAction` attribute are specified, then the WSDL default rules for the `wsa:Action` element kick in. When invoked, these rules essentially generate a unique value for the `wsa:Action` element by combining the target namespace, port type (or interface) name, operation name, message name.

In the following message, for example, the `wsam:Action` attribute is defined for the input message, but not for the output message:

```
<definitions targetNamespace=
  "http://actioncon.com/contract/po" ...>
  ...
  <portType name="ptPurchaseOrder">
    <operation name="opSubmitOrder">
      <input message="tns:msgSubmitOrderRequest"
        wsam:Action="http://actioncon.com/action"/>
      <output message="tns:msgSubmitOrderResponse"/>
    </operation>
  </porType>
  ...
</definitions>
```

Example 19.13

A WSDL operation contains an `input` element with the `wsam:Action` extensibility attribute. However this attribute is not added to the `output` element.

As a result, when the input message is generated, the `wsa:Action` MAP header will contain the pre-defined value, as follows:

```
<soap:Header>
  . . .
  <wsa:Action>
    http://actioncon.com/action
  </wsa:Action>
</soap:Header>
```

Example 19.14
The populated `wsa:Action` header.

…whereas, when the output message is created, the `wsa:Action` MAP element will contain the following auto-generated value:

```
<soap:Header>
  . . .
  <wsa:Action>
    http://actioncon.com/contract/po/
    ptPurchaseOrder/msgSubmitOrderResponse
  </wsa:Action>
</soap:Header>
```

Example 19.15
The `wsa:Action` element value, auto-generated based on default rules that concatenate the WSDL target namespace value, port type name, and message name.

The `wsa:Action` Element and HTTP

As explained in Chapter 15, the action value of a SOAP message can be expressed via the `SOAPAction` HTTP header when using SOAP 1.1 or the `action` parameter value of the `Content-Type` HTTP header, when working with SOAP 1.2. The WS-Addressing `wsa:Action` MAP element has the same purpose as both of these HTTP headers, which is to simply express the action value of a message.

The WS-I Basic Profile 1.2 deprecates any reliance on the `SOAPAction` HTTP header value when using SOAP 1.1 and WS-I Basic Profile 2.0 deprecates any reliance on the `action` parameter value of the media-type when using SOAP 1.2. What this means is that the WS-I is recommending that you avoid relying on either HTTP header to set the action value of a SOAP message. Instead, it is considered preferable to use the WS-Addressing `wsa:Action` SOAP header block whenever possible.

However, this does not avoid the fact that the HTTP headers will still likely be used. After all, the `wsa:Action` header is part of the SOAP envelope which, in turn, is wrapped in the HTTP message. Therefore, we need to understand how the `wsa:Action` header can co-exist with the HTTP headers.

Here are the basic rules:

- With SOAP 1.1, when using the `wsa:Action` element together with the `SOAPAction` HTTP header, it is required that either they both have the same value or the value of the `SOAPAction` HTTP header be set to an empty quoted string ("").

- Similarly with SOAP 1.2, the `action` parameter value of the `Content-Type` HTTP header and the `wsa:Action` value must be the same. The only exception is when the `action` parameter is absent.

Note that when a SOAP message is encrypted, its HTTP headers may still be exposed. This means that while the `wsa:Action` header will be encrypted, the `SOAPAction` HTTP header may not be. Therefore, as a security precaution when using an encrypted `wsa:Action` element, it is considered a good practice to always set the `SOAPAction` HTTP header value to an empty string and to avoid the optional `action` parameter altogether, in order to prevent accidentally revealing the action value.

A Reference Table for Action Values

Because there are several action-related attributes and elements that can be involved with WSDL, SOAP, and WS-Addressing, it can get a bit confusing at times to sort them out. Provided here is a reference table that summarizes what each attribute or element does and what restrictions are applied to it.

SUMMARY OF KEY POINTS

- The `wsa:Action` header element is always required to help support transport independence and interoperability across Web services.

- There are several rules and preferences that need to be taken into account to ensure that Action settings in the WSDL definition and, eventually, in the HTTP headers are in alignment with and do not conflict with the `wsa:Action` value of a message.

Name	What is it?	Purpose	Restrictions
SOAPAction	HTTP header (SOAP 1.1)	Conveys message intention in an HTTP header and informs non-XML processors and firewalls that the payload is a SOAP message.	Required for HTTP request message when used with SOAP 1.1. When used with WS-Addressing, it must either be empty or the same as the wsa:Action element value.
action parameter	Content-Type parameter associated with the media-type application/soap+xml (SOAP 1.2)	Conveys message intent	This parameter is optional when using SOAP 1.2. When used with WS-Addressing, it must either be the same as the wsa:Action element value or it cannot be present.
wsa:Action	WS-Addressing MAP element	Conveys the message intent in a transport- and protocol-independent manner inside the SOAP envelope.	When used with SOAP 1.1, this element must match the value of the SOAPAction HTTP header (if the SOAPAction value is not empty). When used with SOAP 1.2 and the action parameter is present, the two values must be the same.
soapAction	WSDL SOAP binding attribute	Specifies the value for the SOAPAction HTTP header.	If used together with wsam:Action, the two must have the same value.
wsam:Action	WSDL extension attribute for WS-Addressing	Specifies the value for the wsa:Action MAP element.	If used together with soapAction, the two must have the same value.

Table 19.2

A summary and comparison of various action-related attributes and elements.

19.4 WS-Addressing SOAP Faults

The WS-Addressing standard defines the following SOAP fault elements for WS-Addressing-related error conditions:

- `InvalidAddressingHeader` – Indicates that one of the MAP header elements is incorrect with respect to its syntax, cardinality, or semantics.

- `MessageAddressingHeaderRequired` – Is generated when a required MAP header element is missing.

- `DestinationUnreachable` – Is used to communicate that the Web service endpoint specified in the `wsa:To` element is not reachable.

- `ActionNotSupported` – This fault is generated when the value specified for the `wsa:Action` element is not supported.

- `EndpointUnavailable` – When a targeted endpoint is unavailable this fault is used, which means that this could indicate a temporary problem (in which case a retry interval can be specified).

The SOAP binding for WS-Addressing provides the following pre-defined value for the `wsa:Action` element, which must be used whenever one of the previously listed faults is generated:

```
http://www.w3.org/2005/08/addressing/fault
```

Additionally, the following pre-defined value is assigned to the `wsa:Action` element when WS-Addressing headers raise regular SOAP faults (such as `VersionMismatch` and `MustUnderstand`):

```
http://www.w3.org/2005/08/addressing/soap/fault
```

Note that although this value can also be used when generating custom fault messages, it is best to create your own action values for this purpose.

19.5 WS-Addressing Policy Assertions

You might recall that in the previous WS-Policy chapters (10, 16, and 17), we repeatedly used the `wsam:Addressing` policy assertion in examples. Let's briefly recap the purpose of this assertion and also introduce two related policy assertions that can optionally be used with `wsam:Addressing` as nested assertions.

The `wsam:Addressing` Policy Assertion

In order to convey that a Web service supports and may even require the use of WS-Addressing, the `wsam:Addressing` assertion can be added to a WS-Policy expression, as follows:

```
<wsp:Policy ...>
  <wsam:Addressing wsp:Optional="true">
    <wsp:Policy/>
  </wsam:Addressing>
</wsp:Policy>
```

Example 19.16
A policy that says WS-Addressing is supported but not required.

In this example, the `wsp:Optional` attribute indicates that consumers of the service may opt not to provide WS-Addressing-enabled SOAP messages. Removing this attribute would make the use of WS-Addressing headers required by all consumers.

The `wsam:AnonymousResponse` Policy Assertion

The `wsam:Addressing` assertion can be further extended with the `wsam:Anonymous` `Response` nested assertion, as follows:

```
<wsp:Policy ...>
  <wsam:Addressing>
    <wsp:Policy>
      <wsam:AnonymousResponse/>
    </wsp:Policy>
  </wsam:Addressing>
</wsp:Policy>
```

Example 19.17
A nested policy with the `wsam:AnonymousResponse` value.

This assertion requires the use of the following anonymous value for the `wsa:ReplyTo` and `wsa:FaultTo` elements of the request message that was explained in the *EPR Vocabulary* section from Chapter 18:

```
<wsa:Address>
  http://www.w3.org/2005/08/addressing/anonymous
</wsa:Address>
```

Example 19.18

The anonymous value that has a special meaning when used with SOAP over HTTP as part of the `wsa:ReplyTo` and `wsa:FaultTo` MAP elements of a request message.

The use of this policy assertion therefore requires that a synchronous exchange be followed and thereby disallows asynchronous interaction. This can be useful in situations when the service (due to security or infrastructure limitations) does not have the option of opening a separate HTTP connection for the response message.

The `wsam:NonAnonymousResponse` Policy Assertion

Alternatively, the `wsam:NonAnonymousResponse` nested assertion can be used to require that the response message *must* be sent asynchronously. This assertion therefore has the exact opposite requirement of the previously explained anonymous assertion, in that it explicitly disallows response messages from using the HTTP response channel.

Here is the corresponding example:

```
<wsp:Policy ...>
  <wsam:Addressing>
    <wsp:Policy>
      <wsam:NonAnonymousResponse/>
    </wsp:Policy>
  </wsam:Addressing>
</wsp:Policy>
```

Example 19.19

A nested policy with the `wsam:NonAnonymousResponse` value.

> **NOTE**
>
> When neither nested assertion is used, the `wsam:Addressing` assertion indicates that the response to the WS-Addressing-enabled message can be carried out synchronously or asynchronously, without any limitations. Also, when one of these nested assertions is used, the other cannot be added to the same policy alternative.

CASE STUDY EXAMPLE
Adding a WS-Addressing Policy Assertion

Back in Chapter 9, the WSDL 2.0 version of the service contract for the Purchase Order service was created to accommodate a specific subset of consumers. These consumer programs are being built by partner organizations with the specific requirement that all communication be asynchronous in nature.

Steve knows that data exchanges via this version of the WSDL definition are fully geared toward processing asynchronous MEPs, but he wants to safeguard this Web service contract from other potential consumers that may want to use it for traditional, synchronous exchanges (for which alternative contracts already exist).

He therefore decides to make asynchronous interaction mandatory by adding the nested `wsam:NonAnonymousResponse` assertion directly into the WSDL 2.0 document, as follows:

```
<description targetNamespace=
  "http://actioncon.com/contract/po"
  xmlns="http://schemas.xmlsoap.org/wsdl/"
  xmlns:tns="http://actioncon.com/contract/po"
  xmlns:po="http://actioncon.com/schema/po"
  xmlns:soapbind="http://www.w3.org/2006/01/wsdl/soap/"
  xmlns:wsam="http://www.w3.org/2007/05/addressing/metadata"
  xmlns:wsp="http://www.w3.org/ns/ws-policy"
  xmlns:wsu="http://docs.oasis-open.org/wss/2004/01/
    oasis-200401-wss-wssecurity-utility-1.0.xsd">
  <wsp:Policy wsu:Id="AsyncOnly">
    <wsam:Addressing>
      <wsp:Policy>
        <wsam:NonAnonymousResponse/>
      </wsp:Policy>
    </wsam:Addressing>
  </wsp:Policy>
  ...
  <service name="svPurchaseOrder" interface="ifPurchaseOrder">
    <endpoint name="purchaseOrder-http-soap12"
      binding="tns:bdPO-SOAP12HTTP" address=
      "http://action.com/services/soap12/purchaseOrder">
      <wsp:PolicyReference URI="#AsyncOnly"/>
    </endpoint>
  </service>
</description>
```

Example 19.20

A WS-Policy expression added to a WSDL 2.0 contract, requiring the use of asynchronous WS-Addressing communication.

SUMMARY OF KEY POINTS

- A WS-Addressing policy assertion can be used to specify whether WS-Addressing is required or supported.

- The WS-Addressing standard provides pre-defined policy assertion values that can be used to specify whether responses are sent synchronously over the same HTTP connection as the request or asynchronously over a new HTTP connection.

Part III

Service Contract Versioning

Chapter 20

Versioning Fundamentals

After a Web service contract is deployed, consumer programs will naturally begin forming dependencies on it. When we are subsequently forced to make changes to the contract, we need to figure out:

- whether the changes will negatively impact existing (and potentially future) service consumers

- how changes that will and will not impact consumers should be implemented and communicated

These issues result in the need for versioning. Anytime you introduce the concept of versioning into an SOA project, a number of questions will likely be raised, for example:

- What exactly constitutes a new version of a service contract? What's the difference between a major and minor version?

- What do the parts of a version number indicate?

- Will the new version of the contract still work with existing consumers that were designed for the old contract version?

- Will the current version of the contract work with new consumers that may have different data exchange requirements?

- What is the best way to add changes to existing contracts while minimizing the impact on consumers?

- Will we need to host old and new contracts at the same time? If yes, for how long?

The upcoming chapters address these questions and provide a set of options for solving common versioning problems. This chapter begins by covering some basic concepts, terminology, and strategies specific to service contract versioning in preparation for what's ahead.

> **NOTE**
>
> One aspect of versioning that we do not cover in this book is the introduction of new organizational roles. There are separate service, schema, and policy custodian roles that can exist, especially in larger environments. The responsibilities associated with these roles, how they can be combined or distributed across individuals, and how they relate to other governance processes will be covered in the book *SOA Governance* currently in development as part of the *Prentice Hall Service-Oriented Computing Series from Thomas Erl.*

20.1 Basic Concepts and Terminology

The Scope of a Version

As we've established many times over in this book, a Web service contract can be comprised of several individual documents and definitions that are linked and assembled together to form a complete technical interface.

For example, a given Web service contract can consist of:

- one (sometimes more) WSDL definitions
- one (usually more) XML Schema definitions
- some (sometimes no) WS-Policy definitions

Furthermore, each of these definition documents can be shared by other Web service contracts.

For example:

- a centralized XML Schema definition will commonly be used by multiple WSDL definitions
- a centralized WS-Policy definition will commonly be applied to multiple WSDL definitions
- an abstract WSDL description can be imported by multiple concrete WSDL descriptions or vice versa

So when we say that we're creating a new version of a contract, what exactly are we referring to?

Of all the different parts of a Web service contract, the part that establishes the fundamental technical interface is the abstract description of the WSDL definition. This represents the core of a Web service contract and is then further extended and detailed through schema definitions, policy definitions, and one or more concrete WSDL descriptions.

When we need to create a new version of a Web service contract, we can therefore assume that there has been a change in the abstract WSDL description or one of the contract documents that relates to the abstract WSDL description. How the different constructs of a WSDL can be versioned is covered in Chapter 21.

The Web service contract content commonly subject to change is the XML schema content that provides the types for the abstract description's message definitions. Chapter 22 explores the manner in which the underlying schema definitions for messages can be changed and evolved.

Finally, the one other contract-related technology that can still impose versioning requirements but is less likely to do so simply because it is a less common part of Web service contracts is WS-Policy. How policies in general relate to contract versioning is explained as part of the advanced topics in Chapter 23.

Fine and Coarse-Grained Constraints

Versioning changes are generally related to the increase or reduction of the quantity or granularity of constraints. Therefore, let's briefly recap the meaning of the term constraint granularity in relation to a type definition.

Note the highlighted parts of the following example:

```
<xsd:element name="LineItem" type="LineItemType"/>
<xsd:complexType name="LineItemType">
  <xsd:sequence>
    <xsd:element name="productID" type="xsd:string"/>
    <xsd:element name="productName" type="xsd:string"/>
    <xsd:any minOccurs="0" maxOccurs="unbounded"
      namespace="##any" processContents="lax"/>
  </xsd:sequence>
  <xsd:anyAttribute namespace="##any"/>
</xsd:complexType>
```

Example 20.1

A `complexType` construct containing fine and coarse-grained constraints.

As indicated by the bolded text, there are elements with specific names and data types that represent parts of the message definition with a fine level of constraint granularity. All of the message instances (the actual XML documents that will be created based on this structure) must conform to the these constraints in order to be considered valid (which is why these are considered the absolute "minimum" constraints).

The red text shows the element and attribute wildcards also contained by this complex type. These represent parts of the message definition with an extremely *coarse* level of constraint granularity in that messages do not need to comply to these parts of the message definition at all.

The use of the terms "fine-grained" and "coarse-grained" is highly subjective. What may be a fine-grained constraint in one contract may not be in another. The point is to understand how these terms can be applied when comparing parts of a message definition or when comparing different message definitions with each other.

20.2 Versioning and Compatibility

The number one concern when developing and deploying a new version of a service contract is the impact it will have on other parts of the enterprise that have formed or will form dependencies on it. This measure of impact is directly related to how compatible the new contract version is with the old version and its surroundings in general.

This section establishes the fundamental types of compatibility that relate to the content and design of new contract versions and also tie into the goals and limitations of different versioning strategies that we introduce at the end of this chapter.

Backwards Compatibility

A new version of a Web service contract that continues to support consumer programs designed to work with the old version is considered *backwards-compatible*. From a design perspective, this means that the new contract has not changed in such a way that it can impact existing consumer programs that are already using the contract.

A simple example of a backwards-compatible change is the addition of a new operation to an existing WSDL definition:

```
<definitions name="Purchase Order" targetNamespace=
  "http://actioncon.com/contract/po"
  xmlns="http://schemas.xmlsoap.org/wsdl/"
  xmlns:tns="http://actioncon.com/contract/po"
  xmlns:po="http://actioncon.com/schema/po">
  ...
  <portType name="ptPurchaseOrder">
    <operation name="opSubmitOrder">
      <input message="tns:msgSubmitOrderRequest"/>
      <output message="tns:msgSubmitOrderResponse"/>
    </operation>
    <operation name="opCheckOrderStatus">
      <input message="tns:msgCheckOrderRequest"/>
      <output message="tns:msgCheckOrderResponse"/>
    </operation>
    <operation name="opChangeOrder">
      <input message="tns:msgChangeOrderRequest"/>
      <output message="tns:msgChangeOrderResponse"/>
    </operation>
    <operation name="opCancelOrder">
      <input message="tns:msgCancelOrderRequest"/>
      <output message="tns:msgCancelOrderResponse"/>
    </operation>
    <operation name="opGetOrder">
      <input message="tns:msgGetOrderRequest"/>
      <output message="tns:msgGetOrderResponse"/>
    </operation>
  </portType>
</definitions>
```

Example 20.2

The addition of a new operation represents a common backwards-compatible change.

In this example we're borrowing the abstract description of the Purchase Order service that was initially built at the end of Chapter 7. By adding a brand new operation, we are creating a new version of the contract, but this change is backwards-compatible and will not impact any existing consumers.

An example of a change made to a schema for a message definition that is backwards compatible is the addition of an optional element:

```
<xsd:schema xmlns:xsd="http://www.w3.org/2001/XMLSchema"
  targetNamespace="http://actioncon.com/schema/po"
  xmlns="http://actioncon.com/schema/po">
  <xsd:element name="LineItem" type="LineItemType"/>
  <xsd:complexType name="LineItemType">
    <xsd:sequence>
      <xsd:element name="productID" type="xsd:string"/>
      <xsd:element name="productName" type="xsd:string"/>
      <xsd:element name="available" type="xsd:boolean"
        minOccurs="0"/>
    </xsd:sequence>
  </xsd:complexType>
</xsd:schema>
```

Example 20.3

In an XML Schema definition, the addition of an optional element is also considered backwards compatible.

Here we are using a simplified version of the XML Schema definition for the Purchase Order service. The optional `available` element is added to the `LineItemType` complex type. This has no impact on existing consumers because they are not required to provide this element in their messages. New consumers or consumer programs redesigned to work with this schema can optionally provide the `available` element.

Changing any of the existing elements in the previous example from required to optional (by adding the `minOccurs="0"` setting) would also be considered a backwards-compatible change. When we have control over how we choose to design the next version of a Web service contract, backwards compatibility is generally attainable. However, mandatory changes (such as those imposed by laws or regulatations) can often force us to break backwards compatibility.

> **NOTE**
>
> Both the Flexible and Loose versioning strategies explained at the end of this chapter support backwards compatibility.

Forwards Compatibility

When a Web service contract is designed in such a manner so that it can support a range of future consumer programs, it is considered to have an extent of *forwards compatibility*. This means that the contract can essentially accommodate how consumer programs will evolve over time.

The most common means by which forwards compatibility is attempted in message definitions is through the use of wildcards:

```
<xsd:schema xmlns:xsd="http://www.w3.org/2001/XMLSchema"
  targetNamespace="http://actioncon.com/schema/po"
  xmlns="http://actioncon.com/schema/po">
  <xsd:element name="LineItem" type="LineItemType"/>
  <xsd:complexType name="LineItemType">
    <xsd:sequence>
      <xsd:element name="productID" type="xsd:string"/>
      <xsd:element name="productName" type="xsd:string"/>
      <xsd:any namespace="##any" processContents="lax"
        minOccurs="0" maxOccurs="unbounded"/>
    </xsd:sequence>
    <xsd:anyAttribute namespace="##any"/>
  </xsd:complexType>
</xsd:schema>
```

Example 20.4

To support forwards compatibility within a message definition generally requires the use of XML Schema wildcards.

In this example, the `xsd:any` and `xsd:anyAttribute` elements are added to allow for a range of unknown elements and data to be accepted by the Web service contract. In other words, the schema is being designed in advance to accommodate unforeseen changes in the future. Chapter 22 explains in detail how wildcards can be used in support of forwards compatibility.

There are limited options in support of forwards compatibility when it comes to WSDL definitions. These are discussed at the end of Chapter 21.

It is important to understand that forwards compatibility is by no means an exact science. A service with a forwards-compatible contract will often not be able to process all message content. It's contract is simply designed to accept a broader range of data unknown at the time of its design.

NOTE

Forwards compatibility forms the basis of the Loose versioning strategy that is explained at the end of this chapter.

Compatible Changes

When we make a change to a Web service contract that does not negatively affect its existing consumers, then the change itself is considered a *compatible change*.

> **NOTE**
>
> In this book, the term "compatible change" refers to backwards compatibility by default. When used in reference to forwards compatibility it is further qualified as a *forwards-compatible change*.

A simple example of a compatible change is when we set the `minOccurs` attribute of an element from "1" to "0", effectively turning a required element into an optional one, as shown here:

```
<xsd:schema xmlns:xsd="http://www.w3.org/2001/XMLSchema"
  targetNamespace="http://actioncon.com/schema/po"
  xmlns="http://actioncon.com/schema/po">
  <xsd:element name="LineItem" type="LineItemType"/>
  <xsd:complexType name="LineItemType">
    <xsd:sequence>
      <xsd:element name="productID" type="xsd:string"/>
      <xsd:element name="productName" type="xsd:string"
        minOccurs="0"/>
      <xsd:element name="available" type="xsd:boolean"
        minOccurs="0"/>
    </xsd:sequence>
  </xsd:complexType>
</xsd:schema>
```

Example 20.5

The default value of the `minOccurs` attribute is "1". Therefore because this attribute was previously absent from the `productName` element declaration, it was considered a required element. Adding the `minOccurs="0"` setting turns it into an optional element, resulting in a compatible change.

This type of change will not impact existing consumer programs that are used to sending the element value to the Web service, nor will it affect future consumers that can be designed to optionally send that element.

Another example of a compatible change was provided earlier in Example 20.3, when we first added the optional `available` element declaration. Even though we extended the type with a whole new element, because it is optional it is considered a compatible change.

Here is a list of common compatible changes that we will be discussing in the upcoming chapters:

- adding a new WSDL operation definition and associated message definitions (Chapter 21)

- adding a new WSDL port type definition and associated operation definitions (Chapter 21)

- adding new WSDL binding and service definitions (Chapter 21)

- adding a new optional XML Schema element or attribute declaration to a message definition (Chapter 22)

- reducing the constraint granularity of an XML Schema element or attribute of a message definition type (Chapter 22)

- adding a new XML Schema wildcard to a message definition type (Chapter 22)

- adding a new optional WS-Policy assertion (Chapter 23)

- adding a new WS-Policy alternative (Chapter 23)

We will also be exploring techniques whereby changes that are not normally compatible can still be implemented as compatible changes.

NOTE

Compatible Change is also the name of a versioning design pattern that is based on the techniques described in this book for preserving backwards compatibility when modifying a service contract. See Appendix E for a description of this pattern.

Incompatible Changes

If after a change a contract is no longer compatible with consumers, then it is considered to have received an *incompatible change*. These are the types of changes that can break an existing contract and therefore impose the most challenges when it comes to versioning.

NOTE

The term "incompatible change" indicates an absence of backwards compatibility. When referring to incompatible changes that affect forwards compatibility, this term is qualified as *forwards incompatible change*.

Going back to our example, if we set an element's `minOccurs` attribute from "0" to any number above zero, then we are introducing an incompatible change:

```
<xsd:schema xmlns:xsd="http://www.w3.org/2001/XMLSchema"
  targetNamespace="http://actioncon.com/schema/po"
  xmlns="http://actioncon.com/schema/po">
  <xsd:element name="LineItem" type="LineItemType"/>
  <xsd:complexType name="LineItemType">
    <xsd:sequence>
      <xsd:element name="productID" type="xsd:string"/>
      <xsd:element name="productName" type="xsd:string"
        minOccurs="3"/>
      <xsd:element name="available" type="xsd:boolean"
        minOccurs="3"/>
    </xsd:sequence>
  </xsd:complexType>
</xsd:schema>
```

Example 20.6

Incrementing the `minOccurs` attribute value of any established element declaration is automatically an incompatible change.

What was formerly an optional element is now required. This will certainly affect existing consumers that are not designed to comply with this new constraint, because adding a new required element introduces a mandatory constraint upon the contract.

Common incompatible changes that are explained in the next set of chapters include:

- renaming an existing WSDL operation definition

- removing an existing WSDL operation definition

- changing the MEP of an existing WSDL operation definition

- adding a fault message to an existing WSDL operation definition

- adding a new required XML Schema element or attribute declaration to a message definition

- increasing the constraint granularity of an XML Schema element or attribute declaration of a message definition

- renaming an optional or required XML Schema element or attribute in a message definition

- removing an optional or required XML Schema element or attribute or wildcard from a message definition

- adding a new required WS-Policy assertion or expression

- adding a new ignorable WS-Policy expression (most of the time)

Incompatible changes cause most of the challenges with Web service contract versioning.

20.3 Version Identifiers

One of the most fundamental design patterns related to Web service contract design is the Version Identification pattern. It essentially advocates that version numbers should be clearly expressed, not just at the contract level, but right down to the versions of the schemas that underlie the message definitions.

The first step to establishing an effective versioning strategy is to decide on a common means by which versions themselves are identified and represented within Web service contracts.

Versions are almost always communicated with version numbers. The most common format is a decimal, followed by a period and then another decimal, as shown here:

```
version="2.0"
```

Sometimes, you will see additional period + decimal pairs that lead to more detailed version numbers like this:

```
version="2.0.1.1"
```

The typical meaning associated with these numbers is the measure or significance of the change. Incrementing the first decimal generally indicates a major version change (or upgrade) in the software, whereas decimals after the first period usually represent various levels of minor version changes.

From a compatibility perspective, we can associate additional meaning to these numbers. Specifically, the following convention has emerged in the industry:

- A minor version is expected to be backwards compatible with other minor versions associated with a major version. For example, version 5.2 of a program should be fully backwards compatible with versions 5.0 and 5.1.

- A major version is generally expected to break backwards compatibility with programs that belong to other major versions. This means that program version 5.0 is not expected to be backwards compatible with version 4.0.

This convention of indicating compatibility through major and minor version numbers is referred to as the *compatibility guarantee*. Another approach, known as "amount of work," uses version numbers to communicate the effort that has gone into the change. A minor version increase indicates a modest effort, and a major version increase predictably represents a lot of work.

These two conventions can be combined and often are. The result is often that version numbers continue to communicate compatibility as explained earlier, but they sometimes increment by several digits, depending on the amount of effort that went into each version.

There are various syntax options available to express version numbers. For example, you may have noticed that the declaration statement that begins an XML document can contain a number that expresses the version of the XML specification being used:

```
<?xml version="1.0"?>
```

That same `version` attribute can be used with the root `xsd:schema` element, as follows:

```
<xsd:schema version="2.0" ...>
```

You can further create a custom variation of this attribute by assigning it to any element you define (in which case you are not required to name the attribute "version").

```
<LineItem version="2.0">
```

An alternative custom approach is to embed the version number into a namespace, as shown here:

```
<LineItem xmlns="http://actioncon.com/schema/po/v2">
```

Note that it has become a common convention to use date values in namespaces when versioning XML schemas, as follows:

```
<LineItem xmlns="http://actioncon.com/schema/po/2010/09">
```

In this case, it is the date of the change that acts as the version identifier. In order to keep the expression of XML Schema definition versions in alignment with WSDL definition versions, we use version numbers instead of date values in the examples throughout the upcoming chapters. However, when working in an environment where XML Schema definitions are separately owned as part of an independent data architecture, it is not uncommon for schema versioning identifiers to be different from those used by WSDL definitions.

Regardless of which option you choose, it is important to consider the Canonical Versioning pattern that dictates that the expression of version information must be standardized across all service contracts within the boundary of a service inventory. In larger environments, this will often require a central authority that can guarantee the linearity, consistency, and description quality of version information. These types of conventions carry over into how service termination information is expressed (as further explored in Chapter 23).

> **NOTE**
>
> Of course you may also be required to work with third-party schemas and WSDL definitions that may already have implemented their own versioning conventions. In this case, the extent to which the Canonical Versioning pattern can be applied will be limited.

20.4 Versioning Strategies

There is no one versioning approach that is right for everyone. Because versioning represents a governance-related phase in the overall lifecycle of a service, it is a practice that is subject to the conventions, preferences, and requirements that are distinct to any enterprise.

Even though there is no de facto versioning technique for the WSDL, XML Schema, and WS-Policy content that comprises Web service contracts, a number of common and advocated versioning approaches have emerged, each with its own benefits and tradeoffs.

In this chapter we're going to single out the following three known strategies:

- *Strict* – Any compatible or incompatible changes result in a new version of the service contract. This approach does not support backwards or forwards compatibility.

- *Flexible* – Any incompatible change results in a new version of the service contract and the contract is designed to support backwards compatibility but not forwards compatibility.

- *Loose* – Any incompatible change results in a new version of the service contract and the contract is designed to support backwards compatibility and forwards compatibility.

These strategies are explained individually in the upcoming sections and referenced throughout the remaining chapters.

The Strict Strategy (New Change, New Contract)

The simplest approach to Web service contract versioning is to require that a new version of a contract be issued whenever any kind of change is made to any part of the contract.

This is commonly implemented by changing the target namespace value of a WSDL definition (and possibly the XML Schema definition) every time a compatible or incompatible change is made to the WSDL, XML Schema, or WS-Policy content related to the contract. Namespaces are used for version identification instead of a version attribute because changing the namespace value automatically forces a change in all consumer programs that need to access the new version of the schema that defines the message types.

This "super-strict" approach is not really that practical, but it is the safest and sometimes warranted when there are legal implications to Web service contract modifications, such as when contracts are published for certain inter-organization data exchanges. Because both compatible and incompatible changes will result in a new contract version, this approach supports neither backwards nor forwards compatibility.

Pros and Cons

The benefit of this strategy is that you have full control over the evolution of the service contract, and because backwards and forwards compatibility are intentionally disregarded, you do not need to concern yourself with the impact of any change in particular (because all changes effectively break the contract).

On the downside, by forcing a new namespace upon the contract with each change, you are guaranteeing that all existing service consumers will no longer be compatible with any new version of the contract. Consumers will only be able to continue communicating with the Web service while the old contract remains available alongside the new version or until the consumers themselves are updated to conform to the new contract.

Therefore, this approach will increase the governance burden of individual services and will require careful transitioning strategies. Having two or more versions of the same service co-exist at the same time can become a common requirement for which the supporting service inventory infrastructure needs to be prepared.

The Flexible Strategy (Backwards Compatibility)

A common approach used to balance practical considerations with an attempt at minimizing the impact of changes to Web service contracts is to allow compatible changes to occur without forcing a new contract version, while not attempting to support forwards compatibility at all.

This means that any backwards-compatible change is considered safe in that it ends up extending or augmenting an established contract without affecting any of the service's existing consumers. A common example of this is adding a new operation to a WSDL definition or adding an optional element declaration to a message's schema definition.

As with the Strict strategy, any change that breaks the existing contract does result in a new contract version, usually implemented by changing the target namespace value of the WSDL definition and potentially also the XML Schema definition.

Pros and Cons

The primary advantage to this approach is that it can be used to accommodate a variety of changes while consistently retaining the contract's backwards compatibility. However, when compatible changes are made, these changes become permanent and cannot be reversed without introducing an incompatible change. Therefore, a governance process is required during which each proposed change is evaluated so that contracts do not become overly bloated or convoluted. This is an especially important consideration for agnostic services that are heavily reused.

The Loose Strategy (Backwards and Forwards Compatibility)

As with the previous two approaches, this strategy requires that incompatible changes result in a new service contract version. The difference here is in how service contracts are initially designed.

Instead of accommodating known data exchange requirements, special features from the WSDL, XML Schema, and WS-Policy languages are used to make parts of the contract intrinsically extensible so that they remain able to support a broad range of future, unknown data exchange requirements.

For example:

- The `anyType` attribute value provided by the WSDL 2.0 language allows a message to consist of any valid XML document.

- XML Schema wildcards can be used to allow a range of unknown data to be passed in message definitions.

- Ignorable policy assertions can be defined to communicate service characteristics that can optionally be acknowledged by future consumers.

These and other features related to forwards compatibility are discussed in upcoming chapters.

Pros and Cons

The fact that wildcards allow undefined content to be passed through Web service contracts provides a constant opportunity to further expand the range of acceptable message element and data content. On the other hand, the use of wildcards will naturally result in vague and overly coarse service contracts that place the burden of validation on the underlying service logic.

> **NOTE**
>
> All three strategies will be referenced in upcoming chapters as we explore how versioning can be accomplished with the WSDL, XML Schema, and WS-Policy languages.

Summary Table

Provided here is a table that broadly summarizes how the three strategies compare based on three fundamental characteristics.

The three characteristics used in this table to form the basis of this comparison are as follows:

- *Strictness* – The rigidity of the contract versioning options. The Strict approach clearly is the most rigid in its versioning rules, while the Loose strategy provides the broadest range of versioning options due to its reliance on wildcards.

- *Governance Impact* – The amount of governance burden imposed by a strategy. Both Strict and Loose approaches increase governance impact but for different reasons. The Strict strategy requires the issuance of more new contract versions, which impacts surrounding consumers and infrastructure, while the Loose approach introduces the concept of unknown message sets that need to be separately accommodated through custom programming.

- *Complexity* – The overall complexity of the versioning process. Due to the use of wildcards and unknown message data, the Loose strategy has the highest complexity potential, while the straight-forward rules that form the basis of the Strict approach make it the simplest option.

Throughout this comparison, the Flexible strategy provides an approach that represents a consistently average level of strictness, governance effort, and overall complexity.

	Strategy		
	Strict	**Flexible**	**Loose**
Strictness	high	medium	low
Governance Impact	high	medium	high
Complexity	low	medium	high

Table 20.1

A general comparison of the three versioning strategies.

Chapter 21

Versioning WSDL Definitions

Whereas changes to message definition types and policies are often supplementary and less evident, alterations made to a WSDL document will have the most visible impact.

The following sections document a series of common change types for definitions within both abstract and concrete descriptions with an emphasis on the Strict and Flexible versioning approaches. Compared to the schema versioning scenarios covered in Chapter 22, there is not as much opportunity to support forwards compatibility. Hence, techniques related to the Loose approach are summarized at the end of this chapter in the *WSDL Definitions and Forwards Compatibility* section.

21.1 Version Identifiers and WSDL Definitions

As with any contract-related document, a WSDL definition can be subject to compatible and incompatible changes. Based on your versioning strategy and conventions, you can decide how to best apply the identifiers explained in Chapter 20 to express new WSDL definition versions. In the upcoming sections (and throughout the remaining versioning chapters), we will follow the "significance of change" approach to version numbering, plus we will incorporate the use of namespaces.

Unlike the XML Schema `xsd:schema` element, the WSDL `definitions` element does not provide a built-in `version` attribute for us to use. We'll therefore use the WSDL `documentation` element to store the version number instead.

Here are the conventions for our versioning scheme:

- Minor and major contract version numbers will be expressed using a `documentation` element that follows the opening `definitions` element. The version numbers will be displayed after the word "Version," as follows:
  `<documentation>Version 1.0</documentation>`

- Major version numbers will be appended to the WSDL definition's target namespace and prefixed with a "v" as shown here: `http://actioncon.com/contract/po/v2`

- The exception to the preceding rule is when the first version of a WSDL definition is released. In this case, no version number is added to the namespace.

- A compatible change increments the minor version number and does not change the WSDL definition's target namespace.

- An incompatible change increments the major version number and results in a new target namespace for the WSDL definition.

The following example shows how version 2.1 of a WSDL definition would be expressed, based on our version identification strategy:

```
<definitions name="PurchaseOrder" targetNamespace=
  "http://actioncon.com/contract/po/v2"
  xmlns="http://schemas.xmlsoap.org/wsdl/"
  xmlns:tns="http://actioncon.com/contract/po/v2"
  xmlns:po="http://actioncon.com/schema/po"
  xmlns:xsd="http://www.w3.org/2001/XMLSchema">
  <documentation>Version 2.1</documentation>
  ...
</definitions>
```

Example 21.1
The `definitions` element with a target namespace that indicates that this is the second version of the Web service contract.

Note that this approach to version identification is used regardless of where compatible or incompatible changes originated. We are not limiting ourselves to only expressing version numbers in the WSDL header area. In fact, we are usually required to add further version identification to the part of the Web service contract that triggered the change.

For example, an incompatible change to the XML Schema type associated with a message definition will require us to increment version numbers within the schema in addition to the major version number in the WSDL definition's target namespace and `documentation` element. Also as we will shortly explore, it sometimes makes sense to further embed version numbers within the names of specific WSDL elements.

Base Example

The upcoming sections add a variety of changes to the existing Web service contract for the Purchase Order service. The majority of these changes impact the abstract description.

Provided here is a base example of the Purchase Order WSDL definition containing the original abstract description that we designed in prior chapters plus the new versioning identifiers explained in the previous section. Our base example therefore represents version 2.1 of the Purchase Order service contract. Upcoming changes to this example will be highlighted using red or bolded text.

```xml
<definitions name="PurchaseOrder" targetNamespace=
  "http://actioncon.com/contract/po/v2"
  xmlns="http://schemas.xmlsoap.org/wsdl/"
  xmlns:tns=" http://actioncon.com/contract/po/v2"
  xmlns:po="http://actioncon.com/schema/po"
  xmlns:xsd="http://www.w3.org/2001/XMLSchema">
<documentation>Version 2.1</documentation>
<types>
  <xsd:schema>
    <xsd:import namespace="http://actioncon.com/schema/po"
      schemaLocation=
      "http://actioncon.com/schema/purchaseOrder.xsd"/>
  </xsd:schema>
</types>
<message name="msgSubmitOrderRequest">
  <part name="PurchaseOrder" element="po:purchaseOrder"/>
</message>
<message name="msgSubmitOrderResponse">
 <part name="Acknowledgement" element="po:acknowledgement"/>
</message>
<message name="msgCheckOrderRequest">
  <part name="PONumber" element="po:poNumber"/>
</message>
<message name="msgCheckOrderResponse">
 <part name="Status" element="po:status"/>
</message>
<message name="msgChangeOrderRequest">
  <part name="PurchaseOrder" element="po:purchaseOrder"/>
</message>
<message name="msgChangeOrderResponse">
 <part name="Acknowledgement" element="po:acknowledgement"/>
```

```
  </message>
<message name="msgCancelOrderRequest">
  <part name="PONumber" element="po:poNumber"/>
</message>
<message name="msgCancelOrderResponse">
 <part name="Acknowledgement" element="po:acknowledgement"/>
</message>
<portType name="ptPurchaseOrder">
  <operation name="opSubmitOrder">
    <input message="tns:msgSubmitOrderRequest"/>
    <output message="tns:msgSubmitOrderResponse"/>
  </operation>
  <operation name="opCheckOrderStatus">
    <input message="tns:msgCheckOrderRequest"/>
    <output message="tns:msgCheckOrderResponse"/>
  </operation>
  <operation name="opChangeOrder">
    <input message="tns:msgChangeOrderRequest"/>
    <output message="tns:msgChangeOrderResponse"/>
  </operation>
  <operation name="opCancelOrder">
    <input message="tns:msgCancelOrderRequest"/>
    <output message="tns:msgCancelOrderResponse"/>
  </operation>
</portType>
  ...
</definitions>
```

Example 21.2

The abstract description of version 2.1 of the Purchase Order WSDL definition prior to being impacted by further changes that impose additional versioning requirements.

SUMMARY OF KEY POINTS

- The version identification approach used in the upcoming examples requires that major and minor numbers are displayed in the **documentation** element and that major numbers are incorporated in the WSDL target namespace.

- The following examples will demonstrate versioning scenarios that modify a common base example.

21.2 Versioning Operation Definitions

The majority of changes on the WSDL definition level are generally centered on operations. This, the largest section in this chapter, covers the following range of common
operation-related changes:

- adding a new operation

- renaming an existing operation

- removing an existing operation

- changing the MEP of an existing operation

- adding a fault message to an existing operation

As mentioned at the beginning of this chapter, these changes are discussed for both the
Strict and Flexible versioning approaches. Additional methods in support of the Loose
versioning strategy are discussed at the end of this chapter.

Adding a New Operation

Appending a WSDL Definition with an Operation as a Compatible Change (Flexible)

When a WSDL definition is already implemented and in use, consumer programs will
have likely formed dependencies on existing operation definitions. Extending the contract by adding a new operation definition will not impact these dependencies and is
therefore considered a backwards compatible change by default.

As shown by the highlighted text in the following example, the newly added `operation`
construct and its related `message` constructs do not affect any other part of the WSDL
definition, except for the version number:

```
<definitions name="PurchaseOrder" targetNamespace=
  "http://actioncon.com/contract/po/v2"
  xmlns="http://schemas.xmlsoap.org/wsdl/"
  xmlns:tns="http://actioncon.com/contract/po/v2"
  xmlns:po="http://actioncon.com/schema/po"
  xmlns:xsd="http://www.w3.org/2001/XMLSchema">
<documentation>Version 2.2</documentation>
<types>
  <xsd:schema>
    <xsd:import namespace="http://actioncon.com/schema/po"
      schemaLocation=
      "http://actioncon.com/schema/purchaseOrder.xsd"/>
```

```
    </xsd:schema>
  </types>
  <message name="msgSubmitOrderRequest">
    <part name="PurchaseOrder" element="po:purchaseOrder"/>
  </message>
  <message name="msgSubmitOrderResponse">
   <part name="Acknowledgement" element="po:acknowledgement"/>
  </message>
  <message name="msgCheckOrderRequest">
    <part name="PONumber" element="po:poNumber"/>
  </message>
  <message name="msgCheckOrderResponse">
   <part name="Status" element="po:status"/>
  </message>
  <message name="msgChangeOrderRequest">
    <part name="PurchaseOrder" element="po:purchaseOrder"/>
  </message>
  <message name="msgChangeOrderResponse">
   <part name="Acknowledgement" element="po:acknowledgement"/>
  </message>
  <message name="msgCancelOrderRequest">
    <part name="PONumber" element="po:poNumber"/>
  </message>
  <message name="msgCancelOrderResponse">
   <part name="Acknowledgement" element="po:acknowledgement"/>
  </message>
  <message name="msgGetOrderRequest">
    <part name="PONumber" element="po:poNumber"/>
  </message>
  <message name="msgGetOrderResponse">
   <part name="PurchaseOrder" element="po:purchaseOrder"/>
  </message>
  <portType name="ptPurchaseOrder">
    <operation name="opSubmitOrder">
      <input message="tns:msgSubmitOrderRequest"/>
      <output message="tns:msgSubmitOrderResponse"/>
    </operation>
    <operation name="opCheckOrderStatus">
      <input message="tns:msgCheckOrderRequest"/>
      <output message="tns:msgCheckOrderResponse"/>
    </operation>
    <operation name="opChangeOrder">
      <input message="tns:msgChangeOrderRequest"/>
      <output message="tns:msgChangeOrderResponse"/>
    </operation>
    <operation name="opCancelOrder">
      <input message="tns:msgCancelOrderRequest"/>
```

```
      <output message="tns:msgCancelOrderResponse"/>
    </operation>
    <operation name="opGetOrder">
      <input message="tns:msgGetOrderRequest"/>
      <output message="tns:msgGetOrderResponse"/>
    </operation>
  </portType>
</definitions>
```

Example 21.3

A new `operation` construct along with new `message` constructs are simply appended to an existing WSDL definition.

The manner in which the new operation was added in the preceding example supports the Flexible versioning approach in that it allows a compatible change to be made without forcing a new major contract version.

Forcing a New Contract Version when Adding an Operation (Strict)

When following the Strict approach, the addition of the new operation and message definitions will increment the contract version number to "3.0" and also change the WSDL target namespace value to reflect the new version, as follows:

```
<definitions name="PurchaseOrder"
  targetNamespace= "http://actioncon.com/contract/po/v3"
  xmlns="http://schemas.xmlsoap.org/wsdl/"
  xmlns:tns="http://actioncon.com/contract/po/v3"
  xmlns:po="http://actioncon.com/schema/po"
  xmlns:xsd="http://www.w3.org/2001/XMLSchema">
  <documentation>Version 3.0</documentation>
  ...
</definitions>
```

Example 21.4

The same changes made to the WSDL definition in Example 21.3 force a new contract version when carrying out the Strict approach.

Renaming an Existing Operation

If the value of the `name` attribute of an existing `operation` element needs to be changed after the WSDL document has been deployed, then this will clearly impact any consumers that have already been designed to use this operation.

There are two common ways of handling this type of change:

1. Force a new major version of the contract.

2. Add the renamed operation to the existing contract.

Because renaming an operation represents an incompatible change, the first method is compliant with both Strict and Flexible versioning strategies. The second technique proposes a way of renaming an operation as a compatible change and is therefore intended for the Flexible approach (although it can also technically be used as part of a Strict approach).

Forcing a New Major Contract Version (Strict, Flexible)

If the existing operation name must be modified, then the contract is subjected to an incompatible change that will require that a new major version of the contract be created, as follows:

```
<definitions name="PurchaseOrder" targetNamespace=
  "http://actioncon.com/contract/po/v3"
  xmlns="http://schemas.xmlsoap.org/wsdl/"
  xmlns:tns="http://actioncon.com/contract/po/v3"
  xmlns:po="http://actioncon.com/schema/po"
  xmlns:xsd="http://www.w3.org/2001/XMLSchema">
  <documentation>Version 3.0</documentation>
  <types>
    <xsd:schema>
      <xsd:import namespace=
        "http://actioncon.com/schema/po"
        schemaLocation=
        "http://actioncon.com/schema/purchaseOrder.xsd"/>
    </xsd:schema>
  </types>
  <message name="msgSubmitOrdersRequest">
    <part name="PurchaseOrder" element="po:purchaseOrders"/>
  </message>
  <message name="msgSubmitOrdersResponse">
    <part name="Acknowledgement" element="po:acknowledgement"/>
  </message>
  <message name="msgCheckOrderRequest">
    <part name="PONumber" element="po:poNumber"/>
  </message>
  <message name="msgCheckOrderResponse">
    <part name="Status" element="po:status"/>
```

```
    </message>
    <message name="msgChangeOrderRequest">
      <part name="PurchaseOrder" element="po:purchaseOrder"/>
    </message>
    <message name="msgChangeOrderResponse">
     <part name="Acknowledgement" element="po:acknowledgement"/>
    </message>
    <message name="msgCancelOrderRequest">
      <part name="PONumber" element="po:poNumber"/>
    </message>
    <message name="msgCancelOrderResponse">
     <part name="Acknowledgement" element="po:acknowledgement"/>
    </message>
    <message name="msgGetOrderRequest">
      <part name="PONumber" element="po:poNumber"/>
    </message>
    <message name="msgGetOrderResponse">
     <part name="PurchaseOrder" element="po:purchaseOrder"/>
    </message>
    <portType name="ptPurchaseOrder">
      <operation name="opSubmitOrders">
        <input message="tns:msgSubmitOrdersRequest"/>
        <output message="tns:msgSubmitOrdersResponse"/>
      </operation>
      <operation name="opCheckOrderStatus">
        <input message="tns:msgCheckOrderRequest"/>
        <output message="tns:msgCheckOrderResponse"/>
      </operation>
      <operation name="opChangeOrder">
        <input message="tns:msgChangeOrderRequest"/>
        <output message="tns:msgChangeOrderResponse"/>
      </operation>
      <operation name="opCancelOrder">
        <input message="tns:msgCancelOrderRequest"/>
        <output message="tns:msgCancelOrderResponse"/>
      </operation>
      <operation name="opGetOrder">
        <input message="tns:msgGetOrderRequest"/>
        <output message="tns:msgGetOrderResponse"/>
      </operation>
    </portType>
</definitions>
```

Example 21.5

The opSubmitOrder operation name is changed.

In this example, the `opSubmitOrder` operation is renamed to "`opSubmitOrders`" to indicate that it has been redeveloped to support the simultaneous submissions of multiple purchase orders at the same time.

This could easily impact the message definitions and their underlying schema types that now must support messages that can contain one or more entire purchase order documents. In this case, the imported schema itself may also need to undergo a versioning change reflected in the new XML Schema target namespace shown here:

```
<definitions name="PurchaseOrder" targetNamespace=
  "http://actioncon.com/contract/po/v3"
  xmlns="http://schemas.xmlsoap.org/wsdl/"
  xmlns:tns="http://actioncon.com/contract/po/v3"
  xmlns:po="http://actioncon.com/schema/po/v3"
  xmlns:xsd="http://www.w3.org/2001/XMLSchema">
  <documentation>Version 3.0</documentation>
  <types>
    <xsd:schema>
      <xsd:import namespace=
        "http://actioncon.com/schema/po/v3"
        schemaLocation=
        "http://actioncon.com/schema/purchaseOrder.xsd"/>
    </xsd:schema>
  </types>
  ...
</definitions>
```

Example 21.6
The target namespace of the imported XML Schema definition is changed in response to incompatible changes made to the underlying schema content.

Extending the Contract with the Renamed Operation (Flexible)

Depending on the reasons behind the name change, it might make sense to simply preserve the existing contract and add a new operation definition with the new name.

In the following variation of the previous example, the `opSubmitOrders` operation is added alongside the original `opSubmitOrder` operation:

```
<definitions name="PurchaseOrder" targetNamespace=
  "http://actioncon.com/contract/po/v2"
  xmlns="http://schemas.xmlsoap.org/wsdl/"
```

```
xmlns:tns="http://actioncon.com/contract/po/v2"
xmlns:po="http://actioncon.com/schema/po"
xmlns:xsd="http://www.w3.org/2001/XMLSchema">
<documentation>Version 2.2</documentation>
<types>
  <xsd:schema>
    <xsd:import namespace=
      "http://actioncon.com/schema/po"
      schemaLocation=
      "http://actioncon.com/schema/purchaseOrder.xsd"/>
  </xsd:schema>
</types>
<message name="msgSubmitOrderRequest">
  <part name="PurchaseOrder" element="po:purchaseOrder"/>
</message>
<message name="msgSubmitOrderResponse">
 <part name="Acknowledgement" element="po:acknowledgement"/>
</message>
<message name="msgSubmitOrdersRequest">
  <part name="PurchaseOrder" element="po:purchaseOrders"/>
</message>
<message name="msgSubmitOrdersResponse">
 <part name="Acknowledgement" element="po:acknowledgement"/>
</message>
<message name="msgCheckOrderRequest">
  <part name="PONumber" element="po:poNumber"/>
</message>
<message name="msgCheckOrderResponse">
 <part name="Status" element="po:status"/>
</message>
<message name="msgChangeOrderRequest">
  <part name="PurchaseOrder" element="po:purchaseOrder"/>
</message>
<message name="msgChangeOrderResponse">
 <part name="Acknowledgement" element="po:acknowledgement"/>
</message>
<message name="msgCancelOrderRequest">
  <part name="PONumber" element="po:poNumber"/>
</message>
<message name="msgCancelOrderResponse">
 <part name="Acknowledgement" element="po:acknowledgement"/>
</message>
<message name="msgGetOrderRequest">
  <part name="PONumber" element="po:poNumber"/>
</message>
<message name="msgGetOrderResponse">
```

```
    <part name="PurchaseOrder" element="po:purchaseOrder"/>
  </message>
  <portType name="ptPurchaseOrder">
    <operation name="opSubmitOrder">
      <input message="tns:msgSubmitOrderRequest"/>
      <output message="tns:msgSubmitOrderResponse"/>
    </operation>
    <operation name="opSubmitOrders">
      <input message="tns:msgSubmitOrdersRequest"/>
      <output message="tns:msgSubmitOrdersResponse"/>
    </operation>
    <operation name="opCheckOrderStatus">
      <input message="tns:msgCheckOrderRequest"/>
      <output message="tns:msgCheckOrderResponse"/>
    </operation>
    <operation name="opChangeOrder">
      <input message="tns:msgChangeOrderRequest"/>
      <output message="tns:msgChangeOrderResponse"/>
    </operation>
    <operation name="opCancelOrder">
      <input message="tns:msgCancelOrderRequest"/>
      <output message="tns:msgCancelOrderResponse"/>
    </operation>
    <operation name="opGetOrder">
      <input message="tns:msgGetOrderRequest"/>
      <output message="tns:msgGetOrderResponse"/>
    </operation>
  </portType>
</definitions>
```

Example 21.7

A new `opSubmitOrders` operation is added as a compatible change.

In this scenario, the addition of the new operation actually demonstrates the application of the Contract Denormalization design pattern that allows operations with overlapping functionality to exist in the same service contract.

> **NOTE**
>
> The aforementioned technique can be applied when following the Strict approach as long as it forces a new contract version. In this case, it is equivalent to adding a new operation as explained previously in the *Forcing a New Contract Version when Adding an Operation (Strict)* section.

Operation Termination

In the case that the renamed operation represents exactly the same underlying functionality as the original operation, this approach can be considered "transitionary." It is similar to forcing a new version of a contract and then hosting both old and new contracts simultaneously, in that the port type will host old and new versions of the same operation.

As when having separate contracts, a retirement strategy will likely be required for the original operation. In the following example, an annotation is added to communicate the target termination date:

```
<portType name="ptPurchaseOrder">
  <documentation>
    opSubmitOrder is Scheduled for Terminatation on 01/12
  </documentation>
  <operation name="opSubmitOrder">
    <input message="tns:msgSubmitOrderRequest"/>
    <output message="tns:msgSubmitOrderResponse"/>
  </operation>
  ...
</portType>
```

Example 21.8
The `opSubmitOrder operation` construct is annotated to indicate its termination date.

NOTE

Techniques for expressing various types of termination information are provided in Chapter 23.

Removing an Existing Operation

The actual removal of an operation definition from a contract will predictably impact consumers that have formed dependencies on it because after the operation has been removed, calls to that Web service operation will predictably fail.

As with renaming an operation, there are two common approaches to accommodate this change:

1. The operation definition is deleted, forcing a new major version of the contract.

2. The operation definition is preserved as a functional stub.

Unlike renaming an operation, we do not have an option whereby the operation can be removed from the contract as a compatible change. Therefore, both techniques impose an incompatible change, regardless of whether we are following a Strict or Flexible approach.

Removing the Operation and Forcing a New Major Contract Version (Strict, Flexible)

The `operation` construct and its associated `message` constructs are removed, and a whole new WSDL definition is released, as indicated by the incremented major version numbers:

```
<definitions name="PurchaseOrder" targetNamespace=
  "http://actioncon.com/contract/po/v3"
  xmlns="http://schemas.xmlsoap.org/wsdl/"
  xmlns:tns="http://actioncon.com/contract/po/v3"
  xmlns:po="http://actioncon.com/schema/po"
  xmlns:xsd="http://www.w3.org/2001/XMLSchema">
  <documentation>Version 3.0</documentation>
  <types>
    <xsd:schema>
      <xsd:import namespace=
        "http://actioncon.com/schema/po"
        schemaLocation=
        "http://actioncon.com/schema/purchaseOrder.xsd"/>
    </xsd:schema>
  </types>
  <message name="msgSubmitOrderRequest">
    <part name="PurchaseOrder" element="po:purchaseOrder"/>
  </message>
  <message name="msgSubmitOrderResponse">
   <part name="Acknowledgement" element="po:acknowledgement"/>
  </message>

  <!-- msgCheckOrderRequest Removed 01/12 -->

  <!-- msgCheckOrderResponse Removed 01/12 -->

  <message name="msgChangeOrderRequest">
    <part name="PurchaseOrder" element="po:purchaseOrder"/>
  </message>
  <message name="msgChangeOrderResponse">
   <part name="Acknowledgement" element="po:acknowledgement"/>
  </message>
  <message name="msgCancelOrderRequest">
```

```
      <part name="PONumber" element="po:poNumber"/>
   </message>
   <message name="msgCancelOrderResponse">
    <part name="Acknowledgement" element="po:acknowledgement"/>
   </message>
   <message name="msgGetOrderRequest">
      <part name="PONumber" element="po:poNumber"/>
   </message>
   <message name="msgGetOrderResponse">
    <part name="PurchaseOrder" element="po:purchaseOrder"/>
   </message>
   <portType name="ptPurchaseOrder">
     <operation name="opSubmitOrder">
       <input message="tns:msgSubmitOrderRequest"/>
       <output message="tns:msgSubmitOrderResponse"/>
     </operation>

     <!-- opCheckOrderStatus Removed 01/12 -->

     <operation name="opChangeOrder">
       <input message="tns:msgChangeOrderRequest"/>
       <output message="tns:msgChangeOrderResponse"/>
     </operation>
     <operation name="opCancelOrder">
       <input message="tns:msgCancelOrderRequest"/>
       <output message="tns:msgCancelOrderResponse"/>
     </operation>
     <operation name="opGetOrder">
       <input message="tns:msgGetOrderRequest"/>
       <output message="tns:msgGetOrderResponse"/>
     </operation>
   </portType>
</definitions>
```

Example 21.9

An `operation` construct and its corresponding `message` constructs are deleted from the WSDL definition.

The highlighted comments indicate when the operation-related content was removed from the contract. This may be helpful as a historical reference for consumer designers.

Turning the Operation into a Functional Stub and Forcing a New Major Contract Version (Strict, Flexible)

One way to delete the functionality of the operation while reducing (but not eliminating) the impact upon consumers is to turn the original operation definition into a stub:

```
<definitions name="PurchaseOrder" targetNamespace=
  "http://actioncon.com/contract/po/v3"
 xmlns="http://schemas.xmlsoap.org/wsdl/"
 xmlns:tns="http://actioncon.com/contract/po/v3"
 xmlns:po="http://actioncon.com/schema/po"
 xmlns:er="http://actioncon.com/schema/po/errors"
 xmlns:xsd="http://www.w3.org/2001/XMLSchema">
 <documentation>Version 3.0</documentation>
 <types>
   <xsd:schema>
     <xsd:import namespace=
       "http://actioncon.com/schema/po"
       schemaLocation=
       "http://actioncon.com/schema/purchaseOrder.xsd"/>
   </xsd:schema>
   <xsd:schema targetNamespace=
     "http://actioncon.com/schema/po/errors">
     <xsd:element name="statusError" type="xsd:string"/>
   </xsd:schema>
 </types>
 <message name="msgSubmitOrderRequest">
   <part name="PurchaseOrder" element="po:purchaseOrder"/>
 </message>
 <message name="msgSubmitOrderResponse">
  <part name="Acknowledgement" element="po:acknowledgement"/>
 </message>
 <message name="msgCheckOrderRequest">
   <part name="PONumber" element="po:poNumber"/>
 </message>
 <message name="msgCheckOrderResponse">
  <part name="StatusError" element="er:statusError"/>
 </message>
 <message name="msgChangeOrderRequest">
   <part name="PurchaseOrder" element="po:purchaseOrder"/>
 </message>
 <message name="msgChangeOrderResponse">
  <part name="Acknowledgement" element="po:acknowledgement"/>
 </message>
 <message name="msgCancelOrderRequest">
   <part name="PONumber" element="po:poNumber"/>
 </message>
 <message name="msgCancelOrderResponse">
  <part name="Acknowledgement" element="po:acknowledgement"/>
 </message>
 <message name="msgGetOrderRequest">
   <part name="PONumber" element="po:poNumber"/>
```

```
  </message>
  <message name="msgGetOrderResponse">
   <part name="PurchaseOrder" element="po:purchaseOrder"/>
  </message>
  <portType name="ptPurchaseOrder">
    <operation name="opSubmitOrder">
      <input message="tns:msgSubmitOrderRequest"/>
      <output message="tns:msgSubmitOrderResponse"/>
    </operation>
    <operation name="opCheckOrderStatus">
      <input message="tns:msgCheckOrderRequest"/>
      <output message="tns:msgCheckOrderResponse"/>
    </operation>
    <operation name="opChangeOrder">
      <input message="tns:msgChangeOrderRequest"/>
      <output message="tns:msgChangeOrderResponse"/>
    </operation>
    <operation name="opCancelOrder">
      <input message="tns:msgCancelOrderRequest"/>
      <output message="tns:msgCancelOrderResponse"/>
    </operation>
    <operation name="opGetOrder">
      <input message="tns:msgGetOrderRequest"/>
      <output message="tns:msgGetOrderResponse"/>
    </operation>
  </portType>
</definitions>
```

Example 21.10

The "removed" operation is preserved but its behavior is changed.

The msgCheckOrderRequest message remains unchanged, allowing the opCheckOrder Status operation to continue accepting the same input message. But instead of returning the status value, it responds with an error message that indicates that the status value is no longer available with this operation.

The type for this message is (in this case) embedded within the types construct as a separate schema so as not to impose versioning requirements upon the purchaseOrder.xsd schema document (and also because this is considered a contract-specific message).

You can decide whether you want the error message to comply with the schema type so that it is successfully validated by the consumer, or whether it should be based on a different type in order to deliberately fail validation.

Even though this might appear to be a quasi-compatible change, the fact that the behavior and data associated with the opCheckOrderStatus operation have been significantly augmented will almost always make this an incompatible change, thereby requiring a new major contract version (along with a new namespace).

NOTE

This will also likely be a temporary measure until the operation is fully retired and then actually removed from the contract, in which case termination information can also be added.

Changing the MEP of an Existing Operation

Consumers form a dependency on the MEP established by the input and output message definitions associated with an operation as much as they do on the underlying types of the individual messages. Therefore, adding an input or output message to an operation or changing the order of these message definitions is considered an incompatible change that will break the contract.

Changing the MEP and Forcing a New Major Contract Version (Strict, Flexible)

In the following example, the opCancelOrder operation is changed from a request-response to a one-way MEP by removing the output message:

```
<definitions name="PurchaseOrder" targetNamespace=
  "http://actioncon.com/contract/po/v3"
  xmlns="http://schemas.xmlsoap.org/wsdl/"
  xmlns:tns="http://actioncon.com/contract/po/v3"
  xmlns:po="http://actioncon.com/schema/po"
  xmlns:xsd="http://www.w3.org/2001/XMLSchema">
  <documentation>Version 3.0</documentation>
  <types>
    <xsd:schema>
      <xsd:import namespace=
        "http://actioncon.com/schema/po"
        schemaLocation=
        "http://actioncon.com/schema/purchaseOrder.xsd"/>
    </xsd:schema>
  </types>
  <message name="msgSubmitOrderRequest">
    <part name="PurchaseOrder" element="po:purchaseOrder"/>
  </message>
```

```xml
<message name="msgSubmitOrderResponse">
 <part name="Acknowledgement" element="po:acknowledgement"/>
</message>
<message name="msgCheckOrderRequest">
  <part name="PONumber" element="po:poNumber"/>
</message>
<message name="msgCheckOrderResponse">
 <part name="Status" element="po:status"/>
</message>
<message name="msgChangeOrderRequest">
  <part name="PurchaseOrder" element="po:purchaseOrder"/>
</message>
<message name="msgChangeOrderResponse">
 <part name="Acknowledgement" element="po:acknowledgement"/>
</message>
<message name="msgCancelOrderRequest">
  <part name="PONumber" element="po:poNumber"/>
</message>

<!-- msgCancelOrderResponse Removed 01/12 -->

<message name="msgGetOrderRequest">
  <part name="PONumber" element="po:poNumber"/>
</message>
<message name="msgGetOrderResponse">
 <part name="PurchaseOrder" element="po:purchaseOrder"/>
</message>
<portType name="ptPurchaseOrder">
  <operation name="opSubmitOrder">
    <input message="tns:msgSubmitOrderRequest"/>
    <output message="tns:msgSubmitOrderResponse"/>
  </operation>
  <operation name="opCheckOrderStatus">
    <input message="tns:msgCheckOrderRequest"/>
    <output message="tns:msgCheckOrderResponse"/>
  </operation>
  <operation name="opChangeOrder">
    <input message="tns:msgChangeOrderRequest"/>
    <output message="tns:msgChangeOrderResponse"/>
  </operation>
  <operation name="opCancelOrder">
    <input message="tns:msgCancelOrderRequest"/>
  </operation>
  <operation name="opGetOrder">
    <input message="tns:msgGetOrderRequest"/>
    <output message="tns:msgGetOrderResponse"/>
```

```
    </operation>
  </portType>
</definitions>
```

Example 21.11
The `output` message element is removed from the `opCancelOrder operation` construct.

In this example, the corresponding `msgCancelOrderResponse` message definition is also removed, as it is no longer required. The result is an incompatible change that forces a new major contract version and a new target namespace for the WSDL definition.

Extending the Contract with the Operation Containing the Modified MEP (Flexible)

An alternative technique is to simply append the WSDL definition with a new operation definition that contains the new MEP. This allows the operation with the modified MEP to reside alongside the original operation, as follows:

```
<definitions name="PurchaseOrder" targetNamespace=
  "http://actioncon.com/contract/po/v2"
  xmlns="http://schemas.xmlsoap.org/wsdl/"
  xmlns:tns="http://actioncon.com/contract/po/v2"
  xmlns:po="http://actioncon.com/schema/po"
  xmlns:xsd="http://www.w3.org/2001/XMLSchema">
  <documentation>Version 2.2</documentation>
  <types>
    <xsd:schema>
      <xsd:import namespace="http://actioncon.com/schema/po"
        schemaLocation=
        "http://actioncon.com/schema/purchaseOrder.xsd"/>
    </xsd:schema>
  </types>
  <message name="msgSubmitOrderRequest">
    <part name="PurchaseOrder" element="po:purchaseOrder"/>
  </message>
  <message name="msgSubmitOrderResponse">
   <part name="Acknowledgement" element="po:acknowledgement"/>
  </message>
  <message name="msgCheckOrderRequest">
    <part name="PONumber" element="po:poNumber"/>
  </message>
  <message name="msgCheckOrderResponse">
   <part name="Status" element="po:status"/>
  </message>
```

```
<message name="msgChangeOrderRequest">
  <part name="PurchaseOrder" element="po:purchaseOrder"/>
</message>
<message name="msgChangeOrderResponse">
 <part name="Acknowledgement" element="po:acknowledgement"/>
</message>
<message name="msgCancelOrderRequest">
  <part name="PONumber" element="po:poNumber"/>
</message>
<message name="msgCancelOrderRequest">
  <part name="PONumber" element="po:poNumber"/>
</message>
<message name="msgCancelOrderResponse">
 <part name="Acknowledgement" element="po:acknowledgement"/>
</message>
<message name="msgCancelOrderNotifyRequest">
  <part name="PONumber" element="po:poNumber"/>
</message>
<message name="msgGetOrderRequest">
  <part name="PONumber" element="po:poNumber"/>
</message>
<message name="msgGetOrderResponse">
 <part name="PurchaseOrder" element="po:purchaseOrder"/>
</message>
<portType name="ptPurchaseOrder">
  <operation name="opSubmitOrder">
    <input message="tns:msgSubmitOrderRequest"/>
    <output message="tns:msgSubmitOrderResponse"/>
  </operation>
  <operation name="opCheckOrderStatus">
    <input message="tns:msgCheckOrderRequest"/>
    <output message="tns:msgCheckOrderResponse"/>
  </operation>
  <operation name="opChangeOrder">
    <input message="tns:msgChangeOrderRequest"/>
    <output message="tns:msgChangeOrderResponse"/>
  </operation>
  <operation name="opCancelOrder">
    <input message="tns:msgCancelOrderRequest"/>
    <output message="tns:msgCancelOrderResponse"/>
  </operation>
  <operation name="opCancelOrderNotify">
    <input message="tns:msgCancelOrderNotifyRequest"/>
  </operation>
  <operation name="opGetOrder">
    <input message="tns:msgGetOrderRequest"/>
```

```
        <output message="tns:msgGetOrderResponse"/>
      </operation>
    </portType>
  </definitions>
```

Example 21.12

The red text indicates a new `opCancelOrderNotify` operation that is added to the WSDL definition along with a new message definition. The bolded text represents the original `opCancelOrder`-related elements that are preserved.

The motivation behind this approach is to allow the operation MEP to be modified while avoiding an incompatible change. The primary limitation is that because the modified operation is effectively added as a new operation, it is required to have a different name.

> **NOTE**
>
> This technique is most commonly considered when following a Flexible versioning strategy. However, if you should need to follow this approach as part of a Strict versioning initiative, then it will force a new contract version the same way as if you were adding a new operation (as explained in the *Forcing a New Contract Version when Adding an Operation (Strict)* section).

Adding a Fault Message to an Existing Operation

As explained in Chapters 7 and 11, operations can be further assigned a pre-defined fault message that is transmitted by the Web service when certain exception conditions are encountered. The requirement for this change can occur when an operation in an established Web service contract did not previously need a fault message, but a new consumer wanting to use this operation introduces this requirement.

> **NOTE**
>
> You could argue that adding a fault message changes the MEP of the operation. However in WSDL 1.1, the four fundamental MEPs are not affected by the presence of the `fault` element.

Adding a Fault Message (Strict, Flexible)

This type of specific change may raise the question as to whether the addition of a fault message will affect the contract's overall backwards compatibility. Technically it should because we are making a significant change to both the contract and the behavior of an existing operation, as shown here:

```
<definitions name="PurchaseOrder" targetNamespace=
 "http://actioncon.com/contract/po/v3"
 xmlns="http://schemas.xmlsoap.org/wsdl/"
 xmlns:tns="http://actioncon.com/contract/po/v3"
 xmlns:po="http://actioncon.com/schema/po"
 xmlns:ft="http://actioncon.com/schema/po/faults"
 xmlns:xsd="http://www.w3.org/2001/XMLSchema">
 <documentation>Version 3.0</documentation>
 <types>
   <xsd:schema>
     <xsd:import namespace="http://actioncon.com/schema/po"
       schemaLocation=
       "http://actioncon.com/schema/purchaseOrder.xsd"/>
   </xsd:schema>
   <xsd:schema targetNamespace=
     "http://actioncon.com/schema/po/faults">
     <xsd:element name="poFault" type="xsd:string"/>
   </xsd:schema>
 </types>
 <message name="msgSubmitOrderRequest">
   <part name="PurchaseOrder" element="po:purchaseOrder"/>
 </message>
 <message name="msgSubmitOrderResponse">
  <part name="Acknowledgement" element="po:acknowledgement"/>
 </message>
 <message name="msgSubmitOrderFault">
   <part name="POFault" element="ft:poFault"/>
 </message>
 <message name="msgCheckOrderRequest">
   <part name="PONumber" element="po:poNumber"/>
 </message>
 <message name="msgCheckOrderResponse">
  <part name="Status" element="po:status"/>
 </message>
 <message name="msgChangeOrderRequest">
   <part name="PurchaseOrder" element="po:purchaseOrder"/>
 </message>
 <message name="msgChangeOrderResponse">
  <part name="Acknowledgement" element="po:acknowledgement"/>
 </message>
 <message name="msgCancelOrderRequest">
   <part name="PONumber" element="po:poNumber"/>
 </message>
```

```
<message name="msgCancelOrderResponse">
 <part name="Acknowledgement" element="po:acknowledgement"/>
</message>
<message name="msgGetOrderRequest">
  <part name="PONumber" element="po:poNumber"/>
</message>
<message name="msgGetOrderResponse">
 <part name="PurchaseOrder" element="po:purchaseOrder"/>
</message>
<portType name="ptPurchaseOrder">
  <operation name="opSubmitOrder">
    <input message="tns:msgSubmitOrderRequest"/>
    <output message="tns:msgSubmitOrderResponse"/>
    <fault message="tns:msgSubmitOrderFault"/>
  </operation>
  <operation name="opCheckOrderStatus">
    <input message="tns:msgCheckOrderRequest"/>
    <output message="tns:msgCheckOrderResponse"/>
  </operation>
  <operation name="opChangeOrder">
    <input message="tns:msgChangeOrderRequest"/>
    <output message="tns:msgChangeOrderResponse"/>
  </operation>
  <operation name="opCancelOrder">
    <input message="tns:msgCancelOrderRequest"/>
    <output message="tns:msgCancelOrderResponse"/>
  </operation>
  <operation name="opGetOrder">
    <input message="tns:msgGetOrderRequest"/>
    <output message="tns:msgGetOrderResponse"/>
  </operation>
  </portType>
</definitions>
```

Example 21.13
For this example, the contract designer decided to add the required type for the fault message definition by embedding a contract-specific schema into the `types` construct.

However, in some environments, the result of issuing a fault message to a consumer that isn't expecting it is negligible. The fault message is transmitted, fails, and an error is recorded, but the consumer is never bothered by this event and therefore is not impacted by this change. Whether this is an option depends on the behavior of the runtime platform hosting both the Web service and the consumer.

Although these circumstances may make it feasible to classify this change as compatible (and therefore only increase the minor contract version number), this is not a recommended approach. Future platform or other technology-related changes could alter the behavior of fault message processing, resulting in unpredictable results.

Extending the Contract with the Operation Containing the Fault Message (Flexible)

As with the change to operation MEPs, the alternative to simply adding a fault-capable version of the same operation definition also exists:

```
<portType name="ptPurchaseOrder">
  ...
  <operation name="opSubmitOrder">
    <input message="tns:msgSubmitOrderRequest"/>
    <output message="tns:msgSubmitOrderResponse"/>
  </operation>
  <operation name="opSubmitOrderWithFault">
    <input message="tns:msgSubmitOrderRequest"/>
    <output message="tns:msgSubmitOrderResponse"/>
    <fault message="tns:msgSubmitOrderFault"/>
  </operation>
  ...
</portType>
```

Example 21.14
The new **opSubmitOrderWithFault** operation containing the fault message is added to the WSDL definition.

Note that in this example, the opSubmitOrder and opSubmitOrderWithFault operations share the same message definitions for their input and output messages. If you intend to do this, be sure to read up on message dispatch issues that this can cause and the need to perhaps further supplement messages with hints as SOAP Action values (see Chapter 15 for more details).

SUMMARY OF KEY POINTS

- Some operation-level changes, such as adding a new operation, are backwards compatible.

- Most changes to operations, however, are incompatible unless alternative techniques are used, such as making a new change while preserving the original operation.

21.3 Versioning Port Type Definitions

This section explores how the versioning of a WSDL definition in general can affect the port type definition and also how a single contract can be evolved by acting as a container for multiple portType constructs (each representing a different version).

Adding a Version Identifier to the Port Type

To explicitly communicate the version of all operations within a given portType construct, you can embed the major version number in the portType element's name attribute and update it every time the WSDL definition's target namespace is updated.

```
<definitions name="PurchaseOrder" targetNamespace=
  "http://actioncon.com/contract/po/v3"
  xmlns="http://schemas.xmlsoap.org/wsdl/"
  xmlns:tns="http://actioncon.com/contract/po/v3"
  xmlns:po="http://actioncon.com/schema/po"
  xmlns:xsd="http://www.w3.org/2001/XMLSchema">
  <documentation>Version 3.0</documentation>
  ...
  <portType name="ptPurchaseOrder-v3">
    ...
  </portType>
  ...
</definitions>
```

Example 21.15
The portType name is modified to reflect the major version of the WSDL definition.

Versioning with Multiple Port Types (Flexible)

One alternative to creating a whole new WSDL definition document every time an incompatible change is applied to the abstract description is to create a new portType construct instead. Because a single WSDL definition can host multiple portType constructs, you can create a multi-interface WSDL document.

In the following example, the WSDL definition contains three portType constructs, each of which includes one of the incompatible changes described in the previous *Versioning Operation Definitions* section.

```
<definitions name="PurchaseOrder" targetNamespace=
  "http://actioncon.com/contract/po"
  xmlns="http://schemas.xmlsoap.org/wsdl/"
```

```
xmlns:tns="http://actioncon.com/contract/po"
xmlns:po="http://actioncon.com/schema/po"
xmlns:xsd="http://www.w3.org/2001/XMLSchema">
<documentation>Versions 1.0, 2.0, 3.0</documentation>
<types>
  <xsd:schema>
    <xsd:import namespace="http://actioncon.com/schema/po"
      schemaLocation=
      "http://actioncon.com/schema/purchaseOrder.xsd"/>
  </xsd:schema>
</types>
<message name="msgSubmitOrderRequest">
  <part name="PurchaseOrder" element="po:purchaseOrder"/>
</message>
<message name="msgSubmitOrderResponse">
 <part name="Acknowledgement" element="po:acknowledgement"/>
</message>
<message name="msgCheckOrderRequest">
  <part name="PONumber" element="po:poNumber"/>
</message>
<message name="msgCheckOrderResponse">
 <part name="Status" element="po:status"/>
</message>
<message name="msgChangeOrderRequest">
  <part name="PurchaseOrder" element="po:purchaseOrder"/>
</message>
<message name="msgChangeOrderResponse">
 <part name="Acknowledgement" element="po:acknowledgement"/>
</message>
<message name="msgCancelOrderRequest">
  <part name="PONumber" element="po:poNumber"/>
</message>
<message name="msgCancelOrderResponse">
 <part name="Acknowledgement" element="po:acknowledgement"/>
</message>
<message name="msgGetOrderRequest">
  <part name="PONumber" element="po:poNumber"/>
</message>
<message name="msgGetOrderResponse">
 <part name="PurchaseOrder" element="po:purchaseOrder"/>
</message>

<!-- For ptPurchaseOrder-v2 -->
<message name="msgSubmitOrdersRequest">
  <part name="PurchaseOrder" element="po:purchaseOrders"/>
</message>
```

```
<message name="msgSubmitOrdersResponse">
 <part name="Acknowledgement" element="po:acknowledgement"/>
</message>

<portType name="ptPurchaseOrder-v1">
  <operation name="opSubmitOrder">
    <input message="tns:msgSubmitOrderRequest"/>
    <output message="tns:msgSubmitOrderResponse"/>
  </operation>
  <operation name="opCheckOrderStatus">
    <input message="tns:msgCheckOrderRequest"/>
    <output message="tns:msgCheckOrderResponse"/>
  </operation>
  <operation name="opChangeOrder">
    <input message="tns:msgChangeOrderRequest"/>
    <output message="tns:msgChangeOrderResponse"/>
  </operation>
  <operation name="opCancelOrder">
    <input message="tns:msgCancelOrderRequest"/>
    <output message="tns:msgCancelOrderResponse"/>
  </operation>
  <operation name="opGetOrder">
    <input message="tns:msgGetOrderRequest"/>
    <output message="tns:msgGetOrderResponse"/>
  </operation>
</portType>

<portType name="ptPurchaseOrder-v2">
  <operation name="opSubmitOrders">
    <input message="tns:msgSubmitOrdersRequest"/>
    <output message="tns:msgSubmitOrdersResponse"/>
  </operation>
  <operation name="opCheckOrderStatus">
    <input message="tns:msgCheckOrderRequest"/>
    <output message="tns:msgCheckOrderResponse"/>
  </operation>
  <operation name="opChangeOrder">
    <input message="tns:msgChangeOrderRequest"/>
    <output message="tns:msgChangeOrderResponse"/>
  </operation>
  <operation name="opCancelOrder">
    <input message="tns:msgCancelOrderRequest"/>
    <output message="tns:msgCancelOrderResponse"/>
  </operation>
  <operation name="opGetOrder">
    <input message="tns:msgGetOrderRequest"/>
```

```
      <output message="tns:msgGetOrderResponse"/>
   </operation>
 </portType>

 <portType name="ptPurchaseOrder-v3">
   <operation name="opSubmitOrder">
     <input message="tns:msgSubmitOrderRequest"/>
     <output message="tns:msgSubmitOrderResponse"/>
   </operation>
   <!-- opCheckOrderStatus Removed 01/12 -->
   <operation name="opChangeOrder">
     <input message="tns:msgChangeOrderRequest"/>
     <output message="tns:msgChangeOrderResponse"/>
   </operation>
   <operation name="opCancelOrder">
     <input message="tns:msgCancelOrderRequest"/>
     <output message="tns:msgCancelOrderResponse"/>
   </operation>
   <operation name="opGetOrder">
     <input message="tns:msgGetOrderRequest"/>
     <output message="tns:msgGetOrderResponse"/>
   </operation>
 </portType>
 ...
</definitions>
```

Example 21.16

A single WSDL definition containing three `portType` constructs, each representing a different version of the abstract Web description.

Because major versioning is represented by new port types, the target namespace of the `definitions` element remains unchanged from its original value and the major version numbers are incorporated into the `portType` element's `name` attributes instead. The `documentation` element keeps track of supported versions by providing a list of version numbers.

NOTE
Due to the fact that multiple `portType` constructs with different names exist, corresponding `binding` constructs will need to be defined. While providing multiple contract versions in a self-contained document, this approach can lead to extremely large-sized WSDL definitions that may become difficult to govern.

Using Prefixes to Associate Versions

When adding new XML Schema types in support of different port type versions, namespace prefixes can be labeled to indicate version numbers.

The following example shows different version 2 and 3 `portType` constructs, each containing an operation that requires a new type that does not exist in the purchaseOrder.xsd schema:

```
<definitions name="PurchaseOrder" targetNamespace=
  "http://actioncon.com/contract/po"
  xmlns="http://schemas.xmlsoap.org/wsdl/"
  xmlns:tns="http://actioncon.com/contract/po"
  xmlns:po="http://actioncon.com/schema/po"
  xmlns:v2="http://actioncon.com/schema/po/errors"
  xmlns:v3="http://actioncon.com/schema/po/faults"
  xmlns:xsd="http://www.w3.org/2001/XMLSchema">
<documentation>Versions 1.0, 2.0, 3.0</documentation>
<types>
  <xsd:schema>
    <xsd:import namespace=
      "http://actioncon.com/schema/po"
      schemaLocation=
      "http://actioncon.com/schema/purchaseOrder.xsd"/>
  </xsd:schema>
  <xsd:schema targetNamespace=
    "http://actioncon.com/schema/po/errors">
    <xsd:element name="statusError" type="xsd:string"/>
  </xsd:schema>
  <xsd:schema targetNamespace=
    "http://actioncon.com/schema/po/faults">
    <xsd:element name="poFault" type="xsd:string"/>
  </xsd:schema>
</types>
<message name="msgSubmitOrderRequest">
  <part name="PurchaseOrder" element="po:purchaseOrder"/>
</message>
<message name="msgSubmitOrderResponse">
 <part name="Acknowledgement" element="po:acknowledgement"/>
</message>
<message name="msgSubmitOrderFault">
  <part name="POFault" element="v3:poFault"/>
</message>
<message name="msgCheckOrderRequest">
  <part name="PONumber" element="po:poNumber"/>
```

```
    </message>
    <message name="msgCheckOrderResponse">
     <part name="Status" element="po:status"/>
    </message>
    <message name="msgCheckOrderResponseErr">
     <part name="StatusError" element="v2:statusError"/>
    </message>
    <message name="msgChangeOrderRequest">
      <part name="PurchaseOrder" element="po:purchaseOrder"/>
    </message>
    <message name="msgChangeOrderResponse">
     <part name="Acknowledgement" element="po:acknowledgement"/>
    </message>
    <message name="msgCancelOrderRequest">
      <part name="PONumber" element="po:poNumber"/>
    </message>
    <message name="msgCancelOrderResponse">
     <part name="Acknowledgement" element="po:acknowledgement"/>
    </message>
    <message name="msgGetOrderRequest">
      <part name="PONumber" element="po:poNumber"/>
    </message>
    <message name="msgGetOrderResponse">
     <part name="PurchaseOrder" element="po:purchaseOrder"/>
    </message>

    <portType name="ptPurchaseOrder-v1">
      <operation name="opSubmitOrder">
        <input message="tns:msgSubmitOrderRequest"/>
        <output message="tns:msgSubmitOrderResponse"/>
      </operation>
      <operation name="opCheckOrderStatus">
        <input message="tns:msgCheckOrderRequest"/>
        <output message="tns:msgCheckOrderResponse"/>
      </operation>
      <operation name="opChangeOrder">
        <input message="tns:msgChangeOrderRequest"/>
        <output message="tns:msgChangeOrderResponse"/>
      </operation>
      <operation name="opCancelOrder">
        <input message="tns:msgCancelOrderRequest"/>
        <output message="tns:msgCancelOrderResponse"/>
      </operation>
      <operation name="opGetOrder">
        <input message="tns:msgGetOrderRequest"/>
        <output message="tns:msgGetOrderResponse"/>
```

```
    </operation>
  </portType>

  <portType name="ptPurchaseOrder-v2">
    <operation name="opSubmitOrder">
      <input message="tns:msgSubmitOrderRequest"/>
      <output message="tns:msgSubmitOrderResponse"/>
    </operation>
    <operation name="opCheckOrderStatus">
      <input message="tns:msgCheckOrderRequest"/>
      <output message="tns:msgCheckOrderResponseErr"/>
    </operation>
    <operation name="opChangeOrder">
      <input message="tns:msgChangeOrderRequest"/>
      <output message="tns:msgChangeOrderResponse"/>
    </operation>
    <operation name="opCancelOrder">
      <input message="tns:msgCancelOrderRequest"/>
      <output message="tns:msgCancelOrderResponse"/>
    </operation>
    <operation name="opGetOrder">
      <input message="tns:msgGetOrderRequest"/>
      <output message="tns:msgGetOrderResponse"/>
    </operation>
  </portType>

  <portType name="ptPurchaseOrder-v3">
    <operation name="opSubmitOrder">
      <input message="tns:msgSubmitOrderRequest"/>
      <output message="tns:msgSubmitOrderResponse"/>
      <fault message="tns:msgSubmitOrderFault"/>
    </operation>
    <operation name="opCheckOrderStatus">
      <input message="tns:msgCheckOrderRequest"/>
      <output message="tns:msgCheckOrderResponse"/>
    </operation>
    <operation name="opChangeOrder">
      <input message="tns:msgChangeOrderRequest"/>
      <output message="tns:msgChangeOrderResponse"/>
    </operation>
    <operation name="opCancelOrder">
      <input message="tns:msgCancelOrderRequest"/>
      <output message="tns:msgCancelOrderResponse"/>
    </operation>
    <operation name="opGetOrder">
      <input message="tns:msgGetOrderRequest"/>
      <output message="tns:msgGetOrderResponse"/>
```

```
    </operation>
  </portType>
  ...
</definitions>
```

Example 21.17
Namespace prefix labels are named to reflect port type versions.

SUMMARY OF KEY POINTS

- Because a WSDL definition can contain multiple port types, you have the option of versioning multiple abstract descriptions within the same overall Web service contract.

- When versioning multiple port types, prefixes can be labeled with version numbers to associate namespace values with parts of the WSDL definition related to different port type versions.

21.4 Versioning Concrete Descriptions

As mentioned earlier in this chapter, when making changes to `operation` and `portType` elements, you will always impact the concrete description because these elements are mirrored in the `binding` construct. However, in cases where there is more than one concrete description for a given abstract description, the `binding` and `service` constructs themselves can be versioned separately.

In Chapter 14 we discussed how the modularization features of the WSDL language allow one WSDL definition document to import another. The case study example in that chapter's *Modularization Mechanisms* section explained how two different concrete descriptions in separate WSDL documents could be designed to import the same abstract description. If we imagine that one concrete description was released as a newer version of the other, then we introduce the need to add versioning identifiers.

Because the concrete descriptions exist in individual WSDL definitions, we have the opportunity to assign them separate target namespace values. Here we revisit this example by adding the appropriate version identifiers:

```
<definitions targetNamespace=
  "http://actioncon.com/contract/po/binding/v1"
  xmlns:tns=" http://actioncon.com/contract/po/binding/v1"
  xmlns:abs="http://actioncon.com/contract/po"
```

```
  xmlns="http://schemas.xmlsoap.org/wsdl/"
  xmlns:po="http://actioncon.com/schema/po"
  xmlns:soap11="http://schemas.xmlsoap.org/wsdl/soap/">
  <import
    namespace="http://actioncon.com/contract/po"
    location="http://actioncon.com/contract/po.wsdl"/>
  <documentation>
    Binding Version 1.0 for SOAP 1.1 Support
  </documentation>
  <binding name="bdPO-v1" type="abs:ptPurchaseOrder">
    ...
  </binding>
  <service name="svPO-v1">
    <port name="portPO-v1" binding="tns:bdPO-v1">
      <soap11:address location=
        "http://actioncon.com/services/po/soap11/"/>
    </port>
  </service>
</definitions>

<definitions targetNamespace=
  "http://actioncon.com/contract/po/binding/v2"
  xmlns:tns=" http://actioncon.com/contract/po/binding/v2"
  xmlns:abs="http://actioncon.com/contract/po"
  xmlns="http://schemas.xmlsoap.org/wsdl/"
  xmlns:po="http://actioncon.com/schema/po"
  xmlns:soap11="http://schemas.xmlsoap.org/wsdl/soap/"
  xmlns:soap12="http://schemas.xmlsoap.org/wsdl/soap12/">
  <import
    namespace="http://actioncon.com/contract/po"
    location="http://actioncon.com/contract/po.wsdl"/>
  <documentation>
    Binding Version 2.0 for SOAP 1.2 Support
  </documentation>
  <binding name="bdPO-v2" type="abs:ptPurchaseOrder">
    ...
  </binding>
  <service name="svPO-v2">
    <port name="portPO-v2" binding="tns:bdPO-v2">
      <soap12:address location=
        "http://actioncon.com/services/soap12/purchaseOrder"/>
    </port>
  </service>
</definitions>
```

Example 21.18

Two separate WSDL definitions, each containing a different concrete description that imports the same abstract description.

In these examples, the name attribute of the binding, service, and port elements have also been modified to include the version number. This helps explicitly communicate the versioning identifier throughout the WSDL definition.

SUMMARY OF KEY POINTS

- Different versions of a WSDL concrete description can import the same abstract description.

- When following this approach, version numbers can be further embedded within the name of binding, part, and service elements.

21.5 WSDL Definitions and Forwards Compatibility

This chapter has intentionally focused on how changes to a WSDL definition tie into Strict and Flexible versioning approaches because options for supporting the Loose strategy are limited. The majority of changes we've explored so far have no direct bearing on enabling forwards compatibility and therefore support the Loose strategy only to the extent to which they affect backwards compatibility. However, some design options for enabling forwards compatibility do exist and are explained in these remaining sections.

Decreasing Operation Granularity Levels

The only way to really design a WSDL definition to accommodate a wider range of potential future consumers is to reduce its granularity levels so that they are more coarse and less fine.

An extreme example is simply collapsing finer-grained operations into a single coarse-grained operation, as shown here:

```
<definitions name="PurchaseOrder" targetNamespace=
  "http://actioncon.com/contract/po"
  xmlns="http://schemas.xmlsoap.org/wsdl/"
  xmlns:tns="http://actioncon.com/contract/po"
  xmlns:po="http://actioncon.com/schema/po">
  ...
  <portType name="ptPurchaseOrder">
    <operation name="opDoSomething">
      <input message="tns:msgRequest"/>
```

```
        <output message="tns:msgResponse"/>
      </operation>
    </portType>
</definitions>
```

Example 21.19
Forwards compatibility on the WSDL level may result in the need for overly coarse-grained operations.

In this case, one operation is designed to accept a wide range of input message data. You could probably assume that the underlying message types would be using wildcards to accommodate such a design.

Alternatively, you could add the opDoSomething operation onto the portType construct displayed previously in Example 21.17 to accommodate future consumers that, for whatever reason, cannot use the existing, finer-grained operations. However, this type of design is not common.

Using the WSDL 2.0 #any Attribute Value

Another example of building an extent of forwards compatibility into the WSDL definition is using the #any value provided by WSDL 2.0. As explained in Chapter 15, this special value allows an operation to be designed to receive (and respond with) any kind of message comprised of a valid XML document.

```
<operation name="opSubmitOrder"
  pattern="http://www.w3.org/ns/wsdl/in-out">
  <input messageLabel="In" element="#any"/>
  <output messageLabel="Out" element="po:Acknowledgement"/>
</operation>
```

Example 21.20
The opSubmitOrder operation with the **element** attribute of the **input** element set to "#any."

Here is an example of how the WSDL 2.0 version of the base Purchase Order Web service contract can be augmented in support of forwards compatibility:

```
<description targetNamespace=
  "http://actioncon.com/contract/po/v2"
  xmlns="http://schemas.xmlsoap.org/wsdl/"
```

```
 xmlns:tns="http://actioncon.com/contract/po/v2"
 xmlns:po="http://actioncon.com/schema/po"
 xmlns:soapbind="http://www.w3.org/ns/wsdl/soap">
 <documentation>Version 2.2</documentation>
 <types>
   <xsd:schema>
     <xsd:import namespace="http://actioncon.com/schema/po"
       schemaLocation=
       "http://actioncon.com/schema/purchaseOrder.xsd"/>
   </xsd:schema>
 </types>
 <interface name="ifPurchaseOrder">
   <operation name="opSubmitOrder"
     pattern="http://www.w3.org/2006/01/wsdl/in-out">
     <input messageLabel="In" element="#any"/>
     <output messageLabel="Out" element="po:acknowlegement"/>
   </operation>
   <operation name="opCheckOrderStatus"
     pattern="http://www.w3.org/2006/01/wsdl/in-out">
     <input messageLabel="In" element="po:poNumber"/>
     <output messageLabel="Out" element="po:status"/>
   </operation>
   <operation name="opChangeOrder"
     pattern="http://www.w3.org/2006/01/wsdl/in-out">
     <input messageLabel="In" element="#any"/>
     <output messageLabel="Out"
       element="po:acknowledgement"/>
   </operation>
   <operation name="opCancelOrder"
     pattern="http://www.w3.org/2006/01/wsdl/in-out">
     <input messageLabel="In" element="po:poNumber"/>
     <output messageLabel="Out"
       element="po:acknowledgement"/>
   </operation>
 </interface>
 ...
</description>
```

Example 21.21

The values for the `element` attributes of the input message for both the `opSubmitOrder` and `opChangeOrder` operations are changed from `po:PurchaseOrder` to `#any`.

This change is considered both backwards and forwards compatible because it does not impact existing consumers and will enable future consumers to send a broader range of input values to the two affected operations.

Provided next is another variation of the WSDL 2.0 base example where instead of decreasing the constraint granularity of existing operations, the contract is extended with a new, extremely coarse-grained operation that uses the #any attribute value for both input and output messages:

```
<description targetNamespace=
  "http://actioncon.com/contract/po/v2"
  xmlns="http://schemas.xmlsoap.org/wsdl/"
  xmlns:tns="http://actioncon.com/contract/po/v2"
  xmlns:po="http://actioncon.com/schema/po"
  xmlns:soapbind="http://www.w3.org/ns/wsdl/soap">
  <documentation>Version 2.2</documentation>
  <types>
    <xsd:schema>
      <xsd:import namespace="http://actioncon.com/schema/po"
        schemaLocation=
        "http://actioncon.com/schema/purchaseOrder.xsd"/>
    </xsd:schema>
  </types>
  <interface name="ifPurchaseOrder">
    <operation name="opSubmitOrder"
      pattern="http://www.w3.org/2006/01/wsdl/in-out">
      <input messageLabel="In" element="po:purchaseOrder"/>
      <output messageLabel="Out" element="po:acknowlegement"/>
    </operation>
    <operation name="opCheckOrderStatus"
      pattern="http://www.w3.org/2006/01/wsdl/in-out">
      <input messageLabel="In" element="po:poNumber"/>
      <output messageLabel="Out" element="po:status"/>
    </operation>
    <operation name="opChangeOrder"
      pattern="http://www.w3.org/2006/01/wsdl/in-out">
      <input messageLabel="In" element="po:purchaseOrder"/>
      <output messageLabel="Out"
        element="po:acknowledgement"/>
    </operation>
    <operation name="opCancelOrder"
      pattern="http://www.w3.org/2006/01/wsdl/in-out">
      <input messageLabel="In" element="po:poNumber"/>
      <output messageLabel="Out"
        element="po:acknowledgement"/>
    </operation>
    <operation name="opProcessOrder"
      pattern="http://www.w3.org/2006/01/wsdl/in-out">
      <input messageLabel="In" element="#any"/>
```

```
      <output messageLabel="Out" element="#any"/>
    </operation>
  </interface>
  ...
</description>
```

Example 21.22

The coarse-grained `opProcessOrder` operation is added.

This type of operation can provide a broad "catch all" allowing practically any range of input data and also being able to respond with just about any form of output message.

SUMMARY OF KEY POINTS

- There aren't many ways to support forwards compatibility using the WSDL language.

- One option is to use the `#any` attribute and another approach is to simply reduce operation granularity levels.

Chapter 22

Versioning Message Schemas

No part of the Web service contract demands as much versioning-related attention as the XML Schema definitions that form the basis of input, output, and fault messages. Introducing changes to existing type definitions and data structures used by WSDL message definitions can be relatively simple and uneventful, or it can produce a ripple effect across consumers that (especially with agnostic services) can impose significant impact.

In the upcoming sections, we'll be exploring the following three common change types:

- adding a new schema component

- removing an existing schema component

- renaming an existing schema component

- modifying the constraint of an existing schema component

This chapter contains three sections that correspond to the Flexible, Loose, and Strict versioning strategies we introduced in Chapter 20. Each one of these sections explains how these change types can be carried out in accordance with the rules of the versioning strategy.

NOTE

Because some of the versioning practices in this chapter incorporate the use of XML Schema wildcards, you might want to revisit the *Wildcards* section in Chapter 12 before proceeding.

22.1 Basic Terms and Concepts

Re-Introducing the "Component"

Back in Chapter 6 we briefly introduced the term "component" as it is commonly referenced when discussing XML and XML Schema. Essentially, a component, from an XML Schema perspective, represents a fundamental part of the schema and is commonly used to refer to an attribute or element. So far in this book we haven't really used this term in order to avoid confusing XML Schema components with component-based programs used by most Web services to host the underlying service logic.

However, given that we're focused solely on contract versioning from hereon, and because several versioning techniques apply to both elements and attributes, we're bringing the term back. You will sometimes see this term further qualified as *schema component*.

Content Sets

The following new terms allow us to make a distinction between the parts of a message schema that do and do not provide formal component declarations:

- *Defined Set* – This represents the part of a message definition that has been pre-defined via declarations in its underlying schema. The defined set corresponds to the minimum constraints and requirements that messages must comply with in order to be considered valid.

- *Allowed Set* – The maximum range of what a message can contain to remain compatible with the message definition's type. The allowed set encompasses the defined set. If the schema does not use wildcards, the allowed set is equivalent to the defined set. If wildcards are used, then the allowed set will exceed the defined set to whatever extent the wildcards allow.

- *Unknown Set* – This simply represents the gap (if any) between the defined set and the allowed set of a given message definition. It refers to the range of unknown (not pre-defined) data that a message can contain while still remaining valid.

- *Recognized Set* – When message recipients are designed to accommodate a measure of content that is part of the unknown set, we end up with another classification that corresponds to the total amount of content recognized. The recognized set always encompasses the defined set and may encompass some or all of the unknown set. We don't actually begin discussing the recognized set until the *Working with Unknown Content* section in Chapter 23, where the distinction between recognized and allowed content becomes relevant in relation to determining processing options for content that is part of the allowed set but not part of the recognized set.

Let's take a look at our example to determine how these terms apply:

```
<xsd:schema xmlns:xsd="http://www.w3.org/2001/XMLSchema"
  targetNamespace="http://actioncon.com/schema/po"
  xmlns="http://actioncon.com/schema/po">
  <xsd:element name="LineItem" type="LineItemType"/>
```

```
<xsd:complexType name="LineItemType">
  <xsd:sequence>
    <xsd:element name="productID" type="xsd:string"/>
    <xsd:element name="productName" type="xsd:string"/>
    <xsd:element name="available" type="xsd:boolean"
      minOccurs="0"/>
    <xsd:any namespace="##any" processContents="lax"
      minOccurs="0" maxOccurs="unbounded"/>
  </xsd:sequence>
  <xsd:anyAttribute namespace="##any"/>
</xsd:complexType>
</xsd:schema>
```

Example 22.1

A sample complex type with wildcards helps us sort out the difference between a defined set and an unknown set, which together comprise the overall allowed set.

All of the code highlighted in red belongs to the defined set because it establishes pre-defined structure and declarations. The bolded text represents the part of the schema classified as the unknown set because it allows a wide assortment of undefined (unknown) data to be accepted. Finally, both the red and the bolded text is considered the allowed set because the combination of the defined and unknown sets represent the range of allowable message content.

> **NOTE**
>
> The recognized set was not represented in the preceding example because it is dependent on the service implementation.

Versioning and the UPA Rule

In Chapter 12 we briefly introduced the Unique Particle Attribution (UPA) rule that is part of the XML Schema specification. This rule dictates that every element must be attributed to exactly one "particle" (or construct) in a schema.

What this refers to specifically is the use of optional elements together with wildcard elements. You cannot design a schema in which an optional element is followed by a wildcard element that allows the same namespace as the optional element. This is because by having an optional element and a wildcard in the same namespace, you essentially establish two parts of the same complex type that would validate the same element value.

This rule primarily exists to improve the efficiency of parsers. Without the UPA rule, a parser might need to "look ahead" in a type definition to determine if an optional element declaration exists for a given element value or whether the value should be associated with the wildcard. Having to do this for every possible wildcard value can burn up a lot of processing cycles. The UPA rule essentially prevents the need for such a look ahead.

An Example of a UPA Violation

In the following example, there is a conflict because the `po2:available` element instance is valid under both the optional `po2:available` element and the `##other` wildcard. The possibility of the element matching two or more "particles" violates the unique part of the UPA rule.

```xsd
<xsd:schema xmlns:xsd="http://www.w3.org/2001/XMLSchema"
  targetNamespace="http://actioncon.com/schema/po"
  xmlns="http://actioncon.com/schema/po">
  <xsd:element name="LineItem" type="LineItemType"/>
  <xsd:complexType name="LineItemType">
    <xsd:sequence>
      <xsd:element name="productID" type="xsd:string"/>
      <xsd:element name="productName" type="xsd:string"/>
      <xsd:element ref="po2:available" minOccurs="0"/>
      <xsd:any namespace="##other" processContents="lax"
        minOccurs="0" maxOccurs="unbounded"/>
    </xsd:sequence>
    <xsd:anyAttribute namespace="##other"/>
  </xsd:complexType>
</xsd:schema>

<xsd:schema xmlns:xsd="http://www.w3.org/2001/XMLSchema"
  targetNamespace="http://actioncon.com/schema/po2"
  xmlns:po2="http://actioncon.com/schema/po2">
  <xsd:element name="available" type="xsd:boolean"/>
</xsd:schema>
```

Example 22.2
An illegal schema due to the fact that it violates the UPA rule.

The UPA rule is relevant to schema versioning because of the restriction it places on the use of optional elements and wildcards, both of which represent fundamental tools to enable backwards and forwards compatibility.

Base Example

Each of the upcoming versioning techniques will be demonstrated on the same base schema sample:

```xsd
<xsd:schema xmlns:xsd="http://www.w3.org/2001/XMLSchema"
  targetNamespace="http://actioncon.com/schema/po"
  xmlns="http://actioncon.com/schema/po"
  elementFormDefault="qualified"
  version="1.0">
  <xsd:element name="LineItem" type="LineItemType"/>
  <xsd:complexType name="LineItemType">
    <xsd:sequence>
      <xsd:element name="productID" type="xsd:string"/>
      <xsd:element name="productName" type="xsd:string"/>
    </xsd:sequence>
  </xsd:complexType>
</xsd:schema>
```

Example 22.3

The `LineItem` element comprised of the `LineItemType` complex type representing the ID and name of a product.

This code was borrowed from the Purchase Order service schema first described in Chapter 6, and then simplified for use in these versioning chapters. It shows a relatively basic complex type comprised of two elements with simple content.

As part of a SOAP message, an instance of this schema might look like this:

```xml
<LineItem xmlns="http://actioncon.com/schema/po">
  <productID>AY2345</productID>
  <productName>Service Blaster 2000</productName>
</LineItem>
```

Example 22.4

An XML document instance of the base schema.

In the upcoming versioning scenarios, the `LineItemType` complex type is extended with an `available` element that represents a Boolean property of a game product that indicates whether the product is currently available.

Versioning Conventions for Examples

Based on the version number provided in the `version` attribute and the fact that there is no version identifier in the namespace, you can assume that this base schema is version "1.0" in relation to any version numbers you will see hereafter.

As with the convention we used with the WSDL examples in Chapter 21, major versions will be represented in the schema target namespace. With the WSDL definitions we kept track of minor version increments using the WSDL documentation element. We could actually do the same with XML Schema by adding the `xsd:annotation` and `xsd:documentation` elements, as shown here:

```
<xsd:schema xmlns:xsd="http://www.w3.org/2001/XMLSchema"
  targetNamespace="http://actioncon.com/schema/po"
  xmlns="http://actioncon.com/schema/po">
  <xsd:annotation>
    <xsd:documentation>
      Version 1.0
    </xsd:documentation>
  </xsd:annotation>
  ...
</xsd:schema>
```

Example 22.5
Major and minor version numbers presented within the `xsd:documentation` construct.

However, given how bulky this makes our schemas, we're opting for the version attribute of the schema element itself, as follows:

```
<xsd:schema xmlns:xsd="http://www.w3.org/2001/XMLSchema"
  targetNamespace="http://actioncon.com/schema/po"
  xmlns="http://actioncon.com/schema/po"
  version="1.0">
  ...
</xsd:schema>
```

Example 22.6
The `xsd:schema` element's `version` attribute used to express our major and minor version numbers.

SUMMARY OF KEY POINTS

- A schema is comprised of content sets that represent defined, allowed, unknown, and recognized content.

- Defined content plus unknown content is equal to allowed content. Recognized content is specific to the service implementation.

- UPA rule violation is a constant consideration when designing schemas for forwards compatibility.

- This section establishes a base schema that will be used as the basis for upcoming examples.

22.2 XML Schema and WSDL Target Namespaces

In this chapter we'll be repeatedly discussing how major version changes result in a change to the XML Schema definition's target namespace value. This approach is based on common conventions we use in our examples and does not preclude other methods that do no involve namespaces at all. However, because we use this approach, we need to establish how the creation of new XML Schema target namespace values relates to the types of changes that we covered in the previous chapter, which result in the need for new WSDL target namespaces.

The rule of thumb is quite straightforward. If an XML Schema definition undergoes a change that requires a new target namespace for that schema, that change will propagate to the WSDL level, resulting in a new target namespace for the WSDL definition as well.

The best way to understand this relationship is to simply view the XML Schema content as an extension to the WSDL document. We can just as easily embed the XML Schema types and element declarations into the WSDL types construct as we can import them. Therefore, their physical location has no bearing on the fact that these definitions collectively represent the final Web service contract.

Note that one consideration related to XML Schema definitions that exist as separate files is when those schemas are shared (as per the Schema Centralization pattern). This is explored further in Chapter 23.

NOTE

Minor version number changes in XML Schema definitions can optionally also be reflected in the corresponding WSDL definition in order to communicate the change in both documents.

22.3 Strict Versioning

The rules of the Strict versioning approach are very simple: Any type of change forces a new contract version. Therefore, the different code examples in the following sections have pretty much the same end result.

Adding a New Schema Component

Here we can see a sample version 2 of the base schema. The `available` element declaration was added to the `LineItemType` complex type, requiring that the namespace value be changed.

```
<xsd:schema xmlns:xsd="http://www.w3.org/2001/XMLSchema"
  targetNamespace="http://actioncon.com/schema/po/v2"
  xmlns="http://actioncon.com/schema/po/v2"
  version="2.0">
  <xsd:element name="LineItem" type="LineItemType"/>
  <xsd:complexType name="LineItemType">
    <xsd:sequence>
      <xsd:element name="productID" type="xsd:string"/>
      <xsd:element name="productName" type="xsd:string"/>
      <xsd:element name="available" type="xsd:boolean"/>
    </xsd:sequence>
  </xsd:complexType>
</xsd:schema>
```

Example 22.7

The `available` element is added, forcing a change in the namespace value.

In the preceding example the addition of the `available` element introduced an incompatible change because the element was required.

As per the rules of this versioning approach, even a compatible change would require a new namespace value, as shown here:

```
<xsd:schema xmlns:xsd="http://www.w3.org/2001/XMLSchema"
  targetNamespace="http://actioncon.com/schema/po/v2"
  xmlns="http://actioncon.com/schema/po/v2"
  version="2.0">
  <xsd:element name="LineItem" type="LineItemType"/>
  <xsd:complexType name="LineItemType">
    <xsd:sequence>
```

```
      <xsd:element name="productID" type="xsd:string"/>
      <xsd:element name="productName" type="xsd:string"/>
      <xsd:element name="available" type="xsd:boolean"
        minOccurs="0"/>
    </xsd:sequence>
  </xsd:complexType>
</xsd:schema>
```

Example 22.8

The `available` element is added with the `minOccurs` attribute set to "0," making this an optional element, but still requiring a change to the namespace.

Removing an Existing Schema Component

Deleting a component from an existing message schema naturally results in an incompatible change that requires the issuance of a new target namespace value, as follows:

```
<xsd:schema xmlns:xsd="http://www.w3.org/2001/XMLSchema"
  targetNamespace="http://actioncon.com/schema/po/v2"
  xmlns="http://actioncon.com/schema/po/v2"
  version="2.0">
  <xsd:element name="LineItem" type="LineItemType"/>
  <xsd:complexType name="LineItemType">
    <xsd:sequence>
      <xsd:element name="productID" type="xsd:string"/>
      <!-- productName Removed 09/12 -->
    </xsd:sequence>
  </xsd:complexType>
</xsd:schema>
```

Example 22.9

The `productName` element declaration is deleted, resulting in a new major version of the schema.

In this case, the removal of the element declaration is logged via a human-readable comment for future reference purposes.

Renaming an Existing Schema Component

Renaming an established element will have the same impact as any other change, as follows:

```
<xsd:schema xmlns:xsd="http://www.w3.org/2001/XMLSchema"
  targetNamespace="http://actioncon.com/schema/po/v2"
  xmlns="http://actioncon.com/schema/po/v2"
  version="2.0">
  <xsd:element name="LineItem" type="LineItemType"/>
  <xsd:complexType name="LineItemType">
    <xsd:sequence>
      <xsd:element name="productID" type="xsd:string"/>
      <xsd:element name="productName2" type="xsd:string"/>
      <xsd:element name="available" type="xsd:boolean"/>
    </xsd:sequence>
  </xsd:complexType>
</xsd:schema>
```

Example 22.10

The productName element is renamed to productName2, forcing another change to the namespace value.

Furthermore, because you do not need to rely on the use of optional elements or wild-cards, message exchanges are always predictable and validated to whatever extent necessary at the contract level.

Modifying the Constraint of an Existing Schema Component

Due to the rules of the Strict approach, changes that result in either an increase or decrease of a component's constraint granularity will force a new version of the schema.

For example, the following changes make each of the previously required elements optional:

```
<xsd:schema xmlns:xsd="http://www.w3.org/2001/XMLSchema"
  targetNamespace="http://actioncon.com/schema/po/v2"
  xmlns="http://actioncon.com/schema/po/v2"
  version="2.0">
  <xsd:element name="LineItem" type="LineItemType"/>
  <xsd:complexType name="LineItemType">
    <xsd:sequence>
      <xsd:element name="productID" type="xsd:string"
        minOccurs="0"/>
      <xsd:element name="productName" type="xsd:string"
        minOccurs="0"/>
      <xsd:element name="available" type="xsd:boolean"
        minOccurs="0"/>
```

```
    </xsd:sequence>
   </xsd:complexType>
</xsd:schema>
```

Example 22.11
The minOccurs attribute set to "0" on all elements within the LineItemType complex type.

Even though these are all considered compatible changes, a new schema version is still required, as indicated in the target namespace. Similarly, making an incompatible change (such as making an optional element required) will have the same result.

SUMMARY OF KEY POINTS

- The Strict versioning approach requires a new target namespace in response to any change to the message schema content.

- The end result of applying this approach is pretty much the same for most types of changes, regardless of whether they are compatible or incompatible changes.

22.4 Flexible Schema Versioning (Using Optional Components)

When applying the Flexible strategy to schema versioning, we look for ways to leverage features of the XML Schema language that can help us implement different types of changes while continuing to maintain backwards compatibility. The following set of examples explores a range of techniques for accommodating both compatible and incompatible changes.

Adding a New Schema Component

The addition of a new component to an existing schema is considered an incompatible change if the new component is required, and a compatible change if it's optional.

As with the Strict approach, the addition of a new required element declaration forces a new major schema version:

```
<xsd:schema xmlns:xsd="http://www.w3.org/2001/XMLSchema"
  targetNamespace="http://actioncon.com/schema/po/v2"
  xmlns="http://actioncon.com/schema/po/v2"
```

```
version="2.0">
  <xsd:element name="LineItem" type="LineItemType"/>
  <xsd:complexType name="LineItemType">
    <xsd:sequence>
      <xsd:element name="productID" type="xsd:string"/>
      <xsd:element name="productName" type="xsd:string"/>
      <xsd:element name="available" type="xsd:boolean"
        minOccurs="1"/>
    </xsd:sequence>
  </xsd:complexType>
</xsd:schema>
```

Example 22.12

The highlighted declaration is added making the `available` element a required part of the `LineItemType` complex type.

In order to accomplish consistent backwards compatibility, the Flexible versioning strategy encourages us to make any new element or attribute declarations optional. In the following example, we extend the base schema with an optional `available` element and also indicate the change by incrementing the minor version number value in the `version` attribute:

```
<xsd:schema xmlns:xsd="http://www.w3.org/2001/XMLSchema"
  targetNamespace="http://actioncon.com/schema/po"
  xmlns="http://actioncon.com/schema/po"
  elementFormDefault="qualified"
  version="1.1">
  <xsd:element name="LineItem" type="LineItemType"/>
  <xsd:complexType name="LineItemType">
    <xsd:sequence>
      <xsd:element name="productID" type="xsd:string"/>
      <xsd:element name="productName" type="xsd:string"/>
      <xsd:element name="available" type="xsd:boolean"
        minOccurs="0"/>
    </xsd:sequence>
  </xsd:complexType>
</xsd:schema>
```

Example 22.13

The `available` element is added with the `minOccurs` attribute set to "0," making the existence of the element in message instances optional.

The addition of a new schema component now allows messages to optionally include the available element, as follows:

```
<LineItem xmlns="http://actioncon.com/schema/po">
  <productID>AY2345</productID>
  <productName>Service Blaster 2000</productName>
  <available>true</available>
</LineItem>
```

Example 22.14

An instance of a message document that contains the new `available` element.

Placing New Component Declarations into Separate Schemas

Note that the new available element could have been declared in a separate schema that can be referenced from the base schema, as shown here:

```
<xsd:schema xmlns:xsd="http://www.w3.org/2001/XMLSchema"
  targetNamespace="http://actioncon.com/schema/po"
  xmlns="http://actioncon.com/schema/po"
  version="1.1">
  <xsd:element name="LineItem" type="LineItemType"/>
  <xsd:complexType name="LineItemType">
    <xsd:sequence>
      <xsd:element name="productID" type="xsd:string"/>
      <xsd:element name="productName" type="xsd:string"/>
      <xsd:element ref="available" minOccurs="0"/>
    </xsd:sequence>
  </xsd:complexType>
</xsd:schema>

<xsd:schema xmlns:xsd="http://www.w3.org/2001/XMLSchema"
  targetNamespace="http://actioncon.com/schema/po"
  xmlns="http://actioncon.com/schema/po">
  <xsd:element name="available" type="xsd:boolean"/>
</xsd:schema>
```

Example 22.15

The `LineItemType` complex type in the first schema contains an element that references another in a separate schema.

This approach may be preferable when new elements need to be governed by separate custodians, or if the new elements need to be placed into a different namespace as follows:

```
<xsd:schema xmlns:xsd="http://www.w3.org/2001/XMLSchema"
  targetNamespace="http://actioncon.com/schema/po"
  xmlns="http://actioncon.com/schema/po"
  xmlns:ext="http://actioncon.com/schema/po/extension"
  version="1.1">
  <xsd:element name="LineItem" type="LineItemType"/>
  <xsd:complexType name="LineItemType">
    <xsd:sequence>
      <xsd:element name="productID" type="xsd:string"/>
      <xsd:element name="productName" type="xsd:string"/>
      <xsd:element ref="ext:available" minOccurs="0"/>
    </xsd:sequence>
  </xsd:complexType>
</xsd:schema>

<xsd:schema xmlns:xsd="http://www.w3.org/2001/XMLSchema"
  targetNamespace=
    "http://actioncon.com/schema/po/extension"
  xmlns="http://actioncon.com/schema/po/extension">
  <xsd:element name="available" type="xsd:boolean"/>
</xsd:schema>
```

Example 22.16
The externally referenced element is placed into a separate namespace.

Removing an Existing Schema Component

The removal of a component declaration from an existing XML Schema definition results in an incompatible change that forces a new schema and WSDL definition version. Therefore, when carrying out the Flexible versioning strategy, this change has the same results as with the Strict approach, as explained earlier in the corresponding *Removing an Existing Schema Component* part of the previous *Strict Versioning* section.

Renaming an Existing Schema Component

By default, changing the name of an existing component will result in an incompatible change that requires a new schema target namespace and a new corresponding contract version:

```
<xsd:schema xmlns:xsd="http://www.w3.org/2001/XMLSchema"
  targetNamespace="http://actioncon.com/schema/po/v2"
  xmlns="http://actioncon.com/schema/po/v2"
  elementFormDefault="qualified"
```

```
version="2.0">
  <xsd:element name="LineItem" type="LineItemType"/>
  <xsd:complexType name="LineItemType">
    <xsd:sequence>
      <xsd:element name="productID" type="xsd:string"/>
      <xsd:element name="productName2" type="xsd:string"/>
    </xsd:sequence>
  </xsd:complexType>
</xsd:schema>
```

Example 22.17

The LineItem element comprised of the LineItemType complex type representing the ID and name of a product.

This type of change would make the following message instance invalid:

```
<LineItem xmlns="http://actioncon.com/schema/po">
  <productID>AY2345</productID>
  <productName2>Service Blaster 2000</productName2>
</LineItem>
```

Example 22.18

An instance of a message document in which an element name has been changed.

However, with the Flexible strategy, schema components can be renamed as part of a compatible change by using the xsd:choice group element to preserve the old element name alongside the new one:

```
<xsd:complexType name="LineItemType">
  <xsd:sequence>
    <xsd:element name="productID" type="xsd:string"/>
    <xsd:choice>
      <xsd:element name="productName" type="xsd:string"/>
      <xsd:element name="productName2" type="xsd:string"/>
    </xsd:choice>
    <xsd:element name="available" type="xsd:boolean"/>
  </xsd:sequence>
</xsd:complexType>
```

Example 22.19

The productName and productName2 element declarations are wrapped in a choice group.

Modifying the Constraint of an Existing Schema Component

Adjusting the validation rules for a given component is a common type of change, especially when the validation logic is tied to business policies or rules. In the following example, the data type for the `productID` element has been changed to `xsd:integer`, and the `maxOccurs` attribute for the `productName` element has been set to "unbounded," allowing multiple occurrences of the element to exist:

```xsd
<xsd:schema xmlns:xsd="http://www.w3.org/2001/XMLSchema"
  targetNamespace="http://actioncon.com/schema/po/v2"
  xmlns="http://actioncon.com/schema/po/v2"
  elementFormDefault="qualified"
  version="2.0">
  <xsd:element name="LineItem" type="LineItemType"/>
  <xsd:complexType name="LineItemType">
    <xsd:sequence>
      <xsd:element name="productID" type="xsd:integer/>
      <xsd:element name="productName" type="xsd:string"
        maxOccurs="unbounded"/>
    </xsd:sequence>
  </xsd:complexType>
</xsd:schema>
```

Example 22.20

The `type` attribute of the `productID` element declaration is changed from `xsd:string` to `xsd:integer`, and the `maxOccurs` attribute of the `productName` element declaration is changed to a value of "unbounded."

The change made to the `productID` element is incompatible because the `xsd:integer` data type is more restrictive than the original `xsd:string` type, whereas the addition of `maxOcccurs="unbounded"` is a compatible change that will not impact existing consumers.

As a result, the following message sent to the new schema will fail validation:

```xml
<LineItem xmlns="http://actioncon.com/schema/po">
  <productID>AY2345</productID>
  <productName>Service Blaster 2000</productName>
  <productName>Service Blaster 2010</productName>
</LineItem>
```

Example 22.21

A message instance that does not comply with the preceding schema.

The multiple `productName` elements are legal, but the value of the `productID` element is no longer valid, since it does not comply with the `xsd:integer` type.

Similarly, some or all of the previously existing schema types can be designed with increased flexibility by also becoming optional and by increasing their allowable occurrences. In the following example, we decide that the only required element should be `productID`, and therefore also make the `productName` element optional:

```
<xsd:complexType name="LineItemType">
  <xsd:sequence>
    <xsd:element name="productID" type="xsd:string"/>
    <xsd:element name="productName" type="xsd:string"
      minOccurs="0"/>
    <xsd:element name="available" type="xsd:boolean"
      minOccurs="0"/>
  </xsd:sequence>
</xsd:complexType>
```

Example 22.22
The `productName` element is made optional by setting its `minOccurs` attribute to "0."

We might then discover that game products can be renamed several times, but that they are required to retain old names together with any new names. In this case we need to allow the `productName` element to occur more than just once (which is the default). Therefore, we add the `maxOccurs` attribute to the element with a setting of "unbounded," as shown here:

```
<xsd:complexType name="LineItemType">
  <xsd:sequence>
    <xsd:element name="productID" type="xsd:string"/>
    <xsd:element name="productName" type="xsd:string"
      minOccurs="0" maxOccurs="unbounded"/>
    <xsd:element name="available" type="xsd:boolean"
      minOccurs="0"/>
  </xsd:sequence>
</xsd:complexType>
```

Example 22.23
The `productName` element has the `maxOccurs` attribute set to "unbounded," allowing this element to repeat.

We could have made these changes to the productName element in advance, but we also had the option of adding these attribute values subsequent to the initial deployment of the Purchase Order service, because they retained backwards compatibility.

Earlier we demonstrated the use of the xsd:choice group to accommodate component name changes. Note that due to restrictions in the XML Schema language, this group cannot help us overcome changes to schema component constraints in the same way.

For example, the following is not allowed:

```
<xsd:complexType name="LineItemType">
  <xsd:sequence>
    <xsd:choice>
      <xsd:element name="productID" type="xsd:string"/>
      <xsd:element name="productID" type="xsd:decimal"/>
    </xsd:choice>
    <xsd:element name="productName" type="xsd:string"/>
    <xsd:element name="available" type="xsd:boolean"/>
  </xsd:sequence>
</xsd:complexType>
```

Example 22.24

An invalid choice group comprised of two element declarations that only differ in the values of their type attributes.

NOTE

Overuse of minOccurs="0" and maxOccurs="unbounded" can result in vague Web service contracts with reduced capacity to validate incoming and outgoing data. This shifts the responsibility of performing the actual validation into the service logic, further requiring the service to contain exception handling routines for responding to invalid messages.

SUMMARY OF KEY POINTS

- When following the Flexible versioning strategy, most schema changes can be backwards-compatible via the use of the minOccurs attribute.

- Incompatible changes, such as renaming or removing existing XML Schema components, will likely force a new major version unless special techniques are used.

22.5 Loose Schema Versioning (Using Wildcards)

The added goal of supporting forwards compatibility within our schema designs makes this the most challenging approach to follow. The following sections demonstrate how various extents of forwards compatibility can be achieved through the use of XML Schema wildcards.

Adding a New Schema Component

An alternative approach to managing message type changes is with the use of wildcards. Because a wildcard will accept a wide range of elements, this approach has the potential to enable Web service contracts to be designed in support of both backwards and forwards compatibility.

> **NOTE**
>
> As explained in Chapter 12, additional elements that are added and then validated against wildcards are referred to as *replacement elements*.

In the following example, we've extended our base XML schema to add the xsd:any and xsd:anyAttribute wildcard declarations:

```
<xsd:schema xmlns:xsd="http://www.w3.org/2001/XMLSchema"
  targetNamespace="http://actioncon.com/schema/po"
  xmlns="http://actioncon.com/schema/po"
  elementFormDefault="qualified"
  version="1.0">
  <xsd:element name="LineItem" type="LineItemType"/>
  <xsd:complexType name="LineItemType">
    <xsd:sequence>
      <xsd:element name="productID" type="xsd:string"/>
      <xsd:element name="productName" type="xsd:string"/>
      <xsd:any namespace="##any" processContents="lax"
        minOccurs="0" maxOccurs="unbounded"/>
    </xsd:sequence>
    <xsd:anyAttribute namespace="##any"/>
  </xsd:complexType>
</xsd:schema>
```

Example 22.25

The base schema is extended with xsd:any and xsd:anyAttribute wildcards. Our assumption is that we designed these extensions into version 1.0 of our base schema in support of future Loose versioning.

In this case, the wildcards are added to the end of the `LineItemType` construct, which means that all changes and extensions to that type will need to be implemented via wildcards. As a result, the initial defined set (comprised of the `productID` and `productName` element declarations) will never be allowed to grow.

For the previously displayed schema, the following message would still be valid because it simply complies with the types in the defined set:

```
<LineItem xmlns="http://actioncon.com/schema/po">
  <productID>AY2345</productID>
  <productName>Service Blaster 2000</productName>
</LineItem>
```

Example 22.26
A basic XML document instance that conforms to the original element declarations.

And, the same message extended with a previously undeclared element would also be considered valid:

```
<LineItem xmlns="http://actioncon.com/schema/po">
  <productID>AY2345</productID>
  <productName>Service Blaster 2000</productName>
  <available>true</available>
</LineItem>
```

Example 22.27
An extended XML document instance that conforms to the schema because of its use of wildcards.

Using Wrapper Elements for Wildcards

An alternative design to the previously displayed schema is to wrap the wildcard into a separate optional element, as follows:

```
<xsd:schema xmlns:xsd="http://www.w3.org/2001/XMLSchema"
  targetNamespace="http://actioncon.com/schema/po"
  xmlns="http://actioncon.com/schema/po"
  version="1.1">
  <xsd:element name="LineItem" type="LineItemType"/>
  <xsd:complexType name="LineItemType">
    <xsd:sequence>
      <xsd:element name="productID" type="xsd:string"/>
```

```
      <xsd:element name="productName" type="xsd:string"/>
      <xsd:element name="extension" type="ExtensionType"
        minOccurs="0"/>
    </xsd:sequence>
  </xsd:complexType>
  <xsd:complexType name="ExtensionType">
    <xsd:sequence>
      <xsd:any namespace="##targetNamespace"
        processContents="lax" minOccurs="0"
        maxOccurs="unbounded"/>
    </xsd:sequence>
    <xsd:anyAttribute namespace="##any"/>
  </xsd:complexType>
</xsd:schema>
```

Example 22.28

The `xsd:any` and `xsd:anyAttribute` wildcards wrapped in a separate `extension` element declaration.

This approach is desirable when you want to isolate replacement elements into a separate construct within the message document. For example, the previous message would now need to be structured like this:

```
<LineItem xmlns="http://actioncon.com/schema/po">
  <productID>AY2345</productID>
  <productName>Service Blaster 2000</productName>
  <extension>
    <available>true</available>
  </extension>
</LineItem>
```

Example 22.29

A message instance containing the required extension wrapper element in order to conform to the preceding schema.

Schemas for Replacement Elements

Example 22.15 in the *Flexible Schema Versioning* section demonstrated how a new element can be declared separately in its own schema and then referenced from the base schema via the use of the `ref` attribute of the `element` element.

When working with wildcards, in either of the schema designs we just explored (with and without wrapper elements), the `available` element can also be declared in a separate schema definition, as shown here:

```
<xsd:schema xmlns:xsd="http://www.w3.org/2001/XMLSchema"
  targetNamespace="http://actioncon.com/schema/po"
  xmlns="http://actioncon.com/schema/po"
  version="1.1">
  <xsd:element name="LineItem" type="LineItemType"/>
  <xsd:complexType name="LineItemType">
    <xsd:sequence>
      <xsd:element name="productID" type="xsd:string"/>
      <xsd:element name="productName" type="xsd:string"/>
      <xsd:any namespace="##any" processContents="lax"
        minOccurs="0" maxOccurs="unbounded"/>
    </xsd:sequence>
    <xsd:anyAttribute namespace="##any"/>
  </xsd:complexType>
</xsd:schema>

<xsd:schema xmlns:xsd="http://www.w3.org/2001/XMLSchema"
  targetNamespace="http://actioncon.com/schema/po2"
  xmlns:po2="http://actioncon.com/schema/po2"
  version="1.0">
  <xsd:element name="available" type="xsd:boolean"/>
</xsd:schema>
```

Example 22.30

An XML schema in the same target namespace as the preceding schema, providing the element declaration for the `available` element.

You will notice the absence of a `ref` attribute in the base schema. This attribute is not supported with wildcard elements. Several processors are smart enough to associate the two schemas automatically at runtime by using the replacement element name as the primary point of reference. However, you should confirm this support before basing your contracts on this design. Alternatively, you can try to use the standard XML Schema import or include statements to either join one schema with another or have them both pulled into a WSDL definition.

Note that in the previous example, the allowed target namespace values for the replacement element schema are determined by the `namespace` attribute setting of the wildcard element, which also provides the `processContents` attribute that enables us to set whether the schema will actually be used for validation processing. Both of these attributes are explained in detail in the upcoming *Modifying the Constraint of an Existing Schema Component* section.

Removing an Existing Schema Component

If you run into the requirement to remove a component declaration from an established
defined set of a Web service contract, then there are several options you can explore in
order to avoid turning this into an incompatible change. When working with wildcards,
these options relate to the vicinity of the component declaration to the wildcard, as
explained in the following two sections.

Removing an Element Preceding a Wildcard

In this example, we need to remove the declaration for the productName element:

```
<xsd:schema xmlns:xsd="http://www.w3.org/2001/XMLSchema"
  targetNamespace="http://actioncon.com/schema/po"
  xmlns="http://actioncon.com/schema/po"
  version="1.0">
  <xsd:element name="LineItem" type="LineItemType"/>
  <xsd:complexType name="LineItemType">
    <xsd:sequence>
      <xsd:element name="productID" type="xsd:string"
        minOccurs="0"/>
      <xsd:element name="productName" type="xsd:string"/>
      <xsd:any namespace="##any" processContents="lax"
        minOccurs="0" maxOccurs="unbounded"/>
    </xsd:sequence>
    <xsd:anyAttribute namespace="##other"/>
  </xsd:complexType>
</xsd:schema>
```

Example 22.31

The productName element declaration has been identified as an XML Schema component that needs to be
removed.

Because the element declaration for productName is immediately followed by the wild-card, we can simply delete the highlighted line of text, as shown here:

```
<xsd:schema xmlns:xsd="http://www.w3.org/2001/XMLSchema"
  targetNamespace="http://actioncon.com/schema/po"
  xmlns="http://actioncon.com/schema/po"
  version="1.1">
  <xsd:element name="LineItem" type="LineItemType"/>
  <xsd:complexType name="LineItemType">
    <xsd:sequence>
      <xsd:element name="productID" type="xsd:string"
        minOccurs="0"/>
      <!-- productName Removed 09/12 -->
      <xsd:any namespace="##any" processContents="lax"
        minOccurs="0" maxOccurs="unbounded"/>
    </xsd:sequence>
    <xsd:anyAttribute namespace="##other"/>
  </xsd:complexType>
</xsd:schema>
```

Example 22.32
The LineItemType construct after the productName element declaration has been removed.

The removal of the productName element declaration was a simple compatible change because the wildcard can now continue to accept the productName element in messages from existing consumers, while allowing new consumers to no longer have to provide this formerly required element.

Removing an Element Not Preceding a Wildcard

It is more difficult to remove an element declaration that does not directly precede a wildcard declaration. In the following example, we want to remove the productID element, which is located at the beginning of the sequence construct and precedes the productName element declaration:

```
<xsd:schema xmlns:xsd="http://www.w3.org/2001/XMLSchema"
  targetNamespace="http://actioncon.com/schema/po"
  xmlns="http://actioncon.com/schema/po"
  version="1.0">
  <xsd:element name="LineItem" type="LineItemType"/>
  <xsd:complexType name="LineItemType">
    <xsd:sequence>
```

```
      <xsd:element name="productID" type="xsd:string"/>
      <xsd:element name="productName" type="xsd:string"/>
      <xsd:any namespace="##any" processContents="lax"
        minOccurs="0" maxOccurs="unbounded"/>
    </xsd:sequence>
    <xsd:anyAttribute namespace="##other"/>
  </xsd:complexType>
</xsd:schema>
```

Example 22.33

The product ID element declaration is identified as having to be removed from this schema.

In this case, simply replacing the element with a wildcard (as per the previous section) would result in a UPA rule violation.

As an alternative, we can preserve the productID element declaration and simply "relax" its constraints by changing its type to xsd:anyType and adding minOccurs="0", as follows:

```
<xsd:schema xmlns:xsd="http://www.w3.org/2001/XMLSchema"
  targetNamespace="http://actioncon.com/schema/po"
  xmlns="http://actioncon.com/schema/po"
  version="1.1">
  <xsd:element name="LineItem" type="LineItemType"/>
  <xsd:complexType name="LineItemType">
    <xsd:sequence>
      <xsd:element name="productID" type="xsd:anyType"
        minOccurs="0"/>
      <xsd:element name="productName" type="xsd:string"/>
      <xsd:any namespace="##any" processContents="lax"
        minOccurs="0" maxOccurs="unbounded"/>
    </xsd:sequence>
    <xsd:anyAttribute namespace="##other"/>
  </xsd:complexType>
</xsd:schema>
```

Example 22.34

The value of the type attribute of the productID element is changed to "xsd:anyType."

While this technique does not actually physically remove the productID element declaration, it decreases its constraint granularity to a point where it resembles a wildcard and it further limits the impact to a compatible change.

> **NOTE**
>
> This may, in fact, not be the best example for the use of the `xsd:any-Type` type because most of what's allowed by `xsd:anyType` is also allowed by the `xsd:string` data type. A more effective scenario would be one where the original `productID` element declaration contained more restrictive constraints.

Renaming an Existing Schema Component

When having to rename an established component within a schema, the techniques covered in the corresponding *Renaming an Existing Schema Component* part of the *Flexible Schema Versioning* section can be applied.

Modifying the Constraint of an Existing Schema Component

The examples we covered in the corresponding *Modifying the Constraint of an Existing Schema Component* part of the *Flexible Schema Versioning* section also apply to the Loose versioning approach in how they support backwards compatibility for the defined set. Beyond existing component declarations, there are additional considerations related to the constraint granularity of wildcard declarations based on the special attributes used with XML Schema wildcards.

Let's revisit the `xsd:any` wildcard to study its attribute settings:

```
<xsd:any namespace="##any" processContents="lax"
  minOccurs="0" maxOccurs="unbounded"/>
```

The purpose of the `minOccurs` and `maxOccurs` attribute settings is pretty straight forward in that they clearly indicate that additional elements beyond the defined set are optional and can be added as many times as you want.

What's of particular interest to use in relation to Loose versioning are the `namespace` and `processContents` attributes that we first introduced back in Chapter 12. The following two sections recap the allowed values for these attributes and discuss how they relate to versioning options.

The `namespace` *Attribute*

The `namespace` attribute determines the namespaces that replacement elements can belong to, as follows:

- `##any` – (the default value) any namespace or no namespace
- `##other` – any namespace other than the target namespace

- `##targetNamespace` – the target namespace of the schema document

- `##local` – no namespace

- one or more specific namespaces, separated by whitespace

If the replacement element is associated with a namespace other than what is allowed by this attribute, the validation will fail. Therefore, we need to take a closer look to explore the impact of these values on a versioning strategy.

The `namespace="##any"` setting is clearly the most flexible option in that the replacement elements can belong to any namespace. Although it provides the greatest range of replacement elements that can be accepted by a given service contract, it also increases the chances of generating UPA violations if the last part of the defined set is optional.

The use of the `namespace="##other"` setting forces all replacement elements to be associated with a namespace that is different from the existing schema's target namespace. This can introduce more design effort to ensure that new namespace values are always used for replacement elements, but it also guarantees that the UPA rule is consistently adhered to.

If you are employing a versioning approach that is part of a tightly controlled governance program, then you can alternatively use the option whereby the namespace attribute is populated with a specific list of allowed namespaces. This way, messages must always comply with namespaces that are issued by a custodian, and the `namespace="##targetNamespace"` and `namespace="##local"` settings can be used to support specific requirements and conventions that are part of a controlled governance effort.

To understand these attribute settings better, let's take a look at some examples. In the following scenario, the original schema has a wildcard element with a namespace value of "##other" and a possible replacement element is separately declared in a schema that shares the same target namespace as the base schema:

```xsd
<xsd:schema xmlns:xsd="http://www.w3.org/2001/XMLSchema"
  targetNamespace="http://actioncon.com/schema/po"
  xmlns="http://actioncon.com/schema/po"
  version="1.1">
  <xsd:element name="LineItem" type="LineItemType"/>
  <xsd:complexType name="LineItemType">
    <xsd:sequence>
      <xsd:element name="productID" type="xsd:string"/>
      <xsd:element name="productName" type="xsd:string"/>
```

```
      <xsd:any namespace="##other" processContents="lax"
        minOccurs="0" maxOccurs="unbounded"/>
    </xsd:sequence>
    <xsd:anyAttribute namespace="##other"/>
  </xsd:complexType>
</xsd:schema>

<xsd:schema xmlns:xsd="http://www.w3.org/2001/XMLSchema"
  targetNamespace="http://actioncon.com/schema/po"
  xmlns="http://actioncon.com/schema/po"
  version="1.0">
  <xsd:element name="available" type="xsd:boolean"/>
</xsd:schema>
```

Example 22.35

The ##other attribute value used to require that elements belonging to the unknown set reside in a namespace other than the target namespace of the primary schema document. However, the second schema document is still using the same target namespace.

This example would raise an error because the use of the namespace="##other" setting requires that replacement elements exist in a separate namespace. For this to work, either the namespace attribute of the wildcard needs to be changed to a value of "##any" or "##targetNamespace" or it needs to be populated with the actual namespace value.

Here's a correct example of how the schema that declares the available element can work with the primary schema from Example 22.35:

```
<xsd:schema xmlns:xsd="http://www.w3.org/2001/XMLSchema"
  targetNamespace="http://actioncon.com/schema/po/extension"
  xmlns="http://actioncon.com/schema/po/extension"
  version="1.0">
  <xsd:element name="available" type="xsd:boolean"/>
</xsd:schema>
```

Example 22.36

The secondary schema has been corrected to use a new target namespace.

The processContents Attribute

The setting of this attribute allows you to determine the extent to which replacement elements will be validated, as follows:

- `strict` – (default) Elements must be declared and validated. If they are invalid or no declarations are found, an error is raised.

- `lax` – The processor will look for declarations for those elements (based on their names) and if it finds them, it will validate them (if it doesn't find them, it will not raise an error).

- `skip` – No validation will be performed on the replacement elements.

A value of "`strict`" requires that an element declaration exists for any replacement element. In this case, separate schemas will likely need to be created with namespace values that comply with the `namespace` attribute setting. When wildcards are in frequent use by a range of different consumer programs, it is not uncommon for the same base schema that establishes the defined set to be potentially extended with a variety of different schemas.

Similarly, the "`lax`" setting will use existing schemas to validate replacement elements. However, the absence of any required schemas will not cause replacement elements to be rejected.

> **NOTE**
>
> With both the "`strict`" and "`lax`" settings, the processor will usually attempt to locate the appropriate schemas based on the replacement element name values.

The value of "`skip`" will simply tell the processor to allow any replacement elements that comply with the `namespace` attribute setting to pass through to the core service logic.

As an example, the following schema definition for the available replacement element will be ignored:

```
<xsd:schema xmlns:xsd="http://www.w3.org/2001/XMLSchema"
  targetNamespace="http://actioncon.com/schema/po"
  xmlns="http://actioncon.com/schema/po"
  version="1.1">
  <xsd:element name="LineItem" type="LineItemType"/>
  <xsd:complexType name="LineItemType">
    <xsd:sequence>
      <xsd:element name="productID" type="xsd:string"/>
      <xsd:element name="productName" type="xsd:string"/>
```

```
        <xsd:any namespace="##other" processContents="skip"
           minOccurs="0" maxOccurs="unbounded"/>
       </xsd:sequence>
       <xsd:anyAttribute namespace="##other"/>
      </xsd:complexType>
 </xsd:schema>

 <xsd:schema xmlns:xsd="http://www.w3.org/2001/XMLSchema"
    targetNamespace="http://actioncon.com/schema/po"
    xmlns:po2="http://actioncon.com/schema/po2"
    version="1.0">
    <xsd:element name="available" type="xsd:boolean"/>
 </xsd:schema>
```

Example 22.37

The processContents attribute of the xsd:any wildcard declaration set to a value of "skip."

How these attribute values affect your versioning approach depends on how much control you need to exercise over how replacement elements are defined. It is often advisable to begin with a setting of "strict" and to then only reduce it to "lax" or even "skip" when absolutely required. This way, you maintain a measure of control over replacement element definitions for as long as possible.

Once you move from "strict" to "lax" or from "lax" to "skip," you are effectively decreasing the constraint granularity of the operation. This means that you cannot reverse this setting without risking impact upon consumer programs.

SUMMARY OF KEY POINTS

- In support of the Loose versioning strategy, XML Schema wildcards can be used to allow a schema to accept unknown content.

- When making changes to schemas that include wildcards, UPA violations are a constant factor.

- The setting of the xsd:any element's namespace and processContents attributes help determine the range of allowable unknown content.

Chapter 23

Advanced Versioning

This chapter begins by covering policy versioning and continues with a collection of guidelines, techniques, and considerations for solving a range of different versioning problems that relate to WSDL, XML Schema, and WS-Policy.

23.1 Versioning Policies

A policy is a part of the service contract just as much as a schema is, and changing it is subject to the same types of governance issues. Therefore, when working with WS-Policy expressions and definitions, it is important to understand your options when it comes to versioning, because improper or ad-hoc transitions from one version of a policy to another can lead to significant interoperability issues.

Even though the WS-Policy language is comprised of a modest vocabulary of elements, it does provide some features that are very useful when it comes to managing versions of policies. Before we explore these, let's establish a base example that represents version 1.0:

```
<!-- Purchase Order Policy v1.0 -->
<wsp:Policy>
  <wsa:UsingAddressing/>
</wsp:Policy>
```

Example 23.1
Version 1.0 of a simple policy expression.

Adding an incompatible change to this policy would increment the major version number, as follows:

```
<!-- Purchase Order Policy v2.0 -->
<wsp:Policy>
  <wsa:UsingAddressing/>
  <wsrmp:RMAssertion/>
</wsp:Policy>
```

Example 23.2
A new policy assertion is added to the policy expression, thereby incrementing its version number.

On the other hand, a compatible change would only increment the minor version number. The upcoming sections will show some examples of compatible changes.

Alternatives

The fact that you can create optional policy alternatives lends itself extremely well to supporting backwards compatibility. For a given Web service contract, you could start out with the base policy expression from Example 23.1, and when the requirement comes along that you need to change the current policy assertion or add a new policy assertion, you can simply design this as a separate policy expression as part of a `wsp:ExactlyOne` policy alternative construct:

```
<wsp:Policy>
  <wsp:ExactlyOne>

  <!-- Purchase Order Policy v1.0 -->
    <wsp:All>
      <wsa:UsingAddressing/>
    </wsp:All>

  <!-- Purchase Order Policy v1.1 -->
    <wsp:All>
      <wsa:UsingAddressing/>
      <wsrmp:RMAssertion/>
    </wsp:All>

  </wsp:ExactlyOne>
</wsp:Policy>
```

Example 23.3
Version 1.1 of the policy expression which now provides an alternative containing two assertions.

You can continue adding new versions of a policy as additional alternatives. Each new policy expression is considered a compatible change because the alternative construct continues to preserve backwards compatibility.

Optional Assertions

The `wsp:Optional` attribute provides a convenient way to extend a Web service contract by adding an optional policy assertion as a compatible change.

In the following example, the `wsrmp:RMAssertion` policy assertion is inserted into an existing policy expression. Because it is tagged with `wsp:Optional="true"`, it provides optional functionality that can be disregarded by older consumers, and therefore is considered backwards compatible.

```
<!-- Purchase Order Policy v1.1 -->
<wsp:Policy>
  <wsa:UsingAddressing/>
  <wsrmp:RMAssertion wsp:Optional="true" />
</wsp:Policy>
```

Example 23.4
Version 1.1 of a policy expression that has been extended with an optional assertion.

As explained in Chapters 16 and 17, the `wsp:Optional` attribute is simply a shortcut that allows for simplified policy notation. A policy expression containing an optional assertion can also be expressed as a policy alternative, which makes a distinction between using `wsp:Optional` and creating a policy alternative construct somewhat irrelevant (especially considering that runtime processors convert expressions with this attribute to policy alternative structures, as explained at the end of Chapter 17).

However, from an interpretation perspective, it can be effective to use the `wsp:Optional` attribute to explicitly mark an assertion as optional for versioning purposes.

Ignorable Assertions

In Chapter 16 we explained that the primary difference between `wsp:Optional` and `wsp:Ignorable` is that the former indicates a non-mandatory processing option that consumers can choose to use or not, whereas the latter typically indicates a piece of processing that will be carried out, regardless of whether it is acknowledged by the consumer.

Taking this into consideration, is the addition of an ignorable assertion compatible or incompatible? Because you are expressing new functionality (which, presumably, corresponds to new behavior) about an existing Web service, extending the contract with an ignorable assertion usually warrants an incompatible change that will force a new major version number.

```
<!-- Purchase Order Policy v2.0 -->
<wsp:Policy>
  <wsa:UsingAddressing/>
  <custom:LogMessage wsp:Ignorable/>
</wsp:Policy>
```

Example 23.5

Version 2.0 of a policy expression that has been extended with an ignorable assertion considered an incompatible change.

Having stated that, though, it is really up to your discretion. Let's say you have an existing service with ten different consumers and you add a logging function to it that quietly logs certain types of data exchanges. You incorporate an ignorable assertion into your existing policy expression to indicate that logging does occur but that it will not change how your consumers currently interact with the service.

This scenario may justify an incompatible change when those consumers represent external business partners that need to reconsider their relationships with your Web service now that you are logging their transactions. On the other hand, in a modestly sized service inventory, you may have a controlled environment wherein you govern both the services and consumers. Would the addition of this ignorable assertion require you to produce a new Web service contract and subject all of your consumers to a new round of versioning? It really depends on the parameters established by your current policy standards.

Different Endpoints

An option other than using policy alternatives is to attach different policy versions directly to parts of the WSDL definition that can have more than one occurrence.

In the following example, version 1 of the `port` construct contains a policy without logging, whereas version 2 contains a policy with the ignorable logging assertion. This allows consumers to choose which version of the port they can bind to without forcing a whole new contract version due to the addition of the logging assertion.

```
<service name="svPurchaseOrder">
  <port name="purchaseOrder-http-soap12-v1"
    binding="tns:bdPO-SOAP12HTTP">
    <wsp:Policy>
```

```
      <wsam:Addressing>
    </wsp:Policy>
    <soap12:address location=
      "http://actioncon.com/services/soap12/po"/>
  </port>
  <port name="purchaseOrder-http-soap12-v2"
    binding="tns:bdPO-SOAP12HTTP">
    <wsp:Policy>
      <wsam:Addressing>
      <custom:LogMessage wsp:Ignorable/>
    </wsp:Policy>
    <soap12:address location=
      "http://actioncon.com/services/soap12/po"/>
  </port>
</service>
```

Example 23.6

A policy expression is attached to a second `port` element within a `service` construct.

Propagating Major Version Changes to WSDL Definitions

As with incompatible changes made to XML Schema components, incompatible WS-Policy changes will force a new contract version. This can have various results, depending on how and where the policy expression triggering the incompatible change is located.

NOTE

Be sure to revisit the *Designing External WS-Policy Definitions* section in Chapter 16 in order to re-familiarize yourself with how policy content can be separated into individual definition documents.

Attached Inline

If the policy is embedded within the WSDL definition, then it is a simple extension of the Web service contract, and an incompatible change results in a new contract version expressed in a new WSDL target namespace.

Independent Policy Definition

When policies are separated into separate definition files, they can be shared across multiple WSDL documents. This approach is usually taken when applying the Policy Centralization pattern.

In this type of architecture, the individual policy expressions may not belong to their own target namespace, resulting in the need to track policy version numbers using regular comments (as we have been doing in our examples so far). An incompatible change to one policy externally attached to one or more WSDL definitions will then need to be propagated to each WSDL document in order to increment the overall contract version and force a new WSDL target namespace.

Policy Definition Wrapped in a WSDL Definition

One alternative when creating independent policy definitions is to place policy expressions into separate WSDL definitions. This is sometimes done out of necessity when a platform does not support a regular policy definition document. However, this approach also provides us with the benefit of being able to assign the policies their own target namespaces, as per the `targetNamespace` attribute of the WSDL `definitions` element that contains the policy expressions.

In this case, incompatible changes to policies will result in a change to the policy definition's target namespace (which belongs to the WSDL document wrapping the policies), which will then impact any WSDL definition that imports the policy definition. The import statement will need to be updated, plus the incompatible change will further need to be propagated to the WSDL definition's own target namespace as well.

SUMMARY OF KEY POINTS

- Policy alternatives naturally support policy expression versioning by allowing different versions of the same expression to be presented as different alternatives.

- Similar to optional XML Schema components, adding optional assertions is considered a backwards-compatible change.

- Even though adding or modifying an ignorable assertion may not affect some consumers, it is typically classified as an incompatible change because the assertion is likely expressing a new or changed behavior of the service.

23.2 Defining "Non-Ignorable" Unknown Elements

As we explained in the previous chapter, extension features, like the use of wildcards, enable us to establish extensibility points within a type definition that can allow a broad range of unknown elements and data to be considered valid.

The service logic behind a Web service contract with extensibility points can be designed to process all possible variations of this unknown message content, or it can simply choose to ignore it.

This option makes Web service contract versioning flexible but also introduces other limitations. For example, what if we have a business requirement that disallows an element that is part of the unknown set to be ignored by the service? In this case we need to borrow a feature from the SOAP language that allows us to tag a given element as one that must be understood.

In this section we'll explore two techniques for tagging content as "non-ignorable."

Using a Custom `mustUnderstand` Attribute

As explained back in Chapter 11, SOAP provides a `mustUnderstand` attribute that can be attached to header blocks to force recipients to either process the header or raise a fault if they do not recognize it.

Following this concept, we can define a `mustUnderstand` attribute in our schema, allowing messages to add this attribute to unknown elements, as follows:

```xsd
<xsd:schema xmlns:xsd="http://www.w3.org/2001/XMLSchema"
  targetNamespace="http://actioncon.com/schema/po"
  xmlns="http://actioncon.com/schema/po">
  <xsd:element name="lineItem" type="LineItemType"/>
  <xsd:complexType name="LineItemType">
    <xsd:sequence>
      <xsd:element name="productID" type="xsd:string"/>
      <xsd:element name="productName" type="xsd:string"/>
      <xsd:any namespace="##any" processContents="lax"
        minOccurs="0" maxOccurs="unbounded"/>
    </xsd:sequence>
    <xsd:attribute name="mustUnderstand" type="xsd:boolean"/>
    <xsd:anyAttribute namespace="##any"/>
  </xsd:complexType>
</xsd:schema>
```

Example 23.7

An `xsd:attribute` declaration establishing the definition for the `mustUnderstand` attribute. Other attributes, can be optionally added to any element that is validated against the wildcard, as per the `xsd:anyAttribute` declaration.

The presence of this attribute definition enables messages to optionally include this attribute for any elements that are part of the unknown set.

An example of a message that takes advantage of the mustUnderstand attribute is provided here:

```
<LineItem xmlns="http://actioncon.com/schema/po">
  <productID>AY2345</productID>
  <productName>Service Blaster 2000</productName>
  <available mustUnderstand="true">
    true
  </available>
</LineItem>
```

Example 23.8
The available element with a custom mustUnderstand attribute set to "true."

Note that naming this attribute identically to the SOAP mustUnderstand attribute was simply our decision. It is a custom-defined attribute that can be named "cannotIgnore" or "acceptThis" or anything you like.

This also makes this a proprietary extension of a schema, meaning that any consumer programs that want to use it need to contain custom programming. The proprietary nature of this technique further limits the interoperability potential of any Web service contract that relies upon it.

Using the soap:mustUnderstand Attribute

Another approach altogether is to actually separate the unknown element from the message body and place it into a SOAP header. This way, it can be accompanied with the industry-standard soap:mustUnderstand attribute, as follows:

```
<soap:Envelope
  xmlns:soap="http://www.w3.org/2003/05/soap-envelope"
  xmlns="http://actioncon.com/schema/po">
  <soap:Header>
    <available soap:mustUnderstand="true">
      true
    </available>
  </soap:Header>
```

```
  <soap:Body>
    <lineItem>
      <productID>AY2345</productID>
      <productName>Service Blaster 2000</productName>
    </lineItem>
  </soap:Body>
</soap:Envelope>
```

Example 23.9

The `available` element being passed in a `soap:Header` construct, allowing it to use the standard `soap:mustUnderstand` attribute provided by the SOAP language.

To enable this message structure, the `available` element needs to be bound to the SOAP header within the WSDL `binding` construct:

```
<binding name="bdPO-SOAP12HTTP" type="abs:ptPurchaseOrder">
<soap12:binding style="document"
  transport="http://schemas.xmlsoap.org/soap/http"/>
  operation name="opSubmitOrder">
  <soap12:operation soapAction=
    "http://actioncon.com/submitOrder/request"
    soapActionRequired="true" required="true"/>
    <soap:header message="po:available" use="literal"/>
    <input><soap12:body use="literal"/></input>
    <output><soap12:body use="literal"/></output>
  </operation>
  ...
</binding>
```

Example 23.10

The binding syntax required to allow the `available` element to be passed as a SOAP header.

Although this approach may seem a bit out of the ordinary, it does provide a few benefits:

- The `LineItem` type definition does not need to be touched and does not require wildcards.

- The `available` element can be targeted for processing by intermediaries via the use of the `soap:actor` and `soap:role` features.

- Additional extension elements can be added in separate SOAP headers (each with their own `mustUnderstand` setting).

And, as previously mentioned, the fact that `available` and any other extension elements are transmitted together with the industry-standard `soap:mustUnderstand` attribute, the interoperability of the service is improved by avoiding the use of proprietary processing attributes. However, this approach can impose more complex message design and runtime processing requirements.

SUMMARY OF KEY POINTS

- There is no fully standardized way of communicating what part of the unknown content cannot be ignored.

- A custom `mustUnderstand` attribute can be used, or the content can be placed into a SOAP header, thereby allowing it to use the `soap:mustUnderstand` attribute.

23.3 Versioning and Schema Centralization

The Schema Centralization pattern advocates centrally positioning schemas that represent shared types, such as those related to common business documents like invoices and purchase orders. This way, an official data model for each business document can be expressed as a centralized schema that can then be shared by multiple Web service contracts.

As we explained in Chapter 22, any change that forces a new major version in a schema should do the same in its corresponding WSDL definition. But what happens if your XML Schema document is reused by several different WSDL definitions? As a general rule, the same versioning approach of propagating a new target namespace from a schema to any WSDL definition that imports that schema should be followed.

However, a case can be made to loosen this rule for schema types not associated with a service's functional context. This leads us to a distinction between primary and secondary schemas:

- *primary schema* – An XML Schema definition providing types that are directly related to a service's functional context. For example, Invoice and Invoice History schemas will likely be primary schemas for an Invoice service.

- *secondary schema* – A service may use types from an XML Schema definition that is not directly related to the service's functional context. In this case, the schema is considered a secondary schema in relation to that service. For example, a Purchase Order service using a type from the Invoice schema could classify the Invoice schema as secondary.

For primary schemas, the aforementioned rule should always be followed, even when service contracts do not use all of the types provided by the primary schema. For secondary schemas, however, there is a circumstance under which alternative methods can be considered.

For example, let's imagine we have a large centralized Invoice schema that contains many type definitions related to invoice documents. Our Purchase Order Web service contract imports this schema because it needs access to only one of the types that expresses one of the invoice header details.

In this case, depending on your versioning strategy, it may be considered reasonable to not force a new major version upon the Purchase Order WSDL definition when changes to types not used by that WSDL are made.

Instead, you could consider the following options:

- Separate commonly used secondary types into their own schema that acts as a module of a main schema used as a primary schema but that can also be imported independently as a secondary schema. In this case, the secondary schema module can exist in its own namespace. (When exploring this method, be sure to study the transitory limitations documented in Chapter 14.)

- Do not use namespaces when versioning secondary schemas and consider using `version` attributes that are propagated instead.

- Employ a manual system whereby namespaces are still used to force new major versions when incompatible changes are made to schema types, but each secondary schema is assessed prior to propagating the new version to the WSDL level to see if the change does, in fact, impact the message definitions in that WSDL document.

Other approaches can also be created, including the use of automated versioning tools that resolve dependencies between XML Schema and WSDL definitions.

NOTE

The management effort imposed by this approach can sometimes outweigh its benefits. Having to constantly determine what is and isn't included and dependent can turn into a significant governance responsibility.

23.4 Expressing Termination Information

As established by the Termination Notification design pattern, a proven method for supporting the smooth transitioning of one service version to another is to provide a standardized means of expressing termination information about the older service version.

Publicly available Web services published by organizations like Google and Yahoo often have retirement timeframes of three months or less. In corporate IT enterprises, it is not uncommon to give a Web service six months or more before permanently removing it. The amount of time allocated for retirement is often based on a number of factors, including:

- the amount of consumers currently using the service

- how many different consumer custodians or owners will be affected by the transition

- estimated cost of transitioning consumers to a new service version

- estimated risk and disruption resulting from the transition

Another circumstance under which the termination of a Web service needs to be planned ahead is when a service is intentionally only made available for a specific period of time. Perhaps it represents a "leased" service that is scheduled for termination on the date that the lease expires, or it could be a service that provides a temporary access point for an environment while the primary system is still in development.

Either way, once a termination date has been determined, it is ideally added to the actual Web service contract. The easiest and most primitive way to accomplish this is to simply annotate the WSDL definition using the documentation element:

```
<definitions name="PurchaseOrder" targetNamespace=
  "http://actioncon.com/contract/po" ...>
  <documentation>
    This service is scheduled for termination on Jan 31, 2010.
  </documentation>
```

```
...
</definitions>
```

Example 23.11

A human-readable annotation with termination details added via the **documentation** construct.

Although this is a simple approach, it limits the interpretation of the termination date to humans only. In order to make this information accessible to the service consumer, we can express it using a custom policy assertion.

Ignorable Termination Assertions

Termination identification lends itself well to the format of an ignorable policy assertion because it provides supplementary information to the consumer that it can decide to process or disregard, as shown here:

```
<wsp:Policy ...>
  <custom:termination wsp:Ignorable="true">
    Jan-31-2010
  </custom:termination>
</wsp:Policy>
```

Example 23.12

Termination information expressed via an ignorable policy assertion.

With this type of assertion, the consumer can be designed to check for the termination date prior to sending a request message to the service. But regardless of whether this assertion is processed or acknowledged, the service will terminate on the provided date. Additionally, the syntax of such a policy assertion is clear enough so that humans reading the contract can also understand it.

The ignorable termination assertion can further be incorporated into a policy alternative so that it only applies to the alternative that represents the old version of the policy, as shown here:

```
<wsp:Policy ...>
  <wsp:ExactlyOne>
    <wsp:All>
      <wsa:UsingAddressing/>
      <custom:termination wsp:Ignorable="true">
```

```
      Jan-31-2010
    </custom:termination>
  </wsp:All>
  <wsp:All>
    <wsa:UsingAddressing/>
    <wsrmp:RMAssertion/>
  </wsp:All>
  </wsp:ExactlyOne>
</wsp:Policy>
```

Example 23.13

The `custom:termination` assertion as part of a policy alternative.

One risk associated with using ignorable termination assertions is that consumers not designed to process the assertion can ignore it and therefore may attempt to use the service after its termination date. This is a problem that can be solved by making the termination assertions mandatory, as explained next.

Mandatory Termination Assertions

In a controlled environment, and especially when building a service inventory from the ground up, a strong case can be made to require that all Web service contracts use mandatory termination assertions.

Here is our example with a non-ignorable termination assertion:

```
<wsp:Policy ...>
  <custom:termination wsp:Ignorable="false">
    Jan-31-2010
  </custom:termination>
</wsp:Policy>
```

Example 23.14

A custom termination assertion that is not ignorable. (In this case, the `wsp:Ignorable` attribute could have been omitted altogether because it has a setting of "false" by default.)

Requiring the use of termination assertions on all Web services contracts accomplishes the following:

- All services acting as consumers within the service inventory boundary must be designed to acknowledge and process the termination assertion.

- The required use of this assertion enables any consumer to programmatically determine whether a service upon which it has formed a dependency will become unavailable. In response to this information, the consumer can issue a notification to its custodian or take other action.

- A Web service contract that has expired could remain published along with its termination assertion. This enables a consumer to check the assertion prior to attempting a data exchange with the service. If the termination date is later than the current date, the consumer could simply cease its attempt at invoking the service and thereby avoid an exception condition (and perhaps also issue a notification to its human custodian).

Establishing this type of convention across all services within an inventory can support their eventual governance by making versioning a process that is accommodated in advance as part of each service design.

To achieve this clearly requires a design standard that is consistently enforced. Furthermore, Web service contracts that are not scheduled for termination will still need to be equipped with this assertion, along with a special value that indicates their status:

```
<wsp:Policy ...>
  <custom:termination wsp:Ignorable="false">
    nil
  </custom:termination>
</wsp:Policy>
```

Example 23.15
An example of a custom value that expresses that the service has no current termination date.

Terminating Individual Operations

When extending a single Web service contract to support more than one version, it may become necessary to terminate an operation associated with a previous version. In this case, the same type of termination policy assertion we have been describing needs to be attached to the operation instead, as follows:

```
<binding name="bdPO" type="abs:ptPurchaseOrder">
  <operation name="opSubmitOrder">
    <wsp:Policy>
      <custom:termination wsp:Ignorable="true">
```

```
        Jan-31-2010
      </custom:termination>
    </wsp:Policy>
    <soap12bind:operation
      soapAction="http://action.com/submitOrder/request"
      soapActionRequired="true" required="true"/>
    <input>
      <soap12bind:body use="literal"/>
    </input>
    <output>
      <soap12bind:body use="literal"/>
    </output>
  </operation>
  <operation name="opSubmitOrders">
    <soap12bind:operation
      soapAction="http://action.com/submitOrder/request"
      soapActionRequired="true" required="true"/>
    <input>
      <soap12bind:body use="literal"/>
    </input>
    <output>
      <soap12bind:body use="literal"/>
    </output>
  </operation>
    ...
</binding>
```

Example 23.16

The ignorable `custom:termination` policy assertion attached to a specific operation.

In Chapter 21 we explained how different concrete descriptions can be versioned. In this type of contract architecture, each `binding` construct could be associated with a termination date. Additionally, you could have the option of terminating individual operations within the same `binding` construct on different dates, as demonstrated in the following example:

```
<definitions targetNamespace=
  "http://actioncon.com/contract/po/binding/v2"
  xmlns:tns=" http://actioncon.com/contract/po/binding/v2"
  xmlns:abs="http://actioncon.com/contract/po"
  xmlns="http://schemas.xmlsoap.org/wsdl/"
  xmlns:po="http://actioncon.com/schema/po"
```

```
xmlns:soap11="http://schemas.xmlsoap.org/wsdl/soap/">
<import
  namespace="http://actioncon.com/contract/po"
  location="http://actioncon.com/contract/po"/>
<binding name="bdPO-v2" type="abs:ptPurchaseOrder">
  <operation name="opSubmitOrder">
  <wsp:Policy>
    <custom:termination wsp:Ignorable="true">
      Jan-31-2009
    </custom:termination>
  </wsp:Policy>
  <soap12bind:operation
    soapAction="http://action.com/submitOrder/request"
    soapActionRequired="true" required="true"/>
  <input>
    <soap12bind:body use="literal"/>
  </input>
  <output>
    <soap12bind:body use="literal"/>
  </output>
</operation>
<operation name="opSubmitOrders">
  <wsp:Policy>
    <custom:termination wsp:Ignorable="true">
      Mar-07-2010
    </custom:termination>
  </wsp:Policy>
  <soap12bind:operation
    soapAction="http://action.com/submitOrder/request"
    soapActionRequired="true" required="true"/>
  <input>
    <soap12bind:body use="literal"/>
  </input>
  <output>
    <soap12bind:body use="literal"/>
  </output>
</operation>
  ...
</binding>
</definitions>
```

Example 23.17

Separate ignorable policies attached to different `operation` elements. Each assertion expresses a different termination date.

SUMMARY OF KEY POINTS

- Termination information can be expressed using human-readable annotations or ignorable policy assertions.

- Assertions can communicate the termination date of a service or its individual operations.

23.5 Working with Unknown Content

The Loose versioning technique introduced in Chapter 20 and further described in Chapter 22 is heavily based on the use of wildcards in support of both backwards and forwards compatibility. When basing a versioning strategy on this approach, you will inevitably run into situations where services and consumers will receive unknown content that is well beyond the contract's original defined set.

In this case, there are two clear options when it comes to how the recipient of a message with unknown content can behave:

- It can ignore the content and limit its processing to the content in the defined set.

- It can be designed to accommodate a specific subset of the unknown content. In this case it will process content that complies with the defined set or this subset, and will ignore anything else.

In both cases, the message recipient will need to decide what to do with the content it does not recognize or does not want to process. The default behavior when ignoring unknown content is to simply discard it. This may be appropriate in situations where a message recipient has firm limitations on what it needs from a given message.

However, there are often cases when this content can actually turn out to be meaningful. In these situations, services and consumer programs can be designed to follow the "accept and retain" technique.

Accept and Retain Unknown Content

In you refer back to the beginning of Chapter 22, you'll find the original definitions for the terms associated with content sets. The defined set represents content that corresponds to predefined schema components, whereas the unknown set represents unknown content that can be accepted as a result of the use of wildcards. We now finally get a chance to explore the recognized set, which refers to the defined set plus whatever part of the unknown content a program has been designed to accept.

When following the "accept and retain" approach, we are essentially extending the design of a service or consumer so that, after accepting both defined and recognized content, it does not discard the remaining unknown content. Instead, it stores it somewhere for future reference.

There are several reasons why it may be a good idea to retain this "extra" data:

- The data may provide additional context information that further adds meaning to the recognized content that has been accepted.

- The data may be meaningful in the future or it may be useful to other parts of the solution.

- The data may serve as a valuable logging reference.

- There may only be one opportunity to capture the data.

Especially when using Web services to exchange data with external organizations, being able to collect all information in a message beyond the recognized set may prove to be valuable.

Let's revisit our familiar message design where the base `LineItem` element has been extended with the `available` element:

```
<lineItem>
  <productID>AY2345</productID>
  <productName>Service Blaster 2000</productName>
  <available>true</available>
</lineItem>
```

Example 23.18
The `available` element extending the `LineItem` construct.

To keep things simple, let's imagine that our service is not designed to process anything outside of the defined set. This means that the `available` construct is beyond the recognized set and therefore falls into the category of unknown content that we can discard or retain.

By choosing to keep this information, we need to create a repository capable of storing unknown data. A simple database table design that allows us to effectively store any excess content into a generic field is shown here:

Any unknown data that is beyond the recognized set can be placed into a generic Extensions column, which allows this data to remain associated with the recognized set.

ProductID	ProductName	Extensions

AY2345	Service Blaster 2000	`<available>`
		`    true`
		`</available>`

Table 23.1
A Line Item table with an Extensions column.

By retaining the extra data, the service can be later evolved to "understand" extension elements, such as `available`, by adding new columns in the table to represent these elements, as follows:

What Table 23.2 essentially represents is an implementation of version 2 of a Web service that now includes `available` as part of its recognized set.

ProductID	ProductName	Available	Extensions
AY2345	Service Blaster 2000	true	

Table 23.2
An Available column added to the preceding Line Item table.

One thing we lose by separating the data in this manner is any further context information related to the original structure of the XML document. If you feel this might also be worth retaining, you can consider the following table design instead:

Even though this table duplicates some data, it preserves the original XML hierarchy and any significance this structure may have.

ProductID	ProductName	Raw

AY2345	Service Blaster 2000	`<lineItem>`
		`    <productID>`
		`        AY2345`
		`    </productID>`
		`    <productName>`
		`        Service Blaster 2000`
		`    </productName>`
		`    <available>`
		`        true`
		`    </available>`
		`</lineItem>`

Table 23.3
The Line Item table with a Raw column that can contain entire XML documents.

> **NOTE**
>
> Over time, this approach can consume large amounts of storage space, which may make it unsuitable for some environments.

Using a mustRetain Flag

Earlier in this chapter we introduced the mustUnderstand attribute that can be added to unknown content in a message in order to require that recipients process the content or reject the message altogether.

You can apply a similar approach in support of designing services with the retain and accept model. Messages that include unknown content can be further equipped with a mustRetain flag that indicates that services capable of capturing and storing data beyond the recognized set do so. This can then be applied to select pieces of content that the message designer considers relevant.

When consistently used with services throughout a service inventory, this type of attribute can act as a "catch all" by ensuring that certain types of unknown data are never lost.

Of course, as with the mustUnderstand attribute, the use of the mustRetain flag represents a proprietary extension to the XML Schema language, and therefore relies on the consistent use of design standards and custom programming.

```
<lineItem>
  <productID>AY2345</productID>
  <productName>Service Blaster 2000</productName>
  <available mustRetain="true">
    true
  </available>
</lineItem>
```

Example 23.19
The available element extended via a custom mustRetain attribute.

SUMMARY OF KEY POINTS

- Unknown content that is not understood by a message recipient can still be retained for future use.

- A custom mustRetain attribute can be used to indicate which part of the unknown content needs to be kept and stored.

23.6 Partial Validation

With agnostic services especially, service contracts often need to be designed in a generic manner that allows individual operations to fulfill data exchange requirements that can satisfy multiple different types of service consumers. This is the fundamental approach to achieving the goals of the Service Reusability design principle.

However, a possible side-effect of publishing generic service contracts is that a given operation may provide more functionality or more data than a particular consumer actually needs. This can result in consumers having to validate more message content than necessary.

Knowing this in advance gives us the opportunity to streamline the design of service consumers by taking a closer look at the XML Schema definitions of the services that they need to interact with. On many occasions (and especially with agnostic services), there will be contracts with a defined set that goes beyond the consumer's requirements.

It is in this situation where a pattern known as Partial Validation can be applied. This design technique essentially allows a consumer designer to adjust (usually by reducing) the defined set of a service contract, as it will be validated by a specific consumer program.

Let's revisit our familiar `LineItem` message as an example:

```
<lineItem>
  <productID>AY2345</productID>
  <productName>Service Blaster 2000</productName>
  <available>true</available>
</lineItem>
```

Example 23.20
Only the `productID` element is actually required by the consumer receiving this message.

A consumer designed to invoke the `GetItem` operation of the Purchase Order service will, by default, receive a message like this. However, this particular consumer does not require the product name or information about the product availability. This consumer only needs the product ID, and by applying this pattern, it is designed to behave as follows upon the arrival of this message:

1. Locate the `productID` element (perhaps using an XPath expression).

2. Validate the `productID` value.

3. Disregard and discard the rest of the message.

Although this technique places some extra development effort upon the consumer owner in order to extract the relevant defined set from the original message defined set, it has several benefits, including:

- By limiting validation to a subset of a contract's defined set, this pattern ends up supporting the Service Loose Coupling design principle by decreasing dependencies between consumers and services.

- The impact of subsequent contract versions is reduced due to the increased loose coupling between consumers and service contracts.

Even if incompatible changes inadvertently make their way into an established Web service contract, the risk that they will negatively affect existing consumers is lowered when those consumers are programmatically designed to only retrieve what they need from the contract's defined set. In other words, what would normally be an incompatible change that ends up breaking a contract may, in fact, be a compatible change to some consumers of the contract when those consumers are only dependent on a part of the contract that was not affected by the incompatible change.

It is important to keep in mind that this design approach is intended for consumers only. The golden rule in Web service contract versioning is that services (or service providers) should always maintain the integrity of the defined set that their contracts provide. It is only the individual consumers that have the freedom of choosing what parts of that defined set they want to accept and process.

Validation by Projection

When subsequent versions of a contract are created, each can extend the scope of the underlying schemas. The previous sections and chapters have shown us many examples of this. We've also seen how regardless of whether a schema is extended via a compatible or incompatible change, it can result in the issuance of messages that contain extra content represented by the unknown set.

A form of Partial Validation known as "validation by projection" is based on a technique whereby a consumer only validates the defined set of a message and ignores all unknown content. It accomplishes this by simply removing unknown content from the message prior to validation.

In the following example, a message with unknown content is generated:

```
<lineItem xmlns="http://actioncon.com/schema/po"
  xmlns:po2="...">
  <productID>AY2345</productID>
  <productName>Service Blaster 2000</productName>
  <po2:available>true</po2:available>
</lineItem>
```

Example 23.21
The content represented by the `po2:available` element is not part of the defined set.

The consumer receiving this message transforms the message so that unknown content is removed, resulting in a message that only contains content that corresponds to the contract's defined set:

```
<lineItem xmlns="http://actioncon.com/schema/po">
  <productID>AY2345</productID>
  <productName>Service Blaster 2000</productName>
</lineItem>
```

Example 23.22
The subset of the previous message (minus the `po2:available` content) is considered the "projection" of the original message.

This approach is suitable for consumers that simply do not require any more from a given message than what is expressed in the defined set. By applying the validation by projection technique, these consumers always strip messages down to their defined set irrespective of the version of the contract that the message was generated from.

This essentially guarantees that a consumer will always remain in compliance with a specific version of the contract as long as that contract remains supported by the Web service. The result is a baseline level of interoperability between a service and some of its consumers that is never impacted by future versioning, as long as the defined set does not change.

> **NOTE**
>
> This approach assumes that the consumer is in full control over the message when it arrives over the wire. Some toolkits promote the creation of client stubs based on a service contract, and will not deliver an entire message to the consumer. Instead they turn it into native objects, in which case this approach will not work with messages that contain unknown content.

SUMMARY OF KEY POINTS

- Service consumer programs can be designed to only validate and recognize the parts of a message that are relevant to them.

- This approach is formalized by the Partial Validation pattern.

23.7 Versioning Message Instances

> **NOTE**
>
> The following section is not directly related to contract versioning, but is provided simply to demonstrate the use of version identifiers for runtime message versioning purposes. Feel free to skip over this section if you want to continue reading about contract versioning.

An age-old challenge associated with updating a database is dealing with concurrent access. If you have more than one program updating data in the same table, you run the risk of compromising the integrity of that data.

There are pessimistic locking approaches that freeze a table or a row in a table until a particular program has completed an update. For performance reasons, some prefer the optimistic method that allows multiple programs to access the same data and relies on a different means of sorting out a clash.

One way to support the optimistic locking approach is to leverage some of the versioning identifiers we introduced back in Chapter 20. In this case, we're not versioning the Web service contract; instead, we apply version numbers to different *instances* of a message. These version numbers are then further stored by the service (either in memory or alongside the actual data, in the database) and are used to ensure that only updates to the correct version of the data can occur.

Let's study the following sequence of events related to a series of messages based on the `lineItem` element. In this scenario we have two consumers accessing the same data via the same service.

This first message is what consumer #1 retrieves:

```
<lineItem xmlns="http://actioncon.com/schema/po/v1"
  version="1.0">
  <productID>AY2345</productID>
```

```
   <productName>Service Blaster 2000</productName>
</lineItem>
```

Notice how the service has attached the `version="1.0"` attribute setting. The consumer can update the data in this message, but is not allowed to change this attribute.

Next, we have consumer #2 retrieving the same data:

```
<lineItem xmlns="http://actioncon.com/schema/po/v1"
  version="1.0">
  <productID>AY2345</productID>
  <productName>Service Blaster 2000</productName>
</lineItem>
```

Here again, the `lineItem` instance contains the `version="1.0"` setting because the data has not yet changed.

Now consumer #1 changes the data by adding the `available` element, as follows:

```
<lineItem xmlns="http://actioncon.com/schema/po/v1"
  version="1.0">
  <productID>AY2345</productID>
  <productName>Service Blaster 2000</productName>
  <available>true</available>
</lineItem>
```

After the preceding change is made, consumer #2 attempts to submit its own change, which includes an updated `productName` value.

```
<lineItem xmlns="http://actioncon.com/schema/po/v1"
  version="1.0">
  <productID>AY2345</productID>
  <productName>Service Blaster 2006</productName>
</lineItem>
```

However, in the meantime, the service processed the update from consumer #1 and incremented the version number associated with this data set to "1.1." Therefore, when the updated data from consumer #2 is received, the service realizes that the version number is still "1.0" and rejects the message in order to avoid a clash.

In response to having its update rejected, consumer #2 retrieves the new version of the data, which now has the `version="1.1"` attribute setting attached to it:

```
<lineItem xmlns="http://actioncon.com/schema/po/v1"
  version="1.1">
```

```
  <productID>AY2345</productID>
  <productName>Service Blaster 2000</productName>
  <available>true</available>
</lineItem>
```

With the latest data set on hand, consumer #2 makes its change to the productName element and re-submits the update:

```
<lineItem xmlns="http://actioncon.com/schema/po/v1"
  version="1.1">
  <productID>AY2345</productID>
  <productName>Service Blaster 2006</productName>
  <available>true</available>
</lineItem>
```

The service matches the "1.1" version number in the message with the "1.1" number it has on record for this data set and accepts the update. Subsequently, the version number is incremented to "1.2" for the next message exchange.

This preceding example demonstrates one possible application of this design technique. Other variations can certainly be developed. In the end, though, this again relies on a custom attribute (or perhaps a custom header) that requires a corresponding amount of custom programming in both services and consumers.

SUMMARY OF KEY POINTS

- Version identifiers can be incorporated into message content when performing data access functions.

- This approach can be used to support optimistic database locking.

23.8 Customizing a Versioning Strategy

The past four chapters have explored versioning from the perspective of three common approaches. As mentioned back in Chapter 20, these strategies can be considered a starting point and you have the ability to fully customize them to suit your own versioning (and governance) requirements.

These remaining sections provide some examples of known strategies that are variations of the strategies and techniques we've covered so far, followed by a brief discussion of some alternative version identification conventions.

Custom Strategies for Schema Versioning

Compatible and Incompatible Changes in New Namespaces

This strategy is based on the following rules:

1. When a compatible change occurs, existing XML Schema components remain in their existing namespace.

2. When a compatible XML Schema component is added, that component is associated with a new namespace.

3. When any type of incompatible change is made, then a new namespace is created for the existing components and any new components.

In order to enforce these rules, a design standard must be in place that requires that any new incompatible schema component (such as the addition of a new required element or the increase of constraint granularity) results in a new target namespace for the entire schema of the message definition. Also, wildcards must use the `namespace="##other"` setting that requires that all new compatible schema components be placed into a new namespace.

Compatible Changes in Existing Namespaces, Incompatible Changes in New Namespaces

This strategy is based on the following rules:

1. When a compatible change occurs, existing components remain in their existing namespace.

2. When a compatible schema component is added, that component is associated with the existing namespace.

3. When any type of incompatible change is made, then a new namespace is created for the existing components and any new components.

In order to enforce these rules, one design standard is needed to ensure that any new compatible schema component is placed in the same namespace, and another design standard is required to guarantee that when an incompatible change occurs, a new target namespace is created for the entire schema of the message definition. Also wildcards must use the `namespace="##any"` setting that allows newly added compatible schema components to be placed into the existing namespace but also enables them to exist in different namespaces, if required.

Version Identification Conventions

Part of an overall versioning plan will include a standard means of identifying and expressing version numbers. The convention we've been using so far simply requires the use of annotation elements for major and minor versions and namespaces for major version numbers only.

Other conventions may be based on the standardized use of custom elements or attributes to express version numbers along with the optional use of namespaces. Alternatively, namespaces may be disallowed altogether for versioning purposes in order to avoid having to break XPath and XQuery statements that might be embedded in programming code used to search or parse message documents.

When defining version identification conventions, it is important to ensure that these standards are compatible with your overall versioning strategy. You can determine this by exploring whether there are conflicting limitations. For example, the version identification option we just described that disallowed the use of namespaces cannot be combined with either of the two preceding custom strategies. However, it may be compatible with the Strict or Flexible approaches, as long as they are carried out without the use of namespaces.

SUMMARY OF KEY POINTS

- The three versioning approaches explored over the past four chapters can be further customized.

- A custom versioning strategy will typically be comprised of rules that govern major and minor version increases plus version identification conventions.

Part IV

Appendices

Appendix A

Case Study Conclusion

Throughout the chapters in this book, Steve from ActionCon has applied different technologies and techniques to the design of the Purchase Order and Game Web service contracts in support of the following ActionCon business goals:

- Establish a Web presence for increased access to information about game products.

- Establish an online contact point that can facilitate orders submitted by larger retailers, such as MegaEuroMart.

These goals need to be achieved in alignment with the overarching SOA adoption initiative that is underway at ActionCon.

As a result of his experiences, Steve was able to accomplish the following:

- Design balanced data representation models for individual message exchange requirements using basic and advanced features of the XML Schema Definition Language.

- Design the foundation of the Web service contracts using the appropriate version and feature set of the Web Services Description Language.

- Extend the Web service contracts with policies via the use of the WS-Policy Framework.

- Design fundamental message body and header sections using the SOAP language.

- Extend the message designs using features from and patterns associated with the WS-Addressing language.

- Establish an appropriate versioning strategy for the WSDL, XML Schema, and WS-Policy content that comprises the Web service contracts and that accommodates the goals and preferences of the ActionCon IT enterprise.

The eventual deployment of the Purchase Order and Game Web services will lay the foundation for the consistent delivery of future Web service contracts, as a result of the following factors:

- Numerous design standards and conventions will have resulted from the research and development of these initial services.

- ActionCon has the opportunity to leverage the experiences of Steve and others involved in the design of the Web service contracts in order to create formal service-oriented design processes that are tuned for ActionCon's environment and preferences. This can result in a custom methodology that will accommodate the consistent delivery of many future Web services.

- By further determining an effective versioning strategy, ActionCon is well underway toward establishing a long-term governance plan that will help them deliver numerous services as part of a larger service inventory.

- As a result of exploring the potential application of technical policies via the use of the WS-Policy standard, ActionCon will be able to further refine their governance plan in relation to policy expression and administration (which can also carry over into the determination of what will and will not be included in human-readable SLAs).

- With the knowledge of the industry standards and contract-related technologies gained by Steve and others, ActionCon will be able to better assess SOA-related tools, products, and platforms for future services they intend to build as Web services.

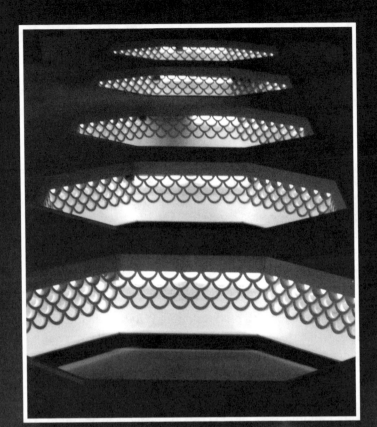

Appendix B

How Technology Standards are Developed

The W3C is an international consortium focused on developing Web-based industry technology standards. Its mission is to lead the World Wide Web to its full potential by developing protocols and guidelines that ensure long-term growth for the Web as a multi-purpose medium.

Tim Berners-Lee founded the W3C in 1994, as risks of segmentation across the Web were becoming apparent (especially with multiple versions of HTML being worked on simultaneously). Ever since, the W3C has made it a priority to develop core Web technologies (HTML, XML, etc.) and related styling languages (CSS, XSLT, etc.).

Today, Web services are heavily reliant upon W3C-developed technologies. The following Web services technologies described in this book have been produced by W3C committees:

- XML Schema 1.0

- WSDL 1.1, 2.0

- SOAP 1.1, 1.2

- WS-Addressing 1.0

- WS-Policy 1.5

How Standards are Developed

In order to fully appreciate Web service technologies, it is important to understand the processes used to develop technology specifications into ratified industry standards.

It all begins with an idea for a new technology. When there is sufficient interest in the community for this idea, the W3C holds an open workshop. Interested parties gather to discuss the scope of the problem addressed by the technology and the proposed solutions offered by the technology.

When it comes to Web services, vendor organizations typically advocate technologies that they developed independently or in partnership. Although these technologies usually address issues that are important to those vendors, there is a desire to make them part of the non-proprietary Web services framework. If there is sufficient agreement among W3C participants, the proposed technology becomes the basis for creating an industry standard.

The Standards Development Process

The first step in the lifespan of a W3C technology specification is the formation of a working group responsible for defining the target standard. This group will be comprised of W3C members, which are generally a mix of vendor representatives and practitioners. The W3C also provides supporting technical staff that help ensure that the technology will fully complement the rest of the already developed industry standards.

This group then develops a specification through the following phases:

1. *Working Draft* – This is a snapshot of the specification that is released regularly to keep the community aware of the direction taken by the working group and to gather early comments.

2. *Last Call Working Draft* – When the working group believes that the specification meets all of its original requirements, it will issue this document and formally request comments from the community. This step typically lasts at least three weeks.

3. *Candidate Recommendation* – Having incorporated feedback from the previous phase, the working group calls for the implementation of the specification to ensure that it is in fact implementable and interoperable.

4. *Proposed Recommendation* – Having demonstrated that the specification has been successfully implemented in an interoperable way, it is presented to the W3C Advisory Committee for ratification. This step lasts a minimum of four weeks.

5. *Recommendation* – The specification is approved as a W3C Recommendation, which is commonly referred to as an "industry standard."

The duration of the whole process varies depending on the scope and complexity of the specification being developed. From the moment a working group is formed, it could take anywhere from 18 months to several years to deliver a W3C Recommendation.

Throughout these stages, the public may comment on the technology specification being developed by submitting feedback to which the working group is obligated to respond. All communication between working group members and all deliverables created by the group are published for open, public access.

> **NOTE**
>
> While these steps are arranged in a natural and progressive order, a specification may be returned to an earlier phase if major issues arise.

There are two other types of W3C documents worth mentioning:

1. *Working Group Note* – This is an informal specification developed by a working group not required to go through the standards ratification process. Notes can address a range of issues and are often created to supplement existing standards efforts.

2. *Member Submission* – This is an externally created specification submitted by W3C members for consideration by the W3C. The W3C technical team always writes a comment to formally acknowledge the document and to give some perspective on the specification. Sometimes, submission documents become the starting point for the previously described standards development steps.

One particularity of the W3C is that its process is based on consensus, meaning that the whole working group needs to agree on a solution before making a decision. Votes are taken only in case of deep disagreement, and any decision taken via a vote is generally scrutinized during the remainder of the process.

> **NOTE**
>
> To learn more about the W3C and other standards organizations, visit www.soaspecs.com.

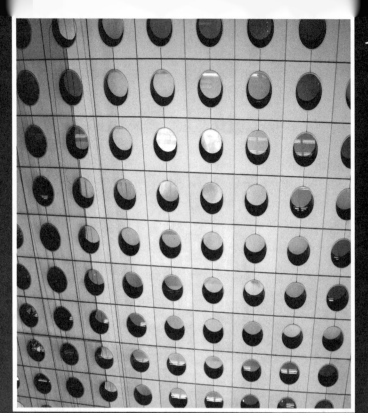

Alphabetical Pseudo Schema Reference

Pseudo schemas provide a representation of elements and attributes from different languages via a common industry-standard expression syntax based on a special set of symbols. This format is helpful for reference purposes to provide an abstract view of a given component that explains how it can be potentially structured and populated.

The symbol convention used is as follows:

- The ? symbol indicates that a component can occur zero or once.
- The * symbol indicates that a component can occur zero or multiple times.
- The + symbol indicates that a component must occur once or multiple times.
- The [and] symbols are used to represent groups.
- The | symbol represents a choice.

The remainder of this appendix provides a master list of almost all the language components described or referenced in this book. The components are organized in alphabetical order by their component name. For clarity's sake, common prefixes have been omitted.

Action Element (WS-Addressing 1.0)

```
<Action>
  xsd:anyURI
</Action>
```

Address Element (WS-Addressing 1.0)

```
<Address>
  xsd:anyURI
</Address>
```

All Element (WS-Policy 1.5)

```
<wsp:All>
 [wsp:Policy |
  wsp:All |
  wsp:ExactlyOne |
  wsp:PolicyReference |
  ElementFromOtherNameSpace]*
</wsp:All>
```

`all` Element (XML Schema 1.0)

```
<all minOccurs="0|1"? maxOccurs="1"?>
  <element/>*
</all>
```

`any` Element (XML Schema 1.0)

```
<any processContents="lax|strict|skip"?
  namespace="##any|##other|##local|##targetNamespace|
  list of uris"?
  minOccurs="integer"? maxOccurs="integer|unbounded"?
/>*
```

`anyAttribute` Element (XML Schema 1.0)

```
<anyAttribute processContents="lax|strict|skip"?
  namespace="##any|##other|##local|##targetNamespace|
  list of uris"?
/>*
```

`attribute` Element (global declaration, child of `schema`) (XML Schema 1.0)

```
<attribute name="NCName" type="QName"?>*
  <simpleType/>?
</attribute>
```

`attribute` Element (local declaration, child of `complexType`) (XML Schema 1.0)

```
<attribute name="NCName" type="QName"?
  use="required|optional"?>*
  <simpleType/>?
</attribute>
```

`attribute` Element (local reference, child of `complexType`) (XML Schema 1.0)

```
<attribute ref="QName" use="required|optional"?/>*
```

`binding` Element (WSDL 1.1)

```
<binding name="NCName" type="QName">*
  <documentation/>?
  <-- extension -->*
  <operation name="NCName"/>*
</binding>
```

`binding` Element (WSDL 2.0)

```
<binding name="xsd:NCName" interface="xsd:QName"?>*
  <documentation/>?
  <fault ref="xsd:QName"/>*
  <operation ref="xsd:QName"/>*
  <-- extension -->*
</binding>
```

`Body` Element (SOAP 1.1)

```
<Body>
  xsd:any*
</Body>
```

`Body` Element (SOAP 1.2)

```
<Body>
  xsd:any*
</Body>
```

`choice` Element (XML Schema 1.0)

```
<choice minOccurs="integer"? maxOccurs="integer|unbounded"?>
  [ <sequence/> | <choice/> | <element/> | <group/> ]*
</choice>
```

`Code` Element (SOAP 1.2)

```
<Code>
  <Value>
    [soap:DataEncodingUnknown |
     soap:MustUnderstand |
     soap:Receiver |
     soap:Sender |
     soap:VersionMismatch]
  </Value>
  <Subcode>
    ...
  </Subcode>?
</Code>
```

`complexContent` Element (XML Schema 1.0)

```
<complexContent>?
  <extension base="QName">
  [ <sequence/> | <choice/> | <all/> | <group/> ]?
    <attribute/>*
  </extension>
</complexContent>
```

`complexType` Element (global definition, child of `schema`) (XML Schema 1.0)

```
<complexType name="NCName" mixed="boolean"?>*
  [ <sequence/> | <choice/> | <all/> |
    <complexContent/> | <simpleContent> | <group/>  ]?
  <attribute/>*
</complexType>
```

complexType Element (local definition, child of element) (XML Schema 1.0)

```
<complexType mixed="boolean"?>?
  [ <sequence/> | <choice/> | <all/> |
    <complexContent/> | <simpleContent/> | <group/> ]?
  <attribute/>*
</complexType>
```

definitions Element (WSDL 1.1)

```
<definitions name="NMToken"? targetNamespace="anyURI"?>
  <documentation/>?
  <import/>*
  <types/>?
  <message/>*
  [<portType/> | <binding/> | <service/>]*
  <-- extension -->*
</definitions>
```

description Element (WSDL 2.0)

```
<description>
  <documentation/>?
  [<import/> | <include/> | <-- extension -->*]*
  <types/>?
  [<interface/> | <binding/> | <service/>
   | <-- extension -->* ]*
</description>
```

detail Element (SOAP 1.1)

```
<detail>
  xsd:any*
</detail>?
```

Detail Element (SOAP 1.2)

```
<Detail>
  xsd:any*
</Detail>
```

element Element (global declaration, child of schema) (XML Schema 1.0)

```
<element name="NCName" type="QName"?>*
  [ <simpleType/> | <complexType/> ]?
  [ <key name="NCName"/> | <keyRef name="NCName"
    refer="QName"/> ]*
</element>
```

element Element (local declaration, child of sequence, choice or all) (XML Schema 1.0)

```
<element name="NCName" type="QName"?
  minOccurs="integer"? maxOccurs="integer|unbounded"?>*
  [ <simpleType/> | <complexType/> ]?
</element>
```

element Element (local reference, child of schema) (XML Schema 1.0)

```
<element ref="QName"
  minOccurs="integer"?
  maxOccurs="integer|unbounded"?/>*
```

endpoint Element (WSDL 2.0)

```
<endpoint name="xsd:NCName" binding="xsd:QName"
  address="uri"/>*
  <documentation/>?
  <-- extension -->*
</endpoint>
```

EndpointReference Element (WS-Addressing 1.0)

```
<EndpointReference>
  <Address>
    xsd:anyURI
  </Address>
  <ReferenceParameters>
    xsd:any*
  </ReferenceParameters> ?
  <Metadata>
    xsd:any*
  </Metadata>?
</EndpointReference>
```

enumeration Element (XML Schema 1.0)

```
<enumeration value="anyType"/>*
```

Envelope Element (SOAP 1.1)

```
<Envelope>
  <Header>
    xsd:any*
  </Header>?
  <Body>
    xsd:any*
  </Body>
</Envelope>
```

`Envelope` Element (SOAP 1.2)

```
<Envelope>
  <Header>
    xsd:any*
  </Header>?
  <Body>
    xsd:any*
  </Body>
</Envelope>
```

`ExactlyOne` Element (WS-Policy 1.5)

```
<ExactlyOne>
  [wsp:Policy |
   wsp:All |
   wsp:ExactlyOne |
   wsp:PolicyReference |
   ElementFromOtherNameSpace]*
</ExactlyOne>
```

`extension` Element (child of `complexContent`) (XML Schema 1.0)

```
<extension base="QName">
  [ <sequence/> | <choice/> | <all/> | <group/> ]?
  <attribute/>*
</extension>
```

`extension` Element (child of `simpleContent`) (XML Schema 1.0)

```
<extension base="QName">
  <attribute/>*
</extension>
```

`Fault` Element (SOAP 1.1)

```
<Fault>
  <faultcode>
    xsd:QName
  </faultcode>
  <faultstring>
    xsd:string
  </faultstring>
  <faultactor>
    xsd:anyURI
  </faultactor>?
  <detail>
    xsd:any*
  </detail>?
</Fault>
```

Fault Element (SOAP 1.2)

```
<Fault>
  <Code>
    ...
  </Code>
  <Reason>
    <Text xml:lang="xsd:string">
      xsd:String
    </Text>+
  </Reason>
  <Node>
    xsd:anyURI
  </Node>?
  <Role>
    xsd:anyURI
  </Role>?
  <Detail>
    xsd:any*
  </Detail>?
</Fault>
```

fault Element of **binding** Element (WSDL 2.0)

```
<fault ref="xsd:QName">*
  <documentation/>?
  <-- extension -->*
</fault>
```

fault Element of **interface** Element (WSDL 2.0)

```
<fault name="xsd:NCName" element="xsd:QName"?>*
  <documentation/>?
  <-- extension -->*
</fault>
```

faultcode Element (SOAP 1.1)

```
<faultcode>
  xsd:QName
</faultcode>
```

faultstring Element (SOAP 1.1)

```
<faultstring>
  xsd:string
</faultstring>
```

FaultTo Element (WS-Addressing 1.0)

```
<FaultTo>
  wsa:EndpointReferenceType
</FaultTo>
```

field Element (XML Schema 1.0)

```
<field xpath="string"/>
```

fractionDigits Element (XML Schema 1.0)

```
<fractionDigits value="integer"/>?
```

From Element (WS-Addressing 1.0)

```
<From>
  wsa:EndpointReferenceType
</From>
```

group Element (global definition, child of schema) (XML Schema 1.0)

```
<group name="NCName">*
  [ <sequence/> | <choice/> | <all/> ]
</group>
```

group (Element reference, descendant of a complexType) (XML Schema 1.0)

```
<group ref="QName"
  minOccurs="integer"? maxOccurs="integer|unbounded"?/>*
```

Header Element (SOAP 1.1)

```
<Header>
  xsd:any*
</Header>
```

Header Element (SOAP 1.2)

```
<Header>
  xsd:any*
</Header>
```

Ignorable Attribute (WS-Policy 1.5)

```
<Assertion Name wsp:Ignorable="xsd:boolean"?>
  ...
</Assertion Name>
```

import Element (WSDL 1.1)

```
<import namespace="uri" location="uri">*
  <documentation/>?
</import>
```

import Element (WSDL 2.0)

```
<import namespace="uri" location="uri">*
  <documentation/>?
  <-- extension -->*
</import>
```

import Element (XML Schema 1.0)

```
<import namespace="uri" schemaLocation="uri"?/>*
```

include Element (XML Schema 1.0)

```
<include schemaLocation="uri"/>*
```

interface Element (WSDL 2.0)

```
<interface name="xsd:NCName" extends="list of xsd:QName"?
  styleDefault="list of xsd:anyURI"?>*
  <documentation/>?
  <fault name="xsd:NCName" element="xsd:QName"?/>*
  <operation name="xsd:NCName"
    pattern="xsd:anyURI"
    style="list of xsd:anyURI"?
    wsdlx:safe="xsd:boolean"?/>*
  <-- extension -->*
</interface>
```

key Element (XML Schema 1.0)

```
<key name="NCName">*
  <selector xpath="string"/>
  <field xpath="string"/>+
</key>
```

keyref Element (XML Schema 1.0)

```
<keyref name="NCName" refer="QName">*
  <selector xpath="string"/>
  <field xpath="string"/>+
</keyref>
```

length Element (XML Schema 1.0)

```
<length value="integer"/>?
```

maxExclusive Element (XML Schema 1.0)

```
<maxExclusive value="anyType"/>?
```

maxInclusive Element (XML Schema 1.0)

```
<maxInclusive value="anyType"/>?
```

maxLength Element (XML Schema 1.0)

```
<maxLength value="integer"/>?
```

`message` Element (WSDL 1.1)

```
<message name="NCName">*
  <documentation .../>?
  <part name="NMToken" element="QName"? type="QName"?/>*
</message>
```

`MessageID` Element (WS-Addressing 1.0)

```
<MessageID>
  xsd:anyURI
</MessageID>
```

`Metadata` Element (WS-Addressing 1.0)

```
<Metadata>
  xsd:any*
</Metadata>
```

`minExclusive` Element (XML Schema 1.0)

```
<minExclusive value="anyType"/>?
```

`minInclusive` Element (XML Schema 1.0)

```
<minInclusive value="anyType"/>?
```

`minLength` Element (XML Schema 1.0)

```
<minLength value="integer"/>?
```

`Node` Element (SOAP 1.2)

```
<Node>
  xsd:anyURI
</Node>
```

`NotUnderstood` Element (SOAP 1.2)

```
<NotUnderstood QName="xsd:QName"/>
```

`operation` of `binding` Element (WSDL 1.1)

```
<operation name="NCName">*
  <documentation/>?
  <-- extension -->*
  <input>?
    <documentation/>?
    <-- extension -->*
  </input>
  <output>?
    <documentation/>?
    <-- extension -->*
```

```
    </output>
    <fault name="NMToken">*
      <documentation/>?
      <-- extension -->*
    </fault>
</operation>
```

operation of portType Element (WSDL 1.1)

```
<operation name="NCName">*
  <documentation/> ?
  <input name="NMToken"? message="QName">?
    <documentation/> ?
  </input>
  <output name="NMToken"? message="QName">?
    <documentation/> ?
  </output>
  <fault name="NMToken" message="QName">*
    <documentation/> ?
  </fault>
</operation>
```

operation Element of binding Element (WSDL 2.0)

```
<operation ref="xsd:QName">*
  <documentation/>?
  <input messageLabel="xsd:NCName"?>*
    <documentation/>?
    <-- extension -->*
  </input>
  <output messageLabel="xsd:NCName"?>*
    <documentation/>?
    <-- extension -->*
  </output>
  <infault ref="xsd:QName" messageLabel="xsd:NCName"?>*
    <documentation/>?
    <-- extension -->*
  </infault>
  <outfault ref="xsd:QName" messageLabel="xsd:NCName"?>*
    <documentation/>?
    <-- extension -->*
  </outfault>
</operation>
```

operation Element of interface Element (WSDL 2.0)

```
<operation name="xsd:NCName" pattern="xsd:anyURI"
  style="list of xsd:anyURI"?
  wsdlx:safe="xsd:boolean"?>*
  <documentation/>?
```

```
  <input messageLabel="xsd:NCName"?
    element="xsd:QName|#any|#none|#other"?>*
    <documentation/>?
    <-- extension -->*
  </input>
  <output messageLabel="xsd:NCName"?
    element="xsd:QName|#any|#none|#other"?>*
    <documentation/>?
    <-- extension -->*
  </output>
  <infault ref="xsd:QName" messageLabel="xsd:NCName"?>*
    <documentation/>?
    <-- extension -->*
  </infault>
  <outfault ref="xsd:QName" messageLabel="xsd:NCName"?>*
    <documentation/>?
    <-- extension -->*
  </outfault>
  <-- extension -->*
</operation>
```

`Optional` Attribute (WS-Policy 1.5)

```
<Assertion Name wsp:Optional="xsd:boolean"?>
  ...
</Assertion Name>
```

`pattern` Element (XML Schema 1.0)

```
<pattern value="string"/>*
```

`Policy` Element (WS-Policy 1.5)

```
<Policy
  Name="xsd:anyURI"?
  [wsu:Id="xsd:ID" | xml:id="xsd:ID"]?
  xlmns:wsp="http://www.w3.org/ns/ws-policy">
  [wsp:Policy |
   wsp:All |
   wsp:ExactlyOne |
   wsp:PolicyReference |
   ElementFromOtherNameSpace]*
</Policy>
```

`PolicyAttachment` Element (WS-Policy 1.5)

```
<PolicyAttachment>
  <wsp:AppliesTo>
    [x:DomainExpression+ | wsp:URI]
  </wsp:AppliesTo>
```

```
[<wsp:Policy/> | <wsp:PolicyReference/>] +
  <wsse:Security/>?
  ...
</PolicyAttachment>
```

PolicyReference Element (WS-Policy 1.5)

```
<PolicyReference URI="xsd:anyURI"
  Digest="xsd:base64Binary"
  DigestAlgorithm="xsd:anyURI"?>
  ElementFromAnyNamespace
</PolicyReference>
```

port Element (WSDL 1.1)

```
<port name="NCName" binding="QName">*
  <documentation/> ?
  <-- extension -->*
</port>
```

portType Element (WSDL 1.1)

```
<portType name="NCName">*
  <documentation/>?
  <operation name="NCName"/>*
</portType>
```

Reason Element (SOAP 1.2)

```
<Reason>
  <Text xml:lang="xsd:string">
    xsd:string
  </Text>+
</Reason>
```

ReferenceParameters Element (WS-Addressing 1.0)

```
<ReferenceParameters>
  xsd:any*
</ReferenceParameters>
```

RelatesTo Element (WS-Addressing 1.0)

```
<RelatesTo RelationshipType="xsd:anyURI"?>
  xsd:anyURI
</RelatesTo>
```

ReplyTo Element (WS-Addressing 1.0)

```
<ReplyTo>
  wsa:EndpointReferenceType
</ReplyTo>
```

restriction Element (child of simpleType) (XML Schema 1.0)

```
<restriction base="QName">
  <length value="integer"/>?
  <minLength value="integer"/>?
  <maxLength value="integer"/>?
  [ <minExclusive value="anyType"/> |
    <minInclusive value="anyType"/> ]?
  [ <maxExclusive value="anyType"/> |
    <maxInclusive value="anyType"/> ]?
  <totalDigits value="integer"/>?
  <fractionDigits value="integer"/>?
  <enumeration value="anyType"/>*
  <pattern value="string"/>*
</restriction>
```

Role Element (SOAP 1.2)

```
<Role>
  xsd:anyURI
</Role>
```

schema Element (XML Schema 1.0)

```
<schema targetNamespace="uri"
  elementFormDefault="qualified|unqualified"?
  version="string"?>
  [<import/> | <include/> ]*
  [<element/> | <attribute/> | <complexType/> |
   <simpleType/> | <group/> ]*
</schema>
```

selector Element (XML Schema 1.0)

```
<selector xpath="string"/>
```

sequence Element (XML Schema 1.0)

```
<sequence minOccurs="integer"? maxOccurs="integer|unbounded"?>
   [ <sequence/> | <choice/> | <element/> | <group/> ]*
</sequence>
```

service Element (WSDL 1.1)

```
<service name="NCName">*
  <documentation/>?
  <port name="NCName" binding="QName"/>*
  <-- extension -->*
</service>
```

`service` Element (WSDL 2.0)

```
<service name="xsd:NCName" interface="xsd:QName">*
  <documentation/>?
  <endpoint name="xsd:NCName" binding="xsd:QName"
    address="uri"/>*
  <-- extension -->*
 </service>
```

`simpleContent` Element (XML Schema 1.0)

```
<simpleContent>?
  <extension base="QName">
    <attribute/>*
  </extension>
</simpleContent>
```

`simpleType` Element (global definition, child of `schema`) (XML Schema 1.0)

```
<simpleType name="NCName">*
  <restriction base="QName">
    <!-- see restriction (child of simpleType) -->
  </restriction>
</simpleType>
```

`simpleType` Element (local definition, child of `element` or `attribute`) (XML Schema 1.0)

```
<simpleType>?
  <restriction base="QName">
    <!-- see restriction (child of simpleType) -->
  </restriction>
</simpleType>
```

`SoapAction` Element (WS-Addressing 1.0)

```
<SoapAction>
  xsd:anyURI
</SoapAction>?
```

`Subcode` Element (SOAP 1.2)

```
<Subcode>
  <Value>
    xsd:QName
  </Value>
  <Subcode>
    ...
  </Subcode>?
<Subcode>
```

`Text` Element (SOAP 1.2)

```
<Text xml:lang="xsd:string">
  xsd:string
</Text>
```

`To` Element (WS-Addressing 1.0)

```
<To>
  xsd:anyURI
</To>
```

`totalDigits` Element (XML Schema 1.0)

```
<totalDigits value="integer"/>?
```

`types` Element (WSDL 1.1)

```
<types>?
  <documentation/>?
  <xsd:schema targetNamespace="xsd:anyURI"?/>*
  <-- extension -->*
</types>
```

`types` Element (WSDL 2.0)

```
<types>
  <documentation/>?
  [<xsd:import namespace="xsd:anyURI"
   schemaLocation="xsd:anyURI"?/>
   |<xsd:schema targetNamespace="xsd:anyURI"/>
   |<-- extension -->* ]*
</types>
```

`Upgrade` Element (SOAP 1.2)

```
<Upgrade>
  <SupportedEnvelope qname="xsd:QName"/>+
</Upgrade>
```

`URI` Element (WS-Policy 1.5)

```
<URI>
  xsd:anyURI
</URI>
```

Appendix D

Namespaces and Prefixes Used in this Book

For your reference, the following tables contain a list of all the namespace prefixes that are used in this book. The first table lists custom namespaces that were defined for case study examples and the second table contains industry standard namespaces.

Custom Namespaces		
Namespace	**Prefix**	**Description**
http://actioncon.com/referenceIDs	act	custom EPR header
http://actioncon.com/schema/arespguarantee	argt	custom policy
http://actioncon.com/schema/common	common	common schema
http://actioncon.com/policy/custom	custom	custom policy assertion
http://actioncon.com/schema/po/errors	err	custom error message
http://actioncon.com/schema/po/extension	ext	custom extension schema
http://actioncon.com/schema/po/faults	ft	custom fault message
http://actioncon.com/schema/gameinfo	game	custom game schema
varies	ns	represents "namespace" (Chapter 5 only)
http://actioncon.com/schema/po	po	custom purchase order schema
http://actioncon.com/contract/po	po, abs	custom purchase order WSDL definition
http://actioncon.com/schema/po2	po2	custom extension schema
http://actioncon.com/security	sec	custom security header
varies	tns	represents a target namespace
different URI for each prefix	v2, v3	custom versioning references
http://schemas.xmlsoap.org/wsdl/	–	WSDL 1.1
http://www.w3.org/ns/wsdl	–	WSDL 2.0
urn:ean.ucc:align:entertainment: electronic_games:2	eg	GS1 industry schema

Standardized Namespaces		
Namespace	**Prefix**	**Description**
http://schemas.xmlsoap.org/ws/2003/03/business-process/	`bpws`	WS-BPEL business process extensibility elements
http://schemas.xmlsoap.org/wsdl/http/	`httpbind`	HTTP binding
http://schemas.xmlsoap.org/wsdl/mime/	`mimbind`	MIME binding
http://schemas.xmlsoap.org/ws/2003/05/partner-link	`plnk`	WS-BPEL partner link extensibility elements
http://www.w3.org/2004/08/representation	`rep`	RRSHB representation
http://schemas.xmlsoap.org/soap/envelope	`soap, soap11`	SOAP 1.1
http://www.w3.org/2003/05/soap-envelope	`soap, soap12`	SOAP 1.2
http://schemas.xmlsoap.org/wsdl/soap/	`soapbind, soapbind11`	SOAP 1.1 binding
http://schemas.xmlsoap.org/wsdl/soap12/	`soapbind, soapbind12`	SOAP 1.2 binding
different URN for each prefix	`udt, cbc, cac, ext, mmo`	UBL
http://www.w3.org/ns/wsdl/http	`whttp`	HTTP binding for WSDL 2.0
http://schemas.xmlsoap.org/ws/2004/08/addressing	`wsa`	WS-Addressing
http://www.w3.org/2007/05/addressing/metadata	`wsam`	WS-Addressing policy assertions
http://docs.oasis-open.org/ws-tx/wscoor/2006/06	`wscoor`	WS-Coordination
http://www.w3.org/ns/wsdl-instance	`wsdli`	WSDL instance
http://www.w3.org/ns/wsdl-extensions	`wsldx`	WSDL extensions
http://schemas.xmlsoap.org/ws/2004/09/policy	`wsp`	WS-Policy

(continues)

(continued)

Standardized Namespaces		
Namespace	Prefix	Description
http://docs.oasis-open.org/ws-rx/wsrm/ 200702	`wsrm, wsrmp`	WS-ReliableMessaging
http://docs.oasis-open.org/wss/2004/01/ oasis-200401-wss-wssecurity-secext-1.0.xsd	`wsse`	WS-Security
http://docs.oasis-open.org/wss/2004/01/ oasis-200401-wss-wssecurity-utility-1.0.xsd	`wsu`	WS-Security utility schema
http://www.w3.org/2001/XMLSchema	`xsd, xs`	XML Schema

NOTE
All of these standard namespaces are subject to change. A newer version of a standard will always have a new namespace value that will often contain its version identifier or creation date.

Appendix E

SOA Design Patterns Related to this Book

This appendix contains a set of profile tables for the following contract-related design patterns referenced in this book:

- Canonical Expression
- Canonical Schema
- Canonical Versioning
- Compatible Change
- Concurrent Contracts
- Contract Centralization
- Contract Denormalization
- Decomposed Capability
- Decoupled Contract
- Distributed Capability
- Messaging Metadata
- Partial Validation
- Policy Centralization
- Proxy Capability
- Schema Centralization
- Service Messaging
- Termination Notification
- Validation Abstraction
- Version Identification

These summaries were borrowed from the book *SOA Design Patterns,* which documents a master pattern catalog for SOA. The upcoming profiles provide only summarized descriptions of the patterns.

For descriptions of the individual profile table fields and to view profile tables for all SOA design patterns, visit www.soapatterns.org.

Canonical Expression

How can service contracts be consistently understood and interpreted?

Problem	
Service contracts may express similar capabilities in different ways, leading to inconsistency and risking misinterpretation.	
Solution	
Service contracts are standardized using naming conventions.	
Application	**Impacts**
Naming conventions are applied to service contracts as part of formal analysis and design processes.	The use of global naming conventions introduce enterprise-wide standards that need to be consistently used and enforced.
Principles	**Architecture**
Standardized Service Contract, Service Discoverability	Enterprise, Inventory, Service

Canonical Schema

How can services be designed to avoid data model transformation?

Problem	
Services with disparate models for similar data impose transformation requirements that increase development effort, design complexity, and runtime performance overhead.	
Solution	
Data models for common information sets are standardized across service contracts within an inventory boundary.	
Application	**Impacts**
Design standards are applied to schemas used by service contracts as part of a formal design process.	Maintaining the standardization of contract schemas can introduce significant governance effort and can introduce cultural challenges.
Principles	**Architecture**
Standardized Service Contract	Inventory, Service

Canonical Versioning

How can services within an inventory be versioned with minimal impact?

Problem	
Services within the same inventory that are versioned differently will cause numerous interoperability and governance problems.	
Solution	
Versioning rules and the expression of version information are standardized within a service inventory boundary.	

Application	Impacts
Governance and design standards are required to ensure consistent versioning of service contracts within a service inventory.	The creation and enforcement of the required standards introduces new governance requirements.

Principles	Architecture
Standardized Service Contract	Inventory, Service

Compatible Change

How can a service contract be modified without impacting consumers?

Problem
Changing an already-published service contract can impact and invalidate existing consumer programs.
Solution
Some changes to the service contract can be backwards-compatible, thereby avoiding negative consumer impacts.

Application	Impacts
Service contract changes can be implemented by extending an existing contract or loosening existing constraints or by applying the Concurrent Contracts pattern.	Compatible changes still introduce versioning governance effort, and the technique of loosening constraints can lead to vague contract designs.

Principles	Architecture
Standardized Service Contract, Service Loose Coupling	Service

Concurrent Contracts

How can a service facilitate multi-consumer coupling requirements and abstraction concerns at the same time?

Problem	
A service's contract may not be suitable or applicable for all of the service's potential consumers.	

Solution	
Multiple contracts can be created for a single service, each targeted at a specific type of consumer.	

Application	Impacts
This pattern is ideally applied together with the Service Façade pattern to support new contracts as required.	Each new contract can effectively add a new service endpoint to an inventory from the service consumer's perspective, increasing corresponding governance effort.

Principles	Architecture
Standardized Service Contract, Service Loose Coupling, Service Reusability	Service

Contract Centralization

How can direct consumer-to-implementation coupling be avoided?

Problem	
Consumer programs can be designed to access underlying service resources using different entry-points, resulting in different forms of implementation dependencies that undermine strategic SOA goals associated with loose coupling.	

Solution	
Access to service logic is limited to the service contract, forcing consumers to avoid implementation coupling.	

Application	Impacts
This pattern is realized through formal enterprise design standards and the targeted application of the Service Abstraction design principle.	Forcing consumer programs to access service capabilities and resources via a central contract can impose performance overhead and on-going standardization effort.

Principles	Architecture
Standardized Service Contract, Service Loose Coupling	Composition

Contract Denormalization

How can a service contract facilitate consumer programs with differing data exchange requirements?

Problem
Services with strictly normalized contracts can impose functional and performance constraints on some consumer programs.

Solution
Service contracts can include a measured extent of denormalization, allowing multiple capabilities to redundantly express core functions in different ways for different types of consumer programs.

Application	Impacts
The service contract is carefully extended with additional capabilities that provide functional variations of a primary capability.	Overuse of this pattern on the same contract can dramatically increase its size, making it difficult to interpret and unwieldy to govern.

Principles	Architecture
Standardized Service Contract, Service Loose Coupling	Service

Decomposed Capability

How can a service be designed to minimize the chances of capability logic deconstruction?

Problem
The decomposition of a service subsequent to its implementation can require the deconstruction of logic within capabilities, which can make the preservation of a service contract problematic.

Solution
Services prone to future decomposition can be equipped with a series of granular capabilities that more easily facilitate decomposition.

Application	Impacts
Additional service modeling is carried out to define granular, more easily distributed capabilities.	Until the service is eventually decomposed, it may be represented by a bloated contract that stays with it as long as proxy capabilities are supported.

Principles	Architecture
Standardized Service Contract, Service Abstraction	Service

Decoupled Contract

How can a service express its capabilities independently of its implementation?

Problem	
For a service to be positioned as an effective enterprise resource, it must be equipped with a technical contract that exists independently from its implementation yet still in alignment with other services.	
Solution	
The service contract is physically decoupled from its implementation.	
Application	**Impacts**
A service's technical interface is physically separated and subject to service-orientation design principles.	Service functionality is limited to the feature-set of the decoupled contract medium.
Principles	**Architecture**
Standardized Service Contract, Service Loose Coupling	Service

Distributed Capability

How can a service preserve its functional context while also fulfilling special capability processing requirements?

Problem	
A capability that belongs within a service may have unique processing requirements that cannot be accommodated by the default service implementation, but separating capability logic from the service will compromise the integrity of the service context.	
Solution	
The underlying service logic is distributed, thereby allowing the implementation logic for a capability with unique processing requirements to be physically separated, while continuing to be represented by the same service contract.	
Application	**Impacts**
The logic is moved and then represented by a service façade, much like a Proxy Capability.	The distribution of a capability's logic leads to performance overhead associated with remote communication and the need for a separate façade component.
Principles	**Architecture**
Standardized Service Contract, Service Autonomy	Service

Messaging Metadata

How can services be designed to consume activity state data at runtime?

Problem
Because messaging does not rely on a persistent connection between service and consumer, it is challenging for a service to gain access to the state data associated with an overall runtime activity.

Solution
The message contents can be supplemented with activity-specific metadata that can be interpreted and processed separately at runtime.

Application	Impacts
This pattern requires a messaging framework that supports message headers or properties.	The interpretation and processing of messaging metadata at runtime increases the performance overhead of messaging-based communication.

Principles	Architecture
Service Loose Coupling, Service Statelessness	Composition

Partial Validation

How can unnecessary data validation be avoided?

Problem
The generic capabilities provided by agnostic services sometimes result in service contracts that impose the receipt of unnecessary data and validation upon some consumer programs.

Solution
A consumer program can be designed to validate the relevant subset of the data and ignore the remainder, thereby avoiding unnecessary validation.

Application	Impacts
The application of this pattern is specific to the technology used for the consumer implementation. With Web services, XPath can be used to filter out unnecessary data prior to validation.	Extra design-time effort is required and the additional runtime data filtering-related logic can introduce processing overhead.

Principles	Architecture
Standardized Service Contract, Service Loose Coupling	Composition

Policy Centralization

How can policies be normalized and consistently enforced across multiple services?

Problem
Policies that apply to multiple services can introduce redundancy and inconsistency within service logic and contracts.

Solution
Global or domain-specific policy assertions can be isolated and applied to multiple services.

Application	Impacts
Up-front analysis effort specific to defining and establishing reusable policy assertions is recommended and an appropriate policy enforcement framework is required.	Policy frameworks can introduce performance overhead and may impose dependencies on proprietary technologies. There is also the risk of conflict between centralized and service-specific policies.

Principles	Architecture
Standardized Service Contracts, Service Loose Coupling, Service Abstraction	Inventory, Service

Proxy Capability

How can a service subject to decomposition continue to support consumers affected by the decomposition?

Problem
If an established service needs to be decomposed into multiple services, its contract and its existing consumers can be impacted.

Solution
The original service contract can be preserved, even if underlying capability logic is separated, by turning the established capability definition into a proxy.

Application	Impacts
Façade logic needs to be introduced to relay requests and responses between the proxy and newly located capabilities.	This pattern results in service contract-level denormalization.

Principles	Architecture
Service Loose Coupling	Service

Schema Centralization

How can service contracts be designed to avoid redundant data representation?

Problem
Different service contracts often need to express capabilities that process similar business documents or data sets, resulting in redundant schema content that is difficult to govern.

Solution
Select schemas that exist as physically separate parts of the service contract are shared across multiple contracts.

Application	Impacts
Upfront analysis effort is required to establish a schema layer independent of and in support of the service layer.	Governance of shared schemas becomes increasingly important as multiple services can form dependencies on the same schema definitions.

Principles	Architecture
Standardized Service Contract, Service Loose Coupling	Inventory, Service

Service Messaging

How can services interoperate without forming persistent, tightly coupled connections?

Problem
Services that depend on traditional remote communication protocols impose the need for persistent connections and tightly coupled data exchanges, increasing consumer dependencies and limiting service reuse potential.

Solution
Services can be designed to interact via a messaging-based technology, which removes the need for persistent connections and reduces coupling requirements.

Application	Impacts
A messaging framework needs to be established and services need to be designed to use it.	Messaging technology brings with it quality of service concerns such as reliable delivery, security, performance, and transactions.

Principles	Architecture
Standardized Service Contract, Service Loose Coupling	Inventory, Composition, Service

Termination Notification

How can the scheduled expiry of a service contract be communicated to consumer programs?

Problem	
Consumer programs may be unaware of when a service or a version of a service contract is scheduled for retirement, thereby risking runtime failure.	
Solution	
Service contracts can be designed to express termination information for programmatic and human consumption.	
Application	**Impacts**
Service contracts can be extended with ignorable policy assertions or supplemented with human-readable annotations.	The syntax and conventions used to express termination information must be understood by the consumer in order for this information to be effectively used.
Principles	**Architecture**
Standardized Service Contract	Composition, Service

Validation Abstraction

How can service contracts be designed to more easily adapt to validation logic changes?

Problem	
Service contracts that contain detailed validation constraints become more easily invalidated when the rules behind those constraints change.	
Solution	
Granular validation logic and rules can be abstracted away from the service contract thereby decreasing constraint granularity and increasing the contract's potential longevity.	
Application	**Impacts**
Abstracted validation logic and rules needs to be moved to the underlying service logic, a different service, a service agent, or elsewhere.	This pattern can somewhat decentralize validation logic and can also complicate schema standardization.
Principles	**Architecture**
Standardized Service Contract, Service Loose Coupling, Service Abstraction	Service

Version Identification

How can consumers be made aware of service contract version information?

Problem
When an already-published service contract is changed, unaware consumers will miss the opportunity to leverage the change or may be negatively impacted by the change.

Solution
Versioning information pertaining to compatible and incompatible can be expressed as part of the service contract, both for communication and enforcement purposes.

Application	Impacts
With Web service contracts, version numbers can be incorporated into namespace values and as annotations.	Version information is expressed in a proprietary manner that needs to be understood by consumer program designers.

Principles	Architecture
Standardized Service Contract	Service

About the Authors

Thomas Erl

Thomas Erl is the world's top-selling SOA author, Series Editor of the *Prentice Hall Service-Oriented Computing Series from Thomas Erl*, and Editor of the *SOA Magazine* (www.soamag.com). With over 100,000 copies in print world-wide, his books have become international bestsellers and have been formally endorsed by senior members of major software organizations, such as IBM, Microsoft, Oracle, BEA, Sun, Intel, SAP, and HP.

His most recent titles *SOA Design Patterns* (www.soapatterns.com) and *Web Service Contract Design and Versioning for SOA* were co-authored with a series of industry experts and follow his first three books *Service-Oriented Architecture: A Field Guide to Integrating XML and Web Services*, *Service-Oriented Architecture: Concepts, Technology, and Design*, and *SOA: Principles of Service Design* (www.soaprinciples.com).

Thomas is the founder of SOA Systems Inc. (www.soasystems.com), a company specializing in SOA consulting and training services with a vendor-agnostic focus. Thomas is also the founder of the internationally recognized SOA Certified Professional program (www.soacp.com and www.soaschool.com). Thomas is a speaker and instructor for private and public events, and has delivered many workshops and keynote speeches. Articles and interviews by Thomas have been published in numerous publications, including *The Wall Street Journal*.

For more information, visit: www.thomaserl.com

Anish Karmarkar

Anish Karmarkar, Ph.D., is a Consulting Member of Technical Staff at Oracle and is part of the standards and strategy team responsible for SOA, Web services, and Java specifications. He has 17 years of research, development, and standards experience in various aspects of distributed systems and protocols.

Anish is a co-editor of various Web services standards, including SOAP 1.2, WS-ReliableMessaging, WS-ReliableMessaging Policy, WS-MakeConnection, WS-I Basic Profile, WS-I Reliable Secure Profile, WS-I Attachments Profile, Resource Representation SOAP Header Block (RRSHB), among others. He is also a co-editor of the Service Component Architecture (SCA) set of specifications including SCA Assembly Model, SCA Web Service Binding, and various Java-related SCA specifications.

As an active participant and a founding member in various Web services and SOA-related Working Groups, Technical Committees, Expert Groups in W3C, OASIS, Java Community Process (JCP), and Open Service Oriented Architecture (OSOA) collaboration, he has played a significant role in the development of Web services and SCA standards and specifications.

Anish has been on the Board of Directors of the OSGi Alliance since 2006, co-chair of the OASIS SCA BPEL Technical Committee, and Oracle's alternate representative on the Java Community Process (JCP) "Big Java" Executive Committee. He has also served as the vice-Chair of WS-I Basic Profile Working Group. He received his Ph.D. in Computer Science from Texas A&M University in 1997.

Priscilla Walmsley

Priscilla Walmsley is a software consultant and Managing Director of Datypic, a consultancy specializing in XML architecture and implementation. She has helped organizations large and small design and implement all things XML, including Web services, enterprise application integration, content management, searchable content repositories, large scale data conversion, and Web publishing. She has over 15 years experience as a consultant, software architect, data architect and developer. She has held positions at RELTECH Group, Platinum technology, XMLSolutions Corporation (as a VP and co-founder), and Vitria Technology.

Walmsley was a member of the W3C XML Schema Working Group from 1999 to 2004, where she served as an Invited Expert. She was also a member of the W3C XML Schema Patterns for Databinding Working Group. She is the author of *Definitive XML Schema* (Prentice Hall PTR, 2001), and *XQuery* (O'Reilly Media, 2007). In addition, she co-authored the book *XML in Office 2003* with Charles Goldfarb (Prentice Hall PTR, 2003).

Hugo Haas

Hugo Haas grew up in the French Alps. He studied engineering at Ecole Centrale Paris in France and computer science at the University of Cambridge in England. As a student, he participated in the creation of the VideoLAN video streaming project, which gave birth to the popular VLC media player, and actively contributed to the Debian GNU/Linux project.

Hugo worked at 3Com in Hemel Hempstead, England, before joining the W3C Technical Team at the Massachusetts Institute of Technology (MIT) in Cambridge, MA, USA in June 1999. At the World Wide Web Consortium, he led the Web Services Activity, and participated in the design of SOAP 1.2, WSDL 2.0, and WS-Addressing 1.0.

He was the primary author of the Common User Agent Problems document (www.w3.org/TR/cuap), which was used by various browser vendors to address issues in their implementation. He was one of the editors of the W3C Web Services Architecture (www.w3.org/TR/ws-arch) and Glossary (www.w3.org/TR/ws-gloss), as well as WSDL 2.0 (www.w3.org/TR/wsdl20-adjuncts).

Hugo gave keynotes and presentations in numerous conferences in various countries (Australia, Brazil, France, Japan, Sweden, USA, etc.), including the International World Wide Web conference, the IEEE European Web Services conference, the IDG Web Services conference, and the IDEAlliance XML USA and XTech conferences.

He currently works for Yahoo! as the Web services platform architect, defining guidelines and tools to expose functionality with HTTP-based services in a reliable, secure, reusable, and interoperable manner.

Hugo lives in California with his wife Nicole. When he's not in front of a computer, he's typically playing with electronic gizmos, listening to music, taking photos, running with his dog, or catching up on European soccer—sometimes all of the above at the same time.

Umit Yalcinalp

L. Umit Yalcinalp is a research architect at SAP Labs. She currently leads a team investigating emerging technologies for enterprise systems focusing on SOA and Web 2.0. She is an author of several technical papers and specifications, an editor of several standards and a speaker at conferences. She has actively contributed to various specification developments at W3C, JCP and OASIS on SOA, Web services and Java(™), including but not limited to WS-Policy, SCA Policy, WS-ReliableMessaging, WS-Addressing, WSDL 2.0, and Enterprise Java Beans 2.0. She has a Ph.D. in Computer Science from Case Western Reserve University.

Canyang Kevin Liu

Canyang Kevin Liu is Solution Architecture Manager with SAP's co-innovation lab in Palo Alto, California, focusing on innovative solutions that leverage SOA and SAP NetWeaver technology. An experienced architect for enterprise business applications and a longtime evangelist for SOA, Kevin helped build many of the Web services technology standards including WSDL, WS-BEPL, WS-I Basic Profile, and RosettaNet Web Service profiles.

David Orchard

For the latest information about this author, visit the blog site: www.pacificspirit.com.

Andre Tost

Andre Tost works as a Senior Technical Staff Member in the IBM Software Group, where he consults with IBM customers world-wide on establishing service-oriented architectures. His special focus is on Web services, Enterprise Service Bus and Business Process Management technology. In this position, he has led a number of successful SOA projects with customers worldwide. Before his current assignment, he spent ten years in various partner enablement, development and architecture roles in IBM software development, most of them related to the WebSphere family of products.

Andre has spoken at many industry conferences worldwide on topics related to SOA and is a frequent publisher of articles and papers. He is also a coauthor of several books on Web services and related technologies.

Originally from Germany, Andre now lives and works in Rochester, Minnesota. In his spare time, he likes to spend time with his family and play and watch soccer whenever possible.

James Pasley

James Pasley is an architect on Workday's Integration On Demand team. James specializes in the customer facing aspects of Workday's integration architecture such as Workday's public Web services. James is editor of Workday's developer Web site and also creates much of the material for Workday's integration related training courses. James joined Workday via the acquisition of Cape Clear Software.

James joined Cape Clear Software in 2001 as a lead developer for Cape Studio. In 2003, James was appointed Chief Architect for Cape Clear, where he oversaw the development of Cape Clear's Enterprise Service Bus. In 2005, James became Chief Technology Officer for Cape Clear Software. Cape Clear was recognized by Gartner and Forrester as the leading Enterprise Service Bus delivering proven on-demand integration reliability, scalability, and performance to connect any content, services or software across the internet using Web services technologies.

Prior to joining Cape Clear Software, James worked for Siemens Nixdorf, developing secure X.400 messaging and public key infrastructure (PKI) solutions for a range of products.

James lives in Leixlip, Ireland with his wife Patricia and children Rebecca, James, Robert, Hannah, and Alyssa. He holds a B.A. (Moderatorship) in Computer Science from Trinity College, Dublin.

For more information, visit: www.jpasley.com

Index

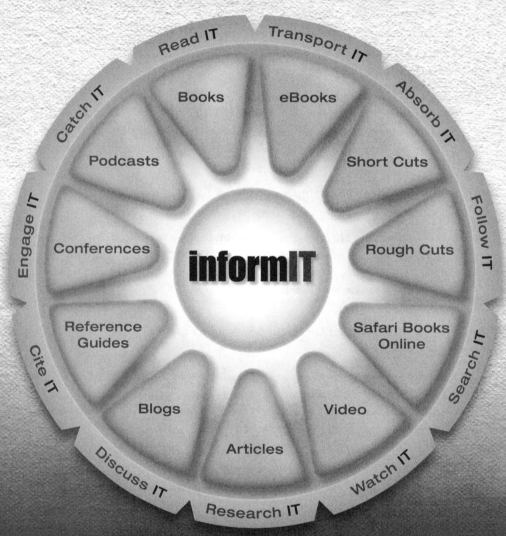

FREE Online Edition

Your purchase of **Web Service Contract Design & Versioning for SOA** includes access to a free online edition for 45 days through the Safari Books Online subscription service. Nearly every Sams book is available online through Safari Books Online, along with over 5,000 other technical books and videos from publishers such as Addison-Wesley Professional, Cisco Press, Exam Cram, IBM Press, O'Reilly, Que, and Sams.

SAFARI BOOKS ONLINE allows you to search for a specific answer, cut and paste code, download chapters, and stay current with emerging technologies.

Activate your FREE Online Edition at
www.informit.com/safarifree

> **STEP 1:** Enter the coupon code: YMIEDFH.

> **STEP 2:** New Safari users, complete the brief registration form.
> Safari subscribers, just login.

If you have difficulty registering on Safari or accessing the online edition, please e-mail customer-service@safaribooksonline.com